Perceptions of Jewish History

Perceptions of Jewish History

Amos Funkenstein

UNIVERSITY OF CALIFORNIA PRESS

Berkeley / Los Angeles / Oxford

University of California Press
Berkeley and Los Angeles, California

University of California Press
Oxford, England

Copyright © 1993 by The Regents of the University of California

Library of Congress Cataloging-in-Publication Data

Funkenstein, Amos.
    Perceptions of Jewish history / by
Amos Funkenstein.
        p.   cm.
    Includes bibliographical references and index.
    ISBN 0-520-07702-4
    1. Jews—Historiography.   2. Jews—History—Philosophy.
I. Title.
DS115.5.F96   1993
909'.04924—dc20   91-41634
                                                                CIP

Printed in the United States of America

1 2 3 4 5 6 7 8 9

To my children
Daniela and Jakob

Contents

Preface

Historical reasoning and theories of history have interested me since my graduate work. My doctoral dissertation, written more than twenty-five years ago, dealt with their varieties during the Middle Ages. Most of the essays collected in this book have been written since. While they manifestly form a coherent body of work, they also bear evidence of changing opinions, emphasis, and taste. I left the substance of the articles unchanged even where my position is different today, while updating them as best I could.

I owe thanks to many friends and colleagues with whom I discussed the issues over the years: Robert Alter, Keith Baker, Sabine MacCormack, Jehuda Elkana, François Furet, Carlo Ginsburg, David Hartman, Susannah Heschel, Robert Kirshner, Yemima and Hanina Ben-Menachem, Jürgen Miethke, Richard Popkin, Aviezer Ravitsky, Peter Reill, and Hayden White. They have read some or all of the articles. Their comments, especially where they disagreed with me, were invaluable.

I owe Saul Friedländer special thanks. Several of the articles published have appeared first in volumes of essays on different subjects edited by him, or in *History and Memory* of which he is likewise the editor. Not only did he prompt me to write them: he worked hard to make each of them as clear and plausible as possible. He is a true friend. Abraham Shapira, of Tel-Aviv University and Am Oved Publications, was the editor of the Hebrew version of this book: it was his idea to collect these articles into a coherent whole, and his energy which overcame hurdles in doing so.

My former and present students in Jewish history at five universities—UCLA, Tel-Aviv, Stanford, the École des Hautes Études, Berkeley—have enriched my knowledge and my judgment: Jody Ackerman, Rachel and David Biale, Stephen Benin, Nina Caputo, Isaia Dimant, Gil Graf, Martin Kohn, Bat-Zion Araki-Klorman, Josef Mali, Marc Lee Raphael, Perrine Simon-Nahum, Amnon Raz-Krakockin, Joel Rembaum, and Steve Zipperstein. They will find in the book many ideas we discussed together and many ideas they developed on their own. For the privilege of being their teacher I am very grateful.

Stanley Holwitz, of the University of California Press, helped in all stages of the book; Michelle Nordon and Gregory McNamee edited it faithfully and meticulously. Sylvia Berman typed and corrected the manuscript with much dedication and care.

Princeton University Press permitted me to repeat a few pages of a former book, *Theology and the Scientific Imagination From the Middle Ages to the Seventeenth Century* (1986). A list of the original place of publication of all previously published essays of this book is to be found below.

Without the prompting and support of my wife, Esther Micenmacher, I would never have found the courage to collect and rework the materials in this book and in its shorter Hebrew version. She also helped me to clarify many of the ideas. For her support I owe many thanks also to my sister, Moria Brautbar.

The book is dedicated to my children Daniela and Jakob. The years I raised them were happy and full of purpose.

Previously Published Essays

"Collective Memory and Historical Consciousness." *History and Memory* 1, 1 (Spring-Summer 1989): 5–26.

"History and Historical Facts in the Middle Ages." *Zemanim, Historical Quarterly* 2 (1980): 38–42.

"History, Counterhistory and Narrative." In Saul Friedlaender (ed.), *Probing the Limits of Representation: Nazism and the "Final Solution"* (Harvard University Press, Cambridge: 1992), 66–81.

"Job Without a Theodicee." *Ha'arets* 2.10 (1988).

"The Book of Jona: A Prophet Who Was Not a Prophet." *Ha'arets* 28.9 (1990).

"A Schedule for the End of the World." In Saul Friedlaender, G. Holton, L. Marx, E. Scolnikoff (eds.), *Visions of Apocalypse-End or Rebirth* (Holmes and Mayer, New York: 1985), 44–60.

"The Scriptures Speak the Language of Man: The Uses and Abuses of the Medieval Principle of Accommodation." *Philosophes Médiévaux* xxvi (1986): 92–101.

"Maimonides: Political Theory and Realistic Messianism." *Miscellanea Medievalia* 11 (1970): 81–103.

"Nachmanides' Typological Reading of History." *Zion* 45, 1 (1980): 35–59.

"Changes in the Patterns of Christian Anti-Jewish Polemics in the 12th Century." *Zion* 33, 3–4 (1968): 125–144.

"The Political Theory of Jewish Emancipation from Mendelssohn to Herzl." *Jahrbuch des Instituts für deutsche Geschichte* Beiheft 3 (1980): 13–28.

"Das Verhältris der jüdischen Aufklärung zur mittelalterlichen jüdischen Philosophie." *Aufklärung und Haskala Wolfenbüttler Studien zur Aufklärung* 14 (1990): 13–21.

"The Genesis of Rosenzweig's 'Stern der Erlösung': 'Urformel' and 'Urzelle'." *Jahrbuch des Instituts für Deutsche Geschichte* Beiheft 4 (1983): 17–29.

"An Escape from History: Rosenzweig on the Destiny of Judaism." *History and Memory* 2, 2 (1990): 117–135.

"Interpretations théologiques de l'holocauste: Un bilan." In *L'Allemagne Nazie et le génocide Juif* (Paris: Gallimard: 1985), 465–495.

"Zionism and Science: Three Aspects" (Rehovot: Yad Chaim Waitzman: 1985).

1

Introduction

The Themes

Few cultures are as preoccupied with their own identity and distinction as the Jewish. It asserted and reasserted its uniqueness in every mode of creative expression, not least in the liturgy, which includes a daily thanksgiving to the Creator "that he did not make us like all the nations of the lands, and did not set us up like other families of the earth. That he did not set our inheritance like theirs and our lot like their multitude."[1] The uniqueness of the nation was seen as a condition for its duration—whether in theological terms or, since the crisis of secularization, in alternative idioms. It served as an explanation for the sufferings inflicted on Jews and as a rationale for sufferings they

---

1. On the antiquity of *alenu*, see Josef Heinemann, *Prayers in the Period of the Tana'im and Amora'im: Its Nature and Patterns* (Jerusalem, 1978), pp. 173–75. *Alenu* was taken from the *mussaf* to New Year's liturgy and introduced into the everyday morning prayer in the thirteenth century. Parts or all of it were censored in the West and altered in the ashkenazic liturgy. See Ismar Elbogen, *Der jüdische Gottesdienst in seiner geschichtlichen Entwicklung* (1st ed., Leipzig, 1913; 3rd ed. Frankfurt am Main, 1931), pp. 63–64. Hebrew trans., Yosef Hainman and Yisra'el Adler, *Hatefila be-Yisra'el behitpatchutah historit* (Tel Aviv, 1972).

occasionally inflicted on others. It stood at the center of Jewish self-reflection.

A culture, a society, may view its existence and distinctive features as a matter of course or as a given part of the furniture of the world, as a natural endowment. Neither was the case with the Jewish culture since biblical times. The continuous assertion and reassertion of its identity and excellence is already an indication that they were not taken for granted. A culture that does not take itself for granted is, by definition, a self-reflexive culture. Historical consciousness became the mode of Jewish self-reflection. I do not mean to suggest that Jews, at least until the nineteenth century, entertained any doubts about their place in the world or about their future existence; both were guaranteed as a divine promise and premise. And yet their existence was to them a source of perpetual amazement: it was never viewed as a naturally given datum, and it remained always in need of explanation. The very emergence of Israel as a young culture among older cultures within "historical" times needed explanation—the biblical account of history, we shall see, provided it. The conquest of a land already inhabited by others likewise needed a justification. The ties of Israel to the Holy Land, Rabbi Abraham Isaak Hakohen Kook once said, are "unlike the natural bonds with which every nation and tongue is tied to its country," not organically grown, but instituted.[2] Every further turn in the history of Israel had to be explained, none seemed self-evident—neither in times of prosperity nor, indeed, in times of need.

This, perhaps, is the cardinal difference between an indistinct, more or less always present collective memory and a historical consciousness: the latter is an answer to definite questions asked. Being such an answer, it cannot merely enumerate events, but must weave them into a meaningful narrative, to be interpreted and reinterpreted. The varieties of the perceptions of Jewish history through the ages—of the Jewish historical consciousness—are the subject of this book. The essays included in it were written separately over a long time and can, of course, be read separately. They are nevertheless united by their subject and by some methical and substantial presuppositions which the reader is entitled to know of in advance. Some of the questions posed arise whenever historical narrative and reasoning become an object of inquiry: what is the difference between collective memory and historical awareness? What changes did the perception of history, now an integral

2. Rabbi Abraham Isaak Hakohen Kook, *Iggrot ha Ra'aya* (Jerusalem, 1965) II, p. 194.

dimension of our culture, undergo? Is history—the actual events that happened—reducible altogether to the historical narrative? These and similar questions are treated in the following introductory essays, the first two chapters of the book. They are followed by some detailed studies. Many pertinent and interesting subjects were either not treated at all or only in passing: these essays were not written with a book in mind. All of them do, however, contribute to the main thesis of the book: the realization that, long before the crisis of secularization—in fact, for as long as Jews thought about themselves—their identity, existence, and fate were never a matter of course, never taken for granted, either by themselves or, indeed, by their environment.

Collective Memory and Historical Consciousness

COLLECTIVE MEMORY

"History," wrote Hegel in *Philosophy of History,* "combines in our language the objective as well as the subjective side. It means both *res gestae* (the things that happened) and *historia rerum gestarum* (the narration of the things that happened)." "This is no coincidence," he goes on to explain, for without memory of the past there is no history, in the sense of events which are meaningful to the collective, events experienced by a collective that is aware of them. Collective awareness presumes collective memory. Without it there are no laws and no justice, no political structures, and no collective purposes. Without "history," there is no history and no state.[3]

Hegel is vague, and perhaps deliberately so. Did he refer to the writing of history? If so, then he conserved, unwittingly, the assumption shared by ancient and medieval authors that there is no history without its written preservation, that every event that is "worthy of being remembered" (*dignum memoriae*) has certainly been put into writing by

3. Georg Wilhelm Friedrich Hegel, *Vorlesungen über die Philosophie der Geschichte,* ed. Herman Glockner (Stuttgart, 1927), pp. 97–98. In contrast see Martin Heidegger, *Sein und Zeit,* 9th ed. (Tübingen, 1960): "And thus its presence which governs the detailed historical matter . . . is not in itself proof of histories of an 'era' . . . non-historical eras (*unhistorische Zeitalter*) are not therefore also without time barriers (*ungeschichtlich*)." The contradiction of the opinions depends on different conceptualizations of time and temporality (ibid., pp. 405 ff.).

a witness whom they consider the best of historians.[4] Or was Hegel perhaps referring to that elusive entity known today as "collective memory?" Where does this reside, how is it expressed, and how does it differ from the writing of history or thought about history?

We naturally ascribe historical "consciousness" and "memory" to human collectives—the family and the tribe, the nation and the state. Nations are meant to remember their heroes "forever"; to perpetuate the memory of a person means to have it entrenched in the collective memory, which forgets, perhaps, only failures and sins. In some languages—including Hebrew—there is a special term for this act of memory (*Verewigen, immortaliser, lehantsiakh*). Upon reflection, the notion is confusing. Consciousness and memory can, after all, be attributed only to individuals who act, are aware, and remember. Just as a nation cannot eat or dance, it cannot speak or remember. Remembering is a mental act, and therefore absolutely and completely personal. Even if we were to commit ourselves to an extreme assumption (as did some medieval thinkers)—that we all share a common intellect[5] insofar as our notions or propositions are valid—we would still have to distinguish between personal memories. The memories of people who have experienced a common event are not identical, even if we assume a "unity of the intellect"; for each of them, a concrete memory evokes different associations and feelings.

These reservations aside, "collective memory" is by no means a mistaken or misleading term. It simply needs to be used within clear limitations. Remembering, whether of personal experiences or of events in the past of a society, is a mental activity of a subject who is conscious of performing it. Memory may even constitute self-consciousness, because self-identity presumes memory. On the other hand, even the most personal memory cannot be removed from its social context. When I remember (and none too happily) my first day at school, I recall the city, the institution, the teacher—through and through social entities or constructs. My personal identity was likewise formed with reference to social objects, institutions, offices, value-hierarchies, and events. Even the very act of self-consciousness is far from being isolated from society.

---

4. See below, pp. 22–29.

5. E.g., Ibn Roshd and the Averroeists of the Middle Ages (*unitas intellectus*), as well as the somewhat different assumption of de Malebranche and Spinoza in the seventeenth century; see Amos Funkenstein, *Theology and the Scientific Imagination from the Middle Ages to the Seventeenth Century* (Princeton, 1986), pp. 290–96. In a sense, this is the assumption of all those who construct a "general consciousness," such as Kant.

Again we remember Hegel, who was the first, it seems, to show that self-consciousness requires a social context by virtue of its very conceptualization. The philosophical literature prior to Hegel treated self-consciousness as though it were isolated in its own world and perhaps even "windowless," whether conceived of as a substance (Descartes, Leibniz) or as a function, that is, a point of intersection for the rational organization of the world (Kant).[6] In a famous chapter in *The Phenomenology of the Spirit,* Hegel abandoned this tradition, stating that self-consciousness "is in and for itself (*an-und-für-sich*), in that and because it is for another (*für ein Anderes*) in and for itself; in other words, it exists only as recognized." Because of the paradox in its reference to itself, self-consciousness is divided between recognizing consciousness and recognized consciousness; Hegel used the word *Anerkennen,* which (in contrast to simply *Erkennen*) is distinctly social.[7] The relationship between these two types of consciousness—which actually are one— is both a conceptual and a historical process, a process that threatens to terminate and to eliminate both if a temporary balance were not achieved in a "master-slave" relation.

Hegel thus initiated a trend of interpretation that culminated, against his intentions, in the recent demand to deconstruct the notion of the self, of the subject, as mediating the world or as giving meaning to it and to our language. It should, some say, give way to a much more relative notion of the subject as a construct dependent on suprapersonal structures, for every structure, in an open or concealed manner, both gives and destroys meanings.[8] If this is true of self-consciousness, it is truer yet of memory. No memory, not even the most intimate and personal, can be isolated from the social context, from the language and the symbolic system molded by the society over centuries.

We should not, therefore, abandon the concept of collective memory,

6. Descartes made the "I think therefore I am"—*sum res cogitans*—be it a judgment or a performative—into an attribute of a substance (thought). Descartes assumes without proof or any argument that this one-time act of self-consciousness is identical to a *person* with all its contents and continuity; among its contents is the concept of God. Only out of such an assumption can Descartes reconstruct the world destroyed previously by the "malignant spirit." For Leibniz, the self is a monad, implying by virtue of its very definition all its "states." Kant, who identifies the unity of consciousness with self-consciousness ("The I accompanies all my perceptions"), denies (much as Ryle later) that it can be treated as a substance; but it is still an isolated self.

7. Hegel, *Phänomenologie des Geistes,* ed. J. Hofmeister, *Sämtliche Werke* VI (Hamburg, 1952), pp. 141–50.

8. See Manfred Frank, *Die Unhintergehbarkeit von Individualität: Reflexionen über Subjekt, Person und Individuum aus Anlass ihrer 'postmodernem' Toterklärung* (Frankfurt am Main, 1986).

but must reformulate the relationship between collective memory and the individual act of personal remembering. The following analogy may help. Modern linguistics has developed the fundamental distinction, first introduced by the Swiss linguist de Saussure, between "language" (*langue*) and "speech" (*parole*). Language is a system of symbols and the rules of their functioning: the inventory of phonemes, words, letters, rules of declension and syntactic rules available at all times to the speaker. Yet a language does not exist as an independent abstraction; it exists in that it is instantiated in every actual act of speech. And because every such act differs from the next even where its linguistic components are completely identical, every act of speech also changes the language in some way.[9]

This distinction should be useful in the attempt to define collective memory. The latter, like "language," can be characterized as a system of signs, symbols, and practices: memorial dates, names of places, monuments and victory arches, museums and texts, customs and manners, stereotype images (incorporated, for instance, in manners of expression), and even language itself (in de Saussure's terms). The individual's memory—that is, the act of remembering—is the instantiation of these symbols, analogous to "speech"; no act of remembering is like any other. The point of departure and frame of reference of memory is the system of signs and symbols that it uses.

It is noteworthy that the word *zikaron* or *zekher* (memory) in the infancy of the Hebrew language—and its analog in the infancy of many languages—incorporates both meanings. Alongside the subjective meaning (memory as a mental act)—"Yet did not the chief butler remember (*ve-lo zakhar*) Joseph, but forgot him" (Gen. 40:23)—we also find the objective sense—"this is my name forever, and this is my memorial (*zikhri*) unto all generations" —(Exod. 17:14). Here "memory" is a synonym for "name" or "letter";[10] at times it is difficult to distinguish between the two meanings. The word denoting the masculine gender in Hebrew (*zakhar*) and in Aramaic is etymologically related to memory (*zekher*), as we might expect of a patriarchal society in which "nation," "community," or "assembly," is always exclusive of women.[11] The male alone (*zakhar*) constitutes the memory (*zekher*).

---

9. Ferdinand de Saussure, *Cours de linguistique générale* (Paris, 1916); 4th ed. (Paris, 1949), ed. Charles Bally and Albert Sechehaye; English trans. Wade Baskin, *Course in General Linguistics* (New York, 1959).

10. See, for example, Exod. 13:9; 13:17; Josh. 2:7. In Deut. 24:22 the remembering action *is* "memory."

11. See, for example, Exod. 19:15.

Again in analogy to language, which encompasses relatively closed regions of professional or status-related languages of different groups, collective memory preserves symbols and monuments that no longer "remind" most members of a society of anything. If language can be consciously manipulated,[12] all the more so collective memory: it is not an anonymous-organic development that led to the circumstance that all of Napoleon's victories and not a single defeat are still memorialized in the names of the streets of Paris: Wagram and Marengo, Jena and Austerlitz, Borodino and Aboukir. In the latter, we are presumably called upon "to remember" the continental war against the Turks alone, rather than Nelson's victory.

But the analogy between language and memory is not seamless. We cannot distinguish unmediated and mediated levels of language, whereas collective memory is, in a sense, direct and unmediated in part, namely when individuals recall socially significant events they experienced. A common experience may be shared by a generation.[13] Although here, too, memory is assisted by signs, symbols, and meanings, some of which have received public valorization, we can nonetheless speak of the *relative* absence of mediation. On the other hand, personal memory—as first shown by Augustine of Hippo—is likewise never pure memory. Most of our personal memories are, in that they are, also the memory of memories.[14]

Indeed, Augustine provided Western literature with the first in-depth analysis of memory as related to knowledge, desire, and personal identity. Like Plato, Augustine saw in every piece of knowledge an act of recall (*anamnesis*); but the Platonic remembrance is that of pure and timeless forms, not of temporal constructs. In the view of Augustine, we remember first and foremost states of our soul, that is, of internal, time-bound events. Wherefore the experience of memory is also a measure of time (time is not merely, as Aristotle believed, "the measure of motion"). The past is the remembered present, just as the future is the anticipated present: memory is always derived from the *present* and from the contents of the soul at present.

This, though expressed in a sociological idiom, was also the fundamental insight of the French-Jewish sociologist Maurice Halbwachs.

12. See, for example, Viktor Klemperer, *"LTI" Die Unbewältigte Sprache; aus dem Notizbuch einen Philologen* (Darmstadt, 1966).

13. Peter Loewenberg, "The Psychohistorical Origins of the Nazi Youth Cohort," *American Historical Review*, vol. 76/5 (1971): pp. 1457–1502; Karl Mannheim, *Ideology and Utopia: An Introduction to the Sociology of Knowledge*, trans. Louis Wirth and Edward Shils (New York, 1936).

14. Aurelius Augustinus, *Confessiones*, X, 10,17; X, 16,14.

Students of historical consciousness cannot afford to overlook his work; he was the first to treat collective memory systematically. Halbwachs stressed the link between collective and personal memory and contrasted both to the historical memory—that is, reconstruction of the past by historians whose craft leads them to deviate from, or to question, accepted perceptions.[15] Both personal and collective memory are primarily a projection of the present and its structure, composed of contents and symbols from here and now. Collective memory is, almost by definition, a "monumental" history in the Nietzschean sense—and it needs the "plastic power" of the collective to keep it alive.[16] The historian demands that we ignore the present and its meanings as much as possible, that we avoid anachronisms and the tendency to "project our concepts on the conditions of the past."[17] Collective memory, by contrast, is completely insensitive to the differences between periods and "qualities of time"; its time is monochromatic; its interests are throughout topocentric. People, events, and historic institutions of the past serve as prototypes for the collective memory; none of them are recognized by their uniqueness.

Halbwachs, however, does not always refrain from hypostatizing the collective memory, even though he is aware that only the individual remembers *sensu stricto*. The tendency to ascribe an independent existence to collective mentality, to the "spirit of the nation," or to language itself, which thinks, as it were, by means of the individual, is clearly a romantic heritage. It ignores the fact that every change in language or in the symbolic system and functions that comprise the cognitive organization of the world (whether in high or local folk culture) begins with the speaking, acting, recognizing individual. Halbwachs, like Durkheim, was aware that only the individual thinks or remembers; nevertheless, he (like Durkheim or the members of the *Annales* school to this day) endows the collective memory with attributes that transcend the concrete historical narrative.

Halbwachs ignores the fact that the historical narrative—the historian's finished creation, or part of it—may itself become an integral part of the collective memory, like the Scriptures or Homer. Now you may argue that historiography, or any type of historic reasoning before the

15. Maurice Halbwachs, *La mémoire collective* (Paris, 1950), pp. 35–79, particularly p. 74; cf. also J. Assman, "Kollektives Gedächtnis und kulturelle Identität," in Jan Assmann and Tonio Hölscher, eds., *Kultur und Gedächtnis* (Frankfurt am Main, 1988), pp. 9–19.

16. See Friedrich Nietzsche's essay "Vom Nutzen und Nachteil der Historie für das Leben," in *Werke,* ed. Karl Schlechta (1874: München, 1960), vol. 1.

17. Cf. chapter 2, n. 14.

onset of historicism and the professionalization of history, was rather naive and much closer to the collective memory, while historiography since the nineteenth century became critical, reflective, and very conscious of the uniqueness of times and periods; wherefore Halbwachs's attribution to collective memory of characteristics of precritical historiography (such as Christian typological thought) is significant and telling. This it is, but the transition from precritical historiography to historicism, however revolutionary, was not altogether sudden. Several indications of its coming can be discerned within the presumably naive historical consciousness that preceded it, including the distinction between one "spirit of the time" and another (*qualitas temporum* in the medieval language).[18] And even ancient authors were aware of varying linguistic uses: "before time in Israel, when a man went to enquire of God, thus he spoke, Come, and let us go to the seer: for he that is now called a Prophet was before time called a Seer" (I Sam. 9:9). The poet, Cicero tells us, may use linguistic archaism.[19]

On the other hand, even the modern historian, whose calling it is to do so, seldom abandons the horizon of his collective memory altogether, because he does not hasten to destroy social norms, least of all those he is unaware of. More often than not the historian's writing reflects the past images shared by his larger community—people of his generation and location, images he embellishes and endows with scholarly respectability.

In order, therefore, to refrain from postulating an unbridgeable gap between collective memory and the recording of history, and at the same time not to blur the differences between them, we need an additional interpretative dynamic construct to explain how the second arises *out* of the first. Unlike the relationship between "language" and "speech"—and even in contradiction to it—reflection on the contents of collective memory gives rise to increasing *freedom* in their individual instantiation. In other words, the more a culture permits conscious changes and variations of the narrator in the contents, symbols, and structures of collective memory, the more complex and less predictable the narrative of history becomes. The liturgical incantations of the list of tribal leaders in a sacred ceremony differ in kind from the poetry of

18 See Funkenstein, *Theology and the Scientific Imagination*, pp. 202–89, and chapter 2 on historical facts below.

19. Cicero, *De oratore* III, 153. Earlier, Aristarchus of Samos formulated the basic interpretative rule that Homer should be explained by Homer alone. See Rudolf Pfeiffer, *History of Classical Scholarship from the Beginnings to the End of the Hellenistic Age* (Oxford, 1968), pp. 225–30.

Homer or the narrative of the Book of Judges; and both again differ from the Book of Kings or Herodotus. I introduce the term "historical consciousness," in this precise meaning, as such a dynamic heuristic construct—the degree of creative freedom in the use of interpretation of the contents of collective memory. This degree differs at different times in the same culture or at different social environments at any given time within the same culture.

Halbwachs's ideas were recently revived by Yosef Hayim Yerushalmi in his fascinating book on Jewish historiography and collective memory. He, too, confronts historiography with collective memory, and both of these with the work of historical interpretations since the beginning of the *Wissenschaft des Judentums* in the nineteenth century. His point of departure is the question why historiography virtually disappeared from the Jewish culture between Josephus Flavius and the nineteenth century, even though it was saturated with historical memories, despite the fact that as early as the Scriptures, liturgical memory was established in the command to "remember," *Zakhor*.[20] The short outbreak of historiographic creativity in the seventeenth century, he says, was an exception. And, he argues, the interest in history was never identical to the historical memory. Until the nineteenth century, Jews were never interested in history *qua* history. Political events of their own time did not seem important to the Jews in the Diaspora. The Scriptures served them as an archetypical pattern for all events in the present, for themselves and for the generations after them. Paradoxically, it was at the beginning of Jewish studies, when historical consciousness and historical research became the backbone of the new methodical study of Judaism, that the split occurred between critical historical consciousness and collective memory.

HISTORICAL CONSCIOUSNESS

Awareness of history in Jewish culture and its environment is also the explicit subject of this book. My points of disagreement with Yerushalmi's perspectives are a quick way to summarize the unifying themes underlying the essays collected here.

First, lacking the mediating category of historical consciousness (which is not at all confined to historiography proper), Yerushalmi, like Halbwachs before him, inevitably polarizes the contrast between his-

20. Yosef Hayim Yerushalmi, *Zakhor: Jewish History and Jewish Memory* (Seattle, 1982). On the commandment to remember, which he rightly stresses, cf. A. Momigliano, *Essays in Ancient and Modern Historiography* (Middletown, 1977), pp. 179–204.

torical narrative and "collective memory." It is my contention that, with or without historiography proper, creative thinking about history—past and present—never ceased. Jewish culture was and remained formed by an acute historical *consciousness,* albeit different at different periods. Put differently, Jewish culture never took itself for granted.

Second, the Jewish historical consciousness articulated, in endless variations, the perception of the distinctness of Israel. Polemical and apologetical exigencies, together with awareness of new cultures, sharpened this perception. A more secularized age then translated it from a divine, transcendent premise and promise into an immanent-historical vocabulary. To concentrate on the liturgical-collective memory only means to lose sight of this main theme of the Jewish historical reasoning, an incessant astonishment at one's own existence.

Third, historical consciousness and collective memory were never completely alien to each other, not even in the nineteenth and twentieth century. On the contrary; then as before, thinking about history reflected the moods and sentiments of the community in which this thinking took place.

A new type of historical images emerged, in antiquity, out of collective memories: it consisted not only in a reminder of the past in order to forge a collective identity and to maintain it, but in the attempt to understand the past, to question its meaning. That historical consciousness in this precise sense developed first and primarily in ancient Israel and in Greece is, I shall argue in the third essay, not a coincidence: both cultures saw their origins in historical rather than mythical times; both preserved a memory of relatively recent origins, preceded by a nomadic prehistory ("A wandering Aramaean was my father" even became a liturgical formula).

To ancient or primitive societies, in which antiquity or a long pedigree makes for a true aristocracy, youth is a sign of inferiority, and a memory of youth calls for compensatory elements, all the more so if this memory of youth was coupled with a memory of slavery and of otherwise low social status. Israel compensated for its sense of youth with the conviction of being a nation chosen by a monogamous god as his only family: Israel is God's "territory" and "property," God takes an active part in Israel's fortunes. The sense of a *recent* beginning in historical times and the consciousness of chosenness, of distinction among others, albeit older nations, are intertwined throughout the Bible.

Greeks, too, suffered from such a sense of youth, and admired—as we are told both in Herodotus and in Plato's *Timaeus*—civilizations older and richer than theirs, such as Egypt's. Greeks, too, compensated for this sense of inferiority in some respects with a sense of superiority to others: theirs was not a cultural or religious but a political superiority. They were distinguished from the bulk of enslaved Oriental nations by their freedom, a freedom possible only in the framework of the *polis*.[21]

Both cultures, the Israelite and the Greek, developed historiography into a high, reflexive art. To say that the aim of the one was to endow history with "meaning" while the aim of the other was to detect "causes" is somewhat misleading: causes and meaning are present in both. "Meaning" in the biblical sense is the work of providence in history; in the Greek sense, it is the uncovering of those mechanisms of human society that are always the same, as human nature is always the same. What Greek historiography—or, for that matter, Greek science—articulated for the first time is the ability to "stand aside" and observe without overtly taking sides, to distinguish between the *questio facti* and the *questio iuris*.

Awareness of the unity of history as a whole also has its dual origin in Israel and in Greece. The image of historical *time* as well-defined historical "periods," originated in the Jewish apocalyptic literature. The apocalyptic literature, whether sectarian (such as the Dead Sea Scrolls) or not, viewed this "world" (αἰών) as a temporary span of time, beginning with the sin of Adam and culminating in cosmic destruction, and an entirely new world to which only a few selected souls would escape. It viewed the present as being on the verge of the end of days, and sought proof of this both in the structure and the course of history, a structure revealed both through an idiosyncratic-actualizing "decoding of Scriptures," and in apocalypses proper, that is, prophecies after the event. This is the subject of the fourth essay. The image of the theaters of history—i.e., historical *space*—as a whole whose parts interact, originated in the philosophical and historical thought of Hellenistic-Roman antiquity. Much as the Stoa saw the entire world as one state (*cosmopolis*), so also Polybius wrote the history of the *oikoumene*, the history of the settled world, as a gradual process of the unification of the world under the best and most balanced of governments.[22]

21. Charles N. Cochrane, *Christianity and Classical Culture: A Study of Thought and Action from Augustus to Augustine,* 2nd edition (New York, 1957), esp. ch. 12.

22. Polybius, *Historiae,* I, 4.1–2 (ed. F. Hultsch). See Kurt von Fritz, *The Theory of the Mixed Constitution in Antiquity: A Critical Analysis of Polybius' Political Ideas* (New York, 1954), pp. 184–219; F. W. Walbank, *Polybius* (Sather Classical Lectures 42, Berkeley and Los Angeles, 1972), pp. 130–56, esp. 131–37.

These two images of the unity of history, the temporal and the spatial, were integrated in the thought of some Christian Fathers from the
third century onwards. From early on, the Christian apologetics faced
several almost contradictory tasks: facing the Jews, they had to prove
the difference of the New from the Old Testament; facing pagans outside and heretics within their own ranks (Marcion, Gnosis), they had
to prove the continuity between the New and Old Testaments, as the
continuous revelation of the one God. And then: toward its own members, the Church insisted that they must live in the pagan culture and
its institutions as "resident aliens" (*peregrini*),[23] while toward the imperial masters it developed a veritable political theology, according to
which the Empire and Christianity were and are destined for each
other.

Out of these contrasting perspectives grew various modes of interpreting history. They are, in part, the subject of the fifth and sixth essay.
From the apocalyptic literature, Christian writers borrowed the method
of "decoding" old prophecies to make them refer in detail to the present. They likewise developed the typological reading of history—identifying institutions, events, and persons of the Old Testament as prefigurations of their parallels in the New Testament. They appropriated the
history of Israel until the coming of Christ in that they viewed it as a
gradual "preparation": God's providential acts, they maintained, are
"accommodated" to the different capacity of humans at different times
to perceive and to follow them. Since Eusebius of Caesarea, profane
history, the history of the Empire, was likewise so appropriated as an
evangelical preparation.

Contrasting the Jewish (or Christian) and the Greek perception of
history, some scholars characterize the one as "linear," the other as "cyclical." Neither is the case. Where and when do we find, for the first
time, an explicit insistence on the uniqueness of historical events—or
on the uniqueness of history as a whole? Perhaps not before Augustine.
Against Origenes's doctrine of subsequent worlds (aeons) emerging
each after the destruction of the other, in each of which the redeemer
appears again, Augustine held with Paul that Christ came but once and
for all times.[24] If this is true of the central event in history, it is likewise

---

23. Tertullian, *Apologeticus* 19, 7 CCSLI, 121; Loeb Classical Library 250, p. 98:
peregrinandum est in historias et litteras orbis.

24. Augustine, *De civitate Dei* XII, 21 CCSL 48, p. 376. Cf. Origenes, *Contra Ceslum*
II, 3, 4; ed. Kötzschau I, p. 338; *De principiis* IV, p. 68 f., ed. Klostermann, GCS Orig.
V, p. 119. Clearly, Augustine slightly distorted the views of Origenes.

true of the entire history of the "city of God wandering (*peregrinans*) on earth," a history that unfolds "like a grand symphony."[25]

Augustine's emphasis on the uniqueness of history may also be linked to his notion of time. The Aristotelian notion of time was that of a physicist—time measures external, repeated processes, such as the motion of the sphere of the fixed stars; Aristotle defines it as "the measure of motion according to the prior and posterior." To Augustine, by contrast, time measures both motion and rest— it is not the index of motion, but of experience and memory, much like Bergson's *durée*.[26] Augustine's time is the internal time: as experience, it refers not to repetitive events or processes, but rather that which is distinct by its novelty and uniqueness. Kant may have been the first to unite both traditions of the perceptions of time.

I shall try to show how these ways of historical thinking in Christianity—the typological and the accommodative—were taken out of their original, purely exegetical context in the twelfth century to become modes of interpreting recent and present history. Until the twelfth century, Christian Europe did not view present events as significant events within the *sacra historia:* from early Christianity to the second coming of Christ, to his second "presence" (παρουσία), the world was deemed to be in its sixth age, an age in which all that happens is that it "grows old." Theologians and historians in the twelfth century discovered that the events of their time were significant, worthy of "interpretation" no less than the events of the Old and New Testaments. No century in the Middle Ages was richer and more abundant in historical speculation and historiographic creativity than the twelfth.

In ancient times as in the Middle Ages, the writing of history— whether sacred or secular history—was guided by the implicit assumption that the historical fact is immediately given: it does not need to be *interpreted* in order to be meaningful except at the deeper theological level (*spiritualis intelligentia*). The eyewitness thus seemed to them the most reliable historian, as I try to argue in the fourth essay.

Somewhere between the sixteenth and eighteenth century, a revolution occurred that was no less radical than the concurrent scientific revolution. It brought about a new *contextual* understanding of history, in which historical fact became "understood" or meaningful only through the context in which it is embedded. This applies to both historical texts and any other monument of the past. The historian must

25. Augustine, *Epistulae* 138 I, 5, ed. Goldbacher, CSEL 44 p. 130 (*veluti magnum carmen . . . excurrat*).
26. See n. 14.

reconstruct the context, and the reconstruction is always linked to his or her "point of view" in the present.

This contextual perception was anticipated to some extent in the medieval concept of accommodation mentioned above, in that it also deems some institutions "fit" or "unfit" for their time, and distinguishes periods according to different "qualities of time" (*qualitas temporis*). But only in the seventeenth century was the idea transferred from the religious domain to the secular. Not until the nineteenth century did history become the primary discipline of all human sciences.

Such, in rough outlines, seems to me the emergence of historical consciousness in Europe. The Jewish historical consciousness was both part of it and different from it in important ways.

JEWISH HISTORICAL CONSCIOUSNESS, TRADITIONAL AND MODERN

It is indeed a fact that from the canonization of the Scriptures until the nineteenth century, Judaism lacked a continuous historiographic tradition. The books of the Hasmoneans constituted an exception. Flavius Josephus wrote for a foreign audience; a fragmentary Latin paraphrase (the Josiphon) was translated only in the tenth century into Hebrew (the Book of Josiphon). Yerushalmi explains this absence of historiography in that the scriptural history provided the *tana'im*, *amora'im*, and generations after them with more than enough archetypical patterns to perceive the events of their time. These generations, at least until Ibn Verga's *The Rod of Judah*, saw no specific significance or identity in the events of their time. They viewed the characters of the Scriptures—another sign of typological perception—as ubiquitous.[27]

But up to the eleventh century, historical conceptions in the Jewish horizon did not differ substantially from those of Christianity in this respect. Christian historiography in antiquity, with few exceptions (such as Orosius) was likewise little more than the chronology of the Church, written to establish the "chain of tradition" or the apostolic succession. Genuine historical narratives were still relatively rare in the early Middle Ages. Most authors of annals until the eleventh century did not regard the events of the present as truly *digna memoriae* except for the history of the Church.[28] Only from the eleventh century onward do we find new attempts to link sacred and recent profane history into

27. Yerushalmi, *Zakhor*, pp. 8–10, 35–36, 47 ff., 108 n. 5.
28. Only Church historians emphasized the unbroken continuity of historiography; see chapter 2 on history as continuum.

one vision of the enfoldment of a divine plan. And while Jews did see in their present humiliation in dispersion a definite divine intention to purge Israel from its sins, details mattered only little—they but added more of the same. Profane history per se was of no interest, even the profane history of biblical times. Rabbi David Kimchi informs us that "the chronicles of the Kings of Israel were recorded in a book. But this book did not join the Sacred Scriptures because the [northern] Kingdom of Israel did not last, and also in the future only the kingship of the house of David will be resurrected."[29]

Moreover, the secular historiography in Europe was, until the nineteenth century, first and foremost political historiography; it focused on the clear bearers of political power, on rulers and their actions. Here the communities of Israel, in the Diaspora and in Israel "in Arabian chains," saw themselves as political objects rather than subjects. Wherefore the political events of their own history as it developed did not seem to them "worthy of memory": it was not their history.

Yet despite this—and perhaps because of it—the medieval Jews were not inclined to the typological vision and extreme typological interpretations that were common in their Christian environment. In emphasizing the typological element in traditional Jewish historical consciousness, Yerushalmi exaggerates:[30] it exists principally in the analogy between the pristine time of the united Kingdom and the messianic period. We find only few typologies in Jewish liturgy (The Ninth of Av, Purim)—in contrast to their abundance in the Christian literature. A famous exception, the subject of the eighth essay in this book, proves the rule: Ramban (Nachmanides) developed a detailed typological vision of history in his exegetical works. But barely anyone imitated his method, in spite of the immense popularity of his commentary.

Though historiography hardly existed in the traditional Jewish literature, and even if the midrash provided a paradigm for completely ahistorical interpretations, a modicum of historical awareness existed none-

29. In the introduction to his commentary of the *Book of Chronicles,* he explains why they omit continuous references to the Israelite kings. Cf. Sara Japhet, *The Ideology of the Book of Chronicles and Its Place in Biblical Thought* (Jerusalem, 1977), pp. 264–77, esp. n. 169.

30. As does also Jacob Neusner, *Judaism and Christianity in the Age of Constantine* (Chicago and London, 1987), pp. 29–58. Neusner postulates—but does not prove—that *Genesis Rabba* was seen as a typological blueprint for all subsequent history. Cf. chapter 4, "History and Typology." Attention should, however, be given to his suggestion that many facets of the Jewish messianic imagery came in reaction to the ascendancy of Christianity.

theless elsewhere—namely in the domain of legal reasoning. I do not mean Moses Maimonides's historical-accommodative interpretation of the "reasons for the commandments," the subject of the tenth essay, but rather the halakhic discussion itself throughout the ages. Here we find clear distinctions of time and place throughout: distinctions concerning customs and their context, exact knowledge of the place and time of the messengers and teachers of *halakha*, the estimated monetary value of coins mentioned in sources, the significance of institutions of the past. In the realm of halakha, every "event" was worthy of preserving, including minority opinions.

Once again we should not be in haste to see in all this an exclusively Jewish achievement. Interpreters of Roman law since antiquity paid careful attention to the *circumstantiae* of legal texts, their period, their location, and the usage of words that changed over the periods; their technique may have begun in rhetoric and philology. We recall that Aristarchus of Samos demanded that one "understand Homer with the aid of Homer alone,"[31] and that pagan polemicists (such as Porphyrius) used the sense of anachronisms to question the authenticity of Jewish and Christian sacred writings. The degree of historical awareness of the commentators and creators of the halakha was approximately the same as the degree of historical awareness of the interpreters of Roman law in the Middle Ages prior to the development of the *mos gallicus*. To be more precise: the historical awareness of the sages of the halakha was restricted mainly to *realia* incorporated in rabbinical law and to questions of authenticity (such as the authenticity of the Zohar).[32]

I do not mean to say that legal reasoning was ipso facto historical reasoning. Some of its elements enhanced differential awareness of historical circumstances; others did not. An impediment to a true sense of anachronisms was the ubiquity of legal opinions: the legal discussion was a discussion across generations, in which all participants, past and present, met on one level of continuous presence. The homiletic imagination expressed this ubiquity when it made even some of Abraham's ancestors into heads of academies.[33]

31. See n. 19. Cf., for example, T. Y. *Kiddushin,* ch. 1, 5.
32. See chapter 8, n. 17. (Emden, as before him Jehuda of Modena).
33. Yerushalmi, *Zakhor,* p. 138, n. 21 (*Genesis Rabba* 46, 4; 63, 7). The tendency to see all of history from the vantage point of the school is nowhere more pronounced than in the remark, in *Echa Rabbati* 2, "Bar Cochba said: I am the king messiah. The sages sent [a messenger to him] to see whether he could judge by smell [*meriack veda'in;* a realization of the metaphor in Isaiah 11:31]. When they realized that he could not, they killed him."

Another facet of legal reasoning relevant to the perception of history, to its uses and abuses, was the deliberate employment of legal historical fictions. One such conscious fiction appears in the very beginning of the Sayings of the Fathers: "Moses received the Torah from Sinai and passed it on to Joshua, and Joshua passed it on to the elders, and the elders to the prophets, and the prophets to the members of the Great Knesset." And where are the priests? Are not priests those whom the Scriptures designate to be the authorized commentators on the law— "And thou shalt come unto the priests and Levites, and unto the judge that shall be in those days" (Deut. 17:9)? But the interests of the *tana'im* required a line of tradition of lay interpreters of the law.

Another example is no less instructive:

On that same day [that Rabban Gamliel was demoted from the presidency at the court of Yavne] Yehuda, an Ammonite convert, came and asked to join the congregation. Rabbi Gamliel said to him: "You are forbidden, as it is said: 'No Ammonite or Moabite shall join the congregation of God.'" Rabbi Joshua [b. Chananya] said to him: "Do Moab and Ammon remain in their place? Sanherib came and mixed up all the nations, as it is said: 'And I will remove the boundaries between nations and ruin their reserves.'"[34]

The time was shortly after the destruction of the Temple. Yavne tried to impose its legal authority and reduce to a minimum the internal barriers between groups—such as the demand for ethnic purity required by priests so as to enable them to intermarry with nonpriestly families. "The priests agree to create distance but not to bring closer."[35] For the sake of removing barriers, Rabbi Joshua b. Chananya was willing to ignore explicit scriptural evidence, such as the demand of Ezra to divorce Moabite and Ammonite women—an event which Joshua b. Chananya surely knew occurred after Sanherib.

Over and beyond these examples the basic fact remains plain: normative Judaism did not preserve a continuous record of political events in the form of chronicles or historical studies. It did, however, preserve a continuous and chronological record of legal innovations, and until the nineteenth century, Jews viewed the raison d'être of their nation in the halakha. Innovations of halakha were genuine "historical" happenings, and the term "innovation" (*chidush*) itself indicates that every halakhic ruling had to have historical, even if fictitious, legitimation.

My main aim in this brief review is to argue that historical conscious-

34. Mishna, *Seder Toharot,* Tractate *Yadayim,* ch. 4.
35. Ibid., *Seder Nezikin, Eduyot,* chapter 8,3 (*almanat ha'issa*).

ness, throughout the ages, does not contradict collective memory, but is rather a developed and organized form of it. The same holds true of historiography proper. While it is true that during the nineteenth century historiography became professionalized and, therefore, less accessible to the reading public, it is likewise true that at the same time the historian was given a special position as a high priest of culture, responsible for the legitimation of the nation-state. Historical studies, even the most technical, often reflected the problems of identity of the nation-state and other wishes and aspirations of the society in which the historian was embedded. Alexis de Tocqueville wanted to prove the continuity of French history since the *ancien régime* and thus to restore the Revolution to French history; German historians debated whether Heinrich the Lion, Duke of Saxony, was right to refuse to participate in King Friedrich I's invasion of Italy, or whether Heinrich IV was indeed defeated by Pope Gregory VII at Canossa.

In the nation-state of the nineteenth century, "collective memory" was in part constructed by historians and found its way into society through textbooks, speeches, lectures, and symbols. Even the meta-theoretical debate over the limits and unique means of cognition of the humanities—empathetic "understanding" as opposed to causal-rational "explanation"—reflected the feeling that writing history can best be done from the inside, while in the exact sciences one does not have to be a triangle in order to prove the Pythagorean theorem. The crisis of the nation-state in and after the First World War was also a "crisis of historicism."[36]

The same holds true for Jewish studies since the nineteenth century. How deeply did the radical historicization of Judaism separate scholars from "collective" Jewish memory? Yerushalmi thought that this separation became almost total. I doubt it. The collective memory of the community in which the *Wissenschaft des Judentums* was embedded shows a high degree of consonance in their fears and aspirations. Even if we grant that the majority of traditional Jews in France, Austria, and Germany were not aware of the full scope of the achievements of the *Wissenschaft,* its results nevertheless faithfully reflected the desires and the self-image of nineteenth-century Jews craving for emancipation, the mood of the "perplexed of the times." The vast majority of German and French Jews wanted to adopt the culture of their environment and at

36. Dilthey developed the main points of his teaching prior to the First World War. Troeltsch published his book after it: Ernst Troeltsch, *Der Historismus und seine Probleme* (Tübingen, 1922).

the same time to preserve their special nature as a subculture.[37] What suited that desire more than a presentation of the history of Israel as "the history of one and the same idea—the idea of [ethical-rational,] pure monotheism?" In the consciousness of the Jews until the nineteenth century, what made them unique among the nations of the world was their difference from others: they alone had been given the revealed law, they alone are bound to observe all its precepts. Their difference secured their existence, the "eternity of Israel." While other nations are subjects to the laws and contingencies of nature, "Israel has no guiding star." The last essays in this book try to show how, in the nineteenth century, this consciousness had been turned upside down; for the generations of gradually emancipated and secularized Jews, the uniqueness of Israel came to mean its *universality*. The learned studies of historians reflected the desire of their community and at times even shaped the "language" itself. Both Geiger's *Urschrift* and the Reform prayer book—that is, both historiography and "collective memory"— reflected the very same mentality and the same image of the past that wished to view contemporary Judaism—and Judaism at all times in the past—as a liberal-bourgeois ideology open to its environment and to change. If Geiger interpreted the conflict between Sadducees and Pharisees as the clash of a national-conservative aristocracy and a democratic party open to change (of which Jesus was also an heir), only his scholarly acumen makes his interpretation more interesting for us today than the somewhat ridiculous homily in which "our forefather Jacob" appears as "an exemplary member of a municipal council" (*unser Erzvater Jacob—das Vorbild eines Stadtverordneten*).

The nation-state replaced the sacred liturgical memory with secular liturgical memory—days of remembrance, flags, and monuments. The national historian, who in the nineteenth century enjoyed the status of a cultural priest, and whose work, even professional, was still read by a wide stratum of the educated public, made the symbols concrete. It even created some of them, some almost from nothing, such as the legend of Hermann, the Cheruskian hero. A comprehensive critical study of the symbols and signs related to Jewish collective memory today, in Israel and outside it, has yet to be written. The pioneering article

37. Amos Funkenstein, "Hermann Cohen: Philosophie, Deutschtum und Judentum," in *Jahrbuch des Instituts für Deutsche Geschichte,* Beiheft 6, pp. 355–65 (Tel Aviv, 1984); David Sorkin, *The Transformation of German Jewry, 1780–1840* (New York, 1987).

by Saul Friedländer,[38] on the memorialization of the Holocaust and the revival, is a good starting point for such studies. They will, I believe, lead to the conclusion that the distance between secular Jews (or secular Israeli culture) and traditional Judaism was created not by the lack of historical knowledge and symbols, but by their alienation from texts and textual messages, the *halakha* and the *midrash*. At any rate, in the history of Zionism and the Jewish settlement of Palestine, historiography likewise reflected the accepted norms and ideals of the society it served.

This is not meant to deny the critical role of the historian in modern society or to view his critical achievements as mere lip service. On rare occasions, the historian runs against the current and combats distorted "collective" images of the past; even more rarely, he succeeds in creating a new discourse beyond his professional domain. Nevertheless, the critical argument itself can become a pattern of "collective memory," as did the Marxist or the psychoanalytical idiom. Even the most aware and critical of historians is bound by assumptions, not all of which he is fully conscious of.

The fact that the historian is always influenced by the "point of view" of time and place,[39] from which he or she cannot be altogether detached, does not necessarily impede the historical understanding. At times it adds a dimension that was entirely absent in the horizon of discourse of the period the historian wants to understand: the medieval period did not record its own economic history. Historical consciousness begins with the data of the present; the object of historical interpretation is never "completely determined," and every interpretation that does not contradict an agreed-upon factual basis adds to our "understanding."

But this is not the place to develop a comprehensive epistemology of historical interpretations. I have tried only to examine briefly the relation of historical consciousness to collective memory and historical writing, and thus to contribute to the demystification of collective entities. And I have also indicated what I believe is the main theme of historical reflection among Jews: the grounding of their uniqueness *in* an understanding of history.

38. Saul Friedländer, "Die Shoah als Element in der Konstruktion israelischer Erinnerung," *Babylon* 2 (1987): pp. 10–22.
39. See chapter 3, n. 20.

2

History, Counterhistory, and Narrative

Perceptions of Historical Fact

HISTORICAL FACTS

Dealing as we shall with thoughts about history, some preliminary remarks about the epistemological foundations of the engagement with the past are nonetheless called for. As a necessary background, let me sketch what I believe to be the ancient and medieval perception of historical facts—and how it differs radically from ours. My starting point is a famous text: the definition of history in Isidore of Seville's *Etymologies or Origins,* a book that served as nearly the only comprehensive encyclopedic reference work from the seventh to the thirteenth century.

His definition of history runs thus:

History is the narration of things done by which what was done in the past is known. The Greek word derives from "historein," meaning to see or know.

Among the ancients, nobody wrote history unless he was present and saw those matters which were to be written.[1]

Needless to say, the Greek ἰστορεῖν meant much more than "to see or recognize": it also meant to inquire and account.[2] But the bias that the eyewitness is the best historian was shared by the Greeks, and in fact was as strong a preconception, and as durable, as the assumption of the perfectly circular orbits of planets from Eudoxus to Kepler. Did Isidore—or those pondering on historical methodology before and after him—not take into account the possibility that an eyewitness be lying? Indeed they did; truth, they say, is the *proprium* of the historian as against the poet who may do with verisimilitude,[3] but, *if* truthful, the eyewitness is the best historian. It did not cross their minds that propositions about so-called historical facts may not be subsumed under the principle of excluded middle, that a historical account may be neither true nor false because the eyewitness—or for that matter, the historian—is unwillingly a captive of his own point of view. He may sincerely intend to tell the truth "wie es eigentlich gewesen" but his eyesight and account are blurred or blocked by deep cultural, even linguistic structures that bind him to his time and place. *Tertium datur.*

In other words: for ancient or medieval authors, historical facts

1. Isidore of Seville, St., *Etymologiarum sive origenum libri* XX, I, 41, 1, ed. W. M. Lindsay (Oxford, 1911: Reprint 1957). About his sources see Marie Schulz, *Die lehre von der historischen Methode bei den Geschichtsschreibern des Mittelalters* (VI–XIII.Jh.), (Berlin und Leipzig, 1909), p. 20, n. 2, and R. Schröder, "Studien zur varronischen Etymologie," *Abhandlungen der Akademie der Wissenschaften u. Literatur Mainz, Geistes-u. Sozialwiss. Klasse* 12 (Wiesbaden, 1959), esp. p. 86.

2. Karl Keuck, *Historia: Geschichte des Wortes und seine Bedeutung* (Ph.D. diss., University of Münster, 1934), pp. 12 ff; Charles N. Cochrane, *Christianity and Classical Culture: A Study of Thought and Action from Augustus to Augustine,* 2nd ed. (New York, 1957), pp. 485 ff. (refers to Heraclitus, frag. 129, and Herodotus II, 45, and discusses history as against logography). As to Isidore's use of *historia* in other contexts, cf. Funkenstein, *Heilsplan und natürliche Entwicklung. Formen der Gegenwartsbestimmung im Geschichtsdenken des hohen Mittelalters* (München, 1965), p. 187, n. 2.

3. E.g., *Cnutonis regis gestae: sive, Encomium Emmae reginae auctore Monacho Sancti Bertini. In usum scholarum ex Monumentis Germaniae historicis recudi fecit,* ed. Georgius Heinricus Pertz (Leipzig, 1955), p. 1; cf, M. Schulz, *Die Lehre,* p. 6, and there also further references. See also G. Simon, "Untersuchungen zur Topik der Widmungsbriefe mittelalterlicher Geschichtsschreibung bis zum Ende des 12. Jahrhunderts," *Archiv für Diplomatik* 4–6 (1958–60): pp. 52 ff., 73 ff. Clinging to the truth meant also writing *neque amore quisquam et sine odio* (Tacitus, *Hist.* I, 1, 3); for the original (restricted) meaning of *sine ira et otudio* see T. J. Luce, "Ancient Views on the Causes of Bias in Historial Writing," *Classical Philology* LXXXIV (1989), pp.16–31; for medieval reassertions of this *topos* see Funkenstein, *Heilsplan,* p. 188, n. 7.

were, so to say, atomic entities that are immediately perceivable and understandable, and hardly in need of interpretation. Indeed, in the medieval idiom, *sensus historicus* is synonymous to *sensus litteralis*:[4] the historical fact can in and of itself be "seen or recognized," and therefore the eyewitness is indeed the best historian—if truthful. Only on the theological level does history reveal deeper meaning, *spiritualis intelligentia*, in that the events point beyond themselves—say, Rachel and Leah "prefigure" the Church and the Synagogue, or the twelve tribes, the twelve apostles. History itself is simple—*simplex narratio gestarum*.[5] Some of this notion still echoes in the words of Jacob Burckhardt in one of his letters: "Historia scribitur ad narrandum, non ad probandum."[6]

The Roman commentator Servius, who was one of Isidore's sources, distinguished between the genre of history, which seeks to explain events, as against annals which only record them. Isidore gives up even this distinction: for him, as for the rest of the Middle Ages, annals are the ideal form of history-writing.[7] It reflects, as many authors will later say, the *ordo naturalis* of the events as against a manipulated *ordo artificialis*.[8] The demand that a historian should stick to the annalistic form remained strong even when it became a purely conventional fiction

4. Gregory the Great, MG. E pp. 1, 223; Isidore of Seville, *de ordine creaturarum*, Migne, PL 83, col 939–40: "historialiter factasunt, et intellectualiter Ecclesiae mysteria per haec designantur." Hugh of St. Victor, *Didascalicon* I, 6, 3 Migne, PL 176, col 801: "Si enim huius vocabuli [historia] significatiore largins utimur . . . non tantum rerum gestarum narrationem, sed illam primam significationem [esse didicimus]." Cf. id., *De scripturis* 3, Migne, PL 175, col. 12A; *De sacramentis,* prologus c. 4, Migne, PL 176, col 185. And even in the sixteenth and seventeenth century we read of history: "dicitur simplex, hoc est 'pura,' quoniam non habet sensum alium, nisi quem verba primo exprimunt, et in hoc differet a parabola . . . Solius tamen sacrae historiae est alios sensus admittere mysticos." Tommaso Campanella, "Historiographia, Rationalis philosophiae" p. V c. 1, ed. L. Firpo. *Tutte le opere di T. C.* (Turin, 1954) I, p. 1226. For other references see Henri de Lubac, *L'Exégèse médiévale: les quatre sens de l'criture* (Paris, 1959–1964), vol. II, pp. 425, 428, n. 6, 474.

5. Besides the references in n. 4, see P. Lehmann, "Die Heilige Einfalt," *Historisches Jahrbuch 1938* (58), p. 305 for "simplicity" as a rhetorical device, as well as Eduard Norden, *Die antike Kunstprosa: Vom VI. Jahrhundert V. Chr. bis in die Zeit der Renaissance* (Leipzig, 1915–1918: reprint, Darmstadt, 1958), vol. I, pp. 529 ff.

6. Jakob Burckhardt, *Briefe,* ed. Max Burckhardt, IV (1960), p. 130 (letter of 1863 to Wilhelm Vischer). Burckhardt evidently alludes to Quintilian, *Institutio Oratoria* X, 1, 31 ed. L. Rademacher (Leipzig, 1959) II, p. 239.

7. Keuck, *Das Wort Historia* (as above n. 2); Isidore, *Etym.* I, 44, 1: "Annales sunt res singulorum annorum. . . . Historia autem multorum annorum," etc. History, in the context of Servius, is the collection of annals.

8. M. Schulz, *Die Lehre,* pp. 104, 127–28. It relates to the question whether historians should rewrite history.

which was tearing at all the seams, for example, in the annals of Lampert of Hersfeld in the eleventh century.[9] Time and again medieval authors ask: Is it permissible to alter the "natural order" of events or the words of an older historian on your own for the sake of a point to be made? And they agree that it is highly undesirable except, perhaps, for stylistic corrections.

Now, against this perception of historical facts as self-evident—a perception shared, I repeat, by ancient and medieval authors alike—stands our modern perception of history, beginning with the "historical revolution" of the sixteenth and seventeenth century. In this modern perception, no historical fact is in and of itself meaningful: only its context endows a historical fact with meaning and significance. The context of historical facts is not at all given: it must be reconstructed by the historian from other facts. This is a veritable hermeneutical circle.[10] The eyewitness is certainly no longer regarded as the best historian, ever captive of "point of view" and time. So is the historian, but the historian is aware of it, aware that every generation reinterprets the past with its biases but also with its new canon of fruitful questions.

The origins of this new, contextual mode of understanding belong to many disciplines, though historiography was not one of them. The lawyer of the sixteenth century who extolled national or even local customs against the *lois écrites* (read: Roman law) began arguing that Roman legal institutions were meaningful and functional only in the original context of their setting: "Quid hoc edicto praetoris?" was Cujas's standard question.[11] From a historical interpretation of Roman law, the humanistic jurisprudence advanced to the historical reconstruction of post-Roman legal institutions—the origins and the career of "feudal" law. Again, classical philologists paid ever greater attention to the Roman *realia* to explain their texts; some used their new acumen for po-

9. Lampert of Hersfeld, *Annales,* ed. Oswald Holder-Egger, *Lamperti monachi Hersfeldensis opera,* MG SS in usu schol., 1894. cf Isidore, *Etym* I, 44, 1 (Annales).

10. For the following, see Funkenstein, *Theology,* pp. 205–10 and id., "Gesetz und Geschichte. Zur historisiernden Hermeneutik bei Moses Maimonides und Thomas von Aquin," *Viator* I (1970), pp. 147–78, and chapter 5 (and n. 47).

11. Wilhelm Dilthey, "Weltanschauung und Analyse des Menschen seit Renaissance und Reformation," in *Gesammeltte Schriften,* vol. 2 (Stuttgart, 1961), pp. 11 ff, 113; Donald R. Kelley, *Foundation of Modern Historical Scholarship: Language, Law, and History in the French Renaissance* (New York, 1970), pp. 106–112; Julian M. Franklin, *Jean Bodin and the Sixteenth-Century Revolution in the Methodology of Law and History* (New York, 1963), esp. pp. 48–58 (Hotman); John Greville Agard Pocock, *The Ancient Constitution and Feudal Law: A study of the English Historical Thought in the Seventeenth Century* (Cambridge, 1957), esp. ch. 1.

lemical political purposes, beginning with Valla's deconstruction of the *Donatio Constantini*.[12] Biblical criticism was likewise a mighty contributor to the newly emerging historical consciousness. Protestants insisted on relying on Scriptures, but without the interpretive mediation of the Church—*sola scriptura*. Nothing underscores the difference between their attitude to the Scriptures and that of Catholicism better than the words of Augustine, who once claimed that he would not even believe the Evangelist unless moved to do so by the authority of the Holy Church ("*nisi auctoritas Sanctae Ecclesiae me commoverit*").[13] Catholic intellectuals like Richard Simon were eager to show that the Bible is far from being self-explanatory.

By the beginning of the seventeenth century it became a truism to ridicule those who "form their notions of ancient matters according to the conditions of their own times" ("de rebus antiquissimis secundum sui temporis conditionem notiones forment").[14] Ancient and medieval historiography, literature, and art had by contrast no idea and consequently no fear of anachronisms. Thus, in the eleventh century, the hagiographer Rimbert lets his hero, Anskar, have a vision in which he beholds his savior "clothed as a Jew" (*more Iudaico vestitus*[15])—needless to say, a contemporary Jew. Only sometimes, when it comes to distinguish periods of faith, do we find some notion of institutions that are obsolete: "aptum fuit primis temporibus sacrificium, nunc non est ita," says Augustine.[16] To the Christian period *ante legem* corresponds the Moslem period of ignorance (*Jahiliyya*),[17] and Maimonides tells us that

12. Kelley, *Foundations*, pp. 38 ff.

13. Augustine, *Contra Epistulam Manichaei* 5, CSEL 25 p. 1971.22. Heiko Augustinus Oberman, *The Harvest of Medieval Theology: Gabriel Biel and Late Medieval Nominalism* (Cambridge, Mass., 1963), gave it too strong a psychological interpretation. Lucien Paul Victor Febvre (*Le problème de l'incroyance au XVIe siècle: la religion de Rabelais* [Paris, 1942]; English trans. Beatrice Gottlieb, *The Problem of Unbelief in the Sixteenth Century: The Religion of Rabelais* ([Cambridge, Mass., 1982], p. 117) did not notice that Postel's similar argument stems from Augustine.

14. Quoted in Ludwig Diestel, *Geschichte des Alten Testaments in der christlichen kirche* (Jena, Mauke, 1869), p. 463. For further examples, see Funkenstein, *Theology*, pp. 209–10. The history of the notion of anachronism has not as yet been written, but see Thomas M. Greene, "History and Anachronism," in *Literature and History: Theoretical Problems and Russian Case Studies*, ed. Gary Saul Morson (Stanford, Calif.: Stanford University Press, 1986), pp. 205–20; Thomas M. Green, *In the Light of Troy: Imitation and Discovery in Renaissance Poetry* (New Haven, 1982), pp. 37 ff.

15. See chapter 6, n. 12.

16. See chapter 4, Ibn Ezra.

17. Ignac Goldziher, *Vorlesungen über den Islam* (Heidelberg, 1910). The Pauline distinction *ante legem, sub lege, sub gratia* has its parallel in the Jewish tradition. Cf. chapter 3, n. 18; also note 24 (Censorinus) below.

"had someone come to the people in those times [of Abraham] and said: worship God with prayer rather than sacrifices, it would be as if someone came today and said: worship God with meditation rather than prayer."[18] But for theological-historical speculations, no real sense of the *qualitas temporum* develops in the Middle Ages—though the expression is medieval.[19]

The first modern historical thinkers to speak explicitly about the "point of view" of each period—to emphasize the boundedness of the historical perspective to time and society—were the Germans Gattereis and Chladenius in the eighteenth century.[20] They seem to have borrowed the term from Leibniz's monadology. Earlier in the century, Giambattista Vico had already built the many methodical impulses into an impressive "new science" of historical reasoning, a science aware of its own unique mode of interpretation.[21] The historical fact ceased to be self-evident: it became *eo ipso*, in and of itself, interpretation, meaningless without being embedded in its context.

HISTORY AS A CONTINUUM

These sharp distinctions between the perception of historical facts before and after the sixteenth and seventeenth century carry yet further. Isidore of Seville's definition of history, the starting point of our reflections, continues by saying, "haec disciplina ad grammaticiam pertinet, quia quidquid dignum memoriae est, litteris mandatur."[22] Indeed, if the eyewitness is the best historian because the historical facts are self-explanatory, then it is reasonable to assume that significant events never evaded notice and were always recorded. Before you accuse me of reading too much into Isidore's terse remark, consider

18. See chapter 5 on political theory.

19. In the exegetical tradition, e.g., Hildebertus Cenomanensis, *Sermo in Septuagesima*, Migne, PL 177, col. 1073. A similar phrase is *ratio temporum*, e.g., Beda Venerabilis, *Super acta apostolorum*, Migne, PL 92, col. 953 (not in the usual, computistic sense). In the legal tradition cf. D. Kelley, "Klio and the Lawyers," *Medievalia et humanistica*, 5 (1975), pp. 24–49.

20. Reinhart Koselleck, *Vergangene Zukunft: zur Semantik geschichtlicher Zeiten* (1. Aufl. Frankfurt am Main, 1979), pp. 176–207, esp. 183 ff. Peter H. Reill, *The German Enlightenment and the Rise of Historicism* (Berkeley, 1975), pp. 125 ff. (Gesichtskreis); idem., "History and Hermeneutics in the Aufklärung: The Thought of Johann Christoph Gatterer," *Journal of Modern History* 45 (1973), pp. 24–51; Funkenstein, *Theology*, p. 108 (Leibniz).

21. Funkenstein, *Theology*, pp. 202–205, 279–89.

22. Isidore, *Etym.* I, 42, 2; other references: Schulz, *Methode*, pp. 66 ff.

how powerful this notion has been since antiquity—the notion namely that "history" in the sense of *historia rerum gestarum* is coextensive with "history" as *res gestae,* that historiography is an objective continuum of eyewitness reports since the dawn of human society. Later we shall see that the author of the biblical Book of Chronicles entertained the idea of the continuity of history-writing by prophets.[23] The famous Roman encyclopedist Varro is quoted by Censorinus to have divided human history into three periods (*tria discrimina temporum*):

First from the beginning of man to the first cataclysm, which, because of ignorance, is called "adelon"; second from the first cataclysm to the first olympiad, which is named "mythical" because much of it is told in fables; third from the first olympiad to us, which is called "historical" since things that happened in it are contained in true histories.[24]

"Historical time" is thought of as a continuum of true records, a chain of genuine traditions. Such a chain, an Egyptian priest tells Solon in Plato's *Timaeus* 21*e*–25*d,* existed in Egypt but not in Greece; because of natural catastrophes the Greeks forgot their origins as "a magnificent noble race" and were cast into renewed childhood. They therefore lack a collective memory. In Egypt, by contrast, every "beautiful or interesting" event was kept on record in the temples.[25] Flavius Josephus, the historian of Jewish antiquities and of the revolt against Rome, alluded to this passage when he explained the inferiority of Greek historiography compared to the Near Eastern: in Egypt, Judean and Chaldean priests kept annual records of the past, while the Greeks had to write their history every generation anew.[26]

   The integrity of their historical tradition, being without a gap, has ever been a powerful polemical argument of Jews and Christians against pagan authors. Should you object that nobody, after all, witnessed the

23. See below, pp. 56–57.
24. Censorinus, *De die natali* c. 21 ed. F. Hulfsch (Leipzig, 1897), pp. 44–45, says of Varro that he distinguished three ages (*tria discrimina temporum*), namely "primum ab hominum principio ad cataclysmum priorem, quod propter ignorantiam vocatur adelon, secundum a cataclysmo priore ad olympiadem primam, quod multa in eo fabulosa referentus mythica nominatur, tertium a prima olympiade ad nos, quod dicitur historicon quia res in eo gestae veris historiis continentur." On its relation to other schemes of periodization cf. my *Theology and the Scientific Imagination,* p. 205, n. 11.
25. See also Günter Röhr, *Platons Stellung zur Geschichte: eine methodologische Interpretationsstudie* (Berlin: Junker, 1932), p. 108; A. Häussler, "Vomp Urrung und Wandel des Lebensaltervergleiches," *Hermes,* 92 (1964), pp. 313 ff., esp. 325.
26. Flavius Josephus, *Contra Apionem* I, 3–7, *Opera* ed. B. Niese (Berlin, 1956) V, pp. 5 ff; "Chaldeans" as in, e.g., Daniel 2:2. See also below n. 49.

creation of the world and that no history was written until Moses, Ambrose of Milan has an answer: Moses was an eyewitness of sorts to the act of creation because the Pentateuch was dictated to him by the Lord.[27] And an old Jewish midrash states: "Seven enveloped the whole world. Methuselah saw Adam; Shem saw Methuselah; Jacob saw Shem; Amram saw Jacob; Ahia the Silonite saw Amram; Elijah saw Ahia the Silonite and he is still living."[28]

Turning now to medieval historiography, we note how its authors, particularly those writing Church history, are at pains to emphasize the continuity of historiography. They are merely continuing where their predecessors left off. This is true of Evagrius, Isidore of Seville, the Venerable Bede. John of Salisbury, who wrote the history of the Church (or rather the Papacy) in the twelfth century, assures us that the later biblical books are an epilogue to the New Testament; they reach to the beginning of the Church. They were continued by Lucas, who "composed [*texuit*] the infancy of the nascent church; whose follower was . . . Eusebius of Caesarea, who told the sequence of the adolescent church, leading it to its virile age."[29]

John of Salisbury names Hugh of St. Victor, whose world chronicle reaches Innocent II and Louis VII, and states, *secutus est eum Sigebertus Gemblensis monachus.* He is to write up to the time of the council of Rheims. Note that he does not distinguish world-chronicles from Church histories: all belong to one continuous record. "Erit enim continua historia mundi," we find Melancthon still saying in the sixteenth century.[30] We have very nearly reached the medieval sense of "collective memory."

HISTORY AND MEMORY

Whether and in what sense there is a collective memory and what we mean by it I have discussed above. Here I am rather concerned with ancient and medieval conceptions and perceptions. We re-

27. Ambrose of Milan, *Hexaemeron* I, 7, ed. C. Schenkel, CSEL 32 = Ambrosino I, p. 6.

28. BT, *Baba Batra* 121b; cf. Isaak Heinemann, *Darche ha'aggada,* 2nd ed. (Jerusalem, 1954), p.206, n. 12.

29. *The Historia pontificalis of John of Salisbury,* trans. and ed. Marjorie Chibnall (Oxford and New York, 1986), pp. 1 ff.

30. Philipp Melancthon *Chronicon Carionis,* ed. Carlus Gottlieb Bretschneider, *Corpus Reformatorum* 12, halle IS (1844), p. 714. Cf. A Klempt, *Die Säkularisierung der universal-historischen Auffassung* (Göttingen, 1960), pp. 67 ff.

member that in many languages, "memory" stands, originally, not only for the mental act of remembering, but also for the objective continuity of one's "name"—the name of a person, a family, a tribe, or a nation.[31] In this context we ought to place the belief in the continuity of history, Varro's "historical time," and in this context belongs Isidore's remark that whatever was worthy of memory was indeed recorded. By contrast, unrecorded periods in the infancy of humanity were periods "without memory," in the individual as in the whole human race. In his famous comparison of the ages of the world to the ages of man, Augustine says so explicitly: infancy is without public acts because it is without memory (*sine memoria*).[32]

This being the case, it had to occur to some ancient and medieval authors—as indeed it did—that the historian, rather than being a mere spectator, possesses a *ius vitae nocendi* of sorts over that which he should record. He or she can make and unmake history, can obliterate names, events, identities by not recording them, for evil or good purposes. Activity and memory belong together: without memory, the political activity cannot affect future generations. "Public deeds die with their agents unless recorded in writing," says Wipo in the eleventh century, quoting Macrobius.[33] The historian, by recording political acts, preserves and intensifies their impact. Conversely, he can suppress memory. "In that year," Jerome once remarked, "Arianic Bishops persecuted the Church. We do not tell their story because they were the Savior's enemies."[34] And Isidore of Seville, in his short world-chronicle, says of the Roman emperor Helius Pertinax that he reigned one year, and *nihil habet historiam*.[35] Ancient and medieval historians were supposed to be mere spectators, eyewitnesses in the ideal case who record what is *dignum memoriae:* under their hand, this assumption turned almost of itself into its opposite, into the conviction that the historian makes history by deciding to record or abstain from it.

31. See above, pp. 6–7.

32. Augustine, *De Genesi contra Manichaeos* c. 24, Migne, PL 34, col. 193–94. Cf. Funkenstein, *Heilsplan* pp. 39, 155, nn. 200–204.

33. "Acta vero rei publicae mori simul cum eius rectoribus arbitrati sunt, nisi quod accidit notaretur": Wippo, *Gesta Chuonradi* ed. H. Bresslau, *MG Script. in usu schol.* (1915) p. 6 (there the reference to Macrobius).

34. "Ariani episcopi ecclesiam opprimerunt, quorum temporum non digerentur, quia hostes Chrisiti indicantur": Hieronymus (ex Eusebio), Migne, PL 27, col. 498; found again in several medieval chronicles—e.g. Hermann of Reichenau, *Chronicon* ed. G. H. Pertz (1844), MG Script. V. ad ann. 328.

35. Isidore, *Etym.* V, 39, 30; cf. ibid. V, 39, 31: "Macrinus ann. I. Huius brevita vita nihil gestorum habet."

This strange dialectics of memory and action served Isidore in another section of his *Etymologies* to define time. Time, he says, "is not perceivable by itself but rather through human actions." Then he explains further: midnight is called timeless because it sees no action.[36] These curious remarks can also be understood as the background of Augustine's famous doctrine of time. Against Aristotle's definition of time as the measure of motion (and meaningless without motion), Augustine's time was to be a measure of both motion and rest because it was internal time. Memory and anticipation express it because it is structured by introspection.[37] Such was the dialectical, unstable unity in the mind of ancient and medieval authors between history as recording and history as a concatenation of significant events, even while this unity was seldom formulated by them. The first to have done so was, I believe, Hegel, in his remark that it is not by coincidence that the word "history" means both the *res gestae* and the *historia rerum gestarum*.

It is time to sum up. In several of his essays, Montaigne pretends to be merely telling a story: "Les autres forment l'homme: je le recite" ("I do not instruct. I just record.").[38] "L'homme" means the man Montaigne himself, in his changing modes and unique temperament, predilections and contradictions. Montaigne speaks, of course, with tongue in cheek. His style is ironic. He knows well that his description of himself is replete with biases and judgments that depend on time, place, and mood; he says so explicitly. For this reason he refrains from systematic discourse and offers us, as he says, only "rhapsodic" impressions. He is also well aware of the circumstance that by telling about himself, he acts upon himself; he changes, educates, and shapes his own person. There was, by contrast, no irony in the claim of ancient and medieval authors that they merely tell a simple story, *res gestae ut gestae*. But an unintended irony was there after all: they wanted merely to describe and, paradoxically, found themselves admitting that by writing, they act upon history: they share the events by recording them. Of this contradiction they were, though, unaware. At the moment at which historical reasoning found the courage to admit freely the interpretive, shaping character of the historian's work, at that moment it left its naive

36. *Etym.* V, 31, 9 ff: "Nam tempus per se non intellegitur, nisi per actus humanos . . . medium autem noctis actus caret" (and is therefore called *intempestum*).

37. See above, pp. 7–8.

38. "Les autres forment l'homme; je le recite": Michel de Montaigne, *Essais* ed. Maurice Rat, 2nd ed. (Paris, 1962), vol. III; see E. Auerbach, *Mimesis. Dargestellte Wirklichkeit in der abendländischen literatur,* 2nd ed. (Bern, 1959), ch. XI; and H. Friedrich, *Montaigne,* 2nd ed. (Bern and Munich, 1967).

epoch. Insight breeds pain: the loss of naiveté was bought at the price of an overt paradox, the hermeneutical circle ever present in every interpretive endeavor that is aware of itself and its methods.

History, Counterhistory, and Narrative

HISTORY AND NARRATIVE

It is one thing to call to mind the basically narrative character of history-writing as an antidote against the hypertrophy of analysis. "Historia scribitur ad narrandum, non ad probandum," Burckhardt said in one of his letters, quoting Quintilian, and added: "aber wenn sie dann durch ihre bloße Wahrheit der Darstellung beweist, so hat sie um so größeren wert."[39]

But it is another matter altogether to claim that there is nothing to history but narrative, that history as *res gestae* collapses completely into history as *narratio rerum gestarum*. Now, there is one sense in which this claim is true—namely in that the distinction between events and the narrative reflecting them is an untenable distinction, or at least not an absolute one. There is another sense in which this claim, taken to the extreme, is preposterously false: namely, if we take it to mean that there is no criterion by which to discern a true from a false narrative, or a precise from a sloppy one; that only literary or social categories are applicable in judging historical narratives. Hayden White, whose work I admire, has more or less taken this position.[40] I want to take some time, before introducing my theme proper, to argue against it.

There is, indeed, a sense in which history, beginning even with personal history, is *eo ipso* narrative. My acting in the world—be it the social world, or be it the world of nature which always is "humanized nature"[41]—is the continuous plotting of a narrative. Acting in the world involves and construes my identity continuously, and my identity

39. See n. 6.
40. It was not as yet the argument of Hayden White's *Metahistory: The Historical Imagination in Nineteenth-Century Europe* (Baltimore, 1973), but became so in his *The Content and the Form: Narrative Discourse and Historical Representation* (Baltimore and London, 1987). Cf. n. 45.
41. Karl Marx, "Economic and Philosophic Manuscripts of 1844," in *Writings of the Young Marx on Philosophy and Society,* ed. and trans. Loyd D. Easton and Kurt H. Guddat (Garden City, N.Y., 1967), p. 335.

is a narrative. In the very same sense in which telling my narrative is a speech act, my actions, my involvement with the world are an act of speech, a building up of a continuous story. "Ich wünschte ich wäre eine Beethovensche Symphonie oder sonst etwas, was geschrieben ist" said the young Rosenzweig in one of his letters; "das geschrieben werden tut weh."[42] It is this dialectics of memory and history, self-identity and purposeful action which Hegel had in mind in a famous passage in his "Philosophy of History," in which he said that the word *history* has both a subjective and an objective meaning. "It means both the *res gestae* and the *historia rerum gestarum*, and it is no coincidence," because there is no history without historical memory.

Are the narratives we tell—by word or act—arbitrary? Neurologists tell us that some patients with Korsakov's disease exhibit an uncanny confabulatory ingenuity. In rapid succession, the patient changes identities from butcher to pastor to scientist; every identity is narrated with convincing details, a "thick description" of sorts:

But Mr. Thompson, only just out of the hospital—his Korsakov had exploded just three weeks before, when he developed a high fever, raved, and ceased to recognize all his family—was still on the boil, was still in an almost frenzied confabulatory delirium (of the sort sometimes called "Korsakov psychosis," though it is not really a psychosis at all), continually creating a world and self, to replace what was continually forgotten and lost. Such a frenzy may call forth quite brilliant powers of invention and fancy—a veritable confabulatory genius—for such a patient must literally make himself (and his world) up every moment. We have, each of us, a life-story, an inner narrative—whose continuity, whose sense, is one's lives. It might be said that each of us constructs and lives, a "narrative," and that this narrative is us, our identities.[43]

You may object that Sacks's Mr. Thompson and similar cases discussed by Luria were deficient precisely because they could not stick to one narrative. If only they would, who could tell whether it were authentic? Yet schizophrenics often do stick to a false identity. It is false because it does not allow them an orientation within the world, either ours or even theirs. Reality is absent both from the confabulated narrative sequences of Korsakov patients and from continuous false identities of schizophrenics. In the first case it leads to indifference ("equation"), in the second, to anxiety; in both, it is a contrived, false meaning imposed on the world. Narratives are historical in that they are not arbi-

42. Franz Rosenzweig, *Briefe*, ed. Edith Rosenzweig (Berlin, 1935), p. 19.
43. Oliver Sacks, *The Man Who Mistook His Wife For a Hat and Other Clinical Tales* (New York, 1985), p. 110; and the literature quoted there (Luria).

trary, inasmuch as they are true, that is to say, historical. The "truth" or authenticity of a historical narrative—if we strip off the subjective categories and points of view of the narrator—is, like the "je ne sais quoi" of eighteenth century esthetic theoreticians, or like Kant's "intuition" (*Anschauung*), evasive, incapable of isolation, yet ever present; triggered—we do not know how—by "things in themselves" we cannot define except to say that they are, and are of necessity. Troeltsch still spoke of the "unvertilgbarer Rest der Anschaulichkeit" without which no historical narrative is authentic.[44] Beyond the modes of narrative, the mythopoetic intensity of the narrator, the intervening subconsciousness and superego, there is also that which can never be isolated yet is all-pervasive—the constraints of reality.

At this point you may wish to accuse me of confusing form with content. Historical accounts do indeed choose a certain mode of narrative—romance, tragedy, comedy, satire—which is sustained by certain tropes (metaphor, metonomy, synecdoche, irony) and correspond to a quaternity of ideological stands or of "world hypotheses." But all of this, you will hold against me, has nothing to do with the *quaestio facti*, only with the categories by which we perceive and order the facts. For "unlike literary fictions . . . historical works are made up of events that exist outside the consciousness of the writer."[45] Now this would be, on your part, an illicit turn in the argument. Form and content, imposed categories and received facts, cannot easily be separated—or rather, they cannot be separated at all. White's *Metahistory* had such a wide echo precisely because our choice of a "form of narrative" dictates the facts we select to fit into it. Indeed, in a sense it creates the facts. Facts are not atomic entities out there which declare their own importance; such was the medieval view of historical facts, which led to the conviction that the eyewitness is the best historian. This naive view of historical facts was replaced, after the seventeenth century, with the growing insight that "facts" gain their meaning and even their very factuality from the context in which they are embedded, a context reconstructed solely by the historian. His narrative makes and shapes the

44. Ernst Troeltsch, *Der Historismus und seine Probleme* (Tübingen, 1922), p. 36; Friedrich Meinecke, "Klassizismus, Romantizismus und historisches Denken im 18. Jahrhundert," in *Werke* IV, ed. Eberhard Kessel (Stuttgart, 1965), p. 264.

45. White, *Metahistory*, p. 2, n. 5. White later also found this position untenable. An even more fundamental quaternity than the "tropes" is the quaternity of logical connectives "and" ($\wedge$) "or" ($\vee$) "if . . . then" ($\supset$) "if and only if" ($\leftrightarrow$). Why not characterize the modes of historical category formation as such that give weight to synchrony ("and"), argument ("or"), causality ("if then"), contextuality ("iff")? I raise this possibility to show that of quaternities there is no end, though I do not doubt their heuristic value.

fact. "Historical events" have no unequivocal referent or *denotatum*, unlike tables, crocodiles, or even the number two (which refers to the set of all sets of two members). Herein lies the core of the celebrated hermeneutical circle. The narrative does not simply "represent" facts, it participates in their making. Its form matters.

Now you are bound to claim that you have caught me contradicting myself shamelessly. Did I not say, on the one hand, that the historical event when spoken of has no clear *denotatum*—and, on the other hand, that it must be reality-oriented? Let me, then, explicate what I mean by reality. I do not advocate naive realism, nor a theory of truth as *adequatio rei ad intellectum*. "The real" is spoken of in two contradictory, yet complementary, senses. On the one hand, real is that which escapes our control, which forces itself upon us whether or not we welcome it; on the other hand, real is only that which we make relevant, construct, manipulate: *verum et factum convertuntur*. It is this dual, dialectical nature of the real which Fichte tried to capture and tame in his "original insight" into the nature of the self-setting "I". What we call a "fact" is, inasmuch as it is independent of us, made by us—and first and foremost among these facts is the self. Our memory, our narrative of the self (and hence of all that is non-self) is both given and constructed, both already constructed and constructing. Its authenticity is not arbitrary, nor does it reside in mere formal consistency or, alternately, in the mere narrative. Only because I recognize the constraint of "reality" can I manipulate "it."

I hope that I do not sound more mysterious than absolutely necessary. I do not think that the metahistorical debate between "realists" and "narratologists" differs in principle from similar debates in philosophy of science between "realists" and "conventionalists" (or instrumentalists) or, in general, from epistemological debates that intend to clarify the constraints and the freedom of the interpreter of nature, of history, of texts. It is wholesome to call into question the absolute dividing line between "facts" and "hypotheses," "text" and "context," set by positivists old and new. It is also wholesome to realize that this does not make facts into arbitrary fictions of the mind, even if you are an instrumentalist or a neo-Kantian.[46]

But rather than lose ourselves in epistemological distinctions, let me

46. Cf. my article "The Persecution of Absolutes: On the Kantian and Neo-Kantian Theories of Science," *The Kaleidoscope of Science: The Israel Colloquium for the History and Philosophy of Science*, I (1986), pp. 329–48. Many of the fundamental insights of Ludwig Fleck or Karl Popper owe their origins to the neo-Kantian heritage. Cf. chapter 8 on Franz Rosenzweig and the *Wissenschaft des Judentums*.

try to exemplify the issue by drawing your attention to a form of historical narrative (and, *eo ipso,* action) which is more often than not an inauthentic narrative and a pernicious action, destructive and self-destructive. I shall call it, for the sake of brevity, the counterhistory.[47]

COUNTERHISTORY: ANCIENT
TO EARLY MODERN

Counterhistories form a specific genre of history written since antiquity; it is curious that they have not been identified as such in treatises on historiography sooner. Their function is polemical. Their method consists of the systematic exploitation of the adversary's most trusted sources against their grain—"die Geschichte gegen den Strich kämmen."[48] Their aim is the distortion of the adversary's self-image, of his identity, through the deconstruction of his memory.

A counterhistory in this precise sense was once Manetho's hostile account of Jewish history, based largely on an inverted reading of biblical passages: Manetho had, so to say, turned the Bible on its head.[49] Does not the Bible admit that the people of Israel lived secluded in the Egyptian province of Goshen, because "breaking bread with them was an abomination in the eyes of Egyptians"; that Moses grew up an Egyptian nobleman; that a rifraf (*asafsuf*)—a "mixed multitude" (*erev rav*)— accompanied the Hebrews on the flight out of Egypt; that they conquered Canaan by brute force, driving out its indigenous inhabitants?

47. The term was used by David Biale, *Kabbala and Counterhistory* (Cambridge, Mass., 1979); and in a somewhat different sense here and in an article of mine, "Anti-Jewish Propaganda: Pagan, Medieval and Modern," *The Jerusalem Quarterly,* 19 (Spring, 1981): pp. 56–72.

48. In Benjamin's felicitous phrase. Walter Benjamin, *Illuminations,* ed. Hannah Arendt, trans. Harry Zohn (New York, 1969), p. 257 ("Theses on the Philosophy of History," VII).

49. Manetho, *Aegyptiaca,* Fragment 54 (from Josephus, *contra Apionem* I, sec. 26–31, sec. 227–87), (Cambridge, Mass.: Loeb Classical Library, 1940), pp. 118–46, pp. 62–86 (Manetho). Also in Menachem Stern, *Greek and Roman Authors on Jews and Judaism* (Jerusalem, 1976), vol. I, pp. 389–416. By contrast, Josephus reiterates, in his rebuttals, what Manetho "concedes" as if *malgré lui,* for example, I, 252: δέδυκε γὰρ οὗτος ἡμῖν καὶ ὡμολόγηκεν ἐξ ἀρχῆς τὸ [Niese: τὲ] μὴ εἶναι τὸ γένος Αἰγυπτίος, ἀλλ᾽ αὐτοὺς ἐξωθέν ἐπελθόντας κρατῆσαι τῆς Αἰγύπτου καὶ πάλιν ἐξ αὐτῆς ἀπελθεῖν. Much later, medieval scholastics formalized such arguments into the logical exercise of the "obligations." See Eleanore Stump, "Obligations," in *The Cambridge History of Later Medieval Philosophy: From the Rediscovery of Aristotle to the Disintegration of Scholasticism, 1100–1600,* ed. Norman Kretzman et al. (Cambridge; New York, 1982), pp. 315–34.

Indeed, the Bible admits that much, because—here begins Manetho's deconstruction—the Hebrews started as an Egyptian leper colony, secluded and despised, until they called to their aid the Semitic Hyksos tribe and established an absolute reign of terror for over a century (Joseph?). Expelled by Iachmes I, the Hyksos, together with those outcasts, were led by a renegade Egyptian priest named Osarsiph (Josef? Moses? or both). He gave them a constitution that was, in all respects, a plagiarized, inverted mirror-image of Egyptian mores.[50]

The last point was one of the most repeated *topoi* in the ancient anti-Jewish polemics. The Jews in antiquity enjoyed religious and political autonomy—to the point of exemption from the cult of *divus Caesar*—because they were regarded and esteemed as an ancient people with an old, venerable, homegrown constitution. The Romans did not seek to destroy what is old and venerable: they loathed *homines rerum novarum cupidi*. This is the reason why Jewish communities remained *collegia licita*[51] while Christianity, by its own admission not only Jewish (which was bad enough, though a tolerable evil) but, on top of that, Judaism with a *new* dispensation, was persecuted. Manetho's propaganda was the archetype of many similar claims that the Jews are neither a genuine nation (*gens*) nor is their constitution original: "Moses . . . introduced new laws contrary to those of the rest of mankind. Whatever is sacred to us, is profane to them; and what they concede, we negate as sacrilege." A millennium and a half later, John Spencer, whose *De legibus et moribus Iudaeorum* is often praised as a first antecedent to a modern, historical-comparative science of religion, still wanted to show the same thing—that nothing in Jewish law is original, that all of it is an inverted mirror-image of Egyptian law.[52] There was again, among

50. Ibid. Cf. Tacitus, *Historiae* V, 4 ed. Kenneth Wellesley: "Moyses quo sibi in posterum gentem firmaret, nouos ritus contrariosque ceteris mortalibus indidit. Profana illic omnia quae apud nos sacra, rursum concessa apud illos quae nobis incesta." Cf. Jochanan Levy, *Studies in Jewish Hellenism* (Jerusalem, 1960), (Hebrew), pp. 60–196.

51. *Religio licita* was never a legal term; it was first used by Tertullian. But Jewish religious rights were tolerated, be it by virtue of their being a *natio* (λαός) or a permitted collegium. Cf. Theodor Mommsen, *Historische Zeitrschift,* 64 (1890), pp. 389–419; Tertullian, *Apologeticus,* ed. Jean-Pierre Waltzing (Louvain, 1910), p. 125 (and the editor's comment); Jean Juster, *Le Juifs dans l'empire Romain: leur condition juridique, economique et sociale* (Paris, 1914), I, pp. 413–24, denies that synagogues were *collegia.*

52. John Spencer, *De legibus Hebraeorum ritualibus* (Cambridge, 1685), for example, p. 223. Cf. Julius Guttmann, "John Spencers Erklärung der biblischen Gesetze in ihrer Beziehung zu Maimonides," in *Festskrift i anleding af Professor David Simonsen 70-årige fødelsodag* (Copenhagen, 1923), pp. 258–76. Shmuel Ettinger, "Jews and Judaism as Seen by English Deists of the Eighteenth Century," *Zion,* 29 (1964), p. 182.

humanists and Puritans, too much admiration for the ancient *res publica judaeorum,* manifested by the proliferation of seventeenth century treatises by this title.

Manetho's counterhistory continues with its narrative of how the Hebrews conquered Canaan by force (again, an appropriation of the biblical narrative) and established there a commonwealth worthy of former lepers and outcasts, a constitution calculated to perpetuate the law of their origin—a rebellious spirit nourished by the hatred of the human race (μισανθρωπία, *odium humani generis*). Indeed, Manetho's description of the way in which outcasts preserve their sense of value by constructing a (sometimes pathological) counterideology, interpreting their discrimination as a sign of special chosenness, is strongly reminiscent of what some modern sociologists of knowledge described as the formation of a "counter-identity." The hypothetical case discussed by Berger and Luckmann is, by a curious coincidence, a leper colony.[53]

Other examples of counterhistory come to mind. That Roman history, read *in malam partem,* is not a story of justice and world-pacification, was a point not lost on Roman authors. They knew of accusations that Romans "create a desert and call it peace" (*solitudinem faciunt, pacem appellant*).[54] Augustine's *De Civitate Dei* wove many such traditions into a veritable counterhistory of Rome. Cicero had once written his *De Republica* with the intent to show (against his better knowledge) that the history of Rome is the history of the gradual enfoldment of *iustitia.* Augustine uses the same and other Roman sources to show, to the contrary, that it is the history of greed, of lust for power (*libido dominandi*). Lust for power was necessary if a semblance of peace was to be established among humans *post lapsum;* but it is neither just nor ever stable. *Remota iustitia, quid sunt imperia nisi magna latrocinia?*[55] Justice exists only in the *Civitas Dei*—both the one in heaven and its projected counterpart on earth, the *civitas Dei peregrinans in terris.* There is no bridge or link between the latter and the earthly city, the *civitas terrenea:* there is only a coincidence of important events in both (Abraham/Ninus-Nimrod; Jesus/Augustus) which heightens the sense of contrast between them. Augustine, in other words, not only *wrote* a counterhistory (in the sense of *historia rerum gestarum*): he also per-

53. Peter L. Berger and Thomas Luckmann, *The Social Construction of Reality* (New York, 1966), pp. 166–67.

54. Tacitus, *Agricola* 30. See Harald Fuchs, *Der geistige Widerstand gegen Rom in der antiken Welt* (reprint: Berlin, 1964), esp. pp. 17, 47 (n. 53).

55. Augustine, *De Civitate Dei* II, 21; IV, 4. CCSL 47, p. 52.

ceived the progress (*processus*) of the city of God as a counterhistory (in the sense of *res gestae*) to the history of the Worldly City (*civitas terrena*).[56]

A counterhistory was also the seventh-century (?) Jewish "Narrative of the History of Jesus" (*Sefer Toldot Yeshu*).[57] Again, it employed the sources of the adversary—in this case, the Gospels—in order to turn Christian memory on its head. Jesus, it tells us, was the son of an illicit affair. He became a magician, having acquired by ruse possession of the explicit divine names (*shem hameforash*), and thus he turned into a powerful seducer of the unlearned multitude (*mesit umediach*). The Jewish legal establishment (the Sanhedrin), at the end of its wits, knew no better remedy than to have one of its own ranks volunteer to infiltrate the heretical movement in disguise and destroy it. The name of this hero was Judas Iscariot. The Gospel's heroes turn into villains, its villains into heroes.

A later continuation of the *Sefer Toldot Yeshu* attends to the early history of the Church. Again the Jewish establishment, it tells us, was searching for a strategy how to separate unequivocally between Christians and Jews. A heroic rabbi, Petrus by name, volunteered to pretend to be a Christian. Once he became a leader, he persuaded Christians that separation from Judaism is in the best interest of their new religion. It seems that the fabulator confused the roles of Peter and Paul.

Not all counterimages of the other are negative, ancient or modern. Herodotus's image of Egypt, in which everything is done the opposite

56. See Amos Funkenstein, *Heilsplan und natürliche Entwicklung*, pp. 43–50; more briefly: idem, *Theology and the Scientific Imagination*, pp. 256–61; against, for example, Alois Wachtel, *Beiträge zur Geschichtstheologie des Aurelius Augustinus* (Bonn, 1960). On Augustine's sources see Heinrich Scholz, *Glaube und Unglaube in der Weltgeschichte Ein Kommentar zu Augustins De civitate Dei* (Leipzig, 1911). Cf. also below, pp. 298–301 (Rosenzweig).

57. It was edited by Samuel Kraus, *Das Leben Jesu nach jüdischen Quellen* (Berlin, 1902). Cf. Joseph Dan, *Hasipur ha'ivri biyme habenayim* (Jerusalem, 1974), pp. 122–32. Morton Smith, *Jesus the Magician* (San Francisco, 1978), elaborated one of the narrative's main themes. In a way he, too, wrote a counterhistory (to all *Leben Jesu* versions of modern Protestant theology). It is worthwhile noting, in passing, the difference between this or similar references to Jesus in the orthodox Jewish literature and the treatment of Jesus in the post-emancipatory climate of acculturation, say in the nineteenth century *Wissenschaft des Judentums*. The orthodox, traditional account agrees with Christians in the question of fact, but differs from Christianity in the evaluation: true, we killed Jesus, but he deserved it as a heretic and a magician. Nineteenth century Jewish historians or theologians—say Geiger or Baeck—disagree about the facts: Jesus was a good Jew (a Pharisee to boot!), and we could not have killed him. But they agree in his evaluation with liberal Protestant theologians: he was the embodiment of ethics.

way than among the Hellenes; or Tacitus's image of the Germans, written as a critique of his own society[58]—both do not seek to destroy the self-identity of the other. But Manetho, Augustine, and the author of the *Sefer Toldot Yeshu* did. What was the methodical rationale, the self-justification, for such an inversion of the adversary's account (*eversio*)?

CHANGES IN EARLY MODERN TIMES

In the previous chapter, I tried to show in what sense the ancient or medieval notion of "historical fact" differs from ours. The premodern perception of historical fact was atomic: facts of history—such that are *digna memoria*—are immediately recognizable, distinct, and accessible to the truthful eyewitness, without need of interpretation; wherefore the eyewitness, if only truthful, is the best historian.[59] "Literal" and "historical" meanings of a text were synonymous to the medieval exegete, who recognized a deeper sense only in the theological perspective (*spiritualis intelligentia*). And since events *digna memoria* were evident and always recorded, world history is a continuous claim of eyewitness reports.

What if the eyewitness lies? Then, only then, it is the *officium* of the later historian to debunk the narrative—indeed, to create a "counter-history" out of the falsified narrative, guided by the assumption that every good lie contains a germ of truth. Ancient and medieval historiography—or rather, historical methodology—obeyed strictly the principle of excluded middle: a story is either true or false, *tertium non datur*. To say (as we do) that an account—either of an eyewitness or of a remote narrator, is subjectively true yet objectively distorted, that everyone is a captive of his individual, or local, or temporal "point of view" and preconception—to say all that, as we do, is to recognize that the "historical fact" is not at all self-evident, that it needs interpretation, that it obtains its meaning from a context which the historian, ever caught in a hermeneutical circle, must reconstruct. History ceased, for us, to be a *simplex narratio gestarum:* it became *eo ipso* interpretation subject to time, place, and the point of view of the interpreter. Such was the insight advanced by the humanists since the sixteenth century, which induced a veritable revolution in philology, biblical studies, legal

58. Herodotus, *Histories* II, 34–35, Tacitus, *Germania*.
59. The following is a summary of pp. 22–32 above on the ancient and medieval perceptions of historical facts.

interpretation (the *mos gallicus*) and, finally, historical studies proper.

The genre of counterhistory that we identified as a well-defined, literary-polemical genre in antiquity and in the Middle Ages, likewise changed with the "historical revolution" of the sixteenth century. It focused on an explicit reinterpretation, rather than inverted exploitation, of sources. Consider, for example, the Pietist Gottfried Arnold's counterhistory of the Church, first published in 1698.[60]

Protestant historiography was driven, from its beginning, toward the construction of a counterhistory of the Church. It called to its aid the new art of philological-historical criticism already cultivated by generations of humanists. Gottfried Arnold's history of Christianity was such a critical counterhistory, examining the sources directly rather than as, in our examples hitherto, referring to them obliquely and surreptitiously. He called it an "Unparteyische Kirchen und Ketzerhistorie," but he is hardly impartial when it comes to decide between Church and deviants. Paul's words "heresies are necessary" (*oportet ut haereses esse*),[61] had acquired in the Middle Ages historical-providential connotations. Heresies were seen as a providential challenge which the Church, inspired by the Holy Spirit, answered by the development of dogmas, by the rejuvenation of the Church through new orders. Heresies, like Goethe's Mephisto, are "ein teil von jenem Geist, der stets das Böse will doch stets das Gute schafft." Gottfried Arnold turned this evaluation on its head. Sectarians and so-called heretics were the only historical vestiges of Christianity during the long night of its decay, of the eclipse of truth. Examining the sources, he could show that, whenever the corrupt establishment defined a movement as heretical, it did so because it abhorred being reminded of the true, spiritual, nondogmatic and non-ceremonial origins of Christianity, that Christianity was internal and apolitical by the very "scandalous" paradigm of its founder. Arnold, then, went back *ad fontes* both in the historiographic and in the religious sense of the word, and meant his "history" to be an incentive for all Christians to do so. He did not seek reason in history: he rather put his trust in the continuous, subterranean instances of true *Innerlichkeit*, of defiance of the world and its wisdom, which always was the trade-

60. The best study is still that of Erich Seeberg, *Gottfried Arnold: Die Wissenschaft und die Mystik seiner Zeit*, (1923; reprint Darmstadt, 1964). See also Biale, *Gershom Scholem: Kabbala and Counterhistory* (Scholem and Arnold), pp. 199–201.

61. H. Grundmann, "Oportet ut haereses esse: Das Problem der Ketzerei im Spiegel der Mittelalterlichen Bibelexegese," *Archiv für Kulturgeschichte*, 45 (1963), pp. 129–64.

mark of martyrs and sectarians alike. Jesus himself stood trial as a heretic.[62] The "true" sacred history of Christianity was a secret private history, even after the age of Luther. The public history of Christianity is,
by contrast, a secular history—a history of involvement with this world
(*saeculum*), of entanglement with power and greed, and hence a history
of a falsification.

COUNTERHISTORY IN MARX

Arnold expressed, like most early Protestant thinkers, a
disdain of history, which is basically a history of human deprivation
and error. His use of history is critical. Historical thought during the
Enlightenment was far more optimistic, but history still served basically
as a foundation of ahistorical arguments about human nature. With the
triumph of the historical dimension of discourse in the nineteenth century came also a different mode of counterhistory, of which Marx is an
excellent example.

Every aspect of Marx's thinking and planning is dominated by the
now all-pervasive historical discourse. At the very core of his economic
theory lies the realization that "the laws of the market" are historical,
rather than natural, laws. There exists no natural drive to barter in humans, nor do commodities own a "nature" dictating their (exchange)
value (the "fetishization of the ware"). Both reflect historical conditions
of social relations shaped by modes of production. If Hobbes changed
the course of modern political theory by systematically denaturalizing
the state—it is a human artifact, not a result of social inclinations—
Marx did the same to the *homo economicus,* except that his interpretation
presupposes a coherent historical narrative.

Marx's interpretation of history is, of sorts, a protracted exercise in
counterhistory. Bourgeois historians, as seen from the Marxist—even
from Marx's—perspective, tell the history of modern times, since the
rise of the bourgeoisie, as a history of growing freedom, human rights,
equality before the law. The driving force of this progress is the pursuit
of individual, economic self-interests, whereby "private vices" generate
of themselves "public virtues."[63] The French Revolution, with its dec-

62. Gottfried Arnold, *Unparteyische Kirchen und Kezerhistorie,* (Schaffhansen, 1740),
I, sec. 9, p. 24; Cf. Seeberg, *Gottfried Arnold,* pp. 24, 224, 219–21.

63. On the origin and various fortunes of Mandeville's phrase see Walter Euchner,
Egoismus und Gemeinwohl: Studien zur Geschichte der bürgerlichen Philosophie (Frankfurt
am Main, 1973); and my *Theology and the Scientific Imagination,* pp. 202–205.

laration of the *droits de l'homme* and equality before the law, legitimized the achievements of the third estate; the modern national state is its fortunate outcome. Standing above all parties and interest-groups, the state only watches that individual, healthy antagonisms do not grow out of the rules of the game.[64]

But this "political emancipation," the liberal ideal of the bourgeoisie, only appears to be also a human emancipation; in reality even the celebrated *droits humains* epitomize the opposite. They guarantee the maximal exploitation of the dispossessed, they strip the individual of all bonds—feudal or corporate—so as to make him free to sell himself, that is to say, his labor, everywhere as a commodity in the market. The modern state just appears to stand above the parties: in reality, it ensures the maximal antagonization and atomization of society. The civil society is indeed a society in which everything, including human labor, has become a commodity obeying the "laws of the market"; the logic of capitalism demands that this commodity be there in superabundance, forming "the reserve army of the Capital" out of these atomized, seemingly free individuals. The social paradox latent in every commodity—that if it represents abstract labor, then it does not represent abstract labor—becomes transparent, explosively so, when labor itself turns into a commodity.[65] "Private vices" will lead to catastrophe rather than to a stable, uniform increase of wealth. The dialectics of *Wesen* and *Erscheinung*, the theme of Hegel's *Wesenslogik*, dominates Marx's analysis of the state, of commodity, of history.[66] Essence turns *eo ipso* into appearance, and vice versa. This saves Marx's counterhistory from being merely the revision of history from the point of view of the oppressed,

64. The following after Karl Marx, "Zur Judenfrage," in *Karl Marx, Friedrich Engels. Werke* (Berlin, 1956) I, pp. 247–377. See also below, pp. 229–232.

65. Karl Marx, *Das Kapital* I, 1 (Hamburg, 1890–1894). It is a variant (Marx would say: a concretization or a turning-on-its-feet) of the idealistic formula for the identity-cum-difference of the I and the non-I, A = B, Identity and difference in the *Wesenslogik*. The "metaphorical" character of the commodity, to which White, *Metahistory* (see next note) draws attention, has its origin here.

66. Georg Wilhelm Friedrich Hegel, *Wissenschaft der Logik* (Nürnberg, 1812–1816). The most lucid explication of its moves was given by Dieter Henrich, "Hegels Logik der Reflexion," in *Hegel im Kontext* (Frankfurt am Main, 1971), pp. 95–156. I hope to develop this interpretation of Marx further at a later date. See also White, *Metahistory*, pp. 285–330, which shows in fact this dialectic (but without reference to Hegel's *Wesenslogik* or *Reflexionslogik*). The only mistake of this chapter is the assumption that "socially necessary time of labor" measures value of usage. The latter has no measure: "Als Gebrauchswerte sind Waren vor allem verschiedener Qualität, als Tauschwerte können sie nur verschiedener Quantität sein, enthalten also kein Atom Gebrauchswert" (Marx, *Das Kapital*), ibid.

a revision worthy of utopian socialists. Rather, his is the account how the "slave" inevitably becomes, through his labor, the true "master"— and how, by knowing it, he revolutionizes history. Marx truly turned the bourgeois vision of state and history on its head—or back on its feet.

NAZISM AND REVISIONISM

Let me move to my last examples of counterhistory, *cum ira et cum studio*. All anti-Semitic ideologies, since the end of the nineteenth century, have this in common, that they are directed less against traditional, orthodox Jews who can be recognized as Jews, and much more against Jews who are well acculturated and assimilated. Assuming, as anti-Semitic ideologues did, that being Jewish is an unobliterable, indelible, innate character, the assimilated Jew deceives, in the best case, both himself and others; in the worst, his assimilation is a conspiratorial pretense, so as to undermine the healthy texture of society from within. Even extreme anti-Semites until the 1930s did not go beyond the suggestion to undo the emancipation, to return the Jews from a status of citizen to the former status of mere subjects. This program was thoroughly implemented during the first seven years following the Nazi *Machtergreifung* in Germany.

But the National Socialist ideology contained the germ of a much more ruthless "solution of the Jewish question." In its dramatic-apocalyptic reading of world history, Jews were the hypostatized negation of sanity, creativity, health, and order, a secularized Antichrist described in hygienic-pseudobiological terms. If other "races," say the Slavs (or, indeed, the Semites) were subhuman (*Untermenschen*), the Jews throughout history were unhuman (*Unmenschen*), a counterrace to the *Herrenrasse*, a vermin, a bacillus. To have exterminated them would even be worth a German catastrophic defeat, Hitler said at the end of the war.

Now observe how this constructed counteridentity of Jews was made into a reality in the concentration camps. The Jews, themselves lice in the Nazi terminology, had to be deliced (*entlaust*) entering the camp; they were made into vermin, deprived of identity, dehumanized even in their own eyes, and finally exterminated as lice. Symbolism and reality become almost one, exactly as in Kafka's *Metamorphosis*.

Indeed I believe that many of Kafka's texts deal with the dissolution of identity, yet none so explicitly as the *Metamorphosis*, in which Gregor

Samsa wakes up one day to find himself "ein ungeheures Ungeziefer."[67] At first, his physical and mental behavior is still more human: slowly, gradually, through a subtle interaction between his family and himself, he acquires more and more the mentality of a bug; and dies like one. At the end of the story we discover that, in a sense, he was always a bug, even before the narrative commenced: the family, only seemingly once dependent on him totally, gets along splendidly without him. He always was superfluous; "becoming" a bug was no coincidence after all, but rather the continuous translation of a symbol or metaphor into reality.

Earlier we attended to the sense in which history (as *res gestae*) is *ipso facto* narrative: namely inasmuch as deeds, no less than words, are the continuous construction of the self-identity of agents—be the agents individuals or collectives.[68] The systematic destruction of self-identity of inmates in concentration camps was also the attempt to destroy their narrative of themselves. Inasmuch as the history of a period ultimately depends on the identity of its agents, the reconstruction of a coherent narrative of the experience of the victims, individual and collective, is an almost insurmountable task, much harder than the refutation of the collective counterhistory that Nazi ideology tried to reify.

An offshoot of the Nazi counterhistory still lives forth in the various apologetic-polemical exercises known as "revisionist" literature. It is a name given (*inter alia*) to a distinct group of writings—books, articles, pamphlets—that deny the fact of the Nazi genocide of the Jews.[69] Of the various examples of counterhistories, this is the most recent and vicious. They qualify as counterhistories *par excellence,* not only because the "revisionists" deny that the victim is a victim, but because most of them also accuse—explicitly or implicitly—the victim of being the perpetrator, and this in two ways.

First, some authors, while denying the existence of extermination camps, do not deny the existence of concentration camps; in those, they say, Jews (Kapos) did kill other Jews in large numbers. This is all there is to the legend of mass killings. If there was any, it was perpetrated by

67. Franz Kafka, "Die Verwandlung," in *Kafkas Erzählungen,* ed. Brigitte Flach (Bonn, 1967).

68. For a minimal construction of the meaning of "collective memory" see chapter 1.

69. The following relies on Pierre Vidal-Naquet, "Theses on Revisionism," in *Unanswered Questions: Nazi Germany and the Genocide of the Jews,* ed. François Furet (New York, 1989), pp. 304–20.

the Jews themselves, the assumption being that they were given genuine autonomy. Of course there have also been accidental civilian casualties—among Jews just as among every population. Why had the Jews to be "concentrated" to begin with? Because they declared war on Germany (rather than vice versa), be it with the general economic boycott of the thirties, be it in a speech of Weizmann's of 1938 in which he said that Jews are at war with Germany, be it by armed rebellion.

Second, the victims become perpetrators also *ex post facto:* the legend of genocide is a world-conspiracy of Jews, some revisionists add, in order to enable them to gain a state after the war. The "world conspiracy" of Jews is a motif that continues in anti-Jewish European literature, as I have shown elsewhere, since the twelfth century. Then and there, I believe I have proven, Judaism lost the image it had hitherto in Christian eyes of an anachronistic yet transparent religion—"noluerunt ipsi Judaei mutari cum tempore"[70]—and acquired instead the image of a religion adhering to the Old Testament only seemingly, while in fact committed in secret to a new, satanic law ("pugnasti tanto tempore diabolicis libris divinos libros"—Peter the Venerable). Some added: a religion committed also to the shedding of Christian blood; every year their rabbis convene in secret and choose another community to shed Christian blood on Passover, for otherwise, they believe they would not be redeemed (Thomas of Monmouth). It is one continuous tradition which leads from here to the *Protocols of The Elders of Zion;*[71] its latest version is the revisionist account of the Jewish anti-German character assassination—a spiritual genocide, as it were.

How does one deny a fact? By arguing it away. Argument (rather than narrative) is the preferred discourse of revisionists. Two modes of argument prevail in particular, and Pierre Vidal-Naquet has exposed them brilliantly. It is either a *reductio ad impossibile* or an argument from analogy. The concentration camps, we are told, could not have been death camps; the alleged gas chambers, for example, were engineered so that, had they contained poison gas, it would have poisoned everything around for miles. Analogy is used, for example, when we are admonished to remember that already once, during the First World War, rumors of German atrocities were cultivated which proved after the war to have been widely exaggerated for propaganda purposes.

Almost every facet of this revisionist literature is present in another

70. See chapter below, pp. 189–196.
71. On the *Protocols* see Norman Cohn, *Warrant for Genocide* (London, 1967); and below chapters 6 and 9.

recent brand of revisionist literature, the attempt to deny the genocide of Armenians during the First World War. It is hard (and redundant) to establish who influenced whom; minds intent at similar tasks argue alike. Again we are told that at best there were a few local pogroms blown out of proportion. The deportations were understandable in view of the Armenian insurrection at Van; besides, they were ordered for the Armenians' own benefit, for they lived along the exposed shores of Syria. The myth of genocide is kept alive by hopes that it will prompt the bad conscience of the nations of the world to grant independence to the Armenians; they evidently took heart in the success of the Jews to turn their national catastrophe into an instrument to gain independence (it is this latter argument which George Steiner made into a fictitious last speech of Hitler's in *The Portage of A. H. to San Cristobal*).[72]

At one crucial point, the revisionists' counterhistories are prompted and aided by a genuine paradox of the subject matter. Many of us say that the Nazi crimes were "incomprehensible," that the sheer limitless inventiveness in degradation in killing of that regime defy all of our historical explanatory schemes: it certainly did not spring out of self-interest or *raison d'état*.[73] Precisely this incomprehensibility of the crimes makes their denial into a much more rational account of a possible world (better than ours)in which people act out of rational, or at least predictable, motivations. "Aber die Wirklichkeit, die ist nicht so."

Which brings us back to our initial question—what makes a story more "real" than another? Or, in another variation, what distinguishes a legitimate revision from a revisionist confabulation? Some counterhistories—by no means all of them—present us with a limit case; from the limit case something may be learned for less clearcut cases. They are inauthentic, unreal, not because their authors lie consciously—this may or may not be the case—but rather because they are through and through derivative, altogether dependent in every detail on the story they intend to overthrow. Reality, we said, is an elusive notion, perhaps even a paradoxical one. No historiographical endeavor may presume to "represent" reality—if by representation we mean a corresponding system of things and their signs. Every narrative is, in its way, an exercise in "worldmaking." But it is not arbitrary. If true, reality, whatever its definition, must "shine through it" like Heidegger's Being—and, like

72. George Steiner, *The Portage of A. H. to San Cristobal* (New York, 1982). Of him we may say, with the medieval Archipoeta, "Quaero mihi similis \ et adjungor pravis."
73. I have argued against the "incomprehensibility" in "Theological Responses to the Holocaust," chapter 9 below.

the latter, without ever appearing directly. Nothing in the counterhistories of Manetho, of the *Sefer toledoth Yeshu,* of the "revisionists," "shines through": everything in them is a reflexive mirror image. (Augustine, Arnold, Marx are different.) Closeness to reality can neither be measured nor proven by a waterproof algorithm. It must be decided from case to case without universal criteria. Everything in a narrative—factual content, form, images, languages—may serve as indicators.

MORALITÉ

This, then, is the final lesson I want to draw from our long preoccupation with counterhistories, ancient or modern. In their most vicious forms, they deprive the adversary of his positive identity, of his self-image, and substitute it with a pejorative counter-image. But how could we discriminate between a genuine narrative and a counter-narrative unless by a criterion outside the narrative? You are not an old nation with ancient, venerable institutions, but rather lepers imitating our institutions, said Manetho to the Jews; you and your history are not a paradigm of justice and virtue, but rather of greed and *libido dominandi,* said Augustine to the pagan Romans; you and the founders of your religion were and are magicians, said the Jews to the Christians; you are not real Jews, said medieval Christians to the Jews; you are not Christians, said Arnold to the Catholics; you are not the protagonists of freedom, but of its opposite, of exploitation and dehumanization, said Marx to the liberals of his time; you are not human at all, said the Nazi ideologues to the Jews, and tried as much as they could to actually dehumanize them even in their own eyes before killing them. You are not even victims of atrocities, say the "revisionists" to the Jews.

In both the case of some mental diseases which I discussed at the beginning, and in the more vicious case of counterhistories, identities are destroyed: except it may seem as if the schizophrenic, or the one who suffers from Korsakov's psychosis, has his own identity destroyed, while in the case of counterhistories, personal or collective, it is the self-identity of the *other* which is under attack. Yet both lost contact with reality—both aspects of its involuntary constraint which enables the effective manipulations of our world. Because of that, every serious counterhistory that will try to become reality turns at the end to destroy not only the identity of the other, but also the self-identity of the destroyer. And it is self-destructive of necessity, if only because the forger of a counteridentity of the other renders his own identity to depend on it. In this "Kampf um Leben und Tod"[74] both identities are inevitably destroyed if the counteridentity succeeds in its aim to destroy the self-identity of the other. This is no solace: because while this happens, the guilty and the unguilty alike suffer; both may be destroyed.

"At the threshold lies sin" (Gen. 4:7). In the beginning, Zionist ideology labored hard to construct a new, positive Jewish self-image, to restore a Jewish "self-respect" (Pinsker) so as to achieve "autoemanci-pation." It was a noble and timely endeavor, which at its worst could be blamed for disregarding the fact that the land of Israel was not empty and barren, that it was already populated by indigenous Arabs. By now, however, the collective self-identification of many Israelis—not of all—is inextricably tied to a downright negation of the national identity of the Palestinians. "There is no Palestinian nation," Golda Meir once said. A standing political argument has it that the Palestinian—or even Arab nationalist movements—are not authentic, that they are a mere mirror image of the emergence of a Jewish national consciousness and a reaction thereto; as if the genesis of a national identity really matters. Another political argument has it that Arab immigration to Palestine swelled only after the Zionist efforts made the land attractive. Deper-sonalization of the Palestinians, denial of their personal and political self-identity, has become an oppressive political reality. As a Zionist and as a historian, I fear these developments and abhor their consequences. By destroying the identity of the other we, too, will destroy our own. It need not happen. It is upon us not to let it happen.

74. Hegel, *Phänomenologie des Geistes.* The significance of these famous pages is, among other things, that they are the first *philosophical* treatment of self-consciousness as a through-and-through social phenomenon. Cf. chapter 1, "Collective Memory."

3

Biblical and Postbiblical Perceptions of History

The Leading Images of the Historical Narrative

YOUTH AND CHOSENNESS

When the most High divided to the nations their inheritance, /
when he separated the sons of Adam, / he set the bounds of the
people / according to the number of the children of Israel. / For the
Lord's portion is his people; / Jacob is the lot of his inheritance

(Deut. 32:8–10).

With a reminder of the confusion of languages, the author of the historical poem begins his review of the dramatic relations between the nation and its God. He seems to assume that, when many of the nations were formed, Israel did not exist yet; only God kept in mind its future borders as a yardstick to the distribution of land among the rest of the nations. Whether or not this is the exact meaning of the verses,[1] the

---

1. IV. Q. reads *lemispar bene el* instead of *lemispar bene yisrael*, and so does the LXX (κατὰ ἀριθμὸν ἀγγέλων θεοῦ). That this should be the correct reading has been argued

consciousness of youth—an awareness of having its beginning in fairly recent, historical times—accompanied the Israelite religion from early on. To the Jahewist, the putative Judean author of the first layer of the biblical historical narrative, Israel was transformed from a clan into a nation only in Egypt, and the exodus from Egypt happened no more than half a millennium ago:

> And it came to pass in the four hundred and eightieth year after the children of Yisra'el were come out of the land of Mizrayim, in the fourth year of Shelomo's reign over Yisra'el, in the month Ziv, which is the second month, that he began to build the house of the Lord (I Kings 6:1).

Such a concession of youth was remarkable in its time. Most societies of the ancient Near East—indeed, most ancient societies I know of—traced their origins back to mythical times, to the creation of the world and of the human race. *In illo tempore* they were founded by gods or demigods with all of their institutions. The myth of "Enuma Elish" concludes with the foundation of the city-state of Babylon by Marduk.[2] "Mythical" I call the time in which a culture sees the world and society as having been in all respects different from what they are today and much more immediate to the gods. The author or editor of Genesis interspersed the "genealogy of men" (*tol'dot ha'adam*) with stories that indicate how the human race slowly shed, one by one, the features that once it shared with the "children of God" (*bene 'elohim*): first driven out of the toil-free life in the Garden of Eden, then learning to murder, then again having its lifespan limited to about a hundred and

---

by G. von Rad, *Deuteronomy: A Commentary* (Philadelphia, 1960), pp. 196–200, and others. This would suggest an elaborate myth of the allotment to each nation (except Israel) of a supervising angel. I prefer to read the phrase with the masoretic text, without such an elaborate myth. Cf. J. M. Grinz, "Ben Ugarit lekummran," *Eshkolot* IV (1962): pp. 146–61; another interpretation: S. A. Loewenstamm, "Nahalat hashem," *Studies in the Bible dedicated to the Memory of U. Cassuto*, ed. Loewenstamm (Jerusalem, 1977), pp. 149–72. The song itself has sometimes been dated early—the "wicked nation" that is to punish Israel for foreking God identified with the Philistines: O. Eissfeldt, *The Old Testament: An Introduction*, trans. P. R. Ackroyd (New York and Evanston, 1965), p. 227. To me it rather seems in line with the prophetic theodicy (below) and the dimensions of the predicted catastrophe better fits the Assyrians. Elements of wisdom-literature have been observed by von Rad, ibid.

2. J. B. Pritchard, ed., *Ancient Near Eastern Texts Relating to the Old Testament*, 2nd ed. (Princeton, 1955), p. 68 l. 47–p. 69 l. 73. Consciousness of youth may be a common feature of invading societies which retain the memory of having been nomads. On older forms of historical remembrance see Jan Assman, "Guilt and Remembrance: On the Theologization of History in the Ancient Near East," *History and Memory* 2, 1 (1990), pp. 5–33.

twenty years, thereafter the contractual stabilization of nature after the flood, finally the dispersion of languages and people.[3] The term "mythical" itself as a learned designation for a period came up only in later antiquity.[4]

And though Ever, the eponymous ancestor of the Hebrew, was close to the mythical second start of humankind after the flood, the nation of Israel emerged much later. Very few ancient societies confessed to their fairly recent origins, but the ancient Israelites, and so to a measure the Greeks (and Romans), admitted it. Both suffered, each in his way, from an acute historical sense of youth. The origins of Israel took place *in* history, indeed in recent history.

In and of itself, such a consciousness of being a relatively young nation must have been a burden rather than an asset, a blemish that made their own community inferior to others of an older pedigree. True nobility is recognized by its old vintage. Not only was Israel conscious of its youth, but it also held in memory its low origin from a status of slavery in Egypt. Some of the pejorative connotations of "Hebrew" as the designation for a person of lower status (rather than as a designation for an ethnic group) were preserved in the legal traditions of the Pentateuch—as, for example, the consistent references to a "Hebrew slave" (*eved ivri*) against references to the "[free] man of Israel" (*ish yisrael*).[5]

But the blemish was turned into a virtue. True, Israel is much younger than most nations,[6] and much smaller. Yet this circumstance is amply compensated for by the fact that God has *chosen* this particular nation. *He* had made it into a nation. Historical consciousness and the Israelite version of monotheism went, from the outset, hand in hand. The certainty of being under the continuous, special tutelage of God operating in history—a god mightier than all other gods—compensated for the historical reminiscence of recent origin.

God's involvement in the fortunes of Israel from the exodus to the time of the Judges is depicted as a real physical presence. With "signs and demonstrations" (*otot umoftim*) he guided and delivered. Where

---

3. Proximity and the distancing of human beings from the *bene elohim* is the recurrent concern of the latter (and of God) throughout these stories; cf. Gen. 3:22; Gen. 6:3–4; Gen. 11:6–7.

4. See chapter 2, n. 24.

5. A. Alt, "Die Ursprünge des Israelitischen Rechts," *Kleine Schriften* (München, 1953) I, pp. 291–94; R. de Vaux, *Ancient Israel* (New York and Toronto, 1965) I, p. 83; *Encyclopedia Mikrait* s.v. "Ivrim."

6. Cf. Hosea 11:1 כי נער ישראל ואהבהו וממצרים קראתי לבני.

his presence is less immediate, his spirit "descends" (*tsolachat*) on leaders (judges) to save or again he confounds the enemies of his nation with a "bad spirit" (*ruakh ra'a*).[7] Less immediate is God's presence in the biblical historiography of the monarchy. In the semi-official narrative of Shelomo's accession to the throne (2 Sam. 5–1 Kings 3), Gerhard von Rad saw the first known instance in any known culture of a genuine historiography that is more than annalistic or anecdotal.[8] The narrative has a coherent, intricate plot, a climax and an anticlimax. It serves a function—to prove the legitimacy of Shelomo's succession to David's throne. Without any active interference or machinations on his part, Solomon's more legitimate rivals disappear one after the other by their own wrongdoings. Concurrent with his story, the author employs a new theology, a more subtle version of God's interference in history. Hitherto, God extended his aid by manifest acts, as when the walls of Jericho fell down or when the sun stood still at Gibeon. By now, God interferes rather indirectly, by planting or removing thoughts in the mind of historical agents:

And Absalom and all the men of Israel said, The counsel of Hushai the Arcite is better than the counsel of Ahithophel.

For the Lord had ordained it to defeat the good counsel of Ahithophel, to the intent that the Lord might bring evil upon Absalom. (2 Sam. 17:14)

THEOLOGY AND DOOM

The pride with which the historian living in the Golden Age of the united monarchy viewed the God-guided political ascendance of Israel up to his own times contrasts sharply with the sense of doom prevailing between the fall of the northern monarchy (721 B.C.) and the destruction of Judea (586). The discrepancy between the claim of Israel to be God's unique, chosen nation and its present powerlessness became evident, and called for a new justification for the belief in God's providence. The later prophets introduced such a new and revo-

---

7. *Judges* 9:23: וישלח אלהים רוח רעה בין אבימלך ובין בעלי שכם. This is a counterpart to the "descending" of God's spirit, recognized by Weber as the mark of charismatic leadership.

8. G. von Rad, "Die Anfänge der Geschichtsschreibung im alten Israel," *Archiv Für Kulturgeschichte* 32 (1944), pp. 1–42. Note the date of the article's original appearance. Also the rest of the volumes of the AKuG is replete with implicit and explicit repudiations of the racist theories. Evidently, the Nazi regime did not compel scholars to pay lip service to its ideology. One could at least remain silent, at times even—as here—express distancing.

lutionary, almost dialectical, theodicy. They inverted the common belief that the measure of the power of a deity is the success of the community obliged to worship it by the bonds of *religio*. The very powerlessness of Israel, they held, was proof of God's immense power, which manifests itself by his using the biggest empires, Assyria, Babylon and Egypt, as "the rod of his wrath" (*mate za'am*, Isa. 10:5–8) to chastise Israel and to purify it. Yet these world-powers are unaware of it, of their historical mission (*vehu lo chen yedame*), and attribute their success to their very own strength and to their God's. Here, perhaps, we encounter the earliest, original version of reading into history "the cunning of God" or "the cunning of reason," of which more will be said in later chapters: by following their own, blind urge for power, the nations of the world unknowingly serve a higher design.[9]

The poetic review of Israel's history, with which we started our considerations, also continues with the collective punishment for the collective transgression:

> They have moved me to jealousy with a god of no account;
> they have provoked me to anger with their vanities:
> and I will move them to jealousy with a people of no account
> I will provoke them to anger with a vile nation.
>
> (Deut. 32:21)

And it concludes with a vision of redemption, a vision both akin to the popular hopes for "the day of Jahave" and different from them:

> Rejoice, O nations, with his people:
> for he will avenge the blood of his servants,
> and will render vengeance to his adversaries
> and will forgive his land, and his people.
>
> (Deut. 32:43)

The "land" spoken of here is the same that was earlier designated as the "portions" and "inheritance" at once of God and of his chosen people.[10]

I have sketched the transformations of the biblical-historical consciousness hitherto with references to concrete, individual (even if anonymous) literary documents. What, in all of these images, pertains to "collective memory" at its time? Here, the ground we tread is much

9. See chapters 5 and 7 and my *Theology and the Scientific Imagination*, pp. 202–13, 245, 251–73.

10. Cf. the formulaic call for rebellion in 2 Samuel 20:1 and 1 Kings 12:16: מה לנו חלק בדוד ולא נחלה בבן ישי. נחלה, חלק are legal terms.

more slippery and observations must remain highly speculative. We know, of course, that most Israelite cult festivals had of old a historical meaning grafted onto their perhaps earlier reference to the cycles of nature. We know further that the recitation of historical formulas such as those in Leviticus was part of the cult. Periods of religious-national awakening were at times expressed as an attachment to a particular festival. A sense of typological identification with the period that first experienced this festival *in illo tempore* is particularly evident in two cases in which the same formula seems to be repeated:

And the king commanded all the people, saying, Keep the passover to the Lord your God, as it is written in the book of the covenant. Surely there no such passover was held from the days of the kings of Israel, nor of the kings of Judah. (2 Kings 23:21–22)

And then:

And all the congregation of those who were come back out of the captivity made booths, and dwelt in the booths [*sukot*]: for since the days of Yeshua the son of Nun to that day the children of Israel had not done so. And there was very great gladness. (Neh. 8:17)

Note that, to the reformers of the seventh century not only the time of the united monarchy but also the time of the judges appeared as a golden age[11]—against its characterization in the Book of Judges as a time in which "each man did what was right in his eyes." Needless to say, the exodus from Egypt served as the archetype of the future redemption.[12]

---

11. If the quoted verse from Kings means that throughout the time of the monarchy no proper passover was celebrated, it may be an allusion (as is Neh. 8:17) to Joshua 5:9–10. King Joshiyahu may, then, have been also conceived as he who "lifted the shame of Egypt" from the nation. The parallel to Joshua 5 suggests, however, a much more plausible reading: that the time of the united monarchy (the kings that ruled over Judea and Israel) was still a golden age in which Israel was truly free and passover was still a living symbol of that freedom. The united monarchy, as much as the time of the judges, was seen as an *aurea aetas* of sorts. Cf. n. 13.

12. S. A. Loewenstamm, *Massoret yetsi'at mitsrayim behishtalsheluta* (Jerusalem, 1968; 1972), pp. 16, 103. Recently, M. Fishbane, *Biblical Interpretation in Ancient Israel* (Oxford, 1985), pp. 350–79, has suggested a host of other instances of typological structures in the biblical narrative, some of them already recognized by the early *Midrash* (cf. chapter 4, "Nachmanides"). Without denying their presence and importance, it must be kept in mind (a) that they are largely literary devices and (b) that they are not the product, as in Christianity, of a conscious, continuous search. See now also Yair Zakovitch, *"And You Shall Tell Your Son . . .": The Concept of the Exodus in the Bible* (Jerusalem, 1991), esp. pp. 15–45.

Identification with portions of the distant past went hand in hand with an awareness of its distance. None of the names of the Patriarchs, of the generations of the exodus, or of the *Landnamma* remained in use throughout biblical times. Some of them reappeared in later antiquity, others only in the Middle Ages. "Collective memory" could thus be seen as close to historical documents as it is far from it.

A new perception of history marked the first generations of settlers in Judea who returned from the Babylonian exile. They did not find the land unoccupied; neither was the entire Israelite population exiled in 721 B.C.E., nor the whole Judean population in 586 B.C.E.[13] Those who remained did not take part in the transformation of religion and religious practices among the Jews exiled to Babylon, visible even in a new practice of name-giving (Haggai, Zacharia, Sabbatai). To the returners, the indigenous population seemed alien: easily they called them so and created a historical narrative to justify their perception. According to this narrative, all Israelites and all Judeans were exiled by the Assyrians or by the Babylonians.[14] In their stead, the land was colonized by other people from far and nearby—Samaritans, Moabites and Ammonites. The "holy seed" (*zera kodesh*) should not mix with these "people of the land" (*am ha'arets*)[15]—and when they did, Ezra demanded that they divorce the alien wives. Never before was the demand for ethnic purity as emphatic as it was then. It was ironic indeed that the grand biblical images of history concluded with a self-serving fiction to uphold a no less fictitious ethnic purity.

Sometime during the Persian rule—perhaps in the interim after the return to the land and before the construction of the Temple—the author of the Book of Chronicles reworked all sources of Jewish history available to him so as to create a consistent, albeit schematic, vision of the pre-exilic monarchy. Its elements have recently been discussed by Sarah Japhet.[16] For the first time, one finds in it a clear distinction between sacred and profane history—a circumstance of which the *Redak* was aware.[17] Hand in hand with this conception of a sacred, temple and

---

13. As might be inferred not only from the Assyrian and Babylonian practices of exiling only the upper strata of society in rebellious territories, but also from internal scriptural evidence, e.g. 2 Chron. 30:1–9. Note esp. v. 5 בכל קול להעביר דבר ויעמידו ישראל מבאר שבע ועד דן לבוא לעשות פסח ליהוה אלהי ישראל בירושלים כי לא לרוב עשו ככתוב.

14. 2 Kings 17:6; 24–41: 28:26.

15. Ezra 9:1–2.

16. See chapter 1, n. 29. Still indispensable is G. v. Rad, *Das Geschichtsbild des Chronistischen Werkes* (Stuttgart, 1930).

17. Ibid. (introduction to the Book of Chronicles).

service-centered history went the assumption of a *continuity* of Israelite historiography that verifies its tradition: the *prophets* of every generation wrote down the history of the kingdom in their time.[18] The recurrent driving forces of events are merit and sin, reward and punishment, God's trials of his faithful servants and their ability to withstand them. The exile to Babylon was an expiation of man and land alike: Israel was to atone for its sins for as long as it took to redeem the unobserved sabbatical years. "Return"—*vaya'al*—is the concluding phase of Cyrus' decree and of the book.

The Historical Novel as Reflexive Literature

THE BOOKS OF RUTH AND ESTHER

Among the latest biblical documents are several for which the name "reflexive literature" is appropriate. They consist of a conscious reflection upon earlier scriptural institutions, conditions or values. Some of them—the books of Ruth, Job, Jonah, and Esther—are cast in the form of a historical novel of sorts, probably the first of its kind in our literature. They were written between the fifth and second centuries B.C.E., and some of them do, while others do not, contain a hidden agenda.

The Book of Ruth seems to contain such a hidden agenda, in its last verses. It has often been discussed, of late, in the fine commentary of Yair Zakovits.[19] Set in the time of the judges, which, as we saw (in contrast to the Book of Judges), was later sometimes seen as a golden age, an idyllic picture is drawn of social harmony in a community living by the law and caring for the poor and the alien. Ruth, an alien Moabite, here marries into the family of her deceased husband—as if the law that

an Ammonite or Moabite shall not enter into the congregation of the Lord; even to their tenth generation shall they not enter into the congregation of the Lord for ever (Deut. 23:4)

18. 1 Chron. 29:29; 2 Chron 9:29; 12:15; 13:22; 20:34; 26:22; 32:32; 33:19. Japhet, ibid. p. 429, n. 19, who gathered references, did not recognize that they express a testimony of the continuity of historiography, a *topos* we discussed in chapter 2, "History as a Continuum." She does refer to the instances in the midrash in which the prophets are said to have composed the historical works of the Bible. But the Book of Chronicles does not claim that.

19. Y. Zakovitch, *Sefer Ruth* (Tel Aviv, 1990).

did not exist. And indeed it did not: it was an addition, if not an interpolation, of those circles who, under the leadership of Ezra, called for the divorce from "Ammonite and Moabite" wives—meaning the indigenous population not exiled to Babylon and returned. Against them, the author of our historical novel shows how David himself descended from a pious Moabite woman. Earlier we saw how the later sages in times of need likewise ignored the very same rules of purity of the stock.[20]

A historical novel recreating past conditions is also the Book of Esther—it, too, may hide a political message, namely the importance of Jews living in the Diaspora at the courts of the high and mighty. There was room for such a message particularly during the climax of the Hasmonean state, a period that saw widespread antagonism between Jews and other citizens of Greek πολεῖς throughout the Middle East. The story is, among other things, an etiological legend to explain the origins of the popular festival of lot-casting (*purim*): it so happens that this festival fell a day after the Hasmonean festival of victory, the *Yom Nikanor*.[21] And so it is well possible that the clash of two festivals embodied a clash of two ideologies, a Judea-centered and a diaspora-centered. But I shall deal with this highly speculative possibility on another occasion.

The Books of Job and Jonah attract our attention because they reflect upon basic components and values of the Scriptures—the trial of the just, the meaning of prophecy—and they do so in the framework of recreating the past. To them we now turn.

THE BOOK OF JOB

The Book of Job never ceases to fascinate its readers. A leading Israeli literary journal recently carried an interesting controversy over the meaning of the book—or rather, over the meaning of God's final answer from the storm. Opinions diverged radically, yet all of them shared one presupposition as a matter of course: all of them joined the tradition of Jewish and Christian exegesis which sees in God's response, at the end of the book, an answer to a question, the

---

20. See chapter 1, nn. 33–34.
21. As we know from *Megillat Ta'anit*. If this (highly speculative) interpretation is correct, the book would have been written very late indeed. Fascination with and knowledge of details of the Persian court—especially when mixed with misinformation and exaggeration—is no indication of time or place, as can be seen from Herodotus.

general-abstract problem "whence evil," *unde malum*. How can evil be accounted for—in ethical, cosmic or esthetic terms? What is its place in the texture of being at large? It is a long exegetical tradition indeed which started with medieval philosophy and ended with Tur-Sinai, Jung and Buber, Kafka, and Hanoch Levin. Within this tradition it is assumed that Job's question is that of "the suffering of the righteous" (*tsadik ve'ra lo*); the problem of sin and punishment, the origins of or response for evil or even the question of cosmic balance that it raises—"since all that is created is created out of being and nothingness" (Ibn Ezra).[22]

I doubt not only their interpretation of the answer, but also the traditional views about the nature of the question. I doubt even the very assumption that the book contains a question to which God answers. Such assumptions were natural and appropriate within the ahistorical, philosophical-medieval exegesis whose time has passed. It seems to me that the interpretations of the text as a theodicy—so evident to the Middle Ages—misses its point altogether. The Book of Job, and the Scriptures in general, cannot be adapted to the tradition of the philosophical problem "from Ionia to Jena" without contortion. Job's "question," such will be my argument, is not a question but a desire and at times even a performative speech-act. Job demands of God, implores him to take him to a trial-court, and in the meantime he lays down his grievances as if he could precipitate such a trial date by his very complaints. He insists on his right to have his public "day in court" in the presence of God, well knowing that his chances to prevail and prove his righteousness are small—God being his judge and prosecutor at once. Job is certain that he did no wrong, but his response to the general-abstract moralizing of the "friends" who came to console him is concrete and personal. Their speeches and consolations were deficient not because they were wrong in principle, but because they were out of place and did not address his personal predicament. They said what Job knew anyhow. Seldom does he doubt the abstract justice of the conduct of God in the world.

None of Job's responses objects to the generalizations or declarations of principle contained in the speeches of the "friends." He rather wishes to silence them because their words bring no solace, or he denies categorically any known or unknown wrongdoing on *his* part.

---

22. In the introduction to his commentary. The recent discussion referred to was published in subsequent issues of *Moznayim* (1988/89).

I know it is so: but how should a man be just before God? . . . Lo, he goes by me, and I see him not: he passes on also, but I perceive him not. . . . the helpers of Rahav [*ozre rahav*] stoop under him. (Job 9:2–13)[23]

Not only does Job know that "it is so" (i.e., that Bildar the Shuchite spoke the truth); note that he downright anticipates God's "answer" to him out of the storm at the end of the book—including the reference to God's taming of primordial cosmic monsters (*rahav*) as proof of God's power and man's ignorant impotence. And he continues:

How much less shall I answer him . . . Whom, though I were righteous, yet would I not answer, but I would make supplication to him who contends with me. (Job 9:14–15)

For he is not a man, as I am, that I should answer him, and we should come together in judgment. There is no umpire between us, who might lay his hand upon us both . . . then I would speak, and not fear him. (Job 9:32–34)

The demand for a quasi court hearing occurs time and again: Job wants to talk to God, to argue with him (Job 12:4; 17:21; 19:6; 31:36):

Behold now, I have ordered my cause; I know that I shall be vindicated. Who is he that will contend with me? for then I would hold my tongue and die. (Job 13:18–19)

As indeed it was to happen later—a confrontation with God in which Job was silenced.

Oh that I knew where I might find him! that I might come even to his seat! I would order my cause [*mishpat*] before him, and fill my mouth with arguments. (Job 23:3–4)

In short: Job is not seeking an abstract understanding of God's providence. He wants a court hearing before God to argue his *own* case.

Corroborating evidence for such a nontheodicean interpretation I find in the very language of the book. Job does not ask "questions," nor do the other *dramatis personae* give "answers" in the fashion of a Platonic dialogue. We rather encounter a series of speeches and counter-

---

23. On *rahav, Leviathan, tanin* and other mythical-cosmic primordial animals cf. Marvin H. Pope, *The Anchor Bible: Job* (Garden City, NY, 1965), pp. 276–278. The *tanin*, another of those primordial creatures tamed by God in prebiblical (extrabiblical) ancient Israelite mythology and mentioned in Job 7:12, appears in Genesis 1:21 as having been created on the fifth day. The context suggests indirect polemics: the name *tanin* appears not in the command-formula, but only in the fulfillment-formula; and it is the only case, except for man, that a definite species is mentioned. Cf. U. Cassuto, *From Adam to Noah. A Commentary on the First Chapters of Genesis* (Jerusalem, 1944), pp. 25–26, 79. This is remarkable, because myths seldom polemicize against other myths.

speeches, each of which begins with the words "*vaya'an . . . vayomer.*" Habitually translated "and he answered . . . and said," it actually means: spoke emphatically, declared. Some medieval commentators were aware of it at least in Job's first speech—cursing the day he was born—which also begins with *vaya'an* without any speech or "question" to precede it. In the commentary attributed to Rashi we read: "Vaya'an: and he shouted, because every *aniya* in the Scriptures is but a phrase indicating the raising of one's voice, and the paradigm for all is 'and the Levites shouted [*ve'anu*] with a loud voice'" (Deut. 26). God's "answer from the storm" should likewise be understood not as an answer to a question but as a declarative reaction.

Should you ask: does not Job accuse God of consistent, general injustice? Indeed he does, but he uses the style of Jeremiah, a fact rightly interpreted as a literary allusion to that prophet's bitter altercation with God.

Why do the wicked live, become old, yea, grow mighty in power? Their seed is established in their sight with them (Job 21:7–8).

Right wouldst thou be, O Lord, if I were to contend with thee: yet I will reason these points of justice with thee: Why does the way of the wicked prosper? why are all they happy that deal very treacherously? Thou hast planted them, indeed, they have taken root (Jer. 12:1–2).

Job's cursing of the day in which he was born is an allusion to Jeremiah 11:14. Which is to say: it is not a theoretical doubting of God's justice, but a complaint born out of his personal situation. His more general accusations of cosmic injustice are but a short-lived response to the various declarations of his friends. Where they provoked him with general assurances of the manifest or latent justice of God's providence, he responds by refuting them. Sometimes he even defines God's justice as valid by definition, like Plato's Euthyphro or Occam, who claimed that the good or just is by definition that which God chose to do. My reading of the "friends" may be the same as that of the contemporary poet:

Job can trust his friends
Who, when time comes, will turn in for a visit,
Asking serious questions with a bent head,
Expressing the justice of this world . . .
They will complement each other
And if they complicate matters with a few repetitions
They are after all friends and not a formulating-team.

(M. Wieseltier)[24]

24. M. Wieseltier, *Davar optimi assiyat shirim* (Tel Aviv, 1976) (my translation).

Here may be the right place to consider the frame-narrative. It is a historical novel in the sense defined earlier. Much as the Book of Ruth reconstructs the days of the Judges, the author of Job reconstructed the days of the Patriarchs. Job is "impeccable" (*tamim*) as Jacob, possessor of cattle and camels, and the balance of his life after his trial was a hundred and four years. Both the classical sages and Abraham Ibn Ezra noticed this similarity when they speculated that Job may have been Nachor's grandchild—"and it seems most plausible to me that he was of the children of Esau" (Ibn Ezra to Job 15:1). The reconstruction of the patriarchal period serves as a stage for an event of the kind of another event which the story of Genesis attributes to Abraham: Job, too, is tried by God and withstands the trial (*nissayon*).[25]

The terms of this trial are known to the reader only, not to the one who is tried: Will Job curse God to his face? In the words of his wife, "Dost thou still retain thy integrity? curse God, and die" (Job 2:9), it is hinted that if Job were to curse God he would be relieved by immediate death from his affliction. And Job indeed "wishes his soul to die" (Job 7:15–21) but not at the price of cursing God. He refuses throughout his trial "to bless God," wherefore he "did not sin with his lips" and withstood his trial.

Indeed, God's response "from the storm" contains nothing which has not been said before either by the friends (e.g., Job 37:15–24) or by Job himself (e.g., Job 28–29). But if it does not constitute an "answer" in an informative sense, it constitutes nonetheless an act of reparation with a moral lesson, a *moralité*. Job got what he asked for—his "day in court," a chance to put forth his case in God's presence. But the altercation he wished for did not take place after all. Job himself was not up to it. God emphasizes what Job knows, what he often expressed earlier—namely the majesty of God and the wonders of his acts. God invites Job to put his case forth. To the first speech of God Job responds briefly: "Behold, I am vile; what shall I answer thee? . . . Once I have spoken; but I will not answer: yea, twice; but I will proceed no further" (Job 40:4–5) (meaning, I presume, the speeches he made to his friends). To God's second speech he responds:

I know that thou canst do everything. . . . I have uttered that which I did not understand; things too wonderful for me, which I knew not. Hear, I beseech thee, and I will speak: I will demand of thee, and declare thou unto me. I have heard of thee by the hearing of the ear: but now my eye sees thee. Wherefore I abhor myself, and repent in dust and ashes. (Job 42:3–6)

25. S. A. Loewenstamm and J. S. Licht, "Nissayon," *Encyclopedia Mikra'it* (Jerusalem, 1950–76) V, pp. 879–83.

Now that he experienced the Divine Presence as he wished he would, he has no power to list his complaints, to make his case.

And the *moralité*? It is both complex and concrete. The Book of Job, much as the Book of Jonah, is a late reflection on basic phenomena of scriptural realities. Just as Jonah reflects on the nature of prophecy and on the link between a prophet and his prophecy, the Book of Job reflects on the nature of the "trials" through which God tries human beings and their complex conflicts while tried. The book is certainly no theodicy: the reader knows from the outset that Job does not suffer aimlessly. The justice of God in the biblical sense of the word—the acknowledgment that it is God's right to do with Job whatever he likes, that God does not owe Job anything—is doubted neither by Job nor by his friends. What, then, was the error of his friends? Why does God scold them for not having "spoken of the thing which is right, like my servant Job" (Job 42:8)? Because they did not comprehend the meaning of a trial. They held to the dichotomy: *if* God is just, if "the judge of all earth" has passed his sentence in word or deed, *then* Job must have sinned; if Job had not sinned, he would not have been afflicted. Job, too, is certain of his innocence and asks for justice—but as the one who is tried and afflicted he has the right to do so, the right to scream and demand to be listened to by the judge.

But we, the readers, know that this dichotomy is erroneous, or that, as God says to Job, "Wilt thou also disavow my judgment? wilt thou condemn me, that thou mayst be in the right?" (Job 40:8–9). Even if Job's afflictions are not a punishment for wrongdoing, God's justice is not disrupted. Beyond the ethical category of crime and punishment stands another category from a totally different realm. The "trial" of Job, as that of Abraham in his time, is the bursting of the numinous into this world, beyond the rules of justice valid in everyday life.[26] In other words, the Book of Job is not a theodicy in the sense that it does not seek a comprehensive answer to the presence of sufferings, evil, ugliness, or privation. The book assumed that its readers accept the existence and the validity of divine justice that need not be proven. It rather tries to reconstruct the thoughts and acts of humans where our notions of divine justice—which are far from being mistaken—do not

26. J. S. Licht, *hanissayon bamikra u-ba-yahadut shel tekufat habayit hasheni* (Jerusalem, 1973). He defines the trial in the Bible as a divine examination to find out whether the tried one obeys God's commands and laws; while already in the apocrypha, God wants to examine faith and piety. Japhet, *Emunot vedeot,* pp. 166–72, places the Book of Chronicles in the midst of the transition from one notion of trial to another, and shows the centrality of the notion in the metahistorical framework of the book. A comparable middle position may be ascribed to the Book of Job.

correspond to the divine aims, and God's "trying" of his faithful is such a situation. Indeed the innocent—especially the innocent—may be cast into that situation. And the book also delineates the limits of the permissible and the impermissible to the one who is tried: he may argue against God and demand that justice be done, he even may exaggerate, but he may not curse God.

Perhaps we should say: Abraham and Job are the biblical paradigms of a trial of the faithful, and the latter is a conscious reflection of the former. What, then, is the difference between them? Abraham, it seems, is the realization of the maximum of "faith" in the biblical sense of the word, which is trust.[27] Job represents the minimum of faith to which a person can hold and still withstand his trial. Abraham, in the words of Kierkegaard, was "the knight of faith," Job a pawn. Abraham stayed silent in the face of his trial, Job rebelled, but still "kept his innocence." Abraham and Job are the poles in a person's being "just" (*tsadik*) in the biblical sense of the word.

I was prompted to publish this interpretation by some recent discussions; it occurred to me as a youngster, when I first read Heinrich von Kleist's *Michael Kolhaas*. The novel illuminated for me the character of Job, who also wanted his day in court. Only Job's end—to our taste much too sweet and banal—was better than that of Kolhaas. Lonelier than both was Josef K. in Kafka's *Trial*—likewise a figure inspired by Job. For he, too, looks for his judges and court of justice, but without a god, without friends—be they phony—and without words. But this is a matter for another discussion.

THE BOOK OF JONAH

No biblical book abounds with ironical, even satirical, elements as much as the Book of Jonah. In the repentance-scene of Nineveh's citizens they even border on the caricature: "but let man and beast be covered with sackcloth, and cry mightily to God: and let them turn everyone from his evil way" (Jon. 3:8).[28] Indeed, some modern

27. Martin Buber, *Zwei Glaubensweisen* (Heidelberg, 1950).
28. It would appear less grotesque if we assume, in the biblical perception, a link between the social and the animal order such that the one reflects the other; an assumption defended skillfully by H. Eilberg-Schwartz, *The Savage in Judaism: An Anthropology of Israelite Religion and Ancient Judaism* (Bloomington, 1990), pp. 115–217. Whether or not the donkey always represents the stranger is debatable: cf. Genesis 49:14 (יששכר חמור גרם).

scholars were so engrossed in the labor of uncovering those ironic elements that they neglected any other aspect of the book. In studies about irony in the Scriptures, the book certainly holds a place of honor.[29] Some view it as a satire or as a parody of prophecy. Focusing on these elements certainly stands in contrast to the traditional exegesis. The fathers of tradition included the book of Jonah in the prayer-cycle of the day of atonement. The following remarks do not intend to refute the modern approaches altogether or to vindicate tradition, but rather to pay attention to the kerygmatic-religious content of the book which almost disappeared from present discussions.

The Scriptures, we know, are replete with intertextual allusions or even internal pieces of exegesis. They have recently been the subject of a comprehensive study by M. Fishbane.[30] An intertextual understanding is particularly called for in that group of later writings which we called the biblical "reflective" literature; most of them employ elements of the historical novel. The Book of Job, we have argued, is a reflection on the phenomenon of the "trial"—such as Abraham's trial in bounding Isaac for sacrifice. It is set in the time of the Patriarchs and employs the style of the Book of Genesis in order to show how "a righteous and innocent man, God-fearing and abstaining from evil," who is not of the stature of Abraham, may conduct himself faced with a trial no less severe than Abraham's. The Book of Jonah, I want to argue, is a reflection on matters of prophets and prophecy. Its author constructed a mental experiment of sorts in which he asked a hypothetical question: what would happen to an average person, without special divine grace or inspiration, if she or he were burdened with a prophecy, that is, with a divine task? What is prophecy, what does it mean to be a prophet, and what makes a person into a true prophet?

Among the many literary allusions within the Book of Jonah—most of them to the prophets and other later Scriptures such as Nahum, Joel, Job—there is one which eluded attention.

And the Lord saw that the wickedness of man was great in the earth. . . . And the Lord repented [*vayinachem*] that he had made man on the earth (Gen. 6:5–6).

And God said to Noah, The end of all flesh is come before me; for the earth is filled with violence [*hamas*] through them (Gen. 6:13).

29. E. Good, *Irony in the Old Testament* (Philadelphia, 1965), pp. 38 ff.; A. Band, "Swallowing Jonah: The Eclipse of Parody," *Prooftexts* 10 (1990): pp. 177–95.
30. Above n. 12.

The children of Nineveh in our book likewise must

turn [*shavu*] everyone from his evil way [*chamas*], and from violence that is in their hands. Who can tell? God may turn [*yashuv*] and relent [*venicham*], and turn away [*veshav*] from his fierce anger, so that we perish not. (Jon. 3:8–9)

And Nineveh "was an exceeding great city of three days' journey in extent." (Jon. 3:3). The allusion is evident, and so is the circumstance that the Nineveh spoken of in Jonah is not the historical Nineveh which embodied iniquity and continued to do so, but rather a symbolic Nineveh, a city representing the whole inhabited, cultivated earth which "in forty days will turn upside down" (*nehefekhet*) much as the world was turned upside down in the deluge.

Indeed, outside this symbolic Nineveh everything is desert, a *terra inculta* without a shadow.[31] Jonah sought refuge in his tent (*sukka*) outside town as Noah once found refuge in his ark "till he might *see* what would comes to pass in the city" (Jonah 4:5), much as Noah sent a dove (Jonah!) to *see* "whether the waters abated." The deluge and the shaking (*mahapekha*) of Sodom and Gomorrah are the archetypes of Nineveh's ordained fate. From the duty to pronounce this divine decree Jonah fled, once to the sea—inside the ship—and a second time to his tent in the desert. But unlike Noah, Jonah finds no relief—a "shadow" (*tsel*) in a double and triple sense of the metaphor—in both places. Contrary to the story of the deluge, humanity repents and is spared; but like the story of the deluge, God gives up his intent to destroy all. In short, it is at once an analogy and its inversion.

God mercifully reconsiders (*nicham*); indeed He is "merciful and forgiving" (*rachum vechanun*). In Noah himself—Noah's very name alludes to it—God "reconsiders" his regret of having made humankind; at the end he concludes with Noah the covenant of the rainbow in the sky. Jonah testifies about himself that he fled to Tarsus,

for I knew that thou art a gracious God, and merciful, slow to anger, and great in love, and repentest of the evil [*venicham 'al hara'a*] (Jon. 4:2).

Now this is the angle upon which our story turns. Jonah is angry over God's reconsideration of Nineveh's lot. But why? Some medieval commentators answered: because he felt shamed. But the text does not reveal it. The matter is worthy of further consideration.

The author of the Book of Jonah named his antihero with a name

31. On the importance of this topos in medieval literature see W. Berges, "Land und Unland in der mittelalterlichen Welt," *Festschrift für Hermann Heimpel zum 70. ten Geburtstag* (Göttingen, 1972) III, pp. 399–439.

known already from the Book of Kings. Jeroboam II, king over the northern kingdom of Israel,

departed not from all the sins of Yarov'am the son of Nevat. . . . He restored the border of Israel from the entrance of Hamat to the sea of the 'Arava, according to the word of the Lord God of Israel, which he spoke by the hand of his servant Jonah, the son of Amittay, the prophet, who was of Gat-hefer. For the Lord saw the affliction of Israel that it was very bitter . . . . For the Lord had not said that he would blot out the name of Israel from under the heavens: but he saved them by the hand of Jeroboam the son of Jehoash (2 Kings 14: 24–27).

Note that Israel would have deserved—as later the Ninevites in the Book of Jonah—to have "its name eradicated," yet it did not happen.[32] The fictitious Nineveh is like the historical Israel spoken of in this passage of the Book of Kings. Again, however, the analogy becomes inverted. The children of Israel did not repent, and therefore the name of Israel—of the kingdom and the ten lost tribes—was eventually wiped out by the Assyrian king, that is, by the Lord of Nineveh.

The historical narrative does not add anything about the figure of the historical Jonah or the content of his speeches. The historical fiction of the Book of Jonah places him in the situation both analogous and inverted. In both cases, strict justice is not carried out, the due sentence is mitigated. In both, the norm "the soul that sins, it shall die" (Ezek. 18:4) is not fulfilled. But the children of Nineveh repented in a dramatic, almost grotesque public act.

In the historical narrative the prophet remains a mere name. The author of the historical fiction filled the gap, beginning with the facts known to him from 2 Kings: the "word of God" to Jonah. The fictitious Jonah is also a "servant of God" (*eved Jahve*), but a servant who flees from his master *because* he is a prophet who knows in advance that his publicly uttered prophecy will *not* come true due to God's mercy. This is a paradoxical situation, not unlike the paradoxes of self-reference such as that of the Cretan Epimenedes, who says of all Cretans that they are liars. If Jonah is a prophet (i.e., knows the consequences of his prophecy) then he is not a prophet (i.e., his prophecy of doom will fail to be realized). This, and not shame, seems to be the situation from which Jonah wanted "to flee" and could not do so. All of the book of Jonah swarms with paradoxes, and this one tops them all: an inverted world. But why did the author need such striking disharmonies?

The paradox of self-reference is a formal paradox. Indeed, the ficti-

---

32. Cf. above, p. 6 (name and memory).

tious Jonah is a prophet only in the formal sense of the word—and precisely because of this he found himself in a paradoxical situation. A corroboration of this reading we find not only in the response he gave to God, but also in the extreme brevity of his explicit prophecy—a mere five words!—a brevity that befits someone who prophesies against his wish and will. Now, that a prophet be "heavy of mouth and heavy of tongue" (Exod. 4:11) and "cannot speak" (Jer. 1:6) are traditional *topoi* of the prophetic literature. Prophets are often depicted in awe of their task, wishing to flee from it, but eventually they identify with their prophetic role and their prophecy becomes part of them, "like a fire burning in their bones," and the source of their eloquence. Jonah, in contrast, is a prophet who is no prophet: his prophecy is and remains alien to him. He detests it throughout the story, throughout his mission.

Lest we think poorly of Jonah as a shallow figure without redeeming features or merits, the answer he gave to the sailors of the ship he fled to testifies to his faith: "I am a Hebrew and fear the God of the heavens who created the sea and the earth." His prayer from the belly of the fish is likewise a testimony of his piety. I fail to comprehend how one modern interpreter could read it as a parody. Among the biblical hymns of prayer it is one of the most sublime and beautiful. Herman Melville appraised it correctly as a "noble canticle" and observed further, "for sinful as he is, Jonah does not weep or wail for direct deliverance . . . he leaves all his deliverance to God."[33] The prayer expresses his certainty that he will be delivered. Because of this, and because it uses the past tense ("I have cried . . . he responded to me") some viewed it as a later, alien addition to the story. I do not think so. On the contrary, the prayer seems to me to be the original nucleus around which at least the first part of the story was written. At any rate it shows Jonah to be a true "servant of God." But is he also a prophet?

Perhaps we ought to say: the author of the book asked himself and his readers how an *average* pious person would react if burdened with prophecy and with all the oddities and dangers of prophecy. How might he feel knowing himself set "over the nations and over the kingdoms, to root out, and to pull down, and to destroy and to throw down, to build, and to plant" (Jeremiah 1:10). The author concludes at the end of his story: a prophet of the kind of Jonah is not a true

33. Herman Melville, *Moby-Dick; or the White Whale* (New York, 1962), p. 62 (ch. 9). For a different opinion of the prayer as ironical, see Band (n. 29).

prophet. Indeed, nowhere in the story is Jonah called a prophet—in sharp contrast to his historical counterpart in the Book of Kings. Jonah is not a prophet for two reasons: one, because he fails to identify with his prophecy (i.e., his prophetic mission), which is forced upon him; second, because when, at the end, he does prophesy, he identifies with his prophecy (i.e., its contents) too much in a narrow, formalistic sense. A true prophet is a prophet by virtue of his personality and by virtue of the divine charisma descending upon him, not by virtue of this or that speech and whether it comes true. Such a prophet does not wish for a punitive divine decree to be fulfilled, but wrestles with God, asking him to rescind the impending catastrophe, as Abraham did before Sodom or Moses after the sin of the sacrifice to the golden calf. Like God himself, the true prophet has mercy on "more than one hundred and twenty thousand persons that cannot discern between their right hand and their left hand; and also much cattle" (Jon. 4:11).

Here, at the conclusion of the story, we also find the technique of inverted analogies observable throughout the text. Jonah himself was delivered from the storm and the belly of the fish because of his prayer. This means that God had mercy on him and accepted his repentance. Yet Jonah does not want what was done to him to be done to others, does not want it to be a norm of divine conduct. He became "very angry" over the acceptance by God of Nineveh's repentance. And finally: unlike most biblical stories, the end of this story remains wide open. Did Jonah comprehend and accept God's last answer to him? In that the author remained mute he may have wanted to indicate that it does not matter at all either way. Jonah's final fate bears no relevance to the substance of the story—the story of the response of a prophet who lacks the spirit of prophecy, to whom prophecy is nothing but a burden.

The ancient rabbinical authorities, who had a very keen eye for differences in styles and conceptions in the various parts of the Bible, once summarized these differences as follows:

Wisdom was asked: what is the punishment of a sinner? and answered: sinners will be prosecuted by [their own] vice. Prophecy was asked: what is the punishment for the sinner? and answered "the soul that sins, it shall die" [Ezek. 18:4]. God was asked: what is the punishment of the sinner? and answered: let him do repentance [teshuva] and be expiated.[34]

34. J. T. Makkot 6, 2. Note that each section of the Bible "answers" in its own language.

The divine point of view does not always converge either with that of the later scriptures (wisdom, *ketubim*) or with that of the prophetic scriptures (*nevi'im*) or even with the point of view of the Pentateuch (*tora*). And perhaps this, too, was on the mind of those who included the book of Jonah in the prayers for the day of atonement.

History as Predestination: The Apocalyptic Mentality

THE APOCALYPTIC VISION

Quoniam festinans festinat saeculum pertransire: "Our world," says the Ezra apocalypse, "hurries toward its end." Written about a generation after the catastrophic end of the first Jewish revolt against Rome (A.D. 71), the vision restates the motifs common to all apocalyptic visions: the end of the world is very near; only a few will survive it to see the outbreak of a new, magnificent eon. The old world is full of "sorrow and pain"; it will crumble under the weight of its own wickedness. The new world will be new in all respects: a new society, a new cosmic order; "all periods and years will then be destroyed, and hereafter will exist neither month nor day, nor hours."[35] The new order of things, albeit anticipated and prophesied, will come "like a thief in the night," sudden and terrible.[36] Very little can be done by anyone, including those who know, to precipitate the end or to prevent it. Its exact time is known to God only: it has been set in a divine plan, written "in heavenly tablets" preceding history and predestinating its course.[37] This blueprint for the course of history is immutable, and so

35. 4 Ezra 4:26, 27, in B. Violet, ed., *Die Esra-Apokalypse*, vol. 1, *Die Überlieferung* (Leipzig, 1910), p. 36; vol. 2, *Die dritische Ausgabe* (Leipzig, 1927), p. 17. For references hereinafter to 4 Ezra or the Ezra Apocalypse, see Violet, "Die Esra-Apokalypse," or G. H. Box, "4 Ezra," in R. H. Charles, ed., *The Apocrypha and Pseudepigrapha of the Old Testament*, 2 vols. (1913; Oxford, 1963), vol. 2, pp. 542–624. On apocalyptic "pessimism," see Rudolf Bultmann, *Das Urchristentum im Rahmen der antiken Religionen*, 2nd ed. (Zürich, 1954), p. 79; and W. Bousset, *Die Religion des Judentums im späthellenistischer Zeitalter*, ed. H. Gressmann, 3rd ed. rev. (Tübingen, 1926), pp. 11–15.

36. Matthew 24:3–51; 2 Peter 3:10; 4 Ezra 4:34 ff.; see Funkenstein, *Heilsplan und natürliche Entwicklung*, pp. 11–15.

37. Ethiopian Enoch 81:2, 93:2, Jubilees 1:29; Funkenstein, *Heilsplan und natürliche Entwicklung*, p. 123, n. 2. For references hereinafter to the Ethiopian Enoch or the

is the end of history. It will come soon, but "not by the hands of man" (Dan. 2:45).[38] A passive, predestinarian posture allowed the apocalyptic visionary to withdraw from this world and to cast all hope on the other world. And though passivity does not always characterize the apocalyptician—the Dead Sea Scrolls, for example, anticipate a final battle between the "children of light" and the "children of darkness"—he is, whether active or passive, filled with a profound sense of alienation within this world. His political resignation, caused by internal persecution and external loss of political autarky since the end of the Hasmonean (Maccabean) dynasty, was complete: nothing in this world seemed to him worth amending or ameliorating.

Apocalypticism was a new and well-defined phenomenon in the history of the Jewish religion since the second century B.C. It was also the main source for future Jewish and Christian eschatological images, images concerning the "last things." Both the novelty and the uniqueness of apocalypticism are far from being self-evident. After all, visions of cosmic doom and delivery are not confined to the Jewish and Christian traditions. They appear in just about all cultures and societies in times of want as well as in times of affluence. Every culture seems to harbor thanatic fears of an ultimate catastrophe and hopes of rebirth of a new world. It is hard to overlook the ties between the myth (and cult) of the yearly regeneration of the earth out of darkness and barrenness and the myths of a future, final recreation of the world out of immense chaos and pain. "Millennarian" movements in different and disparate cultural horizons employ similar myths of rebirth.[39] Even if this is all these were to say of apocalypticism—which is not the case—apocalypticism would be a watershed in the history of the Jewish religion. On a very basic level, its novelty consists in the renewal of the almost severed umbilical cord of the Jewish religion to the domain of creative mythology. The mythopoetical imagination of the apocalyptician re-

---

Ethiopic version of the Book of Enoch, see Charles, *The Apocrypha and Pseudepigrapha of the Old Testament,* vol. 2, pp. 163 ff.; for the Book of Jubilees or the Ethiopic version of the Hebrew Book of Jubilees, ibid., vol 1, pp. 1–82.

38. See Aage Bentzen, *Handbuch zum Alten Testament,* edited by Otto Eissfeldt, 2nd ed. (Tübingen, 1952), p. 33. For exceptions to this passive ideology, see Funkenstein, *Heilsplan und natürliche Entwicklung,* p. 124, n. 6; and, on the Hasmoneans, J. Efron, *Studies of the Hasmonean Period* (Tel Aviv, 1960), pp. 30–34, 41–125.

39. Mircea Eliade, "Cosmic and Eschatological Renewal," in his *The Two and the One,* translated by J. M. Cohen (Chicago, 1962), pp. 125–59, and *Cosmos and History: The Myth of the Eternal Return* (New York, 1959).

mythologized, in a sense, both cosmos and history. His language, his symbols are mythical through and through: unlike the prophets he not only employs current residues of myth, but rather creates a new mythical imagery to express the cosmic battle between good and evil, order and chaos, God and primordial beasts.

Yet if we attend only to the mythopoetical aspect of apocalypticism, important as it is, we shall hardly appreciate its uniqueness. For the sake of clarity, I wish to introduce the (ideal) distinction between apocalyptic imagery and apocalyptic knowledge: the significance of apocalypticism lies not only in the fact that the apocalyptician envisions the end of the world in very vivid images; no less important is the manner in which he proves the veracity of his visions, convinces himself and his community that the end is inevitable and inevitably close. Only with the aid of this distinction can the paradox of apocalypticism be understood—that it enhanced at one and the same time a sense of myth and a sense of history as a distinct unity.

Apocalyptic visions of a final universal trial took the place of the older prophetic visions of an ultimate "day of Jahweh." The later prophets did not invent hopes of a sudden, miraculous delivery. Such hopes were part of popular beliefs during the last one and a half centuries of both monarchies, Israel and Judea, when internal disintegration and political impotence generated hopes for a miraculous relief, prefigured by the exodus from Egypt.[40] The prophets rather tried to cut such hopes down to size. Vis-à-vis the professional optimists of their times, the "false prophets," they did not deny the coming of the "day of Jahweh" but insisted that it would be a time of "darkness, and not light" (Amos 5:20) which would precede the future redemption.[41] The catastrophe could not be avoided; only a radical devastation would atone for internal corruption. Their message also demanded a new theodicy. Then as now, it was difficult to maintain allegiance to a God who seemed incapable of protecting his chosen people; cults are covenants which bind two sides. Could it be that Israel's God was powerless against the gods of mighty Egypt and Assyria? The prophets introduced a revolutionary, dialectical theodicy, an inversion of the popular

40. Isaiah 11:15–16. See S. A. Loewenstamm, *Massoret yetsiat mitsrayim behishtalsheluta,* 2nd ed. (Jerusalem, 1968), pp. 16, 103. On other typologies of reenactment in the Bible, see Amos Funkenstein, "Nachmanides's Typological Reading of History," *Zion* 45:1 (1980), p. 37, and chapter 4, "History and Typology."

41. See Gerhard von Rad, *The Message of the Prophets,* translated by D. M. Stalker (New York, 1972), pp. 95–99.

belief that the measures of power of a deity are the success and prosperity of the community obliged to that deity by the bonds of *religio*.
They insisted, to the contrary, that God's immense, universal powers
were manifested by the very plight of the chosen people: only God
could employ the mightiest empires as a "rod of wrath" to purge Israel,
while these empires were unaware of their role in the divine plan, of
their objective role in history (Isa. 10:5–7).[42] The "remnant of Israel"
(Zeph. 3:13) that survived the day of judgment imposed on all nations
would also witness a new and just order of things.

Many of the leading prophetic images reappear in the apocalyptic
literature—exaggerated almost to the point of an involuntary caricature, and without the strong realistic sense which permeated the writings of the prophet. At times—though by no means always—the
apocalyptic vision of history is rooted within a sectarian counterideology.[43] The Qumran sect, for example, regarded only itself as the "holy
community." The establishment, particularly "the wicked priest and his
community," constituted the "city of vanity"; other Jews were either
part of the adversary or, at best, "fools."[44] And while the prophetic
visions of ultimate doom and delivery were addressed to the whole of
Israel, including the lost tribes, the Qumran sect seems to have written
off most of Israel. They alone are "the remnant," the avant-garde of the
new eon in the midst of the old, doomed one. They alone are the true
Israel, preparing for and knowing about the imminent final war between light and darkness. Their eschatological hopes were confined to
their own group, while the rest of Israel would have to share, so it
seems, the lot of other nations.

The period between the last Hasmoneans in the first century B.C.
and the revolt against the Romans (A.D. 66–71) was more sectarian
than any other period of Jewish history. All over the Hellenistic-Roman
world (*oikoumene*), old religious, social, and political institutions were
disintegrating. The classical political ethics of the Greeks gave way to
the individual ethics of the Hellenistic period: the individual, not the
city, strove now to attain autarky.[45] Traditional, national, or local cults
were replaced by consciously syncretistic cults which centered around

42. See above, pp. 53–54.
43. Peter L. Berger and Thomas Luckmann, *The Social Construction of Reality* (Garden City, N.Y., 1966), pp. 116–17.
44. See J. Licht, "Mata'at olam ve'am pedut el," *Mechkarim bemagilot hagnuzot, Sefer
zikaron le A. L. Sukenik* (Jerusalem, 1951), pp. 49–75; and David Flusser, *Judaism and
the Origins of Christianity* (Tel Aviv, 1979), pp. 324–32, 335–37.
45. W. W. Tarn, *Hellenistic Civilisation*, 3rd ed. (London, 1959), pp. 327 ff.

newly formed groups striving for individual salvation through true knowledge (*gnosis*).[46] Even normative Judaism was affected by the spirit of individualization, at a time which lacked a firm central religious-legal authority, was all the more affected. A century later, this lack of consensus at the eve of the revolt was blamed as the chief cause of the catastrophe, so much so that, according to a learned legend, even a small, insignificant incident could lead to the destruction which neither the Roman Emperor nor the Jews wanted: "The Temple was destroyed because divisions multiplied in Israel."[47]

THE APOCALYPTIC MODES OF PROOF

Before they became widespread and watered down, some apocalyptic visions were a part of sectarian or quasisectarian interpretations of history. A peculiar unity of form and content is likewise the distinctive mark of authentic apocalyptic writings, and both are subservient to the actual social role of apocalypses. The apocalyptic visionary employed three modes of proof for his contentions: first, "uncovered" prophecies (apocalypses in the strict sense); second, a new method by which to "decode" old, well-known prophecies (*pesher*); and third, a technique of "interpreting" the course of history itself "typologically." All of these modes have in common the indication of secret knowledge.

The invention of "rediscovered" or "uncovered" prophecies reveals an unspoken assumption which the apocalyptician shared with normative Judaism of his time, namely, that the age of authentic new prophecies had ended sometime at the very beginning of the second Temple period in the sixth century B.C. Then and there prophecy ceased to be an active social, public institution and was relegated to "the deaf, the dumb, and the minor" only.[48] For the same reason, normative Judaism refused to add any recent books, no matter how valuable, to the canon of sacred Scripture: ancientness was the prime principle of canonization. At the same time, the legal portion of the Talmud (*halakha*) insists on its legitimate disregard of inspiration. The apocalyptician, on the other hand, ascribed his prophetic writings to famous biblical figures. The biblical Book of Daniel, perhaps generated in the circle of "the first

46. Gilbert Murray, *Five Stages of Greek Religion* (3rd ed. [Boston, 1951]. Reprint. Garden City, N.Y., 1955), pp. 119 ff., esp. 154 ff.; Hans Jonas, *Gnostic Religion,* 2nd ed. (Boston, 1963).

47. B. T. *Gittin* 55*b*–56*a*. Cf. chapter 6, "The Rationalization of Polemics."

48. See E. E. Urbach, "When Did Prophecy Cease?" *Tarbiz* 17 (1947), pp. 1–11, and in *The Sages,* 2nd ed. (Jerusalem, 1978), pp. 502–13.

pious man" in the beginning of the Hasmonean era, came first and became the paradigm for a host of similar prophecies-after-the-event. Daniel supposedly lived during the Babylonian exile and experienced four apocalyptic visions. Later visions were ascribed to seven earlier figures, back to Adam and Adam's grandson Enoch, in part in order to enhance veneration toward the apocalypse, in part to convey the growing sense within the apocalyptic tradition that all of history, from the first entanglement in sin down to the ultimate end of this world, is predestined and follows an immutable course. Sealed and concealed by their illustrious authors, these prophecies were destined to be rediscovered by the right persons at the end of days. The circumstance that most of the events prophesied in an apocalypse, in symbols transparent to contemporaries, were already fulfilled, vouched for its authenticity even more.[49] The very fact that an apocalypse was rediscovered proved that the end was close indeed, and that those who found it were what they claimed to be—the small avant-garde of the new world within the old, whose function now was to spread the knowledge about the end:

> And I heard, but I understood not; then said I: "O my lord, what shall be the latter end of these things?" And he said: "Go thy way, Daniel; for the words are shut up and sealed till the time of the end. Many shall purify themselves, and make themselves white, and be refined; but the wicked shall do wickedly; and none of the wicked shall understand; but they that are wise shall understand . . . . But go thy way till the end be; and thou shalt rest, and shalt stand up to thy lot, at the end of the days" (Dan. 12:8–13)

Should we call apocalypses forgeries? Could it be that the authors of pseudoepigraphic materials believed that they were merely recreating, by inspiration, an ancient ideal codex? Such questions may be addressed to the books of Daniel and Enoch no less than to the Book of Mormon, the most recent genuinely apocalyptic text.

More subtle than apocalypses proper, was the apocalyptic decoding of already well known canonical prophecies. The technical term employed for their exegetical acrobatics—*pesher*—was once used to indicate the technique of decoding dreams (Gen. 41:12; Dan. 2:26) by identifying their symbolic contents. The apocalyptician is convinced that all prophecies of old are latter-day prophecies. The prophet himself may not have understood what he was prophesying; he may have (subjectively) believed he was prophesying the approximate events of his

49. See now also Jacob Licht, "The Attitude to Past Events in the Bible and in Apocalyptic Literature," *Tarbiz* LX, 1 (1990): pp. 1–18.

time, whereas in reality he was predicting the events of our days, events close to the end of history. Again, as in the case of apocalypses, the proof of the method is a vicious circle, a proof by self-reference. The fact that the apocalyptician was given a key to unlock the hidden meaning of ancient texts, the fact that God "announced" to the "teacher of righteousness"—the founding father of the sect—"all the secrets of his servants the prophets"[50] proves the proximity of the end and the chosenness of the sect. For only close to the end will "wisdom," that is, knowledge about the end, multiply (Dan. 12:8–13). The apocalyptical exegesis develops great ingenuity in identifying even the smallest details of present history in ancient prophecies: the Book of Habakkuk, for example, referred to the Roman consuls and senate. Formally, the actualizing exegesis of apocalypticians may not differ much from the Midrash of normative Judaism in its methods, but the latter exposition is conscious of violating the grammatical meaning of the Scriptures and does so with a grain of salt, at times even with self-mockery.[51] No trace of humor or relativization will be found in the apocalyptician when he exploits the Scriptures. He is as dead earnest as his subject.

His subject, his obsession, was the end of the world. He was called by later adversaries "a calculator of the end." Self-produced prophecies and a new key to decode old prophecies helped him to ascertain how close the end was. His technique of interpreting history, his method of reading it, his technique of interpreting history typologically served the same purpose. Nowhere before was historical time, the course of history as a whole, so strongly perceived as a unity structured by very precise periods.

The periods, albeit distinct, follow the same pattern; they are the eon in miniature. The Book of Enoch distinguishes clearly three periods of cosmic weeks: the first two from the creation to the "first end," the deluge, five others to the present, and three additional weeks to prepare for the "grand eternal judgment." The Ezra apocalypse has five periods which repeat the same new beginning followed by the triumph of evil: from Adam to Noah, Noah to Abraham, Abraham to Moses, Moses to David, and David to the first destruction. The Baruch apocalypse sees its twelve periods in an antithetical order: a "bright" stream

---

50. *Pesher Habakuk* 7:1–5 (the prophet himself did not understand the meaning of his prophecy; God revealed to the "teacher of righteousness" את כל רזי עבדיו הנביאים. Cf. Matthew 13:35 (as in Proverbs 98:2): κεκρυμμένα ἀπὸ καταβολῆς.

51. B. T. Sanhedrin 90b: [הנך שוכב עם אבותיך] "הנך שוכב עם אבותיך וקם". ודילמא: "וקם העם הזה וזנה"?

is always followed by a "dark" one; only the time before the end will witness the boundless reign of evil.[52] Guided by the analogy between the number of days of creation and periods of the world, and armed with a realization of the biblical metaphor "for a thousand years in your eyes are like one day," apocalyptic calculations find a scriptural rationale for ancient Iranian-Babylonian traditions of a "grand year": "six thousand years the world endures, and is devastated for one thousand"; "six thousand years the world endures, of which two thousand are chaos, two thousand law, and two thousand the messianic days." The treatise Sanhedrin of the Babylonian Talmud, which mentions the last two traditions, also lists many more—probably in order to discard them. The list concludes with the dictum, "Let the spirit of those who calculate the end expire."[53]

The fascination with historical time and its structure was the most important contribution of the apocalyptic mentality to the Western sense of history. The apocalyptician grasped all of history as a structured, well-articulated, meaningful unity. His detailed account of the future drama of the end, down to days, hours, and precise actors, was drawn from the background of his perception of the whole of history as a dramatic struggle between the forces of good and evil.

With these methods, the apocalyptic visionary "proved" his contentions. Visions of an end, as was said above, have also occurred in other cultures at different times. In classical antiquity, however, I know of only two variants which required a proof: the Greek anticipation of the periodic devastation of the world (*apokatastasis, ekpyrosis*) and the apocalyptic expectation of the transition of eons. The difference between these two is not that one views history as cyclical while the other, as has been sometimes contended, endorses a linear view of history—this distinction is a recent scholarly invention. It is very clear that the apocalyptic tradition does not exclude eternal return, at times even alludes to it under the influence, perhaps, of Iranian tradition. Nor indeed does the Bible exclude eternal return—it simply is outside the horizon of biblical imageries. The *uniqueness* of history, or at least of its central event, became thematic only in the Christian horizon. Against Origenes's theory

52. Ethiopian Enoch 93:3–10, 91:12–17; Bousset, *Die Religion des Judentums*, p. 281; recently, Devorah Dimant, "Election and Laws of History in Apocalyptic Literature," in *Chosen People, Elect Nation and Universal Mission*, edited by Sh. Almog and M. Heyd (Jerusalem, 1991), pp. 59–70, and Licht (as in n. 49).

53. B. T. *Sanhedrin* 97a, *Avoda Zara* 9a. On similar Christian traditions (*ante legem, sub lege, sub gratia*), see Funkenstein, *Heilsplan und natürliche Entwicklung*, p. 129, nn. 27–29. Cf. also below, p. 187.

of world succession, Saint Augustine (A.D. 354–435) insisted that Christ came only once for all time. The difference is rather that the apocalyptic relies on astronomical-cosmological speculations.[54] And, of course, for the Greek scientist as well as for the modern, the cosmic end is not so pressing, so urgent an issue as it was to the apocalyptician, who lived in the tense, daily expectation of the end to come. The life of the apocalyptic community revolved around this expectation.

THE JEWISH TRADITION

"Let the spirit of those who ponder upon the end expire." The rabbinical establishment had good reasons to suspect apocalyptic fantasies even when they ceased to be sectarian. Jewish apocalypticism proper died out somewhere during the second century A.D. A strong religious-legal leadership, formed after the first revolt against Rome (A.D. 66–71) and consolidated after the second (A.D. 132–135), systematically eradicated sectarian subcultures. It placed national unity above all other concerns, even the integrity of the priesthood.[55] It also feared messianic-apocalyptic eruptions. The suspicion was well grounded. Christianity grew out of a messianic-apocalyptic heresy into a formidable adversary. The second, or Bar Kokhba, revolt against the Roman Empire was a catastrophe greater than the first revolt: it left Judea depopulated and the Jews barred from Jerusalem.[56] Beyond the danger of promoting uncontrollable messianic eruption, apocalypticism was suspicious on another count. It smacked of mythology, of a mythopoetic mentality. And even though apocalyptic images, traditions, and motifs, taken out of their original context, survived and continued to be embellished, the invention of authentic new apocalypses ceased almost entirely.

Normative Judaism, however, could not rid itself of apocalyptic motifs altogether, because it was, and remained, committed to a utopian ideal, no matter how "realistic" its interpretation. A utopian mentality[57] is an integral component of the Jewish religion: a belief in the ultimate redemption of the nation by a messiah, the restoration of sovereignty

54. See, for example, Eliade, *Cosmos and History*, pp. 112–37; also M. Pohlenz, *Die Stoa*, 2 vols. (Göttingen, 1959), vol. 1, pp. 79 ff., and vol. 2, pp. 47 ff.

55. See chapter 1, nn. 33–34.

56. M. Avi-Yonah, *Biyme Roma u-'Bizantion* (Jerusalem, 1946), pp. 1–4.

57. Karl Mannheim, *Ideology and Utopia*, translated by Louis Wirth and Edward Shils (1929; New York, 1955).

for the rest of the historical time, the return of all Jews from exile, the rebuilding of the Temple at its place, the establishment of peace and justice throughout the world. In view of the ever-present danger of a messianic eruption out of unrestrained apocalyptic fantasies and expectations, the normative attitude toward messianism was a continuous balancing act between affirmation and caution. As a result, no normative interpretation was formulated at all. The rabbinical establishment may have felt instinctively that the best messianic doctrine was no doctrine at all; otherwise, if definite characteristics of the Messiah and his age were given, no matter how restrictive, a generation pregnant with acute messianic hopes would find it all the easier to identify such criteria with the present age and with some present contender. The vaguer the criteria, the less room there was for an actualizing interpretation—such as Christianity—to develop out of the apocalyptic tradition.

Against apocalyptic fantasizing, normative Judaism consolidated the distinction between "the messianic days" and "the world to come" and warned against exaggerated, premature hopes for the former. From the triple repetition of the formula "I beseech you, the daughters of Jerusalem, in the name of the gazelles of the fields, not to hasten nor to precipitate love until it desires," the sages inferred that an oath was laid upon Israel not to precipitate the end nor to rebel against "the nations of the world"; while another oath was laid upon the kingdoms of the world "not to subjugate Israel too much."[58] The "messianic days" entail only the restitution of sovereignty, according to a famous dictum of Mar Shemuel; even poverty will not be abolished, for it is said that "the poor shall never cease out of the land" (Deut. 15:11).[59] Rather than a binding doctrine concerning the last things, the rabbinical sayings amount to the warning not to expect too much and not to expect it too soon. Within the whole Talmud, only one genuine, new apocalypse is mentioned, and even the discovery of this one is ascribed to a Persian soldier.[60]

"When you see empires in conflict, expect the footsteps of the Messiah."[61] The conquest of the land of Palestine by the Persians in A.D. 614, its brief reconquest by Byzantium, and its final conquest by the Muslim Arabs in A.D. 637 incited the renewed production of apocalyptic visions, all the more so since, for a very short while, it seemed as if

58. B. T. *Ketubot* 3a; Song of Songs 2:7; 5:8; 8:4; cf. chapter 9 on Yoel Taitelbaum.
59. B. T. *Berakhot* 34.
60. B. T. *Sanhedrin* 97a.
61. *Genesis Rabba* 52.

the Persians were allowing a Jewish administration of Palestine. Some of the disappointment and the expectations are attended to in the Book of Zerubbabel, an intermediary between ancient and medieval apocalypticism. To the gallery of dreadful events at the end of days, the Book of Zerubbabel adds, both under Christian influence and in an anti-Christian vein, a Jewish version of the Antichrist, the last Roman emperor!

And as I heard his words I fell on my face and said: reveal me the truth about the leader of the sacred people. And he held on to me and brought me to a church and showed me a statue in the image of a woman whose appearance was very, very beautiful . . . and he said to me: upon this stone will rise and reign terror, the dominion of Satan his father. These are his signs, his hair is green as gold, his hands reach his heels, his face a finger in breadth, his eyes irregular, and he has two skulls; everyone will flee him [but] all the nations of the world will follow him to heresy, except for Israel which will not believe in him. And he will attack the saints in Jerusalem with mighty force.[62]

During the First Crusade (1096–1099), there was a resurgence of apocalypses, at times mixed with astrological-astronomical speculations.[63] On the whole, however, it is astonishing how few genuine apocalypses were produced throughout the Middle Ages, all the more so in view of the fact that apocalyptic images and motifs persisted as an integral part of messianic folklore. In other words, medieval apocalypticism, unlike ancient apocalypticism, ceased by and large to be a science, the systematic secret knowledge it once was. "Calculations of the end" are here and there carried forth—by scholars, at times even with astronomical-astrological reasoning—but it is not in the strict sense apocalyptical. Apocalyptic images, on the other hand, permeate the popular fantasy; they are always ready to nourish acute messianic hopes, but they are not part of a secret system of knowledge.

How much this is so we learn from the latest and widest messianic eruption, the Sabbatai Zvi movement in 1665–66. The famous letter in which Nathan of Gaza, the prophet and the moving force behind the Sabbatean propaganda, first argues for the messiahship of the Jewish

62. Jehuda Eben-Shmuel, *Midreshe Geula* (Jerusalem, 1952), p. 79. On the Christian attributes of this Jewish Antichrist, combined with attributes of Christ himself as some Jewish traditions saw him, e.g., "The Book of History of Jesus" in S. Krauss, *Das leben Jesu nach judischen Quellen* (Vienna, 1902). It seems likely that the Apocalypse was written in Byzantium; Byzantium was also the place where rabbinical authority was weakest.

63. I. Baer, "Ein Jüdische Messias-Apocalypse aus dem jahre 1186," *Monatshefte zur Geschichte und Wissenschaft des Judentums* (MGWJ) 70 (1926), pp. 113 ff.

mystic, Sabbatai Zvi, has two almost disconnected parts.[64] In the first part, the whole battery of Lurianic kabbalism is adduced to prove why belief in Sabbatai Zvi and in the fact that the new eon has already begun is the litmus test of Judaism today. The language and symbols are Lurianic, not apocalyptic. In the second part of the letter, a timetable is set for the further deeds of the messiah in the coming years. There is less Lurianic material here, rather a repetition of apocalyptic images— all of which are expected and need no proof, and none of which is tied to kabbalistic symbols.

THE CHRISTIAN TRADITION

The recent realization that the Christian community may have begun as an apocalyptic Jewish sect has thrown Protestant theology into a severe crisis. All reform movements wished a return to the *ecclesia primitiva,* to the original Christian community; this is the leading connotation of *reformatio* even prior to the Reformation in the sixteenth century. But the early Christian community was neither committed to humanistic-ethical ideals as such, nor did it wish to make the whole world a better place to live in. It seems to have been a world-withdrawn Jewish sect which expected the end of this world any day. Its earliest written documents attest the possession of certified knowledge about the stages of the end-of-the-world drama and the establishment of the Kingdom of Heaven in the new world to come. Christ's first presence on earth imitated the new eon, the Kingdom of God; his imminent Second Coming would bring its triumph. In the meantime, the community may have lived in urgent expectation, and all that could be done while this world still prevailed was to spread the good message of Christ's life, sacrifice, and Second Coming.[65]

From previous and contemporary Jewish apocalyptic sects, the earliest Christian writings inherited most of their leading motifs, albeit with shifts of emphasis. In contrast to the Dead Sea sect, for instance, Christianity deemphasized priesthood and was from the outset an open community. Their apocalyptic knowledge of the latter-day drama was

64. Jacob Sassportas, *Sefer Tsitsat Novel Tsvi,* edited by J. Tishbi (Jerusalem, 1956); included in Gershom Scholem, *Sabbatai Sevi,* translated by R. Zwi Werblowski (Princeton, 1973), pp. 270–75.

65. On the balance between apocalyptic expectations and life in the present with its obligation, and on the danger of overexaggerating the one against the other moment, see David Flusser, *Judaism and the Origins of Christianity* (Tel Aviv, 1979).

likewise grounded on a predestinarian, dualistic vision of history as a battleground between good and evil. The Christian community also inherited, perhaps even in a mitigated form, the hatred of priests, scribes, and Pharisees.[66] In Jewish apocalypticism, the Qumran sect regarded the belief in the "teacher of righteousness" as a condition for salvation, for belonging to the community of the elect. Christianity demanded belief in the messiahship of Christ in spite of his overt failure and ignoble end, a paradoxical belief—"et ressurexit die tertio, certum est, quia impossibile est," according to Tertullian. With other apocalyptic sects, early Christianity expected daily the outbreak of the Heavenly Kingdom.

Christian literature also inherited some of the apocalyptic modes of expression such as "decoding" old prophecies and the periodization of world history; but it did not hurry to produce apocalypses of its own. On the whole, early Christianity was much less fascinated with the written word than other apocalyptic movements. Instead of a written revelation, it possessed a living one: the life of Christ, his acts and teachings. In them, Christianity recognized the "fulfillment" of the open and secret message of the prophets. The events of Christ's life and events of the community were prefigured by all the cardinal events and figures in Jewish history. He was Moses, David, and a new Adam in one. He came to establish a new priesthood "after the order of Melchizedek."[67] The community awaited daily for the descent of the "heavenly Jerusalem" to replace the corrupt one.

But Christ failed to come again, and a community cannot live for much more than one or two generations in the tense climate of urgent expectation. Sooner or later it had to adjust to life in the interim, to lose some of its apocalyptic sense of utter alienation in this world, even without abandoning the belief in the close end altogether. At the same time it needed a rationale to explain why the end of this world, the Second Coming of Christ, had been postponed. With its spread and mission, Christianity became more world oriented. Indeed, since the end is not in sight, it must have been postponed, because there still is a mission to be fulfilled on earth. The good message has to reach everywhere; everyone must be given the chance to be among the saved. With the mission and spread of Christianity, with its growing Hellenization,

66. Amos Funkenstein, "Anti-Jewish Propaganda: Ancient, Medieval and Modern," *Jerusalem Quarterly* 19 (1981): pp. 60–61, and below, pp. 315–316.

67. Funkenstein, "Nachmanides's Typological Reading of History," pp. 35–39. Cf. chapter 4, below.

came also the shift away from collective toward individual eschatology and the watering down of apocalyptic motifs. Instead of the revolutionary expectation of a sudden, radical end to this world came the evolutionary conception of a gradual advance of humanity within history toward an ultimate (pristine) perfection. The new version of the sacred history of humankind pertained not only to Jews: Jews and Greeks alike "prepared" the coming of Christ, as did also the political unification of the *oikoumene* under one empire.

The Apocalypse of John, the first genuine Christian apocalypse, was written close to the end of the first century A.D., probably to fortify and comfort the community under the persecutions of the Roman emperor Domitian. To the martyrs and martyrs-to-be, the Book of Revelation promises, before the final end of the world, a millennium of "the new Jerusalem" here on earth—a distinction similar to the recent Jewish distinction between "the messianic days" and "the world to come." But it is different from the older apocalyptic tradition in that its author does not hide his identity or his knowledge; neither, more important, does he speculate on the date of the end. He only describes its essential phases with as rich and colorful symbols as the apocalyptic tradition he draws from, and he projects the fears and hopes of his generation upon the end: even the millennium will conclude with a general lapse, a temporary triumph of Satan. It may be an exaggeration to call it a non-apocalyptic apocalypse: it has nourished Christian apocalyptic fantasies until today, but it lacks a most essential ingredient of apocalypses—an exact timetable for the end-of-the-world drama.

Normative Judaism, we have seen, neutralized the apocalyptic tradition by refusing to formulate a methodology to discern the signs of the end and of the messiahs; it relegated the apocalyptic motifs to the level of folklore. Christianity went the opposite way, with similar intents and similar results. It absorbed both the content and the methods of apocalypticism by giving them new meanings. In part it formulated a precise doctrine of the last things and forbade other expectations; in part it allegorized apocalyptic images, as when Origenes (A.D. 185?–254?) rails against those who identify the descent of the "heavenly Jerusalem" with the millennium too literally.

To those, however, for whom too much philosophical allegorization seemed just as pernicious for Christian doctrine as apocalypticism itself, Saint Augustine showed how to utilize every single apocalyptic motif or method as building blocks for a deapocalypticized philosophy of history. *The City of God (De civitate Dei)* employs an apocalyptic image in its title: the confrontation of "the earthly city" and the city of God throughout history is the theme of Augustine's *magnum et arduum opus*. The tale of the two cities is a tale of contrast in spite of similarities. The subjects of both cities may adore one and the same God: the earthly so as to use Him, the heavenly so as to be of use to Him. Both of them strive for peace—the one for an earthly peace which is imitable because it can be achieved by power, the other for eternal peace. Membership in the one or the other is in part a matter of will,[68] in part a matter of predestination known to God only. But the inhabitants of God's city while on earth are, in a legal as well as metaphysical sense, resident aliens (*peregrini*) in the earthly state: they neither obstruct it nor do they contribute to it.

Augustine denies categorically the attempts to tie the history of Christianity to the prosperity of the Roman (or any earthly) Empire. The bankruptcy of such "imperial theologies" became evident with the very real chance of an end to the Roman Empire, and Augustine wrote his essay in part so as to make it very clear that the end of the Roman Empire was not, as many Christians thought, the end of the world. The end of the world is unpredictable; the city of God counts its progress "not by years, but by steps."

An old apocalyptic tradition fixed the duration of the world at six thousand years, analogous to the six days of Creation together with the realization of the psalmist's metaphor, "For a thousand years in Thy sight / Are but as yesterday when it is past / And as a watch in the night" (Ps. 90:4).[69] This calculation of the end found its way into both Jewish Midrash and Christian literature. How deliberately Augustine tried to deapocalypticize apocalyptic images can be seen from the way he tampered with this tradition. On the one hand, he elaborates the analogy between the days of Creation and the periods of history far beyond the inherited images: he shows in great detail how the contents of each day of Creation prefigure the events in the corresponding period of history. On the other hand, the very elaboration of the analogy enables him to shift emphasis from the duration of the world (which nobody can calculate) to the structure of history. Under his hand, the analogy became a commonplace for every future Christian philosophy of history.

Analogies such as this one (between the days of Creation and the

---

68. Funkenstein, *Heilsplan und natürliche Entwicklung,* pp. 45–46; and below, chapter 8 (Rosenzweig and Augustine).

69. Ibid., p. 27.

period of the world) belong to the domain of figurative-symbolic reasoning. Since antiquity, Christian theologians have exposed the structure and meaning of sacred history with the aid of immanent historical symbols called "types" or "figures": events, persons, and institutions of the Old and New Testament are matched to each other; one is seen as the "prefiguration" of the other. Cain and Abel, Leah and Rachel are "prefigurations" of the synagogue and the Church. The Twelve Tribes prefigure the Twelve Apostles; Melchizedek and David prefigure Christ as priest and king. A figure is not merely an image or a metaphor; it constitutes a symbolic unity between two separate events or persons within the various periods of history.

The typological mode of reading history was part of apocalyptic knowledge (as distinguished from apocalyptic imagery) since antiquity. The detachment of "apocalyptic science" from "apocalyptic myth" (or imagery) culminated in Augustine's philosophy of history. While apocalyptic images were suppressed, the typological exegesis became a central mode of cognition. In the twelfth century, a new sense of the importance of the immediate presence within God's plan of salvation incited new interest in historical speculations. The men of this century of the War of Investiture, the Second and Third Crusades, and the rediscovery of classical science believed that there is more to present history than merely "the aging of the world" between the First and Second Coming of Christ. Present events seemed to them as pregnant with meaning, worthy of detailed exegesis as biblical history. The new speculative moment culminated in the vision of Joachim of Fiore (c. 1132–1202): to each person of the Trinity he attached one period of history. The period of the Old Testament was the period of the Father, that of the New Testament was the period of the Son, and he predicted the outbreak soon of a new period of "eternal testament" and a nonhierarchical church—the period of the Holy Ghost.[70] This expectation was based not on divination, but on a meticulous study of analogous persons, institutions, events, and sequences of events within each period of history. The structure of the imminent millennium could thus be deduced from the course of history. Some radical Franciscan spiritualists after Joachim saw in him and his writing the very eternal Testament which he anticipated: his influence on millennial movements in the later Middle Ages was profound.

The authority of Augustine, the official stand which the Church took

70. See Herbert Grundmann, *Studien über Joachim von Fiore* (Leipzig, 1927).

against apocalypticism, was not strong enough to suppress altogether the creation of new apocalypses. But these remained scattered and un-imaginative, a mere rearrangement of inherited motifs.[71] Yet, while apocalyptic imagery declined, apocalyptic science, employed by the Church itself, became an ever more imaginative tool, and eventually came to serve in its new garb the very same utopian mentality from which it originally embarked. In the speculations of Joachim and the Joachimites I see the only creative, genuine apocalypticism in the Middle Ages—in spite of the fact that no single "apocalypse" emerged from them; apocalypses continued to be applied to present events. But never again, not even during the Reformation, did the apocalyptic men-tality rise to become a creative force, either socially or intellectually. The utopian mind found other forms of expression, bound to new cultural configurations.

A full history of Jewish and Christian end-of-the-world visions is outside the scope of this chapter. Yet we can argue one main point, that even if apocalyptic motifs, images, methods, and texts persisted, their career in Judaism and Christianity was that of elements taken out of an original context. Apocalypticism in the full sense of the word, a balance of myth, method, and way of life, existed only for about two hundred years, and formed a unique mentality. The reader ought to be warned that this is not a commonly accepted view; the terms *apocalypse* and *apocalyptic* are loyally and lavishly employed in current studies. It has been argued that secular utopian movements, even Marxism, are legiti-mate heirs of apocalypticism. I disagree, although lack of familiarity with Muslim apocalypticism and Iranian sources, as well as lack of space, prevents me from giving a detailed proof of my thesis. I do not mean to deny the enormous impact and influence of the apocalypticism of Judaism and Christianity. On the contrary: because apocalypticism was so captivating, it has remained a constant theme. Yet the history of its reception has been the history of its constant dilution. Apocalypti-cians were the first who were believed to possess a unique key for un-locking "the secrets of the times." Other keys have since been found and discarded, but we need not identify all of them with apocalypticism just because they retained general similarities, or simply because apoc-alypticism came first, or even because they assume some demands from the apocalyptic tradition. Our fears and dreams of the end of the world

71. On various apocalypses, see Norman Cohn, *The Pursuit of the Millennium* (Lon-don, 1957).

are different in color, method, and alas, in their chance for realization, from those of other times. To quote the German poet Rainer Maria Rilke:[72]

O Herr, gib jedem seinen eigenen Tod.
Das Sterben, das aus jenem Leben geht,
darin er Liebe hatte, Sinn und Not.

Lord, to everyone his own death grant,
The act of dying, which departs that life
Wherein he once had meaning, love, and hardship.

72. Rainer Maria Rilke, *Die Gedichte* (Frankfurt am Main, 1990), p. 293.

4

Medieval Exegesis and Historical Consciousness

History and Accommodation: Ibn Ezra

DIBRA TORA KILESHON BENE ADAM

Medieval Jewish and Christian exegesis shared the hermeneutical principle of accommodation: the assumption that the divine revelation adjusted itself to the capacity of man to receive and perceive it. Out of the exegetical topos grew various philosophies of history which saw in the course of history an articulation of the adjustment of divine manifestations and divine institutions to the process of intellectual, moral and even political advancement of man. It is astonishing that so little has been written about a principle that was so fundamental to medieval reflections on God and man, nature and history.

The *exegetical* career of the medieval principle of accommodation, by which I mean its function within the interpretation of the Bible, is often tied to a phrase: "The Scriptures speak the Language of man." The Latin phrase—*Scriptura humane loquitur*[1]—is a verbal translation from

1. E.g., Thomas Aquinas, *Summa Theologiae*, 1–2, 1u. 98, a 3: *secundum opinionem populi loquitur Scriptura;* Nicole Oresme, *Le livre du ciel et du monde*, II.25, ed. A. D.

the Hebrew: *dibra tora kileshon bene adam*. In Jewish sources it appears at first in a legal context, and has little to do with its later employment.[2]

Rabbi El'azar ben Azaria, the first *tana* to invoke the rule, refused to read into the laws concerning the discharge of Hebrew slaves the provision to endow the slave, whether or not he profited the household, just because the biblical verse reduplicates the verb: *ha'anek ta'anik*. The reduplication has no specific legal parts. Similar differences arose between Rabbi Akiba, who searched for (*darash*) the legal meaning of every seemingly redundant particle of speech, and Rabbi Yishmael, who was much more ready to admit that rabbinical provisions cannot be deduced from the Scriptures: at best they can be related to a hint.

Z. Lauterbach believed in a Saducean origin of the formula.[3] But he should have known better: he himself has drawn attention to the fact that, against their distorted Tanaitic image, the Sadducees indeed possessed oral traditions of their own, an oral law pertaining to their domain—the *ius circa sacra*. If we must look for origins, I would see in the adverse positions of Yishmael and Akiba a continuation of diverging exegetical approaches going back to Hillel and Shamai. Be that as it may, what to the ancients was primarily a *legal* hermeneutical principle became under the hands of medieval exegetes a general rule to justify or to limit the philosophical allegoresis. In this sense it is employed in the Geonitic literature as well as by Sa'adia or other early medieval philosophers.

The numerous anthropomorphic expressions of the Bible could more or less easily be translated into a less offensive idiom; the right [hand] of God (*yemin adonai*) could be made to mean God's power. Even those who deny that God can be spoken of with positive attributes could still claim that all scriptural predicates of God are reducible to attributes of action or negations of a privation. Still, the very original

---

Menut and A. J. Denomy (Madison, 1968), p. 530: "L'en diroit que elle se conforme en ceste partie a la maniere de commun parler humain."

2. *Talmudic Encyclopedia* (Jerusalem, 1968), (Hebrew) s.v. *dibra tora*. Isaak Hirsch Weiss, *Dor dor vedorshav*, 6th ed. (Wilno, 1911) I, p. 203, uses a reference in Eusebius, *Praeparatio Evangelica* 8, 10, to argue that the principle was used already by the tana'im in a wider sense; but this is an outside witness. A similar principle was, at times, invoked in classical literature to interpret older text, e.g., Homer, as in Strabo I.2, 33 (σχήματι συνήθει χρῆται).

3. Z. Lauterbach, "The Sadducees and Pharisees," in *Rabbinic Essays* (Cincinnati, 1951), p. 31 ff., n. 11. As to my suggestion (the origin of the formula is the school of Hillel), it may also be supported by an inverted analogue: Hillel used hermeneutical principles, it says, even on secular texts: *haya doresh leshon hedyot*.

presence of prima facie anthropomorphism in the Bible was embarrassing and called for a justification. The reason they are employed is to accommodate the lesser capacity for abstraction of the masses. The law was given to all in a language to be understood by all (Maimonides).

Gradually, the heuristic horizon of the principle broadened; it came to explain more than only anthropomorphisms. Evidently the cosmology of the Bible differed from the last world of scientists—in the Middle Ages no less than today. But Scripture cannot be mistaken: rather, it speaks the language of everyday man, or of primitive man. Now at this very point in the career of the principle, "the Scripture speaks in human terms" splits into two possible approaches: a *maximalistic* and a *minimalistic* employment of the formula.

The maximalist will see the whole body of science and theology—needless to say, *his* science and *his* metaphysics—epitomized in the Bible. The Bible may not *read* as a general encyclopedia, but it is one to him. The scientific information is clothed in metaphors so as to remain understandable to the masses. The task of the interpreter is to decode the biblical phrases and show that nothing worth knowing evaded the notice of the revealed text. This was done by the mainstream of medieval Jewish exegetes *mutatis mutandis:* Sa'adia, the Ramban, Sforno. The Ramban (Nachmanides) went as far as to claim that the philosophical allegoresis actually constitutes the simple, literal sense of the Scriptures, while allegoresis is the kabbalistic dimension of understanding, in which the whole Scripture is nothing but a continuous name of God.[4] As against it, the literal sense embraces the whole range of rational science rather than merely colloquial speech.

IBN EZRA'S MINIMALISM

The merits of Abraham Ibn Ezra's exegesis can be partly measured on the basis of this, the maximalistic extension of the Scriptural principle of accommodation. Ibn Ezra himself polemizes against this approach—the first among his list of five exegetical methods[5] (of which the first four are wrong or useless). It is neither true nor false, but often irrelevant. "If you want to learn the sciences, go to the Greeks." The Geonim in their philosophical allegorization invoke at

---

4. See my discussion of Nachmanides below.

5. Abraham Ibn Ezra, *Perush hatora* (Hebrew), ed. by A. Weiser (Jerusalem, 1976), vol. I, pp. 1 ff. (text).

best the results of, say, astronomy, not its proofs; and likewise unscientific, by implication, would be the Bible itself if it were to be read as an encyclopedia. But this would be a far cry from real science.

Ibn Ezra suggests, instead, a minimalistic approach. It may be that he was preceded in it by some of the extreme rationalists in Spain, such as Rabbi Isaak, but of him we know only through Ibn Ezra. "The Scriptures speak a human language"[6] means simply that Scriptures adapt themselves to the point of view of the multitude. They do not contradict science, but neither do they contain all of it. Indeed, nowhere is this minimalistic interpretation of the principle of accommodation more evident than in Ibn Ezra's exegesis of Genesis 1. To quote a few examples, on Genesis 1:1, he explicates:

"The Heavens": with a definite article, to indicate that he speaks of those [heavens] seen. ["Heaven" and "earth" he will later interpret as referring to sublunar elements only.] "And void" [*vabohu*]: for Moses did not speak about the world of Celestial Bodies [*olam Haba*: the otherwise eschatological term is used here in an astronomical sense, spatial rather than temporal] which is the world of angels [*hamal'akhim*, here in the sense of intelligences, but only about the world of generation and corruption (*olam hahavaya vehahash'chata*—the medieval, Aristotelian equivalent for the sublunar realm].[7]

Time and again, Ibn Ezra emphasizes that Genesis is not a scientific, comprehensive account of the creation of the universe *ex nihilo,* but rather the account of the formation of the sublunar realm through natural processes, that is, laws. Genesis only tells the facts immediately pertinent to the formation and status of man. Even the celestial bodies appear in the narrative of creation only from the vantage point of the average man, not with any reference to their essence or true nature. "And should one ask," he explains Genesis 1:16,

Did not astronomers [*chakhme hamidot*] teach that all planets excepting Mercury and Venus are bigger than the moon, and how could it be written [in the Scriptures] "the big ones"? The answer is that the meaning of "big" is not in respect to bodily size but in respect to their light, and the moon's light is many times [stronger] because of its proximity to the earth.

That the moon is called a great luminary, while the bigger planets are only called stars—this mode of speech corresponds merely to our point of view. "The speaker is a man [Moses], and so are the listeners," he

6. Ibid., to *Genesis* 1:26, edited by Weiser, vol. I, p. 18: ואחר שידענו שהתורה דברה כלשון בני אדם, כי המדבר אדם גם כן השומע.

7. Ibid., p. 13 (text).

says elsewhere.[8] Further hermeneutical devices were not even needed to reconcile the Copernican theory with Scriptures. Nicole Oresme, in the fourteenth century, already discarded the exegetical arguments against the motion of the earth as the least disturbing parts of the geodynamic hypothesis (which he eventually rejected). It may be that *Scriptura humane loquitur,* even where it appears to hold to a geostatic cosmology. Galileo would later use a similar argument to defend the Copernican heliocentric system[9] and even Cardinal Bellarmine had to admit that if anthropomorphisms in the Scriptures could be allegorized away, so could the seemingly geocentric references; moreover, one must allegorize anyway even if one accepts Ptolemy.

The narrative of creation is, according to Ibn Ezra, the narrative of the creation of objects immediately perceived in proportion to the way in which they are perceived. If not to give an adequate cosmology, what, then, is its purpose? For one thing, because the sublunar world, of which only it speaks, was created for the sake of man, unlike the supralunar world of which the story of Genesis is mute:

And now let me pronounce a principle. Know that Moses our Master did not give the laws to the philosophers [*chakhme halev*] only but to everybody. And not only to the people of his generation but for all generations. And he did not refer in the story of creation to anything but the sublunar world which was created for the sake of man.[10]

Moreover, the story of Genesis 1 shows how man is at one and the same time subject to necessities of matter and above them: man represents the material universe and participates in the realm of the intelligences (Ibn Ezra seems to have endorsed a *unitas intellectus*). Man is a microcosm, just as God is the Macrocosm—this is Ibn Ezra's neoplatonic, almost pantheistic interpretation of "in our image and likeness" (Gen. 1:26).[11]

All this is not to say that Scripture does not contain metaphysical allusions, but that the exegete should be careful when, where, and how to look for them or to refrain from it. Ibn Ezra, just like Spinoza at the beginning of early modern biblical criticism, established a most fruitful

8. See n. 6.
9. S. Sambursky, *Three Aspects of the Historical Significance of Galileo,* Proceedings of the Israel Academy of Sciences and Humanities, II (1964); Robert Wesman, "The Copernicans and the Church," in *God and Nature: Historical Essays on The Encounter of Christianity and Science* (Berkeley-Los Angeles, 1986), pp. 76–113.
10. Ibn Ezra, ibid., p. 14.
11. Ibid., p. 18.

methodological principle. Whether a biblical imagery has to be interpreted literally or metaphorically cannot be decided arbitrarily from a point of view outside the text, but rather immanently. In other words: Ibn Ezra delimits the borderline between permissible and impermissible allegorization. As we shall see later, it is with this principle more than in any detail of his interpretation that Ibn Ezra influenced Spinoza's exegetical approach.[12] Against Sa'adia he sees in references to the word of God—"and God said"—not a substitute for "God's will" but the image of a king commanding his servants. The work of creation was effortless since God operated through "servants"—laws of nature or natural elements.[13] Ibn Ezra, in his grammatical as well as in his allegorical interpretations, looks for the *context* of the *explanandum*.[14]

With the exception of the proper name of God, Ibn Ezra looks for a deeper meaning (*sod*)—astronomical or metaphysical—not in the biblical formulations, but in the things—objects and events—which they refer to, a principle reminiscent of the exegetical revolution which Christian exegesis underwent in the thirteenth century.[15]

And, just as Maimonides and Thomas Aquinas after him, Ibn Ezra founds his doctrine of permissible allegorization on the properties of language. Language is, by its nature, ambiguous and analogical: we project the familiar onto the unfamiliar "above us and below us." Indeed, Ibn Ezra develops an exegetical doctrine of *analogia entis* to explain the creation of man in "God's image and likeness." But the elaboration of his reasoning would lead us beyond the scope of this lecture.

In short, as an exegetical principle, "The Scripture speaks the language of man" eventually referred to a body of theories concerning the properties of the sacred language. The language of revelation uses elements of the familiar and natural in order to transcend them—and this procedure is in itself a property of the language of man, which operates through analogies and metaphors.

12. One should, therefore, not mistake Ibn Ezra for a biblical critic in the style of the seventeenth century. He did preserve critical arguments or suggestions of more radical rationalists (cf. Ibn Ezra on Gen. 36:11), but only to reject them. Many of the questions that were the starting point of biblical criticism (cf. below) were anyway already asked by traditional exegetes, for example, the different names of God used in the two narratives of creation. Only the answers differed.

13. Ibid., p. 14.

14. Thus, for example, he accepts Rashi's interpretation of Gen. 1:1 (*bereshit*) as a construct-case, but rejects Rashi's contention that it is always a construct-case: the context ought to decide.

15. B. Smalley, *The Study of the Bible in the Middle Ages* (Notre Dame, 1964), pp. 281–355.

ACCOMMODATION IN HISTORY

Now, even though the exegetical principle of accommodation as hitherto discussed was profoundly ahistorical, it is easily understandable how it could serve historical speculations. The historiosophical principle of accommodation developed first in Christianity.

In one of Augustine's better known letters,[16] we find a classical statement of the principle of accommodation as a historical principle. The very name for this principle is probably derived from an often quoted passage in this letter:

It befitted God to request sacrifices in earlier times, now however things are different, and he commands that which befits [*aptum fuit*] this time. He, who knows better than man what belongs by accommodation to each period of time [*quid cuique tempori accommodate adhibeatur*], commands, adds, augments or diminishes institutions . . . until the beauty of the whole of history [*saeculum*], whose parts these periods are, unfolds like a beautiful melody [*veluti magnum carmen*].

In question was the wisdom of the sacrificial rituals. The pagans ask: if they were not good, why were they instituted? Does it befit a God to change his mind (*consilium*)? Note that here, as elsewhere, the intellectual pagan in later antiquity has no quarrel with the monotheistic stand of either Christianity or Judaism; on the contrary, he believed that *una est religio in varietate rituum*. This was well known to the Church Fathers, as well as to the Tana'im and Amora'im. "You and I know that idolatry has no substance to it, Gentiles abroad are not idolaters: they merely follow the customs of their fathers."[17] The pagan philosopher cannot digest the idea of a special providence, of a God acting arbitrarily in history, changing, as it were, his mind. Special providence, Celsus once said, is a "frog and rainworm perspective."[18] Augustine tells him that the process of history, rather than being arbitrary, is as much a beautiful whole as the cosmos, and for the same reason: the parts fit into the whole. In accord with his aesthetical theory, Augustine

16. *Ep.* 138, I, 5, Goldbacher, ed., CSEL 44, 130; Funkenstein, *Heilsplan und Natürliche Entwicklung*, pp. 40–41 and n. 210; cf. also S. D. Benin, "Thou Shalt Have No Other God Before Me: Sacrifice in Jewish and Christian Thought" (Ph.D. diss., University of California, Berkeley, 1980); Idem, "The Cunning of God and Divine Accommodation: The History of an Idea," *The Journal for the History of Ideas*, 45 (1984): pp. 179–91.

17. B. T. *Tractate Avoda Zara*, 55a; *Hulin*, 13b.

18. Origenes, *Contra Celsum*, IV, 23, ed. Kötzschau, GCS 30, Orig. I, p. 281; C. Andresen, Logos und Nomos, *Arbeiten z. Kirchengeschichte*, edited by K. Aland, 30 (Berlin, 1935), pp. 226 ff.

distinguishes here, as in other instances, between the "fitting" and the "beautiful" (*aptum—pulchrum*). The parts of a whole are never, in themselves, "beautiful." They at best can be attributed with "fitness." But the whole is only beautiful inasmuch as the parts in it fit to each other. In another place, he concedes to each single period in the life of man or in the process of world history "its own beauty"—*pulchritudo sua*—because the institutions and signs of each period fit to each other and are adjusted to the capacity of humans to perceive or to live by them.[19]

Augustine only reformulated a principle which guided Christian reflections on history since Irenaeus of Lyons.[20] With this principle of accommodation the Pauline contention that the Old Dispensation is a παιδαγωγὸς εἰς χριστόν gained a positive meaning. Some hints of similar earlier Jewish interpretations, especially of the sacrifices, cannot compete with the breadth and manifold usage of this principle in the Patristic literature. The divine revelation adjusted itself to speak of a mutual process of adjustment (*adaequatio*) of God and man.[21] And the principle will continue to dominate Christian philosophy of history down through the ages. It was invoked to answer a variety of problems, from the question *quare non ante venit Christus* (Augustine), to the question, specific of the twelfth century, *quare tot novitates in ecclesia hodie fiunt* (Anselm of Havelberg). It underlies the ecclesiological considerations of opportunity even today.

Interestingly enough, the passage quoted from Augustine, and similar Christian interpretations of the function of the sacrifices since the second century, have their roots in Jewish traditions. Of Lev. 17:7 we read,

R. Pinhas in the name of R. Levi: A simile to a prince whose heart [reason] has forsaken him and who was used to eating carcasses and forbidden meat. Said the king, let these dishes be always on my table, and of himself he will get weaned. So also, since Israel was eagerly attached to idolatry and its sacrifices in Egypt . . . God said: Let them always bring their sacrifices before me in the tabernacle and thus they will detach themselves from idolatry and be saved.[22]

Out of such scattered hints, Maimonides in his doctrine of "the rationale for the commandments" (*ta'ame hamitsvot*) developed one of

---

19. Augustine, *De div. quaest.*, XLIV, MPL 40, 28 (*Habet autem decorum suum . . . singula quaeque aetas*); *Adv. Jud.*, III, r, MPL 42, 53 (*ut rerum signa suis quaeque temporibus conveniant*).
20. A. Funkenstein, op. cit. (n. 15), pp. 17–22.
21. Ibid., pp. 25–26.
22. *Levit. Rabba*, 22:6, ed. Margulies (Jerusalem, 1956), t. III, pp. 517 ff.

the most ingenious medieval versions of the divine accommodation through history.[23] The divine "ruse"—(*tallatuf fi allahi*), not unlike Hegel's *List der Vernunft*—operates within the laws of nature, not against them. Rather than changing the polytheistic mentality of the nascent Israel all of a sudden by miracle—*natura non facit saltus*, "human nature cannot change from one extreme to another suddenly"— God preferred to use some elements of the then universal polytheistic cult of the Sabeans in order to turn these elements against their original intent. He concedes anthropomorphic images and usages in order to guide Israel towards a deanthropomorphized monotheistic religion. Again I must cut short; I have dealt with these matters elsewhere. Maimonides uses the principle of accommodation in order to reconstruct the original and forgotten meaning of precepts. In doing so he anticipates one of the fundamental methods of the modern "historical" revolution of the sixteenth century—a method of understanding through alienation and reconstruction.

SPINOZA AND THE SECULARIZATION
OF ACCOMMODATION

This leads us to the last station of the principle of accommodation—the phase of secularization. Let us again distinguish between the exegetical and historiosophical principle. Spinoza's *Theological-Political Treatise* contains one of the earliest documents of biblical criticism. The borderline between exegesis and criticism is not always sharp. For a preliminary definition, it suffices to say that biblical criticism is not concerned with the authentication of the Bible as a superhuman document.[24] Now Spinoza, here as elsewhere, does not oppose outright the theological terms and principles of the Middle Ages. His strategy is more subtle: to use them in an adversarial meaning. "Gen-

23. A. Funkenstein, *Gesetz und Geschichte.* "Zur historisierenden Hermeneutik bei Moses Maimonides und Thomas von Aquin," *Viator,* I (1970): pp. 147–78, and chapter 5, "Maimonides."

24. Pagan critics of the Bible such as Celsus and Porphyrius in antiquity provided a good starting point to the critics of the seventeenth and eighteenth centuries. See, e.g., Milton V. Anastos, "Porphyry's Attack on the Bible," in *The Classical Tradition: Literary and Historical Studies in Honor of Harry Kaplan,* edited by I. Wallach (Ithaca, N.Y., 1966), pp. 421–50. Their arguments were kept alive in the Jewish medieval polemics: see Joel Rembaum, "The New Testament in Medieval Jewish Anti-Christian Polemics" (Ph.D. Diss., UCLA, 1975). On Islamic arguments against the Bible (the Scriptures as forgery, Ezra as the author of the Old Testament) see Hava Lazarus-Yafeh, "Ezra-'uzayr: Metamorphosis of a Polemical Motif," *Zion* LV, 3 (1986): pp. 359–80.

eral" and "special" providence, he says, are legitimate terms—but only if understood as two kinds of universal laws of nature![25] Likewise, "the Scripture speaks the language of man" is a legitimate principle—but only if understood so that, since the author is human, the contents of the Scriptures are his language.[26]

Whether Moses or Ezra, the author of the Scriptures was a man reflecting the world view of his age. The exegete should not assume a priori what this world view is, or force it to conform with true metaphysics. Take, for example, Moses' image of God.[27] In Deuteronomy 4:24 we read: "For Jahweh your God is consuming fire, a jealous God." Should this verse be interpreted literally or allegorically? Is it anthropomorphic or not? No external philosophical viewpoint should guide us. We rather ought to establish, from the context, an internal principle of permissible allegorization. Now we know that the Pentateuch rejects bodily images of God; *esh okhla* could be allegorized, all the more so since fire stands elsewhere as a metaphor for jealousy and vengeance; *'el kana* refers to a psychical attribute, and nowhere do we find scriptural objections to psychical attributes. It has to be interpreted literally. Moses' image of God is the image of a God without a body, but with a soul—an unphilosophical image indeed, since *ordo rerum idem est ordo idearum.*[28] There can be no soul without a corresponding body, for both denote one and the same constellation of acts.

The Bible is a book written by primitive man in his own language, which he could not escape. It is a historical rather than a perennial document: this is Spinoza's use of the exegetical principle of accommodation. As to the historical principle of accommodation, it too underwent a process of secularization, most evident in Vico's use of *providentia*[29] to show how man transformed, by himself, his brutal nature into a human one in the process of history. "Accommodation," for Vico, means the fitting together of all manifestations of the human

---

25. Spinoza, *Tractatus Theologico-Politicus,* edited by C. Gebhardt, t. III (Heidelberg, 1926), pp. 45–47. *Auxilium Dei externum,* is the chain of causation which determines the actual internal balance of motion (mv) or, in simple bodies, the law of inertia. So also in states: the *auxilium externum* their actual fate, the *auxilium internum* their constitution. Cf. also A. Funkenstein, "Natural Science and Political Theory: Hobbes, Spinoza and Vico," *Giambattista Vico's Science of the Humanity,* ed. G. Tagliacozzo (John Hopkins University Press, 1976), pp. 196 ff.

26. Spinoza, TTP, pp. 77–79, p. 263.

27. Ibid., vol. VII, pp. 98–102.

28. Spinoza, *Ethics,* p. II, prop. 7.

29. A. Funkenstein, "Periodization and Self-Understanding in the Middle Ages and Early Modern Times," *Medievalia et Humanistica,* NS, V (1974): pp. 3–23.

spirit (*sensus communis*) in every period of the collective human creativity: the similarity of structure and meaning of poetry, law, institutions of different times—the correspondence of everything belonging to the same *Zeitgeist*.

The principle of accommodation was, throughout the Middle Ages, a bridge between the secular and the sacred, inasmuch as it served to construct a rationalistic exegesis and a rationalistic historiosophy. We shall forego its revival in seventeenth- and eighteenth-century Protestant theology.[30] Apart from that, the principle came, in early modern times, to indicate the emancipation of the secular from transcendental connotations. The theological language, before being abandoned, was vacated from its content. Its history teaches us a lesson about "secularization" in general. Secularization is not a movement that starts against the realm of the sacred but rather within a religious tradition itself.

History and Typology: Nachmanides's Reading of the Biblical Narrative

CHRISTIAN TYPOLOGY

The typological interpretation of history was rich and dominant in the Christian purview, while peripheral and unimaginative in the Jewish. It remained weak even when, in medieval Spain, the Jews recognized the fertility of typological speculations and at times borrowed some of their figures from Christian authors. In the following essay, I shall try to adduce some good reasons why this was so, on the basis of an exception which proves the rule: Nachmanides's typological exegesis. In order to advance my argument, it will be necessary to sketch the development of Christian typological (i.e., analogical) reasoning since antiquity.

A Christian movement called by some "the symbolism of the twelfth

---

30. Cf. G. Horning, in *Wörterbuch der Philosophie*, vol. I, edited by G. Ritter et al. (Darmstadt, 1971), s.v. Akkommodation. It is remarkable that this article starts the history of the concept only with the seventeenth century. On the Protestant use of accommodation in the sixteenth century, cf., e.g., William J. Bousma, *John Calvin: A Sixteenth Century Portrait* (New York, Oxford, 1988), pp. 124–25. On the Jesuits in China see Arnold H. Rowbotham, *Missionary and Mandarin in China: The Jesuits at the Court of China* (Berkeley, 1942).

century"[31] and "speculative biblicism" by others[32] excited intellectuals in a century that also saw the reception of Aristotle, the beginnings of scholastic theology, the revival of Roman law and the return of biblical scholarship to the *veritas hebraica*, that is, solid philology. Of these movements symbolism was the most conservative in method and the most revolutionary in outcome. It culminated in the teachings of Joachim of Fiore, which were proclaimed by some radical Franciscans to be the very *evangelium aeternum* which he anticipated, a new revelation within history.[33] Yet the typological method in itself was not new. Ever since antiquity, Christian theologians had exposed the structure and meaning of history with the aid of immanent-historical symbols called "types" (*typoi*) or "figures" (*figurae*). *Figurae* are symbolical-speculative analogies. Events, persons and institutions of the old and new dispensation are matched to each other: one is seen as a "prefiguration" of the other. Cain and Abel, Jacob and Esau, Rachel and Leah, are the symbolical figures of the *ecclesia* as against the *synagoga*.[34] Adam was the figure of Jesus, the renewed, second man, and so was Moses as the greatest prophet, David as king, Melchizedek as king and priest at once. The sacrifice of Isaac was the figure of Christ's self-sacrifice. The twelve apostles were figured by the twelve prophets and the twelve children of Jacob. The "figure" and its "fulfillment" (*impletio figurae*) stand in a complex relation of identity, contrast and completion—not unlike Hegel's famous "sublation" (*Aufhebung*) which it inspired. In the Christian understanding, these symbols coalesced into an immanent-historical system of parallels. Already the letter to the Hebrews is particularly saturated with figurative arguments.[35] They form a genuine mode of exegesis, the sectarian-apocalyptic consciousness, namely (i) the "apocalypse" proper as a prophecy given long ago, concealed until the end of days and now revealed, and (ii) the "decoding" (*pesher*) of biblical prophecies—to which only the sectarians possess the proper

---

31. Alois Dempf, *Sacrum Imperium* (Munich, 1929), pp. 229–68. The expression was borrowed from the modern literary movement of this name. Cf. also M. D. Chenu, *Nature, Man and Society in the Twelfth Century* (Chicago, 1957), pp. 99–145. An excellent explanation of figurative reasoning can be found in Erich Auerbach, "Figura," in *Scenes from the Drama of European Literature* (New York, 1959), pp. 11–76.

32. Reinhold Seeberg, *Lehrbuch der Dogmengeschichte,* 5 vols. (Berlin, 1930), vol. III, p. 184. It is a much more felicitous name.

33. Ernst Benz, *Ecclesia Spiritualis* (Stuttgart, 1934), pp. 244–55.

34. Cf. chapter 6 below, on the role of prefigurations in the polemical literature.

35. See n. 39.

key.[36] But contrary to the apocalyptic decoding technique, the typological interpretation focuses on symbols rather than metaphors. As a genuine symbol, a figure is not a linguistic expression of a literary analogy, but a concrete piece of historical reality—a thing, an event, a person—which, while referring to something else, still maintains its own identity and does not dissolve completely into that which it signifies.[37] In the fortunate phrase of Iunilius Africanus, a "figure" is "a prophecy by means of things" (*prophetia in rebus, in quantum res esse noscuntur*).[38]

Three moments, we said, were combined in the figurative reasoning into a dialectical unity: the sense of identity with a concrete segment of the past, the sense of contrast to the present, and the sense of the eschatological perfection of the past in the present. Most if not all of these moments can already be found in the pre-Christian Jewish sources. The exodus from Egypt was always perceived as a blueprint for the future redemption.[39] The author of the Book of Kings identified, in a pejorative vein, the sin of the golden calf at Sinai with the construction of a golden calf under the Israelite king Jerobo'am, and had both sinning communities utter the same formula.[40] The exiled Judaeans returning to Zion gave, according to the Book of Nehemiah, a liturgical expression to their sense of identity with the generation of the conquerors of the land.[41] Again we find a specific identification with the last generation to wander in the desert and the first to enter the land among the Dead Sea sectarians, "the exiled unto the desert" (*goley hamidbar*) in their own designation, whose utopian-eschatological organization was to follow

36. See above, pp. 74–78.

37. A sense of hidden identity between symbol and that which it symbolizes ("participation mystique") likewise prevails in many definitions. Others again advance negative determinations: a symbol lacks a one-to-one correspondence with its *significandum;* it stands for something opaque that "shines through" it and is always referentially opaque. In yet other definitions, the difference between metaphor and symbol is quantitative, as if symbols are but consolidated metaphors, sanctioned by repetitive usage. For these and other distinctions, cf. René Wellek and Austin Warren, *Theory and Literature* (New York, 1956), pp. 188–90; Angus Fletcher, *Allegory: The Theory of Symbolic Mode* (Ithaca, 1964), p. 17. I believe that much of the prevailing uncertainty in distinguishing symbols from metaphors is due to the imparity of the terms. The extraordinary range of connotations of "symbol," if not the world itself, is of fairly recent vintage, while a clear definition of metaphors is as old as poetics itself.

38. *Instituta regularia divinae legis,* 2.22, PL 68, col. 34; Grundmann, *Studien über Joachim von Fiore* (Leipzig, 1927), p. 37. Number symbolism has, of course, its place here too, but only as related to content.

39. See chapter 3, n. 12.

40. 1 Kings 12:28; Ex. 32:4.

41. See chapter 3 and n. 11.

tribes, stocks, and camps (*shevatim, matot, machanot*).[42] In general, the apocalyptic literature tends to underline the repetition of events in various well-defined periods so that the structure of history demonstrates, as do the well-decoded prophecies, that indeed the transition from the old to the new cosmic order (αἰών) is very close and that only they, the members of the sect, are the avant-garde of the new world within the old one, only they are worthy of being redeemed.[43] Here and there we encounter typological readings also in the *midrash*—by no means often and without a clear distinction between the interpretation of the text and of the events themselves.[44] In that distinction, we shall see, lies the specificity of typologies.

These and other sporadic examples in the Jewish sources, normative and sectarian, do not compare with the abundant use of typologies in the Christian literature from its earliest beginnings. Why was Christianity so fertile a ground for a symbolic reading of historical events? First and foremost because the very body and life of Christ, not only his words, assumed a central sacral meaning. Already in the New Testament Christ is perceived not merely as fulfilling biblical prophecies (in a manner close to the *pesher* of the Dead Sea Scrolls)[45] but also as repeating and completing events and persons of Israel's past. The forty days of his seclusion and trial in the desert parallel Moses' seclusion at Sinai. Most of the Letter to the Hebrews is dedicated to the proof— perhaps against a Christian sect whose views resembled too much those of Qumran in that it expected a messiah from the lineage of Aaron— that Jesus was indeed a priest and greater than the high priest.[46] While the high priest sacrifices many, Christ sacrificed himself only, once and

42. N. Wieder, "The Law Interpreter of the Sect of the Dead Sea Scrolls: The Second Moses," *JJS* IV (1953), pp. 158 ff.; Yigael Yadin, "Megilot yam hamelach veha'iggeret el ha-'ivriyim," in *Mechkarim bamegilot hagenuzot—sefer zikaron le A. L. Sukenik* (Jerusalem, 1961), pp. 191–208.

43. See chapter 3, n. 44.

44. See Isaak Heinemann, *Darche ha'aggada* (Jerusalem, 1954), esp. p. 149 ("amplifying homilies"). Cf. also above, chapter 1, n. 30 (against Neusner). So as to avoid unnecessary polemics let me reiterate that I do not deny the existence of typological *midrashim* or traditions before Nachmanides. I merely stress their paucity in comparison with the Christian exegetical traditions. An important medieval predecessor of Nachmanides ought, though, to be mentioned. As Sara Kamin, *Jews and Christians Interpret the Bible* (Jerusalem, 1991), pp. 13–58, has shown, Rashi uses the term *dugma* in the sense of τύπος in his Commentary to the Song of Songs—perhaps under the impact of Origenes. But his are not *historical* prefigurations.

45. See chapter 3, n. 50.

46. See Yadin (as above, n. 9) and Flusser, *Judaism and the Sources of Christianity*, pp. 335–37 (the Temple as the figure of the Church).

for all (Heb. 9:25–28). He is, therefore, a priest of another order, after the likeness of Melchizedek (7:15: εἰ κατὰ τὴν ὁμοιότητα μελχισε- δεν) of whom the Psalmist said: "you are a priest forever after the order of Malchizedek" (Ps. 110:4) just as Malchizedek was not of the seed of Aaron but "without father or mother" (7:3 ἀπάτωρ, ἀμήτωρ, ἀγενεαλόγητος) so also Christ. With yet a different intention, Paul sees Adam as a type of Jesus—for Jesus is a renewed man who renewed humanity.[47] The early Jewish community recognized in the desert-generation its "own image" (τύποι ἡμῶν)—though as a negative pattern to be reversed (1 Cor. 10:6).

If the New Testament—and this is particularly true of the Letter to the Hebrews—employed typological arguments to highlight the contrast, within the continuity, of the old and the new dispensation, Church Fathers of the second century had to reverse the emphasis: against Marcion and against the Gnostics they had to prove the continuity—in spite of the diversity—of both Testaments. In his treatise against heretics, which was rightly called the first Christian philosophy of history,[48] Irenaeus of Lyons constructed an entire family of symbols to express one dominating theme—how the life of Christ recapitulates and completes all periods of history up to his advent. The dynamical content of this structure was provided, as I showed elsewhere, by the idea of divine accommodation to the level of understanding of the human race at different times.[49]

The ancient Antiochian exegetes of the fourth to the sixth century systematized the search for prefigurations—in part as an antidote to the danger of unbound allegorizations which characterized the pneumatic exegesis of Alexandria. Systematic typology and the upgrading of the literal sense of the Scriptures went hand in hand, as it did in the twelfth century, with the revival of biblical philology. Their attitude was well formulated by Thomas Aquinas: only biblical events, institutions and

47. Flusser, ibid., p. 377; Gerhart Ladner, *The Idea of Reform* (New York, 1967), pp. 55–59. On typology in the New Testament in general see also Jean Danielou, "The New Testament and the Theology of History," *Studia Evangelica* 1 (1959), 25–34; K. J. Woolcombe, "Biblical Origins and Patristic Development of Typology," *Essays on Typology* (London, 1957), pp. 39–75. Both emphasize, with good reason, the difference between allegory and typology.

48. Wilhelm Kamlah, *Christentum und Geschichtlichkeit* (Stuttgart, 1951), p. 113. Here also is an extensive discussion of his dependence on Theophilus of Antioch.

49. "Renovat hominem et recapitulans in se omnia . . . elevans et pennigerans homines in caeleste regnum": Irenaeus of Lyons, *Libri quinque adversus haereses* III, 2.2 (8), ed. W. W. Harvey, 2 vols. (Cambridge, 1857), vol. II, p. 50. Cf. Funkenstein, *Heilsplan*, p. 22.

persons themselves, not the language referring to them, bear a meaning which transcends their times. Typology and the mystical sense must rest on the solid foundation of philology. "The first [mode of] signification, by which words signify things, pertains to the primary meaning [of Scriptures], which is the historical or literal meaning. The signification however by which things signified by words signify on their part other things is called spiritual understanding, which is founded on the literal and presupposes it."[50] Without this clear sense of the distinction between words and their referents (things), "figures" could never have turned, as they did here, from metaphors into genuine symbols, "a prophecy in things."

The figurative system that was to influence the Latin West most was Augustine's elaborate parallelization of the days of creation to the ages of the world (*aetates mundi*). He made the contents of each day of creation prefigure events of the corresponding period of history.[51] The image was not altogether new. The apocalyptic literature had already invented the realization of the Psalmist's metaphor: "For a thousand years in thy sight are but as yesterday when it is past, or as a watch in the night."[52] It found its way into the midrash as well as into Christian apocalyptic literature. But Augustine differs from this tradition. He deliberately sought to deapocalypticize a hitherto apocalyptic image and shifted the significance of the analogy from the duration of the world (which nobody ought to know) to the structure of history. Hence the great care he took to elaborate the analogy. It became, as mentioned, one of the most used *topoi* of Christian philosophy of history. Eventually, with Abraham bar Chiyya, it was to enter Jewish literature.

50. Illa ergo prima significatio qua voces significant res, pertinet ad primum sensum, qui est sensus historicus vel litteralis. Illa vero significatio, qua res significatae per voces iterum res alias significant, dicitur sensus spiritualis, qui super literalem fundatur et eum supponit. Thomas Aquinas, *Summa Theologiae*, 1–1.9. Cf. Henri de Lubac, *Exégèse médiévale*, 2 parts in 4 vols. (Lyons, 1959–1964), vol. 2, part 2, pp. 272–302. Earlier similar statements are in Alexander of Hales, *Summa Theol.*, part 2, inq. 3, tr. 2, sec. 3.9.1, c. 2, Quarracchi: 4 (1924–1948): pp. 760–62. On the typological tradition since the Antiochians, cf. Herbert Grundmann, *Studien über Joachim von Fiore* (Leipzig, 1927), p. 34.

51. *De Genesi contra Manichaeos*, 1:23, PL, 34:190–92; *De diversis quaestionibus*, 83: PL, 40:43 and many other places. Cf. Alois Wachtel, *Beiträge zur Geschichtstheologie des Aurelius Augustinus* (Bonn, 1960), pp. 57–60 (n. 39).

52. כי אלף שנים בעיניך כיום אתמול כי יעבור וכאשמורה בלילה (Ps. 90:4); B. T. *Sanhedrin* 99. Both the tanna de-bei 'Eliyahu and the Paulinean division of history *ante legem*, *sub lege, sub gratia* are anticipated, e.g., in *Aeth. Hennoch*, 93.3–10; 91.12–17, p. 57. The very same talmudic tradition enabled Christians later to claim that tanna'im and amora'im believed in the messiahship of Christ. See below, pp. 196–198.

To the Church Fathers as to the early Middle Ages, the search for symbolical correspondences in history remained an exegetical device only, part of the *spiritualis intelligentia*. Recent history—their immediate present–had no particular characterization or significance. It was a fraction of the *sexta aetas* in which all that happens is that the world "grows old" (*mundas senescat*), a true "middle age" between the first and second *parousia*. (It is not widely known even among medievalists that the term "Middle Ages" has a theological origin.) This changed in the twelfth century, in which the theological significance of present history was discovered. No century of medieval historical thought and writing was as productive and innovative as this one. Its enchantment with new and richer symbolical schemes of history rested on the discovery that recent history is as worthy of typological exegesis as scriptural history. From Rupert of Deutz through Anselm of Havelberg, Hugh of St. Victor, Gerhoch of Reichersberg down to Joachim of Fiore and the Franciscan Spiritualists,[53] the so-called symbolists dealt with the totality of human history, including posttestamental history, in a manner hitherto reserved for typological exegesis only. By uncovering the structure of history they were able to determine the exact place of their present within the divine plan of salvation. It was a method of prediction without divination.

In Joachim's *Concordia veteris ac novi testamenti* the method found its consummation. To each person of the Trinity he allotted one period of history: the period of the Old Testament (Father), of the New Testament (Son), and of the *testamentum aeternum* (Holy Spirit). Each period revealed the events and persons of the preceding at a higher level. The structure of the imminent millennium could then be deduced from the course of history.[54]

Our summary of the history of typological speculations leads to an interesting conclusion. Many of the images employed and the basis of the method itself had their origin in Jewish and Christian apocalypticism: the *tria tempora* (*ante legem, sub lege, sub gratia*), the four monarchies, the six ages, the parallelism of events and persons. Yet, in the apocalyptic tradition, such images served the sole purpose of calculating the end (or at least demonstrating how close it was). In contrast, the Church Fathers employed these images for other purposes—to define

53. Wilhelm Kamlah, *Apokalypse und Geschichtstheologie* (Berlin, 1935); Peter Classen, *Gerhoch von Reichersberg* (Wiesbaden, 1960); still valuable is Karl Hauck, *Kirchengeschichte Deutschlands*, 5 vols. (Berlin, 1958), vol. 4, pp. 428–70.

54. Grundmann, *Studien*, p. 108.

the continuity and progress from the Old and the New Testaments or even to refute apocalyptical speculations, and at any rate to determine the structure rather than the duration of history. This shift was the cause of the vitality of the typological approach. The less apocalyptic such images become, the more they turned from metaphors into real symbols. The less of a subterfuge for *vaticinia ex eventu* they were, the more multifaceted they grew. Armed with this conclusion, we turn to the examination of Jewish typological attempts, particularly that of Nachmanides.

NACHMANIDES

Nachmanides carries out biblical exegesis on four distinct levels that will be called later, from the time of the *Zohar* onwards, "*peshat, remez, derash, sod*" (*pardes*), undoubtedly under the impact of the Christian readings of the Bible.[55] Nachmanides seems to be the first biblical interpreter to include within the plain sense of scriptures (*peshat*) the full scope of philosophical allegoresis. "In the beginning God created the Heavens and the Earth" means literally, he claims, that at the beginning of cosmic time God created out of nothingness the prime matter of celestial bodies and the prime matter of the realm of generation and corruption.[56] On the one hand, then, Nachmanides disagrees with Ibn Ezra about the scope of philosophical allegoresis: his is a maximalist attitude in the sense discussed earlier; there is no limit to the natural science to be found in the Scriptures. On the other hand, though, he does not regard the philosophical allegoresis as a hidden meaning (as Maimonides did). It is the plain meaning of the Scriptures.

Yet his commentary is not free of contradicting philosophical traditions. Sometimes he interprets the creation of the prime matter of heaven and earth as two distinct instances of *creatio ex nihilo*, while on other occasions he sees the latter emanating from the former which again is derived from the "light of the [divine] garment" (*'or halevush*), a "most subtle matter" (*chomer dak eyn bo mamash*) which precedes both. This neoplatonic version he then grafts upon the kabbalistic dis-

55. Scholem, *Major Trends*, p. 400, n. 15 (there also lit.). Jewish exegetes could employ it with good conscience even while denying any trace of Christian doctrine (cf. below) because the method seemed to them autochtonous.

56. *Perush haramban al hatora*, edited by Ch. D. Chavel (Jerusalem, 1959), vol. I, p. 12 (on Gen. 1:1). See the following note. Unlike Rashi or Ibn Ezra, Nachmanides refuses to read the verse as a construct-case. On the Maimonidean view cf. Sara Klein-Braslawy, *Perush harambam liberi'at ha'olam* (Jerusalem, 1978), pp. 23–34.

tinction between the worlds of "creation, shaping, making" (*beri'a, yet-sira, assiya*).[57] Like every medieval Aristotelian, he struggles with the meaning of the creation of matter out of nothingness if prime matter is a principle of pure potentiality.

Already in his discussion of creation we note Nachmanides's penchant for blurring the dividing lines between nature[58] and miracle. A cardinal problem of Aristotelian meteorology was the question why and how some of the earth is above the water if indeed earth is the heaviest of elements.[59] Nachmanides sees no difficulty: it happens by two divine "decrees" (*gezerot*), that is, "two states of affairs made by the will of God contrary to their nature." Even more remarkable is Nachmanides's contention that the air, rather than the fire, is the most subtle sublunary element and should have naturally taken its place above the fire; only "by the word of God" (*bema'amaro shel hakadosh baruch hu*) does the air (*ruach*) "hover over the water."[60] The order of the upper elements that seemed natural to Aristotle seems to Nachmanides a perpetual miracle! These are not random comments. Nachmanides does augment the use of philosophical allegoresis, but he does so against the intentions of the philosophers. Medieval rationalists wanted to fortify the idea of nature, of what is natural. Nachmanides challenged it. They tended to reduce the number of miracles in the Scriptures to a minimum and to give them a natural explanation, as "miracles of the category of the possible" (*Nissim misug ha'efshari*)[61] while he viewed the

---

57. As against his comment on Gen. 1:1 (above n. 26)—"and know that the heavens and all that is in them are one matter, and the earth and all that is in it is another matter. And God created these two from nothingness and both alone are created [out of nothingness: נבראים] and everything is made out of them"—stands his comment on Gen. 1:8 (Chavel, ibid., p. 20): "But the light or the garment is the first created [thing] and from it came out (יצא) the physical matter of heaven and gave the earth another matter which is not of the subtlety of the first and it is the snow under the throne of [God's] glory (כסא הכבוד). For the throne of glory is created (נברא), and from it became the snow underneath, and from it was made (נעשה) the matter of earth which is third in creation." Note the triad: creation, becoming (יצירה = התהוות), making (עשייה), which correspond to the kabbalistic scheme.

58. The very term *teva* came to mean the same as φύσις or *natura* only in the Middle Ages; in the classical Jewish literature it means imprint or seal.

59. On the fortunes of this problem in Jewish philosophy see Aviezer Ravitsky, "Aristotle's *Meteorologica* and the Maimonidean Exegesis of Creation," *Jerusalem Studies in Jewish Thought* IX (1990), Shlomo Pines Jubilee Volume II, pp. 225–250.

60. Nachmanides, *Perush hatora* vol. I, p. 14, to Gen. 1:9. It may indicate Stoic influences (πνεῦμα), but Nachmanides's point is the utter contingency of the cosmic order. This is all the more impressive since the Scriptures could easily be also accommodated, on this issue, to the Aristotelian cosmology.

61. See the discussion of Maimonides below, pp. 137–144.

entire endeavor as a methodical error. On the contrary: the miracles explicitly mentioned as such in the Bible are but a small sample of those that actually happened, and the task of the biblical interpreter— even on the level of the plain meaning—is to uncover those "hidden miracles," because

> The miracles performed by a prophet prophesying in advance or by a revealed angel in the divine service are mentioned by the Scripture, but those done of themselves to aid the righteous or to crush the wicked are not mentioned in the Pentateuch or in the Prophets . . . all the foundations of the Scriptures are in hidden miracles, and the meaning of the Scriptures in all matter is neither nature nor custom, indeed the tasks of the law consist in signs and miracles because no one will die or be wiped out by nature for transgressing [even] the prohibitions of incest . . . . and the heavens will not become iron if we plant in the sabbatical year . . . . And every success of the righteous . . . and all our prayers are signs and miracles, except that they do not involve a publicized change in the nature of the world.[62]

Here Nachmanides polemicizes especially against Ibn Ezra. Hidden miracles are the mode of operation of God's special providence. If this is true of nature, all the more so of history, be it in the private sphere ("to aid the righteous and crush the wicked") or in public affairs. The interpreter of the Bible ought to pay attention to "God's judgment on earth" (*mishpat elohim ba'arets*). Nachmanides seems to refer to this particular concern as "*derash*" (analogous to the *sensus moralis*). The principle of "God's judgment"—of retribution and reward—manifests itself within history as the habitual exile of an individual or a community from their place as divine punishment: "therefore it is proper that, if a nation goes on sinning, that it be exiled from its place while another nation comes to inherit its land."[63] It is true always and everywhere, but especially in the Holy Land, which is "the choicest place of habitation." Exile and redemption, individual or collective, are the signature

---

62. *Perush hatora*, edited by Chavel, vol. I, p. 254 (to Gen. 46:15). Cf. Nachmanides, *Torat hashem temima*, edited by Chavel; *Kitve haramban* (Jerusalem, 1963), vol. I, p. 155; and Gerschom Scholem, *Hakabala begerona* (Jerusalem: Akademon, 1964). A possible rabbinical source of this doctrine may be found in *Avot de Rabi Natan* 35, 1, "Ten miracles were done to our forefathers in the temple [in Jerusalem]," etc., though Nachmanides does not mention it. Another possible source is the doctrine of "vestiges of his marvels" (זכר עשה לנפלאותיו) in ashkenazic chassidism.

63. To Gen. 1:1; *Perushei ha-torah*, vol. I, p. 10. In his interpretation to the *petikhta* (Gen. R. 1:3): כח מעשיו הגיד לעמו לתת להם נחלת גויים, he reprimands Rashi for giving a wrong interpretation to the midrash on the basis of a faulty text. His own text was better, but Rashi was nonetheless right in giving it a polemical, rather than historiosophic, interpretation.

of God's intervention in history. Where it is not immediately visible, the interpreter ought to expose the "hidden miracles" by way of *derash*.

On the deepest level of scriptural understanding, "the way of truth" (*bederech ha'emet*), the Pentateuch is a code of kabbalistic mysteries. So considered, it contains theosophical mysteries only: it neither narrates events nor prescribes laws but reflects the interactions and counteractions between the divine emanations or forces (*sefirot*). "And know that in the truest sense Scripture speaks of lower matters and alludes to higher matters."[64] The one instance in which the mystical sense (*sod*) is the only rationale of the Scriptures is the sacrifices.[65] Otherwise, *peshat* and *sod* are quite divergent—at times even grammatically so. Thus, we read Genesis 1:1 *literaliter* to mean that, in the beginning of time (for *be-reshit* does not indicate, as it did to Rashi and Ibn Ezra, a construct case), God created *ex nihilo* the prime matter (ὕλη; *hiyyuli*) of heaven and the prime matter of earth. *Mystice* we take "God" to be the grammatical object rather than the subject of the verse. It alludes to the emanation (*bara*) of the third *sefirah* (*binah* = *'Elohim*) from the second (*be-reshit* = *chokhmah*), a reading which, according to B. T. *Megillah* 9*a*, was considered so misleading (= heretical) that it had been altered by the inspired legendary translators of the Pentateuch into Greek.[66] Evidently the early kabbalists believed themselves capable of rescuing suspicious readings and investing them with higher mysteries.

Noteworthy is also how split Nachmanides's position really is. In the course of his disputation with the Dominicans in Barcelona (1263), confronted by the so-called Christological Jewish prooftexts from the midrash, he denied that the midrash has any authoritative character: "Our midrash is nothing more than your sermons."[67] But here, in his biblical

---

64. *Perush hatora*, edited by Chavel, vol. I, p. 15.

65. Nachmanides developed his doctrine of *ta'amey ha-misvot*, and in particular his theory of sacrifices, in contraposition to Maimonides; Lev. I:9: ואמר הרב במורה הנבוכים כי טעם הקרבנות בעבור שהמצרים והכשדים . . . היו עובדים לצאן ולבקר . . . אלו דבריו ובהם האריך והנה אלה דברי הבאי . . . Where the latter sees but pedagogical-historical functions (cf. n. 98 below), the former sees deep mysteries. Sacrifices are at one and the same time theurgical actions and supreme symbols as well as preserving forces of creation (Gen. 2:8). Cf. in detail, Gerschom Scholem, *Hakabbalah;* Ephraim Gottlieb, *Mechkarim be-sifrut hakabbalah*, edited by Joseph Hacker (Tel Aviv, 1976), pp. 93–95; (Gottlieb reOcognizes the magical character of the sentence ודע כי כל גזירת עירין וגו', but does not discuss the typological-figurative context).

66. וכתבו לו אלהים ברא בראשית. The same applies to נעשה אדם which the kabbalah interprets as the collaboration of all *sefirot*. But traditional exegesis forbade such readings which smack of trinitarian implications.

67. *Vikuach haramban* edited by Eisenstadt, *Otsar havikuchim* (New York, 1928), p. 89. And he continues: וזה הספר מי שיאמין בו טוב ומי שלא יאמין לא יזיק. In our context it matters little how reliable his own account of the disputation really is. See I. Baer,

commentary, he wishes to silence those "of little faith who ridicule the words of our sages" by enumerating contradictory *midrashim* to the same phrase. Against these rationalists who felt embarrassed by the classical homilies, Nachmanides shows that the kabbalistic reading unites these seemingly contradictory midrashim into one coherent interpretation. A different Nachmanides appears *in foro interno* than *in foro externo*.

We may call this mystical-theosophical exegesis, *pace* Scholem, "logos-symbolism," for the following reasons. We referred earlier to the *participation mystique* of the symbol and that which it symbolizes. This sense of identity-within-diversity explains the elasticity and fecundity of religious symbols. The more "hidden" their reference, the more they tend to multiply and reflect each other vertically and horizontally; they easily become symbols-of-symbols and symbols-of-symbols-of-symbols.[68] One is reminded, and for good reason, of Plato's paradox of the third man.[69] Thus, for Nachmanides, both the Torah and its contents are symbols. The Torah not only "alludes to" constellations within the divine realm, but is also a part of them. The various manifestations of God are so many metamorphoses of his name. The Torah not only speaks of these names but is actually composed of them: "All of the Pentateuch is nothing but God's names."[70]

THE TYPOLOGICAL READING

But between the *peshat, derash,* and the kabbalistic reading, Nachmanides sometimes interposes an immediate level of symbolic

---

"Lebikoret havikuchim shel Jechiel miparis vehshel rabbi Moshe ben Nachman," *Tarbiz* 2 (1971), pp. 172–77. (See also below, chapter 6, on disputations).

68. This is, I believe, one of the interesting and least discussed characteristics of, e.g., kabbalistic symbols: they easily turn into symbols of symbols, etc., that is, they are, to a high degree, reflexive. In *Zohar* 2:239a, for example, the ascent of the incense symbolizes the ascent of the lower seven *sefirot,* while these again symbolize the ascent of the upper three *sefirot,* that is, their urge to unite with their origin.

69. Its logic is as follows. If $a_1, a_2, \ldots a_n$ can be attributed with A only because of their "participation in" and "imitation of" A (*methexis* and *mimesis*), by virtue of what can A be attributed with A? Of necessity we look for some A such as $[a_1 \ldots a_n, A]$ to participate in and imitate, and so forth *ad infinitum*. Cf. R. E. Allen, "Participation and Prediction in Plato's Middle Dialogues," *Plato* I: *Metaphysics and Epistemology,* ed. Gregory Vlastos (Garden City, 1971), pp. 167–83.

70. *Perushei hatora,* Nachmanides's Preface: *Torat hashem temimah, Kitvei ha-Ramban,* ed. Chavel, p. 167; G. Scholem, *Hakabbalah shel sefer hatemunah veshel Avraham Abulafia* (Jerusalem, 1968), p. 38, emphasizes the still magical character of this dictum in Nachmanides (as against, e.g., the *Sefer hatemunah*).

understanding. He insists far beyond midrashic reminiscences that the events and persons of which the Torah speaks—not the words themselves—are historiosophical symbols whether or not they are also theosophically relevant. They foreshadow, prefigure, and even predetermine events in the future of Israel. I shall call this symbolism, for reasons to be discussed soon, praxis-symbolism.

That Abraham stayed in Shekhem before the land was promised to him (Gen. 12:6) prefigures the premature conquest of the city by his descendants, that is, before they merited it. Abraham's encounter with the four kings (Gen. 14:6) prefigures Israel's encounter with and ultimate victory over the four monarchies, of which Rome and its emperor are the present and last.[71] An anticipation of the four monarchies is also the fourfold expression of Abraham's dread in the covenant between the pieces (*berit bein habetarim*) (Gen. 15:12): "And great darkness fell upon him."[72] Both instances build on the midrash, but Nachmanides adds that the slaughtered lamb, sheep, and ram prefigure the sacrifices. Isaac's involuntary "exile" to Gerar (Gen. 26:1) prefigures the Babylonian exile, and the three wells he dug there (Gen. 26:19–22) prefigure both of the destroyed temples and the third to be and endure. Midrashic, of course, is also the prefiguration of Rome by Esau, but Nachmanides is more specific than the midrash: "All that occurred to our father with his brother Esau will always occur to us with the sons of Esau"[73] (Gen. 32:4). That Jacob sent messengers to Esau unto the land of Sei'r prefigures the unfortunately amicable beginnings of our relations with Rome:

71. On the *topos* of the four monarchies, see Fuchs (below, n. 74); Gerson Cohen, *The Book of Tradition by Abraham Ibn Daud* (Philadelphia, 1967), pp. 223–62; J. W. Swain, "The Theory of the Four Monarchies: Opposition History under the Roman Empire," *Classical Philology* 35 (1940), 1 ff. Cf. nn. 73–74 below. Nachmanides's view on the succession (against Ibn Ezra) at Num. 24:20; Chavel, 2:302.

72. עליו נופלת גדולה חשכה אימה. Ed. Chavel, 1:92. Types of the four monarchies are particularly abundant in the midrash. One example, not used by Nachmanides, is the four paradisiacal rivers (Gen. Rabbah 16:7: 'עתיד הקב"ה להשקות כוס תרעלה לעכו"ם וגו). It is one of the rare cases in which Christian exegesis postponed a historical typology to the Middle Ages. Ambrosius (*De paradiso*, 3:19–21: CSEL, 32:277) following Philo (*legum allegoriae*, 1:19–21) takes them to represent the four cardinal virtues. The first to give the four rivers a historical meaning (*pace* Ambrosius) was Radulfus Glaber, *Historiarum sui temporis libri quinque* 1.1–3, ed. Marcel Prou (Paris, 1896), pp. 4–5.

73. Ed. Chavel, 1:180: כל אשר אירע לאבינו עם עשיו יתארע לנו תמיד עם בני עשיו. On the tradition of the equation of Edom = Rome, cf. Harald Fuchs, *Der geistige Widerstand gegen Rom in der antiken Welt*, 2nd ed. (Berlin, 1964), esp. pp. 68–73, n. 77; G. Cohen, "Esau as Symbol in Early Medieval Thought," *Jewish Medieval and Renaissance Studies*, ed. Alexander Altmann (Cambridge, 1967), pp. 19–48. Cf. Nachmanides to Num. 24:17, Chavel 2:301.

And in my opinion this hints that we initiated our downfall through the hand of Edom. For the kings of the Second Temple [i.e., the Hasmoneans] entered into a treaty with Rome and some of them came to Rome [?] and it was the cause of their falling into their hands; and this is mentioned in the sayings of our sages and noted in books.[74]

Jacob's strategy of survival—the splitting of camps (Gen. 32:9)—prefigures Israel's lot in the diaspora:

And this means that Jacob is aware that his progeny will not all fall into the hand of Esau if one camp can survive. And it also hints that the sons of Esau will not decree that our name be wiped out, but rather oppress some of us in some of their countries. One of their kings decrees in his country concerning our money or our bodies and another king at his place has mercy and rescues refugees. Thus they said in Genesis Rabbah: "If Esau is to come and hit one camp," these are our brothers to the south; "Then the other camp will survive," these are our brothers in the diaspora. They also recognized that the passage refers to generations to come.

The ten princes of Edom (Gen. 36:33) prefigure the last emperors of Rome, of which the last will rule the whole world before the coming of the King Messiah. The ceremony of the dedication of the tabernacle (*chanukkat ha-mishkan*) (Num. 7:11–8:26) symbolizes history from creation to the Messiah, whereby, for example, Aaron's lighting of the candles, seemingly a humble task, prefigures the *chanukkah* at the hand of the Hasmoneans:

But the meaning of this homily is to infer from this passage a reference to the dedication of candles which took place at the Second Temple through Aaron and his sons. And in this wording I found it in the secret tract of R. Nissim who mentioned this homily.[75]

Such and others are the instances of Nachmanides's typological exegesis. Some are marked as his opinion. Many of them are built on midrashic allusions, but Nachmanides makes it clear that they are allusions only, in need of explication. More than that, Nachmanides systematizes them and articulates the methodological assumptions of typologies.

---

74. ועל דעתי זה ירמוז כי אנחנו התחלנו נפילתנו בידי אדום [!] כי מלכי בית שני באו בברית עם הרומיים ומהם שבאו ברומה והיא היתה סבת נפילתם בידם וזה מוזכר בדברי רבותינו ומפורסם בספרים. By *sefarim* he probably means Josiphon. Does Nachmanides refer to the treaty with Rome of the early Hasmoneans? Cf. *Josephon Hebraicus,* ed. J. F. Breithaupt (Gotha and Leipzig, 1710), p. 226. Or does he mean the appeal of Hyrcanus to Pompeius to intervene?

75. Ed. Chavel 2:220: אבל ענין בהגדה הזאת לדרוש רמז מן הפרשה על חנוכה של נרות שהיתה בבית שני ע"י אהרון ובניו. ר"ל כי הם חשמונאי ובניו ובלשון הזה מצאתי במגילת סתרים לרבינו נסים שהזכיר האגדה הזו . . .

The patriarchal story is, he claims, particularly pregnant with figurative implication, and therefore of the nature of the story of creation:

Scripture here concludes the Book of Genesis which is the book of formation concerning the creation [out of nothing] of the world and the formation of everything created and concerning the occurrences of the fathers which [occurrences] are of the category of formation to their progeny because all of their occurrences are figures of events to hint at and to announce all [that will happen in] the future.[76]

The term *tsiyyurei devarim* can only be translated as *figurae*.

The predetermining nature of such prefigurations—which is much more than their mere predictive or metaphorical function in the midrash—becomes evident in the long methodological remark on Genesis 12:6 with which he introduces all following typological speculations. It is worth quoting in full:

I shall tell you a rule you will comprehend in all subsequent passages concerning Abraham, Isaac and Jacob. And it is an important matter which our sages mentioned briefly and said: "Whatever occurred to the fathers is a sign to the sons." Wherefore the Scriptures prolong the story of travels [of the patriarchs] and of the digging of the wells and other occurrences. And one may deem them to be redundant, useless matters. But all are there to teach of the future, because whenever something happens to a prophet of the three patriarchs, he may understand from it that which has been predestined for [literally: decreed upon] his progeny. And know that every divine decision, wherever it turns from the potentiality of a decree into the actuality of a similitude [prefiguration], such a decree will be fulfilled under all circumstances. Wherefore the prophets perform acts in [their] prophecies. . . . And therefore God kept [him, Abraham] in the land [of Israel] and created for them similitudes to whatever he intended to do to his progeny.[77]

---

76. Preface to Exodus, ed. Chavel, 1:279: השלים הכתוב ספר בראשית שהוא ספר היצירה בחדוש העולם ויצירת כל נוצר ובמקרי האבות שהם כענין היצירה לזרעם מפני שכל מקריהם ציורי דברים לרמוז ולהודיע על כל העתיד לבוא.

77. Ed. Chavel, 1:77: אומר לך כלל תבין אותו בכל הפרשיות הבאות בענין אברהם יצחק ויעקב והוא ענין גדול הזכירוהו רבותינו בדרך קצרה ואמרו: על מה שאירע לאבות סימן לבנים. ולכן יאריכו בכתובים בספור המסעות וחפירת הבארות ושאר המקרים. ויחשוב החושב בהם כאילו הם דברים מיותרים אין בהם תועלת וכולם באים ללמד על העתיד כי כאשר יבוא המקרה לנביא משלושת האבות יתבונן ממנו הדבר הנגזר לבוא מזרעו. ודע כי כל גזירת עירין כאשר תצא מכוח הגזירה אל פועל דמיון תהיה הגזירה מתקיימת על כל פנים. ולכן יעשו הנביאים מעשה הנבואות . . . ולפיכך החזיק הקב"ה בארץ ועשה לו דמיונות בכל העתיד לעשות בזרעו והבן זה. Cf. also Nachmanides's sermon *Torat ha-shem temimah, Kitvei rabbenu Moshe Ben Nahman*, ed. Chavel, 1:304. ועניין יעקב ולזה האריך כל כך במעשה האבות, לומר כמה בארות חפרו. אמרו, כל מה שאירע לאבות סימן עם עשיו ולבן. אבל מצאתי בבראשית רבה ענין מתרץ כל זה. להודיע לנביאים מה שעתיד לבוא עליהם ועל זרעם. והיה מוציא הענין מן לבנים וכן היה הקב"ה רוצה הכוח אל הפועל להיות שריר וקיים.

The key word of the passage is *dimyon*. It does not mean "imagination"—what could "the actuality of the imagination" (*po'al ha'dimyon*) mean?—but rather "similitude," just as the *tsiyyur devarim* quoted earlier: in other words, *typos* or *figura*. Nachmanides is visibly searching for a Hebrew equivalent for the Christian term. God arranged that events would befall the patriarchs similar to events which were to come later in the history of Israel. A simile of this kind not only enables prediction. It is, as already quoted, a symbolic creation, wherefore it is binding, determining: "such a decree will be fulfilled under all circumstances." The binding character of figurative occurrences, he says, is the same as the binding force of the symbolical acts performed by the prophets. The anxiety of Moses during the Amalekite war may have been he says, because

everything that Moses and Joshua did to them [the Amalekites] once, Elijah and Messiah ben Joseph will do to their progeny [in the messianic era]; therefore Moses made such an effort in the matter [to keep his hands raised].

We see, then, how at times Nachmanides speaks of prefigurations and their target events as if they were one ("for they were the Hasmoneans and his sons"). Sacrifices, too, have such a symbolic-creative function.[78] Nachmanides linked together prophecy, symbolic practices and figurative events in a strong bond, as strong as can be found in Christian exegesis.

The influence of Christian typology seems to be irrefutable. But Nachmanides's emphasis on the predestining faculty of *dimyonot*—prefigurations—is stronger than I can find in any other text, Christian or Jewish. In searching for an origin or source of inspiration for such emphatic pronouncements, a possible candidate comes to mind. The doctrine of the individual celestial shape, *tselem* or *demut*, especially as it was advanced in Ashkenazic Hasidism, was not a historiosophical doctrine at all, nor did Nachmanides accept it.[79] But he may have translated some of its features from the angelofogical into a historiosophical idiom. The celestial-ideal shape of every man is his preexisting proto-

78. See n. 50 above.
79. G. Scholem, *Major Trends*, pp. 117–118; idem, *Von der mystischen Gestalt der Gottheit* (Zürich, 1962), pp. 249–73; G. Scholem, *Pirqei yesod behavanat hakabbalah u-semaleha* (Jerusalem, 1976), p. 367; Isaiah Tishbi, *Mishnat hazohar*, 2 vols. (Jerusalem, 1957), 2:90, 93. Scholem emphasizes that only later was this doctrine to merge with doctrines of "astral bodies." The most detailed examination of *tselem* in Ashkenazic Hassidism was given by Joseph Dan, *Torat hasod shel chasidut Ashkenaz* (Jerusalem, 1968), pp. 224–29.

type, engraved or depicted in the veil surrounding the seat of God's glory. Eleazar of Worms insists that the fate of each individual is predetermined and transmitted by his ideal shape:[80] "In the day in which God created man he decreed concerning [i.e., predestined] the image."

A curious (and neglected) facet of this doctrine is the further idealized differentiation of all things, even inanimate, into ideal "aspects" or "pictures" (*mar'ot*):

> Everything created has a picture corresponding to it . . . and the pictures are not independent angels but, according to the will of the Creator, what He intends to do He shows [*mar'eh*] to the mind of the prophet in that the Supreme One infuses the knowledge of his intended decrees into the images and the images turn as the decrees do.[81]

The relation between image (*demut*) and picture (*mar'eh*) is opaque; the borderline between them is floating. The *mar'ot* emanate both from divine predestinarian acts and from human actions (sin or merit) inasmuch as both involve objects, and all objects have ideal counterparts. All past or future deeds involving an object are preserved in its picture.

It may be that the etymological affinity between *demut* and *dimyon* is not coincidental. It may be that Nachmanides transformed this angelical-ideal *eidos* into a historical-magical *typos*. It may even be that he did so consciously, as if he were to say: This doctrine of predestining prototypes may not be valid in one sense, but it is true in another. I do not wish to press this mere conjecture any further. Sound philology is guided by the maxim "in dubio contra reum," especially in the domain of images where anything is potentially associable with anything else.

That Nachmanides understood the hermeneutical presuppositions of figurative reasoning is borne out not only by his methodological declarations. A glance at the manner in which he handles his sources corroborates it. Nachmanides, just as the more mature Christian exegetes do, distinguishes clearly between words and images describing an event on the one hand, and the events themselves on the other: typological

---

80. ‏על דמות ‏[!] ‏ביום ברוא אלהים אדם גזר . .‏ Eleazar of Worms, *Sefer chokhmat ha-nefesh*, reprint ed. (Jerusalem, 1967), p. 16*b*.

81. Ibid., p. 18*a–d*: ‏והנפש כל מעשיה למעלה כי בבורא יש לו מראות כנגד כל דבר אם‏ ‏יעשה בבחרותו עוון או זכות. והזכות גם להם יש מראית עין וכי תועבה היא לפני 'ישתה עוונותינו‏ ‏לנגדיך עלומינו למאור פניך' . . . כי כל העבירות והמקומות שחטאו באותן דמיות יש מראות זהו‏ ‏רהיטיו ועציו ואבניו מעידין בו וכתוב 'וכפיס מעץ יעננה.' ואם נשרף קודם שמת אדם או בלה איך‏ ‏יענה ויעידו? אלא כי יש מראות שנבראו כנגד כל דבר שברא . . . והמראות אינם מלאכים שהיו‏ ‏בכח עצמן אלא רצון הבורא מה שחפץ לעשות מראה לדעת הנביא שמכניס העליון דעת מחשבות‏ ‏גזירות בתוך במראות ומתהפכות המראות כפי הגזירות . . .‏

analogies rest only on the latter. His main sources are Genesis Rabbah and Tanhumah. In the former, emphasis is clearly on the similarity of scriptural formulations rather than substance (Gen. R. 40:8): "You find that everything written of Abraham is also written of his sons."[82] This emphasis on formulations, though less strong, is still evident in the comparable passage of Tanhumah.[83] By contrast, Nachmanides omits most of these parallel wordings.

In another case—the interpretation of "a great darkness" mentioned above—where one can hardly found the typology on a basis other than that of the language used, he makes it very clear that he means rather states of mind: "They [the sages] interpreted it as an allusion to the subjugation under the four monarchies, because the prophet [i.e., Abraham] found in his soul dread and thereafter came darkness." Undoubtedly, Nachmanides learned from Christian exegetes that typology refers to things or states, not to words.

In one particular instance, the Christian origin not only of the method but also of the figure itself is well known. Abraham bar Chiyya had already borrowed the Augustinian parallelization of the days of creation to the periods of the world, including the detailed specification of things created and the corresponding events mentioned above. J. Guttmann saw Isidore of Seville as bar Chiyya's immediate source.[84] I rather believe that bar Chiyya was directly acquainted with the doctrines of Augustine himself, though perhaps only from hearsay. It is not only bar Chiyya's *aetates* doctrine that betrays Augustinian influence.

---

82. את מוצא כל מה <u>שכתוב</u> באברהם <u>כתוב</u> בבניו .באברהם כתוב ויהי רעב בארץ. בישראל כתיב כי זה שנתיים הרעב בקרב הארץ. באברהם כתיב וירד אברהם מצריימה . . . בישראל כתיב וירדו אבותינו מצריימה . . . באברהם כתיב וילך למסעיו. בישראל כתיב אלה מסעי בני ישראל 83. (לך לך:) אמר רבי יהושע דסכנין: סימן נתן לו הקב"ה לאברהם שכל מה שאירע לו אירע לבניו. כיצד? בחר באברהם מכל בית אביו שנאמר אתה הוא ה' האלהים אשר בחרת באברהם . . . ובחר מבניו משבעים אומות שנאמר כי עם קדוש אתה לה' אלוהיך ובך בחר . . . לאברהם נאמר לך לך ולבניו נאמר אעלה אתכם מעוני מצרים . . . אברהם נזדווגו לו ארבעה מלכים אף לישראל עתידים כל המלכים להתרגש עליהם; Gen. Rabbah 40:8 (ed. Theodor-Albeck); Tanhuma, Lekh lekha 10 (ed. Buber). Cf. also Gen. Rabbah 84:6: א"ר שמואל בר נחמן אלה תולדות יעקב יוסף . . . מה ת"ל יוסף. אלא שכל מה שאירע לזה אירע לזה. מה זה נולד מהול אף זה נולד מהול. מה זה אמו עקרה אף זה אמו עקרה . . . . וגו'. Here, emphasis is on events, not on language, but without any philosophical-historical implications. The "corporative unity" of the patriarchs has biblical roots and midrashic explications, from which, as is well known, Thomas Mann drew extensively.

84. Abraham bar Chiyya, *Megillat hamegalleh,* eds. Adolph Poznanski and Julius Guttmann (Berlin, 1924), pp. XIII–XIV; Julius Guttmann, *Philosophie des Judentums* (Munich, 1933), pp. 128–31. Except for Nachmanides (with traces in the *Zohar*), the figure was also used by Abarbanel, *Perush ha-torah* (Warsaw, 1862), p. 146. Isaac ibn Latif (cf. S. O. Heller-Wilensky, "Isaac ibn Latif," *Jewish Medieval and Renaissance Studies,* ed. A. Altmann [Cambridge, 1967], p. 218).

The long discourse on time as a subjective yet necessary measure of duration—against (and alongside of) the Aristotelian definition of time as "measure of motion"—is far from being, as M. Wachsmann held,[85] "original." It is Augustinian. Augustinian also is the allusion to *seminales rationes* (*shorshei ha-minim*) and hence to a *creatio continua*.[86] Isidore has none of these in such clarity. And yet bar Chiyya's employment of the *aetates* analogy is thoroughly counter to Augustine's intent, for his sole interest is calculation of the End (*chishuv ha-qets*).

This is still in part true of the usage which Nachmanides made of this figure (Gen. 2:3), but only in part. He is not only interested in redemptory calculations but is also fascinated with the symbolic opportunities offered by the image. The very exegetical setting is significant: Nachmanides employs the image to interpret the *prima facie* pleonasm *bara la'asot:* "And know that in the word 'to do' is also included the fact that the six days of creation are all the days of the world for its duration will be six thousand years wherefore they say that the day of God is a thousand years . . . etc."[87] In the order of creation God prefigured the course of world history, just as, with the order of their occurrences and actions, the patriarchs prefigured the history of Israel. In both cases, Nachmanides sees symbolic creation: they are "of the nature of creation with respect to their progeny."

Here, too, Nachmanides covers the traces leading to the Christian origins of the figure; he rather quotes the Sanhedrin references we mentioned above. Even in philosophical terms and positions Jews refrained from admitting Christian influences, for example, the doctrine of individual forms;[88] how much more so in exegetical matters. How can we expect Nachmanides to admit the influence of a method of reasoning which, more than any other exegetical method, was used to prove the "concordance of the Old and New Testament?"

Indeed, many of Nachmanides's figures are intentionally or unintentionally structured to counter Christian usages. The creation of Adam

85. Meir Wachsmann, "Hamachshavah hafilosofit vehadatit shel Avraham bar Chiyya hanasi," *Sefer hayovel le-H. A. Wolfson*, 3 vols. (Jerusalem, 1965), Heb. sec., pp. 143–47. Gerhard Ladner, *The Idea of Reform* (New York, 1967), pp. 203–206.

86. Augustinus, *De Genesi secundum litteram*, 5:1–4, CSEL, 28.1, pp. 137–50; cf. Ladner, ibid., pp. 459–62.

87. Ed. Chavel, 1:31: ודע כי נחלל עוד במילה לעשות כי ששת ימי בראשית הם כל ימות העולם כי קיומו יהיה ששת אלפים שנה שלכך אמרו יומו של הקב"ה אלף שנים . . . וגו'.

88. Shlomo Pines, "Hasekholastiqah she-'acharei Thomas Aquinas u-mishnatam shel Chasdai Qresqas veshel kodemav," *Proceedings of the Israel National Academy of Sciences* 1 (1966): no. 11, p. 38.

in the sixth day of creation prefigures the coming of the Davidic messiah rather than that of Christ, as Nachmanides's computation shows. Esau prefigures, of course, the nations of the Roman Empire rather than, as Christian exegesis has it, the Jews who lost their legal primogeniture. And except for the *aetates* analogy—where Nachmanides consulted Augustine independently of Bar Hiyya—none of his prefigurations are known to me from Christian exegesis. He was careful in their use and carefully ascribed them whenever he could, to the midrash. These last observations lead us back to our initial problem.

JEWISH AND CHRISTIAN TYPOLOGIES

We asked why Jewish typological traditions are so meager and unimaginative compared to the Christian tradition. Even Nachmanides's typological attempts are limited, despite the promising methodological declarations he made. In a way, these declarations are even more radical than most Christian typologies, namely in his insistence on the theurgical, almost magical, predestining bond between a prefiguration—*tsiyyur devarim, dimyon*—and its target-event. But if we are made to expect very much more of the same, we are disappointed. Although, for the first time in Jewish tradition, he is clearly aware of the specific heuristic possibilities of typologization, he does not carry it very far, hardly beyond the story of the patriarchs. Why? I suggest five interdependent reasons.

1. Caution. Nachmanides was aware of the force of the figurative imagination in Christianity and of its consequences. To awaken the taste for them was a dangerous affair. For this reason, I suspect, Nachmanides confined his typologies to the patriarchal narratives, always avoiding Christian typological commonplaces. In some instances of characteristic Christian targets for figurative readings, Nachmanides even refrains from employing existing midrashic typologies; he makes no use of the Joseph-typology in Tanhumah, nor does he offer one to the *'aqedah*.[89] In fact, it is astonishing how seldom Jews used typologies creatively even for polemical purposes. An exception is the *Sefer Nissahon yashan*, which turns some Christian *figurae* on their heads and in-

---

89. Midrash Tanhuma, *Va-yehi* 10: ואת יהודה שלח, זזז"ה הנני שולח את מלאכי וגו' (מלאכי ג'). בוא וראה כל הצרות שאירע ליוסף אירע לציון. ביוסף כתיב וישראל אהב את יוסף בציון כתיב אוהב ה' שערי ציון . . . On Joseph as "figura Christi," see, e.g., Augustinus, *Contra Faustum* 12:28.

vents others that are anti-Christian,[90] whereas Yair ben Shabbethai of Correggio, in his polemical tract, lets "the Christian" introduce figurative exegesis with the words of Nachmanides: "The sages stated a great principle, that all that has happened to the fathers is a sign for the sons" and refutes the figural reference altogether: "it was not in the mind of the Holy One, Blessed be He, to hint at the [coming of] the Messiah, but rather to test Abraham."[91]

2. Even Nachmanides did not altogether shift the focus from the apocalyptic to the structural implications of figural interpretations, especially of the days of creation. In Christianity, we saw that this shift transformed typological images from allegories into symbols. Indeed the initial impetus that caused such a shift in Christianity never existed in Jewish tradition. Never were Jews compelled to demonstrate the unity-within-diversity of two or more successive revelations. Yet throughout the history of Christian typologies, the *concordia veteris ac novi testamenti* remained the main methodological paradigm.

3. The speculative energies of Nachmanides and his generation were concentrated on theosophical rather than historiosophical issues. The very same figures which serve Nachmanides's typological interpretations also serve him in a much more imaginative, vivid function: they symbolize divine processes and powers. The *yamim* are also *middot*, that is, *sefirot*. The patriarchs and matriarchs symbolize divine constellations: "the patriarchs are the chariot" (Gen. 17:22).

4. Even where the early kabbalah indulges in historical speculations, these are, as in the *Sefer ha-temunah*, much more detached from the content and attached to the form of the Scriptures, to letter-and-name symbolism. But the essence of typologies, we saw, is indeed detachment from language and a focus on the referents of language: things and

---

90. *Sefer nissahon yashan*, in J. Ch. Wagenseil, *Tela ignea Satanae* (Altdorf, 1681), 1:10–11 (Melchizedek), 19–27 (esp. p. 20): רמז לגלות היאך מושכין :ובשל מבושל במיים. 22–66 (Jacob and Esau), esp. p. 23. כדכתיב באנו באש ובמים; אותנו ומבשלים אותנו
על כן כשיש רעמים הם עושים שתי וערב (ר״ל קרייק בל״א) הקול קול יעקב והידים ידי עשיו:
בידיים סימן שידו של עשיו היו רוצחות תמיד. ואין לנו אלא תפילה והזכרת ברכות רמז שקקול
24–66 (Joseph), esp. p. 27: ועוד יש להשיב שוטים למה תדמוהו לשר האופים pp. ליעקב.
תדמוהו לבן־מלך לאבשלום שנתגלה. וכמו שזה גונב דעת בריות שני׳ ויגנב אבשלום את לב אנשי
ישראל אף ישו במו כן. ומה אבשלום מרד באביו אף ישו מרד באביו שבשמיים. cf. also ;
pp. 46–47 passim; (ר״ל מריה) והנה פרח מטה אהרן לבית לוי. אומרים המינים שזה רמז על חריא
שהיתה בתולה כשילדה את ישו . . . ועוד למה כתוב ויגמול שקדים לשון רבים, ואם על ישו רמז
היה לו להיות שקד אחד ועתה משמע שיהיו הרבה ישויים.
91. כלל גדול אמרו חכמים שכל מה שאירע לאבות סימן לבנים . . . לא עלתה על לבו של
הקב״ה עקדת יצחק כדי לרמוז למשיח . . . אלא לנסות את אברהם. :Yair ben Shabbetai da Correggio, *Herev pifiyyot*, ed. Judah Rosenthal (Jerusalem, 1958), pp. 78–80.

events, persons and institutions. As a matter of fact, this is true of all forms of Christian transliteral exegesis: the more they matured, the more they tended toward a praxis- rather than a logos-symbolism. One will recall the definitions of Thomas Aquinas discussed earlier. Yet Jewish exegetical tradition, *derash* and kabbalah alike, was intimately tied to language, script, and even accents of the Scriptures as supreme symbols.

For here we are within a domain in which Jewish speculative imagination was infinitely rich, where Christianity has but faint and feeble beginnings, even if we include the Christian kabbalah. The grand picture drawn in the surrounding of Nachmanides of the Torah changing physical shape from one *shemitah* to another, while in our *shemitat hadin* one letter is missing,[92] stands against the (totally unrelated) tract of one Fulgentius who, in the manneristic mode of later antiquity, wrote biblical history by dividing it into twenty-two periods and narrating the course of each period by omitting one letter successively—"abest a"—from Adam to Noah and so on, a tasteless stylistic device of which he became tired, abandoning it in the middle.[93] Even where Christian kabbalists later shifted from reception to original speculation their endeavors remained meager and imitative,[94] not only because Hebrew is hard to learn. Some Christian scholars learned it well, especially for polemical purposes; Raymund Martin became proficient enough to imitate midrashim so well that we are still in doubt as to whether some of them may not be genuine lost pieces. Yet a kabbalist's work reflects not only his own linguistic proficiencies, but also the tastes of his reading public. Apart, then, from the fact that Hebrew is easy to admire but harder to acquire, there existed no real, wide Christian market for Hebrew letter-and-name speculations, mystical or otherwise. Nor did there exist a real Jewish market for typologies.[95] But above and beyond

92. Gershom Scholem, *Reshit ha-qabbalah* (Jerusalem, 1948), pp. 176–93; *Ursprung und Anfänge der Kabbala* (Berlin, 1962).

93. Fulgentius, *De aetatibus mundi et hominis,* ed. Rudolf Helm, *Fulgentii opera* (Leipzig, 1898), pp. 127–29; R. Helm, "Fulgentius, de aetatibus mundi," *Philologous* 56 (1897): 253–89; Ernst Robert Curtius, *Europäische Literatur und Lateinisches Mittelalter* (Bern, 1956), p. 73.

94. Chaim Wirszubski, *Sheloshah peraqim betoledot haqabbalah hanotserit* (Jerusalem, 1975), p. 24; *Mequbbal notseri qore ba-torah* (Jerusalem, 1977), pp. 22–25.

95. In his study of Abraham Ibn Daud, Gerson Cohen emphasizes the important role of forced symmetries in the *Sefer ha-qabbalah.* Such symmetries also entail a reason for parallel numerical relations between periods, with the aim of uncovering the structure and end of history, G. Cohen, *The Book of Tradition,* pp. 189–222. But admittedly, Ibn Daud does not assert his method: it has to be decoded. And then numerical correspon-

these reasons for difference, we may yet speculate on a more fundamental one.

5. Typologies, and for that matter all forms of historical speculations in Christianity, express a distinct sense of steady progress within history: progress from the old to the new dispensation, progress within the further history of the *ecclesia militans et triumphans,* extensive progress (mission) as well as intensive progress (articulation of faith and dogma).[96] Jews lacked such a sense of progress and hence the desire to show how matters repeat themselves periodically on a higher level. The first progressive Jewish historical speculation came perhaps only with the Lurianic kabbalah. Maimonides's picture of history as a sometimes gradual, sometimes dramatic process of the monotheization of the world, which I will describe below,[97] was exceptional and, in any event, did not see a real development in Judaism since its beginnings: the world advances slowly and without knowing it—guided by divine "cunning"—to our level. In essence, so it was believed, the Jewish people never changed; they always carried the same revelation, in which *netsach Yisra'el* was premise and promise. In this sense, there is more than a grain of truth in Franz Rosenzweig's contention that Jewish existence (as against that of Christianity) is "ausserhalb einer kriegerischen Zeitlichkeit"—outside the turmoil of history. "Das jüdische Volk ist für sich [in its own understanding] schon an dem Ziel, dem die Völker der Welt erst zuschreiten."[98] Christianity proves itself through history and through its success in history. In its own understanding, its meaning is

---

dences are not typologies proper, though the borderline is floating. Finally, the function was still, if we accept this interpretation, *hishuv ha-qets.* Cf. also H. H. Ben-Sasson, "Limegamot hakhronografyah hayehudit shel yemei habeinayim uve'ayoteha," *Historyah veaskolot historiyot* (Jerusalem, 1962). (By "typology" G. Cohen means, of course, something utterly different from that discussed by us, a systematization of social-psychological "types", i.e., characterology.)

96. One of the earliest discussions of nascent scholasticism was "an secundum mutationes temporum mutata sit fides," e.g., Hugh of St. Victor, *De Sacramentis Christianae fidei* 1.10.6; PL, 176:335. Cf. Johannes Beumer, "Der theoretische Beitrag der Frühscholastik zu dem problem des Dogmenfortschritts," *Zeitschrift Für katholische Theologie* 74 (1952): 205 ff. Cf. also Funkenstein, *Heilsplan,* pp. 55–67.

97. See below, pp. 147–153.

98. Franz Rosenzweig, *Stern der Erlösung* (Frankfurt, 1921), p. 416. Rosenzweig was not oblivious to the grounding in history of Jewish religious images. Jehuda Halevi was, in fact, his prime cultural hero. He rather meant to say that, compared to Christianity, the Jewish orthodox, traditional sense of history does not see time as a task. Cf. below, pp. 291–295.

still unfolding. This was not at all the self-perception of traditional Judaism. Not until Krochmal could any Jewish thinker conceive of Jewish history as the unfolding of a concealed content.

History and Providence: Gersonides's Biblical Commentary

RALBAG'S COMMENTARY

Gersonides's biblical commentary does little to ingratiate itself to its readers, be they medieval or modern. It has nothing of Rashi's charm, his unique blend of correct grammatical readings with pedagogically instructive homilies.[99] It lacks the grammatical acumen of Ibn Ezra, who taught us how always to interpret the biblical vocabulary and imagery in context.[100] It also lacks Ibn Ezra's attractive speculative enigmas. It avoids two dimensions of exegesis which made Nachmanides's commentary dear to its readers—the typological-historical hunt for prefigurations and their fulfillment (*remez*) and the allusions to kabbalistic-mystical symbolism (*sod*).[101] Nor was Gersonides endowed with Ibn Kaspi's keen sense for anachronisms, his capacity to place biblical customs and institutions in the context of bygone historical circumstances.[102] His is rather a dry, schematic, repetitive and dogmatic exercise. It is, of course, of some use for the reconstruction of his philosophical and scientific position—but again not excessively so, because Gersonides's main work, his *Perush hatora,* hides nothing. Unlike the *Guide* of his admired Maimonides, Ralbag felt no need to conceal his real opinions or to wrap them in an ambiguous language.

Why, then, bother to examine a somewhat boring commentary? Partly, of course, because it is there—the ultimate rationale for the his-

99. The latter are introduced only inasmuch as they bear directly on the understanding of the meaning and order of scriptural verses; this is Rashi's conception of "peshuto shel mikra ve'aggada hameyashevet peshuto shel mikra davar davur al ofnav" (to Gen. 3:8). Cf. Sara Kamin, *Rashi: Peshuto shel Mikra u-Midrasho shel Mikra* (Jerusalem, 1986).
100. Cf. my *Styles in Medieval Biblical Exegesis* (Tel Aviv, 1990), chs. 3, 4 (Hebrew).
101. See above, pp. 109–117.
102. Isadore Twersky, "Josef ibn Kaspi: Portrait of a Medieval Jewish Intellectual," in *Studies in Medieval Jewish History and Literature,* ed. I. Twersky (Cambridge, Mass., 1979), pp. 231–57, esp. 238–42.

torian. Partly because it fleshes out, in many cases, the details of positions which his main treatise mentions but briefly and with much abstraction, as, for example, the ways in which astrology is relevant to the study of collective fates—to the study of history. In part because the very dryness of this commentary, its decisiveness, is interesting and telling. Let me start with the latter feature.

PHILOSOPHY AS AN EXACT SCIENCE: RALBAG AGAINST MAIMONIDES

In a famous essay, Husserl spoke of "philosophy as an exact science" ("Philosophie als strenge Wissenschaft"). Philosophy, he believed, could become an exact science if it abandons speculation in favor of a systematic search for empirical, a priori, "eidetic" structures. Gersonides, needless to say, was not a precursor of phenomonology; yet, like Husserl or Spencer or Russell, he too was convinced that most philosophical issues can be settled with a good knowledge of the sciences coupled with a methodical application of common sense. While Maimonides left many cardinal metaphysical questions explicitly unsettled—notably the controversy over the *aeternitas mundi*—Gersonides believed in the ability of philosophy to settle them, and, moreover, had no fear that, by settling them, he would unsettle faith.

Comparing the positions of Maimonides and Gersonides in the matter of *creatio ex nihilo* teaches us something about both, and brings us to a point neglected in the ongoing debate about Maimonides's alleged duplicity.[103] Even Strauss (and his followers) cannot deny that Maimonides's *explicit* position amounts to the argument that neither *chidush ha'olam* nor *kadmut ha'olam* can be proven demonstratively; nor, for that matter, can the middle stand be proven, according to which the world is both eternal and "created"—the latter in the sense that it is utterly contingent upon God's will to preserve it. God could have always annihilated it from eternity. Only tradition and plausibility—this is Rambam's overt position—incline him towards the big bang hypothesis. Now even if we concede to Strauss that Maimonides's true, concealed opinion contradicted his declared stance, even if we concede that Rambam really held the world to be eternal and that he disguises

103. A moderate, well-reasoned argument of this point of view can be found in S. Pines's introduction to his translation of Maimonides, *The Guide of the Perplexed* (Chicago, 1963).

his true beliefs *ad usum delphini*—even if we concede all that, we need and cannot argue that he thought the position he allegedly held to be true (in secret) to be capable of a *demonstrative* proof. His arguments in favor of both contradictory positions are too convincing. It is clear that Maimonides put forth the best possible case for either one of them.

The same holds true, *mutatis mutandis*, of the eternity of the soul. It may, or may not, coincide with the eternity of the active intellect—still, one can argue for a sense in which individuality is preserved. The hidden opinion of Maimonides may have been that the prophecy of Moses, the famous eleventh step in the ladder, is capable of a naturalistic explanation—and a case can be made for the hypothesis that Maimonides thought so, but no case can be made for the hypothesis that he thought it could be proven demonstratively one way or the other, except, perhaps, in Moses' own mind.[104] And finally: God, according to Maimonides, constitutes the ultimate enigma; wherefore the discourse about God should be confined to negations of privations and attributes of action that tell you a lot about the world, but nothing about God.[105]

In short: Maimonides's program—the manner in which he thought his book could guide the perplexed—was *not* centered around matter we could not know at all and not even around that which is dubious. It rather focuses, having cleared the ground, around that which we can hold safely, be it much or little. He shows us which theories can be rejected with certainty: theories of emanation and kalam atomism.[106] He constructs a proof for God's existence that is valid whether or not the world is eternal. Like a good physician, Maimonides stresses the confidence in what he does know for certain rather than his doubts about that which he does not know for sure: the latter might only confuse and harm the patient, even the educated one. But again, like a

104. Maimonides, *Guide* II, 32, 36, 39; III, 17.

105. Ibid., I, 52–58, trans. Pines, pp. 114–37. Note that the "negation of a privation" is always ambiguous: it either denies that a subject lacks a property (which by nature is his) or it denies that it is not a category mistake to attribute that property to the subject, but not both. This ambiguity serves Maimonides well in generating ever more specific "negations of privations" down to nonmultiplicity. Whenever a privation is denied, one avoids the assertion of an attribute by descending to a more specific negation of privation. Critics of Maimonides's theory of negative attributes, such as Thomas Aquinas, *Summa Theologiae* I q. 13 a.2, failed to see that negative attributes are by no means all the same. As top attributes of action, they do not say even that God exists—one is tempted to compare their status to a material implication of the sort "If God exists, then the world is created."

106. Maimonides, ibid., II, 73–76.

conscientious doctor, he was keenly aware how little he knows for sure. This, I believe, is a line of interpretation which avoids both the pitfalls of Straussians and anti-Straussians.

Ralbag, by contrast, believed that we have certain knowledge of many more matters than Maimonides believed to be the case—perhaps because his criteria of demonstration were lower. And as to matters we do not have knowledge about (e.g., bodily resurrection), he does not treat them at all. That the world is created (*qua* form) can be proven as strictly as that its matter (*qua* potentiality) is eternal.[107] Of God we can know many things; positive attributes are not at all detrimental to his transcendent unity.[108] His omniscience excludes knowledge of singulars *qua* singulars, past or future contingents: Gersonides assumes, without saying so, that God's knowledge does not differ from ours.[109] Interesting in all of these positions is not only *that* Ralbag held them, but with what ease, lucidity and transparency he did so. He has nothing to hide. His style is, accordingly, precise, highly nonornamental and undramatic—the style of a scholastic *quaestio*. Indeed, the difference between him and Rambam is more than a difference of mentality of persuasion. It is a difference of cultural climates. In the *dar al Islam* philosophy was always on the defense; not so in the Europe of Duns Scotus and Occam, which fought the wars of the Lord with the proper rational arguments; and which has learned that an argument, though short of absolute certainty, can be still held to be good and valid *in physicis*.[110] At any rate, this unidimensionality of Gersonides's thought and style are the ultimate source of the slight effect of boredom it may exude, especially in the biblical commentary to which we now turn.

NATURE, HISTORY, AND SCRIPTURES

Three characteristics distinguish Gersonides's commentary from others: (a) His belief in the relative transparency of the biblical text made him an enemy of mystical or typological readings à la Nachmanides. (b) His belief in philosophy as an exact science led him

107. Levi ben Gershon, *Sefer Milchamot hashem* (henceforth: Gersonides, *Milchamot*) I, 1, 17 (Leipzig, 1866), pp. 362–68. Cf. H. Davidson, *Proofs for Eternity, Creation, and the Existence of God in Medieval Islamic and Jewish Philosophy* (Oxford, 1987), pp. 35, 209–12.

108. Gersonides, *Milchamot*, III, 3, pp. 135–37.

109. Ibid., III, 4, pp. 137–47.

110. See Anneliese Maier, "Das Problem der Eridenz in der Scholastik des 14. ten Jahrhunderts," *Ausgehendes Mittelalter* (3 vol., Rome, 1964–67) II, pp. 367–418.

to stress the rational character of the commandments not only in a negative, but in a positive sense. Philosophical allegory is the *peshat,* and it serves not only to refute and remove wrong opinions but to delineate a complete, correct cosmology (though pedagogically attuned to lesser minds) and metaphysics. This was unlike Ibn Ezra or Maimonides. (c) His belief in the complete, rational, comprehensive nature of the Law led him, again unlike Maimonides, to deny that any of its institutions, including sacrifices, may have a merely contingent-historical reason; and to seek in it the foundation of all Jewish Law, written and oral. Let me elaborate these features at the hand of the Book of Genesis.

The story of creation, according to Ibn Ezra, is *not* a cosmology. It is rather the story of the formation, within the sublunar world, of dry land through natural forces. "The heavens" are not the astronomical heavens (these are called, he says, *shmey shamayyim* rather than *shamayyim*), but rather the air above us.[111] The Genesis-story does not, of course, contain wrong cosmological information; it just tells us as little of it as is necessary to understand the place of humans in their sublunar realm, and that which is told is told "in the language of humans"— *scriptura humane loquitur.* Here and there, Ibn Ezra hints that the true story of creation is a story of emanation. Except for the latter, Maimonides seems to have concurred, all the more so since he was aware of the structural lacunae of science. The Bible is not a scientific treatise. Gersonides thought otherwise.

Nachmanides, by contrast, took a maximalist position: the Bible does contain all the science and wisdom there is. The philosophical *allegoresis* is, to him, the plain sense of the Scriptures. "In the beginning God created the heavens and the earth" means that God has created *ex nihilo* the prime matter of the heavens and the separate prime matter of the earth; and so on. But Nachmanides's ultimate aim, we saw, was to undermine the philosopher's enterprise with their own means. The cosmos and history are full of "hidden miracles" (*nissim nistarim*).[112] Even that which philosophy sees as most natural—the natural place, for example, of the element of fire above that of air—is a miracle *contra naturam,* for air is the most subtle of elements and only by divine decree does it "hover above the waters," as Scripture says, rather than being above the fire. Indeed, the philosophical explication

111. See above, p. 91.
112. See above, p. 107.

is but one of four modes he employs (probably under Christian influence), the *quattuor sensus scripturae*. *Moraliter,* the story of Genesis teaches us a world-historical rule of divine providence—humans are exiled from their place when they sin. *Mystice (bederech ha'emet la'amito),* the story of creation is the story of emanation and interaction of divine names and forces. *Analogice,* the story of creation prefigures the six ages of the world; that which was created each day prefigures the main event of the corresponding age: an Augustinian idea already employed by Abraham bar Chiyya.

Gersonides, by contrast, has no use of the mystical and analogical dimension. The story of creation is a straightforward cosmological account—in which nothing is omitted or hidden. Its precise place is analogous to that of Aristotle's physics in the history of Greek science; philosophy in Moses' time was "very deficient"; people did not distinguish the formal from the material causes (*velo hayu margishim basiba hatsuriyyit kelal*) and held to opinions similar to the pre-Socratic views mentioned by Aristotle.[113]

The formal structure of the cosmos, such was the position of both Rambam and Ralbag, is teleological. In one place, Maimonides even speaks of God as *tsurat ha'olam, forma mundi*—clearly in a teleological sense.[114] (We recall that Amalrich of Bena had his body exhumed and his bones burned to ashes for expressing a similar view in early thirteenth century Paris.[115]) Yet while Maimonides qualified his teleology in that he considered it to be neither anthropocentric nor transparent to us (wherefore it could hardly function as proof of either God's existence or creation), Gersonides, by contrast, insisted on the evident, intelligible character of the teleological hierarchy of forms to the point that it could easily serve to prove even *creatio e nihilo,* and looks for it in the Bible.[116] Similarly, Maimonides denies our ability to construct a physical interpretation to accommodate the astronomical model of celestial orbits.[117] Gersonides asserts his ability to construct an astrophysics, and looks for it in the Bible: the "water above the firmament," for instance, is the *geshem she'eno shomer tsurato,* a plastic ethereal substance

113. Levi ben Gerson, *Perush al hatora al derech habe'ur* (Venice, 1546) f. 9*a* (henceforth: Gersonides, *Commentary*).

114. Maimonides, *Guide* I, 69.

115. F. Überweg, L. Geyer, *Grundriß der Geschichte der Philosophie* (Basel-Stuttgart, 1960), vol. III, p. 251; Funkenstein, *Theology and the Scientific Imagination,* p. 46.

116. Gersonides, *Commentary* f. 9*b*–10*a*.

117. Maimonides, *Guide* II, 19.

in contrast to the rigid substance of planets and stars.[118] With Einstein, Levi ben Gershon could easily say: "Cunning the Lord may be, but he is not devious." Ralbag holds the biblical text to be as intelligible as nature itself: certainly in need of an expert guide, sometimes difficult and cunning, yet never a malicious trickster.

Like Maimonides (or Kant), Ralbag exempts free will—"das Faktum der praktischen Vernunft"—from natural necessities. His interpretation of necessity is at the same time more universal and less problematic than Maimonides's. Not only did Gersonides—in the commentary no less than in the *Milchamot*—recognize only in the sublunar domain the realm of contingency (which Maimonides expanded to all bodies inasmuch as they are material), but he also held astral constellations, an anathema to Maimonides, to be the source of necessities, governing sublunar fates, individual as well as collective.[119] On the other hand, however, since he did not fear the confinement of God's knowledge to universals (i.e., necessities) only, leaving singulars *qua* singulars out of God's horizon, free will posed no paradoxes to him. What, however, about special providence? Gersonides endows it with a dialectical meaning: it amounts to the degree of participation (*hitdabkut*) in the agent intellect and, consequently, knowledge of ways to avoid the vagaries of chance: either through knowledge of astral constellations, or, better, sticking to right beliefs and divine precepts.[120] The first of those in Genesis is the commandment of procreation, for the human species is the only species which could—how right he was—destroy itself, through a consent to abstain from procreating.[121] By contrast, losing God's special providence amounts to being left to the forces of nature, necessary and contingent.[122] Most of this is well known. In the following we shall see how Gersonides applied it to Jewish history. My aim

118. Gersonides, *Commentary* f. 9a–b. See Gad Freudenthal, "Cosmogonie et physique chez Gersonides," REJ 145 (1986), pp. 295–314.

119. Gersonides, *Milchamot* II, 6, pp. 104–108.

120. Gersonides, *Commentary* f. 56b (*dvekut Moshe*); f. 71a.

121. Ibid., f. 13a (אם תשלם ההסכמה בין אנשים להימנע להוליד).

122. Gersonides, *Milchamot* II, 6, p. 111, sees free will interfering with celestial influences (*im hejotam efshariym mitsad habechira*). In *Commentary* 71a–b he says more specifically that Israel's foes (*amalek*) are victorious "from the vantage point of the constellations" (*mitsad hama'arekhet*) if not for God's help (*lule azar hashem yit'ale*). The importance of this passage in the *Commentary* is heightened by the circumstances that the biblical narrative deals here with "the wars of the lord" (*milhama la'adonay ba'amalek midor dor*, Exod. 13:16)–the verse that lent the title to Gersonides's main philosophical work.

was only to show how style and content, views about nature and exegetical method, are tied together. Because Gersonides believed nature to be so much less opaque than did Maimonides—his astronomy is the ultimate witness to this position—he also believed the biblical text to be straightforward and intelligible.

GENERAL AND PARTICULAR PROVIDENCE

Let us now turn to the story of the patriarchs and of Israel. Again we find the contrast to Nachmanides flagrant and, I believe, conscious. Nachmanides maintained that one ought to understand both the story of creation and the story of the patriarchs typologically, that is, as prefigurations: just as God prefigured world history (the Augustinian *sex aetates mundi*) in the six days of creation, the patriarchs prefigured Jewish history with their acts and events.[123] The method is clearly borrowed from Christian exegesis, and so are its technical terms. If not for their typological import, one might justly deem the stories of the patriarchs "redundant matters without any purpose" (*devarim meyutarim 'en bahem to'elet*). Gersonides, by contrast, stresses *ad nauseam* the "purpose" or "usage" (*to'elet, to'aliot*) of the biblical narratives.[124] The choice of the same term may not be coincidental. Each section of his commentary commences with an "interpretation of the words" (*perush hamilot*), continued by "the narrative" (*sipur*) and followed by a detailed, elaborated list of sometimes up to a dozen or more "*to'aliot*" ("uses"), alternating between ethical purposes (*midot*) and instructional (*de'ot*). The *Tora* is everyman's comprehensive philosophy—theoretical, practical and political. There is no need for mystery-dimensions in the text.

Among the many prefigurations mentioned by Nachmanides, the war against the Amalekites deserves particular notice. It prefigures the wars of the Messiahs against the fourth world monarchy, i.e., Christianity = Edom. Moses had to keep his arms raised—he knew that whatever he does, the king messiahs will do in the future.[125] For Gersonides, the significance of the story is likewise eschatological, but not in the way of symbolic acts or prefigurations; rather, it instructs us about the relation of special and general providence. The Amalekites, needless to say, were well versed in astrology, and were also cunning enough to

123. See above, p. 126 ff.
124. Some go up to twenty-four (*Commentary* f. 29a).
125. Nachmanides, *Perush hatora*, I, p. 372 (on Ex. 17:9).

choose a time for war in which the astral constellation favored its victory (*hitchakem 'amalek lehilachem al yisrael ba'et shehaya ra'uy lenatse'ach mitsad hama'arakhot*).[126] The only exception to general astral laws and influences is human free will. In this case, only Israel's belief in God's help and victory could turn the war, wherefore Moses left the actual campaign to be led by Joshua and stood where he was visible by all to make the victory sign, fortifying Israel's belief. The lesson: God helps only those who help themselves by believing in God's help—then, now, and at the end of tribulations. The very help of God consists in this belief in his help and that which it does to the souls. God, we remember, does not even know present and future contingents—precisely because of the fact of human freedom. By the same token, Israel's clamor to God effected their delivery from the Egyptian yoke "before the proper time" (*lifney heyot hazeman harauy*)—prior to the astrologically proper καιρός. This was made possible by educating Israel towards perfection (*Shlemut*), that is by obeying God and his laws.[127] This was Gersonides's version of the dictum *eyn mazal leyisra'el,* a motif which, from Jehuda Halevi to Nachman Krochmal, stood for Israel's exemption for those laws of nature which govern other nations.

RALBAG'S RATIONALISM

Almost all post-Maimonidean rationalists accepted Rambam's theory of the reasons for the precepts, including the historico-pedagogical rationale for sacrifices and the dietary laws. Gersonides, too, accepted it in part; but he could not acquiesce with a rationale which is only historically contingent. True, the sacrifices were introduced as a concession to polytheistic usages in order to wean Israel away from them. But sacrifices have also a positive function. Not only do they educate in giving: the incense affects the senses to heighten the mind's capacity for detachment (*hitbadlut*), a necessary precondition for prophetic meditation.[128] Of the same category are the symbolic acts of Prophets. Here, again, the contrast to Nachmanides is sharp.

I shall not go into the details of Gersonides's rational reconstruction of Jewish law from Scriptures—it remained, of course, a program only.

126. Cf. above, n. 122.
127. Gersonides, *Commentary* f. 54*b.*
128. Ibid., 55*b;* 115*b;* 114*a* (*hitbodedut*); cf. M. Idel, "Hahitbodedut keikuz' bafilosofia hayehudit," *Mechkare Yerushalayim beMachshevet Yisrael* 7 (1988): pp. 39–60, esp. p. 50.

The very law and obedience to the law *are* Israel's special providence—such was the lesson we drew already.

Rationalism has many faces, and escapes definitions. If I had to characterize dogmatic rationalism, medieval or modern, in one formula, I would say: a rationalist is a thinker who refuses to be surprised; nothing seems mysterious. Now even if we view the proposition that $2 + 2 = 4$ as logically necessary, it is still a great wonder why nature behaves accordingly: why, when one adds two stones and one, a fourth is not created out of nothingness to make a set of four, or why is it universally true of birds no less than of stones. A rationalist has no such problems; he expects nature to be always consistent and "true to itself" (Newton). A mystic, by contrast, sees the world full of mysteries: τὸν κόσμον μῦθον εἰπεῖν, as Sallust once said.[129] Of all medieval Jewish philosophers of the first rank, Gersonides came closest to being a dogmatic rationalist. This was the source of his confidence as an astronomer, but also the source of the slight boredom which his commentary exudes. He saw at best riddles, but no mysteries, either in heaven, or on earth, or in the biblical text.

129. A. D. Nock (ed.), *Sallustius Concerning the Gods and the Universe* (Cambridge, Mass., 1926), p. 4, lines 9–11.

5

Law, Philosophy, and Historical Awareness

Maimonides: Political Theory and Realistic Messianism

REALISTIC MESSIANISM

"Realism" is a vague term, and at least as an attribute of political theories it means little more than the rejection of utopian models. Giambattista Vico summed up the classical tradition of political realism in a succinct (though borrowed) phrase. Plato and Grotius, he said, construed their ideal constitution to fit "man as he should be." While sharing their aspirations, Vico nonetheless concurs with their adversaries from Aristotle through Tacitus to Machiavelli and Hobbes in the search for the best constitution to accommodate "man as he is, in order to turn him to good uses in human society. Out of ferocity, avarice and ambition . . . it makes civil happiness."[1] All varieties of

---

1. Giambattista Vico, *La Scienza Nuova* (1744), ed. F. Nicolini, *Opere* IV (Bari, 1928), vol. I, pp. 75–76; *Autobiography,* trans. T. G. Bergin and M. H. Fisch (Ithaca, New York, 1944), p. 138. Cf. "De Universo iuris uno principio et fine uno," *Opere*

political realism share the belief that no form of social organization is capable of changing the basic ingredients of human nature. No constitution, they maintain, could produce a better species of man. Campanella, a most interesting forerunner of the modern brand of secular-totalitarian utopianism, recognized better than others the continuity of the realistic attitude in its diverse manifestations: *exiit machiavellismus ex Peripatetismo*.[2] If neither the cosmos nor man can ever be changed, what else is left *in politicis* but the despicable logic of *raison d'état*? And indeed, already Aristotle insists against Plato that even an imaginary constitution must not transgress the realm of human possibilities.[3] In response, the modern utopian will answer that a change to the better of the human condition is possible or even an inevitable historical necessity; and that he, the utopian, is in fact the true realist. He foresees the inevitable outcome of history. Such are the contours of a dialogue which dominates a good portion of the classical history of political theories in the West.

The Jewish occupation with designs for the best constitution or with discussions concerning the relative merit of forms of government—the core of political theories until the nineteenth century—was very modest indeed. While the Christian reception of Aristotle secured for his politics an influence even stronger and longer than the profound influence of his metaphysics or natural philosophy, Jewish medieval thought knew Aristotle—*the* philosopher—mainly in the nonpolitical portions of his doctrine. Being without a sovereign state, what little of political theory may be found in the Jewish tradition is linked to the mythical past or to the eschatological future. *In illo tempore* Israel had a state and believed that it would have one again. But with or without a political theory Judaism did not miss the fruitful confrontation between the uto-

---

II, 1 (ed. Nicolini, Bari, 1936), p. 32; and my essay "Natural Science and Social Theory: Hobbes, Spinoza and Vico," in *Giambattista Vico,* ed. G. Tagliacozzo (Baltimore, 1975). The phrase "man as he is" etc., is taken from Machiavelli or Hobbes or Spinoza.

2. T. Campanella, *Atheismus triumphatus* (Paris, 1636), p. 20; cf. *Metafisica* ed. G. Napoli (Bologna, 1967), vol. I, p. 22; vol. III, p. 114; F. Meinecke, *Die Idee der Staatsraison, Werke* I 2nd ed. (Munchen, 1960), pp. 115–29; and recently G. Bock, *Thomas Campanella, politisches Interesse und philosophische Spekulation* (Tübingen, 1974), pp. 229–98, esp. pp. 265 ff.

3. E.g. Aristotle, *Politics,* 1.1288b 25–40; 11.129a 25–30; H, 4.1324b 34–40; even the imaginary constitution must still be possible. The best study of utopian designs in antiquity is still R. v. Poehlmann, *Geschichte der sozialen Fragen u. des Sozialismus in der antiken Welt,* 2 vol. (München, 1912).

pian and the realistic mentality. Both found their expression in the very domain of utopian images, in the difference between the utopian and the realistic Messianism.

Maimonides was the first theoretician of a "realistic Messianism"; but he only gave a systematic expression to a deep-rooted, yet hitherto ill-articulated tradition of attitudes towards messianic images. Vis-à-vis the professional optimists in the last decades of Jehuda and Israel, the prophets did not deny the coming of the "day of *Jahwe*,"[4] but insisted that it will be a time of "darkness, not light" (Amos 5:18) which will precede the future redemption. Vis-à-vis the apocalyptic expectations that the new αἰών would bring both a cosmic and social revolution, the famous dictum of Shmu'el (Babylon, third century) insists that "nothing distinguishes this world from the messianic days except for the subjugation under Kingdoms."[5] Wherever the dictum appears, it includes the reference to Deut. 15:11 "for the poor will not vanish from the land." The long array of so-called calculation of the end (*chishuvei hakitsin*) in *Sanhedrin* XI (Chelek), if it is not a mere presentation of various traditions, seems to have been gathered merely to prove their extreme divergence and unreliability; it concludes with the curse: "Let the spirit of those who calculate ends expire." Among the famous three oaths inferred from the triple repetition of the verse "I bequeath you the daughters of Jerusalem . . . not to awaken love until it desires" (Song of Songs 2:7) one oath construes the obligation not to push for the end (*shelo lidchok et hakets*).[6] Indeed, these and simi-

---

4. Whether or not one agrees with the deemphasis of *Amos 5:18,* it certainly is directed against the *vulgi opinio.* Cf. G. v. Rad, *The Message of the Prophets* (New York, 1962), pp. 95–99. See chapter 3, "The Christian Tradition."

5. B. T. *Sanhedrin* 91*b*, 99*a*; *Sabat* 63*a*, 151*b*; *Berakhot* 34*b*. It is interesting to note that while the intrinsic reference is to a change of social order, the extrinsic reference to the dictum by later Amora'im is in relation to changes of cosmic order. On the tana'itic and amora'itic messianic attitudes in general see E. E. Urbach, *Chazal: Pirke emunot vedeot* (Jerusalem, 1969), pp. 585–623; here also the expression "realistic conception of redemption"—an equivalent to G. Scholem's "restorative" type of messianism (n. 19).

6. B. T. *Ketubot* 111*a; Cant. Rabba* 2, 7. It is not necessarily an admonition against calculation of the end, but against political activity which aims to precipitate the end, without, of course, casting any doubt of its eventual (or even immediate) coming. Literally the formula is not an oath, but a playful imitation of one; wherefore the invocation of God (*el shadai*) is replaced by a phonetic simile (*aylot ha'sade*). Cf. R. Gordis, "The Song of Songs," *Mordechai M. Kaplan Jubilee Vol.* (JIS, New York, 1953), pp. 281–397, esp. 307–309. No study of the history of the topos exists, yet it is the main reference for all protagonists of a strictly passive messianism. A review of the tradition, with a strong polemical-ideological intent, can be found in the polemical tract of J. Taitelbaum, *Vayoel Moshe* (New York, 1952). See chapter 9, below (Taitelbaum).

lar traditions do not yet constitute a theory or even a doctrine. They amount to the admonition not to expect too much and not to expect it too soon.

The lack of a theory is all the more astonishing in view of the natural suspicion extended by the legal establishment (or, if you wish, the rabbinical leadership) towards messianic eruptions. It was a well-grounded suspicion. Christianity grew out of a messianic heresy. The Bar Kokhba revolt was a catastrophe greater than the big revolt of A.D. 66–67: it left Judea depopulated.[7] The Abu-Issa movement was, or grew into, a syncretistic heresy.[8] Messianism was often the hotbed of antinomian trends. Yet precisely this very suspicion may in part explain the lack of a normative messianic doctrine. Whenever definite characteristics of the Messiah and the messianic age were given, no matter how restrictive, a generation pregnant with acute messianic hopes found it all the easier to recognize such criteria in the present age and in some present contender. The more vague the criteria, the less room there is for an actualizing interpretation. The archetype of actualizing interpretation, the apocalyptic *pesher* or "decoding" of old prophecies which we know from the Qumran documents, is based on the systematic exploitation of such concrete suggestive identifications.[9] The rabbinical establishment may have felt instinctively that the best messianic doctrine is no doctrine at all. Yet in response to repeated messianic eruptions, a position had repeatedly to be taken.

MAIMONIDES AS A REALIST

Maimonides raised this very desire to refrain from detailed doctrines to the level of a theory. The influence of his theory on

7. M. Avi-Yonah, *Biyme Roma u'Bizantion* (Jerusalem, 1946), pp. 1–4. Maimonides himself invokes, in the *Iggeret Teman,* a long list of heresies and tribulations which resulted from messianic contentions: *Iggeret Teman* (henceforth IT) ed. J. Kapah (Jerusalem, 1952), pp. 21 f, 53–56.

8. A. Z. Eshkoli, *Jewish Messianic Movements* (Hebrew) (Jerusalem, 1956), pp. 117–28 (Sources); S. Baron, *A Social and Religious History of the Jews* (New York, 1952–), vol. V, pp. 193–94. We must, here as in other applications of the term, distinguish between conscious and unconscious "syncretism." The latter is, in several degrees, the mark of all creeds; the former is a particular attitude towards other religions which is in itself a part of a religion. Such attitudes characterize, since antiquity, a good many religious communities, among them Manichaeism and Islam. It is based on the assumption that one's own religion received the best from, or is the crowning and the ideal of, many true elements in former or other religions. Abu Issa commanded his followers to stay in their respective religions, and recognized Mohammed and Jesus as true prophets.

9. See above, pp. 74–78.

Jewish life and thought was considerable indeed. In his letter to the Yemenite community, recently afflicted by a messianic contender, he clarifies first and foremost the duty of the rabbinical leadership when confronted with messianic aspirations.[10]

> But regarding what you [Jakob ben Nethan'el] said in the matter of this man claiming to be the messiah, the truth is that I was not astonished about him or his followers. Not about him, for he is undoubtedly a madman, and the sick do not bear guilt . . . nor about his followers, for due to the hardship of the situation and their ignorance in the subject of the Messiah and his high status they imagined what they did. . . . But I was astonished at *your* words—for you are the sons of the *tora,* and have learnt the dicta of the sages—(in that you said) "perhaps this is true". . . . *What proof* did he advance for his lies?

Skepticism is not a mark of disbelief in the coming of the Messiah, but rather the foremost duty of the learned. He should not give in to the natural inclination of hoping "perhaps it is true." The normative leadership can never afford the luxury of a protracted illusion.[11] Its very function in the midst of a messianic eruption is to voice extreme criticism. The rabbinical authority is, by nature, anticharismatic both *in foro interno* and *in foro externo,* or at least opposed to any charisma which is not derived from law and learning. The critical duty of the learned legal expert is, paradoxically, his very eschatological function. Maimonides sincerely believed that his age was close to redemption. The rapid increase of false messiahs is in itself a sign of the end.[12] By suppressing

10. Moshe ben Maimon, *Iggeret Teman* (IT), chapter 4, p. 50, Cf. also Eshkoli, pp. 178–82. Our following remarks do not yet distinguish the style and content of the Yemenite letter from the other instances in which Maimonides expounded his Messianic doctrines, i.e., *Mishne Tora, Hilkhot Teshuva* (HT); ibid., *Hilkhot Melakhim* (HM); *Ma'amar Techiat Hametim* (Ma'amar); *Perush Hamishna* (PH). We shall rather treat all of Maimonides's assertions in the matter as part of one comprehensive theory, and we shall discuss the possible evolution of these doctrines below.

11. Maimonides succeeded here in identifying a pattern of reaction of the rabbinical leadership which will occur time and again in similar situations. During the height of the Sabbatai Zvi Movement, Rabbi Jacob Sassportas was particularly enraged by letters from colleagues in Italy who urged him to keep his opposition silent, for one should wait and see the outcome of the movement and, besides, an opposition too harsh will damage the positive trend of teshuva which came in the wake of the movement. Rabbi Jacob Sassportas, *Sefer tsitsat novel tsvi* (Jerusalem, 1954), pp. 58–60; G. Scholem, *Sabbatai Sevi: The Mystical Messiah,* trans. S. Werblowsky (Princeton, 1973), p. 498.

12. IT, chapter 4 (ed. Kafih p. 55): "And in this matter a prophetic stipulation preceded . . . that when days of the true Messiah will draw close, claimers and imitators of Messianity will multiply." On the other hand, Maimonides refers to a well-guarded tradition in his family for eschatological renewal of prophecy to come in the year 1210, a tradition to which he gives some credence (ibid., chapter 3, pp. 48–49). But he quotes this tradition only as a possibility, and warns against its publication.

false messiahs, the rabbinical authorities perform, so to say, an escha-tological role, their role at the end of tribulations.

Maimonides establishes three categories of signs for the veracity of the Messiah. The first category is a negative one. The Messiah will not change an iota of the law. An antinomian attitude is the clearest indi-cation of an imposter. The second category includes a few positive spe-cific signs. The Messiah cannot but arise in the land of Israel, the forum of his actions.[13] He will emerge out of obscurity, but must be nonethe-less most learned in the law, the utmost synthesis of charisma and legal expertise. The third category is the most decisive of all. His main and only proof will be his ultimate success; success in the restitution of the sovereign kingdom: "If he acted successfully and built the temple at its place and gathered the dispersed of Israel, he is in certainty a Messiah."[14]

The transition to the messianic age will be revolutionary. But will it also be miraculous? The Messiah, Maimonides admonishes, does not have to perform miracles to prove his messianity.[15] But he must accom-plish extraordinary things indeed. The restoration of sovereignty and the gathering of the exiles are but the beginnings of his deeds. The Messiah will establish, through fame of invincibility, the hegemony of Israel over the nations, a *pax aeterna* in which all nations have embraced monotheism as the only religion and look up to Israel for law and ar-bitration.[16] It is true that Maimonides warns against the apocalyptic ornamentation of *yemot hamashiach*. The messianic days will neither bring a change in the cosmic order nor an egalitarian society. "And the wolf shall dwell with the lamb" should be understood allegorically.[17]

13. IT, chapter 4, p. 52; not repeated in the HM, in which Maimonides refrains, as much as possible, from the dogmatic assertions.

14. HM, chapter 11, p. 4. Whereas if the future Davidic king only achieves sover-eignty and leads the state within the rule of the law ("tora"), he is yet only a *potential* Messiah (*bechezqat mashiach*). On the revolutionary character of the "first phase" of the messianic days, below, pp. 101 ff. (This, also, against Scholem, below n. 19.)

15. Ma'amar chapter 6, p. 76; HM chapter 11, p. 3.

16. IT chapter 4, p. 52; HM chapter 11, p. 4. Even an ultimate political hegemony of Israel is not invoked directly except for the *Perus Hamishna* (Sanhedrin, Helek): "and all the nations will make peace with him and all the lands will serve him in his abounding righteousness."

17. HM chapter 12, p. 1. In his critical notes (*hasagot*), the Raabad of Posquiers objected that the extermination of predatory animals is, after all, mentioned in the Pen-tateuch itself; that is, one may allegorize, if at all, only prophetical passages. Cf. Abraham ben haRambam, *Milchamot Hashem*, ed. R. Margaliot (Jerusalem, 1953), p. 65, and the editor's note (n. 79).

But is not a perpetual peace of the kind Maimonides envisages in itself a miracle, a change in human nature?[18] And even if we agree with G. Scholem that the messianic age of Maimonides only actualizes man's natural potentialities, we cannot fully agree with Scholem's following characterization of the messianic age as being merely restorative.[19] The messianic days are at least a *reformatio in melius* and they exceed in perfection any age known before. It seems, then, as if we face an ambiguity in Maimonides's messianic images. But we ought to study them within the context of his social theories as a whole, and pay specific attention to the meaning and role of miracles in history. We shall see how and why Maimonides regarded the laws of nature, the laws of society and the course of history as successive instances of divine *accommodation* to an ultimately contingent world.

HISTORY AND NATURE:
THE REASONS FOR THE COMMANDMENTS

In the *More Nevukhim* III, 26–56, Maimonides unfolds his philosophy of law, the doctrine of "reasons for the commandments."[20] Against the Sa'adianic disjunction between commandments of obedience (*mitsvot shim'iyot*) and of reason (*sikhliyot*), a disjunction which combined the Kalam terminology with Midrashic reminiscences,[21] Maimonides holds that every single precept has a dual structure and may be seen as both a commandment of reason and a commandment of obedience. Every commandment serves a rational design: "The law of God is perfect" (*torat hashem temima*). But the right obedience to every commandment should not be dictated by insight into

---

18. A contemporary of Maimonides, R. Eliezer of Beaugency, went even further, and assumed the perpetuation of national tensions even in the messianic age, in which Israel will be assigned the role of an arbiter. H. H. Ben-Sasson, "Yichud am yisrael leda'at bne hame'a hashtem esre," *Peraqim le'cheqer toldot yisrael* II (HUC 1971), pp. 212–14.

19. G. Scholem, *The Messianic Idea in Judaism* (New York, 1971), pp. 24–32.

20. Henceforth MN. We use the edition of S. Munk, Moise ben Maimon, *Dalalat al Hairin* (3 rol., 1856–1866) and the translation of S. Pines, *The Guide of the Perplexed* (Chicago, 1963). The following pages are in part a summary, in part a modification of my earlier article "Gesetz und Geschichte. Zur historisierenden Hermeneutik bei Moses Maimonides und Thomas von Aquin," *Viator* I (1970), pp. 147–78.

21. The Midrash furnished the name for the discipline (*ta'ame hamitsvot*, e.g., *Numeri Rabba* 16:1, 149a; and some of the paradigms (the red heifer). Cf. I. Heinemann. *Ta'ame hamitsvot besifrut Yisrael* (Jerusalem, 1959), vol. I, pp. 22–35; E. E. Urbach, op. cit. (above n. 5), pp. 320–47.

its purpose: it must be based on the *potestas coactiva* of the law, the fact that it is the will of the sovereign.[22] Maimonides is thus forced to look for a specific rationalization of those commandments—the ceremonial and dietary laws—to which Sa'adia assigned only a generic rationale. A perfect constitution, Sa'adia held, must include some irrational commandment as an opportunity for the subjects to profess blind loyalty; and Sa'adia, in the endeavor to demonstrate that the written and oral law form a perfect constitution, valid for all societies and all times, had to limit the number of such pure "commandments of obedience" to a minimum. Maimonides, who questioned this very axiom of Sa'adia's legal philosophy, needed a new starting point. He started, as so often, by trying to define anew the meaning of old questions.

What do we really look for when we ask for the *reason* of a commandment? Must a rationale for a specific law cover every part and detail of that law? In a preliminary answer, Maimonides draws a strict analogy between laws of nature and social laws.[23] In the second part of the *Guide*, Maimonides developed one of the most original philosophies of science in the Middle Ages. There he proved that not only are laws of nature (the ordering structures of nature) in themselves contingent upon God's will; but that each of them must include, by definition, a residue of contingency, an element of indeterminacy. No law of nature is completely determining, and no natural phenomenon completely determined (*omnimodo determinatum*), not even in God's mind.[24] To illustrate the matter, allow me to invent an example. Assume that tables

---

22. Even in the domain of obligations pertaining to non-Jews (*sheva mitsvot bne Noah*) Maimonides insists that insight into their rationality (*hekhra hada'at*) does not suffice to characterize an obedient gentile, a "pious from among the nations," but only the fulfillment of these commandments because they are the will of God (HM VIII, 11). Cf. also J. Levinger, *Maimonides' Techniques of Codification* (Hebrew) (Jerusalem, 1965), esp. pp. 37 ff.; J. Paurs, "The Basis for the Authority of the Law According to Maimonides," *Tarbiz* 38, 1 (1969): pp. 43 ff. (Hebrew). I disagree with Paurs's assumption that, contrary to Sa'adia, Maimonides could not have developed an equivalent to the concept of a *lex naturalis*. The classical theories of the *lex naturalis* separate between the rationality and the *potestas coactiva* even of natural law.

23. MN III, 26, trans. Pines, p. 509: "This resembles the nature of the possible for it is certain that one of the possibilities will come to pass," that is, which necessitates the actualization of one of the possibles within a material substrate. Cf. MN II, 25, as well as our following notes.

24. Maimonides does not say so explicitly, but it follows clearly from his discussion of the particularization of precepts and of natural phenomena. The Maimonidean theory of nature, and in particular his doctrine of contingency, have not yet received due emphasis. But cf. J. Guttmann, "Das Problem der Kontingenz in der Philosophie des Maimonides," *MGWJ* 83 (1939), pp. 406 ff.

should all be made out of wood; assume that the kind of wood most suitable to make tables from is mahogany, and that the best mahogany can be found only in a remote forest in Indonesia. A carpenter who wishes to make a perfect table has good reasons to choose mahogany and to travel all the way to the said forest. But there and then he will ultimately be confronted with two or more equally reasonable possibilities. Should he choose the tree to his right or to his left? He must choose one, and both are equally suitable. The purpose can never determine the material actualization in all respects, down to the last particular; a "thoroughgoing determination" is ruled out by the very material structure of our world. In the very same way, there may (indeed must) be a purpose to the universe; but it does not govern all particulars. The purpose of the universe may require the circular orbit of the celestial bodies. But it does not account necessarily for the different velocities or colors of the planets.[25]

Technically, Maimonides seems to have recognized[26] that the Aristotelian concept of matter (ὑποκαίμενον, ὕλη) carried two different explanatory burdens. It was both a principle of potentiality and a *principium individuationis*. Maimonides abandons the second connotation of matter; matter becomes for him the source of contingency throughout the universe, and not only in the sublunar realm. Between essential forms (laws, necessities) and matter *qua* mere potentiality (contingency, possibility) lies a hierarchy of contingent structures—*causae finales*—which account for the individuation (i.e., particularization) of all singulars. The natural world is thus a continuum of instances of the accommodation of divine planning to indifferent if not resilient substrates. The influence of parts of this doctrine on scholastic philosophy was considerable. One may or may not agree that Maimonides prepared the way for the Scotistic suggestion of individual forms no less than Ibn Gebirol. Certain and more important is the impact of his view

---

25. MN II, 19 (Pines, pp. 302–14). On similar examples in the Kalam, H. Davidson, "Arguments from the Concept of Particularization," *Philosophy East and West* 18 (1968), pp. 299 ff., esp. 311 ff., 313, n. 50 (Maimonides). On the Aristotelian concept of contingency (e.g., *De generatione animalium*, 3.778b, pp. 16–18), cf. J. Hintikka, *Time and Necessity: Studies in Aristotle's Theory of Modality* (Oxford, 1973), pp. 27–40, 93–113, 147–75.

26. MN II, 19, discusses Aristotle's failure to account for the particularization of terrestrial as well as celestial bodies; the failure is then converted into a virtue—namely that matter can never be *omnimodo determinatum*, because it is, by definition, a principle of potentiality (cf n. 22). Of prime importance for the understanding of this chapter is the distinction between necessity and purpose.

of physical (or contingent) necessities on the confrontation of the *po-tentia dei absoluta et ordinata*, a backbone issue of later scholasticism. I have shown elsewhere how the Thomistic interpretation of the *potentia dei ordinata* mirrors the Maimonidean theory of contingency and at times relies on it explicitly.[27] In a sense, Maimonides's principle of indeterminacy is closer to modern physics than to the Newtonian: modern physics likewise assumes a principle of indeterminacy not as a limit to our knowledge, but as an objective indeterminacy within nature itself.[28]

His principle of indeterminacy and the corresponding principle of accommodation allowed Mainmonides to rephrase that which Kant later was to call the "physico-theological argument," the proof for God's existence from the order of the universe. If the universe were to be well-ordered throughout, it would be of itself necessary and would not imply an ordering hand. The physico-theological argument assumes neither that the universe is completely ordered nor that it is com-

27. E.g., Thomas Aquinas, *De potentia* q.3.a.17 (ed. Marietti, p. 103): "Cum autem de toto universo loquimur educendo in esse, non possumus ulterius aliquod creatum invenire ex quo possit sumi ratio quare sit tale vel tale; unde cum nec etiam ex parte divinae potentiae quae est infinita, nec divinae bonitatis, quae rebus non indiget, ration determinatae despositionis universi sumi possit, oportet quod eius ratio summatur ex simplici voluntate producentis, ut si quaeratur, quare quantitas caeli sit tanta et non major (cf. Maimonides, MN III, p. 26: 'veheyot misparo echad') non potest huius ratio reddi nisi ex voluntate producentis. Et propter hoc etiam, ut Rabbi Moyses dicit, divina Scriptura inducit homines ad considerationem caelestium corporum (cf. Maimonides, MN II, 19:24), per quorum dispositionem maxime ostenditur quod omnia subjacent voluntati et providentiae creatoris. Non enim potest assignari ratio quare talis stella tantum a tali distet, vel aliqua hujusmodi quae in dispositione caeli consideranda occurunt, nisi ex ordine sapientae dei." From these and similar references (e.g., *Summa Theologica* 9.25 a 5 resp. 3), we obtain the following structure of the "Potentia-ordinata" relation: whatever is not self-contradictory ("per se impossibile") falls under *potentia absoluta* even if it is not well ordered. Under the *potentia ordinata* falls not only our world, but also every other well-ordered possible universe, and it is futile to ask why this or that universe has been chosen to be created—for the questions could be repeated ad infinitum: it is a voluntary act. From here, the road to Scotus's proof of contingency is not very long; cf. Duns Scotus, *Opus Oxoniense* dist. 8 q. 5. (ed. Quarracchi, I, 665) and id. 39. 3n. 14 (ibid., I, 1215); and E. Gilson, *Johannes Duns Scotus* (Düsseldorf, 1959), pp. 280 ff. On the influence of Maimonides in the West, and in particular on Thomas, cf. J. Guttmann, *Das Verhältniss des Thomas von Aquino zum Judentum und zur jüdischen Literatur* (Göttingen, 1891); W. Kluxen, "Literaturgeschichtliches zum lateinischen Moses Maimonides," *Rech. theol. anc. et méd.* xxi (1954), pp. 23–50.

28. Niels Bohr, "Discussion with Einstein on Epistemological Problems in Atomic Physics," in *Albert Einstein: Philosopher Scientist,* ed. P. A. Schilpp, 3rd ed. (London, 1949), vol. I, pp. 199–241. Here and there, "indeterminacy" is not a limit to our understanding, but a limit within nature itself.

pletely disconnected (in the manner of the extreme nominalism of the *Isharia*), but that its order is imposed on the heterogenous elements which of themselves do not demand or imply this particular order.[29] The argument from particularization has been used already by the Kalam; Maimonides gave it the balanced form in which it was to remain effective until Kant.

CONTINGENT HISTORICAL REASONS: THE CUNNING OF GOD

The principle of indeterminacy allowed likewise to introduce most miracles—or, more generally, instances of special providence—without violating laws of nature.[30] Miracles are mostly, but not always, taken from the reservoir of the remainder of contingency on all levels of nature. Maimonides calls such miracles "miracles of the category of the possible (*moftim . . . misug ha'efshari*).[31]

And precisely the same figure of thought is used by Maimonides to clarify what we look after in the search for "reasons of the commandments" (*ta'ame hamitsvot*). Take, for example, the sacrifices. We may be able to explain, in view of their purpose, why sacrifices should have been instituted in the first place; "but the fact that one sacrifice is a lamb and another a ram; and the fact that their number is determined—to this one can give no reason at all, and whoever tries to assign a rationale enters a protracted madness."[32] Rather than look for an always determining principle for each law, we should look for a contingent rationale. Maimonides found such a contingent rationale in the concrete historical circumstances under which these laws were given to the nascent Israel. Sacrifices and the bulk of the dietary laws are not in them-

---

29. I. Kant, *Kritik der Reinen Vernunft,* ed. W. Weischedel, *Werke* (Wiesbaden, 1956), vol. IV, p. 552 (B654 A626): "Den Dingen der Welt ist diese zweckmäßige Anordnung ganz fremd und hängt ihnen nur zufällig an, d.i. die Natur verschiedener Dinge konnte von selbst, durch so vielerlei sich vereinigende Mittel, zu bestimmten Endabsichten nicht zusammenzustimmen, wären sie nicht durch ein anordnendes vernünftiges Prinzip . . . dazu ganz eigentlich gewählt und angelegt worden."

30. MM II, 48 and Ma'amar 10 ed. Kafih, pp. 98–101. The words "Shekol ze taluy bechiyuv chokhma sheen anu yod'im ba me'uma, velo od ela she'anu hizkarnu kevar ofen hachokhma bekhakh," whose meaning eluded the translator and editor, may be taken as reference to the divine "cunning," that is, to purpose rather than necessity.

31. Maimonides, *Ma'mar,* ibid., p. 98.

32. Maimonides, MN III, p. 26. (Pines, p. 509; ours is a translation from the Hebrew).

selves beneficial for every society at every time. The former are in particular suspicious, because they invoke anthropomorphistic associations of a smelling or an eating deity. Considering the vigor with which Maimonides eradicated even the most abstract positive attributes of essence from the concept of God,[33] the institution of sacrifice must have been to him unworthy of a truly monotheistic community. And indeed he interprets it as a remnant of the universal polytheistic culture of the Sa'aba which prevailed in the times of Abraham and Moses. So deep-rooted and pervasive[34] were its abominable creeds that they could not be eradicated altogether in one sweeping act of revelation and legislation. Human nature does not change from one extreme to another suddenly (*Lo yishtnae teva ha'adam min hahefekh el hahefekh pit'om: natura non facit saltus*). Had anyone demanded of the nascent Israel to cease the practice of the sacrifices, it would be just as impossible a demand as if "someone demanded today (of a religious community) to abandon prayer for the sake of pure meditation." Only a miracle could have transformed the polytheistic mentality immediately into an altogether monotheistic one: but God does not wish to act *contra naturam*. He rather prefers to act with the aid of nature, to accommodate his plans to existing, contingent circumstances, to use contingent elements within nature in order to change it. Rather than eradicating all polytheistic inclinations among the emerging monotheistic community from the outset in a miraculous act, he preferred to use elements of the polytheistic mentality and culture in order to transform this very mentality

33. The doctrine of negative attributes, as we wish to prove on another occasion, should not be taken as a mechanical, indefinite enumeration of negations, but rather as the constructive generation of one "negative attribute" from another until we reach the ultimate, transcendental "unity" of God (i.e., the negation of multiplicity). This movement, described in MN I, 58, is a dialectical one, and employs the negation of privations rather than simple negations. Without explicitly saying so, Maimonides commits himself to the exemption of the divine attributes from the principle of excluded middle; to say that God is "not unjust" is not the same as saying that he is just—or, if "∞" stands for privation, we may write:

$$\exists(x, y)\langle[\sim\sim A(y) \equiv A(y)\wedge\sim[\sim\infty A(x) \equiv A(x)]\rangle$$

But once we have established such a negation, we try to invest it with meaning, and produce a more precise "negative attribute," aided by our knowledge of science. The most convincing interpretation of this doctrine was therefore given by Hermann Cohen, precisely because he relied on his theory of "infinite judgment" as a generative logic.

34. Maimonides calls these practices and beliefs "an abomination (*to'eva*) to human nature ('*altaba 'alanasani*)" (MN III, 29), "against nature" (MN III, 37). On the other hand, he described how mankind lapsed gradually, almost naturally, into such a universal error.

by degrees.[35] Sacrifices were conceded with maximal restrictions and changed intents. They are turned into a fruitful error.[36]

Just as Hegel's *objektiver Geist* uses the subjective, egotistic freedom of man to further the objective goals of history (for otherwise, history would cease to be "Fortschritt im Bewußtsein der Freiheit"),[37] so also Maimonides's God fights polytheism with its own weapons and uses elements of its worship as a fruitful deceit. Maimonides spoke of the "cunning of God" (*'ormat hashem utevunato; talattuf fi'allahu*)[38] where

35. It seems as if Maimonides implies a somewhat similar structure of understanding to explain the polytheistic residues within Islam. In his famous letter to Obadiah the Proselyte he remarks, "Those Ismaelites are not all idolators, of long [idolatry] has been eradicated from their mouth and heart and they unify the exalted God properly. . . . And should one say that the house they worship [the Qa'aba] is a house of idolatry and contains idolatry which their fathers used to worship, so what. Those who kneel against it today have no other intention but towards God [*en libam ela lashamayim*] . . . indeed, the Ismaelites once held in their places three kinds of idolatry, 'pe'or,' 'marqolis' [= Mercurius] and 'khemos,' they admit it today and give them Arabic names. . . . And these matters were clearly known to us long before the emergence of Islam, but the Ismaelites of today say that the fact that we untie our hair and refrain from sewn clothes is so as to submit oneself to God, be he blessed. . . . And some of their sages [*paqachehem*] give a reason and say there were idols there, and we throw stones on the place of idols; that is: we do not believe in the idols which were there and in a manner of despising we throw stones on them; and others say: it is a custom." Here as in the outset of Israel, pagan cults are reinterpreted. R. Moses b. Maimon. *Responsa*, ed. J. Blau (Jerusalem, 1960), vol. II, pp. 726–727. A different but explicit usage of the principle of accommodation to explain the origins of Islam can be found in Petrus Alfunsi, *Dialogi* V, Migne, PL 157, 605 B; cf. below, pp. 187–188.

36. Comparable, perhaps, to Ambrosius's "felix culpa"—except that it lacks the background of a doctrine of original sin. Ambrosius, *De Jacobo* I, 6, 21, CSEL 32, 2, p. 18.

37. This, of course, is a historiosophical projection of the Kantian ethical prescription never to use man as means but only as an end unto itself. Hegel's objective Spirit does not directly use man as means; its "cunning" allows history in its totality to remain ethical without infringing on the "limitless right" of the individual to pursue his goal.

38. Maimonides, MN III, 32, ed. Munk, p. 69: *talattuf alallah wahakhmatah*. (cf. iii, 54 where *talattuf* stands for "practical reason" as against wisdom or *chokhma*); Hegel, *Philosophie der Geschichte*, ed. F. Brunstädt (Reclam, 1961), pp. 78ff. On the further history of this "topos" in early modern historical reasoning, cf. my article "Periodization and Self-Understanding in the Middle Ages and Early Modern Times," *Medievalia et Humanistica* V (1975): pp. 3–23. The resemblance of the Maimonidean to the Hegelian metaphor was noted by S. Pines in the introduction to his translation of the *Guide*. Pines draws attention to Maimonides's use of Alexander of Aphrodisias. But in a sense, one should trace the origin of this historiosophical figure of thought not so much to the Greek notion of harmony—for the Greek harmony is a throughout transparent harmony—but to the prophetic dialectical demonstration of God's omnipotence through the very misery of the people he chose to protect. The prophets introduced a revolutionary theodicy, an inversion of the common belief that the measure of the power of a deity is the success of the community obliged to it in the bonds of a *religio*. God's power manifests itself by using the greatest empires as "rod of his wrath" to purify Israel while

Hegel will speak of the "cunning of reason" ("List der Vernunft")—their point of agreement is at one and the same time the point of their difference. Hegel's "List der Vernunft," much as its forerunners—Mandeville's "private vices, publick benefits" or Vico's "providence" or again the "invisible hand" of Adam Smith and lastly Kant's "geheimer Plan der Natur"—articulate a sense of the absolute autonomy of human history and its self-regulating mechanisms. Maimonides, as all other medieval versions of the divine economy, allows at best a relative autonomy to the collective evolution of man.

Maimonides demonstrates with considerable detail how every single allegedly "irrational" precept is a countermeasure to this or that Sabean practice. Now it matters little that the Sabeans, of whom Maimonides speaks with the genuine enthusiasm of a discoverer, were actually a small remnant of a gnostic sect of the second or third century A.D. rather than a polytheistic universal community[39]—note that Maimonides uses for it the Moslem self-denomination "umma." The mistake in the identification of the background of the Mosaic law led Graetz to discard the Maimonidean explanations as "flat."[40] But it is still possible that the argument of Maimonides is new and reliable in its method rather than in the actual validity of his historical reconstruction.

PRECEDENTS AND ORIGINALITY

Yet the interpretation of sacrifices as a divine concession to polytheistic usages in order to eradicate idolatry all the more forcefully was not altogether new. Vajiqra Rabba (22:6) attributes it to Pinhas ben Levi: "[a simile to] a prince whose heart has forsaken him and who was used to eating carcasses and forbidden meat. Said the king, let these dishes be always on my table, and of himself he will get weaned. So also: since Israel were eagerly attracted to idolatry and its sacrifices in Egypt . . . God said: let them always bring their sacrifices before me in the tabernacle and thus they will separate themselves from idolatry and be saved."[41] The Middle Ages, both Christian and Jewish, gave

---

they are unaware (*vehema lo yada'u*). Cf. chapter 3, "The Leading Images of the Historical Narrative."

39. Pines, *Introduction* (above n. 20); pp. cxxiii–iv.

40. H. Graetz, *Die Konstruktion der jüdischen Geschichte* (Berlin, 1936), pp. 85–86 and the note.

41. *Leviticus Rabba* 22, 6. It seems that a similar Jewish tradition is the source of Theodoret of Cyrrhus, *Questiones in Leviticum*, PG LXXX, 300. Cf. my "Gesetz und Ge-

the broadest meaning to the originally merely legal principle *dibra tora ki'lshon bene'adam* (*Scriptura humane loquitur*). From Theodoret of Cyrrhus and Augustine, through Walahfrid Strabo, to William of Auvergne and Thomas Aquinas, some Christian exegetes interpreted the sacrifices as well as the whole of the *vetus lex* (except the Decalog) not as a mere "burden" but rather as the accommodation of God to the phase of understanding of humanity at that time. "Aptum fuit primis temporibus sacrificium, quod praeceparat deus, nunc vero non ita est, aliud enim praecepit, qui multo magis quam homo novit, quid cuique tempori accommodate adhibeatur" (Augustine).[42] The sacrifices were but "bona in sua tempore" (Hugh of St. Victor), a concession to a primitive mentality, and antidote to Egyptian idolatry. Maimonides himself may have drawn his version of the principle of accommodation from Kirkasani.[43] Paradoxically, a similar figure of thought was exploited earlier by Graeco-Roman anti-Jewish polemicists. The Jewish cult and law—this was the essence of Manetho's counterbiblical reconstruction of Jewish history—were nothing but an inverted mirror of the Egyptian cult and laws.[44]

It seems as if Maimonides's theory is just another variation of the principle of accommodation. Yet consider the following. None of these traditions is actually concerned with the reconstruction of the original meaning of biblical legal and ritual institutions out of their forgotten historical background. Maimonides raised such a reconstruction to a methodical level. His theory not only explains, in detail, how the "forgotten" culture of the Sa'aba accounts for opaque parts of the law. It explains at one and the same time why these original "reasons for the commandments" were forgotten and must now be reconstructed so painfully. The very intention of the lawgiver was to eradicate all the reminiscences of the abominable rites and opinions of the Sabean *'umma*. The fact that the reasons for certain commandments were forgotten is in itself a testimony to the success of the divine "cunning" or pedagogy. Not only among the Jews: the whole inhabited world, Maimonides believes, is by now monotheistic.[45]

---

schichte," (above n. 20), p. 165 and n. 71. For the further references to Christian exegesis cf. my *Periodization and Self Understanding,* pp. 10–14.

42. Augustine. *Ep.* 138 I, 5, ed. Rademacher, CSEL 44, 130.

43. Kirkasani. *Kitab al Anwar,* ed. L. Nemoy (New York, 1939), I, 44: TT, 214; index (s. v. Sabians).

44. See above, pp. 36–38.

45. MN III, 52; Cf. below pp. 97 ff. and nn. 57–67, above n. 35.

In the last few decades, we have learned to pay attention to the "historical revolution" of the sixteenth and seventeenth centuries, the transformation of historical understanding into a genuinely *contextual reasoning*.[46] Among the humanistic commentators of the *Corpus Iuris Civilis* (the so-called *mos Gallicus*) as well as biblical critics we notice a growing awareness to the demand that in order to understand the meaning of ancient institutions, texts or monuments, they ought to be *alienated* from any present connotation and placed in their original context. No historical fact is in itself meaningful unless it obtains meaning from its proper context. This method of "understanding through alienation and reconstruction" matured[47] long before it found its way into historiography proper. Maimonides's reconstruction of the *ta'ame hamitsvot* was a genuine medieval precursor of the revolution of historical reasoning.

A lesson in political theory was closely linked to the new historical reasoning starting with the sixteenth century: that no ideal state can be conceived in a historical vacuum. Even the best of all constitutions must bear the marks of its historical origins. This was the modern contribution to the old tradition of political realism. The political realism of Maimonides seems to be grounded on a similar historical perspective. Even the Mosaic legislation is not an ideal which can be abstracted from its origin to fit all societies at all times. Sa'adia's fault, so Maimonides seems to imply, was his endeavor to uncover an absolutely rational social structure, while he, Maimonides, established methods of contingent rationalization.

Of course, the new perspective was apt to be challenged as dangerous. Did not Maimonides relativize the validity of those precepts which he interpreted against the background of a concrete and now bygone historical situation? Maimonides himself never addressed this problem directly, and the problem was to become one of the main issues in the anti-Maimonidean controversy.[48] Should laws be changed? Maimon-

---

46. For the following, see chapter 2, and nn. 10–12.

47. By the beginning of the eighteenth century, it was already a truism to warn against those who *de rebus antiquissimis secundum sui temporis conditionem notiones forment;* Franz Budde, *Historia Ecclesiastica*, 3rd ed. (Jena, 1726), Praef.; L. Diestel, *Geschichte des Alten Testaments in der christlichen Kirche* (Jena, 1869), p. 463. It is not our contention that Maimonides refrained from anachronisms. To the contrary: his historical remarks are usually full of them, as when he lets Jacob make Levi a *rosh yeshiva:* MT, *hilchot 'Avodat Kohkavim* 1, 3. But his interpretation of the sacrifices is free from them.

48. D. J. Silver, *Maimonides' Criticism and the Maimonidean Controversy*, pp. 1180–1240 (Leiden, 1965), 148 ff., 157 ff.; for criticism of the Book, H. Davidson, *Jewish Social Studies* 30/1 (1968): pp. 46–47. It was, of course, part of the controversy over the *hagsama.*

ides, we have seen, insists on the validity of every iota of the law even in the messianic age. He includes explicitly the restoration of the Temple and its sacrifices in the schedule of messianic deeds. Then, as once, the law will save the masses from a relapse to the superstition to which they are and will remain prone. Maimonides was no "Aufklärer," and he did not believe in an essential "Erziehung des Menschengeschlechts," the capability of the masses to rise to the level of the philosopher.[49] The respect of the masses before the law is founded on their belief in the law's immutability. Which is not to say that the law cannot be modified at all. Again we have to resort to his doctrine of contingency; a good law, this was already the essence of the Aristotelian doctrine of equity ($\dot{\epsilon}\pi\iota\kappa\epsilon\dot{\iota}\epsilon\iota\alpha$),[50] and must be formulated so as to remain flexible enough to meet changed conditions. It must be precise in its "core" and allow for a "penumbra" for indeterminacy. The absolute immutability of the law may be a necessary fiction for the masses, but the legal experts of every generation have the right and the duty to adjust the law *in casu necessitatis*.[51]

MESSIANISM AND HISTORY

The messianic doctrines of Maimonides are therefore only the tip of the iceberg, a part and a consequence of his historical perspective and of his political realism in the sense of our introductory remarks. The emergence of that "eternal peace" which Maimonides envisages should be seen in analogy to the emergence of the Israelite monotheistic community out of an all-pervasive polytheistic environment. Every order, physical or social, contains a residue of contingency. Direct providence operates with this residue of indeterminacy in nature

49. Against Leo Strauss, cf. our remarks in "Gesetz und Geschichte: Zur historisierenden Hermeneutik bei Moses Maimonides und Thomas von Aquin," *Viator* I (1970), pp. 147–78, 162, n. 60. Maimonides, we argue there, depicts, e.g., Abraham as already on the height of wisdom; if there is a relative progress, it consists in the taming of superstitions among the masses. For a similar view of the question *an secundum mutationes temporum mutata sit fides* in the Christian horizon (Hugh of St. Victor) see my *Heilsplan und Natürliche Entwicklung*, pp. 52–53.

50. Cf. Guido Kisch, *Erasmus und die Jurisprudenz seiner Zeit* (Basel, 1960), pp. 18–26, for the Aristotelian origin of the demand to complement law through equity (to cover the necessary residue of indeterminacy in any legislation). My knowledge of the Arabic sources does not suffice to trace the possible vehicles through which Maimonides might have received the doctrine.

51. This interpretation is given by Jacob Levinger, "Hamachshava hahalakhtit shel haRambam," *Tarbiz* 37.3 (1968): pp. 282 ff.

and society; at times man calls such acts miraculous. God used polytheistic images in order to eradicate polytheism in a slow and imperceptible process of "purification," rather than change human nature all of a sudden. Similarly, human nature will not have to change when the entire world will be transformed into a peaceful community.

Again God will first combat the present state of things with its own elements, antagonism and war. "But the removal of strife and war from east to west will not come in the beginning of his [the Messiah's] appearance, but only after the war of Gog."[52] The king Messiah will establish the hegemony of Israel by force and fear. "When he will appear God will frighten the kingdoms of the earth by his fame, their dominion will weaken, they will cease to rebel against him."[53] Only afterwards, when recognized and established, the political dominion of Israel will become an ideological hegemony. While fear secured the establishment of the *pax Iudaica,* the paradigm of the kingdom of Israel and its very preoccupation with the true knowledge of God—the purpose of the utopian society—will secure the conditions for the perpetuation of that peace. The durability of the eschatological body politic is explainable in natural terms: "And there is no cause to be astonished that his kingdom will endure thousands of years, for the philosophers (*chakhamim*) say that once a good body politic is constituted, it does not dissolve easily."[54]

The analogy we drew between the time of Israel's birth and the time to come of its rebirth became under our hand more than a mere analogy. The latter does not only resemble the former, but complements it. The messianic age crowns a didactic and dialectic process which began with the modest establishment of a monotheistic community by Abraham, continued with the fortification through laws of this community after its relapse, advanced with the growing hold of the monotheistic imagery in Israel, and made a decisive progress even in the time of the Diaspora. Even if Maimonides does not go as far as Philo or Jehuda Halevi in seeing the function of the Diaspora as a missionary one—the

52. IT chapter 4, pp. 52–53; less definitive HM, chapter 12.

53. IT ibid. Scholem (above n. 19) denies the revolutionary character of Maimonides's messianic days, and does so by equating revolutions to apocalyptic-cosmical catastrophes only. True, Maimonides deapocalypticized his eschatology; but envisaged nonetheless, in the first phase, the messianic age, a rapid radical change, utmost tribulations and a world war.

54. *Perush hamishna, Sanhedrin* (chelek). In a similar reference to rational causes Maimonides explains there the longevity of life in the messianic days: security and abundance prolong the life expectation of the individual.

Jews carrying the seeds of the logos among the nations[55]—he none-theless recognizes a growing process of monotheization of the entire world. Christianity and Islam are for him "of the nature of a religion," even though the one was founded by a heretic and the other by a lu-natic.[56] It is from the phrase of Maimonides that Hame'iri later bor-rowed the somewhat similar phrase *'umot hagdurot bedarkhe hadatot*.[57] Still in another context Maimonides distinguishes between those na-tions of the world which obey the seven Noachidic laws and should be tolerated, as against those who do not conform to this Jewish counter-part of the *ius naturale* (or rather *ius gentium*) and could be killed.[58] The distinction calls in mind the Moslem distinction between the *ahl al kitab* and the *ahl al maut,* all the more so since Maimonides does not envisage the proselytization of the world even in the messianic days. All he wants is to make the world a safe place to obey God's laws and in-crease the knowledge of him.[59] And finally: in yet another allusion to the divine cunning, Maimonides calls Christianity and Islam outright "road-pavers for the king Messiah"—*Meyashre derekh lamelekh hamashiah*.[60]

These and other scattered passages add up to a distinct view of the course and phases of human history seen as a history of monotheisa-tion. It is a gradual process, which shall be succeeded by an indefinite period of unchallenged, universal monotheism, and was preceded by a likewise gradual process of polytheization. From Enosh to Abraham, the original monotheism of Adam degenerated through polylatrism into polytheism, which then enabled a priestly class to exploit and ter-rorize a superstitious mass.[61] If this sounds as an outright inversion of the evolutionary models of anthropologists since the nineteenth cen-tury, it is due to one basic agreement and another basic disagreement.

---

55. Jehuda Halevi, *Kuzzari* (ed. Zifroni) 4,23; I. Baer, *Galut* (New York, 1947), p. 32; below n. 67.

56. IT, chapter 1, p. 12.

57. Cf. J. Katz, *Ben Yehudim legoyim* (Jerusalem, 1960), pp. 116–28. Katz empha-sizes rightly the halakhic differences between Maimonides and Hame'iri in their treat-ment of Christianity. But the expression itself belongs first and foremost to the philo-sophical tradition and is the medieval version of the "natural religion."

58. MT, HM chapter 6, 1.

59. HM chapter 12, 4; "The sages and prophets did not desire the days of the Mes-siah in order to rule the entire world, nor in order to tyrannize the nations, nor again so that they be elevated by all people, nor in order to eat, drink and be merry—but in order to be free for the to'ra and its wisdom, and so that there be no tyranny over them to cause distraction." Cf. *Perush hamishna,* loc. cit., and HT chapter 9, 2.

60. Cf. below p. 151.

61. MT, *Sefer hamada, Hilkhot avodat kokhavim,* chapter 1, pp. 1–3.

The medieval and modern rationalistic views of the development of (true or false) religions share the dislike of radical mutations; they only disagree as to the starting point of the evolutionary process. To the Middle Ages, the knowledge of God's unity was part of the *lumen naturale*. Not its presence, but any deviation from it called for a historical explanation: all the more so since Adam, as it were, encountered the Almighty frequently and directly, if not always on friendly terms. Schmidt's anthropological arguments for the primacy of the "Ur-monotheismus" are but a modern guise of old theologoumena, for example, Eusebius of Caesarea's description of the gradual corruption of man's "kingly nature" through polytheism and polyarchy and its restitution through universal monarchy and monotheism.[62] Similar questions bothered already the author of the *Wisdom of Solomon;*[63] and of similar scope is also the Maimonidean attempt to reconstruct the prehistory of monotheism.

The second period in the essential history of mankind begins with the establishment of a monotheistic community. The "feeble preaching" of Abraham[64] did not suffice to guard against a relapse of his followers: the masses were, and still are, prone to superstition, and can be held in the boundaries of religion by laws only. These laws, we have seen, were construed by the "cunning of God" so as to utilize polytheistic images and rites with the intent to abolish them. The emergence of a monotheistic mentality was slow and difficult: *tanta molis erat Romanam condere gentem*. Graduality and slowness, we noted already, are the formal marks of natural change—here as in the Christian versions of the principle of accommodation since Irenaeus of Lyons.

If already the transformation of a small nation into a monotheistic community was a slow and difficult process, all the more so the monotheization of the entire oikoumene. This is a dialectical and highly dramatic process, guided again by the operation of the divine ruse. Time and again "the nations of the world" wish to destroy the people of Israel, whose election they envy (even if, one may add, they deny it).[65] They generate successively destructive ideologies—Maimonides calls

---

62. Eusebius of Caesarea, *Historia Ecclesiastica* I, 2, 19, ed. E. Schwarz (Berlin, 1952), pp. 8–9. On the "political theology" of Eusebius, see E. Peterson, "Der Monotheismus als politisches problem," *Theologische Traktate* (München, 1951), pp. 44 ff., 89.

63. *Sap. Salomonis* 14: 12–17, a euhemeristic interpretation.

64. MN III, 32. In his placing of the role of Moses above that of Abraham's Maimonides may also have intended to invest the Moslem historical scale of values, which placed Abraham way above Moses.

65. IT chapter 1, p. 21.

them "sects"—each of greater sophistication than the former, though all of them exist at present, wherefore they correspond only loosely to the "four monarchies" of the Book of Daniel.[66] Having failed in their attempt to extinguish the true religion by force or argumentative persuasion (Hellenization), the nations of the world resort to a ruse. A third sect emerges that imitates the basic idiom of the monotheistic, revelatory religion in order to assert a contradictory law, so as to confuse the mind and thus cause the extinction of both the original and its imitation. "And this is of the category of ruses which a most vindictive man would devise, who intends to kill his enemy and survive, but if this is beyond his reach will seek a circumstance in which both he and his enemy will be killed." Yet inasmuch as this latter sect and those similar to it—Christianity and Islam—do imitate a monotheistic mentality, they help to propagate and prepare the acceptance of the true religion against their will: their stratagem turns, by a divine ruse, against them; or better: their ruse turns out to have been a divine ruse from the outset. The effect of their resistance to the truth is a negative *preparatio messianica* (or, in the fortunate phrase of H. H. Ben Sasson, *preparatio legis*): in this sense, I believe, one has to interpret the phrase that Christianity and Islam are "roadpavers for the king Messiah."[67]

Our attention was drawn repeatedly to some analogies between Maimonides's historical employment of the principle of accommodation and its Christian counterparts. The broad role which Maimonides assigned to the divine (as against the polytheistic adversary) "ruse" also reminds us of one of the most original pieces of historical speculation in the twelfth century, Anselm of Havelberg's *Dialogi*.[68] The *spiritus sanctus* accommodates its historical operations not only to the degree of perception of man, but also to the ever more refined stratagems of Satan: each of the seven successive *status ecclesiae* is characterized by a less obvious and therefore more dangerous opposition of the adversary; in his own, fourth, status ecclesiae Anselm sees Satan penetrating the

---

66. IT, ibid. Maimonides, unlike some Jewish and most Christian philosophers of history, did not pay specific attention to detailed periodizations. Nor was he interested in history as such. Cf. S. Baron, "The Historical Outlook of Maimonides," *History and Jewish Historians* (Philadelphia, 1964), pp. 109–63, esp. 110–13.

67. H. H. Ben-Sasson, op. cit. (above n. 18).

68. Anselm of Havelberg, *Dialogi* I, 10 Migne, PL 188, 1152ff. Cf. W. Kamlah, *Apokalypse und Geschichtstheologie* (Berlin, 1935), p. 64; W. Berges, "Anselm von Havelberg in der Geistesgeschichte des 12. Jahrhunderts," *Jahrbuch für die Geschichte Mittel-und Ostdeutschlands*, 5 (1956): pp. 38 ff., esp. 52 (reference to Hegel's "List der Vernunft"); Funkenstein, *Heilsplan*, pp. 60–67, esp. 66.

church with pretention and imitation, *sub praetextu religionis,* through *falsi fratres*—a move that the Holy Spirit counters by a variety of new, fresh turns of religiosity. Needless to say that such analogies do not suggest direct mutual influence; their interest lies precisely in the circumstance that these figures of thought belong to such disparate cultural horizons. The search for the theological meaning of history was much more a part of Judaism and Christianity than of Islam. A similarity of the problem-situation led, at times, to somewhat similar patterns of answers.

Returning to Maimonides, we note that even though the scheme of each of the "sects" is doomed to failure, they still inflict on Israel severe physical and mental blows. It is the lot of Israel to endure in spite of dispersion and deflection. Among the current types of historical theodicies—attempts to invest meaning into the discrepancy between being the people of God's choice and the present humiliation in dispersion—Maimonides occupies a unique position. His explanation is neither of the cathartic, nor of the missionary, nor again of the soteriological type.[69] Not the purification and punishment for old sins, nor the propagation of the seeds of the logos, nor again suffering for the sins of nations so as to redeem the world, are for Maimonides the essential rationale of the *galut.* His language is rather sacrificial-martyrological. Israel is constantly called to bear witness. Time and again it brings itself as sacrifice, *korban kalil*[70] throughout this long phase of world history.

The last period, namely the messianic age, will finally transform the hostile and implicit recognition of the spiritual primacy of Israel, which most nations share already now against their will and word, into a more or less voluntarily explicit recognition of the community of Israel as a most perfect and paradigmatic society. It will be a time of material affluence and security,[71] but not of total egalitarianism either among men or nations. The messianic age of Maimonides is in all its aspects a part of history, the concluding chapter in the long history of the monotheisation of the world. In the Christian medieval horizon there is only one eschatological doctrine which seems to come nearer to Maimonides in this respect—Joachim of Fiore's version of the *tempus spiritus sancti.* But the similarities are only superficial. Joachim's millennium, even though

69. I have explained this classification in "Patterns of Christian-Jewish Polemics in the Middle Ages," *Viator* 2 (1971), p. 376. Cf. chapter 6, below.

70. IT, chapter 1, p. 30.

71. Above, n. 59.

it is within the boundaries of history, is of an order which altogether transcends historical processes.[72]

IMPLICATIONS

With the impact of Maimonides's theory, practical and theoretical, we shall deal elsewhere. One instance of the later discussions must be mentioned here, for it touches on the very texture of the theory. Did Maimonides envisage, in accord with his messianic views, any practical measures to be taken by those generations which are close to the *eschaton* to precipitate the coming of the Messiah, measures that are in the natural domain of possibilities? We spoke earlier[73] of the negative, critical eschatological task of the legal experts of the last generations—the duty to unmask false contenders, of which the time close to the end will be particularly pregnant. But later admirers of Maimonides took some of his enigmatic remarks concerning the possible renewal of the institution of ordination to mean a positive eschatological task for the legal experts in the preparation for the Messiah. When Jacob Berab attempted the renewal of the *semikha* (1538), he relied on a messianic interpretation of a view which Maimonides expounded first in his *Exegesis of the Mishna* and reiterated later in the *Mishne tora.*[74] With an indication that it is but his personal view, Maimonides considers in both his earlier and later work the possible renewal of the authentic courts through an initial act of ordination by consent of the sages in the land of Israel only. As is well known, the attempt of Jacob Berav failed mainly due to the opposition of the Jerusalemian Rabbis, led by Levi ben Habib.[75]

But Levi ben Habib, out of deference to the authority of "the Rav," had to explain away if not the remark of Maimonides as such, then at least the eschatological implications drawn by Jacob Berav. He did so by introducing an evolution into Maimonides's thought. Eschatological implications, he admits, are present in the *Perush hamishna:* there the renewal of ordination prepares the renewal of the full Sanhedrin of

72. See H. Grundmann, *Studien über Joachim von Fiore*, pp. 56–118.

73. Grundmann, p. 85.

74. *Perush hamishna* to Sanhedrin XI (Heleq); MT, *Hilkhot Sanhedrin* 4, 11.

75. On the ideological background of the Controversy cf. J. Katz, "Machloget hasemikha ben Rabbi Jacob Berav vehaRalbah," *Zion* 17 (1951): pp. 34 ff. In the meantime, some new material has been discovered: H. Z. Dimitrowski, "New Documents Regarding the Semikha Controversy in Safed," *Sefunot* 10 (1966): pp. 115–92.

seventy-one members, which again will precede the first acts of the Messiah. But later, in his code, Maimonides drops both references to the full court and to the coming of the Messiah. He speaks of the renewal of the minimal civil courts only.[76] In other words, Levi ben Habib makes him retract the view allowing for practical, active preparations for the Messianic era.

This is by no means an altogether impossible interpretation. Maimonides of the code is much more cautious, in his assertions concerning the messianic era, than Maimonides of either the *Perush hamishna* or *Iggeret*.[77] And so it may well be that he refrained, in the Code, from making an all too radical judgment pertaining to the renewal of the courts. But there is no reason to assume that he actually gave up the messianic connotation of the renewal of some elements of the pristine judicial system. He just may have chosen not to invoke them as a definite, binding part of the messianic doctrine.

To sum up, it would be wrong to deny a this-worldly character to the processes and even actions of the messianic era, for which the entire history of the dispersion is a preparation of sorts. But it would be equally wrong to relegate the messianic era to the realm of ordinary political processes. The contradistinction of Maimonides's theory to the rationalistic consequences which Josef Ibn Caspi drew from it makes it very clear. S. Pines has shown[78] how Ibn Caspi derived his assertions (which were to be repeated, in another context, by Spinoza) from the

---

76. *Responsa* (Venice, 1565), p. 283*a:* וכפי הנראה שהרב חזר בו בזקנותו ממה שכתב במשנה בשני דברים. Ralbach's feigned deference comes to the fore where he pretends that, of course, Maimonides must have had sources (books) for his opinion, and unless these are recovered, no one can really know what Maimonides meant. But, of course, Maimonides makes it clear that it is his opinion only. Cf. also Dimitrowski, ibid., p. 149.

77. Above n. 13, n. 16.

78. Shlomo Pines, "Joseph Ibn Kaspi's and Spinoza's opinions on the probability of a Restoration of the Jewish State" *Iyyun* 14–15 (1963–64): pp. 289 ff. In a more recent article, the late Sh. Pines objected to some of my interpretations of Maimonides's messianic conceptions. Maimonides spoke of Christianity and Islam as "roadpavers" to the king Messiah, but these are only occasional, insignificant remarks, inspired by similar remarks of Jehuda Halevi (*Kuzzari* IV). See "Al hamunach ruchaniyut ve'al mishnato shel Yehuda Halevi," *Zion* 57:4 (1990), pp. 511–540. But my interpretation (of the messianic days as a period which is not merely restorative, as a climax to the process of slow monotheization of the world) does not depend merely or even mainly on this passage in Maimonides to which Pines referred. Closer to my views is the recent article of Isadore Twersky, "Ha Rambam ve'erets yisrael," in: *Tarbut vechevra betoldot Yisrael biyme habenayyim* (Jerusalem, 1989), pp. 353–381. Relevant and important are also Aviezer Ravitsky, "Lefi koach ha'adam—yemot hamashiach bemishnat ha Rambam," in *Messianism and Eschatology,* ed. Z. Baras (Jerusalem, 1984), pp. 191–221; Jacob Blidstein, *Ekronot mediniyyim bemishnat haRambam* (Ramat Gan, 1983).

peripatetic belief in the recapitulation of similar states of affairs. Just as a political constellation once existed in which a Jewish sovereignty was an actualized possibility, it is probable to assume that again such a constellation will exist in which it may even be in the interest of the nations of the world to have a Jewish monarchy exist. How far from this is the Maimonidean doctrine! True, the messianic age is in the realm of the possible by nature; but it also excels every previous historical period by leaps.

Maimonides does not deny the occurrence of genuine miracles, simple violations of the order of nature. They occurred at the birth of Israel and will occur again biymot hamashiach. But he distinguished them from miracles taken from the domain of the possible. And he regards the Messianic period itself, much as the transformation of Israel from an idolatrous into a monotheistic community, as a miracle in the second sense, miracles taken from the vast residue of contingencies. He is mute concerning genuine miracles. Indeed, there will be a resurrection of the dead—but when and where, whether in the days of the Messiahs or thereafter, he does not know nor, it seems, care too much.[79] Genuine miracles are isolated events of no lasting significance. But their counterpart, "the miracles of the category of the possible" (*moftim misug ha'efshari*) are the inner driving force of human history from each phase to a higher one.

Realistic utopianism is not a contradiction in terms. The modern history of political thought from Vico to Marx differs from the classical or medieval tradition precisely in that it sought to overcome the abyss between "man as he is" and "man as he should be" through possible if not even necessary historical processes. The Jewish utopian tradition knew a meditation between the ideal and the possible earlier. For it was committed to a messianic ideal, but had always to sharpen its critical faculties against it.

The Image of the Ruler in Jewish Sources

THE LEGAL DISCOURSE

I wish to discuss the meaning of absolutism as it is reflected in Jewish medieval and early modern sources. How did the tran-

79. *Ma'amar*, chapter 7, pp. 98–99.

sition of the image of kingship from the early to the late Middle Ages, and then again to early modern Europe, affect Jewish law, political thought, and the popular imagination? Let me start with the law, the *halakha*.

Fritz Kern's monumental book *Gottesgnadentum und Widerstands-recht*[80] is still an indispensable starting point for every discussion of the complex process of transition from early to later medieval perceptions of law and government. In the early European Middle Ages, law was primarily custom-law (*consuetudines*), a law which the ruler could "find out," not create: only ancient law was seen as good law (*altes Recht ist gutes Recht*). How deeply did Pope Gregory VII stun his adversaries when declaring that he is entitled "to make new laws" (*novas leges con-dere*)![81] A precondition for the rise of absolute monarchy was the emergence of positive law in theory and praxis, be it under the direct tutelage of Roman law or only under its influence. Positive law means always new law—down to the absolutistic formula, the so-called *lex-regia* of the *corpus iuris civilis,* that "whatever pleases the ruler has the force of law" (*quod principi placuit, legis habet vigorem*).[82] With the rise of the positive legislation and the absolute monarchy, the right of resistance disappeared, that right which every free noble man had in the early Middle Ages to even take arms against his king[83]—as long as the latter was still conceived as being only first among equals, and his kingship was still won by election and acclamation.

---

80. Fritz Kern, *Gottesgnadentum und Widerstandsrecht im frühen Mittelalter,* 2nd ed. (Darmstadt, 1954), pp. 23 ff.; idem, *Recht und Verfassung im Mittelalter* (reprint: Darmstadt, 1958), pp. 23 ff.

81. Erich Caspar, ed., *Das Register Gregors VII,* MGH, *Epistulae selectae in usum scholarum,* II, 1 (Berlin, 1920: reprint 1967), pp. 202 ff, esp. 203.

82. Inst. I. 2. 6; G I. 5; Dig. I. 4. 31: "Sed quod principi placuit, legis habet vigorem, cum lege regia, quae de imperio eius lata est, populus ei et in eum omne suum imperium et poltestatem concessit." On Ulpian's original formulation see F. Schulz, "Bracton on Kingship," *English Historical Review,* 60 (1945): 136–76. It also seems that the name *lex regia* (rather than *imperatoris*) is no earlier than the third century; nor was there originally a link between it and the concept, of eastern provenance, of the king as νόμος ἐμψυχός. See Chayim Wirszubski, *Libertas as a Political Idea at Rome During the Late Republic and Early Principate* (Cambridge, 1968), pp. 130–36. On the medieval career see Kern, *Gottesgnadentum,* pp. 213–16; Michael J. Wilkes, *The Problem of Sovereignty in the Later Middle Ages* (Cambridge, Mass., 1964), p. 154 and n. 1; Brian Tierney, "The Prince Is Not Bound by the Laws," *Comparative Studies in Society and History,* 5 (1963): pp. 388 ff. Cf. below n. 100 (Manegold of Lauterbach).

83. Kern, *Gottesgnadentum,* passim; Heinrich Mitteis, *Der Staat des hohen Mittelalters,* 5th ed. (Weimar, 1955), pp. 79, 323 f., 400, 422; Otto Brunner, *Land und Herrschaft. Grundfragen territorialen Verfassungsgeschichte Österreichs im Mittelalter* (Wien, 1959); Marc Bloch, *La Société Feodale* (Paris, 1939), chapter IV, 3.

Now, few have paid attention to the repercussions of this complex process in Jewish law. A notable exception is Shemuel Shilo's study on the halakhic principle "the law of the kingdom is [valid] law," *dina demalkhuta dina* (henceforth DMD).[84] On the face of it, no principle seems to symbolize more visibly the loss of Jewish sovereignty than this principle, which is attributed to Mar Shemuel and appears but in four instances in the Babylonian Talmud.[85] But this is far from being the case. For one, the principle extended only to property and business law. And then, Jewish law, in that it accepts the sovereignty by any means. It just recognizes a limited section of the law of the land to be valid *pro tempore,* just as the Carolingian or Salic rulers did not abandon their ultimate legal sovereignty when they granted Jews the right to "live according to their own laws" (*secundum legem suam vivere*).[86] And finally: the principle negates as much as it affirms. From the beginning of its career it served to distinguish between "the law of the land" and "the robbery of the king" (*chamsanuta demelekh*), between valid law and the arbitrary act of a ruler. If a king acts in accordance with the law of his land, the principle DMD obtains, as, for example, if a king confiscates land for which property taxes (*taska*) were not paid. (This is the Talmudic example. It means that, should the king have sold the property to a second party that happens to be Jewish, the original owner has no claim on it—not even in a Jewish court of arbitration.) Where the ruler deviates from the law of the land, there is, from the halakhic point of view, no obligation to obey or accept his act; such as, to follow the same example, if a king confiscated land whose owner failed to pay the head-tax (kharga).[87] (In this case, the original owner has a claim—recognized at least by the Jewish courts.) Which means that the principle DMD, far from demanding blind obedience, entails even a law of resistance of sorts—not active perhaps (taking arms against the ruler), but certainly passive. It is as much a principle of disobedience as it is a principle of obedience.

What is "the law of the land?" How is it recognized and distinguished from possibly illegal acts of a sovereign? According to the ear-

84. Sh. Shiloh, *Dina demalkhuta dina* (Jerusalem, 1975). Cf. also Leo Landman, *Jewish Law in the Diaspora: Confrontation and Accommodation* (Philadelphia, 1968).

85. Babylonian Talmud *Nedarim* 28*a; Gittin* 10*b; Baba Kama* 111*a–b; Baba batra* 54*b–*55*a.*

86. See Lea Dassberg, *Untersuchungen über die Entwertung des Judenstatus im 11 Jahrhunders* (Paris-La Haye, 1965), pp. 60 ff., 73–87.

87. Underlying this discussion is already the assumption that, whenever avoidable, a Jew will not turn to a non-Jewish court: אין פונים לערכאותיהם של גויים.

lier French and German legal experts (*chakhme ashkenaz vetsorfat*), a king who changes the custom of a place or creates a new law acts illegally, and his acts are of the category of "a robbery of a king" (*Rashba*).[88] From the thirteenth century onwards, the distinction between custom (*minhag*) and legislation erodes until it disappears altogether—undoubtedly under the impact of the rise of positive law in Latin Europe which entails the right of the sovereign "to set new laws," *novas leges ponere*. On the other hand, these early ashkenazic sages did not always stick to a further qualifying provision of the principle DMD, namely that a law must be applied without discrimination throughout the kingdom in order to be valid. It must apply to all inhabitants of a country and even to all countries of a given ruler. In the early medieval social and legal reality such a ruling had no meaning or applicability; every region, every stand lived according to its own customs and privileges (*libertates*).

The transition from custom-law to positive-law is also reflected in the Jewish discussion concerning the rationale and legitimation of the principle DMD. In Germany and France some, like Rabbenu Tam, derived it from the principle that "an abandonment to a court of law is irrevocable [valid] abandonment." Some, like Maimonides and Rashbam, derived it from the social contract between a king and his subjects. Some even regard the principle DMD itself to be a custom and therefore like valid law (*minhag dome le-din*). In other climates, it was sometimes derived from the absolute power of the king. R. Nissim Gerundi (Ran) derives it from the absolute dominion which the king has over all real property in his kingdom. Rashba derives it from the status of conquerer which every king inherently has, which puts his subject of definition in the status of conquered. Some derive it by analogy from the status of conquered. Some derive it by analogy from the status of an Israelite king who may judge not according to the written and oral law—a subject we shall soon return to. Rabbi Josef Karo examined all of these positions and came to the conclusion that the principle, however derived, does not deny to the ruler the right to legislate new laws.[89]

---

88. For the following, Shiloh, *DMD*, pp. 70 ff. Aviezer Ravitzky, *Al da'at hamaqom: Studies in the History of Jewish Philosophy* (Jerusalem, 1991), pp. 118 ff. This article ("The law of the King," etc.) originated, as the author remarks (p. 106, n. 4), as a response to a paper of mine of 1986. My paper appears here fairly unchanged, but I shall indicate where I agree or disagree with his comments.

89. Shiloh, *DMD*, pp. 74 ff.

POLITICAL THEORY

This leads us into a more theoretical matter which is only partly linked to the rule DMD. Jewish sources recognize from early on two paradigms of a Jewish kingship: a king from the house of David (*melekh mibet David*) and a king from the house of Israel (*melekh mibet yisrael*). The latter category includes the Hasmonean kings or the Herodian dynasty. Davidic kingship was, since the time of the Second Temple, utopian kingship; Israelite kingship was and remained a real possibility even prior to the advent of the Messiah. Now Maimonides summarized all of his legal sources, sharpened the distinctions and defined the Davidic kingship as a constitutional monarchy, subject to the written and oral law (*din tora*), while the Israelite kings are not subject to any law.

> And one does not seat a king of Israel in the Sanhedrin because it is not permitted to contest him and to disobey his ruling. . . . Kings from the house of David, though not seated in the Sanhedrin, sit to judge the people. And they are sentenced if there is cause. But kings of Israel neither judge nor are judged for they do not submit to the verdict of the law [*she'eynam nichna'im ledivre tora*] and a mishap may [thus] occur.[90]

Among other things, a king may be sentenced even to flogging if he "multiplied wives, horses, gold and silver" (Deut. 17:16–17), but only if he is of the house of David.

As for the authority of every king, it is broad indeed. "Whoever rebels against a king of Israel, the king is permitted to kill him. Even if someone of the people is ordered to go someplace and he did not go, or ordered to stay in his house and he left it, he faces the death-sentence [*chayav mita*]." The word "ordered"—*nigzar*—has the connotation of arbitrariness. And then:

> Whoever kills persons without clear evidence [of murder], or without warning, even if there is but one witness, or it was a foe who killed unintentionally, the king may put him to death and keep the order of the world [*uletaken olam*]

---

90. Maimonides, *Mishne tora* (= MT), *hilchot melachim* XIX, 4. Ravitzky, *Al da'at hamaqom,* p. 109, sees the real origin of the distinction between a constitutional king and a king not bound by law (in Jewish law) in Rabbi Nissim Gerundi, and seems to deemphasize Maimonides's distinction between a Davidic and an Israelite king, which I believe to have been the inspiration for many later elaborations. See also J. Bildstein, "On Political Structures—Four Medieval Comments," *The Jewish Journal of Sociology* 22 (1980). That Gerundi aimed at a separation of state and sacral-religious functions is certainly true, and reflects an ancient perception of the contention of the Pharisees against the Hasmonean kings (די לך בכתר מלוכה, הנח כתר כהונה לזרעו של אהרן).

according to the need of the hour. And he may put many to death in one day and leave their bodies hanging for many days to frighten and break the arm of villains.[91]

These are formidable emergency-powers; but note that they do not exceed the powers which courts also do have. A court may also constitute itself as an emergency court (*mipne darche shalom*) and disregard constitutional law (*din tora*). Maimonides relies here on unambiguous ancient authorities. Which is one more reason to dismiss the debate whether the trial of Jesus by the priestly court was, or was not, held with due process. The court may have acted as an emergency court. At any rate, medieval Jews never doubted that Jesus was sentenced also by Jews: they only added (as in the "Story of the Life of Jesus") that he deserved it.[92] Only much later, in the age of assimilation and emancipation in Western Europe in the nineteenth century, did Jewish scholars try to prove that it could not have been so.

The Maimonidean distinction between a Davidic and an Israelite king does not yet amount to the medieval (and Aristotelian) distinction between an absolute and a constitution-bound king, or even to the early medieval distinction between *rex* and *tyrannus*. But elements of Maimonides's "laws concerning kings" could easily be translated into these Latin political categories without much distortion of the text. We remember that the Ritba indeed deduced the principle DMD by analogy to the powers of an Israelite (as against Davidic) king.

There was in the latter Middle Ages a famous instance of application of European categories of political thought to the Jewish sources. In the generation of the expulsion from Spain, Don Isaac Abrabanel wrote his commentary to the Bible and his messianic treatises. A deep disappointment of kings and their favors speaks from the writings of this last Jewish high official at the Spanish court who chose exile voluntarily. His clear antimonarchical, republican sentiments have been often mentioned.[93] I am raising the issue again because it is far from being a clearcut case.

91. Maimonides, MT, ibid., III, 8; 10.
92. See chapter 3 on the *Sefer Toledot Jeshu*.
93. Of the older literature see I. Baer, "Don Yitschak Abravanel veyachasso el be'ayot hahistoria vehamedina," *Tarbiz,* 5 (1937): pp. 398–416; E. E. Urbach, "Die Staatsauflassung des Don Isaak Abrabanel," MGWJ 81 (1937); Leo Strauss, "On Abravanel's Philosophical Tendency and Political Teaching," *Isaac Abravanel: Six Lectures,* ed. J. B. Trend and H. Loewe (Cambridge, 1937); Benjamin Z. Netanyahu, *Don Isaac Abravanel: Statesman and Philosopher* (Philadelphia, 1953).

Abrabanel's analysis of the biblical institution of kingship is, I believe, informed by the famous scholastic distinction between absolute and ordained power (*potentia absoluta et ordinata*). Already Duns Scotus gave a juridic meaning to this originally theological distinction; he correlated it to the distinction of lawyers between the acts of a ruler *de facto* and *de jure*. With the significance which this distinction had in medieval thought in general, particularly in the emergence of a new concept of nature and its order, I have dealt elsewhere.[94] Inasmuch as it pertains to political theory, the distinction differs considerably from the Aristotelian distinction between law-bound and tyrannical monarchy in that it assumes that a real sovereign can never act illegally even where he disregards his own promulgated laws. Where the law is in *potestate agentis,* the latter never acts *inordinate.*[95]

In his commentaries to the Books of Deuteronomy and Samuel, Abrabanel raises the following question. "You shall put a king upon yourself" seems to be, in Deut. 17:15, a clear commandment. Why, then, did Israel displease God—or even sin against him—when it asked Samuel for a king? To begin with, Abrabanel explains, what seems to be a commandment is but a hypothetical sentence. Crowning a king is only permitted, not commanded upon; the verse merely indicates that if a king is elected, he must be elected "from among your brethren." But the question still remains—why was Samuel's anger raised against the king-seekers? Among the various opinions quoted by Abrabanel is also that of

Don Paulus, Bishop of Burgos . . . namely that the appointment of kings may be in one of two ways. A king may be subject to the sentences and commandments of the law, or a king may be absolute [*behechlet*] to pass the kings of the nations since antiquity, so that they make the laws and keep them at their own will. Now the first kind is the proper one which the *tora* commanded upon . . . while the second king is indeed most detrimental, because a king, due to the absolute power [*yeckolet muchletet*] in his hand, will not preserve true equity and justice in all matters but will do whatever he wishes and who should tell him "what are you doing"? Now the people of Israel when they asked for a

---

94. Funkenstein, *Theology and the Scientific Imagination*, pp. 117–201.

95. Johannes Duns Scotus, *Ordinatio* I:d. 44 q. u. *Opera Omnia*, ed. P. C. Balič et al., 17 vol. (Vatican City, 1950 ff.) VI: pp. 363 ff. See Jürgen Miethke, *Ockhams Weg zur Sozialphilosophie* (Berlin, 1969), pp. 145–49; for the importance of this dialectic in later medieval and early modern political theory see Francis Oakley, *Omnipotence, Covenant and Order: An Excursion in the History of Ideas from Abelard to Leibnitz* (Ithaca and London, 1984).

king did not ask for the first, proper king but rather for the second, detrimental one.[96]

Abrabanel also calls the absolutistic king "a king not subject [*lo nichna*] to any law [*dat*], whom Aristotle, in the third chapter of the *Politics,* called a wicked and arbitrary king, and he is called in their language a tyrant." And, he adds, "indeed we can aid his interpretation in that we shall say that Saul's kingship did not endure because it was of the second king . . . while David's kingship did continue . . . because it was of the first king, a king subject to the law of God and his precepts."

Nevertheless, Abrabanel rejects this interpretation because it assumes the necessity of kingship of some king according to Jewish law. There is, he believes, no such necessity. He continues and proves that kingship is redundant both from the point of view of sound political theory, and from the point of view of political experience—and indeed from the vantage point of the *tora*. The logic of political theory does not demand kingship, because consonant, consistent, leadership by no means depends on it:

For it is not impossible that a nation should have many leaders gathering, uniting and agreeing in one council [*be'etsa achat*]. . . . Why should their governance be temporal, from year to year more or less? . . . And why should their power be limited and ordered [*mugbelet umesuderet = potentia ordinata*] according to laws and constitutions? But why adduce rational [a priori] arguments in this matter, if already the philosopher (Aristotle) taught us that experience prevails over syllogism. Come and see the countries which are governed by kings, and see their abominations and idolatry, each of them does whatever he pleases and the land is full of their iniquity, and who should tell them "what are you doing"? And meanwhile we see today many countries ruled by judges and temporal governors elected at times for three months [only] and God is with them, their constitutional power is ordered and they rule the army so that no one can withstand against them . . . and should one of them transgress in any matter soon another one will come in his stead and the transgressor will be punished. . . . Did you not know, did you not hear of the wicked fourth world-monarchy Rome, which ruled supreme and devoured all the earth and oppressed it while it was ruled by consuls—in consonance though they were many, and thereafter, ruled solely by an emperor, it became subject [to him].

96. Isaac Abrabanel, *Perush hatora* (Warsaw, 1862), to Deut. 17:14 ff.; I Sam. 8, 4–6; Paulus Burgensis, *Additiones ad Nicolai de Lyra Posillas,* to Deut. 17:14 f. Ravitsky (above n. 4), pp. 107ff., derives Paulus of Burgos's distinction from Aristotle's distinction between kings with limited power, kings unlimited by law, and tyrants (Aristotle, *Politics* III, 14–6, 1285*a* 4–5; 1287*a* 10)—which is partly true, but in part not, since the formula *a legibus solutus* derives from Roman law. Important is the reference to Gerundi.

And still today and kingdom [i.e., republic] of Venice is great among the people and a ruler over countries, and the kingdom of Florence is the crown among nations, and the kingdom of Genoa is strong and frightening, and Lucca and Siena and Bologna and other kingdoms have not other than a governance by elected leaders for a definite time. And these are just kingdoms without rebels and nobody to commit criminal acts with impunity, and they conquer alien countries with wisdom, prudence and knowledge. And all this is to teach us that the existence of a king is not necessary and obligatory for a nation, but, to the contrary, is very pernicious and brings great danger to his subjects and servants inasmuch as he can kill and destroy at whim.

Abrabanel concludes by reinterpreting the distinction between an absolute and a constitutional king, as a merely relative-historical distinction, much in the spirit of Scotus's distinction between the *potentia absoluta* and the *potentia ordinata* mentioned above; indeed, Abrabanel also uses the very same terms (*yekholet muchletet—yekholet mesuderet 'umugbelet*).[97] This is not to say that Abrabanel must have read Scotus. It enabled him, however, to realize better than Paulus of Burgos (or Gerundi) that there is no absolute demarcation line between a king and a tyrant:

And from all I said it becomes clear that the matter of kingship is not necessary, neither to improve the commonwealth nor for its unity or continuity or absolute sovereignty [*yekholto*]. And therefore, I think, kings were made at first not by the election of people but by force, the strongest prevailing [*kol de'alim gvar*]. As it is said (Isa. 7:6) "Let us go to Judah and wake her up and crown over it the son of Taba'el." Even then they were appointed as professionals to serve and lead the community but they turned into masters. And when God gave them the earth and its inhabitants, the whole world, this pernicious leprosy spread wide, namely that one person should rise and tame his people and lead them as donkeys. And in this matter also not all kingdoms are equal because in some of them the power of the king is limited as in the kingdom of Aragon, while in some of them it is absolute, and better than both is that it not be at all, as I mentioned.

Therefore it is irrelevant what sort of king the children of Israel really wanted from Samuel. Even if they desired a king of the first kind, of

97. Ravitsky, *ibid.*, refers also to Abrabanel's theological usage of the *potentia absoluta-ordinata* distinction in *Mifalot elohim* 53*a*, yet he errs in assuming that the distinction is the reserve of theologians only; already Scotus linked it to political theory (above n. 14); cf. also Oakley, *Omnipotence*, passim. Moreover: my point was (and remains) that from Scotus, directly or indirectly, Abrabanel learnt that *potentia ordinata et absoluta* are but two aspects of a coextensive set of divine or royal actions where the law is *in potestate agentis*. Neither Paulus of Burgos nor indeed Gerundi taught him that.

itself his kingship was bound to turn into the second, improper kind. The sin of Israel consisted in disregarding altogether Samuel's warning that no king is immune from the danger of turning into a tyrant. It lies in the nature (and origin) of kingship to be, or to become, absolute:

And the sages from among the nations inquired into this interpretation and discussed it and came to the conclusion that one should act in the matter as the [ten northern] tribes acted toward Rehabeam.[98] And I spoke concerning this interpretation [= theory] before kings and their advisors. And I demonstrated that it is illegal and beyond its power for a people to rebel against their king, to depose him, which is a greater crime than any the king can commit (*af yarshi'a al kol dvar pesha*). And I brought in that matter three arguments: one, that the people, when making a king, enter a covenant with him (*kortim lo brit*) to obey him and to follow his words and commands. And this covenant by oath is not conditional but an absolute treaty (*amana muchletet*), wherefore a rebel against the king deserves the death-sentence, no matter whether the king is just or unjust. Because none of the people may distinguish his justice from injustice. And about that may he be blessed said He to Joshua (1 : 18) "whoever disobeys your word will be put to death."[99] From the aspect of the oath and the covenant which the people conclude with the king they are obliged to honor him and have no power to criticize him or to rebel against him.

The social contract theory often served to limit the power of a sovereign—even to argue that he may be deposed—since it was first invoked in the Middle Ages by Manegold of Lauterbach during the investiture-struggle of the eleventh century. Abrabanel abandons this tradition, not out of sympathy to an absolute monarchy but to stress its dangers. Whether or not a king is supposed to be limited by a constitution, in fact he is bound by no laws, his or others: *rex a legisbus solutus est.*[100]

Nevertheless, in spite of his antimonarchical sentiments, Abrabanel

98. In rejecting his kingship. It is interesting to compare Abrabanel's views on monarchy with those of Azaria de Rossi, to whom monarchy is a stabilizing, harmonizing principle among the nations subject to nature: only the Jews did not need it as long as they were under the immediate tutelage of God; hence having a monarch means being "like all other nations." *Meor eynayyim imre bina* 4 ed. Bonfil (Jerusalem, 1991) pp. 264–267.

99. Cf. Ravitsky, ibid., p. 116, n. 41.

100. Another medieval tradition—beginning with Manegold of Lauterbach—drew an opposite conclusion from the *Lex regia,* namely that the people who conferred power to the king may, if he is unjust, depose him: *Libelli de lite,* I, pp. 365, 391 (ch. 30, 67); see Kern, *Gottesgnadentum,* pp. 216–21. Manegold and others often invoked the biblical narrative of confrontation between Samuel and Saul; see the dissertation of my father, Josef Funkenstein, *Das Alte Testament im Kampf zwischen Regnum und Sacerdotium während des Investiturstreits* (Dortmund, 1937); idem, "Samuel und Saul In der Staatslehre des Mittelters," in *Archiv für Rechts-und Sozialphilosophie* XL/1 (1952), pp. 129–140.

is well within the medieval tradition where he envisions a *translatio imperii* from the first world monarchy to the fourth one, Rome;[101] and again from Rome to the kingdom of Israel which will form the fifth monarchy led by the king Messiah. The famous talmudic dictum, also attributed to Mar Shemuel, "nothing distinguishes this world from the messianic days except for the subjugation of the nations," was once generally understood (e.g., by Maimonides) to mean that, in the messianic days, the kingdoms of the world will cease from subjugating Israel. Abrabanel makes "the kingdoms" into an objective genitive and inverts the meaning of the saying to mean that, in the messianic days, Israel will subjugate the nations of the world. The Messiah will be a true "cosmocrator" and impose the law of the *tora* over the world in which there will no longer be a division between sovereign nations.[102] In other words: while the distinction between absolute and constitutional monarchy is a relative one for the duration of historical times, it is an unconditional distinction in utopian times. Put still differently, Abrabanel's antimonarchism pertains only to "this world," not "the messianic days." The latter will witness a truly ideal monarch, a monarch who will never erode his own constitutional basis.

MONARCHY AND THE POPULAR IMAGINATION

A few words are still in order about the popular imagination. The late Gerschom Scholem has convincingly demonstrated the importance of the Lurianic Kabbala in the propagation of the good message about the messianism of Sabbatai Zvi. Some perplexing problems still remain unanswered. First, the correlation between the spread of Lurianic doctrines and the belief in Sabbatai Zvi was not at all coextensive. In some countries, the message of the new Messiah was accepted enthusiastically even though Lurianic doctrines were fairly unknown. Belief in Sabbatai Zvi permeated all levels of Jewish society; it became a truly popular movement even while some learned men, such

101. Werner Goez, *Translatio Imperii. Ein Beitrag zur Geschichte des Geschichtsdenkens und der politischen Theorien des Mittelalters und der frühen Neuzeit* (Tübingen, 1938). Another reference in Jewish literature of the time to the *translatio*-doctrine can be found in Ibn Verga, *Shevet Yehuda*, p. 14.

102. I. Leibowitz, *Emuna, historia, ve'arakhim* (Jerusalem, 1982), pp. 108 ff.; Ravitzky, *Al da'at hamaqom*, p. 123, has convinced me that Abrabanel's conception of the *yemot hamashiach* is transhistorical, unlike that of Maimonides. Indeed, he saw, like the stoics or Augustine, the origin of political power in avarice, luxury, and sin.

as the rabbinical leadership in Jerusalem, remained skeptical or took the posture of waiting and seeing.[103] Glücklen of Hameln still remembered the intensity of expectation. Even a staunch opposer as Rabbi Jacob Sassportas did not dare to challenge the movement in public for the fear of being stoned alive; he only warned rabbinical colleagues time and again and urged them to assume leadership.[104] Now, the populace at large certainly did not think in Lurianic terms. What, then, captured their imagination? Why did the movement not remain, like all earlier messianic movements since later antiquity, a strictly local affair? A promoting factor was, no doubt, the far better advanced network of communication in the seventeenth century. More important, however, was the strong urge for kingship which came to the fore during the Sabbatianic movement and before. All contemporary descriptions of Sabbatai Zvi emphasized his royal demeanor, appearance, and conduct. In all of his letters he writes as king because he is expected to act as one; in captivity in Gallipoli he divided the world between his faithful—a "cosmocrator" such as Abrabanel once envisioned. Such was also the tone of the first prophecy of Nathan of Gaza—"here our king has come, Shabatai Tsvi is his name, he will call for battle and overpower his enemies."[105] New was the emphasis on Sabbatai Zvi's immediate kingship already here and now, not only after his victory; no previous pretender for messianism claimed to be king already in this urge for kingship—or even the belief that the Jews ought to have a king somewhere already now. I also see the secret to the success of David Hareubeni after 1524, appearing as he did from virtually nowhere with the claim to be the brother of the Reubenite king of Chevar (probably imagined in the Arabian peninsula) and with the diplomatic mission to call for a joint Christian-Jewish war against the Turks.[106] Astonishing is the combination of realism and fantasy: Hareubeni did not claim to be a Messiah, he called for the redemption of the land of Israel here and now by earthly military means. Astonishing is also the credulity brought towards him by Jews and non-Jews alike—the family of Abrabanel, Pope Clemens VII, the Portuguese king living in the age of absolutistic monarchy. The Jews, too, were impatient to have a monarch, and at least stressed this aspect of their redemption more than others. The subject still calls for deeper scrutiny.

103. See above, p. 135.

104. Jacob Sassportas, *Sefer tsitsat novel tsvi,* ed. I. Tishby (Jerusalem, 1954). pp. 18 ff., 41 f., etc.

105. Scholem, *Sabbatai Sevi,* p. 206.

106. A. Z. Eshkoli, ed., *Sipur David Hareubeni.*

Two conclusions may be drawn from our brief study. First, "political theory" in the narrow sense of the word found its expression, in Western Europe, in instructional treatises for kings and princes (*speculum regale*), treatises about ideal government, commentaries on Aristotle's ethical-political writings or treatises on contemporary political issues (such as the *Libelli de lite*). In this narrow sense, Jewish literature lacked a specific genre, a place in which to articulate political reasoning so to say *ex officio*. We may speculate on the lack of this genre in Jewish literature, and may ascribe it in part, as we did with the lack of historiography proper,[107] to the loss of sovereignty. In both cases, it seems, reflection about the state—ideal and real—were relegated, in the Jewish literature, to the mythical past or the mythical future. *In illo tempore* (to use Eliade's terms) we had a state and will have one once again. But again, just as the lack of historiography did not mean absence of historical reflection, the lack of treatises dedicated to matters political does not mean the absence of political theory. The Jewish philosophical literature may have treated political matters only in passing. The halakhic and exegetical literature abounds with them. There we find a genuine confrontation with political theory as well as practical questions, intentionally and in an ordered manner. It reflects the problems of the societies within which Jews lived and the problem of Jews within these societies. Because the materials are so scattered, we do not as yet have a systematic history of Jewish political thought, though there are some pioneering studies in the field—such as those of my late friend and teacher, H. H. Ben Sasson.

Second, among the most dubious recent theses on Jewish history is the contention that Jewish law in its development became apolitical or antipolitical, unable to cope with matters of the state. This dubious heritage of the nineteenth century (in which, for example, the Pharisees were at times depicted as an apolitical movement) itself serves political aims in its present forms, aims which I partly endorse without endorsing their wrong historical rationale. True, the *halakha* neglected to develop as rich a *Staatsrecht* as other aspects of the law, but it is not apolitical. Isaiah Leibowitz strongly emphasized the growing distance between the *halakha* and state-law, but he never claimed that it is, in principle, unable to accommodate itself to a sovereign political Jewish life. On the contrary—he demanded of the rabbinical leadership of today (at least in the beginning of his public career) to develop such a law with the same flexibility that Jewish law was capable of when coping

107. See above, p. 15f.

with other pressing social problems. His discussion of the problem was strongly polemical and at times radical, but never aprioristic or ignorant of historical facts. Not so some of his secularizing followers who turned his arguments into an a priori, so to say metahistorical characterization of Jewish law.[108] There can be no greater mistake. Precisely because I, too, wish the total separation of state and religion in the state of Israel, I am careful not to ground my arguments on a false historical perspective. Precisely because a halakhic state is a real concrete possibility, I fight all attempts to realize it.

108. I. Leibowitz, *Dat umedina;* Gerschon Weiler, *Theokratia Jehudit.*

6

Polemics, Responses, and Self-Reflection

Confrontation and Polemics

Anti-Jewish propaganda has a very long past. But a long past does not necessarily make for an interesting history. Why should a literary genre so repetitious and unsavory be studied? Literary polemics is not even a true reflection of popular biases and emotions. As for these, how could a historian be expected to explain them? Hatred has no history: hatred of individuals or of groups is part of the most basic human emotional endowment. We should rather turn to the psychologist or sociologist to tell us how and why a minority, cognitive or other, becomes the target of hatred.

But if indeed the historian fails to explain the brute fact of hatred because it evades historical differentiation, he can nonetheless add to the understanding of its manifestations in various cultures—or at different times in the same culture. The historian can uncover the mechanisms of suppression through which a culture may try to inhibit the radical acting-out of aggression and hatred not only among its members, but even towards the alien. The Christian society of the Middle Ages, in spite of its growing hostility towards Jews, could hardly conceive of genocide; it took the Church over a thousand years even to find the right formula for sanctifying war against infidels as a holy mission.[1] Not that the mass killings—such as the Saxonian wars of Charlemagne—did not occur, but the systematic conception of genocide, employing a Christian idiom, was outside the horizon of discourse.

Not as documents of hatred, but rather as a source for the study of cultural confrontation, religious polemics is of importance. It articulates—and be it as caricature—the image of the other culture, and the changes in that image, because Judaism and Christianity were indeed confrontational cultures in a precise sense of the word. The conscious rejection of values and claims of the other religion was and remained a constitutive element in the ongoing construction of the respective identity of each of them. Indeed, I know of no other two religions tied to each other with such strong mutual bonds of aversion and fascination, attraction and repulsion. This astonishing symmetry of ambivalence can hardly be explained as a necessary consequence of the circumstance that both were monotheistic religions with an absolute claim for the truth living in one place: Judaism and Islam were much less interested in each other. Against a host of Jewish-Christian polemical treatises—hundreds in number—stands the paucity of Moslem-Jewish polemical works, a handful at most.[2] Judaism and Islam regarded each other with an indifference bordering on contempt. Hostility towards Jews never translated into hostility towards Judaism. Judaism and Islam were *not* confrontational cultures.

The Jewish-Christian confrontation, on the other hand, took many forms. It was far less theological in genesis and nature than commonly assumed. I take it upon myself to find a Jewish equivalent to just about any and every central Christian dogma—not always at the center of Jewish thought and tradition, but respectable enough to make the point (and prove also the profound attraction of Christianity to Jews). This holds true even for the doctrines of trinity or original sin. Indeed, no written or oral commandment forbids an orthodox Jew even now to believe in the messianity of Christ. The confrontation between the religions was first and foremost a *historical* process of alienation and antagonism rather than a dogmatic-theological clash of beliefs.

1. Carl Erdmann, *Die Entstehung des Kreuzzugsgedankens* (1935, reprint Stuttgart 1955), pp. 1–29. Up until the Crusades, even the justified killing of an enemy in a just war (*bellum iustum*) required absolution.

2. M. Steinschneider, *Polemische und apologetische Litteratur in arabischer Sprache zwischen Muslimen, Christen und Juden* (Leipzig, 1877); M. Perlman, *Ibn Kammua's Examination of the Three Faiths* (Berkeley-Los Angeles, 1971), pp. 8–9, knows only of three responses to this, most penetrating example of Jewish anti-Moslem polemics.

Religious polemics—the subject of this chapter—hardly reflects, therefore, the whole gamut of attitudes of one religion towards the other. For one thing, the written treatises seldom reflect the situations and arguments of a live altercation.[3] And then, written polemics focuses, overemphasizes, dogmatic issues; it tends to reflect the normative, official stand of each camp. Officially, as we shall see, both Judaism and Christianity developed a doctrine of relative tolerance towards each other: Judaism (in Christian terms) was to remain as a testimony for the veracity of Christianity until the end of days; Christianity (in Jewish terms) was eventually classified as a monotheistic religion of sorts—at least removed from the category of idolatry. How different, though, were the less official voices! The very language of the *tossafists* deciding that Christians are not idolatrous testifies to the rift between reason and sentiment: "As to today's idolaters, we hold it that they do not worship idolatry."[4] An entire semantics of hatred towards each other was part of the everyday attitude that seldom comes to the fore in the stylized polemical tracts.[5] Nor does it reflect the considerable fascination of each to the other.[6]

3. A welcome incursion into the domain of popular polemics is the study of Ora Limor, *The Disputation of Maiorca* (Ph.D. Diss., Jerusalem, 1986). In his autobiography, Hermannus quondam Judaeus, *Opusculum de conversione sua*, MGH, *Quellen zur Geschichte des Mittelalters,* ed. G. Niemeyer (Weimar, 1963), recalls a disputation he had while still a Jew, with the famous Rupert of Deutz. His main argument—much in contrast to the written polemical treatises—was the idolatrous nature of Christian image-worship. Recently, the authenticity of the *Opusculum* has been questioned by Avrom Saltman, "Hermann's Opusculum de Conversione sua: Truth or Fiction," *REJ* 147, 1–2 (1988), pp. 31–56. The arguments are not cogent: "Jewish" elements are present precisely where Saltman denies them, namely in the dream of a white horse: B. T. *Berachot* 56b, *Sanhedrin* 93a; cf. Arnaldo Momigliano, "A Medieval Jewish Autobiography," in *Essays in Honor of H. R. Trevor-Roper,* ed. H. Lloyd-Jones et al. (Oxford, 1981), pp. 30–36, esp. 33. Inexactitudes, even pure inventions, are not proofs of inauthenticity, but of distance and tendentiousness.

4. B. T. *Avoda Zara* 2a and the *tossafot* ad locum: נראה דטעם ההיתר משום דעכו"ם שבינינו קים לן בגוייהו דלא פלחו לעבודת־כוכבים. On the issue, see Jacob Katz, *Exclusiveness and Tolerance: Studies in Jewish-Gentile Relations in Medieval and Modern Times* (Oxford, 1961), pp. 24–47.

5. A cursory reading of the tossafists or early responses—e.g., the tossafists on *Avoda Zara*—reveals a whole network of semantic substitutions to everything sacred to Christians. Christ was referred to as "the hanged one" (התלוי), an allusion to the biblical verse "for the hanged one is a curse of God." Churches were not houses of prayer (*tefila*) but of vain (*tifla*). Relics were "the filth of their bones" (רקב עצמותיהם). Saints (*kedoshim*) were prostitutes (*kdeshim*). The cross was שתי וערב, an illicit mixture. Maria was חריא, and so on.

6. The subject merits an extensive study; I intend to deal with it elsewhere. It is, of course, futile to look for explicit expressions of interest in Christian theologoumena: while freely admitting links to Moslem philosophers, Jews were careful to obliterate traces of influence even of Scholastic philosophy—let alone theology: Pines, *"Hasekholastika"*

With these methodological caveats in mind, we shall nevertheless find much in the polemical literature to teach us about the shifts in images and attitudes. Among other matters it will cure us from the naive, enlightened prejudice, that increased knowledge about each other leads to increased tolerance. The history of medieval polemics testifies to the opposite. The more each culture knew of the other, the more intense were both the rejection and the attraction of the other.

Changes in Christian Anti-Jewish Polemics in the Twelfth Century

THE TRADITIONAL MODES OF ALTERCATION

New patterns of Christian anti-Jewish polemics emerged in Western Europe during the twelfth century. Some of them challenged the way in which the Jews, their religion, and their role in the cosmic-historical order were hitherto perceived. The new may not have replaced older patterns altogether, yet they came to dominate the Christian discourse down to the age of Enlightenment. Towards the end of the Middle Ages, religious polemics became ever more acrimonious. It provided rationales for the burning of the Talmud in France and Italy,[7] hastened missionary activity, and at times orchestrated expulsions or

---

(chapter 4, n. 88). On the other hand, it is common knowledge that the Kabbalah was accused by its Jewish opponents, from its beginning in the thirteenth century, of Christianizing tendencies, which were later sensed also by Christian kabbalists of the Renaissance. See Gerschom Scholem, *Reshit ha-kabbalah* (Jerusalem, 1948), p. 154 (ובסוד דרש בכל / רומם כמו הגמון . . .); Talya Fishman, "New Light on the Dating and Provenance of *Kol Sachal* and Its Timeless Critique of Rabbinical Culture," *Tarbiz* 59 (1989/90), p. 178, n. 33; I. Liebes in *Tarbiz* 60.1 (1990), pp. 133–35. But the Kabbalah was not the only domain of influence: see chapter 4 on Nachmanides and the discussion of Rashi below.

7. S. Baron, in *A Social and Religious History of the Jews* vol. IX, pp. 62 ff., belittled the material implications of the confiscation and burning of the Talmud. He argued that the number of books actually destroyed was much smaller than the number of books lost as the result of natural catastrophes. Even if we disregard the process of intellectual decline of medieval communities affected by the loss of books—cf. E. E. Urbach, *Ba'ale hatossafot, chiburehem veshitatam* (Jerusalem, 1956), pp. 377 ff.—we should not measure the impact of the Talmud trials by their material implications alone. From now onwards, the study of Jewish law was not immune from outside danger in the consciousness of those engaged in it; the knowledge that their own literature became open to systematic Christian scrutiny must in itself have been oppressive to Jews. See D. J. Silver, pp. 11–16. See chapter 5, n. 48.

other oppressive measures. It tended to isolate and alienate the Jews—on all levels and in all of its varieties.[8]

Between the twelfth and thirteenth centuries, Christian polemics falls, I believe, under four categories: (1) The older pattern of altercation, consisting mainly of scriptural proofs for the veracity of Christian doctrines. (2) Rationalistic polemics, the attempt to prove Christian dogmas with the sole aid of reason (*sola ratione*). The twelfth century witnesses even a downright "geometrically demonstrated theology," *theologia more geometrico demonstrata*. The mainstream of scholastic theology abandoned such aspirations later on. They had no room in the thought of Thomas Aquinas, Duns Scotus, or William of Ockham. Raymundus Lullus remained an exception. (3) Accusations against the Talmud, or, rather, against most of the postbiblical Jewish literature. This polemical strategy resulted in the confiscation or burning of maligned books in almost every century following the first Talmud trial in Paris, held in 1240. (4) Attempts to prove not only from the Old Testament, but from the Jewish postbiblical literature itself, from the legal and homiletic traditions, an implicit recognition of the messianity of Christ and other tenets of Christian faith. Needless to say, these basic types of polemical strategies appeared more often than not mixed and together. In the following I shall try to reconstruct the motives and mental attitudes behind these new polemical modes. I leave for another occasion the detailed discussion of the causes and circumstances of the changes and the Jewish response to them. Anselm of Canterbury, Petrus Alfunsi, Abelard, Petrus Venerabilis, and Alanus ab Insulis will be our main witnesses for the transformation of polemical attitudes. It occurred in the twelfth century, though its full dangers became manifest only subsequently, with the growth of the Church's political power and organization.

Polemical arguments in the early Middle Ages were repetitive and stereotypical; Bernard Blumenkranz described them in detail.[9] While

8. The theological polemics, we shall see, differs from the more vulgar only in terminology and level when it comes to the demonization and dehumanization of the Jews, traced by J. Trachtenberg in *The Devil and the Jews: The Medieval Conception of the Jews and Its Relation to Modern Antisemitism* (New York, 1961). The synthetic achievement of the book is also its disadvantage: it lacks a differentiation of polemical kinds, of levels of altercation, and it lacks altogether diachronic considerations. Cf. also Baron, ibid., XI pp. 122 ff.

9. Bernard Blumenkranz, *Les auteurs Chretiens latin du moyen age sur les Juifs et le Judaisme* (Paris, 1963). The review ends with the eleventh century. Our following study is based mainly on Latin sources. See now also the important study by David Rokeah, *Jews, Pagans and Christians in Conflict* (Jerusalem-Leiden, 1982).

no century passed without bequeathing to posterity several "Tractatus contra Judaeos," "Sermones contra Judaeos," "Dialogi cum Judaeis," until the twelfth century none of them contains a new idea or prooftext. Often enough they just copy arguments from the writings of Tertullian, Cyprianus, and Augustine. They list prooftexts from the Old for the veracity of the New Testament and add to them proofs from history—that is, from the present sorry state of the Jews, their humiliation and dispersion. Hardly any of these writings reflects a real occurrence: Tertullian's dialogue is already a mere literary exercise. The "Dialogue with the Jew Trypho," written in Greek by Justin the Martyr in the mid-second century, may have been for a long time to come the last record of a live altercation.[10] For hand in hand with the shift in the missionary activity of the early Church from the Jews to the "God-fearers" (θεοσεβεῖς, yir'ey shamayim)[11] and again from these to utter pagans—a process that ended approximately at the end of the second century—religious polemics likewise changed its nature and aims. Gradually, polemics with Jews became polemics against them,[12] the

10. On the importance of the question see M. Simon, Verus Israel. Études sur les relations entre Chretiens et Juifs dans L'Empire Romain (135–425) (Paris, 1964), pp. 166 ff.; M. Avi-Yonah, Biyme Roma ubizantion (Jerusalem, 1946), p. 101; J. Parkes, The Conflict of the Church and the Synagogue (London, 1934), pp. 71, 98 ff. The "Dialogue with Trypho" evidently contains fictitious elements, but the occurrence of the altercation and its dramatis personae seem to be factual. It is also evident that actual religious altercations occurred later: Cf. Blumenkranz, ibid., pp. 279 ff. (Crispin), but few of them were recorded. The disputation between Herman the Jew (Hermannus quondam Judaeus) and Rupert of Deutz bears the mark of authenticity for precisely the reasons that made A. Soltman doubt it: Herman's Jewish arguments are so different from those we are used to in written compositions.

11. See S. Pines, Hakinuy ha'irani Lenotsrim veyirey hashem, Proceedings of the Israel Academy of Scienceso 2/7 (Jerusalem, 1966), pp. 3–5. On the problems of proselytizing, see B. J. Bamberger, Proselytization in the Talmud Period (Cincinnati, 1939). Rokeah, Conflict, pp. 40 ff., warns correctly against exaggerating the number of either proselytes or god-fearers.

12. The argumentative strategies of early Christians probably differed only little from those of other apocalyptic sectarians, for example, the Dead Sea Scrolls sect, who likewise defined themselves as a "holy community" (adat kodesh) that was given the exclusive "decoding" (pesher) of the Scriptures at the end of the old eon (see chapter 3, "History as Predestination"). Depending on the concrete polemical situation, Christians since Paul developed two arguments. That they are "Israel in the spirit" to whom the choice of God has been transferred from "Israel in the flesh" they justified with an anachronization of the Old Testament as a παιδαγώγος εἰς χριστόν, a praeparatio evangelica. The Old Testament was a historical phase sublated by Christianity. Against Jews and "Judaizing" in its midst, Christian apologists sometimes argued that the law was given to Israel as a burden so as to enhance its sins and punishment (Gal. 3:19–24; 4:1 ff.). Cf. H. D. Wendland, Geschichtsanschauung und Geschichtsbewußtsein im Neuen Testament (Göttin-

product of missionary competition that imposed upon Christians the burden of proving to the pagan intellectuals why they hold to the Old Testament without being Jews.[13] And even while "the empire turned heretical"(*malkhut nehefkha minut*) down to the early Middle Ages, when the Jews in Western Europe (with the exception of Visigothic Spain) were a small minority among other minorities, the Church retained the fear of Jewish influence over *Judaizantes* in its midst. In Spain and Carolingian France the Church feared the social status of Jews, all the more so in that, until even the tenth century, the Christianization of Western Europe was fairly superficial: pagan customs and beliefs were deeply rooted and could be uprooted only by an intensive internal missionary drive. Mainly, however, religious polemics remained vital for the self-definition of the Church. The very fact that Jews' existence with the realm of influence of the *militans ecclesia* caused astonishment, perhaps even admiration, and called for an explanation.

For all of these reasons—and not only because of its lack of intellectual creativity during the early Middle Ages—polemics against Jews was still necessary even in a stereotypic, internalized form which preserved elements of its former apologetic past. The fixed image of the Jews in this polemical literature has been often described in recent literature,[14] though some of the presuppositions underlying this image have not always been clearly stated. The "blindness" (*obcaecatio*) of the

gen, 1938), pp. 23 ff., 30 ff. For such reasons Harnack saw in Marcion's dualistic doctrine merely an exaggeration of a Pauline motif. A. von Harnack, *Marcion: Das Evangelium vom Fremden Gott* (Leipzig, 1924; reprint: Berlin, 1960), pp. 30 ff., 106 ff. Cf. M. Werner, *Die Entstehung des christlichen Dogmas* (Bern-Tübingen, 1953), pp. 201 ff., 207. As to the place of polemics in life, Jewish missionary activity must be assumed to have lasted at least to the time of Hadrian: Simon, *Verus Israel*, pp. 315 ff. Note that Tertullian's disputation is directed against a pagan convert to Judaism (*proselyto Iudaeo*): "Adversus Iudaeos," 1 in *Tertulliani Opera Omnia*, ed. A. Kroymann, CSEL 70 (1942) p. 251. See also Rokeah (see n. 99).

13. Even Eusebius still formulates the objections of pagan intellectuals as follows: if indeed Christians hold to the Jewish religion, why did they make it into a new religion? Eusebius, *Praeparatio Evangelica*, ed. Schwartz, i, 2, 1–4. (His teacher Origenes fought similar objections of Celsus.) In the eyes of a politically minded Roman, Judaism might be a nuisance, but it can be tolerated for the sake of order and, at any rate, it follows a *mos majorum*. A new Jewish religion is an evil without redeeming features. That Christians were persecuted mainly because they were seen as *homines rerum novarum cupidi* has already been Edward Gibbon's opinion: *The Decline and Fall of the Roman Empire* (New York, n.d.) I, pp. 448 ff. See also Rokeah, *Jews, Pagans and Christians in Conflict*, pp. 16 ff.

14. E.g., Adolf Leschnitzer, *Die Juden im Weltbild des Mittelalters* (Berlin, 1934); Rosenthal, JQR 47, pp. 59 ff.; H. H. Ben Sasson, *Perakim betoldot yisrael biyme habenayyim* (Tel Aviv, 1962), pp. 29 ff.

Jews expresses itself in the "obnoxious" tenacity with which they hold to the simple, literal sense of the Scriptures, refusing to discern the hints in the Old Testament for the veracity of the new dispensation, refusing to recognize the fulfillment of prophecies and prefigurations in their own history, to recognize that, with the coming of the Messiah, the precepts of the law became obsolete because their aim was achieved by him. Israel "in the flesh" understands its chosenness and its law "literally" rather than in the proper "spiritual" understanding. We mentioned already the Pauline origin of this terminology. Nonetheless, there is a meaning to the continued existence of Israel in dispersion. In this view, which grew out of a variety of discrepant and contradictory voices to become dominant since the fifth century, the dispersion of the Jews among the nations was not only (if at all) a collective punishment for the collective sin of having crucified the Savior: it acquired also a triple teleological, positive meaning. In their dispersion, the Jews fulfill vital functions in the Christian order, in the divine plan of history. To heretics and pagans they serve as a living testimony to the authenticity and antiquity of the scriptures: Augustine inherited this idea from the earlier Greek apologists and transmitted it to the Middle Ages.[15] Furthermore, until the end of days, the Jewish humiliation in dispersion is a living testimony that chosenness by God has been transferred from Israel in the flesh to Israel in the spirit. Their state demonstrates that, when "Shilo" appeared, "the scepter has ceased from Judah" ("The staff shall not depart from Yehuda, nor the sceptre from between his feet, until Shilo come," Gen. 49:10). And finally: at the end of days, with the second presence ($\pi\alpha\rho o\nu\sigma i\alpha$) of Christ, the remnant of Israel will convert to Christianity in a dramatic act, thus completing and crowning the universal mission of the Church militant: "Thereafter the carnal Jews having passed, their children at the end of days will, as the prophet testifies, believe in Christ."[16]

Evidently, this doctrine reflects the gradual realization of the Church that it is incapable of converting the Jews, at least for the time being. In it, the Church developed a rationale why Jews still exist, and why they should be tolerated, with their "errors," at least conditionally. In

15. Augustine, *De civitate Dei* IV, 34; XVIII, 46; B. Blumenkranz, *Die Judenpredigt Augustins* (Basel, 1946); Baron, op. cit. II p. 34 n. 52, pp. 168 ff.

16. "Transeuntibus quidem istis carnalibus Judaeis, postea in novissimis temporibus filii eorum in Christo credituri sunt, propheta testante": Isidore of Seville, *De fide catholica contra Iudaeos* II, 5, In Migne, PL 83 col. 508 ff. On him see Blumenkranz, *Les auteurs* pp. 80 ff. On the theme of *testamentum aeternum* in Isidore cf. Leschnitzer, op. cit., n. 7.

the terms of canon law, Jews were not heretics as long as they remained Jews; nor were they unbelievers; their status was *sui generis*. Isidore of Seville, for example, opposed the forced conversion of Jews in Visigothic Spain for the reason just quoted, though approving it after the event. But the very same doctrine could likewise provide Christian rulers with reasons for the restriction and oppression of Jews whenever they sought such reasons, that is: whenever they felt that the actual social and political status of the Jews does not match their theoretical "servitude." It was a doctrine of *conditional* tolerance only.

The basic assumption underlying this doctrine of conditional tolerance was, then, the certainty that Jews and Judaism never changed, neither ethnically (for they are Israel in the flesh) nor in their religion; that they kept their blind, literal adherence to the Scriptures with its erroneous consequences in Jewish law. *Secundum carnem* the Jews remained the same through the ages—a fossil; Toynbee merely translated into a secular idiom an old theological bias. In the beginning of the thirteenth century, Joachim of Fiore once expressed this assumption in a succinct phrase: "the Jews refused to change with the times" (*noluerunt . . . ipsi Judaei mutari cum tempore*).[17] The Jews are a historical anachronism. In the more popular imagination Jews did not even change in their outward appearance, in their clothing. And an eleventh century hagiographer tells us in passing (in an altogether nonpolemical context) of a vision that his hero, the missionary and later martyr Anskar, has as a young man. His savior appeared to him "clothed as a Jew"—*more Iudaico vestitus*.[18]

The stone of contention between Jews and Christians was not the "fact" of ethnic continuity—both sides did not doubt it—but rather its meaning. The Christian contention that this ethnic continuity became meaningless with the advent of Christ forced some Jewish apologists to stress the value of this continuity far beyond traditional claims. Jehuda

---

17. Joachim de Fiore, *Super quattuor Evangeliarum*, p. 105, quoted after H. de Lubac, *Exégèse medievale. Les quatre sens de l'écriture* (Lyon-Fournier, 1961), III (II, 1), p. 144, n. 2. It is, of course, a clear literary allusion to Ovid: "tempora mutant et nos in eis." Later, Josef Albo formulated this principle from the Jewish perspective most succinctly: "ואולם אחר היות כל הדתות מסכימות באחת מהן שהיא אלהית, אלא שהן חולקות עליה בשיאמרו שהיתה זמנית וכבר עבר זמנה, הנה נאמר שהוא ראוי לכל בעל דת לחקור על עקרי דתו ואמונתו." Josef Albo, *Sefer ha'iqqarim*, I, 14, ed. J. Husik (Philadelphia, 1946), I, p. 191.

18. Rimbert, *Vita Anskari* 4, ed. G. Waitz, *M. G. in usu Schol.* (Hannover, 1884), p. 24: "cumque ab oratione surrexit, ecce vir per ostium veniebat, statura procerus, Iudaico more vestitus, vultu decorus." Luther was not the first European to recognize "dass Jesus Christus ein Jud gewesen."

Halevi elaborated the biological criterion to define Judaism almost *ad absurdum* in his famous doctrine of the adherence of "the divine matter" (*al'amer al'ilahi, ha'inyan ha'elohi*) to Israel. It adheres, he contended, to those of pure ethnic lineage only; even converts to Judaism are exempt from it.[19]

THE RATIONALIZATION OF POLEMICS: ANSELM OF CANTERBURY

Christian anti-Jewish polemics changed radically in the twelfth century, reflecting historical events and changes in the methods and contents of theology. I shall not deal with the historical causes for the deterioration of the social, economic, and political status of the Jews since the twelfth century. It was a complex process that defies monocausal explanations. Among its main driving moments were the demographic explosion, social differentiation, the war of investitures, the various religious popular movements—legitimate and heretical—since the eleventh century, of which the First Crusade was a part. At the time the Christian religious polemics abandoned its introverted nature, became ever more aggressive and began to serve new social and religious functions.

Two formal characteristics became dominant in the history of learned Christian polemics from now onwards: an increasing rationalization, a turn towards rational-philosophical arguments, and—of greater importance—the fact that Jewish postbiblical literature became known to Christian theologians, at first in fragments, systematically later on. Inasmuch as theologians felt an increasing need to rethink theological issues and redefine systematically basic theological terms, they also changed their views about the aims and possibilities of religious polemics. Scholastics sought to ground the dogmas and the elements of canonic law *auctoritate et ratione;* in their case against Judaism some of them likewise sought to replace the stereotypic repetition of scriptural reference-lists with rational argument. Polemics became creative again.

Anselm of Canterbury's "Cur deus homo?" though arguably not written for immediate polemical purposes,[20] influenced the polemical literature directly and indirectly. His proofs of the necessity of incarnation for the success of God's plan for the salvation of humanity were

19. See below, p. 293.
20. See n. 27.

meant to replace older perceptions of humanity as the "captive" of Satan since the original sin, in need of being "ransomed."[21] Anselm undertook an *Entzauberung* of theology, its emancipation from redundant myths. His argument presupposes that if God wanted to create the world and the completion of the *civitas dei coelestis,* he was obliged to maintain their implicit order: "it does not behoove God to let into his kingdom anything inordinate."[22] Humanity had to compensate God with a proper compensation (*debitum satisfactionis*) for the original sin wherefore the savior had to be human. But the once impaired human will have lost the capacity to want that which God wants, wherefore the savior had to be divine. He had to be at once man and God. This divine necessity does not amount to absolute determination and does not infringe on God's omnipotence, such as, for instance, the *'akl* in the doctrine of the *mu'atazila*. It is rather a consequence of the world's order chosen by God (*ordinatio*). It seems to me that Anselm was the first among medieval thinkers to see clearly the problem known later as the relation between God's absolute and ordained power (*potentia Dei ordinata et absoluta*), a problem that became central to theological discussion after Thomas. God—such is Anselm's answer to Petrus Damiani's contention that the omnipotent God can act *contra naturam*[23]—is

21. These, says Anselm, were allegorical readings only (*quasi quaedam pictura*): Anselm of Canterbury, "Cur deus homo?" I, 4, ed. Schmitt, *Anselmi Opera Omnia* (Edinburgh, 1946), pp. 51 ff. On Anselm's theology at large see E. Seeberg, *Lehrbuch der Dogmengeschichte* III (Darmstadt, 1959), pp. 218 ff.

22. Anselm, *Cur deus homo?* I, 12: "Deum . . . non decet aliquid inordinatum in suo regno dimittere."

23. Petrus Damiani, *De divina omnipotentia,* V, XII, ed. P. Brezzi and B. Nardi, *Editione Nationale dei Classici del pensiero Italiano* 5 (Firenze, 1943), pp. 70 ff., 118 ff. On his sources see A. Enders, *Petrus Damiani und die Weltliche Wissenschaft, Beitrage zur Geschichte der Philosophie des Mittelaters,* ed. C. Baumher VIII, 3 (Munster, 1910), pp. 16 ff., esp. p. 17, n. 1. Anselm joins Augustine, who stated, "Deum, creator et conditor omnium naturarum, nihil contra naturam facit": *Contra Faustum* XXVI, 3, Migne, PL; 42, col. 480. Most theologians of the twelfth century gave a similar answer to the question whether God can act *contra naturam:* cf. Thorndike, *A History of Magic and Experimental Science during the First Thirteen Centuries of Our Era* (New York, 1958) I, pp. 58 ff. On the dialectics of *potentia dei absoluta et ordinata* and its importance in the later Middle Ages much has been written since this article first appeared (1969); see my *Theology and the Scientific Imagination,* pp. 117–52 (with the recent literature). Ibid., p. 126, I traced the origin of the earlier formula *agere per potentiam—agere per iustitiam.* Cf. Gregory of Rimini, *Lectura super primum et secundum sententiarum,* idem, pp. 42–44 q. 1a. 2, ed. A. D. Frapp and V. Marcolino, 6 vols. (Berlin, New York, 1979–84, III, p. 368), on Origenes (e. g., Migne, PG 13 col. 1716). On Anselm and the *potentia absoluta* see also W. Courtenay, "Necessity and Freedom in Anselm's Conception of God," *Analecta Anselmiana* 4.2 (1975), pp. 39–64.

bound at least to the (logical) principle of noncontradiction and to its consequences. Ascribing to God the power to effect two logically contradictory states of affairs weakens God's omnipotence rather than increasing it; without that logical restriction, it would be conceivable that God could annihilate his own existence. Anselm, it seems, wishes to secure God's status as a necessary existent (*ens necessarium*), the ground for Anselm's ontological proof for God's existence.[24] Being confined to the principle of noncontradiction also means that God is bound to the world-order that he wanted for as long as he wants it, and consequently to the immanent logic of this order. The object of God's will must remain consistent. Wherefore God became flesh of necessity and yet out of God's unrestricted will and power.

Anselm's emphasis on the necessity of the incarnation may have made him less prone to acuse Jews, collectively or individually, of having killed their savior. At any rate, he explicitly denies the charge of deicide: "no man can knowingly wish to kill God, wherefore those who killed him out of ignorance did not fall into this infinite sin."[25] Few medieval authors said so, and fewer so explicitly. It fits the general nonpolemical style of Anselm.

In our context it is of little importance whether the dialogue was really written with Jewish arguments in mind, as the result of an actual confrontation or with the intent to induce it.[26] The considerable influence of the treatise on later anti-Jewish polemics, in content and form of argumentation, justifies our attention to it here. Yet the internal logic of the treatise makes it difficult to ascribe to it outright polemical purposes. Though he believed in the power of reason to provide a priori proofs for God's existence and even for the truth of the dogma, he was not a rationalist of the kind that believes in the capacity of the unaided, natural reason to perceive these proofs without divine inspiration. Anselm's notion of evidence has sometimes been erroneously compared to

24. D. Henrich, *Der ontologische Gottesbeweis, sein Problem und seine Geschichte in der Neuzeit* (Tubingen, 1960), pp. 10 ff., has argued that Anselm's proof, accepted in the Middle Ages by only a few, was grounded on the notion of God as *eus perfectissimum* (ens quod majus cogitari non potest), while Descartes revived it with the less ambiguous starting point of the notion of God as *ens necessarium* (*causa sui*). N. Malcolm, "Anselm's Ontological Arguments," *The Philosophical Review* 69 (1960): pp. 41–62, has shown that in fact both forms were anticipated by Anselm. Cf. also my *Theology,* pp. 25–28.

25. Deum occidere nullus homo umquam scienter saltem velle posset, et ideo qui illum occiderunt ignoranter non in illud infinitum peccatum . . . proruerunt: *Cur deus homo* II, 15.

26. Ibid. I, 1; II, 22; ed. Schmitt, pp. 133, 147.

Descartes's.[27] The "evidence" which Descartes ascribes to "clear and distinct" ideas is largely subjective. Only systematic reasons moved him to ascribe absolute certainty to the transition from the "objective" to the "formal" idea of God, yet to deny such certainty to, say, mathematical propositions.[28] The evidence attributed to Anselm to the *rationes necessariae* is, by contrast, an objective evidence. Their certainty reflects and participates in the eternal truth, the eternal light itself, of which every particular truth is a part. Anselm felt, therefore, compelled to try to prove the absolute, a priori validity of God, his goodness, truth—to prove that they are, in the language of Thomas, *nota per se ipsa*. For these reasons, Anselm put forth in the *Proslogion* his ontological proof of God's existence from his very notion—after having developed, in the *Proslogion*, a "physico-theological," a posteriori proof. But these very considerations also moved Anselm, again in contrast to Descartes, to distinguish between objective evidence and subjective certainty (*certitudo*). The latter does not always accompany the truth and may at times be erroneous.[29] Every cognition is rooted in illumination: Anselm could not distinguish between the "natural" and "supernatural light" (*lumen supernaturale*) so as to attribute the former with immanent, innate capacities of judgment.

Anselm's epistemology thus makes it clear why only the one who already believes can be convinced; and it may be the reason why Anselm abstained from religious polemics even while possessing good arguments against "the wicked" (*insipiens*) who "said in his heart there is no God." Yet if he abstained from outright anti-Jewish polemics, his disciples and imitators did not, such as Odo of Cambray[30] or the anony-

27. E. g., R. Allers, *Anselm von Canterbury: Leben, Lehre, Werke* (Wien, 1936), p. 73. Cf. J. Fischer, *Die Erkenntnislehre Anselms von Canterbury,* BGPhM X, 3 (Münster, 1911), p. 647 (valuable only as a collection of materials). No less mistaken is the comparison of Descartes's notion of evidence to that of Sa'adia Gaon who, in many ways, occupies the same positional value in medieval Christian philosophy as Anselm in the development of Christian philosophy.

28. This was recognized already by Arnauld in his response to Descartes's "Meditations": *Meditationes* q. IV, ed. A. Tannery (Paris, 1904), VII, pp. 199–207. See also A. Funkenstein, "Descartes and the Method of Annihilation," *Sceptics, Millenarians and Jews,* ed. D. Katz and J. Israel (Leiden, 1990), pp. 70–75.

29. Seeberg, ibid., III, p. 165; Fischer, ibid., pp. 50–63. Here, again, Anselm anticipated a major turn in fourteenth-century philosophy. See A. Maier, "Das Problem der Evidenz in der Scholastik des 14ten Jahrhundert," *Ausgehendes Mittelalter,* vol. 2 (Rome, 1967), pp. 367–418.

30. Odo de Cambray, *Disputatio cum Judaeo,* Migne, PL 160 col. pp. 1104 ff.; cf. Seeberg, *Lehrbuch* III, p. 237.

mous author of a polemical treatise erroneously ascribed to William of Champeaux. The latter starts his "dialogue" with a declaration that he was unable to convince his Jewish interlocutor with scriptural arguments—that is, with the traditional mode of polemicizing. He was able to do so only with rational arguments.[31] The arguments themselves are a shallow repetition of Anselm's, certainly without the restrictions that Anselm set on their capacity to convince. Had Anselm's epistemological stunt been really accepted, it might have enhanced true tolerance.

That the increased rationalization of disputation could lead to increased tolerance becomes evident even more when one reads Abelard's *Dialogus inter philosophum, Judaeum et Christianum*[32]—a book close in form and content, though not in its intention, to a similar work by Raymundus Lullus in the fourteenth century. Its basic fairness to the Jewish point of view was born out of genuine interest in the Jewish people; it reflects direct contact with, and sympathy for, Jews. Yet the dangers in the invocation of reason were not smaller than its benefit. Peter the Venerable, whose polemics we shall discuss later, set up the following simple syllogism. Man is a rational animal. It is well known that Jews can be convinced neither by scripture nor by reason. They are, therefore, inhuman; their demonic nature drives them to feign lack of understanding.[33] Of the extreme rationalism of the *mu'atazila*, Goldzieher once remarked that "dogmatism, by its very notion, harbors the tendency to intolerance."[34] The part played in Europe by rationalists in the history of intolerance is no smaller than their part in the promotion of tolerance. Radical rationalists tend to identify cognitive errors with moral vicissitude. They often tend to identify reason with faith or at least to prove their compatibility. Abelard revived ancient patristic doctrines (going back to Clement of Alexandria) which viewed Greek philosophy as being no less a *praeparatio evangelica* than the Old Testament. Greek thinkers, Abelard assumed, had already accepted many, if

31. [Ps.] William of Champeaux, *Dialogus inter Judaeum et Christianum*, Migne, PL 163, col. 1041.

32. Petrus Abaelard, *Dialogus inter philosophum, Judaeum et Christianum*, Migne, PL 178, 1609 ff. About the general tone and character of the book see H. Liebeschütz, "Die Stellung des Judentums im Dialog des Peter Abälard," *MGWJ* 83 (47) (1939): pp. 390 ff.

33. Petrus Venerablis, *Tractatus adversus Judaeorum inveteratam duritiem* V, Migne, PL 189, col. 602.

34. "Dem Dogmatismus wohnt vermöge seines Begrittes die Tendenz zur Intoleranz inne": I. Goldzieher, *Vorlesungen über den Islam* (Heidelberg, 1910), p. 117.

not all, tenets of the Christian faith, which forms at its core a rational system; only the fear of ignorant masses made them veil their knowledge in hints.[35] Similar views in Arab and Jewish philosophy are better known. Sa'adia Gaon, in the beginning of the medieval Jewish philosophical tradition, likewise saw in revelation and prophecy a historical-social necessity rather than a matter of principle. The labor of reason is discursive, slow, and prone to be impeded by mistakes and dead-end trials. Therefore the *tora* was given, and so also miracles and prophecy, "because [God] knew in his wisdom that the proposition sought by the work of reason cannot be completed except in time, and if he deprives our knowledge of them in the *tora* we shall remain a long time without it until the labor is completed." Especially the masses are cause for concern: "and perhaps many of us will never complete the work because of the internal defects or lack of talent to deal with it . . . or because of overbearing doubts. . . . And God saved us from all these troubles quickly and sent us his messengers."[36]

REASON AND CONVERSION: PETRUS ALFUNSI

The Christian reaction to these exaggerated hopes of reason came after Thomas, particularly during the fourteenth century. The Jewish reaction grew out of an awareness of the dangers implicit in the emergence of intellectuals to whom differences of faith are but differences of intellectual levels.[37] In Jehuda Halevi's "Kuzzari," the positions of the Muslim and Christian participants in the fictitious dialogue are set in close proximity to that of the "philosopher." This is not a mere theoretical or rhetorical construct. Close to Jehuda Halevi's time and place, Petrus Alfunsi converted to Christianity. In his polemical trea-

---

35. Abaelard, *Dialogus,* Migne, PL 178 col. 1614 ff. Cf. H. Reuter, *Geschichte der Aufklärung im Mittelalter* (Berlin, 1875; reprint: Aalen, 1963), I, pp. 215, 323, n. 1. Reuter's anachronistic hunt for "enlighteners" stretches to John the Scott (Eriugena). The book was written from a Catholic, apologetic point of view at the end of the last century to document the Church's openness to science.

36. Sa'adia, *Sefer ha'emunot vedeot* (Ibn Tibbon's trans.), introduction (New York, 1956), p. 16: מפני שידע בחכמתו כי המבוקשים המוצאים במלאכת העיון לא ישלמו כי אם במדה" מהזמן כי אם ימחה אותנו בידיעת תורתנו עליה נעמוד זמן רב בלא תורה עד שתשלם המלאכה . . . ושמא רבים ממנו לא תשלם בו המלאכה בעבור חסרון שיש בו או שלא ישלם לו להתעסק בה . . . או "מפני שהספקות שולטים עליו . . . ושמרנו הבורא מכל אלו הטרחים במהרה ושלח לנו שלוחיו.

37. J. Katz, *Exclusiveness and Tolerance* (Hebrew) (Jerusalem, 1960), p. 178.

tise—one of the most notorious and influential throughout the Middle Ages—Alfunsi focused on the rational motives leading to his conversion. Only Christianity is the suitable faith for a philosopher. We shall see later how he transformed arguments of Sa'adia Gaon: his acquaintance with Jewish philosophy seems more profound than his knowledge of Christian theology.

Petrus Alfunsi was an early prototype of those Spanish-Jewish upper-class intellectuals who led to the "Taufweller" of the fourteenth century. Their motives were many—economic, social, and religious. As was the case among German Jews in the nineteenth century, many of them may have embarked from the false perception that the measure of tolerance in the Christian society at large resembled the measure of understanding for other religions in the small enlightened circles to which they belonged. Some of them, such as Abner (Paulus) of Burgos later and Petrus Alfunsi, may have felt a genuine attraction to Christianity as a religion of reason that fits the dominant elements of their education better than Judaism. At any rate, Alfunsi was a victim of a more popularized philosophy, of half-digested ideas. I do not see in his polemical treatise an intent to vilify Judaism at all costs, but rather a fairly sincere account of the motives of his conversion.[38] Having converted, the new name he chose was Petrus, to honor the king who was present at his baptism: the conversion of a Jew in the early days of the *reconquista* was still a rare event because the economic situation of a convert was often enough worse than it was as a Jew; he could be dispossessed. In short, I have no reason to doubt Alfunsi's protestations that he was not led by material considerations. He certainly was not led by them.

His treatise is written as a dialogue between himself and his friend Moses. Moses was Alfunsi's name prior to his conversion: the dialogue seems to be an internal dialogue between his new and old self. The explicit intent of the book was the immanent refutation of Judaism with its own weapons, *secundum Hebraicam veritatem*.[39] To that aim, Alfunsi employs extensively the talmudic aggadic materials. He wishes to show that Judaism is confined to primitive, anthropomorphic perceptions of

38. For a different assessment see A. Ashtor, *The History of the Jews in Moslem Spain* (Hebrew) (Jerusalem, 1966), pp. 172–73, 382 nn. 261–67; I. F. Baer, *A History of the Jews in Christian Spain* (Hebrew) (Tel Aviv, 1959), p. 35.

39. Petrus Alfunsi ex Judaeo Christians, *Dialogi* etc. I, Migne, PL 157 col. 536ff. Quotation: col. 339C. Against the view that the *Sefer michamot hashem* of Jacob ben Reuben was written to refute Alfunsi, see J. Rosenthal in the introduction to his edition of *Milchamot hashem* (Jerusalem, 1963), pp. xvii–viii.

God, and that it is necessarily confined to those because it is limited to the literal understanding of its scriptures and its traditions. "You contend that God has a head, arms and a form; if this is so, then, of necessity, you confess that God has the dimensions of altitude and longitude."[40] A. L. Williams and S. Lieberman have traced many of Alfunsi's sources. Like Agobard of Lyons almost two hundred years earlier, he uses heavily the anonymous and esoteric *Sefer shi'ur koma*. Alfunsi himself names the treatise *Berachot* of the (Babylonian) Talmud as his main source: "in the first part of your doctrine, whose name is Benedictions (*benedictiones*)."[41] In the course of his dialogue he develops eclectic theological and cosmological theories that purport to be free of anthropomorphizations. He goes on to refute the Jewish reasons for being scattered in the *Galut* and adds, at the end of the first part, some further examples of the absurdities in the aggadic imagination.

All of this is not to say that Alfunsi objects in principle to concrete illustrations of abstract ideas, to parables and metaphors. In his *disciplina clericalis* he demonstrated the practical-pedagogical value of "philosophical" stories: it was one of the most popular books of anecdotes in the Middle Ages. He opposed the *aggada* because he saw in it not merely odd and infantile elements even where it does not relate miracles, but rather an insult to common sense. Since Jews are incapable of allegorical interpretations—the *sensus spiritualis*—of necessity they read such materials literally. The *aggada* proves that Judaism must essentially stay outside the garden of true philosophy. You may argue: surely he must have known that Jews do practice allegorical and symbolical reading (*derash*). But then again, many Jewish intellectuals of his time were profoundly embarrassed by some of the *midrashim*.[42] His stand differs from theirs only in its radical consequences. The medieval Jewish enlightenment of the Middle Ages also aimed at the sublimation of vulgar anthropomorphism (*hagsama*).

A. L. Williams still thought that one could omit a discussion of Al-

---

40. Alfunsi, *Dialogi* I, Migne, PL 157 col. B–C: "Vos Deum caput, brachia et totam corporis formam habere contenditio. Quod si hoc est, igitur Deum longtitudinis et altitudinis dimensionibus constare necesse est fateamini." This is a clear allusion to the *shi'ur koma*, as if to say: rabbinical legends lead of necessity to the bizarre speculations about the dimensions of God such as in the *shi'ur koma*.

41. Ibid., Migne, PL 157, col. 541–42.

42. Cf. Ramban, *Perush hatora*, ed. Schawel (Jerusalem, 1962), I p. 11 (after enumerating divine and seemingly conflicting midrashic traditions, and harmonizing them kabbalistically): "אבל הזכרתי זה לבלום פי קטני אמונה מעוטי חכמה, המלעיגים על דברי רבותינו" Maimonides was so incensed about the *Shi'ur koma* that he suggested it be better incinerated.

funsi's philosophical theories.[43] Aside from the belittling of medieval philosophy as such, which sounds today much more obsolete than its object, in our case the separation of the religious from the philosophical argument is particularly impractical. One of the main marks of Alfunsi's polemics is the way in which he employed Jewish philosophy—a dominant ingredient in his education. It seems clear to me that he borrowed his proofs for God's existence and attributes—together with its epistemological presuppositions—directly or indirectly—from Sa'adia's "Book of Beliefs and Opinions." Sa'adia distinguished three sources of cognition, "the underlying grounds (*meshachey*) for truth and evidence"; "the first: cognition of the apparent, the second: knowledge of reason, the third: knowledge of that which is necessitated."[44] He means sensual perception, direct intellectual evidence (axioms), and deductive inferences. So also Alfunsi:

To know has three meanings. One, when something is perceived by the bodily senses. Another, when something is known by necessary reason only. Yet another, what is known by analogy to other things.

And he continues and borrows some of Sa'adia's examples for the latter verbatim: that we infer from smoke the presence of fire, and from a human voice the presence of a person.[45] But Sa'adia also admitted a fourth source of knowledge that Alfunsi omits, a source confined to "the community of true monotheists" (*kehal hameyachadim*), namely "trustworthy hearsay" or tradition. Upon it Sa'adia grounds the validity of the "commandments of obedience" in the third part of his book. Alfunsi may have omitted this mode of knowledge because he had no

43. With a curious argument, at least in its conclusion: "These essays must have been intended for the perusal of the upper classes of all educated men of the period. Naturally they are out of date now, and it is not worth the trouble to any but a very few readers to try to understand the philosophy and the science of the period": A. L. Williams, *Adversus Judaeos. A Bird's-Eye View of Christian Apologiae until the Renaissance* (Cambridge, 1935), pp. 233 ff.

44. Sa'adia, ibid. *Meshech* in the sense of underlying matter: cf. D. Kaufmann, *Geschichte der Attributenlehre in der Judischen religiosen Philosophie des Mittelalters von Saadya bis Maimuni* 4 (Gotha, 1877), p. 1, n. 1.

45. Alfunsi, *Dialogi* I, Migne, PL 157 col. 555C; Sa'adia, *Sefer ha'emunot vede'ot*, intro.:

Illud autem quod per simili-	והאחד מהם כי כשאנחני רואים
tudinem percipitur, tale est	עשן שנאמין במציאות האש
ut sicuti vocem audieris,	במציאות העשן כי לא יתום זה
ibi aliquot vocale esse intelle-	כי אם בזה. וכן כאשר נשמע
gis, quamvis minime videas,	בקול אדם מאחורי הפרגוד
vel cum ubilibet fumum	או מאחרי הכותל אנחנו חייבים
conspexerit, ille ignem etsi	שנאמין במציאותו מפי שלא יהיה
non videas esse cognoscis" etc.	קול אדם בלתי אם מאדם נמצא וגו'

need for it—if indeed he saw the merits of Christianity over Judaism in that it has no room for blind obedience. It is a religion of reason.

Be that as it may, Alfunsi undoubtedly knew either Sa'adia's book or parts of it, or perhaps only a paraphrase, in Hebrew or Arabic. His proof for the existence and unity of God are likewise Sa'adia's, and so is his elaboration of the divine attributes. The latter forms the basis for his proof of the Trinity—rather than, as one might guess from other theological writings of his time, the somewhat similar ideas of Augustine.[46] In the short time that he acquired his far from elegant Latin he may not have read Augustine, who was one of the most quoted but less often read of the Church Fathers in the early Middle Ages. Alfunsi's theological education was rather narrow.

In the course of his defense of Christianity, Alfunsi employed another family of ideas that again became popular at the time about the place of various religions in the cultural progress of the world. The idea that Christianity appeared only when the cultural, social, and political development of humanity reached a proper level to perceive and spread it over the whole inhabited world is not the same as the Pauline conception of the sublation of the commandments of the Old Testament and the distinction of periods "before the law, under the law, under grace" (*ante legem, sub lege, sub gratia*). Eusebius combined both lines of thought into one argument so as to defend Christianity as the only religion really befitting the Roman Empire.[47] Others repeated similar arguments in various contexts down to the liberal theology of the nineteenth century. Alfunsi employs them in his classification of Judaism and Islam. The more traditional use of the idea of divine accommodation is his explanation for the now obsolete commandments of the Old Testament:

In the beginning of the world, humans were still bestial and more or less wild, and could not be immediately guided towards obedience to God's precepts. Knowing this, the divine wisdom, unwilling to give them all precepts, gave slowly [*paulatim*] one to Adam . . . another to Noah. . . . When indeed Moses

46. Kaufmann, op. cit., pp. 41 ff., read Augustine's comparison of the three faculties of the soul to the trinity as a mere illustration or allegory; in fact it is more, namely the latter a prototype of the former, and humans a true *imago* of God. Cf. Uberweg-Geyer, *Grundriss der Geschichte der Philosophie* (Basel-Stuttgart, 1960), vol. 3, p. 108.

47. E. Peterson, "Der Monotheismus als politisches Problem: Ein Beitrag zur Geschichte der politischen Theologie im Imperium Romanum," *Theologische Traktate* (München, 1951), pp. 86 ff. On the theme of accommodation in classical and medieval literature see Funkenstein, *Heilsplan*, pp. 31–34; idem, *Theology and the Scientific Imagination*, pp. 256–58; S. D. Benin, "Thou Shalt Have No God Before Me: Sacrifice in Jewish and Christian Thought" (Ph.D. diss., UC Berkeley, 1980).

came, and God wished the children of Israel to join him and be distinguished from other nations, he gave them all his precepts.[48]

Alfunsi could have drawn from the long and rich history of this figure of thought in Christian theology from Irenaeus of Lyons through Augustine to his own times.[49] But he could have also relied on traces of it in the Jewish tradition again down to his time—they are present in Jehuda Halevi's *Kuzzari*.[50] Maimonides was later to work them out into a detailed theory about the origins of some commandment as a partial concession to polytheistic practices so as to invert them. We shall deal with it later.

While discussing the abolition of the pristine law given to Israel, Alfunsi lets his interlocutor, Moses, ask: if indeed he, Alfunsi, wanted the most progressive religion, why did he not turn to the youngest one among the monotheistic creeds? Alfunsi answers by describing the primitive character and origins of Islam:

People in Mohammed's time were lawless, without letters, ignorant of any values except warfare and plowing, seeking luxury, given to gluttony. . . . Had he preached to them in any other way, he would not have moved them towards his law.[51]

In other words, Islam is even further from reason than Judaism. It is worth noting that he assumes the influence of Samaritans and Nestorians on nascent Islam. He also repeats the story of Mohammed's Jewish helpers.

I argued that Alfunsi did not intend a crude defamation of Jews and Judaism. Nowhere did he accuse the postbiblical Jewish literature of blasphemous misrepresentations of Christianity—as other Christian theologians who came to be acquainted with the *aggada* and *halakha*

48. Alfunsi, *Dialogi* V, Migne, PL 157, col. 667 ff., esp. 667B: "Quoniam in mundi exordio quasi silvestres erant adhuc homines et bestiales, nullatenus tam cito possent admoneri ad oboedientiam praeceptis Dei. Quod Dei comperiens sapientia, nequaquam simul omnia eis voluit dare praecepta, imo patulatim unum dedit Adae . . . aliud vero Noe . . . cum vero Moyses venit, et Deus filios Israel secum adjungere et ab aliis gentibus, discernere voluit, praecepta eis sua praecepit." Cf. Sa'adia (above n. 44); Eusebius, *Historia Ecclesiastica* I, 2, 19, ed. Schwartz, 5th ed. (Berlin, 1952), p. 8.

49. Cf. above, pp. 141–145.

50. Jehuda Halevi, *Kuzzari* IV, 3

51. Alfunsi, *Dialogi* V, Migne, PL157, col. 605B (Cf. 603A): "Homines autem temporis Mohameti, sine lege, sine scriptura, totius boni inscii praeter militiam et aratrum, appetentes luxuram, deditique gulae, facile secundum voluntatem eorumdam praedicari poterant. Si enim aliter faceret, non ad legem suam eos impelleret."

did. On the other hand, his materials could be used for baser purposes, and indeed were so used.

THE POLEMICS AGAINST THE TALMUD

From the twelfth century onwards, attacks against the Talmud became a dominant theme in the Christian polemical literature. The term was used to refer to almost the entire postbiblical Jewish literature, of which the legal and homiletic parts—*halakha* and *aggada*—were found to be equally offensive. Accusing Judaism with blasphemy against Christianity was, as I said before, only part of a much broader, much more pernicious accusation of heresy, of deviating from the original and proper form of Judaism. That Jews and Judaism did not change was, as we saw, the assumption underlying the doctrine of conditional tolerance towards Judaism prevalent in antiquity and in the early Middle Ages. That Jews and Judaism did change was the implicit and explicit ground for the trial and burning of the Talmud in 1240 and several times since.[52] Should I be able to show, as I intend to do, that already Petrus Venerabilis of Cluny raised similar accusations about a hundred years earlier than the speculations about the role of the convert Dunin in the Talmud-trial or about the damaging effects of the controversy over Maimonides's philosophical writings may seem much less relevant. Christian theologians were, then, ready and prepared for such allegations long before 1240.

Peter the Venerable was the first to express such views in the twelfth century. Though I doubt whether he was acquainted even with one fully translated talmudic tractate (he claimed to have initiated the translation of the whole Talmud), his source-material was richer than that of any of his predecessors. The change was not merely quantitative: he views the Talmud as a genuine heresy, containing human traditions which are not intended to interpret the Bible but to compete with it. He begins the fifth chapter of his *Tractatus adversus Judaeorum inveteratam duritiem* with solemnity and sarcasm:

I will, in public, show you, O Jew, you beast, your book, I say this book of yours, this Talmud of yours, that venerable doctrine of yours which you prefer to the prophetic books and to all authentic sentences.[53]

52. See n. 72.
53. Petrus Venerabilis, *Adversus Judaeorum inveteratam duritiem*, V, Migne, PL 189, col. 602C–D: "Profero tibi coram universis, O Judaee, bestia, librum tuum, illum, inquam, librum tuum, illum Talmuth tuum, illam egregiam doctrinam tuam, propheticis libris et cunctis sententiis authenticis praeferendam."

Some of the words are not new. They echo, in part, a famous judgment of Jerome. In an often quoted letter, Jerome—who, like Origenes, was well acquainted with Jewish traditions—complained that there are "so many Pharisaic traditions now called 'deuteroseis', like old women's tales."[54] He continues with the argument that, given the fact that the biblical precepts cannot be fulfilled literally, the only proper way to understand them is spiritually; yet the Jews prefer to force the Scriptures to yield their oral laws, such as the laws concerning the walking-limits on the Sabbath, "preferring the doctrines of men to God's doctrine" ("doctrinas hominum praeferentes doctrinae Dei").[55] Yet Jerome never questioned the subjective dependence of the *halakha* on the scriptures. He does not doubt the sincerity of the sages who believed that the oral law represented an interpretation and adaptation of the written law. A similar attitude is reflected in the widely read remarks of Epiphanius a hundred years earlier on the scribes who hold customs and beliefs that cannot be found in the *Tora* (νόμος). But he knows that the scribes and Pharisees regard their laws as a fence around the written law (*syag latora*). Indeed, his use of the word "heresy" is value-free: he distinguishes four hermeneutical "schools" of those who add to the law (Δευτερωται). Similar remarks can be found throughout the Patristic literature in the East and West.[56] Only the Emperor Justinian I drew radical conclusions when he forced on the Jewish community the liturgical use of translations and forbade, in his notorious novella, the use of traditions (δευτερωσεῖς).[57]

We find Jerome's remarks quoted also by Agobard of Lyons in the ninth century. But even while attacking the crude, blasphemous anthropomorphisms of the *Sefer shi'ur koma* or other Jewish *errores et superstitiones*,[58] Agobard, too, does not challenge their subjective dependence

54. Hieronymus, *Epistulae* 121 q. 10, ed. I. Heiberg, CSEL 61, 3 (1918): pp. 48–49: "Quanta traditiones phareiseorum sint, quas hodie δευτερωσεῖς vocant, et quam aniles fabulae, revolvere nequeo."

55. Ibid.: "Solent respondere et dicere: Barkhibas et Symeon et Helles [Akiba, Hillel, Shamai], magistri nostri, tradiderunt nobis . . . doctrinas hominum praeferentes doctrinae dei." At issue are the הלכות תחום שבת.

56. Epiphanius, πανάριος I, 1, 15, Migne, PG 41, col. 242 ff.; cf. id., Ἀνακέφαλον, Migne, PG42, col. 846. As to the term "haeresis" in the sense of "school" or "sect," cf. παν. I, 5, about the lack of differences of beliefs and opinions in the beginning of the world. For others, cf., for example, Augustine, *Contra adversarium legis et prophetarum* II, 1, 1, Migne, PL 42, col. 637.

57. A. Linder (ed.), *Roman Legal Legislation on the Jews* (Jerusalem, 1983), pp. 295–302.

58. Agobard, *Epistola . . . de Judaicis superstitionibus* X, Migne, PL 104, col. 88B–C; on his sources: Williams, *Adversus Judaeos*, pp. 348 ff.; Blumenkranz, *Les Auterus*, pp. 152–67, 195 ff. On Agobard and the *sefer tole'dot Jeshu* see S. Kraus, *Das Leben Jesu*, pp. 5 ff.

on the Bible, and never denies that all the Jews believe they are doing is interpreting the scriptures.[59] The same passage from Jerome's letter was quoted again by Agobard's disciple Amulo of Lyons and others after him.[60] Little, then, seems new in Peter the Venerable's opening remarks: the Jews "prefer" their doctrines to God. But he took it literally to mean that the Jews but pretend to still hold to the Old Testament. He continues:

You wonder, since I am not a Jew, who put into my hand the Jewish *secrets?* Who uncovered your most occult and intimate [matters]? . . . These are your mysteries, O Jews, these your hidden sacraments, your wisdom, which you prefer to all the divine wisdom.

The Talmud is the secret of the Jews revealed by the Savior. It contains their *hidden* doctrines.

It has been shown by Lieberman (against Williams) that most of Peter's materials are drawn from Petrus Alfunsi's dialogue.[61] Yet he changed their context and intent. Like Alfunsi, he is certain that the legends of the Jews are to be taken literally, for Jews are incapable of any but a literal understanding of their texts. But unlike Alfunsi, he wanted much more than to demonstrate the absurdity and backwardness of such legends. To the contrary: so much absurdity points not at error, but deceit. Wherefore Peter focused his attention not so much as Alfunsi or Agobard before him on anthropomorphic Jewish traditions as such, but rather on those anthropomorphic traditions that want, as he thinks, to prove that God himself recognized the superiority of the man-made Talmud. To prove his point, Peter mixes and distorts his sources deliberately. Out of the talmudic anecdote about the controversy over the snakelike oven (*Baba metsi'a* 59b) and another talmudic anecdote about a controversy concerning skin-spots (*ibid* 86a) he weaves one story which aims to prove that, whenever God disputes a matter of law with the earthly courts, the latter prevail. Where the

59. Agobard, ibid., col. 87B. See also G. Scholem, *Major Trends in Jewish Mysticism* (New York, 1946), p. 63, n. 82; Scholem also showed that already Origenes knew some early forms of speculative *midrashim* of the kind known to Agobard; and that he distinguished (unlike Agobard) between them and the δευτερωσεῖς: Scholem, *Jewish Gnosticism, Merkabah Mysticism and Talmudic Tradition* (New York, 1960), p. 38; Origenes, *Prologus in Canticum*, Migne, PG 13, col. 63.

60. Amulo of Lyon, *Liber contra Judaeos*, Migne, PL 116, col. 145; cf. below n. 75. The same passage can also be found in the anonymous treatise ap. Martene Durand, *Thesaurus Anecdotae* III, 1507 ff., mentioned in Williams, *Adversus Judaeos*, p. 396. Similar formulations can be found in Petrus Alfunsi and others.

61. S. Lieberman, *Sheki'in*, pp. 27 ff., esp. p. 33 against Williams, ibid., pp. 384 ff.

death-angel is said to have been "unable to approach Rabba bar Nah-
mani, because his mouth did not cease learning" (*lo hava matsi lemikrav
ley midelo hava ka psik pumey migirsa*), Peter adds, "reading the scriptures
of the Talmud mentioned above, which the Jews say to be so sacred,
that no one can die while reading it."[62] Where God "smiled and said:
my sons won a victory over me" (*chiyekh ve'amar nitsachuni banay*) Peter
brings the following translation: "Then God, blushing somewhat, and
not daring to contradict the testimony of such men, said smilingly
NAZA HUMI BANAI, that is my sons won a victory over me."[63] Of
course, he omits the voice from heaven (*bat kol*) and the hermeneutical
principle "it [the law] is not in heaven" (*lo bashamayyim hi*)—the *Torah*
was given to humans so that they be responsible for interpreting and
applying it. His aim is to construct a conflict between the talmudic
sages and the divine law, a conflict of which they were clearly conscious.
Since the cessation of prophecy, Jews are engaged in the production of
new canonical writings utterly alien to the Old Testament. These writings are kept secret so that their satanic nature remains likewise hidden,
but they are meant to compete with the Scriptures and to suppress
them: "You have fought for so long a time against the divine books
with diabolical books."[64] These were new accusations, never before
raised by Jerome, Augustine, or even Agobard, and certainly not by
Alfunsi. The Talmud is the satanic secret of the Jews: Peter the Venerable took present Judaism out of the framework of the Church doctrine
of conditional tolerance because, as he thought, Jews did change and
hold today to the Old Testament only outwardly. Their purpose is
throughout destructive.

In this context one ought to place two other elements of his polemics. He was, of course, also interested in instances of Jewish defamation
of Christianity, but he ties them again to the Talmud. Lieberman, has
shown that Peter appropriated his story of the ascendance to heaven of
Rabbi Jehoshua bar Levi from the book known as *Alphabeta deben Sira*.
Again, Peter's alterations reveal his purpose. The hero asks his accom-
panying angel upon his way to visit Hell:

62. Petrus Venerabilis, *Adversus Judeaos*, Migne, PL 189, col. 607 ff.: Legentem Talmuth supradictam scilicet scripturam, quam Judaei adeo sanctam dicunt ut nemo, dum
eam legerit, mori possit.

63. Ibid.: Tunc deus aliquantulum erubescencs et contra testimonium tanti viri nihil
dicere audens sic Judaeis secum disputantibus alluendo respondit: NAZA HUMI BE-
NAI, id est vincerunt me filii mei. That he left the Hebrew words show how important
they were to him.

64. Ibid., col. 648 ff.: Pugnasti tanto tempore contra divinos libros diabolicis libris.

Why are the Christians damned? Said he: Don't you know? He answered: I do, but I would to hear it from you. Said he: because they believe in the son of Maria, and do not observe the law of Moses, and chiefly *because they do not believe in the Talmud*.[65]

There is a certain symmetry between this alleged Jewish contention that Christianity's main fault is its failure to recognize the Talmud and the Christian contention that Judaism ought to recognize the New Testament. Implicitly, Peter sees in the Talmud a Jewish, man-made equivalent to the New Testament—a different *nova lex,* and therefore a heresy even in terms of Judaism proper.[66]

On another front, Peter the Venerable—more like Alfunsi and more so—was engaged in polemics against the Koran and in the endeavors to convert Moslems to Christianity. He may have initiated the translation of the Koran; he wrote the first systematic critique of it in the West.[67] In view of the chances of a successful mission, Peter objected to a second crusade and drew instead the attention of the crusaders to "the Jews who are much worse than the Saracens, desecrating contumaciously the name of the savior and everything sacred to the Christians in public . . . and they do not live far from us, but among us."[68] The language is reminiscent of that of the "popular" crusaders in 1096.

---

65. Ibid., col. 636: "Cur Christiani damnati sunt? Ait: tu nescis? respondit: scio, sed a te audire desidero. Ait: Quia credunt in filium Mariae, et non observant legem Moysi, et maxime quia non credunt Talmut." On the source, cf. Lieberman, *Sheki'in,* pp. 31 ff. In the original anecdote we read: "And in that house are ten nations of the nations of the world (מאומות העולם). . . . And one nation says to the other: if we sinned because we failed to accept the *Torah,* what is your sin? They answered: We, too, are like you": A. Jellineck (ed.), *Beth hamidrash* II, p. 50. Here or elsewhere there is no specific mention of the Talmud or even the oral law.

66. Since its publication (1968), my thesis of radical change in Christian polemics—the accusation that Judaism became heretical even on its own premises—has more often than not been accepted. See, e.g., Benjamin Z. Kedar, "Canon Law and the Burning of the Talmud," *Bulletin of Medieval Canon Law,* NS 9 (1979): pp. 79–82. Some modified it, as e.g., J. Cohen, *The Friars and the Jews: The Evolution of Medieval Anti-Judaism* (Ithaca and London, 1982), esp. pp. 51 ff., 129 ff., who concurs in the evaluation of the nature of the change but places it a hundred years later. That the thirteenth century saw the practical consequences of the change was also my contention; it still seems clear to me that Peter the Venerable exhibits the first signs of that change.

67. P. Kritzeck, *Peter the Venerable and Islam* (Princeton, 1964).

68. *Epistulae Petri Venerabilis,* RHFG 15, pp. 641–43; J. Prawer, *A History of the Crusaders Kingdom* (Hebrew) (Jerusalem, 1963) I, p. 226; Prawer shows that objection to the crusade, tolerance towards Moslems (as a missionary target), intolerance towards Jews, belong into one agenda. It was the less irenic aspect of that notorious peacemaker. See now also Gavin I. Langmuir, *Towards A Definition of Antisemitism* (Berkeley-Los Angeles, 1990), pp. 197–208, esp. 201 ff.

Such is the context in which we ought to place the Cluniacenic allegation—which may have grown out of Alfunsi's story about Mohammed's Jewish helpers—that the Jews made Mohammed into a heretic *with the aid of the Talmud*.[69] In short: the new polemical stand of Peter the Venerable carried a strong potential for the erosion of the hitherto existing *modus vivendi* between tolerating Christianity and tolerated Judaism. On a lower, more popular level of discourse, the new attitude found its expression in the first blood libels—very close to Peter's time. Their beginning, much as the allegations against the Talmud in the twelfth century, were not as dangerous as they became later, when they eroded the very physical basis of Jewish existence. While the unequivocal curial stand against them barred blood libels from the subsequent trials against the Talmud, they reflect nonetheless the same tendency to alienate and demonize the image of Jews and Judaism. Underlying the blood libels was likewise the perception that Jews hold to esoteric, satanic traditions beside their exoteric traditions. Thomas of Monmouth, to validate the accusations at Norwich, marshals the testimony of the apostate Theobald: "he told us sincerely that in the ancient writing of their fathers it is stipulated that the Jews can not regain freedom and return to their land without shedding human blood."[70] Thomas continues to describe periodic clandestine rabbinical synods which determine the community whose turn it is to shed Christian blood. His account, he says, is authenticated by the circumstance that a convert revealed to him "the secrets of the enemy."

The twelfth century thus revived the classical pagan polemical tradition that accused Judaism of "misanthropy" (*odium humani generis*), of "secrecy" (*arcana*).[71] Christian apologists, who regarded these traditions as part of their own, were bound to exchange the accusation of secrecy with the claim that the Jews misunderstood their own traditions. Now the classical suspicions of conspiracy and secrecy were revived—and this, too, was an aspect of the "renaissance of the twelfth century."

How efficacious were the allegations against the postbiblical Jewish

69. See N. Daniel, *Islam and the West: The Making of an Image* (Edinburgh, 1960), pp. 62, 84–85, 188 ff.

70. Thomas of Monmouth, *De vita et passione Sancti Wilhelmi Martyris Norwicensis* II, 9, ed. A. Jessop and M. R. James (Cambridge, 1896), p. 93: referebat quidem in antiquis patrum suorum scriptis [!] haberi Iudeos sine sanguinis humani effusione nec libertatem adispisci nec ad patrios fines quandoque regredi. See also Langmuir, *Antisemitism* pp. 209–236 (Thomas of Monmouth).

71. Cf. above, pp. 36–38.

literature? They led, in the thirteenth century, to the trial, confiscation, and burning of the Talmud in France. It has been customary to identify the accusation of blasphemy as the main driving force in these persecutions—perhaps because they became prevalent later.[72] Yet the collection of materials for the trial,[73] as well as the letters of Gregory IX and Innocent IV,[74] show clearly that the "authority" of the Talmud, replacing that of the Bible, as well as its function as a "new law" (*nova lex*) were the primary concerns then.

While charges against the Talmud were not to cease down to the age of counterreformation, their grounds shifted. The accusation of heresy was mostly abandoned. But why? Why did censors and theologians assiduously collect instances of possible defamation of Christianity if they had at their hand a much better, much more fundamental charge? We can but speculate. Perhaps it became clear to the Church that if at all it wishes to tolerate Jews, however conditionally, they must be permitted "to live according to their own laws" (*secundum legem suam vivere* was the standing phrase in all privileges granted to Jews). Or again, it may also be that accusing Jews of heresy on account of the Talmud was dangerous from the Church's own vantage point. Had the Church insisted that Jews must stick to "Scriptures only," that oral traditions

---

72. S. Dubnow, *World History of the Jewish People* (Hebrew trans.: Tel Aviv, 1958) V, p. 21 (defamation of Christianity); I. Baer, "Lebikoret havikuchim shel rabbi Yechiel mi-Paris veshel ha-Ramban," *Tarbitz* 2 (1931): pp. 172 ff.; J. Rosenthal, "The Talmud on Trial: The Disputation at Paris in the Year 1240," *JQR* 47 (1956–57): pp. 58 ff., 145 ff. (emphasizes the role of Karaism in the trial); S. Grayzel, *The Church and the Jews in the XIIIth Century* (Philadelphia, 1933), pp. 250 ff.; B. Z. Dinur, *Yisrael Bagola* II, 2 (Jerusalem, 1967), pp. 507 ff., 521 ff. (Dinur is right in assuming that defamation was not the only charge against the Talmud, but he did not try to assess the role and function of the various charges); Urbach, *Ba'ale hatossafot*, pp. 371 ff; Baron, *Social and Religious History* IX, pp. 62 ff. (recognized the charge of heresy, pp. 64 ff.). J. Katz, *Exclusiveness and Tolerance*, pp. 106–133; Silver (above n. 8); and below n. 73 (Kedar). The Hebrew version of the disputation—R. Jechiel's account—while starting with the charge of blasphemy, soon continues with echoes of the disputation over the authority of the Talmud; *Vikuach Rabbi Yechiel* (Thorn, 1873): ״ויקם החסיל המין הכסיל וישׁאל: . . . . : האתה מאמין בן[!]ארבעה אלה? ויען יועץ הפלא, אני מאמין לכל החוקים והמשפטים הכתובים בהם . . . ונקרא תלמוד ע״ש מקרא ולימדתם את בניכם . . .״

73. Bibliothèque Nationale Ms. lat. 16558, starts with the alleged *auctoritas* that the Talmud has among the Jews. The elaboration of this accusation, as well as the absurdity of talmudic legends, occupies a much greater role in this compilation of talmudic materials—the basis for the trial—than the accusation of blasphemy. See also H. Merchavja, *Hatalmud bire'i hanatsrut* (Jerusalem, 1970), pp. 259 ff.

74. Grayzel, ibid., p. 240, n. 96; p. 250, n. 104. On the reflection in canon law see B. Z. Kedar, "Canon Law and the Burning of the Talmud," *Bulletin of Medieval Canon Law*, NS 9 (1979): pp. 79–82.

distort Scriptures, then the Church would have taken a stand that, in the context of its internal struggles, was the trademark of heretical sectarians, of Wycliffians, Hussites, and Protestants. I do not claim that the Church was always shy to contradict itself, yet raising consciously the principle *sola scriptura* may have constituted a taboo in any context.

POLEMICS AIDED BY THE TALMUD

The third polemical pattern, I said, was the employment of the Talmud (or of Jewish oral traditions in general) to corroborate Christian arguments, to demonstrate that already the Jewish sages of antiquity recognized, however obliquely, the messianity of Jesus and the details of the dogma. The public disputation in Barcelona (1263) already abounded with such arguments, which were then systematized in Raymundus Martini's famous *Sword of Faith* (*Pugio fidei*), a book that became a major sourcebook for anti-Jewish treatises. I added that I can demonstrate the beginning also of this mode of polemics in the twelfth century—a mode that led eventually to a distinction between authentic and inauthentic, valuable and pernicious Jewish traditions.

Indirect, vague knowledge of Jewish messianic traditions can be found in the Latin literature throughout the early Middle Ages.[75] But the first instance of an actual quotation from the Talmud (or the *midrash*) as a prooftext for Christian tenets of faith—or, rather, as a prooftext for the implicit Jewish acceptance of their veracity—occurred in the treatise against heretics of Alanus ab Insulis. The passage, hitherto overlooked, says:

We see among Jews that, in the main part, everything pertaining to the law has ceased: there is no sacrifice among Jews. . . . The law has mainly been abolished. We see, therefore, that the law has no place. In *Sehale* Elija also says, that the world will endure for six thousand years, and two thousand years were emptiness, which refers to the time before the Mosaic law; two thousand years of the Mosaic law, and the following two, of the Messiah. But it is apparent that more than four thousand years have passed. Therefore it is clear that the law has passed and that the Messiah has come.[76]

75. In the seventh century, Julian of Toledo wrote his *De comprobatione aetate sexta* to refute Jewish apocalyptic calculations, but he does not seem to have known the traditions attacked by him from first hand. In the ninth century, Amulo of Lyons (above n. 60) knows of the Jewish tradition of two Messiahs, son of David and son of Ephraim. Cf. Blumenkranz, *Les Auteurs*, pp. 124 n. 39; 197; Williams, *Adversus Iudaeos*, pp. 358 ff.

76. Alanus ab Insulis, *De fide catholica contra haereticos libri quatuor* IV, 3, Migne, PL 210, col. 410: *Videmus etiam apud Iudaeos in magna parte cessare quae ad legem pertinent:*

Alanus recombines here two traditions that indeed may have had once a common origin but then drifted apart: Jewish apocalyptic traditions based on the realization of a metaphor in Psalms 90:4 (for a thousand years in your eyes are as a day that passes) and a parallel between the days of creation and the duration of the old *aeon* on the one hand, and the Pauline division of times before the law, under the law, under grace (*ante legem, sub lege, sub gratia*).[77] Needless to say, Alanus does not quote the addition that follows the passage just quoted in the original—"and because of our sins however many of them have already passed." Alanus's reference to "Sehale" is odd. It may be a metathesis of the Hebrew *chasal*,[78] the anagram for "our sages of blessed memory," in which case his source was probably hearsay.

Distinguishing genuine and valuable from worthless and offensive traditions within the Jewish literature became, after the thirteenth century, a standing practice. It reflects the growing knowledge of Jewish sources among a small group of scholastics, and later among a somewhat larger group of humanists. The distinction is certainly already noticeable in Martini's *Pugio fidei*.[79] While rejecting talmudic law and lore no less vehemently than Peter the Venerable,[80] he also uses talmudic prooftexts as authentic eschatological-christological tradition.[81] His thorough erudition makes it difficult to decide whether some of them

---

non enim est apud Judaeos sacrificium. . . . In maxima parte abolita est lex. Videtur ergo quod lex locum non habeat. In Sehale etiam loquitur Elias, quod mundus durraturus est per six milia annorum, et duo milia fuisse vanitatis, quod refertur ad tempus quod fuit ante legem Mosaicam; duo vero milia legis Mosaicae, sequentia duo milia, Missiae. Sed manifestum est plus quam quattuor annorum milia transiisse, ergo manifestum est legem transiisse, et Messiam venisse. I wonder why Merchavja, *The Talmud*, p. 128, notes that I have been "the last" to discuss the passage; as best I know I first found it. For later polemical usages cf., e.g., Shlomo Ibn Verga, *Shevet Yehuda*, ed. M. Wiener (Hannover, 1924), p. 70.

77. See above, p. 77.

78. Another less plausible explanation is the contraction of the name of the treatise (Sanhedrin) and of the chapter (Chelek): I still prefer my other reading, though Merchavja, ibid., mentions only this one.

79. Raymundus Martini, *Pugio fidei adversus Mauros et Judaeos* (Lipsia, 1687), Praem. p. 3.

80. Ibid. III, 12 p. 931. See J. Cohen, *The Friars and the Jews*, p. 51 ff., 129 ff., while agreeing with me about the nature of Martini's polemics, disagrees in that he sees no anticipation of it in the twelfth century; cf above n. 66. What the book lacks is a thorough comparison of the Talmud trial with other "Lehrprozess" of the thirteenth century. Cf. J. Miethke, "Papst, Ortsbischof und Universität in den Parisent Theologenprozessen des 13ten Jahrhundert," *Miscellanea Medievalia* 10 (1978), pp. 52–94.

81. And at times even illustrates general philosophical principles with rabbinical dicta, e.g., I, 12 p. 246 (human and divine cognition).

are genuine lost midrashim or the product of his creative invention. To some humanists and Renaissance Neoplatonists, the Jewish *kabbala* appeared as such an authentic tradition, a veritable *pristina philosophia,* in contradistinction to the Talmud. Reuchlin used the passage quoted by Alanus—now known as the *vaticinium Eliae*—alongside with other, similar midrashim to defend the preservation of the Talmud against Pfefferkorn.[82] This particular tradition enjoyed a modest popularity in the sixteenth century: Melancthon quoted it approvingly; Jean Bodin made it a basis for historical periodization.[83]

Perhaps there was less danger in this line of argument than in the outright condemnation of the entire postbiblical Jewish literature. But the Christian differentiation between authentic and inauthentic, permissible and impermissible Jewish tradition meant much more than the nuisance of censorship. No longer could a Jewish intellectual feel safe at home, free from the scrutiny of aliens, while engaged in his own tradition. He had to put up with the situation of "being seen."

THE DIALECTICS OF POLEMICS
AND INFLUENCE

The general trend of the later medieval Christian polemics, we said, was that of increasing isolation and alienation. While in the early Middle Ages the Jewish religion appeared at best as an anachronism, in the later Middle Ages the image is rather that of a closed, secret, destructive and diabolical religion. This process went hand in hand with the geographic, social, and economic marginalization of the Jews in Western Europe. The founders of the *Wissenschaft vom Judentum* in the nineteenth century, imbued with the pedagogical ethos of the Enlightenment,[84] believe that information and knowledge about the Jewish culture will of itself remove prejudices. The course of late medieval history teaches an opposite lesson. The growing alienation of Jews in Western Europe happened in spite of the circumstance—if not because of it—that intellectual links between Jews and Christians were almost nonexistent in the early Middle Ages and grew rapidly from the twelfth century onward, and so also did the knowledge of each other.

---

82. Johanus Reuchlin, *Augenspiegel* (Tübingen, 1511), Ratschlag, etc. pp. VII*b* ff.

83. Jean Bodin, *Methodus ad facilem historiarum cognitionem* V (Strassburg, 1907), pp. 108–109, 120. Melancthon: A. Klempt, *Die Säkularisierung der universalhistorischen Auffassung* (Gottingen, 1960), pp. 67–68.

84. See below, pp. 234–238.

As for religious polemics, it changed in quantity and quality alike. It became rationalized. It shows a growing knowledge of the adversary's culture and letters. Of the Christian polemics we saw some examples above. As to the Jewish polemical literature, the *Sefer milchamot hashem* of Jacob ben Reuben is a good example. It was the first thorough critical examination of the New Testament—an immanent analysis in its first eleven chapters, a philosophical refutation in the last chapter. Nor was the intellectual exchange confined to polemics; a growing body of evidence points at more and more instances of mutual influence and parallel cultural movements.

Yet these growing contacts did not increase mutual understanding or tolerance. To the measure to which the similarity between Christian and Jewish patterns of thought grew, so did all the subjective hiatuses between them. If we judge common notions and modes of thought to be evidence of a shared language or cultural idiom, we ought to add that this *common language* served to express *contradictory propositions*. Therefore I find the distinction between altercation and influence highly mechanical. It does not reflect the dialectical reality in which there was no polemics without reception and seldom a reception without a polemical twist. The polemical situation forced of itself the reception and internalization of some of the alien points of view. "Them you answered evasively; but what do you answer us?" asked already R. Simlai's disciples when they listened to his answer to heretics. A telling example of this inner dependence between polemics and reception is Abraham bar Chiyya's speculative doctrine of history. It is well known that he employed the Augustinian allegorical parallelization of the days of creation and the period of history—much as Nachmanides and Abrabanel after him.[85] Bar Chiyya also accepted from Augustine the doctrine of original sin in its strictest predestination sense, and it seems to me that his subjective notion of time is likewise Augustinian:[86] Bar Chiyya uses it to prove the finitude of time through its dependence on thought. The age also saw the revival of speculative historical doctrines in Western Europe. While accepting such doctrines, bar Chiyya uses them against their original intention in a clearly polemical vein. The validity

85. See above, pp. 115–117.
86. M. Wachsman, "Hamachshava hafilosofit hadatit shel Abraham bar Chiyya hanassi," in *H. A. Wolfson Jubilee Volume* (Jerusalem, 1965), argued for the originality of bar Chiyya's notion of time. On the Augustinian notion of time see, e.g., G. Ladner, *The idea of Reform*, 2nd ed. (New York, 1967), pp. 203 ff. On the developments of the notion of time in later antiquity: S. Sambursky, "The Notion of Time in the Late Neoplatonic School," *Proceedings of the Israel Academy of Sciences* II, 8 (Jerusalem, 1967).

of the doctrine of original sin he confines to the "nations of the world" only: Israel is exempt from it. The Augustinian periodization serves him to refute christological doctrines: the Messiah to come, not Christ, is Adam's *impletio figurae*.[87] This was not merely a polemical technique. It can be compared, rather, to the patristic *eversio,* which refuted Gnostic and Manichaean doctrines by transforming them.[88] It was a real acceptance and therefore a polemical one. The same dialectics is also evident in Rashi's appropriation of the Christian interpretations of the "suffering servant" in Isaiah 53: all of Israel is the servant of God, suffering vicariously to expiate the sins of the nations of the world.[89] And perhaps one can argue for traces of this dialectics even in Jehuda Halevi's above-mentioned doctrine of the divine logos (*al'amer al-illahi*). He contrasted it with the Christian doctrine in which only the Messiah is the son of God and incarnate logos (which is the first instance in the *Kuzzari* in which the term appears). The Jewish understanding of God's *logos* is rather such that it pertains to all of Israel, for all children of Israel are "sons of God."[90]

The Jewish image of Christianity likewise underwent considerable changes. From the twelfth century onwards, the legal and philosophical classification of Christianity as a monotheistic religion prevailed. But the gap between the normative position and the popular sentiment was considerable. A semantics of despicatory substitution for any and every sacred matter in Christianity was developed. At the same time, as we saw and will see further, Christianity also had its fascination.[91] The gap between the popular and normative position was greater among Jews than in the Christian polemics, for the latter grew more aggressive

---

87. Abraham bar Chiyya, *Sefer megillat hamegalle,* ed. Poznanski (Berlin, 1924), pp. 39 ff. and above pp. 115 ff. See chapter 4, "History and Typology." On the dialectics of reception and polemics in bar Chiyya and Jehuda Halevi see already I. Baer, "Eine judische Messias prophetie auf das Jahr 1186 und der erste kreuzzug," *MGWJ* 70 (1926), pp. 113 ff., 120 n. 1; idem, *The History of the Jews in Christian Spain* (Hebrew), pp. 39 ff.

88. Funkenstein, *Heilsplan,* p. 140, n. 84 (Irenaeus), p. 36 (Augustine).

89. H. H. Ben-Sasson, *Perakim betoldot hayehudim biyme habeynayim* (Tel Aviv, 1962), p. 258; and Rashi *ad locum.* Cf. also Funkenstein, *Styles in Medieval Jewish Exegesis* (Tel Aviv, 1990), p. 26.

90. Jehuda Halevi, *Kuzzari* I, 4; and, in contrast, I, 95: While for Christians the Savior is the son of God, נאמין בו ובשכנו בתוך בני ישראל לכבוד להם כאשר היה הענין האלהי נדבך בהם the *chaver* shows the adhesion of the *'inyan elohi* in single persons since Adam "וכבר נקרא אצלנו בן אלהים וכל הדומה לו מזרעו—בני אלהים." The polemical intent is clear. To the origin of the notion see Guttmann, *Philosophies of Judaism,* p. 386, n. 353 and H. Davidson, "The Active Intellect in the *Kuzzari* and Halevi's Theory of Causality," *REJ* 131 (1972), pp. 351–96.

91. See above, p. 171 n. 6.

while the former grew more apologetic. Already Raymundus Martini understood well that the growing contacts between the religions resulted in a growing acrimony of their confrontation: "for no foe of the Christian faith is more familiar to us, no one more inevitable than the Jews."[92]

Responses to Adversity

THE CONTINUITY OF ADVERSITY

Modern Jewish historiography has sometimes taken adversity against Jews almost for granted, as if it were a constant, continuous fact of Jewish existence always and nearly everywhere. In a famous article in the *Realenzyklopedie der Altertumswissenschaften,* Isaak Heinemann spoke of "ancient anti-Semitism"—as if, in essence, animosity is one, and only its outer guises changed through the ages.[93] Only recently have we learned to question this alleged continuity and ubiquity without falling back into an absolute denial of the phenomenon, without reducing it to momentary socioeconomic constellations. There is no continuity, we shall argue later,[94] between the pagan and the Christian anti-Jewish propaganda. Christianity was, without doubt, the single most important factor in the conservation of anti-Judaism in Europe; still, it took different, at times discontinuous forms. It was different before and after the twelfth century. It changed radically again with the Reformation.[95] It changed again—in substance, not only in insignificant predicates—with its secularization. And finally, the transition from verbal adversity to systematic extermination could neither have been predicted nor even remotely anticipated.[96]

Hatred towards Jews was and is neither ubiquitous nor continuous. The myth of its inevitability was, however, not a modern-day construct, nor even a medieval one. It was a powerful element in the traditional Jewish self-perception since antiquity. Jews thought of themselves as

---

92. Raymundus Martini, *Pugio fidei* Proem, p. 2: "Nullus autem inimicus Christianae fidei magis fit familiaris, magisque nobis inevitabilis quam Judaeus."

93. Isaak Heinemann, "Antiker Antisemitismus," in Pauli-Wissowa, RE V, col. 389–416.

94. See below, pp. 307–309.

95. See note above.

96. See Shulamit Volkow, *Jüdisches Leben und Antisemitismus im 19ten und 20ten Jahrhundert* (München, 1990), pp. 54–75.

bound to be hated almost by necessity because of their preferred status before God.

CHOSENNESS AND ADVERSITY

The biblical story of Jacob and Esau is a story about the right of primogeniture, the *bekhora*. That Jacob gained it is so much against the sanctioned order of things that it is explained in three complementary ways—as a divine prediction to Rebecca, as a legal transfer in a moment of weakness, as a ruse to obtain Isaac's blessing (Gen. 25:23; 25:31–33; 27:1–41). Already the biblical story speaks of "nations" (*le'umim*) of which Jacob (Israel) and Esau are the eponyms. The Jewish tradition extended Esau to stand for Rome, later for Christianity.[97] When so understood, the discrepancy between promise and reality became oppressively evident, for Esau-Edom rules the world. The Jerusalemian translation, therefore, construed the divine prediction as a conditional one: "and the senior will serve the junior if the law's commandments are watched by the junior" (*im begoy ze'ira natrin pikudayya de'orayta*). And where the Bible narrates that "Esau hated Jacob for the blessing with which he was blessed by his father" (Gen. 27:40) the *midrash* states as an atemporal fact that Esau always hates Israel.[98] The chosenness of Israel is the continuous, constant cause for the adversity of the nations.

To the medieval observer, the link between adversity and chosenness seemed so evident that it needed no further explication. Not self-evident at all, however, was the fact that the choice of Israel was latent rather than manifest, that the Jews were at the mercy of the lesser nations. The discrepancy between the certainty of being God's chosen people and the present humiliation in exile and dispersion called for an explanation, all the more so in the Christian environment in which the Church claimed that with the first coming of Christ, the choice of God has been transferred from "Israel in the flesh" ($\kappa\alpha\tau\grave{\alpha}$ $\sigma\acute{\alpha}\rho\kappa\alpha$) to "Israel in the spirit" ($\kappa\alpha\tau\grave{\alpha}$ $\pi\nu\epsilon\hat{\upsilon}\mu\alpha$).[99] The Church, not Israel, was prefigured

---

97. G. Cohen, "Esau as Symbol in Medieval Jewish Thought," in *Jewish Medieval and Renaissance Studies,* ed. A. Altmann (Cambridge, Mass., 1967). So strong was the tendency to typify the story even more than the text does that Onkelos renders the characterization of Jacob, יושב אהלים־משמש בית אולפנא.

98. הלכה בידוע שעשיו שונא ליעקב: *Sifre to Numeri* 9:10.

99. See recently David Rokéah, "Early Christian-Jewish Polemics on Divine Election," in *Chosen People, Elect Nation and Universal Mission* (Hebrew), ed. Shmuel Almog and Michael Heyd (Jerusalem, 1991), pp. 71–98.

by Jacob, Israel by Esau. Of all the allegations and demonstrations against Jews and Judaism, this was the most painful to listen to and the most difficult to refute. Four main types of answers, of historical theodicies, were advanced by Jews as a response to inner and outer questions of the meaning of their exile (*galut*) of uncertain duration.[100] I shall call them, in turn, (i) the cathartic, (ii) the missionary, (iii) the soteriologic, and (iv) the sacrificial answer.

THE THEODICIES

The oldest, and always dominant, rationale for being in dispersion was the cathartic rationale: "because of our sins we were exiled from our land." The later prophets already reiterated it time and again; it found its way into the liturgy. Exile, then, is a process of expiation and purification. Now the sins of Israel and Judah in biblical times were easy to count, they were anchored in the text: idolatry, syncretism, deviation from the law, injustice. What, though, were the sins warranting the destruction of the Second Temple? The rabbinical tradition was at a loss to name one decisive transgression that could be agreed on by all. More often than not it named futile (internal) hatred (*sine'at chinam*), social injustice or even lack of leadership. Some of these stories tell of accidental, avoidable causes rather than of sins, such as the famous story of the enemies Kamtsa and Bar-kamtsa. One was invited accidently to the banquet of the other and expelled in public, denounced his fellow Jews to the Emperor as rebellious and urged him to test their fidelity with a sacrifice, and mutilated the sacrifical animal so that it could not be accepted. This highly stylized legend ends with the moralité: "the modesty (*'anvetanuto*) of Rabbi Zecharia ben Avkulas destroyed our city, burnt our Temple, exiled us from our land."[101]

100. I. Baer, *Galut* (Berlin, 1934); A. Eisen, *Galut* (Bloomington and Indianapolis, 1986, mainly on recent Jewish thought). A more detailed classification of responses is in Shalom Rosenberg, "Land and Exile in Sixteenth Century Jewish Thought," in *The Land of Israel in Medieval Jewish Thought* (Hebrew), ed. Moshe Challamish and Aviezer Ravitzky (Jerusalem, 1991), pp. 166–192, esp. 169–83.

101. B. T. *Gittin* 55*b*–57*a*. Of the three stories in this famous cycle—"אקמצא" ובר קמצא חריב ירושלים"; "אתרנגול ותרנגולתא חריב טור מלכא"; "אשקא דריספק חריב ביתר"—the first one (on the destruction of Jerusalem) is undoubtedly the richest, and the paradigm of the others. In all of them, a seemingly insignificant incident incites rebellion and destruction. In all of them, the emperor is depicted as rather benevolent, or at any rate not particularly antagonistic to the Jews; it stands in sharp contrast to all other rabbinical stories of the destructions which never fail to curse the wicked Titus or Hadrian (שחיק טמיא). It leads me to believe that the time in which these three stories were

On the lookout for a more substantial collective sin, the rabbis at times focused on Israel's *peccatum originale* as a nation, the sacrifice of the Golden Calf at Mount Sinai. Assuming that all generations past and future were present at this occasion of the true birth of the nation—the giving of the law—each generation had also a share in the sin and had to expiate it by suffering; such, they said, was the meaning of the verse "and in the day I reckoned I shall reckon" (*ubeyom pokdi upakadeti*).[102]

Jacob ben R. Shimeon, the eyewitness and chronicler of the destruction of the Jewish communities of the Rhineland during the First Crusade (1096), used this very rationale to account for the sufferings of his generation. He asked in pain:[103] why did the catastrophe hit this particular community, in a place and time so abundant with exceptionally pious men (*chassidim*)? And he answered: precisely because the generation abounded with pious men it was chosen to take upon itself a larger measure of expiation for the sin of the Golden Calf, thus easing the collective burden to hasten the final redemption. Jewish history so perceived indeed stands outside any ordinary causal chain of events. It is a theater with but two actors—God and his chosen people.

During the sixteenth century, in the Lurianic Kabbala, the catharatic theodicy found its most extreme expression. Israel's exile turned into the symbol and the last stage of a drama within the divine realm, within God himself. God himself undergoes a process of self-purification through self-alienation. The primordial divinity, an infinite, undifferentiated "light" (*or en sof*) harbored a few "roots of sternness" (*shorshey hadinim*), as few as a few grains of sand within a vast ocean. To rid itself of them, a realm of non-divinity, an "empty space" had to be created (*chalal hapanuy*): From a central point within itself, the infinite light contracted itself sideways and an empty space was formed. Into this empty space, a divine light of lesser purity was poured—or, in other versions, remained there after the contraction as a "vestige" (*reshimu*) to form "vessels" or "vehicles" for the divine emancipation. But when the pure divine light penetrated the empty space and filled them, they broke down (*shevirat hakelim*): a catastrophe within God, within the realm of the divine powers (*atsilut*) which are now out of balance. From

---

composed was the only period of *modus vivendi* between the Roman administration and the Jews of Palestine, namely the time of the Severan emperors.

102. B. T. *Sanhedrin* 102*a* (on Exod. 32:34).

103. A. Haberman, *Sefer gezerot ashkenaz vetsorfat* (Jerusalem, 1945), pp. 24 ff.

that moment onwards, the sparks of the divinity held captive by the forces of contamination must be redeemed one by one and returned to their divine origin: it is a slow, accumulative process of "restoration" (*tikkun*) or redemption.[104] Once complete, the divine powers (*sefirot*) will be truly united; their union being then a direct one, "face to face" (rather than, as it is now, "face to back") the divine *élan vitale* will flow uninterruptedly; and the "Shechina will return to the crown of her husband." Redemption will come to Israel, to the cosmos (which exists for the sake of Israel), to God himself.

It was a powerful myth in the original sense of the word—a story about the gods. It places Israel and its redemption within the life, the biography, of God himself as an instrument and symbol at once of the cathartic process—almost deterministic in its evolution—of the divine realm, of God. It may have comforted the generations after the exile from Spain (1492) who yearned for redemption, for finding significance in the momentous events of their present, for radical change.

Side by side with the cathartic theodicy we find, here and there in the classical Jewish literature, a missionary rationale: because of their dispersion, the Jews can and did disperse the knowledge of God among the nations. More often than not, it appeared in a context of close cultural interchange between Jews and their environment, as in Hellenistic Roman Alexandria (Philo) or in Moslem Spain (Jehuda Halevi).[105] It never *replaced* the cathartic theodicy until the liberal theologies of the nineteenth century.

A third type of theodicy—mediating, of sorts, between the other two—may be called soteriologic. Rashi, we saw earlier, interpreted the "suffering servant" in Deuteroisajah as standing for the totality of Israel (rather than for the Messiah); Israel suffers for the sins of the nations of the world. The rejection of the christological reading, we said, went

104. Chayim Vital, *Ets Chayim* (Tel Aviv, 1960) I, p. 27. On the issue see Scholem, *Major Trends*, pp. 244–86; Isaia Tishby, *The Doctrine of Evil and 'Kelippah' in Lurianic Kabbala* (Hebrew) (Jerusalem, 1943), ch. 1; allusions to the (esoteric) doctrine that the roots of sternness were within the primordial deity itself can be found not only in Ibn Tabul but also in Vital, *Ets Chayim* I, p. 28a (ענין הצמצום הזה לגלות שורש הדינים). On earlier views of an impurity within the primordial divine realm (thirteenth century), see Haviva Pedaya, "The Spiritual Versus the Concrete Land of Israel in the Geronese School of Kabbala," in *The Land of Israel in Medieval Jewish Thought*, pp. 233–89.

105. Jehuda Halevi, *Kuzzari* IV, 23. Halevi's positive evaluation of Christianity and Islam as a *praeparatio messianica* turned, in Maimonides, into a negative sort of preparation; see chapter 5, "Contingent Historical Reasons." In the later apologetic literature cf., for example, Yshac Cardoso, *Las Excelencias de los Hebreos* I, 10 (Amsterdam, 1679).

hand in hand with the reception of its premise: vicarious suffering.[106] Finally—without mention of any sin—Maimonides mentions a sacrificial rationale for the *galut:* Israel is a Holocaust, *korban 'ola,* to God.[107] He gave up, one might say, the search for an overwhelming "sin" or for an immanent meaning.

THE TWO REALITIES

Underlying these various rationales for being in exile, exposed to the adversity of jealous and cruel nations, underlying also the expectations for future redemption—be it in the mode of "passive" or "active" messianism, realistic or utopian[108]—we detect a basic, seldom articulated, peculiar and all-pervasive sense of reality. In a precise sense of the word, medieval Jews lived—as orthodox Jews still do—in a world of split realities, an imperfect and a perfect one.

The surrounding world here and now was an imperfect world not because of human shortcomings, wars, and pestilence, but primarily because of the anomalous state of the people of Israel. Being in exile, without the Temple and without sovereignty (judges and leaders), meant being unable to maintain the entire law, to fulfill all commandments. The entire body of the commandments with the institutions pertaining to it was the other reality, always present, well-defined and vivid, albeit parts of it could only be actualized in another place and time. One cannot easily call this other reality "utopian" in any sense given to the term in the history of Europe. It was not in and of itself a hoped for future ideal order imagined by contrast and elimination to elements in the sad present state of affairs. I do not deny that utopian images and expectations enhanced the vision of the complete reality, but they were not its essence—it could be (and was) equally depicted with many of the human wrongs and infirmities still in place.

Of the various biblical terms for divine ordinances—*chukkim, mishpatim, pikkudim, mitsvot*—only the latter prevailed as a generic term for all. It is derived from the verbal root *ts. v. h.* and evokes the image of a king commanding his subjects. The kingdom of God, much as his commandments, was likewise imagined as incomplete in the present reality. True, as the creator of the world God was, is, and will remain king; but only when recognized by all, he "will be king over the whole earth."

106. See above, p. 200.
107. Maimonides, *Iggeret hashemad.*
108. See below, pp. 309–311.

The election of Israel was always imagined as instrumental—dependent on the fulfillment of the commandments, which were very seldom seen as an instrument, but as ends in themselves. The divine commandments were of old imagined as an organism. Each of them was also seen as a real entity, endowed with an ontic status of sorts. It was perhaps this perception that was felt to be most threatened by the instrumental interpretation of the precepts of some medieval philosophers. In this respect the Kabbala, though not less a revolutionary discipline than the philosophical discourse, was much more in tune with prevailing perceptions.

The world in which *all* divine precepts could again be actualized could, of course, be embellished by the utopian fantasy. Its core, however, consisted of an existing, ever present reality—the reality of the commandments themselves: an invisible, yet real, topography, chronology, and order. That Jews lived in both realities needs hardly a proof. Only since the nineteenth century do we find the ongoing effort to reduce both realities into one.

The chosenness of Israel, we said, was never taken for granted or reduced to innate, natural qualities. It was made thoroughly dependent on the acceptance and maintenance of the divine commandment. The imperfect state in which only a part of them could be fulfilled was a rupture in the very order in the world (if not even within the balance of the divine forces themselves). The certainty of redemption was nourished by many sources—prophecy, the "merits of the forefathers" (*zekhut avot*); yet first among them was the perception of the present reality as an incomplete order that does not permit the observance of all ordinances—because "God's inheritance" was invaded by aliens.

My aim is not to deny altogether the presence of utopian elements in the Jewish tradition from the Bible onwards: images of world peace and harmony that could be attached either to the messianic days or to "the world to come." I rather wanted to warn against their exaggeration in the nineteenth and twentieth century, an exaggeration that stemmed from the desire to merge both realities and see the one as a negative mirror image of the other. Genuine utopian ideals were an embellishment, not the core of messianic expectations. The latter could, but again not of necessity, also be the focus of dreams of vengeance or at least compensation.[109] Only in this light can one really understand why

---

109. Haim Hillel Ben Sasson, "Yichud am Yisrael leda'at bene hame'a hashtem esre," *Perakim, The Schocken Institute at the HUC* 2 (1971), pp. 145–218.

Jewish communities in the Diaspora could, on the one hand, perceive their existence as an exile in an alien reality and an alien soul, expect their deliverance daily, easily fall prey to messianic claimants, while, on the other hand, acquiescing with the present state of affairs as long as it was not too oppressive.

History, Apologetics, and Humanism

JEWISH HUMANISM?

A modest revival of Jewish historiography in the sixteenth and seventeenth century coincided with a revival of Jewish apologetic literature, a genre absent from Jewish literature during the Middle Ages. Both genres are linked in more than one way, even while intended for different audiences. Their authors are often seen as "Jewish humanists." While this is, in a sense, true—several Jewish authors of the time can be rightly called Jewish humanists—a Jewish humanism did not exist.

Unlike the Lurianic kabbala, Sabbatianism, Chassidism, the Enlightenment, or the *Tenu'at hamussar*, humanism did not become a Jewish movement, either in an institutional sense or as a well-recognizable family of cognate ideas with which a group of intellectuals could be identified or identify itself. Not even a term for humanists or for their pursuit, the *litera humaniora*, was coined in the Hebrew language of that time. I do not deny the impact of humanism on Jewish letters: the balance of this essay is dedicated to its reexamination. But a movement it was not, not even in Renaissance Italy. The reasons for its absence are primarily sociocultural.

The European humanists tried hard to distance themselves from scholasticism. Nevertheless, humanism and scholastic philosophy shared a common ground. Both were relatively autonomous pursuits, relatively unencumbered by theological demands. The philosophical faculty in medieval universities since the thirteenth century served a preparatory function for those who wished to continue their studies in a higher faculty—theology, medicine, or the law. Nevertheless, the teachers of philosophy or the liberal arts developed a professional pride of their own, pride in their faculty and in its autonomous subject matter. The humanists, too, were committed to the liberal arts (*artes liberales*) even while calling for a pedagogical reform in the ways those were hitherto taught. Many of them were in fact *magistri artium,* determined to purge their discipline of dialectical excesses by returning to the classical. The relative institutional independence of the liberal arts permitted school-men and humanists alike to stake for themselves an intellectual domain that was theologically neutral, even if but few or none of them really espoused the alleged Averroistic doctrine of a "double truth." This, I believe, was the basis for the process which Hans Blumenberg called the "self-assertion" (Selbstbehauptung) of humankind.[110] He saw in it a signature of modernity, but it was no less medieval.

Some humanists, however, developed a distinct ideology to justify this already existing autonomy. Its most radical expression we find in Pico della Mirandola's famous oration on the dignity of man (*De hominis dignitate*). Of all living species, he said, the humankind alone lacks a fixed nature. Being a true microcosm, endowed with the seeds of every kind there is, he can become everything he wills to become:[111]

At last the best of artisans ordained that that creature to whom He had been able to give nothing proper to himself should have joint possession of whatever had been peculiar to each of the different kinds of being. He therefore took man as a creature of indeterminable nature and, assigning him a place in the middle of the world, addressed him thus: "The nature of all other beings is limited and constrained within the bounds of laws prescribed by us. Thou, constrained by no limits, in accordance with thine own free will, shalt ordain for thyself the limits of thy nature . . . thou mayest fashion thyself in whatever shape thou shall prefer. Thou shalt have the power to degenerate into the lower forms of life, which are brutish. Thous shalt have the power . . . to be reborn [*regenerari*][112] into the higher forms, which are divine". . . . It is man who Asclepius of Athens, arguing from his mutability of character and from his self-transforming nature, on just grounds says was symbolized by Proteus in the

110. Hans Blumenberg, *Die Legitimität der Neuzeit* (Frankfurt/Main, 1966), pp. 90 ff., 174 ff., 359 ff. But many of his characteristics can also be attributed to medieval philosophy. For an evaluation of Jewish humanists, at least Azaria de Rossi, similar to mine see Salo W. Baron, *History and Jewish Historians,* pp. 201 ff.

111. Giovanni Pico della Mirandola, *Oratio de hominis dignitate* 3–6, ed. E Garin, *De hominis dignitate, Heptaplus De ente et uno e scritti vari* (Florence, 1946–52). The translation after E. Cassirer, P. O. Kristeller and J. H. Randall, Jr., *The Renaissance Philosophy of Man* (Chicago and London, 1956), pp. 224–27.

112. On Mirandola, his notion of rebirth and its religious and humanistic context, cf. Konrad Burdach, *Reformation, Renaissance, Humanismus. Zwei Abhandlungen über die Grundlage Moderner Bildung und Sprachkunst* (2nd ed., Berlin, 1926, reprint Darmstadt, 1963), p. 168.

mysteries. Hence those metamorphoses renowned among the Hebrews[113] and the Pythagoreans. . . . "Let a certain holy ambition invade our souls, so that, not content with the mediocre, we shall pant after the highest and . . . toil with all our strength to obtain it."

Having no fixed native properties—which is the primary ancient and medieval meaning of both φύσις and *natura*[114]—humans can shape their own nature to become supernatural, divine. A few centuries later, this dialectics of nature to supernature will turn into a dialectics of nature and culture, the latter also being a "second," acquired nature.

I have quoted from Pico's famous passage extensively because it will serve us as a good yardstick to measure what we can, and what we cannot, expect of the Jewish humanists. The question what is "natural" rather than supernatural in the human or Jewish condition and history was indeed very much on their mind, more so than in any medieval sustained reflection. But none of them formulated an ideology of human autonomy. Pico's exaltation of the *prisca theologia* of the ancients—turning the Christian revelation almost redundant—presupposes a cultural-institutional (relative) autonomy of philosophical pursuits mentioned earlier. But neither medieval nor early modern Jewish intellectuals knew such genuinely independent domains of inquiry, independent of religious Jewish concerns. Indeed, most of Jewish medieval philosophical texts are concerned with their own religion and its rational justification. Exceptions prove it. Shlomo ibn Gebirol's *Mekor Chayyim* (*Fons vitae*) disappeared completely from the horizon of Jewish letters not because it voiced heretical or even particularly daring opinions. How much more daring was Gersonides' virtual denial of special providence or the kabbalists' hints that the seeds of evil lay in the primordial divinity! But the *milchamot hashem* survived while the *Fons vitae* did not, because the latter was a purely metaphysical-ontological exercise, without reference to particular Jewish concerns; it does not even bear any hint as to the religious identity of the author.

A sustained Jewish humanistic movement did not develop for the very same reason that no autonomous subculture of pure philosophical

---

113. Only in some kabbalistic traditions. See Gerschom Scholem, *Elements of the Kabbalah and Its Symbolism* (Hebrew, Jerusalem, 1976), pp. 308–57. On Pico's kabbalistic speculations and knowledge see Chaim Wirszubski, *Three Studies in Christian Kabbala* (Jerusalem, 1975).

114. See A. Funkenstein, "The Revival of Aristotle's Nature," in N. Cartright (ed.), *Idealizations and Capacities,* in press.

debate evolved in the medieval Jewish society, nor a sustained interest in the sciences during the scientific revolution. In vain we look for praise of human *curiosity*, though we often find it displayed. Every instance of intellectual activity beyond pure entertainment[115] had to be linked to Jewish religious concerns. Moreover, the Jewish tradition never carried with itself a substantial body of ancient non-Jewish literature that could, in due time, be idealized. It had no *litera humaniora*, a firm basis to glorify the *rerum humanarum eruditio* apart from the *rerum divinarum scientia*.

And yet, some Jews developed a keen interest in the writings of humanists and in the classical literature. They wrote history in a new way. They thought about similar problems in similar modes; in particular, their notion of "human nature," even of "Jewish nature" as shaped by history, bears the mark of encounter with the new world of letters. The Jewish humanist's employment of the term shares all the ambiguities that it exhibits since it became, during the sixteenth century, a much more fluid term than it was before.

JEWISH HISTORIOGRAPHY AND JEWISH "NATURE"

National catastrophes have, since the Peloponnesian Wars, been a mighty incentive for the historical retrospection. The persecution of Jewish communities since the end of the fourteenth century resulted in the disintegration of many of them, in a wave of conversions to Christianity of proportions known never before nor after in Jewish history, followed by the expulsion of Jews from Spain in 1492, followed thereafter by the persecution of *conversos* and the catastrophe of Portuguese Jewry. Spanish Jews had come to love Spain, to view it almost as homeland, far more than Jews did in any other medieval country they lived in. A measure of their bitterness, of the magnitude of the catastrophe in the encoded memory, was the henceforth designation of Spain as "contaminated land" (*adama tme'a*) to which no Jews ought to return.

It stands to reason that, upon reflection, none of the traditional theodicies sufficed to give meaning to the events. The very circumstance

---

115. It is interesting how Ibn Verga, *Shevet Yehuda* (ed. Wiener) saw storytelling—*aggadot*—as a Jewish analogue to instrumental music. On him cf. below.

that the expulsion was not merely a sudden catastrophe—*gezera*—but was preceded by a failure of nerves and the breakdown of leadership called for a specific etiology; that it was a punishment for accumulated sins since the beginning of the nation was too general a formula to explain the exceptional ferocity of recent events. Shlomo ibn Verga, in his "Scepter of Juda,"[116] tried to create a portrait of Spanish Jews as a part of an etiology of their failure. It is not narrative of events in their chronological sequence but an enumeration of catastrophes (*shemad*) and an account of dialogues and disputations woven together.

These dialogues about the fate and fortunes of the Jews are remarkable on several counts. First, most of their participants are not Jews: King Alphonso and his counselor Thomas, a (fictitious) pope and a Jewish apostate. This, as Martin Kohn has shown,[117] is not merely a rhetorical device to safeguard objectivity or impartiality: Ibn Verga tries time and again to portray Jews as they appear to others; he lived, as Sartre would say, in a situation of "être vue," and cared about it, though one may debate to what degree he internalized the point of view of the other. It is the very same impulse which generated, throughout the sixteenth and seventeenth century, an apologetic Jewish literature intended for rulers or for the educated public. Historians and apologists assumed a basic benevolence on the part of the ruling classes towards Jews—be it by virtue of their antiquity (and nobility), be it out of *raison d'état*. They also assumed unbounded hatred on the part of the uneducated masses; those who have never seen Jews, we are told by Eliyahu Capsali, imagine "that he lacked the form of a man."[118]

Second, these dialogues—as many of ibn Verga's positions—are throughout equivocal, often ironic. Irony rather than skepticism is the dominant tone of the book, a kind of basic suspicion of human motives and knowledge of matters divine, a suspicion born out of common sense and experience rather than out of a sustained epistemological argument: the very same "incroyance" which Lucien Febvre described so well at the example of Rabelais. This is how one should read his famous lines, put into the mouth of King Alphonso, that

116. Shlomo Ibn Verga, *Shevet Yehuda*, ed. M. Wiener (Hanover, 1924). About his sources see F. Baer, *Untersuchungen über Quellen und Komposition des Schebet Jehuda* (Berlin, 1923); "He'arot chadashot lesefer shevet yehuda," *Tarbiz* 6 (1933), pp. 152–79, reprint in I. Baer, *Mechkarim* II, pp. 417–52.

117. Martin Kohn, "Jewish Historiography and Jewish Self-Understanding in the Period of Renaissance and Reformation" (Ph.D. diss, UCLA, 1979), pp. 23 ff.

118. Eliyahu Capsali, *Seder Eliyahu Zuta* C.54 (2 vol., Jerusalem, 1975) I, pp. 174–75. Cf. Kohn, "Jewish Historiography," p. 20.

everyone agrees that religious rites [*datot*] do not subsist except by the imagination. The Jew imagines that there is no other religion and no faith but his own, and he who believes in something else is in his eyes like an animal (and I heard that they say, whenever passing our cemeteries, "shame on your mother" etc. [Jer. 50:12]).[119] And the Christian imagines that the Jew is but a human-shaped animal whose soul dwells in the lowest compartment of hell. And should you ask a Moslem he would say of both of us that hell is crowded by us. And in the far islands of the sea there are those who bow before the form an ass and carry on their flag the form of an ass. . . . And when Christians come there they are mocked by saying that we bow before the form of man even if it is the noblest of forms . . . and the God who removed the Jews from all shapes commanded that Cherubim be made in the temple in the form of man.[120]

We are immediately reminded of the then current story of the three impostors.[121] The very same irony is at work when ibn Verga describes "good" kings or,[122] when Alphonso promises Thomas reward in the world to come for his insights, the latter answers "may it [rather] come about that I receive it in this world."[123] Even the name of the book, *Shevet Jehuda,* may be equivocal. It alludes to Genesis 49:10 ("the scepter shall not cease from Juda"), but may also allude to Proverbs 13:24 ("whoever fails to use the stick hates his child"). Viewing afflictions as collective punishment was not a new theme, but the manner in which ibn Verga employed it was.

119. Cf. Ibn Verga, *Sheret Yehuda,* p. 79.

120. Ibid., p. 16. Cf. p. 64 (*po'al hadimyon*). The context of this often-quoted passage is noteworthy. At issue are the dietary laws binding Jews, which Abrabanel, according to Thomas, related to the higher physical status of Jews למעלה ממדרגת האדם, wherefore they need a different diet. Thomas, who elsewhere shows understanding of Jewish rites, becomes angry to the point of "hatred," and is answered by the kind with the above quoted lines. It is, undoubtedly, an implicit argument of ibn Verga against a strand of interpretations that go back to Jehuda Halevi. Placing it in Thomas's mouth would shield ibn Verga from undue criticism. Important in our context is the stress on common, equal share in humanity. Cf. Baer, "He'arot," p. 174; it is, I believe, more than parody, but a dominant theme. On disbelief in general: Lucien Febvre, *Le problème de l'incroyance au xvie siècle: la religion de Rabelais* (Paris, 1968). English translation by B. Gottlieb, *The Problem of Unbelief in the Sixteenth Century* (Cambridge, 1982).

121. The recent monograph of Friedrich Niewöhner, *Veritas sine Varietas: Lessings Toleranzparabel und das Buch Von dess drei Betrügen* (Heidelberg, 1988) is unduly speculative and erratic. On the Western tradition, cf. pp. 251 ff. Cf. Febvre, *The Problem of Unbelief,* pp. 107 ff.

122. See Kohn, "Jewish Historiography," pp. 52 ff., for a well-balanced criticism of Josef Yerushalmi, "The Lisbon Massacre of 1506 and the Royal Image in the Shevet Yehuda," HUCA Supplement (Cincinnati, 1976). Baer, "He'arot chadashot," p. 154, speaks of the abundance of "parabolic joke and religious criticism," which he attributes to the influence of the Italian novel.

123. Ibn Verga, *Shevet Yehuda,* p. 13.

Third, these dialogues pursue—consistently and consciously—the question what, in the sorry condition of Jews, was and is the outcome of "natural cause" (*siba tiv'it*), "the way of nature" (*derech hateva*).[124] The entire Jewish history passes review, but again the verdict is equivocal. To King Alphonso it seemed that the success of the Jews, in their antiquity, was much due to their natural endowments—courage, wisdom, and fecundity. Their failure must therefore be interpreted as a divine, supernatural punishment. To his counselor Thomas—who is, by and large, much better informed about Jewish religious practices and their interpretations—it seems, to the contrary, that Jews were always divine and arrogant; and a small child can still scare a hundred Jews. Their success was a sign of divine favor. While it lasted, Jews trusted it and failed to acquire military prowess, so that, when God "turned his face from them," they found themselves bereft on all counts,[125] and were left to the natural course of the world in which the stronger prevails—which is as true of the physical world as it is of the world of nations.[126] Ibn Verga's concept of "nature," though basically Aristotelian, is already informed by the much more fluid notion of Renaissance philosophers of nature as place of strife and the drive for homogeneity. As for hatred towards Israel, universal factors may be a general rationale, but they are enhanced by the antagonism that Jews generate through their conspicuous display of power and riches.[127] Being queru-

---

124. Ibid., pp. 17, 19, 57 (סדרי העולם והטבע), 79, 95.

125. Ibid., pp. 7–24. Note that the dialogue appears under the heading of "the seventh affliction" (*hashemad ha'shevii*). Neglect of the art of war has already been mentioned by Maimonides as one cause of the loss of sovereignty.

126. Ibid., 79: אמר האפיפיור אין מן הצרות ראיה כי ידוע שאנו מורכבים מארבע יסודות וטבע הפשוטים יש במורכב ומצינו כל יסוד ויסוד בהתגבר מבקש לשאוב חברו ולהפכו לעצמותו כמו שמצינו האש שישרוף כל דבר אם לא ימנעוהו המים . . . וכן בב״ח והעופות והדגים המתגבר בולע את חברו וכן העמים האומה הגוברת מבקשת להפוך האומות האחרות לעצמותה ואלו היה בידי שלא ימשול בעולם אלא אני הייתי שם בזה כל יכולתי וממשלתי וצרת היהודים נמשכת מהתגברות שיש לנו עליהם. while the doctrine of four elements is, of course, Aristotelian and medieval, the idea that there is both strife and a drive for homogeneity fit more into Renaissance philosophies of nature. See Funkenstein, *Theology,* pp. 63–70.

127. Ibid., 11: תשובת טומאש לא ראיתי מעולם בעל שכל שהיה שנאה עם היהודי ואין מי שישנא אותם כי אם כללות העם ויש בזה טעם האחד כי היהודי הוא בעל גאוה ומבקש תמיד המשתרר [להשתרר] ולא יחשבו שהם גולים ועבדים דחופים מגוי אל גוי אבל להפך שיבקשו להראות עצמם אדונים ושרים לכן העם מקנא בהם. ואמר החכם שהשנאה הנמשכת מצד הקנאה אין לה תקנה כל ימי העולם. ויראה אדוננו הנסיון בזה כאשר באו היהודים למלכות אדוננו היו באים כעבדים וגולים לובשי בלויי הסחבות ועמדו שנים רבות שלא לבשו בגד יקר ולא הראו שום התנשאות ובימים ההם האם שמעת אדוננו שהיו מעלילים עליהם אכילת הדם? . . . ועתה היהודי משתרר ואם יש לו מאתיים זהובים מיד לובש בגדי משי ולבניו רקמה מה שלא יעשו השרים אשר . . . להם הכנסת אלף כפולות לשנה. Cf. p. 95 (Ibn Verga's *own* reflection).

lous and proud was, and remained, the characteristics of Jews (*midat hayehudi*).[128] And yet, in explicit contrast to Jewish and non-Jewish allegations of a Jewish nature different even physically from other human beings, Ibn Verga sides with those who assume that all humans have the same share in human nature. And such, mutatis mutandis, was also the claim of Jewish apologists such as Luzzatto: Jews have, and believe others to have, a share in the *commune humanitas*,[129] even though their nature has been "deformed" by oppression and submission.[130]

The dialectics of nature and that which is beyond nature was, then, a leading theme taken from the humanistic discourse—but employed in the context of concrete arguments only, never as an overarching theory that aims to promote the autonomous state of humanity.

HUMANISTIC SCHOLARSHIP

Jewish intellectuals, we said, had no classical religiously neutral *litera humaniora* such as Greek and Latin authors were to the humanists—at least not as a part of their own literature. Inasmuch as they lived also the culture of their environment, in part at least, they also developed a taste and an interest in the classical literature. At times, they made good use of it in their polemical or apologetic arguments, in Hebrew or in the vernacular. The novelty of Azaria de Rossi's "Meor Enayim" was the nonpolemical use he made of the classical literature within the very sanctum of Jewish scholarship: he employed his vast classical erudition mainly for critical purposes—the reexamination of chronology, of aggadic-historical materials, of traditional views of natural matters. He could also reclaim, for Jewish literature, the letter of Aristeas and the forgotten writings of Philo, *Yedidya ha'alexandri*. His intentions have often been discussed, and selected chapters of his book are now available with an excellent, detailed commentary by Reuven Bonfil.[131]

128. Ibid., p. 68: והסכימו כולם שיתחיל דון וידאל בנבנישתי מפני שהיה חכם בחכמות ויודע בטיב לשון לאטין והסכימו ביניהם שלא יהיה עניגם כמידת היהודים המלומדים בישיבותיהם ליכנס כל אחד בדברי חברו ולחרף כאשר לא יודה לו . . .

129. Simone Luzzatto, *Discorso circa il stato degl' Hebrei* (Venice, 1638), p. 52b. See Kohn, "Jewish Historiography," p. 179.

130. Ibid., pp. 152b ff. We remember how Ibn Verga chastised the cowardice of Jews, alongside with their tenacity.

131. Reuven Bonfil (ed.), *Azaria de Rossi, Selected Chapters from Sefer Me'or Einayim and Matsref lakessef* (Jerusalem, 1991). Ibid., pp. 131–33, contains a detailed recent bibliography.

In the limited scope of this essay, I wish to draw attention to but two facets of de Rossi's work. With other Jewish literati of his time, he shares an intense curiosity of things human and natural—to a much higher degree than ever displayed by a medieval author. *Curiositas*, we have learnt from Hans Blumenberg's studies, became a virtue in early modernity.[132] The difference between Jewish and other authors of the time is but a matter of confessing openly their interest in the world surrounding them, including its bizarre, unique creatures or the strange habits of its human inhabitants. Jewish chroniclers still thought it necessary to justify their interest in the history of other nations, even while the impulse for writing was plainly a thirst for information on their part as on the part of their audience. Even narrating their own history required justification.[133] Again, we find both in de Rossi as in other authors lengthy discussion of natural phenomena as if in passing,[134] a genuine sense of amazement and the wish to amaze their readers. But it never becomes systematic or thematic for its own sake. Much attention has recently been given to the Jewish encounter with, or awareness of, the achievements of the scientific revolution.[135] The truth of the matter is that we rather ought to ask why the Jewish participation in it was so minimal and insignificant (in spite of the *Sefer Tuvia,* even in the late eighteenth century the geocentric world-picture was still prevalent among Jewish intellectuals). Perhaps it was because they were remote from some centers of science, such as England and France; but they were present in Holland and Italy. A strong contributing factor was, without doubt, the absence of a sense of the relative autonomy of such

132. Blumenberg, *Die Legitimität der Neuzeit,* pp. 203 ff.

133. Cf. Kohn, "Jewish Historiography," pp. 2 (Zacuto's declared pedagogical and apologetic aims), 42 (Capsali's eschatological lessons), 65 ff. (Josef Hakohen's writing the history of nations as revenge), 126 (Gedalia Ibn Yahya), 140 (David Gans wants to show God's special providence).

134. Even in Ibn Verga, *Shevet Yehuda,* pp. 57 ff. Again, what seemed to Baer as parody reflects rather Renaissance notions (consciously reminiscent of Empedocles) of love and hate as cosmic factors (בהתחלת הבריאה נבראו שמיים וארץ מחומר אחד ולכן הם באהבה כשני אחים מבטן אחד וגו׳). It was the time in which Leone Hebreo wrote his Dialogue on Love. On Telesio cf. my *Theology,* ibid.

135. See, for example, André Neher, "Copernicus in the Hebraic Literature from the Sixteenth to the Eighteenth Century," *Journal for the History of Ideas* 38 (1977), pp. 211–26; id., *David Gans (1541–1613) and His Times,* translated by D. Maisel (Oxford, 1986); B. Goldstein, "The Hebrew Astronomical Tradition: New Sources," *Isis* 72 (1981), pp. 237–51; David B. Ruderman, *Kabbalah, Magic and Science: The Cultural Universe of a Sixteenth-Century Jewish Physician,* Cambridge, 1988).

pursuits as legitimate or even God-willed.[136] And so Azaria, too, sees the necessity to elaborate, at great length, the benefits that will accrue to traditional Jewish learning from alien wisdom.

Nonetheless, underlying many of de Rossi's chronological and textual critical examinations of Jewish traditions was the assumption that in matters other than determining the oral law as God-given, the ancient authorities—*amora'im* or even *tana'im*—could fall prey to honest errors. This is particularly true where the error is a part of a widely shared consensus by ancient Jews and non-Jews alike, at a time in which knowledge from experience was much more limited than it seemed at present. The sphericity of the earth, now a proven fact, was then rather a matter of speculation. Among both Jews and gentiles there were few who argued against the earth being flat.[137] Neither experience nor revelation supported either "hypothesis" at that time. It seems even as if de Rossi assumed the existence, then and now, of a neutral space, a republic of letters in which all erudites have a share and within which all opinions have an equal standing and right to be examined, provided they do not pertain to matters of the written or oral tradition. This had, of course, also been an assumption made by medieval philosophers; but now, it seems, it covered a much wider terrain—opinions, estimates (*umdanot*), even biases. Whether or not Azaria assumed such a religiously neutral space in which reasonable and educated people examined each other's opinions, willing to give up biases, may be debated. It certainly was the assumption of Jewish apologists such as Jehuda de Modena or Simone Luzzatto.[138] Belief in the efficacy of rhetorics, and the demand to create for it a domain of fair play, underlined the humanistic idea of tolerance down to the seventeenth century.[139]

Historical and political writings of the sixteenth and seventeenth centuries are sometimes credited with a larger amount of realism than

136. Robert K. Merton, *Science, Technology and Society in Seventeenth Century England* (New York, 1970). For a discussion of the Merton thesis see Bernard I. Cohen (ed.), *Puritanism and the Rise of Modern Science* (New Brunswick, 1990); John L. Heilbron, "Science in the Church," *Science in Context*, and in the same issue, the essays of Steven J. Harris, Rivka Feldhay and Michael Heyd as well as Merton's answer (pp. 291 ff.).

137. Azaria de Rossi, *Me'or Enayim* (Jerusalem, 1970) I, pp. 160 ff.

138. On him and his arguments from *raison d'état* see Kohn, "Jewish Historiography," pp. 144–86. Of great value is also his analysis of the atomistic psychology of Luzzatto.

139. Gary A. Remer, "Christ as Peitho: Classical Rhetoric and the Humanist Defense of Religious Toleration," Ph.D. diss. (UCLA, 1989).

their medieval counterparts. So are also some Jewish humanists, notably de Rossi. But realism is as elusive a term as the quality it refers to. Otto of Freising's judgments were no less sober than Bodin's or Villani's. Machiavelli's political schemes were much more fantastic than those of Marsilius of Padua. Perhaps one might say that some historians or political thinkers since the Renaissance exhibit a much more profound involvement with the here and now than with the ultimate goals of history; that they are more this-worldly, less shy of consideration of *raison d'état*, less constricted by inherited categories such as the *translatio imperii* among the four monarchies.[140] The Middle Ages found a balance between reason and that which transcends it; this balance was disturbed in the Renaissance, permitting both extreme skepticism or suspicion and utter credulity in the most fantastic stories and schemes, prompting therefore a renewed appeal to common sense, *recta ratio*, practical reason.

Azaria de Rossi's detailed account of the earthquake in Ferrara serves many purposes. It was the occasion at which he learnt of the letter of Aristeas from a Christian scholar. But the extensive description of the quake, and the long enumeration of theories since antiquity that explain the phenomenon in terms of "nature" or wish to see in it a divine portent, allowed de Rossi to draw the conclusion that quakes, while always a natural phenomenon subject to a natural causation, are sometimes a contingent event, sometimes attributable to the special providence of God—except that we are not able to classify any concrete occurrence as being the one or the other.[141] Azaria's protracted critical investigation into the Jewish chronology *ab initio mundi*, introduced as learning for its own sake, has also the function to debunk all "calculations of the end," prevalent at his times as they were earlier. He was committed to common sense.

While we do notice, in de Rossi's writings, not merely a critical attitude toward some veteran traditions but even a modicum of self-assertion of the "moderns" against the "ancients"—of his generation he, too, speaks of dwarfs on the shoulder of giants—we look in vain for traces of the most enduring and significant achievement of humanistic historical thought, namely the clear, articulated realization of which we

---

140. A. Klempt, *Die Säkularisierung der universalhistorischen Auffassung* (Göttingen, 1956); Hans Baron, *The Crisis of the Early Italian Renaissance* (Princeton, 1966), esp. summary, pp. 447 ff. (detheologization).

141. De Rossi, *Me'or Enayim, Kol Elohim*, pp. 187 ff.

spoke earlier that historical events can only be comprehended if one reconstructs the full original context in which they were embedded, a context which endows them with meaning. None of the Jewish humanists had caught up with this novel hermeneutical attitude—most likely because it was an attitude born out of the dialectics of proximity and distance to Greek and Roman literature, art, and law, dialectics of identification and alienation. They were revered as paradigms even while it became ever more evident that they were obsolete. Yet no Jewish scholar could ever say of an ancient Jewish legal institution "Quid hoc edicto praetoris?" The Jewish world of letters had to wait until the nineteenth century to meet conditions that were conducive for a historicizing confrontation with its core traditions.

Most other ingredients of the humanistic movement can be found among some Jewish authors of the sixteenth and seventeenth centuries in one form or another. But these ingredients never coalesced into a conscious, thematic program. These are the reasons that led me to state that, while Jewish humanists then existed, a Jewish humanism did not.

7

The Threshold of Modernity

The Political Theory of Jewish Emancipation

THE JEWISH QUESTION

It is common knowledge that "the Jewish Question" was born in the nineteenth century. It was fathered by the modern, national state, before whose laws all citizens are supposed to be equal. Jews, of course, had caused painful theological problems to their environment earlier; but there was nothing problematic in their political status until the nineteenth century. Throughout antiquity and the Middle Ages they constituted corporations (πολίτευμα, *collegium, universitas*) enjoying better or worse privileges (*libertates*). Very often these privileges included the basic right *secundum legem suam vivere,* to set autonomous courts. No matter, therefore, how "enlightened" or religiously indifferent a medieval Jew may have been, he still could not aspire to obtain equal rights: not because he was discriminated against, but because the very term was outside the medieval political universe of discourse. Equal to whom? The Middle Ages knew only *libertates* and not political *libertas*. The "Freiheit des Christenmenschen" was merely theological. Persons belonged to very different spheres of law according to origin, locality, stand, profession or religious order. Equality before one law was an ideal first conceived under absolutistic regimes, a denominator common to the sovereign and the third estate in their fight against the estates. The ideal began to be concretized with the French Revolution. Then and there the national state needed the emancipation of the Jews no less than the Jews urged for it. By its very raison d'être, the modern national state could not tolerate corporations as a *status in statu*. Since no legal construct could be devised to declare them alien on a soil they often inhabited for longer than the indigenous nation, they could not be naturalized. The emancipation of the Jews could have become a problem only in the nineteenth century.

But why did it become a problem? Nothing in Jewish law really prevents its adjustment to the modern state; it had adjusted before to worse political conditions. Byzantium did not recognize Jewish self-government, the emperor even imposed his judgment over internal religious rules (such as whether the Pentateuch may be used in the vernacular for liturgical purposes). Under such conditions, Jewish law persisted through the inner discipline of the community—*en ponim le'arcka'otehem shel goyyim;* its courts became private arrangements of arbitration. All the easier, it could and did adjust to the modern national state. Indeed, the very legal principle through which Jews recognize the relative validity of "the law of the land"—*dina demalkhuta dina*—also anticipated the modern principle of equality before the law long before its modern career. It distinguishes, as we saw, between *dina demalkhuta* (the law of the kingdom) and *gazlanuta demelekh* (the robbery of a king); the latter is the case if the law is discriminatory, if it does not treat all subjects—even in different provinces (*medinot*)—equally. Theory aside, *historia ipsa docet:* naturalized orthodox Jews live in perfect harmony with the state in America, England, Switzerland. Why, then, a Jewish question?

Because Jews and non-Jews, friend and foe alike, shared a powerful assumption, namely that legal emancipation demands some degree of social and cultural assimilation, and (a compounded confusion) that assimilation will result in social integration. Perhaps Jews cannot change at all and do not merit emancipation? Should emancipation be granted immediately so as to induce change, or should it only be granted after they have assimilated, a prize for good behavior? The confusion between emancipation, assimilation and integration was almost total. Indeed it had profound causes. Two very powerful impulses converged to generate the confusion: one was the almost religious ideology of national homogeneity and loyalty which characterize the nascent national state, the other was the likewise almost religious eagerness of Jews not only to gain civil rights, but to participate creatively in German or French society and be accepted in it. Assimilation was taken for granted in various degrees of consciousness and with various degrees of bad conscience. Few Germans loved German language, culture and political institutions as much as Jews did—a one-sided love that ended catastrophically. The strict orthodoxy was at first even unable to understand this zeal. Why, asks one of the authors of *ele divre haberit*, do you, the Reformers, wish to abolish references to Zion and the Messiah from our prayers? Don't you know that since the destruction of the Temple we are captives of war (*shvuye milchama*) at the hand of princes? It pleased God to make many of them benevolent towards us. They do not demand that we abandon messianic creeds—indeed, they have one of their own—so why then do you, the Reformers, demand what the princes do not demand of us? It did not cross the mind of this rabbi that his assumption was precisely the assumption that the Reformers refused to share: namely that we are captives of war. They wanted to become loyal citizens and were willing to pay that price of assimilation which seemed to them just.

MENDELSSOHN'S "JERUSALEM"

Confused ideas do not make good theories, but the removal of confusion does. The only sound political theories of Jewish emancipation were those which, against the *consensus communis*, argued for the disjunction of emancipation and assimilation. Such theories occurred before, during, and after the acts of emancipation: I mean Mendelssohn's *Jerusalem*, Marx's *Zur Judenfrage* and Herzl's *Judenstaat*; the one an anticipation, the other an admonition, the third a drawing of balance.

The two chapters of Mendelssohn's *Jerusalem*[1] seem to contradict each other. In the first chapter Mendelssohn devotes all of his philosophical energies to separating the state from religion, to stripping religious communities of any vestiges of coercive power, either *in tem-*

1. Moses Mendelssohn, "Jerusalem oder über religiöse Macht und Judentum" (Berlin, 1973), in *Gesammelte Schriften*, ed. G. B. Mendelssohn (Leipzig, 1843–1845), III, pp. 255–362. On the background and causes of publication cf. J. Katz, *Zion* 29 (1964): pp. 112–32, and A. Altmann, *Moses Mendelssohn: A Biographical Study* (Philadelphia, 1973), pp. 502 ff.

poralibus (taxation) or *in spiritualibus* (excommunication). We shall recapitulate his argument soon. Indeed, because no religion has a specific claim for "eternal truths" and Judaism is the only religion in his surrounding which has no dogmas, that is, does not coerce in matters of belief, Judaism is even better prepared to enter the state as it should be than any other Christian denomination. And Mendelssohn is willing to pay the price he demands of all religions in the true civil society—the renouncement of a corporative status. Yet in the second chapter Mendelssohn describes the sovereign Jewish state in antiquity as an inseparable unity of state and religion. He even intensifies the contradiction by deriving the vitality of the Jewish religion after the cessation of sovereignty from this ancient unity of religion and law. But is it not a mere historical coincidence that the Jewish ceremonial and moral precepts still valid have no teeth to them, no *potestas coactiva?* Is this not a temporary condition to be rectified in the messianic days—or even today by outside authorities recognizing Jewish courts?

This contradiction, noted by nearly all readers of Mendelssohn's tract, may be solved in part if we read the thesis of the first chapter, beginning with the examination of the "state of nature," admittedly a *fictio iuris* which already served Hobbes as a limiting case to all political bodies, much as the inertial principle does not describe any actual motion but is a limiting case. Mendelssohn owes to Hobbes the most fundamental insight that marks the birth of modern political theory: that the state, that all social institutions are not an outcome of man's social instincts. Man has none. The state is rather an artifact through and through, a product of man's nature. Previous natural-law theoreticians were at best willing to admit a partial participation of reason and labor in the natural formation of social bodies: "sciendum est quod civitas sit aliquo modo quid naturale eo quo naturalem impetum ad civitatem constituendam: non tamen efficitur nec perficitur civitas nisi ex opera et industria hominum," said Aegidius Colonna.[2] By eliminating the natural social impetus altogether, Hobbes stressed more than anyone before him, it eliminated man's natural desire to barter and reduced all economic relations to human-historical conditions. Mendelssohn accepted this Hobbesian premise that the state is an artifact. But Mendelssohn disagrees, as did Leibniz or Pufendorf before, with Hobbes's perception of the state of nature as a *bellum omnium contra omnes* in which

---

2. Aegidius Colonna ap. O. V. Gierke, *Johannes Althusius und die Entwicklung der naturrechtlichen Staatstheorien* (Breslau, 1913), p. 95, n. 52.

might is right. If no obligations existed in the state of nature, then the social contract could not have the absolutely binding force which Hobbes wants it to have. Granted that man is a rational animal even in the state of nature (Hobbes thought so), that it is his rationality, not brutality, which leads man to be his neighbor's enemy in the state of nature, and that the same rationality leads man to escape constant fear of death by delegating to the sovereign the right to act in his own name: why should man stick to this commitment once his fear abated? If the contract was generated by considerations of expediency, why does Hobbes not allow for considerations of expediency to revoke it? Whence the absolute, univocal character of obligations? Hobbes's exegesis still wrestles with this question: the Warrender-Taylor thesis was an attempt to settle it. Mendelssohn simplifies Hobbes's account of the state of nature so as to refute it more effectively. He insists that even the state of nature must know obligations, albeit only negative ones, comparable to Pufendorf's *obligationes imperfectae*. Negative obligations do not force man to cooperate with his fellowmen (as state laws do); they only prohibit him from harming the person and property of others. The positive obligations of the social compact (and the state) draw their validity from the prohibition to break contracts: *pacta sunt servanda*.

Obligations, however, can by definition pertain to "alienable things," that is, entities which can be given or taken. Opinions, beliefs or sentiments are inalienable and should by definition never become objects of obligations or contracts, as they do now in dogmatic religions. Religion can at best persuade man to enter positive obligations, change his mental state but never enforce it, either in the state of nature or in the political state. Religious organizations are not contractual and ought therefore to have neither the external power of purse nor the internal power of excommunication. Religious organizations cannot be corporations. And, of course, a state-religion is a contradiction in terms. I cannot escape the suspicion that Mendelssohn alludes, in his theory of obligations, to a well-known tradition of Jewish legal thought. We mentioned already the principle *dina demalchuta dina*. According to some medieval Jewish theoreticians, it has its grounding in a social contract and extends only to alienable things (*Rashbam*). If Mendelssohn alludes to this principle, then he implies once more that, indeed, Judaism is better equipped than other religions to enter the modern state, for it already thinks in proper political-legal terms.

The distinction between positive and negative obligations, even the distinction between alienable and inalienable things, is ambiguous at best. But whatever the merits or flaws of Mendelssohn's theory may be, even if accepted, it seems to contradict his later characterization of Judaism as a legal system—unless we read the first chapter hypothetically, that is: as an if-then proposition. Mendelssohn does not describe the only possible formation of political bodies. He should rather be read as stating, if man generates the political state himself out of the state of nature, then the civil state so generated must be separate from religion *toto caelo*. But another origin of political states is also possible. God rather than man may institute the state in an act of revelation. Instead of a social contract, the state may be founded on a covenant in which God himself is the sovereign. Then and then only, religion is the state and the state is religion. Put differently, Mendelssohn denies in any case the possibility of the state to have or to adopt a religion, say in the manner of *cuius regio, eius religio*. If, however, God is the sovereign, then the state *is* religion. This happened only once in history, at Sinai. Why only once, if it is so beneficial? Neither does Mendelssohn raise the question nor can I answer it for him.

Such a revealed constitution existed as an empirical fact. Reason neither necessitates nor contradicts it, it is just that: a *vérité de fait*. It is a unique fact, a historical *hapax legomenon* that "defies cheap labels such as Hierocracy or Theocracy." But a law it was and as such it had coercive powers. A law it still is even if parts of it became obsolete *pro tempore* and all of it lost coercive power. What, then, did Mendelssohn gain? If Judaism is a legal system, even of divine origin, how can it enter the secular, man-made state? This could have been Mendelssohn's dilemma had he really reduced Judaism into a legal system with moral *consilia* in the manner of Spinoza's *Tractatus*. Again Mendelssohn's formulations lead to misunderstandings because of his pursuit of elegant simplicity. Jewish law, he maintains, is not at all a system of functional provisions, a mere constitution, not even an ideal one. Jewish law then and now rather constitutes a system of symbolic acts: whence it follows that *potestas coactiva* is only an accidental property to it.

In a few pages, Mendelssohn sketches a theory of signs in order to distinguish between symbolic images and symbolic acts. These pages are, I believe, the most original and fertile part of the book, and often misunderstood. Again Mendelssohn seems indebted to Hobbes.[3] That which separates man from beast is, according to Hobbes, neither will nor memory but "foresight" and science, derived solely from the capacity to invent and manipulate signs. Man is a symbolical animal. "Signs"

---

3. J. W. N. Watkins, *Hobbes' System of Ideas* (London, 1965), pp. 138 ff.

are, to begin with, physical entities standing for other physical entities through the mediation of "phantasms." Implicit in most medieval and modern theories of language was the Aristotelian distinction between the meaning of a sign (image, concept, λεκτόν, or to Aristotele παθήματα) and its reference: a sign refers to a thing, but evokes a concept; hence Aristotle insists that every sign, even the most natural, such as onomatopoetic words, is artificial inasmuch as it is a sign. Indeed, some signs undoubtedly have their origins in nature—be it through similarity (analogy), association (metonymy) or participation (synecdoche); and the process of abstraction evidently commenced with them, just as writing began with ideograms. With greater abstraction came real detachment of signs from images; later came signs of signs. Thus signs may have their origin in nature, but they obtain their univocity and validity from an arbitrary human act only, not the similarity to the generation of the political state out of the state of nature.

Mendelssohn's analysis incorporates much of this theory with a shift of emphasis towards the ambiguity of natural signs. It takes us back to primitive times when "thought and *praxis*," man and nature, were much closer to each other. Written signs were as yet closer to natural signs, to pictorial images, ideograms, hieroglyphs. In order to identify moral dispositions such as conscience, timidity, love, and hatred, humans used images of animals that seemed to embody them: the lion, the dove, the serpent. Such pictorial signs became means to human self-consciousness. A step further, these images became expressions of divine attributes: a sense of the divine is common to all men, there is an element of spirituality even in crude polytheism (the Ranak may have borrowed his similar idea from Mendelssohn). But due to the ambiguity of natural signs, the process towards greater abstraction could also be reversed. The natural sign stands both for itself and for something else: *significans* and *significandum* can easily be converted to each other. The sign could become a thing, e.g., the lion could be seen as divine rather than as a sign of referring to the divine. What "wisdom" (the capacity of man to elicit signs from nature by analogy and association) has built, "folly" (the tendency to hypostatize and fetishize signs) destroys "by the very same means." Both wisdom and folly have their origin in the ambiguity of natural signs. We note in passing that Mendelssohn's account of fetishization is a forerunner to similar theories of "Verdinglichung" later, for example, Marx's account of the fetishization of the commodity. We notice likewise that interchangeability within a sign-system between significants and significands is the very heart of Derrida's recent structuralist attack of structuralism.

The Egyptian hieroglyphs are Mendelssohn's heuristic paradigm of both the progress toward abstraction and the regress to fetishization. The seventeenth and eighteenth centuries were fascinated by the not yet deciphered hieroglyphs. The hermetic tradition saw them as a depository of profound divine wisdom. To Mendelssohn they offer both a methodical and material model: the manner in which hieroglyphs were eventually simplified into a phonetic alphabet recapitulates the manner in which our concepts advanced from natural-pictorial to arbitrary-abstract signs. That hieroglyphs may have been venerated as sacred signs is again the adverse road of "folly." Mendelssohn's analysis may well be directed against the famous claim of John Spencer that many sacred images of the ancient Hebrews were simply borrowed from the hieroglyphs.[4]

Spencer blended an enriched version of Apion with Maimonides's rationale for the ceremonial law as a concession to the polytheistic mentality of the nascent Israel. Mendelssohn may have wished to destroy all possible links between hieroglyphs and the biblical *ius circa sacra*. At any rate he wishes to establish that while the former are symbolical images, the latter consists of symbolical acts.

If the use of symbolic images leads to a vicious circle between abstraction and fetishization, wisdom and folly, the practical precepts of Jewish law break that circle. They are also signs, but not pictorial: they signify through the acts commanded by them. Mendelssohn may have remembered Nachmanides's symbolic interpretation of the sacrifices which was directed against Maimonides' historical-functional "reasons of the commandments." Inasmuch as these signs are signs rather than images, they are much harder to hypostatize and to fetishize. Because the bond between man and God is not based on nature (*lumen naturale*) but rather on a special and extranatural dispensation, it is not always possible to determine the specific (rather than generic) reason to specific precepts—much as Sa'adia Gaon's "reasons for the command-

---

4. "Si enim Kirchero Hieroglypicorum interpreti non vulgari, credendum sit: Aegyptii Hieroglyphica sua, non ad temporum historias, regum laudes, aut philosophiae arcana; sed res sacras, naturae divinae proprietates, Geniorum et Angelorum ordinem, expiationum rationem, spectantes, posteritati consecrandas adhibuerunt. Cherubinos etiam, ad dei providentiam et potentiam, Angelorum sapientiam, in sacris praesentiam, obsequium Deo paratissimum, et alia similia, significanda, divinitus institutos fuisse, res est apud plerosque extra controversiam posita. Utraque e commistis variorum animalium formis componebantur; nam Cherubini vultu quidem hominem, humeris leonem, alis aquilam, referebant, partibus inferioribus in formam vitulinam vergentibus: Aegyptii etiam sacris animalibus aut eorum formis commistis, tanquam rerum sacratiorum symbolis et hieroglyphicis, utebantur." Johannes Spencer, *De legibus hebraeorum ritualibus et earum rationibus libri tres* (Cambridge, 1685), p. 789.

ments." Our interpretation of a particular precept can therefore never suffice to change it: another revelation only could do that. Judaism is unique not because it contains more or less of "eternal truth," *vérité de raison,* than other religions, but because its expression of the sacred is not based on nature. Nature suggests God's existence in its own, through analogies (images) and concepts, though it may lead to error. (Not necessarily: remember that Mendelssohn was the last defender of the ontological proof for God's existence before its demolition by Kant, "der Alleszermalmer.") The revealed law of the Jews is to Mendelssohn what freedom was to Kant: "das Faktum der praktischen Vernunft," miracle in the sense of a demonstrative empirical fact.

A historiosophic lesson follows from here: Judaism is not a species among other species of religion, not even the highest species, but a *genus* in itself. It cannot be conceived as a phase in the "Erziehung des Menschengeschlechts." It can be neither missionary nor a *praeparatio evangelica.* Indeed, Mendelssohn refuses to see in history at large a history of progress; he must, he says, disagree with his friend Lessing. No Jewish philosopher of religion in Germany until Rosenzweig followed Mendelssohn's lead entirely. Between Mendelssohn's *Jerusalem* and Rosenzweig's *Stern der Erlösung,* German-Jewish philosophies of religion translated "the essence of Judaism"—this ghost of an evanescent quantity—into the one or the other current philosophical or historistic idiom. At times they argued the subsumption of Judaism under pure ethics—ethics' noblest concretization. At times they spoke the language of objective idealism. Sometimes they even argued, à la Schleiermacher, the irreducibility of religious sentiment or, with Schelling, the facticity of revelation. Yet in all of their varieties, they endeavored to distill "the essence of Judaism" and show its accord with the culture they wished to be embraced by. The sole exceptions were Mendelssohn and Rosenzweig, the former with his interpretation of Judaism as a revealed system of symbolic acts, the latter in his distinction between laws (*Gesetz*) and precepts (*Gebot*) and his interpretation of Jewish existence as an act of symbolic procreation—"Zeugung" rather than "Überzeugung," an existence "outside the turmoil of history."[5] This is a remarkable fact: it seems as if German-Jewish philosophy went full circle to return to its point of origin.

A political lesson likewise follows: if the modern state is to accept

5. Franz Rosenzweig, *Briefe,* ed. E. Rosenzweig (Berlin, 1935), pp. 276–81 (to Helene Sommer, 16.1.1918). *Kleinere Schriften* (Berlin, 1937), pp. 357–72 (18.11.1917). Cf. below, pp. 260–270.

Jews as citizens, and according to Mendelssohn it must accept them as Jews, neither Jews nor Judaism have to change in order to fit into one state, that is, in order to be integrated. The state as it is now must change, abandon its endorsement of any religion, and relegate religion "from the public to the private sphere." I do not mean to indicate that there is no trace of the urge to acculturate in Mendelssohn's treatment of Judaism. He could not concede any surplus of "external truths" to Judaism over that which underlies all religions; he has difficulties interpreting the chosenness of Israel as an advantage towards salvation, and one can virtually hear his sigh of relief that many of Israel's once valid constitutional and ceremonial laws became obsolete with the destruction of the Temple, that only "moral precepts" remained in it. He was not altogether free from the apologetic tendencies that were to become dominant later. Perhaps we ought to say, he has not yet reached the point where assimilation or at least accommodation even of religious tenets seemed a necessary price for emancipation into the state, because the state he conceived of was not yet the national state of the early nineteenth century, itself a surrogate for religious fervor. And, for the same reason, he could not yet see the gap between political and social integration.

MARX AND THE JEWISH QUESTION

If our interpretation of Mendelssohn is correct, then he was not a forerunner of the reform, nor was he "der Jüdische Luther" (Heine). His image was distorted by his followers and admirers. The image of Marx in this respect was tainted by himself only. His treatises on the Jewish question[6] are utterly soaked with Jewish self-hatred, and it is hard to penetrate its stench to discover their interesting core. The first treatise answers Bruno Bauer's arguments against the emancipation of Jews. Bauer had woven all traditional negative cliches about Jews into a dialectical tapestry. Jews embody the principle of particularism and self-interest. Their god is therefore a particularistic god, their reward this-worldly, their indifference toward other nations total. Christianity represents the negation of Jewish particularism, but as a universal *ecclesia e gentibus* it has also universalized the Jewish exclusivity:

6. K. Marx, "Zur Judenfrage," in *MEW* (Berlin, 1957), Bd. I, pp. 247–377. On possible changes in Marx's later views see Daniel Gutwein, "Marx on the Relationship Between Jews and Capitalism: From Sombart to Weber," *Zion* LV, 4 (1990): pp. 419–47.

nulla salus extra ecclesiam. True emancipation, a genuine liberation of man, can come only dialectically by way of a negation of the negation, the negation of the universal exclusive claims of Christianity. Because no two steps can be taken at one time in the dialectical ladder, Jews could not be ready for emancipation unless they went through the phase of self-negation, that is: Christianity.

This, Marx explains, is a fallacious argument. It confuses political with social (i.e., human) emancipation. A successful critique not only recognized the mistake of a theory, but also of its origin. The confusion was bound to emerge. It is part of the inherent contradiction within the modern state in which "appearance" (*Erscheinung*) and "essence" (*Wesen*) are at odds by necessity, and political emancipation must appear in the deceptive guise of human emancipation. Marx's essay is a masterful application of the middle part of Hegel's *Wissenschaft der Logik,* the "Wesenslogik," to a concrete historical situation. The central role of the "Wesenslogik" in Marx's thought has hardly been noticed even by those who emphasize Hegel's impact on Marx; the otherwise excellent study of Avineri does not refer to it, even though neither the analysis of the state nor the later analysis of the community can be understood without the dialectics of *Wesen* and *Erscheinung.* Essence and appearance must be one in the sense that their unity or oneness (*Einheit*) is the unity of unity and difference (reality). Now if we wish to say that S appears as X while in effect it is Y, this very appearance is essential while everything we determine as essence is *eo ipso* appearance. The ideal is that the essence of the liberal state is its mediating function between individual self-interests so that, to quote Mandeville, "private vices" will turn into "public virtues." It purports to stand above all particular social interest-groups. In reality, though, it expresses and institutionalizes the atomization of society. The "freedom" or equality which it propagates—the *droits de l'homme*—are nothing but a tool to strip the individual member of society from all bondages, feudal or corporative, so as to make him free to sell himself, his labor, as a commodity in the market. The civil society (*bürgerliche Gesellschaft*) is indeed that society in which man's alienation from his creativity achieves its most radical and therefore transparent, naked forms: everything in this society, including man's labor, has become a commodity obeying the "laws of the market." The social rather than merely conceptual paradoxes latent in every commodity—that if it represents abstract labor, then it does not represent abstract labor—become transparent when labor itself turns into a commodity.

Thus we find that the appearance of the state—as an aggregate of conflicting interest groups—is its essence, while its essence or "ideal" is only appearance. The very discrepancy between essence and appearance is the driving moment of the state. If, however, the bourgeois state is so designed as to guarantee the self-interests of a class without extra-economic inhibitions, why should Jews not be accepted into it as a particular, antagonistic interest group among others? Indeed, they embody the very principle of self-interest in deed and ideas. They represent the very spirit of capitalistic society. Indeed, they cannot but be emancipated into this state, which cannot let either religion or family stand in the way of political emancipation of man: his transformation into a commodity. Only when the inherent contradiction of the atomized, alienated society changes its conflicting elements and transforms it into a human emancipation will all interest groups, including their arche-type Judaism, disappear. "Private vices" are not *eo ipso* and simultane-ously, as classical economists and political theoreticians assumed, "pub-lic virtues." The transformation of the former into the latter is rather a revolutionary, dialectical process. Only at the end of this process will "the emancipation of Jews" be nothing but "the emancipation of soci-ety from the Jews."

It seems as if Marx's argument is a caricaturized version of Mendels-sohn's. It need not be consciously so. It is not the Jews who have to change in order to be granted emancipation, it is the state which has to change and become its true ugly self. When it does, it will have no choice but to remove the corporative status of Jews—relegate religion "von der Sphäre des öffentlichen Rechts zur Sphäre des Privatrechts." Indeed, Marx, like Mendelssohn, also sees the Jews as better fit than any other social segment for the civil state; they are the very incarnation of its true essence, the atomization of society into conflicting economi-cal interest-groups. The civil state is a Jewish state.

Our initial impulse was to separate, methodically, between the ele-ments of self-hatred and the elements of true political insight in Marx's treatise. Indeed, he was almost the only thinker during the struggle for emancipation who did not share the axiom that emancipation and social integration (or acceptance) must go hand in hand. But having carried our methodical isolation of his self-hatred so far we realized that, after all, it is an integral part of this argument. In a peculiar way, Marx thus prefigures the attitudes of both the anti-Semite and the Zionist. The former inasmuch as he gave expression to the worst fears of later anti-Semitism, namely that the modern state is about to become a Jewish state, an incarnation of the "dirty Jewish spirit" of capitalism. The latter inasmuch as he separates emancipation from integration and views emancipation as both necessary and irrevocable, real integration as non-existent and impossible.

ANTI-SEMITISM AND ZIONISM

By the end of the nineteenth century, no great intellectual powers were needed any more to recognize the gap between emancipation and integration. Emancipation was already a fact; integration almost as distant as it was in 1812. I do not mean the considerable vestiges of discrimination only but, first and foremost, Jews continued to be perceived, and to perceive themselves, as a distinct group. They lived in a situation of *être vue,* and cared about it. In spite of almost religious fervor with which they advanced their acculturation and identified with the state, they were still the prototype of the alien. How could these facts be accounted for? *Historia ipsa docet*—emancipation *cum* acculturation did not solve the "Jewish question." If the confusion could not be maintained on its original terms, it could be upheld by virtue of the anti-Semitic distinction between deceptive and true assimilation.

Here I cannot venture into the history of political anti-Semitism. A few phenomenological remarks must suffice. Anti-Semitism is first and foremost an anti-emancipatory movement, and this in the following sense. The anti-Semite—whether moderate or radical—regarded as his prime enemy not the traditional, orthodox Jew, but the Jew who had become almost one of us—the Jew who under the guise of assimilation was about to destroy the healthy texture of society from within. Being a Jew is rather a *character indelebilis,* a matter of nature not to be erased even by conversion; Jews are a force of disintegration, "zersetzendes Element." They may be so subjectively or objectively, knowingly or unknowingly; the radical anti-Semite will assume the former: that the Jews are out to gain incognito and with a conspiratorial master plan the dominion over the nation and perchance the world. The Jews ought to be made recognizable again: their emancipation was a partial or total mistake, because, want it or not, they are not capable of true assimilation.

It is astonishing how many of these assumptions were shared by early Zionist ideologues, albeit with inverted prefixes. If I were to sum up the theoretical essence of the Jewish question in Herzl's *Judenstaat,*[7]

7. Theodore Herzl, *Der Judenstaat* (Wien, 1934).

it would be like this: granted that assimilation did not result in integration, how can one nonetheless defend and maintain the achievements of the emancipation? Herzl all but admits that radical assimilation—the elimination of all distinctive marks—would be the ideal solution to the Jewish question, given sufficient time. Jews are willing and capable of assimilation, but there is no time to complete the process, nor can it progress without profound antagonism.

Herzl's theoretical language is first and foremost the incredibly unsophisticated language of social Darwinism. During their preemancipation ordeal, subjected to harsher conditions of life than any other group, Jews underwent a process of natural selection; the fittest survived. In his words: Jews have acquired enormous energies. The emancipation of the Jews set these energies free: Jews concentrated all of them to gain entry into, and a hold within, civil society, and succeeded in acquiring vast power in areas open to their activity—Herzl exaggerated the extent of Jewish financial and political power no less than his anti-Semitic adversaries. But the very impetus of Jewish entry was bound to awaken anxiety, in particular the anxiety of the bourgeoisie; the more power Jews acquired, the deeper the resistance to their integration. The problem threatens to acquire catastrophic dimensions: therefore Jews should redirect their power; instead of seeking a hold in society they should build a society of their own. The solution of the Jewish question is not social, but national: the only way to conserve and complete the emancipation of the Jews is through a collective autoemancipation, their emancipation as a nation. Then and there Jews will cease to be a threat.

The most ingenious part of Herzl's tract is, in retrospect, not his analysis of the Jewish question but his justification for action. A "society of the Jews" must be formed, an executive which will act as a representative of all; but upon what legitimation? Roman law recognizes, *in casu neccessitatis,* the unauthorized representation by another, the *gestor negotiorum.* If the house of my absent neighbor is on fire, I am permitted and even obligated to intrude on his property and act in his name—extinguish the fire any way I deem necessary. "The house of Israel is on fire." The construct is ingenious not because of its theoretical merits, but because it conveys two insights which were the key to the success of the Zionist movement in its beginning. Herzl recognized the political power vacuum within Jewish society: no group or party was even willing to appear as representative of all Jews, because doing so would imply what most Jews denied—that they must act as a "political subject." Herzl sensed that if such a group were to appear and presume to act in the name of all, it would also be accepted as such by other political subjects, no matter how tiny the minority it actually represented. Herzl was a master of *Als-Ob Politik* at a time when theatrics was just as important as actual power. His political-practical message was, already in 1896, the urge to act "as if."

Herzl's program endeavored to rescue the achievements of the emancipation without assimilation. True emancipation will not come to Jews as individuals, but as a nation. Their integration into the civil state will be the formation of their own state. In a way, he shared the confusion between emancipation, assimilation and integration which characterized his century: in their places, Jews cannot achieve true emancipation because they are not given the chance and the time to assimilate. *Der Judenstaat* presented itself as a pragmatic rather than ideal solution to the "Jewish Question." And albeit the question was a non-question, the ideal of statehood was the sustaining dream in the most horrible hours of Jewish history. The state is here now, but it is still upon us to make it into a good state: *tantae molis erat Romanam condere gentem.*

Haskala, History, and the Medieval Tradition

THE ETHOS OF THE ENLIGHTENMENT

The image of the Middle Ages entertained by the Enlightenment consisted of a series of negative stereotypes. Medieval philosophy was not exempt from this bleak outlook. From the vantage point of the Enlightenment, scholasticism was not less regressive than the feudal institutions, the inquisitional courts and the "gothic"—read barbaric—architecture of the Middle Ages. Did not scholasticism evade the main task of philosophy, namely to sharpen our critical faculties, promote genuine knowledge, and remove prejudices? Instead, it lost itself in subtleties which were nothing more than empty word-games; or as Gassendi once said (quoting Seneca), "philosophy turned into philology."[8]

The Jewish *Haskala* saw itself as part of the Enlightenment. Many of its basic tenets corresponded indeed to those of the "Aufklärer," "phi-

8. Pierre Gassendi, *Exercitationes paradoxicae adversus Aristoteleos* I, 14, ed. B. Rochot (Paris, 1959), pp. 45–46. On other contemporary uses of this quotation from Seneca see A. Grafton, *Defenders of the Text: The Traditions of Scholarship in an Age of Science, 1450–1800* (Cambridge, Mass., 1991), pp. 39–40.

losophes," "illuministi." Yet its attitude towards the medieval tradition of Jewish philosophy was throughout different and positive: so much so that one can, without exaggeration, tie the beginning of the *Haskala* to the renewed interest in medieval religious philosophy. The contrast to the European Enlightenment is blatant and calls for an explanation. I wish to argue that both contradicting postures were rooted in one and the same character of the Enlightenment, that both reflect its fundamental socio-pedagogical commitments. Everywhere in Europe, men of the Enlightenment were striving to reeducate society by means of true knowledge.

Medieval philosophy—or science—was esoteric in an objective and subjective sense of the word. Among the few literates in the medieval society, fewer still devoted themselves to the pursuit of theories. These again developed a strong elitist consciousness, in the Islamic and Jewish cultures even more so than in Christianity. The *vulgus* seemed to them condemned forever to ignorance. It is the duty of the masses, of society at large, to sustain the intellectual, according to Maimonides—but it is not the task of the intellectual to educate the masses, to raise them to his level: the masses (*hamon ha'am*) were, are, and will remain dumb even in the messianic days. The *vita contemplativa*—much as the βίος θεωρητικός of the ancients—is not Everyman's talent. How different was the ethos of the Enlightenment! At the center of its self-understanding stood neither "the revival of paganism" nor science for science's sake, but rather the duty of enlightening, of spreading the light of reason everywhere. The Enlightener of the eighteenth century, contrary to his rationalistic counterpart in the Middle Ages, believed therefore in the capacity of every person, high or low, to be educated, to acquire all knowledge. The very transformation of the term "common sense" signifies the change of attitudes. Originally it stood, as a technical term, for the capacity to coordinate sense-perceptions from the various "senses."[9] Since the seventeenth century it has come to mean—perhaps under Stoic influence—the capacity of each and every person to make sound judgments. Descartes wrote his *Discours* in the vernacular so that even his maid could read it.

Peter Gay, in his reinterpretation of the Enlightenment,[10] seems to have underestimated this fundamental driving force, and hence overes-

---

9. E. Ruth Hervey, *The Inward Wits: Psychological Theory in the Middle Ages and the Renaissance,* Warburg Institute Surveys 6 (London, 1975), esp. pp. 43f. (Avicenna). I closely follow my argument in *Theology and the Scientific Imagination,* pp. 357–60.

10. Peter Gay, *The Enlightenment: A Reinterpretation,* vol. 1, *The Rise of Modern Paganism* (New York, 1960).

timated its break with the Christian tradition, its revival of paganism. In effect, the complex dialectical relation of the Enlightenment to the Christian past overshadows all traces of the spirit of classical antiquity in it. Its ideals were secularized, inverted, Christian ideals "put on their feet" again. The Enlightenment inherited from Christianity its missionary-pedagogical zeal. It substituted the Christian *extra ecclesiam nulla salus* with *extra scientiam nulla salus.* Superstition rather than *superbia* became the cardinal vice, and ignorance was the original sin. The Freemasons became a counter-Church with countersymbols, countersacraments, counterpriests, and counterconfession. Gay developed his thesis against C. Becker[11] and others who exaggerated the eschatological-cum-utopian ingredients of the Enlightenment. In this sense he was right, but not with his paganism thesis. Not apocalyptic, but missionary and pedagogical-social motives were taken from Christianity even where the latter was seen as an adversary. Nothing of the kind existed in antiquity.[12]

Salvation through knowledge was not even a notion totally alien to Christianity. The dangers of an extreme intellectualistic interpretation of Christian doctrines accompanied the Church since the ancient gnostics. This danger tended to emerge whenever intellectuals within the Church entertained an exaggerated consciousness of their autonomy and importance. Such was the case at the University of Paris in the beginning of the thirteenth century. Intoxicated by the newly gained freedom to teach—to discuss every topic provided that the deciding conclusion does not contradict Church doctrines (*disputandi more, non asserendi more*)—teachers seem to have tried every possible theoretical avenue for size. Some, like the Amalricans, claimed that only philosophical knowledge really saves: to the extent to which we have it, God is literally in us, irrespective of any religious denomination; for God is the *forma mundi.*[13] Such elitist views seldom came to the fore in Chris-

11. Carl L. Becker, *The Heavenly City of the Eighteenth Century Philosophers* (New Haven and London, 1932). The argument was later extended to the agents of the revolution: Jacob L. Talmon, *The Origins of Totalitarian Democracy* (London, 1952).

12. It has been argued—notably by A. D. Nock, in *Conversion: The Old and the New in Religion from Alexander the Great to Augustine of Hippo* (Oxford, 1933)—that the Christian theory and praxis of conversion was preceded and influenced by the theories and practices of philosophical schools in antiquity. Even if so, none of them were "missionary" in the sense that Christianity was, seeking to save every soul in every walk of life.

13. Garnerius of Rochefort (?), *Contra Amaurianos,* ed. C. Bäumker (Münster, 1926), pp. 2, 8, 9, 16–17. On David of Dinant, who even claimed that God is the *materia mundi,* see Funkenstein, *Theology,* p. 46.

tian Europe; Amalrich of Bena was banned, his followers declared heretics; but that they appeared at all is significant. Only in the Enlightenment did such views break through publicly. The movement of the
Enlightenment seems to have combined both motives into one: the
theme of salvation through knowledge only and the exoteric, nonelitist
ideal of open knowledge.[14] The Enlightenment was, as it seems to me,
through and through a post-Christian phenomenon.

Not all Enlighteners believed in an evenly progressive "education of
the human race" ("Erziehung des Menschengeschlechts").[15] But all of
them believed in the education of their fellow humans through knowledge that, because of its socio-pedagogical function, must be open,
accessible to all. On the other hand, knowledge itself—that is, science—became, even in the eighteenth century, more and more special-
ized in its methods and content, and thus, in effect, more and more
esoteric. This circumstance likewise distinguishes modern from medieval science. The medieval image of science and its functions may have
been esoteric, but in its content and in its methodology it was a
common-sense philosophy, much like Aristotle's. It is the duty of science, Aristotle once said, to explicate "what everyone knows, only more
clearly."[16] The presuppositions of Aristotelian and scholastic science
were seldom counterintuitive. Aristotelian physics rested firmly on direct generalizations from common sense perceptions, as in its conviction that bodies tend to rest and that "whatever moves is moved by
something else" (*omne quod movetur ab alio movetur*).[17] Indeed, to stand
"against the senses" (*contra sensum*) was the death verdict for any
theory: medieval science, as A. Maier has shown, was too strongly committed to "experience" to develop real "experiment."[18] By contrast,

14. Together with Adin Steinsalz, I have discussed this topic in more detail in our
Sociology of Ignorance (Tel Aviv, 1987). See also G. E. R. Lloyd, *Magic, Reason, and Experience: Studies in the Origins and Development of Greek Science* (Cambridge, 1979), esp.
pp. 246–64, and idem, *The Revolutions of Wisdom: Studies in the Claims and Practice of
Ancient Greek Science* (Berkeley and Los Angeles, 1987).

15. Moses Mendelssohn, *Jerusalem, Schriften*, vol. III, pp. 317 ff. (against Lessing).

16. Aristotle, *De Caelo*, IV, 1; 308*a* 24.

17. On the principle see S. Pines, "omne quod movetur necesse est ab alio movetur,"
Isis 52 (1961): pp. 21–54 (the difference between *ab alio* and *ab aliquo*); R. R. Effler,
"John Duns Scotus and the Principle omne quod movetur ab alio movetur," *Franciscan Institute Publications, Philosophy Series* 15 (1962): pp. 120 ff.; Funkenstein, *Theology*,
pp. 161–71.

18. Anneliese Maier, *Metaphysische Hintergründe der spätscholastischen Philosophie*
(Rome, 1955), p. 405. A history of the notion and practices of precision is yet to be
written. The word *praecise*, though in a more logical-conceptual sense, starts to permeate
the philosophical literature in the fourteenth century.

classical physics in the seventeenth century embarked from counterintuitive propositions—for example, that every body tends to stay in its
state of rectilinear, uniform motion indefinitely, as long as other forces
do not act on it.[19] Entities such as mass, energy, field, electrons, or
quarks are by definition inaccessible to immediate sense-perception.[20]
Modern science thus became increasingly esoteric in its content, methods, and in its drive towards the proliferation of special disciplines—
while the ideal of modern science became, as we saw, increasingly exoteric, an ideal of open science. One could call this state of affairs
outright, the paradox of the Enlightenment, its "scandal." The paradox
was temporarily tamed, and the praxis somewhat harmonized with the
ideal, with the new, mediating notion of "culture" as a middle ground
between ignorance and special knowledge. The Enlighteners often saw
themselves as mediators, as transmitters and popularizers of science
rather than as scientists. Their domain was the creation of the broadest
common denominator of knowledge, the true "formation" (*Bildung*) of
humankind.

Here is not the place to elaborate or prove this very rough sketch of
a theory of the Enlightenment. It serves me only inasmuch as it sheds
light on the attitude of the Jewish Enlighteners, the *maskilim,* toward
the medieval philosophical literature.

HASKALA AND MEDIEVAL PHILOSOPHY

No elaborate proof is needed to convince us that the early
Haskala manifested itself through a renewed dedication to medieval
philosophical writings. A few examples may suffice.[21] Isaac Halevi
Stanow (1730–1803) wrote commentaries to Jehuda Halevi's *Kuzzari,*
to Maimonides's *Guide,* and to the *Book of Principles* (*Sefer ha'ikkarim*)
of Josef Albo. Moses Mendelssohn commented on Maimonides's early
logical treatise (*Be'ur milot hahigayon*). Wolfsohn wrote a commentary
on Sa'adia Ga'on's *Book of Beliefs and Opinions* (1789). Mendel Lepin
retranslated the *Guide to the Perplexed* into Hebrew. If his translation
was much more fluent and accessible to the common reader than the

19. Funkenstein, *Theology,* pp. 161–71.
20. So were atoms in antiquity: but it was precisely this their elusiveness to perception against which Aristotle—and the philosophical tradition after him—raised serious
methodological objections of nonfalsifiability. To counter them, Lucretius, *De rerum natura* II : 114 ff., may have developed his indirect proof.
21. Pinchas Lachover, *Toledot hasifrut ha'ivrit hachadasha* (Tel Aviv, 1927), vol. I,
pp. 85, 90, 132, etc. Mine is by no means an exhaustive list.

medieval translation of Ibn Tibbon, it was also much less precise. And Salomon Maimon's commentary on the first part of Maimonides's *Guide*—we shall take a closer look at it later—remained influential in the nineteenth century. The various periodicals of the *Haskala*— *Sulamith, ha-me'assef, Kohelet mussar*—published continuously laudations and evaluations of medieval philosophers.

The Enlighteners saw in the medieval philosophers their own predecessors. It is interesting to note that such was also the judgment of their early adversaries, notably R. Jacob Emden. The *Guide* was, in his eyes, a dangerous and heretical book whose authorship cannot be reconciled with the formidable authority of the author of the code of law, the *mishne tora*. Emden drew, therefore, the perfectly logical conclusion that the *Guide* must be a pseudoepigraphical machination, the work of a forger who mixed some genuine Maimonidean traditions with many false ones. Emden, we know, used a similar strategy to discredit the authenticity of the *Zohar,* the cannonical text of Jewish mysticism. His analysis pointed at the authorship of Moshe di Leon in the fourteenth century rather than the self-attribution of the text to Shime'on bar Jochai. In this case, he was even right.[22]

No European Enlighteners at the time would have read the history of medieval philosophy as a "history of religious Enlightenment" ("Geschichte der religiösen Aufklärung"). This happened only much later and even then but occasionally for apologetic purposes, for example, in Hermann Reuter's book bearing that same title.[23] Why, then, was it so evident to the Jewish *maskilim* that the medieval rationalists were their forerunners? Five interdependent reasons come to mind.

1. Reasons of Legitimation. The proximity of their endeavor to similar, older elements in the Jewish tradition provided the Enlighteners with a legitimation for their goal—namely to lead Judaism internally on the "way of the world" (*derech erets*). At their time, medieval philosophers also looked for a legitimation, and thus developed their own version of the theory of a *translatio sapientiae ab Hebraeis ad Graecos:*

---

22. R. Jacob Emden, *Mitpachat Sefarim* (Lemberg, 1870), esp. pp. 37–40. On his critique of the *Zohar*, see Isaiah Tishby, *Mishnat haZohar* (Jerusalem, 1957), I, pp. 52–56. One is reminded of Morgenstern's famous lines: "Und er kam zu dem Ergebnis / Dass nur Traum war dies Erlebnis. / Denn, so schloss er Messerscharf, / Nichts kann sein was nicht sein darf."

23. Hermann Reuter, *Geschichte der religiösen Aufklärung im Mittelalter vom Ende des 8ten. bis zum Anfang des 14ten Jahrhunderts* (Berlin, 1875). See chapter 6, "Changes in Christian Anti-Jewish Polemics in the Twelfth Century." And recently Kurt Flasch, *Aufklärung im Mittelalter? Die Verurteilung von 1277* (Mainz, 1989), pp. 19–21.

Plato was a disciple of Moses. The wisdom of the nations of the world—including astronomy—had its origins with the Hebrews; unfortunately, the children of Israel later forgot many of these wisdoms and had to regain them from the borrowers.[24]

2. Reasons of Compensation. To "nations of the world," medieval philosophy testifies to the fact that, even though Israel lived "in the darkness of exile" (*becheskat hagalut*), it nonetheless produced important works of universal value. The *maskilim* were a new phenomenon in the Jewish culture also in that they were permeated with a deep sense of the inferiority of at least the present Jewish culture compared to its environment. The reference to medieval achievements served as a compensation of sorts, and continued to serve as a compensation for the *Wissenschaft des Judentums* in the nineteenth century.

3. Symbolic Reasons. The *maskilim* viewed medieval philosophy as a prefiguration, of sorts, of the age of Enlightenment. Like them, the medieval "enlighteners" also had to fight obscurantists, *viri obscuri*, in their society in their times, and were also occasionally excommunicated by the latter. Was not the Maimonides controversy, which flared up in France in the beginning of the thirteenth century, an example of the struggle between obscurantists and enlighteners?

4. Biographical Reasons. In the life of many *maskilim*, reading medieval philosophers at a young age—more or less clandestinely—was often the first impulse towards involvement in the "external wisdoms" (*chokhmot chitsoniyyot*). It was only natural for the *maskil* to assume that what was good for him must also be beneficial for others.

5. Pedagogy. Weightier than all of these reasons, it seems to me, was the socio-pedagogical value the *maskilim* attributed to the philosophical writings of the Middle Ages. In their eyes, these writings still had in them an enlightening potential, their contents were not at all obsolete. This is the reason why generations of enlighteners kept editing, commenting on, and paraphrasing the medieval texts. But, at the same time, the *maskilim* could hardly avoid noticing the discrepancy between the present-day and the medieval state of philosophy and science. At the hand of two examples—Salomon Maimon and Nachman Krochmal—I shall try to show how the more talented among the *maskilim* reconciled this contradiction and tried to bridge the gap between them and congenial past endeavors.

24. E. R. Curtius, *Europäische Literatur und lateinisches Mittelalter,* 3rd ed. (Bern-München, 1948), pp. 38–39; Funkenstein, *Heilsplan,* p. 219, n. 270.

SALOMON MAIMON

Reverence towards Maimonides speaks from every page of Salomon Maimon's commentary to the *Guide*. Already the name the author chose for himself testifies to his admiration. And yet there is no single theoretical position of Maimonides that is upheld by Maimon. True, Maimon distinguishes between metaphysical and scientific positions of both Aristotle and the Rambam:

> The philosophy that came down to us from Aristotle teaches us clearly that the most perfect mind [*sekhel*], when deprived of the means necessary to investigate the actions of nature, while it may invent new and marvelous things in dialectics and metaphysics, will nonetheless be very limited, of necessity, in its understanding of the science of nature.[25]

The introduction to Maimon's commentary contains therefore a sketch-like history of astronomy and physics down to his present. One may think, then, that at least some of Maimonides's philosophical positions ought to be exempt from the vicissitude of time and change. But Maimon, who was already washed with Kantian waters, knows better than to draw an artificial line between metaphysics and science. He could not have meant the distinction seriously (such as Leibniz's or his own) can thrive only on the fertile grounds of good science. Therefore he corrects not only Aristotle's (and Rambam's) astronomy, physics, and cosmology—which takes up a good part of the commentary—but also further fundamental positions of the *Guide*. Maimon refutes, point for point, Maimonides's detailed refutation of the atomism of the Muslim *kalam*. Maimonides's long discussions for and against the eternity of the world turn to be redundant, considering that time, as Kant has shown, is but a "pure form of intuition" (*eine Form der Anschauung*).[26] Why, then, stick to Maimonides? Why did he bother to correct or reinterpret the details of his theories?

For one thing, Maimon identifies with Maimonides's intention to

---

25. Salomon Maimon, *Giv'at hamore,* ed. S. H. Bergmann and N. Rottsenstreich (Jerusalem, 1965), p. 9. A word may here be in order about Maimon's autobiographic *Geschichte des eigenen Lebens* (Berlin, 1934). It is written as a story of progressive personal enlightenment, whereby his "good, natural disposition" (*Naturanlagen*) prevailed at the end against the adverse conditions of ignorance and superstition within which he grew. Its sources of inspiration, except, of course, Rousseau's *Confessions,* which he imitates throughout, is Flavius Josephus's *vita;* like the latter, Maimon tried all "three schools" of religion in his time.

26. On the importance of "Anschaulichkeit" in the period, see my *Theology and the Scientific Imagination,* pp. 107–108.

reconcile reason and revelation. A good philosopher cannot but turn to a philosophical allegoresis of the Scriptures in the spirit of science. Underlying every such allegoresis is the assumption that "the Scriptures speak a human language" in the sense discussed earlier in this book.[27] Revelation adjusted itself to the capacity of humans to receive and to perceive it. We remember how Maimonides interpreted not only the biblical cosmology guided by this maxim, but also Jewish law itself.[28] Maimon approves of this method, adjusting it (as indeed he must) to the scientific insights of his day.

Not only does he approve of it; he turns it into a tool to save Maimonides himself (rather than the Scriptures only). That which Maimonides presented as a proper philosophical allegoresis is itself only a superficial doctrine, accommodated to the opinions current in his times. So, for example, in the eternal seat of God (*ve'ata adonai le'olam teshev*). Maimonides explained it as a reference to the circumstance that the heavenly bodies remain perpetually unchanged not only in their species but also—unlike sublunar bodies—as singulars. Here Salomon Maimon remarks:

> Now know, enlightened reader, that the truth as illuminated by recent astronomers and philosophers of nature is that even celestial bodies are not a fifth matter [element], as Aristotle believed, but are the same as the matter of the earth. . . . Nonetheless, the explication of verse according to the *Rav* of blessed memory corresponds to reality, in the sense that the Scripture speaks the language of humans. Now, the multitude always senses changes in terrestrial bodies but does not notice changes in the celestial bodies, because that [matter] requires many distinctions and subtle calculations.[29]

In other words, Maimon applies philosophical allegoresis to Maimonides's philosophical allegoresis; he does to Maimonides what Maimonides often did to the ancient *midrash*. Aristotelian cosmology now becomes identified with the common sense of the multitude, which therefore befits the plain sense of the multitude, which therefore befits the plain sense of the Scriptures, which "speak the language of humans."

The distance between the biblical and medieval cosmologies thus appears to the enlightener as being so much smaller than the distance between medieval and modern cosmology. In spite of this, Maimon-

27. See above, pp. 88–98.
28. See above, pp. 141–144.
29. Maimon, *Giv'at hamore*, 46 (ct. p. 134).

ides's cosmological views—and medieval philosophy in general—still maintain a pedagogical value. It eases for the "novice" (*matchil*) access to modern science in that it allows him to start at the level of naive consciousness (which it represents). It also shows him to what heights reason can climb even while possessing only a very limited (or false) knowledge of nature.

NACHMAN KROCHMAL (*RANAK*)

Salomon Maimon measured the progress of the Enlightenment by the yardstick of our true knowledge of nature. A generation later, Nachman Krochmal interpreted the progress of enlightenment as the progress of *historical* consciousness, of "the knowledge of the end of days" (*da'at acharit hayamim*), which is likewise the progress of self-awareness.[30] His major (and only) book, the *More nebuche hazman*, betrays his ambition to provide his time with a "guide to the perplexed" much as Maimonides did once to the perplexed of his time, for the sources of perplexity have shifted. A more facetious way of reading the meaning of the book's title—which anyway was given to it by Zunz, though employing Krochmal's own language—is that it wants to be a guide to those who are perplexed by the phenomenon of time. Whether or not one fancies such reading, there is no doubt that Krochmal saw in time—in historical changes even of Jewish religious expression itself—the source of latter-day puzzlement. On the other hand, once understood, historical insight into changes in time provides, he believed, the only real chance for a revitalization of the religious culture now beleaguered by "mindless observance" (*Werkheiligkeit*), "enthusiasm," and "superstition,"[31] for which read rabbinical pedantry, Chassidism, and popular *kabbala*.

His sources of inspiration—other than Maimonides—are easily

---

30. Nachman Krochmal, "More nebuche hazman," in *The Writings of Nachman Krochmal* (Hebrew), ed. S. Rawsidowicz (Waltham, Mass., 1961), pp. 37–39. On the translation of the eschatological term (*omek acharit hayamim*) into a historical idiom see Jacob Taubes, "Nachman Krochmal and Modern Historicism," *Judaism* 12 (1961): pp. 150–164, esp. 160. The insight is valid even if we do not accept his interpretation of an end of history according to Krochmal. It is worth noting in this context that Azaria di Rossi's *Meor eynayyim*—Ranak's philological precursor and paradigm of the sixteenth century—is, to a large part, an attempt to debunk eschatological "calculations of the end."

31. Ibid., chapter 1. See also Roland Goetschel, "Philon et le judaisme héllenistique au miroir de Nachman Krochmal," *Hellenica et judaica*, ed. A. Laquot et al. (Paris, 1986), pp. 371–83.

identifiable: Azaria di Rossi's *Me'or Eynayyim*, Herder and Hegel.[32] From the former he learned to ask for the exact time and setting of traditions, the method of historical criticism. Like Azaria, Krochmal applied textual criticism to everything but the biblical text: he was a cautious person who even preferred his book to appear posthumously. From Herder and Hegel—in spite of striking similarities, he seems not to have read Vico's *New Science*—he drew the elements of a philosophy of history, its vocabulary. The achievement of Krochmal lies precisely in this two-tiered approach to his subject matter: a conceptual framework cum detailed textual analysis, even if the latter was not always guided by the former (and certainly not vice versa).

The central theme of the book is "the spirit of the nation" (*ruach ha'umma*). The "spirit" of every nation (Herder's *Volksgeist*) embodies a definite, partial aspect of the "absolute spirit" (*haruchani hamuchlat*, Hegel's *absoluter Geist*). The development of each nation brings this aspect to the fore, makes explicit, say, the idea of beauty among the Greeks or of power among the Romans. This process is tied to the biological process of growth and maturation. Once this process of self-explication of the national spirit is completed, a nation will have outlived its world-historical role and purpose. It will, then, of necessity, decay, physically and intellectually. Only the people of Israel are exempt from this inevitable fate because it expresses and embodies the never exhaustible *totality* of the "absolute spirit" rather than only a partial, definite aspect of it. The history of the spirit of Israel is indeed the history of the very idea of God becoming ever clearer but remaining always ineffable. True, the Jewish nation is not altogether exempt from physical regularities; it also underwent several periods that ended in decay; but they always did and will revive, for theirs is a truly *catholic* spirit.

We recognize in this first attempt in the age of Enlightenment to construct a rationale of and for Jewish history—a philosophy of his-

---

32. See Rawidowicz in the introduction to his edition (above n. 25) and his essay "War Nachman Krochmal Hegelianer?" *HUC Annual* V (1928): pp. 535–83; J. Guttmann, *Philosophies of Judaism* (Jerusalem, 1952); N. Rottenstreich, *Jewish Thought in Modern Times* (Hebrew), (Tel-Aviv, 1945). How "Hegelian" Krochmal was depends on definitions. Of course his scheme of periodization, with the biological metaphors underpinning it, are evolutionary rather than dialectical; but there were many other curious self-designated "Hegelians." See Toews, *Hegelianism*. Krochmal's leaning on di Rossi still awaits detailed analysis. For the interpretation of Krochmal's periodization see also Ismar Schosrach, "The Philosophy of History of Nachman Krochmal," *Judaism* 10 (1961), pp. 237–45.

tory—many medieval motives; yet they appear here in an inverted form. The inversion of medieval forms of reasoning was, as I tried to show elsewhere in detail, characteristic of the European "pre-Enlightenment" and Enlightenment.[33] So also here: That Israel is exempt from laws of nature—be they biological (growth and decay) or astral—was a traditional topos that goes back to antiquity: *ein mazal leyisrael,* Israel has no guiding star. The people of Israel stand under the direct, special providence of God, unlike other nations whose fate is subsumed under general laws; wherefore the people of Israel is, like its God (*netsach yisrael*), eternal. Yet Krochmal translated this metahistorical principle into a historical idiom.[34] What for the Middle Ages was a transcendent, divine premise and promise became to him a partially immanent feature provable through and in history. While, to the Middle Ages, Israel proved and adhered to its vocation by being unchangeable, Krochmal proves their excellence through the very changes that even their religion underwent: it is, as Graetz was to say soon afterwards, "the history of one and the same idea—the idea of pure monotheism" in ever clearer articulations in word and deed. There was, of course, also a polemical-apologetical inversion involved in Krochmal's (and Graetz') formula. While Hegel, Bauer, and later Marx emphasized—as did centuries of Christian polemicists earlier—that the Jewish God is a particularistic-nationalistic one, Jewish religious philosophy in the nineteenth century, preceded by Krochmal, emphasized the true universality of Judaism and its God. Among all religions it is, each of them argued in his own way, the most catholic.

An inversion of a medieval topos was also Krochmal's employment of the principle of accommodation discussed in this chapter and ever so often in this book earlier—*dibra tora kileshon bene adam.*[35] For Krochmal, as for Maimonides earlier, it was not only an exegetical, but also a historical principle. The deity of each nation, he maintained, reflects its "national spirit." An intended ambiguity lurks in this statement; depending on our preferred point of view, it can be interpreted objectively as well as subjectively. The objective sense is derived from the ontological superstructure of Krochmal's historical perspective. If every national spirit embodies a partial aspect of the absolute spirit, then the deity of each nation represents this partial aspect. It is worth noting that Krochmal does not shy from slight distortions of rabbinical

33. Funkenstein, *Theology,* pp. 12–18.
34. Krochmal, *MNH,* 37; and chapter 8 below (Rosenzweig).
35. See n. 27.

sources to make them fit his theory. The rabbinical distinction between those who worship "the mountain" (*har*), that is, a physical entity, and those who worship "the spirit of the mountain" (*gada dehar*) serves him to prove that even the ancient sages recognized the true kernel of each religion. But of course he knew the immediately following lines in the text in which the former mode is judged much less pernicious than the latter.[36] It is further worth noting that Krochmal's list of national virtues (or spirits) corresponds to the order of divine powers or emanations in the *Kabbala* (the *sefirot,* whose names were again derived from the Davidic hymn in 1 Chron. 29:11).[37] Krochmal believed that it contained seeds of deep wisdom: he also was one of the first to point to its proximity to the ancient gnosis.

On the other hand, in a more subjective sense, each nation can be said to have created its gods in its image, to reflect its individual mental configuration: for the preponderance of *one* virtue in a nation does not mean the exclusion of all others. In its religion as in other areas of its creativity, a nation comes to recognize itself, its spirit, gradually. And so the principle of accommodation can be read either as a divine accommodation to humans—God revealing himself to each nation to the limits of its mentality—or as a human projection of a collective mentality upon the transcendent in the manner in which already Spinoza inverted the principle of accommodation.[38] Or again you may say: both senses, the subjective and the objective, are one.

That the *Kabbala* articulated all partial aspects of the divine is not a coincidence. Only the nation of Israel progresses towards an understanding of the divine as a totality, or (which is the same) towards its own self-understanding. Krochmal seems to imply, but never says so, that this self-understanding of Israel, when complete, amounts to the understanding that it is an instrument through which the divine totality achieves its own self-consciousness. Now, in Krochmal's view, the Middle Ages already arrived partially at such insight: in the Kabbala, and even more so in the philosophy of Ibn Ezra, "the wisdom of the oppressed" (*chokhmat hamisken*), which Krochmal interpreted in the spirit of his own version of neoplatonic pantheism.[39] In what, then, consists the contribution—or progress—of the *Haskala*? Precisely in

36. Krochmal, *MNH,* p. 29; B. T. *Chullin,* 40*b.*

37. Krochmal, *MNH,* pp. 35 ff. See David Biale, "The Kabbala in Nachman Krochmal's Philosophy of History," *Journal of Jewish Studies* 32 (1981), pp. 85–97.

38. See above, pp. 96–98.

39. Krochmal, *MNH,* pp. 284–394; and Guttman, *Philosophies of Judaism,* pp. 374 f.

the introduction of the historical, evolutionary dimension which these older insights lacked completely. He and his generation have introduced the "knowledge of latter days"—*da'at acharit hayamim,* which is historical knowledge—into the understanding of Israel and its god. Krochmal, who did not distinguish as explicitly as Salomon Maimon between the "metaphysics" and the "science" of medieval authors, seems nonetheless to have taken this distinction much more seriously. And, again in contrast to Maimon, science is to him not first and foremost knowledge of nature, but rather knowledge of history.

Much more can be said about Krochmal's pioneering endeavor, but it would exceed the limitations of this essay. Attention should be paid to the circumstance of this first philosophy of Jewish life and aspirations in Western and Central Europe—the struggle to obtain civil rights, political emancipation. Attention has been paid recently to the profound influence which Krochmal had on Eastern *maskilim* throughout the nineteenth century, as divergent as Abraham Mapu[40] and Achad Ha'am. Our conclusions are confined to the early *Haskala* and to the ways it compares with other European movements of the Enlightenment. Because the *maskil* affirmed the medieval intellectual heritage at least in part, he could draw a much more nuanced picture of the Middle Ages than the one born out of utter rejection; he learned to affirm the medieval tradition without accepting it wholesale, without identifying with it totally. And the ambivalence of the Jewish *maskil* toward medieval philosophy enabled him, more than some of his European counterparts, to realize the ambivalence, or relativity, of his own notion of Enlightenment.

Reform and History: The Modernization of Western European Jews

"MODERNIZATION"

The role of historical reasoning in the "modernization" process of Judaism since the age of Emancipation is the theme of the

40. Dan Miron, *Beyn Chazon le'emet: nitsane haroman ha'ivri vehayiddi beme'a ha-19* (Jerusalem, 1979), pp. 147–57; Abraham Katsh, "The Impact of Nachman Krochmal on the Development of the Zionist Movement," *Proceedings of the Ninth Congress of Jewish Studies* (1986), pp. 233–37.

following observations. Since its spread in the twelfth century,[41] the word *modernus,* which is derived from the classical *modo* for "now," meant "new," "in accord with recent times." To reshape Jewish religion in accord with the present was indeed the program of the founding fathers of reform Judaism since the beginning of the nineteenth century. They were more than ready to change religious perceptions, practices and institutions so as to ease (or even, as they thought, enable) for Jews their adjustment to the culture of their surroundings, to ease their entry into the "civil society" and their incorporation into the national state as equal citizens. But even the adversaries of religious reform, at least in Germany, France, or England, by no means wanted to return to the medieval, corporative community structure with its immunities and autonomy. Whether conservative, orthodox, or liberal, most Jews of Western Europe came to identify unconditionally with the various political states they lived in. Unlike Eastern European (or indeed Near Eastern) Jews, they lost the consciousness of being in the Diaspora—of being, as Rabbi Moses of Pressburg put it, "prisoners of war" in alien lands.[42] The process of turning from subjects into citizens—*Verbürgelichung*—encompassed all variants of German and French Jewry. All of them became, in this sense of the word, "modernized."

Now, "modernity"—however defined—means not only the affirmation of what is new, but also the consciousness of its historical formation and conditioning; it means the recognition of temporality as a cardinal dimension of self-understanding. Not even metaphysical principles of transcendent values were from now on immune against their historicization. Hegel's demand "to determine substance as subject" ("die Substanz als Subjekt zu bestimmen")[43] meant that even the absolute, whole truth converges totally with the envelopment process of its moments. History owed this royal role of hers to the bourgeoisie and its perception of itself and of the national state. The new state was supposed to find its legitimation and its roots in the anonymous past of the creative "spirit of the nation" (*Volksgeist*) rather than in the heroic deeds of individual founders or in the dynastic continuity of the rulers. Patient and industrious labor secured for the bourgeoisie (in its own account) its causal, decisive role in the progress of the civil society. The bourgeoisie saw itself as the inner, driving force of modernity, albeit

41. See W. Freund, *Modernus und andere Zeitbegriffe des Mittlealters* (Köln, 1957).

42. Rabbi Moses of Pressburg, in *Ele divre habrith* (Altona, 1819), p. 26.

43. Hegel, *Phänomenologie des Geistes,* ed. Hofmeister, introduction, p. 18. On Hegel's reinterpretation and employment of Spinoza's doctrine of substance see Klaus Düsing, *Hegel und die Geschichte der Philosophie* (Darmstadt, 1983), pp. 170–93.

late in being recognized as such. Historical scholarship became through and through a bourgeois discipline in a subjective as well as an objective sense. The historian became an industrious citizen, a conscientious laborer on the historical sources that he also made available. Unlike the earlier type of gentleman or court historian, he does not draw from existing earlier materials only as their *arbiter,* nor does he depend on genial insights: he must rather, in painstaking work, unearth and reconstruct his sources, and then detect in them information they did not intend disclosing, and reveal deep trends which the historian of earlier generations inevitably overlooked.

This very self-image of the civil society (*Bürgertum*) also stood in the background of the theoretical concept of individuality that Durkheim formulated at the beginning of his sociological career. He translated the interdependence between the individual and his "milieu," spoken of throughout the nineteenth century, into a precise analysis of the "organical," well-developed social order as against the "mechanical" one.[44] The former, by the very logic of its division of labor, demands the initiative of the enterprising individual as a being that shapes society and is shaped by it. Such were also the anthropological assumptions of literary realism in the nineteenth century, which was (as Auerbach and Lukács have shown)[45] throughout intertwined with the new forms of historical reasoning and with the self-image of bourgeois society. Both the will to modernize society and the fear of this modernization were expressed in the new "science of history" (*Geschichtswissenschaft*).

It is all the more astonishing to realize how marginal the role of the *Wissenschaft des Judentums* was even within the reform movement. Why were, even within the reform, historical arguments employed at best for tactical purposes? A deep frustration, almost desperation, speaks from the letters of Geiger to Derenburg.[46] The considerable scholarly achievements of the "Science of Judaism" were hardly noticed either by the non-Jewish or by the Jewish environment, and certainly not assimilated into the cultural context. The notorious type of "Rabbiner-Doktor" was, in a personal union, rabbi on the Sabbath and private scholar on Sunday. Why was this so?

Only partly can we blame it on the scarcity of academic recognition

44. Émile Durkheim, "L'individualisme et les intellectuelles," Revue bleue 4, 10 (1898), p. 12n. cf. S. Lukes, *Émile Durkheim: His Life and Works* (New York, 1972), pp. 332–49.
45. Georg Lukács, *Der historische Roman* (Berlin, 1955); Erich Auerbach, *Mimesis. Dargestellte Wirklichkeit in der abendländischen Litteratur,* 2nd edition (Bern, 1959), pp. 202–87. See also chapter 10.
46. Abraham Geiger, *Nachgelassene Schriften* (Berlin, 1875–78).

and acceptance. In Germany, it is true, the *Wissenschaft des Judentums* was never represented in universities until the 1950s, but in France it entered the academic institutions at least through the back door of Oriental languages.[47] The primary reason for the isolation should, though, be sought in the conditions under which Judaism, civil society, and historical awareness met. All studies dedicated to the Jewish religion in the age of emancipation—including the outstanding book of Max Wiener by that title[48]—avoided a comparison between Protestantism, Catholicism and Judaism. With this comparison I wish to start.

CATHOLIC, PROTESTANT, AND JEWISH SENSES OF TIME

The confrontation between religious images and the new sense of history took different modes in the different Western European religions. The Catholic Church could maintain its distance from both the civil state and historical criticism, because it possessed, of old, effective weapons to defend itself against secularization. For Protestant denominations, however, history was from the very beginning a source of embarrassment, a σκάνδαλον of immense proportions. As for preemancipatory Judaism, it was indifferent towards history—at least the interval between antiquity and the coming of the Messiah.

The Catholic Church was well fortified against historical relativization long before the emergence of historicism. We had, on previous occasions, many opportunities to study the fortunes of the idea of divine accommodation.[49] To the question of the pagans, why did the Church abolish the institutions of the Old Testament if they were commanded by God, the Church Fathers answered that God adjusted his revelation and his institutions to the capacity of persons at different ages to perceive and to follow them; God knows best "that which applies by adjustment to each age" (*quid cuique tempore accomodate adhibeatur*).[50] To the Middle Ages, we saw, this idea was an unending source of historical observations. So, for instance, for Anselm of Havelberg, a bishop *in*

---

47. See Perrine Simon-Nahum, *La cité investie*. Paris, 1991.

48. Max Wiener, *Jüdische Religion im Zeitalter der Emanzipation* (Berlin, 1933). The same is true of more modern studies, e.g., Michael A. Mayer, *Response to Modernity. A History of the Reform-Movement in Judaism* (Oxford, 1988).

49. See above, pp. 94 ff., 141 ff. (Maimonides), 241 ff. (Salomo Maimon), 243 ff. (Ranak).

50. See above, pp. 94–95.

partibus infidelium, who, as a member of a new order (the Premonstra-
tensians) felt hard pressed to answer the question why Christianity
should have so many recently founded orders. And he answered: Particularly in our present, fourth period of Church history, in which
the Church is not persecuted anymore nor endangered by heretics
but in danger of corruption by *falsi fratres,* the Holy Ghost combats
them with ever new religious impulses.[51] The Church, throughout the
Middle Ages, was aware of its transformation in time, and was even
willing to concede that dogmatic progress was triggered by temporal
circumstances.[52]

In the early modern centuries, the principle of accommodation became even more a principle of opportunism (without any negative connotation). When the Jesuit missionary Ricci adjusted Christianity to
the Chinese mentality by identifying God with the traditional notion
of *shang ti,* his approach became—especially after his death—heavily
disputed.[53] But nobody accused him of heresy or doubted his missionary zeal and achievements. The Church even learned to employ, for
its own purposes, the newly emerging biblical criticism. Against the
Protestant claim to read the Scriptures alone—*sola scriptura*—Richard
Simon advanced his criticism to prove that no unaided reading of
the Bible *sine glossa* is possible. His work was eventually condemned,
but not so the work of Jean Astruck with similar intent and graver
consequences.[54]

In short, the Church was always involved in history, in the double
meaning of the term. It could view the process of secularization in the
nineteenth century as nothing really new, and it had historical categories with which to explain whatever happened recently. It remembered
confrontations with worldly powers since Theodosius and, nearly without interruption, since the War of Investiture. History was for it a
source of solace and courage.

For Protestantism, at least in its main trends, history was, by con-

51. See above, p. 51.
52. On the *questio scholastica* whether faith has changed with the change of times (*an
secundum mutationes temporum mutata sit fides*), see J. Beumer, S.J., "Der theoretische
Beitrag der Frühscholastik zur Problem des Dogmen fortschritts," *Zeitschrift für katholische Theologie* 74 (1952), pp. 105 ff.
53. On the Chinese mission see Arnold H. Rowbotham, *Missionary and Mandarin in
China: The Jesuits at the Court of China* (Berkeley, 1942).
54. A. Lods, *Jean Astruck et la critique biblique au XVIIIe siècle* (Strassburg and Paris,
1924). Astruck wanted, against Spinoza, to defend the authorship of Moses—by identifying his "sources." The documentary-hypothesis was thus born.

trast, a problem. Luther and his contemporaries believed themselves to be close to the end of history, to the second coming of Christ. Looking back on the balance of the history of the Church at least since Augustine, Luther saw a history of corruption, of the eclipse of truth. History unfolded, in his eyes, by no means "like a grand symphony" (*veluti magnum carmen*)[55] as it did to Augustine: it was by no means a source of confidence. Later on, Gottfried Arnold will describe the persecuted heretics throughout the history of the Church as the true believers; Jesus himself was persecuted as a heretic. The domain of public history is the domain of corruption: not even Luther, he believed, could reform the Church by renewing the original Church.[56]

But withdrawal from the world (and its history) was only one component of the Protestant revolution: another was an extreme affirmation of the world, immersion in it, elevating any *Beruf* into a *Berufung*,[57] at times to the point of identifying the Church with the historical success of the civilization in which it was embedded. The liberal-enlightened Protestantism of the eighteenth and nineteenth centuries tended to identify Christianity with cultural progress, *Christentum und Kultur* (Overbeck). In the best case, this attitude led to an anemic interpretation of Christianity as rational ethics, of Christ as a Socratic hero. In the worst cases it led to a *Thron und Altartheologie*—the legitimation of the powers that be. The so-called crisis of Protestant theology came, at the end of the nineteenth century, as an almost inevitable reaction: when it dawned upon historically oriented Protestant theologians that there is no way back (*reformatio*) to the original form or constitution of Christianity, namely back to a Jewish-apocalyptic, world-renouncing sect.[58] Moreover, a Christianity that is too closely identified with the state may lose its substance when placed, as the logic of the national, secularized state demands, in a "market situation of religion" (Berger).[59] History, in the Protestant domain, was a source of incessant self-criticism.

55. See above, p. 94 (Augustine) and n. 16.

56. See chapter 2 (Arnold).

57. Max Weber, *Die Protestantische Ethik und der Geist des Kapitalismus* in *Gesammelte Aufsätze zur Religionssoziologie,* 3 vols. (Tübingen, 1920), vol. I, pp. 17–206, esp. 24 ff.

58. Franz Overbeck, *Christentum und Kultur,* ed. C. A. Bernouli (Basel, 1919), casted doubt over the whole enterprise of a "theology." See Karl Löwith, *Von Hegel zu Nietzsche,* 5th edition (Stuttgart, 1964), pp. 402–15.

59. Peter Berger, *The Sacred Canopy. Elements of a Sociological Theory of Religion* (Garden City, NY, 1967), pp. 105 ff.; Peter Berger and Thomas Luckmann, "Secularization and Pluralism," *Intern. Yearbook for the Sociology of Religion* (1966).

Very different was the role of historical criticism in Judaism. Rosen-zweig's famous judgment that Judaism stands "outside the turmoil of temporality"[60] does, to a measure, fit the traditional Jewish attitude towards recent history. Nothing that happened between the loss of sovereignty and its future regaining seemed "worthy of memory." The Jews, said Rabbi Simone Luzzato in the seventeenth century, are like a river going through different soils: the water remains the same while its color changes. Jews are industrious, adjustable on the outside, without local patriotism—an ideal subject to an absolutistic, mercantilistic prince. They have no history, and do not desire it, for the time being.[61]

The driving force of Protestantism—the yearning for a *reformatio,* for a return to the original shape—had no precise equivalent in the traditional Jewish imagery. The belief in the future coming of the Messiah, who, "even if he procrastinates, will surely come," and the belief in the restoration of the Davidic kingship were not necessarily tied to the hope of a *better* Judaism, a purer community.[62] Traditional Judaism lacked the image of an innocent, pure *Urgemeinschaft* that shall once again be restored. This was already reason enough why the movement of "reform" could by no means intend a "reformation" even while claiming that it did.

Now, it is true that the Jewish law—the *halakha*—developed of old mechanisms of change and adjustment to new circumstances. The famous word-pun of Rabbi Moses of Pressburg—"everything new (*chadash*) is forbidden by law"[63]—was itself "new," characteristic of the reaction against the reform movement. The very term "novelty" (*chidush*) carried, as we said earlier, a highly positive connotation within legal scholarship (*talmud tora*). But changes and adjustments, even radical ones, had to appear under the guise of conservation, of being merely "fences to the law." The reformer of the nineteenth century, on the other hand, denied the sovereignty of Jewish law and wanted to relegate religion, in the phrase of Karl Marx, from the public to the private sphere of law. Both premises were downright unthinkable earlier.

To sum up: the Catholic sense of temporality was evolutionary. The

60. See above, p. 120, and below, pp. 291–295.
61. See above, pp. 15–17.
62. Even the age of the patriarchs did not always seem better: cf. chapter 5 (Maimonides). On the other hand, even the period of the judges, in which "each man did the right thing in his eyes," sometimes did appear as a golden age. Maimonides, we saw, conceived the messianic age as being "better" only in the sense that the whole world will be monotheized.
63. Jacob Katz, *Ben halakha lekabbala* (Jerusalem, 1987).

254   THE THRESHOLD OF MODERNITY

Protestant sense of time was, at least potentially, revolutionary. The traditional Jewish attitude towards time and history was neither affirmative nor negative, but indifferent.[64]

REFORM AND HISTORY

Because the idea of reform was so alien to the traditional Jewish thought, it was not entertained by the preemancipatory enlighteners (*maskilim*) either. They rather opted for two extreme possible solutions for the "amelioration" of "the civil state of the Jews" (the title of Dohm's famous treatise).[65] Some, like Friedländer, envisioned a mass conversion of Jews, but only pro forma. Others, like Mendelssohn, hoped for an internal education of the Jews, bringing them to the cultural level of their environment without changing an iota of the law.[66] A third possibility seemed not to be given.

The demand to change the Jewish religion, and the willingness to do so, did not come from within the Jewish community, but rather as a response to outside pressure. Jews who were eager to acquire civil rights were required to prove that they regard the law of the land as their law in all respects. The reformers therefore wanted first and foremost to denationalize the Jewish religion, to "confessionalize" it, so that one could be a German Jew in precisely the same sense one could be a German Catholic or Protestant. All references or allusions to a national redemption had to be eliminated from the liturgy, which was also to be completely translated into the vernacular. Even those components of the synagogal reform which seemingly had a purely aesthetic function, such as the introduction of the organ into the service, were calculated to blunt eschatological-national aspirations: the reason why choirs and musical instruments were barred earlier was primarily because they were improper expressions of joy after the destruction of the Temple. The rebuilt Temple will again have them. In short: synagogal reform was a

64. Which does not, however, make their history-writing any more detached from the "collective memory" of the Jewish community in which they lived than the historical accounts of other times and places. To say, as Yerushalmi (*pace* Halbwachs) does, that the beginning of scientific historiography marks a growing hiatus between memory and historiography is to beg the question *whose* memory is spoken of. If it is the memory of German Jews, then it certainly was well articulated by Jost, Geiger, and Graetz. See chapter 1, "Jewish Historical Consciousness."

65. Christian Wilhelm Dohm, *über die bürgerliche Verbesserung der Juden* (1781).

66. See above, pp. 222–229.

political act. Dubnow erred when he viewed it as an attempt at a "Jewish reformation"[67]—just as Heine erred when he called Mendelssohn "the Jewish Luther."

Now, in the hour of the nascent reform, it may seem that the proper moment for historical criticism and evaluation of Judaism has come. Such was the hope of the founders of the Gesellschaft für die Wissenschaft des Judentums. Historical reflection was to take the place of traditional modes of legitimation. Historical knowledge was to become the nucleus of a new Judaism. We remember that Nachman Krochmal, by far more traditional in his aspirations, also held the "knowledge of the end of days" (*da'at acharit hayamim*)—that is, historical knowledge—to be the proper mode of reviving religion today.[68] Jost, Zunz, and Geiger were much more explicit: historical consciousness was to be the substitute for the traditional religious imagery *and* praxis.

But what was this historical consciousness to be? Whose image was the new image of history to represent? If the Jews were to be neither a nation nor in any other sense a political subject, all that was left for the new mode of historical criticism to focus on were apologetic or antiquarian concerns. This is not to belittle the enormous achievements of the *Wissenschaft des Judentums* in surveying the existing sources of Jewish history and securing them philologically. Often enough, the reform-scholar looked into the past to find but a mirror of himself, and a legitimation of his doing. To Derenburg, the Pharisees were the prototypes of good republicans.[69] To his friend Abraham Geiger they were the prototype of true reformers. Countless histories of communities proved the antiquity of Jewish settlements. The Jewish "contributions" to world culture were to be highlighted. In short: the new image of history was none. By reflecting the wishes and concerns of the community in which it was embedded, the *Wissenschaft* became in fact as ahistorical as its Orthodox predecessors.

This is even true of Heinrich Graetz. At least, you may argue, he permitted the same subject to be the subject of Jewish history through the ages; he conceded the existence, even to the present, of a Jewish nation. But the raison d'être of the nation was an idea, "the idea of pure monotheism." For its reification, or embodiment, that idea demanded

67. S. Dubnow, *World History of the Jewish People* (Hebrew, Tel-Aviv, 1958), IX, pp. 41–67.

68. See above, pp. 243–247.

69. Cf. Simon-Nahum (as above, n. 47).

a political state at first, a religious community thereafter. Now, however, neither the state nor publicly organized religion is still a *conditio sine qua non* for the Idea to survive in a "philosophical" age.[70]

Should we, perhaps, distinguish between that which the protagonists of the "science of Judaism" wanted as against what they *really* wanted? Perhaps without knowing it, they strove to establish a German-Jewish (or French-Jewish) subculture, both distinct from the environment and yet part of it,[71] without separate political aspirations but with claims for a valid and valuable separate form of life and values. Their paradigm was, therefore, the so-called golden age of Spanish Jews between the tenth and thirteenth centuries, accompanied by the conviction that the emancipation of the Jews was irrevocable, that the end of Spanish Jewry could never happen again in a secularized, cultured Europe.

For all of these reasons, the *Wissenschaft des Judentums* remained without profound impact even on the reform movement—though most of the ideologues of the latter were practitioners of the former. The driving force of the reform movement was first and foremost well-to-do community members, *ba'ale bathim,* and their efforts were half-hearted and variegated. For most of the duration of the nineteenth century, moreover, the majority of Jews—particularly in smaller towns and villages—remained fairly traditional if not orthodox. Agnon's short story "Between Two Cities" sketches a fairly accurate picture of a small Jewish *Landgemeinde* until the First World War: religiously observant and German patriotic.[72]

Indeed, herein lies the transformation that Jews, whether liberal or orthodox, really underwent: all German (or French) Jews came to identify themselves, without reservations, with the state. They came to view the political state as their very own. They lost the sense of being in exile. For most of them, including the neo-orthodox, religion became private matter. The Jewish *kehilla* became a liturgical community, *Kultusgemeinde.* As such, they did not want to have an open-ended, independent history, but only a past.

70. H. Graetz, *Die Konstruktion der jüdischen Geschichte. Eine Skizze.* (Berlin, 1936), pp. 95–96.

71. Shulamit Volkow, "The Dynamics of Dissimilation: 'Ostjuden' and the German Jews," *The Jewish Response to German Culture,* ed. J. Reinharz (London, 1985), pp. 195–211.

72. Shmuel Yosef Agnon, *Ben shtey arim, Collected Stories* (Hebrew), vol. VI (*Samuch venir'e*), pp. 78–91.

8

Franz Rosenzweig and the End
of German-Jewish Philosophy

Introduction

THE THEMES

Seldom can the historian indicate the beginning and the end of a movement with such a precision as in the case of German-Jewish philosophy. It started with Mendelssohn's *Jerusalem* (1783) and ended with Rosenzweig's *Stern der Erlösung* (1921), the subject of the following essay. German Jews continued to write about philosophy after that for a short while (Buber, Brod, Guttmann, Weltsch, Strauss), but even when they wrote in German, their audience ceased to be the German-Jewish *Bildungsbürgertum;* their *Wahlheimat* was irretrievably lost. German Jewry continued to be visible for a while after the catastrophe in language—islands that did not claim or want their own perpetuation in a new land. And so Rosenzweig's very chronological distinction adds significance to the considerable body of thought that was his.

German-Jewish philosophy in the nineteenth century abounded with ingenious constructions and fertile interpretation. For all of the difference between various systems of thought, they and the movement of which they were a part, the critical study of Judaism (*Wissenschaft vom Judentum*), shared nonetheless a high degree of consensus; they reflected the convictions and aspirations of many German Jews during the rise and fall of liberalism. They wanted to eliminate the accidental nature of their existence as both Germans and Jews. They believed that the best of German culture—the *Bildung* to which they were committed—corresponded to the best in their own Jewish tradition. They looked for a true synthesis of "Deutschtum und Judentum" and construed a *Wahlverwandtschaft* between both. All this may strike us today as a paradigm of false consciousness, ridiculous and, considering its end, dangerous. Could they not have read the ominous signs of reflection already during the *Antisemitismusstreit* of 1876? But we ought to refrain from judging the wishes and aspirations of German Jews merely from the point of view of their catastrophic end. The ideals of a German-Jewish synthesis were not idle dreams of a nonexisting entity, because they reflected, and helped to generate, a rich and vital German-Jewish subculture, not unlike Alexandrinian Jewish culture in antiquity or Spanish-Jewish culture in the Middle Ages. This subculture possessed its own press and literature—such as Georg Hermann's novel *Jetchen Gebert,* which could be read by German Jews only. German Jews had their own folklore, their own cultural code, their humor, even their own peculiar habits of speech. Only a German-Jewish *Bildungsbürger* could appreciate or even understand the reference to a good-natured fool as a "Schaute mit vergnügten Sinnen"—an allusion both to the Hebrew-Yiddish "Schote" (fool) and to the beginning lines of Schiller's poem "The Ring of Polycrates":

> "Er stand auf seines Daches Zinnen
> Und Schaute mit vergnügten Sinnen
> Auf das beherrschte Samos hin."[1]

A mark of this German-Jewish subculture was its incessant self-reflection, constant self-occupation, with or without irony. Franz Rosenzweig's "Star of Redemption" was one of the last great instances of this self-reflection. Rosenzweig was as much a part of the aspirations of the German-Jewish *Bildungsbürgertum* as he rebelled against its complacency. His rebellion, unlike the Zionist commitment of some of his

---

1. Friedrich Schiller, "Der Ring des Polykrates," in *Werke.* On the notion of a German-Jewish subculture see D. Sorkin, and my article "Herman Cohen: Philosophie, Deutschtum und Judentum," *Jahrbuch des Instituts für deutsche Geschichte.* Beiheft 6 (1984): pp. 355–65, esp. 356.

generation of intellectuals, was a rebellion from within, a call for re-orientation articulated on many levels.

The following observations and considerations offer three indepen-dent approaches to Rosenzweig's major theological work, *Der Stern der Erlösung:* a biographical, architectonic (or systematic), and a political-interpretive avenue. Each of them consists of a comparison: Rosen-zweig's main tenets, formulated already in 1917, reflect his intellectual biography and can in part be traced to expressions which even precede his famous "conversion." Furthermore, the system finally constructed, when compared to its draft (the "Urzelle"), showed a sudden vigorous employment of Cohen's main epistemological tool, the "principle of beginning"; the way in which Rosenzweig transformed a logical figure into a philosophical allegory says much about the book. And, finally, Rosenzweig's peculiar view of the unhistorical (and apolitical) nature of the Jewish nation will gain by comparison to some German-Jewish thinkers which he respected and rejected. Ours, then, is a biographical approach towards the understanding of Rosenzweig's system, taking as a central point of departure the mentioned early draft, to look from it backwards and forwards. The strength of this approach is also its weak-ness: the strong biographical character of Rosenzweig's thought is un-deniable; but our biographical sources are meager and fragmentary.

AN EXEMPLARY LIFE

A few well-known biographical dates are nonetheless in order.[2] Franz Rosenzweig was born in 1886 to a well-to-do, fairly well assimilated Jewish family, in which Judaism was venerated and affirmed but thought of as an added confessional ornament to a basically Ger-man national identity.

He grew up, in Kassel, without signs of deep religious interests, but decided to learn Hebrew at the age of fourteen—a much better way to spend the obligatory *Religionsunterricht* than the habitual read-ing of uplifting literature. A deep interest in Greek and Roman classics had accompanied him since the *Gymnasium;* after finishing it, he turned first to medical studies, then shifted to history and philosophy, and obtained his doctorate of philosophy under the guidance of Friedrich Meinecke—then in Freiburg—with a doctoral dissertation which is still an indispensable work in the field, "Hegel und der Staat." A religious

2. Nahum U. Glatzer, *Franz Rosenzweig: His Life and Thought,* 2nd ed. (New York, 1961). A comprehensive biographical study is now in preparation by Paul Mendes-Flohr (The Hebrew University, Jerusalem).

crisis—or crisis of identity—made him seriously consider conversion to Christianity; intense debates with his friends, and perhaps the attendance of a solemn Day of Atonement traditional service, caused him to decide "to remain a Jew," and to try to fill this his renewed commitment with a religious and intellectual content. When the First World War broke out, Rosenzweig was drafted in the German Army as an artillery officer, and spent most of the war in the Balkans. Around 1916 or 1917 he started the composition of his *magnum et arduum opus,* the "Star of Redemption."

The war being over, he was not interested in an academic career that was offered to him. He rather saw his mission in the reorganization of Jewish education, the main instrument, he thought, of changing the stagnant religious consciousness and knowledge of German Jews, filling it with substantial and durable content. He founded and for two years directed a new institution of free adult education, the *Frankfurter Lehrhaus,* the meeting place for a young, rebellious Jewish intelligentsia. In 1921, the first signs of a mortal illness—multiple sclerosis—appeared. Soon Rosenzweig was bedridden and completely paralyzed. His intellectual powers were not affected, his courage grew with the challenge; helped by his wife Edith, whom he married shortly before his symptoms broke out, Rosenzweig was capable of sitting, receiving guests, and communicating slowly with the aid of a specially devised typewriter which he could move with the slight movement of his finger, the only movement he could still perform. During this time he translated medieval Jewish poetry, and, with Buber, the Bible into German in a new translation that was meant to capture the sound and rhythm of the Hebrew, and that succeeded in doing so to an astonishing degree. He became a center of admiration and veneration to German Jews—in particular to a new generation of intellectuals committed to Judaism. Franz Rosenzweig died, at home, in 1929.

Toward the System: "Urformell" and "Urzelle"

EARLY PRONOUNCEMENTS

An intellectual biography of Rosenzweig has yet to be written. It is needed if only to understand properly the "Stern der Erlösung," which speaks in part of a personal, almost private language, addressed to a small group of friends who shared similar formative *Bild-ungserlebnisse*. Now it is, of course, a triviality that any philosophical system in some measure objectivizes biographical moments. In the case of Rosenzweig, this is eminently true. He himself asks us to read his philosophy as a "narrative," which must also mean as a personal narrative. And then, the converse is likewise true. From early on Rosenzweig reflected upon his life as a work of art to be shaped or, if you wish, as a philosophical text to be written: "Ich wollte, ich ware eine Beethovensche Symphonie oder sonst irgend etwas, was *fertig* geschrieben *ist*. Das Geschrieben-werden tut weh," he wrote at the age of eighteen.[3] It was more than an ephemeral outburst of a young man yearning for an identity. Then and later he very deliberately set about making his life into a clean, clear, meaningful text, written by himself alone.

But the intellectual biography of Rosenzweig cannot be written on the meager basis of his published letters and diaries. These suffice at best to give us a few clues as to what questions may be asked of the sources once they do surface. If we wish to discern within the *Stern* primary from secondary or even tertiary layers, if we wish to separate as far as possible the architectonic from the fundamental elements in his thought, the best we can do now is to take, as a point of departure, the "Urzelle" together with his correspondence with Rosenstock and to try to compare it with earlier and later positions. What of it, we ask first, expresses previously crystalized attitudes, and under what biographical circumstances were they assumed? What and how much was then added to the "Urzelle" in the *Stern*?

The early letter just quoted testifies to the pain of yearning for a clear, authentic, objective identity; the seriousness with which he pursued it made him, in his own eyes, "ein Mumelgreis von achtzehn Jahren."[4] The language employed is that of the classical-romantic ideal of the heroic personality: he speaks of the tension between his εἶδος and reality, of the fear and the necessity to test and assert the former against the latter. The Goethean ideal of the heroic, self-fulfilled personality was first and foremost a painful constitutive force in his early experience before it appeared as a possible theme on which to write a learned tract[5] and, later, as one of the three "irreducible" ingredients in his system. It

---

3. Franz Rosenzweig, *Briefe*, ed. E. Rosenzweig (Berlin, 1935), p. 19 (12.11.1905). This chapter follows closely my article "The Genesis of Rosenzweig's 'Stern der Erlösung': 'Unformell' and 'Urzelle'" in *Jahrbuch des Instituts für deutsche Geschichte*, Beiheft 4 (1983), pp. 17–29. A new edition of the letters appeared in The Hague, 1979.

4. *Briefe*, p. 16 (22.10.1905).

5. *Briefe*, p. 60 (28.9.1911).

shows (and, in part, also explains) Rosenzweig's early urge for intellectual, professional, and emotional commitments.

It is indeed astonishing how early some of the positions assumed in the "Urzelle" occurred to Rosenzweig, earlier even than his "conversion" in 1913. I do not mean to belittle the impact of his confrontation with Rosenstock, of the preceding crisis and the subsequent months-long struggle with the impulse to convert to Christianity, and of his final decision not to do so, conveyed in a letter to the very same Hans Ehrenberg whom he once encouraged to convert. But I do find that, once the struggle was over, he found himself repeating positions which he had already begun to assume earlier. His own sense of sudden intuitions is, at times, deceiving. In a conversation with Rosenstock, he says that the sense of revelation as an Archimedean point of orientation dawned upon him;[6] the factuality of revelation was hence the cornerstone of his "empirical" philosophy. But already in 1910, we find him writing to Hans Ehrenberg:[7]

Viel Metareligiöses steckt in all diesen Fragen nach dem Ursprung des Bösen, nach Gott und der Geschichte. Das Religiöse selbst ist immer positive Religion, beginnt mit dem factum, nicht mit dem Ursprung und Wesen des Faktums. Gottes "naturas continueri" überließ Luther der Spekulation, "beneficia eius cognoscere" nahm er für sich Anspruch.

Much later, in the *Stern*, he will call the third part of his tract the reconstruction of the "elements" and their "course" into concrete historical religions, that is, the reading of history as a history of God's manifestation, "pattern" (*Gestalt*). Already here, in this letter, he intimates the converse:

Daher weigern wir uns auch, "gott in der Geschichte" zu sehen, weil wir die Geschichte (in religioser Beziehung) *nicht als Bild*, nicht als ein Sein sehen wollen; sondern wir *leugnen* Gott in ihr, um ihn in dem Prozess, durch den sie wird, zu *restaurieren*.

Apparently likewise in 1909 and 1910 questions of religious identity had already troubled him. They were less bothersome when he was out of school, when he merrily commented (again in Goethean vein) on the paganization of his religious sentiment, "denn gewöhnlich werden Luft-und Wettergötter . . . allmählich zu sittlichen Melechs hoalom,

6. *Briefe*, pp. 71–73 (31.10.1913).
7. *Briefe*, p. 53 (26.9.1910).

und nun ists meinem umgekehrt gegangen."[8] Now, about a year after his change of profession, he starts to rethink fundamentals, all the more so in conjunction with the conversion of his close friend, Hans Ehrenberg, to Christianity. So, we already find some very basic formulations on the significance of being Jewish, which contain, *in nuce,* his systematic point of view of later years. In a letter to his parents, Rosenzweig admits that he encouraged Ehrenberg to take this course:[9]

> Wir sind in allen Dingen Christen, wir leben in einem christlichen Staat, gehen in christliche Schulen, lesen christliche Bücher, kurzum: unsere ganze "Cultur" ist ganz und gar auf christliche Grundlage; deshalb gehört für den, der kein hemmendes Moment in sich hat, weiter nichts als der ganz leichte Entschluß . . . dazu, um das Christentum anzunehmen.

He continues, though, with what seems to me to be an assurance to his parents that he, indeed, possesses some "inhibitory moments": "das Judentum kann man im häutigen Deutschland nicht 'annehmen', daß muß einem anbeschnitten, angegessen, angebarmitzwet sein." And, finally:

> Wenn der Jude (der Jude wie ich ihn verstehe, also der Religionsjude) angegriffen wird, dann hat er die Tora nicht als Schild vor sich zu halten, sondern er gehört *vor* die Tora. Nicht die Juden sollen erhalten bleiben, sondern das Judentum.

Already, then, he thinks of Judaism as a biological-cultural community, rather than as a set of creeds;[10] already, then, he ties this insight to the demand for a reform of religious instruction.

I do not wish to leave the impression that the formation of Rosenzweig's attitudes was a smooth, linear progression. The shift from medicine to history must have been a crisis of identity of sorts;[11] it coincided with the profound and lasting impact which Kant made on him, at first as the right philosopher for a natural scientist, the philosopher who ended all nonempirical philosophizing.[12] To Kant he also owes the trichotomy of the reducibles of "experience" in his later system. The historical studies he assumes under Meineke, Rickert, and Wölflin, together with a strong wish to become "ein echter Historiker-

8. *Briefe,* p. 14 (3.4.1905).
9. *Briefe,* p. 45 (6.11.1909).
10. "Zeugung" rather than "Ünberzeugung" is the final formulation in the *Stern der Erlösung.*
11. *Briefe,* p. 35 (4.3.1908).
12. *Briefe,* p. 30 (4.11.1906) as against pp. 33–34 (18.11.1907).

kopf" (he once said just as emphatically, "ich bin kein Historiker!"), failed eventually to satisfy his search for identity. In a later letter to Meinecke, he talks of his "breakdown" in 1913, of a sense of meaninglessness, and of a realization that he used historical studies to satisfy an insatiable hunger for "images"—to nourish, perhaps by confrontation, his self-image, his εἶδος.[13] A conversion there was, but neither his turn to philosophy, nor to Judaism, were as "sudden" as he himself called them at times. The change rather enabled him to fall back on, and to maintain, positions already delineated.

THE ORIGINAL FORMULA

By the time he decided, after months of wrestling with the problem, "to remain a Jew," he also possessed the basic formula which, from now on, would serve him to distinguish Judaism from Christianity. If his letter of November 18, 1917, to Rudolf Ehrenberg was named the "Urzelle" of his *magnum et arduum opus,* I wish to call the following statements of late 1913 the "Urformell" of the *Stern der Erlösung:*[14]

Die Entwicklung des Judentums geht an dem Jesus zu dem die Heiden "Herr" sagen und durch den sie "zum Vater kommen" vorbei; sie geht nicht durch ihn hindurch,

or, a week later,[15]

Es *kommt* niemand zum Vater—anders aber wenn einer nicht mehr zum Vater zu kommen braucht, weil er schon bei ihm *ist.* Und dies ist nun der Fall der Volkes Israel. . . . Das Volk Israel, erwählt von seinem Vater, blickt starr über Welt und Geschichte hinüber auf jenen letzten fernsten Punkt, wo dieser sein Vater, dieser selbe, der Eine und Einzige—"Alles in Allem!"—sein wird.

Later, he will attest to Israel's existence "ausserhalb des kriegerichen Tumults der Zeitlichkeit"[16] and to the contraposition "zum Vater kommen—beim Vater sein," which will remain his basic formula. He learned to express it in a richer idiom.

These two fundamental themes—the factuality of revelation and the

13. *Briefe,* p. 32 (Sylvesternacht 1907/8).
14. *Briefe,* p. 68 (23.10.1913).
15. *Briefe,* p. 71 (31.10.1913).
16. *Briefe,* pp. 276–81; *Der Stern der Erlösung* (The Hague, 1979; text after the edition of Frankfurt/Main, 1921), p. 59: "Das jüdische Volk ist für sich schon am Ziel, denn die Völker der welt erst zuschreiten."

timelessness of Judaism—coexisted in Rosenzweig's thought for the following four years. To each theme he found ever more ingenious "formulations," to each he devoted considerable speculative energies. But he did not yet find a structure to accommodate both, an argument of the kind sustained in the *Stern* to show how, from his understanding of revelation, it follows that it *must* be expressed in two incompatible yet true modes of historical manifestation. Put differently, even though he believed he knew the essential difference between Judaism and Christianity, he could not yet make up his mind whether and in what sense both are necessary.

But even without such a mediating structure, both formulas sufficed, in 1914, to cause Rosenzweig to insist on what Judaism *cannot* be reduced to—namely a nationalistic-secular revival. Thus, in his "Atheistische Theologie,"[17] Rosenzweig was ready to diagnose the problem of Jewish theology: the historical-rational orientation of the *Wissenschaft vom Judentum* threw Jewish theology into the same crisis of identity generated in Protestant theology by the "Leben-Jesu-Forschung." Christianity must restore the relevance of Jesus' historical individuality to religion; Judaism must conceive a theology of revelation which would lend significance to the historical uniqueness of Jews and yet be acceptable to the historical sense of modern man. But how?

Not even in the letters to Rosenstock (until 1916) or in the "Urzelle" did Rosenzweig succeed in establishing that *necessary* mediation between his philosophy of revelation and his contraposition of Judaism against Christianity. Such a necessary connection, formulated in the *Stern,* appears only in 1918, embodied in the metaphor of the star and its radiation as two necessary modes of the star of redemption, as subjective and objective time, as negation and affirmation to be consummated in absolute eternity as a "totality."[18] In the meantime, however, he worked at both ends of the future book. In his continuing correspondence with Rosenstock, we watch the "Urformell" growing, generating a host of derivative distinctions between Judaism and Christianity, of which many found their way verbatim into the final version of the third book of the *Stern.*[19] Parallel to this family of reflections, but

---

17. *Kleinere Schriften,* pp. 278–90. Buber refused to accept the article for *Der Jude.* Cf. also below.

18. On the structure of the argument in the *Stern* see G. Scholem, "Franz Rosenzweig and his 'Stern der Erlösung'," in *Dvarim Bego* (Tel-Aviv, 1976), pp. 407–25; E. Freund, *Die Existenzphilosophie Franz Rosenzweigs* (Berlin, 1959).

19. *Briefe,* Anhang, pp. 64 ff.

still without a tight link to them, Rosenzweig pondered the possibility of a theology of revelation.

In 1917, as a German soldier in the Balkans, Rosenzweig first formulated the contours of his system in a letter to Rudolf Ehrenberg, the famous "nucleus"(*urzelle*) of his book of 1919.[20] The "Urzelle" was written with the enthusiasm of the discovery of an answer. Even though Rosenzweig, *more suo,* speaks again of a sudden intuition, he admits that it consists less in the invention of a new position and much more in the "settling into order" of already assumed points of view: "Nun erwarte Dir aber nichts Neues."[21] He discovered how to fit together various disparate elements of his reflections, learning, and commitments; how dominant themes in the different phases of his development could be merged. We have already identified the "self," "world," and "God" as representing also *biographical* moments in Rosenzweig's life: the preoccupation with his self, with his εἶδος, expressed in Goethean vocabulary; the flight into the "world," the search for a balance between the particular and the general in his historical studies, as well as theoretical and practical experience of the dialectics between ἔθος and κράτος; and, finally, "God"—the sense of religion as founded on revelation and his acceptance of it since 1913. The language which Rosenzweig employs in the "Urzelle" to develop the possibility of an interdependence between these three elements is, to a large extent, that of Schelling. Now, while writing the first draft of his system, he believed himself to be capable of fleshing out the program which Schelling left as mere skeleton in his "Weltalter."[22]

FROM THE ORIGINAL NUCLEUS
TO THE "STAR"

The "Urzelle" commences with the realization that true knowledge can be obtained only if philosophy abandons its dream of the reduction of the manifold to one principle. The ideal of identity of being and thought, prevalent "from Ionia to Jena," rests on the presuppositions of difference between being and thought; it carries its negation within itself. Once that ideal is broken, we are left with three irreducible blocks of experience: God, World, and Man. If these are related, then they do not entail each other logically but as an act, as an event,

20. Rosenzweig, *Kleinere Schriften,* pp. 357–72 (letter of 18.11.17).
21. *Kleinere Schriften,* p. 358.
22. On the links to Schelling see Freund, op. cit., pp. 12–42.

historically rather than conceptually. These relations cannot be thought out, but rather they can be narrated, since they happen in time. The relationship between God and World is an act of creation, which determines the world as contingent. The relationship of God to Man is that of revelation, in which man's tragic-heroic "isolation" is broken, broken not by subsumption of man's singularity under universal (ideal or general) maxims, but rather as a concrete, individual, momentary encounter, *hic et nunc*. God's revelation can be spoken of because it happens through the medium of language: it constitutes language. And he does not subsume the individual under a law (*Gesetz*), but rather manifests his will through precept (*Gebot*) here and now. Language is, therefore, the necessary medium of revelation; revelation institutes it and can, therefore, be spoken of.

So much is already included in the "Urzelle"; only now has Rosenzweig discovered the actual meaning of the most distinctive mark of Jewish existence: "the burden of Law" in the Christian perspective. It is a distorted perspective: Judaism is not a system of laws, but rather a succession of precepts, each of which demands man's full and exclusive attention when it occurs. This became Rosenzweig's Archimedean point, just as Mendelssohn's Archimedean point was the discovery that Judaism is not simply a system of laws, but of symbolic acts, actual manifestations of God's presence.

An argument from silence should persuade us that Rosenzweig's primary concern in this draft was not the development of a theological rationale for his Jewish commitment, but rather the development of a rationale for theological commitments as such. It covers the ground of the first two books of the *Stern*. We note the absence of contraposition between Judaism and Christianity in the "Urzelle" (although it contains a contraposition of both with "paganism"). Now it is not as if he has abandoned his "Urformell" to recover it only in the *Stern*; it was, as we saw, very much on his mind in the correspondence with Rosenstock. We are, rather, led to the conclusion that, for the time being, he still did not possess an overall structure for both themes.

Through all of his many characterizations of Christianity until now he has not yet settled the crucial question, crucial biographically as well as systematically: whether Christianity is a legitimate, a necessary mode of revelation and, if so, why.

Again, as so often, an intense dialogue prepared the coming of a "sudden" insight. An intense correspondence with Hans Ehrenberg in 1918 revolves around this very problem of mediation between Christianity and Judaism.[23] At the beginning, Rosenzweig is only annoyed by Ehrenberg's claim to be a Jewish-Christian of sorts; he must, Rosenzweig insists, be either the one or the other exclusively. Whether Christ was or was not a true Messiah he does not know: only at the end of history will we know it in retrospect. Gradually, annoyance recedes in Rosenzweig's answers, to make room for more than a mere contraposition of Judaism and Christianity. I find a letter of May 11, 1918, particularly significant:[24]

> Ich sehe, ich muß dir das jüdische Verhältnis zum "Zwischenreich" etwas aus größerer Nähe (also etwas dialektischer) auseinandersetzten. Daß der Christ aus dem Anfang, der Jude aus dem Ende des Zwischenreichs lebt—so habe ich dir doch wohl geschrieben—genügt nicht. Also genauer: das christliche Verhältnis zum Zwischenreich ist bejahend, das jüdische verneinend. . . . Wie verneint man ein Zwischen? Schärfen noch: wie drückt man in der Form des Zwischen aus, daß etwas *nicht* zwischen ist? . . . Indem man den Anfang negativ, als noch nicht gewesen [the coming of the Messiah] das Ende positiv, als schon gewesen [kingdom of God] setzt—also Anfang und ende zwar nicht vertauscht, aber umwerkt. Dies ist das Judentum.
>
> Hier muß ich endlich, zum ersten Mal in dieser Auseinanderstzung seit letzten Juni, "danke schön" zu dir sagen. Denn hier hast du endlich maieutisch bei mir gewirkt, und eine ganz entscheidende formulierung bei mir ans Licht gebracht, ein Grundparadoxon, durch das sich wahrscheinlich alles widersprendende in meinem Material ordnet[!] . . . Für dich muß die klare Formulierung der beiden jüdischen Bewußtseins—Grundakte (des nicht gekommenen Messias und des schon wirklichen Gottersreich) und ihrer gemeinsamen und notwendigen Abhängigkeit von dem jüdischen Standpunkt der Verneinung des Zwischenreichs genügen. An der mathematischen Analogie [irrational numbers] siehst du zugleich, wie das Judentum vom Christentum aus erscheint. . . .

Here, I believe, Rosenzweig found a new vantage point. The hitherto mainly polemical antithesis of Judaism and Christianity is given a positive meaning. The most he was willing to concede earlier was the function of Christianity as παιδαγώγος εἰς χριστόν of the "pagans." In the meantime, he has already read Cohen's posthumous work, in which Cohen, as he quotes him, "causally" remarks: "Christus ist wirklich der Messias der Völker"[25]—in the sense that only Christianity could, through its mythical-pagan elements, monotheize pagans. By now Ro-

23. *Briefe*, pp. 302, 304, 309–12, 313–18, 243–332.
24. *Briefe*, p. 316.
25. *Briefe*, p. 317 (11.5.1918). Rosenzweig read Cohen's *Religion der Vernunft* in Ms. in February 1918 (*Briefe*, p. 281–5.3.1918; cf. p. 286—9.3.1918 to Cohen). Only later Rosenzweig turned to read the (earlier) *Logik der reinen Erkenntsis*, cf. *Briefe*, p. 299 (16.4.1918).

senzweig was ready to see much more than that in Christianity: an expression of revelation *sui generis*. It allowed him to view Judaism and Christianity as being at the same time incompatible, necessary, and, to a measure, interdependent. Thesis and antithesis, he will postulate in the *Stern*, are to be resolved in the "totality" at the end.

Our reconstruction suffers from the scarcity of biographical material. One further clue can, however, be elicited from Rosenzweig's "Sprach-denken." Until the time of the letters to Hans Ehrenberg (discussed previously), Rosenzweig admits the truth of Judaism *and* Christianity only *pro tempore:* the messianic days will decide whether the one *or* the other is true—and Rosenzweig has committed himself to assume that the one is, rather than the other. The time of truth will be the time of Judaism *or* Christianity, "yes" or "no."[26] Now, after his correspondence with Ehrenberg, the formula inverted. Our time is the time of Judaism *or* Christianity; one can be only the one *or* the other; the messianic days, the end of the "Zwischenreich," will be the time of Judaism *and* Christianity, of "yes" *and* "no" consummated in one truth. I may, of course, be exaggerating the importance of this correspondence in 1918; at any rate, about four months later (September 4) he sends the outline of the book to Rudolf Ehrenberg and informs him of his "system":[27]

Es ist vor vierzehn Tagen plötzlich [!] dagewesen und seitdem sitze ich unter einer Dusche von Gedanken. Dich geht es besonders an, denn es ist weiter nichts als der ausgewachsen Brief an dich vom vorigen November.

Within a year and a half he then wrote it all, without many revisions.

A final remark regarding Rosenzweig's views on Judaism may be in order. If it is critical, then it is so on Rosenzweig's own grounds only. From the initial formulations down to the *Stern*, the uniqueness and eternity of Israel is described in a language saturated with Christian images and terms. Rosenzweig himself is aware that he turns Christian theologoumena concerning Jews, on their heads: the *caecitas judoearum*, the Jews as scattered and stateless *testimonium aeternum*, their self-centered and world-withdrawn "particularism" against Christian world-oriented "universalism"—in such and more instances, Jewish vices (from a Christian perspective) are interpreted as virtues. His dualistic historiosophy reminds me strongly of Augustine's *De civitate Dei:* I shall deal with it later.[28] Even in the messianic days, Rosenzweig does

26. On the saturation with Christian imagery see below, and Scholem, op. cit.
27. *Briefe*, pp. 345–47.
28. See below, pp. 291 ff.

not grant the Jews political sovereignty: *qua* Jews they have no political aspirations.

Moreover, by definition Jews cannot see that which Rosenzweig concedes—that both Christianity and Judaism are parts of the same truth—since by definition they are antithetical truths. Judaism is a set neither of creeds nor of laws, but a form of existence that in order to reflect upon itself would have to transgress beyond itself—an impossibility which makes it "blind" precisely because it is at the center of a light-giving star. Rosenzweig's preoccupation with Christianity, even his ability to see Christianity and Judaism as "correlative," is, by his own uncomfortable admission, "Christian" rather than Jewish. In a letter to Hans Ehrenberg, he justifies his preoccupation with Christianity biographically, and concludes:[29]

> Du magst ganz recht haben: ohne Christentum wäre das Judentum nicht da (ganz sicher wissen wir das ja erst, wenn—der Messias kommen wird). Soll aber dem Juden diese. . . . Ansicht solche Bedeutung haben, daß sie sich mit seinem "gläubigen Bewußtein" notwending auseinandersetzen müßte? Dieses . . . Wichtignehmen der Welt und Welterkenntnis das du voraussetzt ist doch wiederum christlich, nicht jüdisch.

And "Christian," by implication, is therefore much of what he says, both about Christianity and Judaism in the third part of the *Stern*. This is particularly true of the churchlike images Rosenzweig employs to depict the Jewish community as based on liturgy rather than on law.

In the previous chapter we endeavored to show that Rosenzweig was the first Jewish thinker since Mendelssohn to have emphasized again the incompatibility of Judaism with any other religion, its self-sufficiency. If this is true, then he did it in almost Christian terms, and was aware of it, aware of his paradoxical position.

Hermann Cohen and His Legacy

TERMINOLOGICAL ADAPTIVITY

By isolating, as we did, two thematic concerns in Rosenzweig's thought from others, we were able to show how early and continuous some of his most basic theoretical commitments were. Yet

---

29. *Briefe*, p. 331 (12.6.1918).

against the tenacity with which Rosenzweig held to convictions once formed stands the ease with which he acquired new and independent idioms to express them. He employed the terminologies of Hegel's dialectics, Schelling's *Offenbarungsphilosophie,* Rosenstock's grammatology (*Sprachdenken*), and Cohen's *Ursprungsprinzip,* successively or jointly. On a minor occasion he observed in himself his readiness to identify with a new terminology. After some legal studies, he says, he has learned so well to think and talk like a lawyer that he catches himself being annoyed with laymen.[30] The eagerness to master and appropriate new terminologies is, I believe, as characteristic of Rosenzweig as the fact that, once acquired, he used them to say much the same things.

These heterogenous terminologies are fairly discernible in the *Stern.* How important is each of them to its argument? How well are they integrated? This line of inquiry helps to make the construction of the book comprehensible; I shall follow it in one case only and try to assess the impact of Cohen's terminology. There is no trace either in the "Urzelle" or in any of Rosenzweig's earlier reflections of Cohen's Ursprungsprinzip. External evidence confirms this: in 1918, moved by his admiration of Cohen's posthumous "Religion der Vernunft," which he had just read, Rosenzweig asked his parents to send him Cohen's systematical works, and he studied them for the first time. Yet, the *Stern* employs persistently Cohen's "method of origin." As to Cohen's later philosophical work, Rosenzweig's attitude was somewhat ambivalent. He hails Cohen in a way in which a revolutionary camp will greet a famous veteran general of the *ancien régime* who has decided to join their ranks. He calls him the "Columbus" of his own new way of thinking, who discovered America without knowing it. But, at times, he seems to admire Cohen's posthumous book more than his own. It is easy to see why Rosenzweig recognized the affinity.

COHEN AND KANT

The "method of origin," which Rosenzweig borrowed from Cohen, was gained through a creative interpretation of certain elements in Kant's first critique.[31] Among the "categories" with which

---

30. *Briefe,* p. 134.

31. The following after my article "The Persecution of Absolutes: On the Kantian and Neo-Kantian Theories of Science," in *The Kaleidoscope of Science,* ed. Edna Ullmann-Margalit (Boston Studies in the Philosophy of Science 94) (Dordrecht, 1986), pp. 34–63. Cf. also S. H. Bergmann, "The Principle of Apriority in the Philosophy of Hermann

we structure all experience, Kant recognized the category of *limitation* as the one that allows us to quantify qualities. It underlies our sense of reality (rather than existence) inasmuch as we regard the whole presence of a quality in a subject as "reality," its total absence as (simple) negation, and any degree of it as "limitation." Quality thus constitutes a range that is quantifiable. Now, the categories with which we structure, of necessity, all experience are the preconditions for all possible content of our judgments; the preconditions for our judgments to have content at all. Kant called these preconditions "transcendental logic." Inasmuch as they refer to content, they are tied to our experience which is ultimately grounded in a substrate received by our understanding without identifiable sources outside it. Inasmuch as they refer not to this or that concrete experience but to *all* experience a priori, they are spontaneous, an addition of the understanding subject to that which it receives through the senses, an addition without which no synthesis, no bringing together of elements of experience is conceivable. Inasmuch as they are forms of *judgment,* the categories—or rather their exhaustive list—are secured by the list of all possible judgments as such, regardless of any content—"formal" logic. The qualitative categories are secured by the formal-logical figures of affirmation, negatible and "infinite" judgments: it is the latter which corresponds to the category of "limitation."

"Infinite" judgments are of the form "x is non-y," as when I say that the soul is immortal. A judgment of that kind is affirmative and negative at once: it instructs us that the soul is not mortal and that the soul belongs to the set of all subjects of which mortality cannot be predicated, though other predicates can. It limits the range of predicates that can be predicated of a subject by one.

Predicates that negate but assume a positive form in a judgment were known by Aristotle. He called some of them "privative," when they deny of a subject a property that by its nature belongs to it: as when I say of Socrates that he is blind or unseeing. The importance which Aristotle ascribed to such predicates in the interpretation of the natural world has its origin in his belief that there are many natural kinds—species—each of them with its own "nature." His world is a hierarchy of such "natures" rather than, as the world of early modern physics, one homogeneous, uniform "nature" ruled everywhere by the same laws.

Cohen," *Knesset* (1944); and Werner Marx, *Transzendentale Logik als Wissenschafts Theorie* (Frankfurt am Main, 1977), pp. 103 ff., esp. 119 ff.

Matter, form, and privation are, for Aristotle, the real constituents of every thing. With the rise of modern physics—if not earlier—came the decline of Aristotle's "privations" and the ascendency of another mode of complex negation recognized already by him, namely "indefinite" predicates (ὄνομα ἀόριστα) such as "non-hot," which characterizes the negation of a property which is not one of a pair of mutually exclusive contraries. Boethius once called them "infinite" judgments: Kant joined a tradition that made them replace Aristotle's privation altogether in an age to which the "nature" of a subject was nothing but the sum total of predicates it happens to have.[32]

The infinite judgment (in formal logic) is the prototype of the sense of the less-than-complete presence of a quality (in transcendental logic) which again is projected, or schematized, in our sense of time. It is thus a necessary mode of making experience intelligible by the "understanding." But the infinite judgment governs not only our interpretation of experience as a coherent totality, but also our understanding of the understanding itself—the reflexive effort of "reason" (*Vernunft*) irrespective of experience. Reason forms the notion of a "complete determination" (*durchgängige Bestimmung*) of everything if it is to be real. All possible, simple predicates must either belong or not belong to a throughout determined subject. Simple predicates, predicates that neither include nor exclude others, are never part of our experience: they are a product of speculative reason. Kant calls such predicates, as did others before him, "realities." Reason now hypostatizes all positive predicates into an idea of a sum total of all realities—*the* "Reality" in the singular. Subjects, then, can be ranged according to how many positive realities they have—or how many of the (one) "reality." It is easily seen how the concept of the sum total of realities as a range of all possible predicates generates "naturally" the "hypostatized, later personified" ideal of a most real subject, an *ens realissimum:* God.

The idea of God thus turns to be exorcised from the direct interpretation of nature (through the understanding with its categories), though it remains as a construct of reason. That its existence cannot be demonstrated makes it speculative; that its origin can be traced makes it an almost necessary metatheoretical assumption for employment of our categories. Of Leibniz's and Descartes's methodical function of the ideal of God as a guarantee for the intelligibility of nature thus remained, in Kant's system, only a shadow. Cohen exorcised even this

32. Funkenstein, *Theology,* pp. 347–56.

shadow from the foundations of the exact sciences. This he did by abolishing the demarcation lines between understanding (*Verstand*) and reason (*Vernunft*), thus restituting the Kantian thing-in-itself into the domain of understanding nature. Kant believed in the passive, receptive, though unidentifiable passive element of intuition; because these elements cannot be isolated, things-in-themselves are not objects of our understanding. Cohen denied any *passive* residuum within cognition. Standing in this respect well within the German idealistic tradition, he insisted that *all* components of our cognition (or experience) have their source in the spontaneity of the mind. Yet the manner in which he abolished the dichotomy between the passive sense-data and the spontaneous structure imposed on them differs *toto caelo* from the German idealistic endeavors to develop the manifold contents of the absolute out of its idea. His starting point is not the idea of the absolute, but the actual scientific achievement as a real context embodied in concrete problems.

Within the context of science, Cohen argued, "facts" and "laws" that explain and order them are throughout interdependent. A "fact" or a datum is not something which enters the body of science from the outside, for it is nothing more than the sum total of references to it in the relevant laws. The planets do not exist, he used to say, in reality, but only in the science of astronomy. Nor are "laws" expressions of some rigid structures of the mind, Kant's categories. The latter are rather operative patterns, manners to proceed in the ordering and generating of both facts and laws. The interdependent, contextual character of science ensures its progress. An example is in order.[33]

To the ancients, the contraposition of rest and movement seemed to be immediate sensory perceptions, given facts. On the basis of this "fact" the body of Aristotelian mechanics was construed: the hypothesis that bodies in movement have an inclination towards a point of rest (*inclinatio ad quietem*) and hence that no body can move unless a force is acting upon it constantly (*omne quod movetur ab alio movetur*). But such a discrimination between the given fact and the hypothesis explaining it is artificial. When early modern physics first used (Galileo) and then formulated (Descartes) the principle of inertia, it did not only change a hypothesis, but the very "fact" itself. They recognized the fact to be a *problem* for which an adequate hypothesis was sought. In New-

33. The example is mine, though based on Cohen's remarks, especially in his *Das Prinzips der Infinitissemalmethode und seine Geschichte* (Frankfurt-Main, 1968), esp. pp. 95 ff.

ton's formulation, the inertial principle postulates that a body will continue in its state of either rest or uniform rectilinear motion in a given direction as long as there is no force acting on it. This, of course, is a mere hypothesis, and a counterfactual conditional to boot: for no actual body in the universe could be far enough removed from the force field of other bodies so as to perform an inertial motion, and if it could we would not be able to observe it (the observer being himself a body). Yet with this new hypothesis, the very initial sense datum was altered, for "rest" now became a special case of (rectilinear) uniform motion. It became uniform with the value 0, or the constructive *limiting case* of uniform motions. Uniform motion itself became a special case of accelerated motion, the differential of acceleration, acceleration with the value $a \cdot t$ (if $s = at^2/2$). This enabled, for the first time, the quantification of force as an intrinsic magnitude, Leibniz's *vis viva* (mv^2). The old contraposition of rest and motion was now replaced by the contraposition between uniform and nonuniform motion; until this "fact," too, was changed through the general theory of relativity. Correspondingly, the concept of "body" changed since the ancients from "substance" through "mass points" to a proportion of mass and energy ($E = mc^2$). Science thus creates as much its own "facts" as it creates the hypothesis to explain them: *verum et factum convertuntur* (Vico). Cohen, said Natorp, made the *factum* into a *fieri*, given "facts" into a "process" within the self-asserting mind. But it is time to employ Cohen's own terminology.

Science is a search for ever richer continuities. It finds them by setting one concept (or fact) as the beginning (*Ursprung, principium*) of others, that is, their constructive limiting case, their "differential." The method of origin (*Ursprungsdenken*) was Cohen's most central heuristic device, from the very beginnings of his philosophy of science, through his ethical theory, and down to his latest philosophy of religion. We should perhaps distinguish between the material, analogical, and metaphorical usages of the paradigm of calculus. Concepts that belong to a quantifiable domain in natural sciences use the calculus itself. Epistemology uses it as a methodological analog. In the domain of ethics, Cohen has yet another use for the same principle of origin inasmuch as he employs it, as we shall see, in a more metaphorical vein. The concept or principle is anchored in his reinterpretation of *infinite* (*privative*) judgments. The genuine positive judgement, S is non-P ($S \equiv \infty P$), is not, as Kant wanted it, the paradigm of the category of limitation only, but of every act of synthesis (reasoning). ∞P is both the negation and affirmation of P in the sense that it originates P without being P. ∞P is the limiting-case of P. It is not as if, as Bergmann remarks, Cohen returns to the Aristotelian usage of privation, because no putative "nature" of a subject is involved at all. The infinite judgment is rather a methodological guideline as to how we generate, when we want to define the content of a concept, the closest concept against which it is distinct and thereafter make the second concept into a limiting concept of the first. The very concept of "reality" is but an (infinite) negation of nothingness, that is, position (*setzen*). In every act of reasoning (or "positing") we create a unity within a multiplicity and vice versa. Every act of reasoning is *both* analytic and synthetic. For Leibniz, and even for S. Maimon, this characterized only the divine, infinite mind.

But let us return to our example. We discover a dialectical movement of three steps repeating itself on ever higher levels *ad infinituum*. P and ~P, say rest and motion, are first contraposed as two concrete notions (or, if you wish, facts). They appear as irreducible sensory data, yet they express nothing but this contraposition, while the contraposition itself appears as a law. Once this is realized, we convert ~P into ∞P, the negation of motion into a privation of motion (i.e., look for the law expressing both affirmation and privation as a continuum). But the new, richer concept of $(P \cap \infty P) = S$ cannot abrogate the principle of excluded middle altogether; it must presuppose a contrapositional negation, $S = \sim(P \cap \infty P)$, say uniform motion against acceleration, which again calls for a process of differentiation, and so forth. The "residue of intuition"—or "fact" or, again, "sense-datum" becomes successively an ever more rarified, ever more subtle abstraction. Call all laws (determinations) referring to a not-yet reduced term "thing-in-itself", and call the term itself "rest of intuition" or "sense-datum," then both the thing-in-itself and the sense-datum are complementary aspects of one and the same X; they are correlates. The X is the limiting case ("differential") of our *knowledge of* X. And the more the latter progresses the more hitherto unrelated concepts and facts will be linked to it. If our knowledge of X were complete, it would include all the knowledge there is of other things. Like Leibniz's monads, it would be a *mundus in gutta:* the knowledge of one thing could *reflect* the knowledge of all other things; a single law will mirror all laws of nature.

Once the thing-in-itself returned into the horizon of cognition (as an infinite task, the sum total of all the laws of nature which shall be found to explain the datum, X), the methodological God became superfluous even as a metatheoretical presupposition. For instead of the metatheoretical principle of throughout determination in which things-in-themselves function as abstract, mechanical limits, Cohen uses the correlative principle of infinite negation within the theory. The latter is a constructive version of the former and shows how one predicate (or determination) generates another throughout all possible knowledge. The only ultimate guarantee that the early Cohen thought would be needed for the rationality of our experience was the principle of generative continuity of our consciousness, ensuring that we can proceed from a limit through a limit within the limit and so forth ad infinitum. *Conscientia non facit saltus.*

But absolutes have some nasty habits. Thrown out of the main entrance, they force their way back through the chimney. Cohen could not do without a metatheoretical substitute for Kant's methodological idea of God. He soon had to make the principle of beginning in itself into such an absolute idea. By doing so, he separated the method from the idea of beginning—without admitting it. As a method, the principle assures us: (1) that "thought" can begin the process of generating knowledge (*Erzeugung*) arbitrarily, with any given specific "problem" it sets for itself; (2) that this process is a process of continuous generation of one concept by another through infinite negations; (3) that this process will always leave a seemingly contraposed residue of "intuition"—a new problem to be answered with a new, unpredictable "beginning." Contrary to Hegel's *Wissenschaft der Logik,* Cohen's dialectical process is open-ended. But continuous generation means that no science can have its own principles of beginning as its "objects." It is the critical task of the philosopher to uncover the transcendental structures of sciences, their "categories." Unlike Kant's rigid and discrete categories, Cohen's are but functional a priori structures (directions) and generate each other. The principle of their generation, the dynamic equivalent to Kant's transcendental unity of the apperception, can, however, not itself be a category. It is just that—an idea of the unity, continuity and spontaneity of all knowledge. It is the absolute, never-exhausted paradigm, neither generated by our knowledge nor by itself. This ambiguous duality of method and idea led or may lead to two distinct modifications. In the one, we abandon the idea and keep the method; in the other, we abandon the method and keep some of the idea. In both cases we comb Cohen against his line: moderately in one, violently in the other.

Cohen realized very early that whenever Kant spoke of "experiences" or of "nature" he actually meant our science. Out of this disguised vice,

Cohen made an explicit virtue. But, as a consequence, his science expands like space in modern physics, namely into itself and not "into" another space. It expands by making ever more subtle distinctions and thus creating new facts which again call for even better distinctions, etc. Science is thus a dynamical and self-sufficient context. But in so doing, and in the way he did it, Cohen prepared the relativization of his own theory. Another culture may use an altogether different system of categories to orient itself in this world; if you wish, to create its own knowledge different from ours. Cassirer drew this latter conclusion from Cohen's radical contextualization of science in his *Philosophy of Symbolic Forms*. He abandoned the idea of ultimate unity, which already Natorp downgraded into a mere "task."

More fundamental, however, is the following modification which was only partially drawn by Natorp and later Cassirer. Cohen's principle of beginning is a systematic method of exploiting ambiguities in order to remove them. It is, so to say, a generative grammar of science and culture, ethics and religion. It guides us how to establish continuities, but it is at the same time a hypostatization of the physical principle of continuity, Leibniz's *lex continui*. But the belief in this latter principle as an absolute principle has been shattered in modern physics. In the quantum it found a physical limit to continuities; and in the law of indeterminacy it set a limit to the progressive, continuous refinement of observation or even to any possible determination. Our instruments, no matter how refined, necessitate the distortion of minute objects of observation. It is still possible to express this revolution in Cohen's own terminology, but only against his intentions, perhaps in the following manner. If the principle of continuity is but one device among others in the history of science, then it is a part of a science and generated by it. Against Cohen's intention it becomes a self-referring principle. Self-reference may lead to paradoxes, such as "the set of all sets which are not members of themselves," or the proposition which declares itself to be false. As a matter of fact, the principle of beginning is self-referring, even if we disregard the course of modern physics. Whenever Cohen applies it within science, it refers both to the continuity it has established in this concrete case and to itself. It invites its own abrogation. Cohen thought to avoid the pitfalls of self-reference by making the last instance of the principle into a mere idea, but this is arbitrary. Now, take the principle of continuity as *a* beginning: is not its negation a principle of noncontinuity? Let us now construe, in Cohen's sense, both continuity and noncontinuity as correlative principles. Is the range which does not necessarily entail the establishment of compatibility between two distinct scientific principles, but something else, for example, complementarity.

The excellence of philosophical systems is often recognizable by their ability to dig their own graves. The unique instruments which they create to defend crucial positions prove to be so valuable as to survive the system itself or even help undermine it. Cohen articulated the harmonizing creeds of the nineteenth century in an idiom in which their crisis and breakdown will be declared later. His philosophy of science epitomizes the nineteenth-century *Wissenschaftsgläubigkeit,* the belief in the even, organic growth of scientific knowledge under one and the same canon of rationality. But, inasmuch as Cohen sought to ground this belief on the idea of science as a context in which facts and theories, objects and modalities of cognition are interdependent throughout, he also created tools to deal with the revolution in the foundation of the exact sciences which was soon to break in. Ambiguities, due in part to the ambiguity of Cohen's method of constructive ambiguity, characterize not only his philosophy of science. We meet them also in his ethical theories and in his philosophy of religion. They, too, express the harmonizing creeds of the nineteenth century. Cohen never abandoned the belief in the primacy of rational ethics over religion, or the belief that Judaism is a religion of reason. But his perspectives can be reversed on his own grounds, and in part he started the reversal himself.

It is crucial to Cohen's argument that he apply the principle of beginning only to elements within the totality of nature (science), and not to the totality as such. When, in the domain of nature, Cohen treats concepts as "differentials" he uses an analogy from mathematics. He feels justified in doing so because the analogy is not a mere metaphor. It is a material or methodological analogy: we seek to quantify natural phenomena, we treat the phenomenal realm as a mathematical continuum, or at least like a continuum of discrete concepts. The continuum is not a concept but a method to construct continuity between single concepts. The question, "With what is the whole continuum continuous?" is as nonsensical in the exact sciences as it is in mathematics. But Cohen himself made the illicit jump from the analogical to the metaphorical use of the mathematical differential, and he needed a generating principle for the totality of the universe. Not, indeed, in science, but in ethics.

COHEN ON ETHICS AND RELIGION

Kant, after having destroyed all proofs of God's existence in the first *Critique,* revived God's existence in order to construct his ethical system (in the second *Critique*). God is the only guarantee for betterment of the world, and therefore for the realization of ethics. Cohen, too, revived God for the purposes of rational ethical discourse; yet it was not God as an existent moral personality whom he revived, but God as an *idea.* Once again, the "principle of origin" assumed a leading role. The idea of God is necessary, says Cohen, so as to guarantee the realizability—not the realization—of ethics. It does so by ensuring the duration of nature, that is, of the existence of the world, without which ethics remains abstract, a mere intention. The world, it must be shown, does not prevent ethics from being instantiated, does not obstruct the progressive transformation of humanity into an ethical society. Only this lack of contradiction between ethics and nature is contained in the idea of God. God and nature are, again, shown to be correlative concepts, one being the "beginning" of the other, the "creator," in Cohen's peculiar sense of the word. Put differently: the idea of God is not necessary because without it ethical concepts could not be construed or shown to be valid: on the contrary, any ethical system that claims consistency for itself can be grounded only in the absolute autonomy of ethically responsible agents. Otherwise we easily drift into positions such as Plato's Euthyphro or William of Ockham, namely that it is not so that God chooses to do the good but that what God chooses to do or to command is good by definition, including murder and deception. Already Kant was well aware of this postulate of radical autonomy of humans, but there, too, Cohen believes that Kant was not sufficiently radical or consequential. Kant felt that he had to postulate a *summum bonum* in order to guarantee the realization of a "kingdom of ends" (*Reich der Zwecke*). Cohen, as I said already, has only to show the realizability of ethics, not its actual process of realization: he does not, therefore, need a personal God, only an idea of God. The realizability of ethics means merely that nature does not obstruct ethical interests—that if I intend to feed the hungry by shipping food, nature will not make all modes of transportation impossible. The "intention" must be capable, if it is a true intention, to be the "beginning" or "origin" of its realization. It is the infinite, never to be completed "task" of the autonomous human being—here Cohen speaks the language of the prophets and of the Jewish prayer-book—"to amend the world into the kingdom of God," *Le'taken 'olam be'malchut shaddai*. This, says Cohen, is the essence of ethical monotheism, the essence of Judaism, the essence of German idealism rightly conceived.

Franz Rosenzweig narrates a now famous anecdote. An older, observant Jew once listened to Cohen lecturing on ethics, approached him after the lecture and asked, "But sir, we are commanded to love God; how can one love an idea?" To which Cohen allegedly answered, "How can one love anything but an idea?" Let me count the ways. Or, better yet, let the later Cohen do so.

In 1907 Cohen left his chair at Marburg to go to Berlin, there to teach at the "Hochschule für die Wissenschaft des Judentums." In Berlin he wrote his last work, "Die Religion der vernunft aus den Quellen des Judentums," which appeared posthumously.[34] The key concept of the work is, still, the "principle of origin." We first met it as a guiding principle in Cohen's theory of science as a logical principle that defies the principle of the excluded middle, and legitimizes controlled ambiguity; it arose as an extended analogy to the mathematical notion of a differential. In Cohen's system of ethics, the principle turned from an analogy into a metaphor. Now, however, in Cohen's later philosophy of Judaism is an attempt to interpret rationally the sources (*Quellen*) of Judaism. The term and the notion of a "source" is a cognate of "origin." Our "sources" or "origins"—the written and the oral law (*Torah*)—are not a completed "datum," they are continuously in the making. Interpreting the law amounts to making it, shaping it; in the sources and in their interpretation, our history is constantly made and reflected. Our sources shape us to the measure in which we shape them. We recognize, in this line of reasoning, Heidegger's and Gadamer's later, basic insights on the nature of hermeneutics. Both were, at times, close to the Neo-Kantian school. Our "sources" are the outcome and the origin of the idea of monotheism at one and the same time; the idea is eternally in the making, a *creatio continua*, because, as a true idea, it is an ever-flowing fountain. It means, then, that even the critical-historical study of Judaism is a legitimate continuation and revivification of its sources. And so is the reflection on Judaism enriched by Kant's terminology: all belong to the sources of Judaism.

Yet now, in his later work, Cohen did not believe any more in the reducibility of religion into pure, rational ethics. Herein lies his new

---

34. Herman Cohen, *Die Religion der Vernunft aus den Quellen des Judentums* (Berlin, 1921).

insight, his break with his former philosophy of religion, perhaps under the impact of Feuerbach. Rational ethics must view each human being merely as a representative of the species of humanity, not in their singularity or individuality. Individual human beings with their weaknesses, shortcomings, fear of failure, and fear of death have no room in purely ethical considerations. From the point of view of (pure) ethics, every misdeed or ethical failure is irrevocable and brands its agent as nonethical. Only religion guarantees to the individual the possibility of repentance, of conversion, a chance to return to a moral life—the chance of *teshuva* in the double sense of the word, returning and answering. And religion is capable of giving this guarantee because it conceives God not as a mere idea, but as an existing person with whom humans engage in an I-thou relationship. Only an existing, answering God can assure us the chance to return to good in spite of shortcomings, failures and sins.

That Cohen now, in his latest work, refused to reduce religion into rational ethics does not at all mean that he succumbed to the then fashionable trends of irrationalism; his thought still differs *toto caelo* from the thought of either Buber or Rosenzweig, who owe so much to him. Cohen remained committed to a "religion of reason." Religion was not to be grounded on the shaky foundations of a *je ne sais quoi* such as Otto's "numinous" (*das Numinose*), on a form of reception or a sense *sui generis*. The "sources of Judaism" offer an ever richer access to ethical monotheism, for the individual as well as for the community. The archenemy of true religion and true ethics is the adoration of nature, whether in its primitive, polytheistic manifestations or in its sophisticated guise as philosophical pantheism. What Judaism always possessed, at least in a crude initial beginning, Christianity had to obtain through a hard and long struggle: Christ, said Cohen, "was truly the Messiah of the nations" (*Christus war tatsächlich der Messias der Völker*), because they—the nations—could be converted to monotheism only at the high price of concessions to the spirit and practices of paganism. Only in the sixteenth century did Christianity embark on the long road of the serious effort to rid itself of all vestiges of paganism. The history of the German *Geist* from the Middle Ages through the Reformation to German idealism thus appears to Cohen as a progressive history of de-Teutonization—as a road leading from German paganism through Protestantism to rational ethics, that is, Judaism. Cohen's contemporarian, the celebrated court-theologian Adolf von Harnack, interpreted the same history from paganism to humanistic

Christianity as a gradual progress of de-Judaizing Christianity, ridding it from the vestiges of the Old Testament; wherefore Marcion was his hero. Only Jews spoke of a true synthesis of "Germanhood and Judaism." Even for the more liberal among non-Jewish Germans, Judaism and Jews were an alien if not destructive power (*zersetztend*), useful at best, as Mommsen once said, as "ferment of ethnic decomposition" (*Ferment der nationalen Dekomposition*).

A few concluding words of criticism are in order. Cohen manifests himself, in hindsight, as a prophet *malgré lui* in many domains of thinking. His theory of science replaced the static, permanent a priori judgment that Kant attributed to any rational discourse about nature with a dynamic principle of constructive ambiguities which establishes continuities and links. But the principle in itself proves to be ambiguous when we refer it to itself. It ought not to be absolutely valid and must be so nonetheless; it invites its own abrogation. Cohen prepared for the crisis in the methodology of sciences in a double way. His principle of origin relativizes science; and, if cleansed from false mathematical analogies, the principle is capable of yielding insights into the structure of modern science after its crisis. This I tried to show elsewhere. Likewise ambiguous is the employment of that principle in ethics. Is the idea of God a guarantee from the compatibility of ethics and nature, or is the very notion of this compatibility asserted without proof?

Then, one can also count Cohen's later philosophy of religion as against the grain. The "sources" of Judaism, Cohen wished to show us, are continuously generated and lead towards a genuinely philosophical religion. But the argument can be turned on its head. Christianity, one could argue, was much closer to philosophy since the second century A.D. Christianity is a "dogmatic" religion, Judaism was not. "Dogma" means not only beliefs or opinions, but—in the new, Christian meaning of the older Greek term (which can mean pronouncement or decree)—the precise formulation of beliefs. These formulations were saturated with a philosophical terminology. Therefore, in contrast to Judaism, Christianity had to develop a systematic, rational theology. Philosophy was and remained a constitutive source of Christianity. Not so in the history of Judaism, where philosophy was at best, sometimes, one form of articulation of religious positions among many others, never central and seldom really spontaneous or original. It may be argued that, in the long history of Jewish philosophy since Sa'adia Gaon, only Herman Cohen and Franz Rosenzweig succeeded in developing a genuine "Jewish" philosophy that does not merely translate Jewish concepts and images into another, alien idiom but actually develops Jewish themes in a way that would be impossible without philosophy, and develops philosophy in a way which would be inconceivable without Judaism.

Finally, we notice that Cohen later reflects and repeats a crisis in religious thought that is known to us from Protestant theology since Kirkegaard and Overbeck. Protestant theology discovered that Christianity cannot be reduced to a liberal-rational, humanistic ethics without sacrifice. Protestant theologians discovered that original Christianity was a Jewish-apocalyptic, world-negating sect with no interest in the amelioration of humankind *in hoc saeculo*. Cohen's understanding of Jewish "sources" may just as well lead us to recognize a multiplicity of conflicting principles within Judaism. Perhaps its history is replete with different trends—rational as well as mythical, all of which being equally legitimate "sources." Scholem, who took a similar position, may have derived his notion of Jewish sources as something which cannot be separated from its various interpretations from Cohen; though Scholem denied that he was ever seriously engaged with Cohen's ideas.

COHEN AND ROSENZWEIG

We interpreted Cohen as a prophet *malgré lui*. So did Rosenzweig. It is easy to see why Rosenzweig recognized the affinity between the later phases of Cohen's philosophy and his own aims. The later Cohen reintroduced God as an existence rather than an idea. And, even if he did not abandon the claim of primacy of rational ethics over religion, he nonetheless discovered the irreducibility of religion into terms of pure ethics. Cohen already maintained the insufficiency of pure ethics for the *situation humain:* only an existing God can assure the individual person that his ethical shortcomings do not make him *eo ipso* immoral, that he can revert to his moral self. Such a God must stand to man in an individual I-thou relationship, in an individual dialogue. At the same time, it is clear why Rosenzweig felt admiration, but not a trace of indebtedness to Cohen on these issues. Rosenzweig came to his positions independently of Cohen, and expressed them in a different idiom, an idiom he believed was far more adequate for the "new paradise" of "natural reasoning."[35]

35. Rosenzweig, "Das neue Denken," *Kleinere Schriften* (1925).

The only element of Rosenzweig's thought that was unmistakably derived from Cohen's system—and not even from the "Religion der Vernunft," but from the systematic works—was the principle of beginning. Rosenzweig acknowledges his source at the very first instance in which he invokes the principle:

Hermann Cohen, who was in no way—as he thought of himself or as it may seem from his writings—a mere withdrawal troop within that movement which really came to its end, *only he* discovered in mathematics the instrument [Organon] of thought, precisely because it establishes its foundations not out of the empty nothingness of the one indistinct zero but rather out of the concrete nothing, which fits time and again the element sought after, the nothing of the differential.[36]

Note the exclusive credit he gives to Cohen. It may be intended to exclude precursors, such as Schelling, who also used a form of constructive negation, and even called it "beginning." But whether intended or not, it proves that, in this case, Rosenzweig did not take his cue from Schelling; indeed, we found no traces of the idea even in the "Urzelle," which is saturated with Schelling's vocabulary. This is all the more noteworthy because Cohen may, of course, have taken the name of his method from Schelling, though he could have taken nothing but the name. If at all he had a precursor, it was Salomon Maimon, whose philosophical writings Rosenzweig probably was not acquainted with at all.

We turn now to Rosenzweig, and to the uses he made of Cohen's principle. Rosenzweig's *Stern der Erlösung* has an elaborate architecture. It is a philosophical "system" first and foremost in the sense that its composition is completely structured. But if we expect of it a sustained philosophical argument, we find it at best in the first part (on the elements). When Rosenzweig later commented on the "four styles" of his book, he named the style of the first part only "wissenschaftlich." The other two parts abound in insights and interpretations, but only the first part argues. And here, in the first part, Cohen's impact is strongest.

The argument runs as follows.[37] In the introduction, Rosenzweig *describes* the dissolution of the ideal of an intelligible totality into the "elements," Man, World, God. Man breaks that ideal because of his

---

36. Rosenzweig, *Der Stern*, p. 23 (my translation). *The Star of Redemption*, transl. by William W. Hallo (New York, 1970), p. 20.
37. The following summarizes part I of *Der Stern*.

mortality. No system can explain death or prepare for it. The world cannot be conceived as a totality because the very idea of the identity of being and thought already assumes a plurality. What is left is an idea of the absolute (God) which can be neither man nor the world. Now Man, World, and God are not, as yet, concrete entities; they are rather three ways of negating the totality, three negative concepts, none of which can be reduced to the other. Rosenzweig proceeds, in the first part, to "construct" the elements out of their negative concepts with the aid of Cohen's method of beginning. That is, Rosenzweig finds out everything that can be said of the "elements" without referring to any one of them in terms of the others. At the outset the elements are mere points without conceptual extension, mere negations, albeit concrete negations (the negation of God, of Man, of the World) in the sense that the "being" of each one of them must be thought of in terms of what they are before they are "thought of," a paradox. The elements are, in and of themselves, "differentials"—a *constructive* negation. Wherefore the language of mathematics (i.e., calculus) is the only language adequate to them.

Of God we have only a concrete negative concept. We know "nothing" about him. Now this negative concept, inasmuch as it is concrete, behaves as the differential in calculus. The differential not only combines affirmation and negation (as Cohen saw it) but actually can be split into a negative and a positive concept: a non-magnitude and a not-magnitude. In one sense it is an entity "which has all characteristics of a magnitude except magnitude," in the other sense it is not a magnitude. God, too, is in one sense "not-nothing" and the negation of "nothingness." The affirmative characterization of God as "not-nothing" ($G \equiv \infty N$) assumes an "infinity," the characterization of him as not-nothingness ($G \equiv \sim N$) assumes a finite entity which is negated. $\sim N$ refers to God's activity and freedom—he breaks time and again out of nothingness—while ∞N refers to his essence, his infinity; that both negation ("no") and affirmation ("yes") are united with the particle "and," that is, that God is both ∞N and $\sim N$, accounts for the dialectical movements or "vitality" of God.

"World" and "Man" are constructed in much the same way. ∞N turns to stand for the ubiquity and eternity of the world ("infinity"), i.e., the λόγος. $\sim N$ stands for its "nature," "reality," the particular, the phenomena; the "yes" creates, the "no" generates, the "and" shapes the world (i.e., informs the plurality of phenomena with a λόγος). Again, ∞N stands for the uniqueness, the character, the fate of man, $\sim N$ for his freedom. The terms used throughout these deductions—"infinity," "freedom," "universality," "particularity," "character," "fate," "will"— are not as yet positive terms with the content they have in language. They are rather used in *anticipation* of the connotation they will acquire once the "elements" are brought to interact with each other in the patterns of revelation, creation, redemption. Only then will these terms form sentences, become "experience." For the time being they are, so to say, mere points of orientation, points without extension (content). It seems as if Rosenzweig introduces here an inverted version of Kant's "schematism"; the formal ideas carry with them a monogram of their late experimental content.

A CRITIQUE

So far these are the general outlines of Rosenzweig's argument as I understand it. On its own grounds, it is open to several lines of attack.

To begin with, it seems that Rosenzweig's improvement on Cohen's principle actually destroys it. For Cohen, infinite negation (∞P is our notation) overcomes simple negation ($\sim P$) in a process of scientific synthesis. Synthesis consists in the conversion of $\sim P$ into a "beginning of" P, i.e., into ∞P. For Rosenzweig, both $\sim P$ *and* ∞P are equally independent aspects of a (concrete) "negation." But what kind of a negation are they aspects of? A *third* kind of negation is neither introduced nor desired by Rosenzweig, yet surely he does not mean to say that the one or the other is a partial aspect of itself. It is, of course, true that Cohen's "infinite negation" has a negative and positive aspect, but these aspects are *interdependent* aspects for Cohen, while Rosenzweig wishes them to be independent aspects of an overall "concrete" negation. Cohen does not treat ∞P, the infinite negation (the differential) as an independent term, but as a process starting with $\sim P$ and leading to a richer understanding of P. We may write it as $\infty P_i \equiv (\sim P_{i1} \supset P_{i2})$. Or we may say: for Cohen ∞P_i connotes both $\sim P_i$ and P_i, both denotes neither of them, wherefore $N(P_i) \equiv [\sim P_i \wedge \infty P_i]$; for Rosenzweig, $N(P_i) \equiv [\sim P_i \vee \infty P_i]$. $N(P_i)$, the negation of P_i, denotes both $\sim P_i$ and ∞P_i. We cannot even say that Rosenzweig returned to the Kantian or Hegelian usage.

It seems that this implies an introduction of a third, overall negation in the actual "construction" of the "elements." Rosenzweig's starting point is neither the term "not God" nor "non-God," but rather the concept of God as "not nothingness" and "non-nothingness," respectively, in our notation, $N(P) = [(\sim P_i) \wedge (\sim\infty P_i)]$. Yet "nothingness" is exactly the kind of abstract, empty negation which Rosenzweig believed he had avoided. It stands neither for $\sim G$ nor for ∞G. Again we ask: why did Rosenzweig introduce it? Or, in his own terminology, why did he construe "yes" and "no" as equally primordial particles of speech, dialectical moments of an overall negation? Perhaps because, against his claim, he did not break the "totality" of God, World, and Man into its elements altogether. They have something in common even after the breakdown of the totality and prior to their interaction: they are blocks of immediate experience set against absolute nothingness; they share in a reality beyond which there is only that nothingness which, univocally, God, World, and Man "are not." From the outset Rosenzweig felt about them that which, if true to his principle, he could nevertheless not say; that they are "real" in the same sense of the word: not-nothingness.

We find a similar ambiguity in Rosenzweig's comments about mathematics. Mathematics, he says with Cohen, teaches us how to construct a magnitude out of a non-magnitude ($\blacktriangle x/\blacktriangle y$, 0). Mathematics is also, as a whole, a science that does not deal with "reality"—it has no content but itself—and yet "touches upon" reality (inasmuch, I suppose, as parts of reality are quantifiable). Therefore, mathematics is the language adequate for the elements before their interaction, their manifestation; they, too, are as yet "nothing" as long as they are, *in statu nascendi*, isolated. They have as yet no content, "nothing" can be said about them (except for this concrete nothing, their "differentials"). Evidently, Rosenzweig did not make up his mind whether the "formal" language (symbols) with which he speaks of the element *is* mathematics or is only *like* mathematics. But of course it could only be the latter.

In short, Rosenzweig, like Cohen, wavers here between the employment of the "infinitesimal" as a material or as a methodological analogy.

The very same relation as between mathematics and its reification also prevails between the elements (i.e., as their formal determinations constructed out of "nothingness") and their reification. The abstract elements stand to their reification (coming to be) as rudimentary particles of speech ("yes," "no," "and") to elements of speech (names, adjectives, verbs). This is the theme of the second part of the *Stern;* here Rosenzweig makes a further use of the principle of origin, an allegorical use. World, God, and Man actually *come to be* out of nothingness through their mutual involvement. To Rosenzweig this is not a mere process of philosophical explication, but rather a true account of that which happens. What, then, is the status of the principle of beginning now? For Cohen, much as until now for Rosenzweig, it was a heuristic device, a form of *thought* only. That is, in the second part of the *Stern*, no longer the case. Should we then say that Rosenzweig reverted to the Hegelian mold, in which "negation" was a real force, an actual event, or moment of everything and of every thing? This avenue is also closed to Rosenzweig, who denies the unity of thought and being. Inevitably we must, therefore, conclude that the principle has turned into a symbol or a metaphor. It is used, from now on, metaphorically.

On the one hand, Rosenzweig regards "God," "World," and "Man" as immediately given by experience; on the other hand, he endeavors (in the first part) to construct them. This is not, as one of his interpreters thought, a contradiction. The construction of the elements stands for their being and their being experienced as isolated entities; the full experience of them, as well as their being, happens only when they *involve* each other. The terms with which the various negations of God, World, and Man are determined in the initial "construction" ("infinity," "essence," "freedom," etc.) are not yet the contents of the "elements" but rather anticipations of future contents—a mere monogram, or "mapping into" of the elements which their future interaction will reveal as their content. The idea may well have been taken from Kant's "schematism," which shows how the categories are "mapped into" time-relations (just as three-dimensional figures can be mapped into a plane). Now even if we accept this anticipatory character of the terms used throughout the construction, on which grounds do we justify assigning to ∞G one group of anticipatory terms (infinity, essence) and another group (finitude, freedom) to $\sim G$? Unless $\sim G$ and ∞G already have a vestige of meaning beyond being just formal determinations to correlate them with finitude, freedom, will, and so forth, Rosenzweig's identifications are highly arbitrary—indeed, already here, ∞N and $\sim N$ become metaphors. We saw how Cohen resorted to a metaphorical use of his principle only in some portions of his ethics and, later, in his philosophy of religion: God as the "beginning" of the world. Rosenzweig employs the principle almost exclusively as a metaphor. He began where Cohen had ended.

Cohen's interpretation of mathematics is open to severe criticism. He saw in the calculus the essence of mathematics because of its service to physics; it embodied for him the *lex continui*. This may have been an adequate perspective for an eighteenth-century mathematician, but not for the nineteenth or twentieth century. Rosenzweig's allegorization of the differential is even more removed from real mathematical concerns. Nevertheless, Rosenzweig preserved better than Cohen a Kantian idea which became, independently from Kant and without Rosenzweig's awareness, a cornerstone of modern mathematical logic: that a universe of discourse may be seen as an interpretation of its formal system, and that the metalanguage may even be "mapped into" a language—say, metamathematics into arithmetic with the aid of Gödel-numbers. Seen in this light, there may be merit to the way in which the universe of discourse serves, in the second part of the *Stern,* as an interpretation of the elements, albeit with the aid of allegorizations. Physics is, after all, *an* intepretation of mathematics, and modern physics abounds in metaphors. The second part of the *Stern* interprets the "elements" by identifying their real with their formal structures. Rosenzweig's linguistic remarks corroborate our reading: the formal elements stand to their reification as grammatical structures stand to language (naming). On the other hand, they also constitute language. The appearance of "something"—entities, language out of "nothing"—is, in Rosenzweig's perspective, the essence of the always present "miracle," a *creatio continua.*

FURTHER ARGUMENT

If the second part of the *Stern* interprets the formal determinations of the elements by their reference structures to each other, then the third part invests their mutual reference with a direction or an overall *meaning.* Once again, Rosenzweig invokes the principle of beginning. The movement from "nothingness" to "God, World, and Man" is invested with meaning in the correct order of creation, revelation, redemption as actual movements of God's explication of himself, as the enfoldment of truth. This is, perhaps, the most Hegelian part of the three. All the elements and their deductions in the first part were purely "hypothetical" in the Cohenian sense: they were just that, a mere beginning out of "nothing." The being of God is not completed with the reification of the elements either; it will be completed only at the end of the process in which God, World, and Man will have become one, and God will be "all in all." In this sense, the negation of the totality in the first and second parts of the *Stern* was in itself an act of "beginning" and a driving force toward the goal, the "end." "Negation" and "affirmation," beginning and end, will be consummated in one "truth." The enfoldment of the truth is the real history of God. The principle of beginning, which served as an analogy in the first part and as a metaphor in the second, is thus hypostatized in the third part: it is the biography of God.

At the end Rosenzweig resurrected the totality he had destroyed in the beginning. The becoming of the totality invests it with a "meaning" it could not have at the beginning. This, I believe, is Rosenzweig's intent when he places "epistemology" only at the end of the system, as a "messianic epistemology."[38] We read it as the successive generation of three levels of understanding: formalization, identification (reification), and meaning (unification). Our reading reinforces our initial impression that the "totality" was not totally broken to begin with; some traces of it existed from Rosenzweig's start. In the end, Rosenzweig got out of his elaborate interpretative endeavors exactly what he put into them in the beginning. I believe that even Rosenzweig would agree with this verdict. He saw himself as a common-sense philosopher, not as a wizard who pulls rabbits out of empty hats. Not even God, at least his God, could do that.

An Escape from History: Rosenzweig on the Destiny of Judaism

THE VISION AND ITS SOURCE

Franz Rosenzweig's views on Jewish history and destiny are idiosyncratic. They are also, given his premises, compelling. Like other domains of his thinking, biographical and systematic impulses were fused together into an impressive structure. Put in one succinct formula—and Rosenzweig was addicted to succinct formulas—Rosenzweig denies to Jews and Judaism an active role in history and, in a sense, even denies their historicity. They exist, he says, "outside the bellicose temporality" (*ausserhalb einer kriegerischen Zeitlichkeit*).[39] Their eternity is not a goal, but a presence.

38. "Das neue Denken," *Kleinere Schriften*, p. 394.
39. Franz Rosenzweig, *Der Stern der Erlösung*, p. 368; cf. pp. 332 ff. (the Jewish nation needs no land), p. 450 (Judaism exists "by subtraction"). Christianity, by contrast, exists "in der Spirale der Weltgeschichte" (p. 417)—there is no world history without states (p. 450)—and is therefore essentially involved in the world and in the turmoil of

This is an odd pronouncement to come from a historian, even a renegade one to the profession. What he meant was approximately the following: the "essence of Judaism" was the elusive philosopher's stone sought by the *Wissenschaft des Judentum* from its inception. Rosenzweig does not deny that it exists; he denies that one ought to look for it, because it can be found neither in any particular set of doctrines (a *Weltanschauung*) nor in the body of commandments. Judaism is the very life of Jews, their biological continuity and community: *Erzeugung* rather than *Bezeugung*.[40] Judaism, then, has no historical-political goal which it wishes to implement on earth: it is already, from inception, at its goal. It is, therefore, not interested in a role as a historical agent, nor could it avoid the vagaries of time—of "temporality"—if it were. Judaism is not actively involved in the wars, revolutions, conquests and defeats of this world. Historical agents have historical-political goals: founding states, expanding states, converting others to their own convictions and ways of life, creating a just and better society, obtaining freedom. Judaism is indifferent to all of these goals and other world-historical tasks. Its existence in the Diaspora, in dispersion, agrees with its nature perfectly: having a sovereign state, Jews could not but be again an agent in history, involved in the turmoil of this world. The inner truth of Judaism, unlike Christianity, need not evolve with time: if Christianity represents the rays of "the star," Judaism is at the center of it. The heartbeat of Judaism is community, procreation, ritual life, now as in the messianic days.[41] Judaism has no "history," and it need not fight for redemption because, essentially at least, it already is redeemed.

These are odd views, at odds also with the views and aspirations of just about every Jewish party or group of his time, political or intellec-

history. Note that, by attributing a *contemptus mundi* to Judaism rather than to Christianity (p. 453: *Weltverachtung*), Rosenzweig employs a virtue traditionally extolled by Christianity!

40. Ibid., p. 331 ("Das Bezeugen geschieht im Erzeugen"); pp. 379 ff.: "Sein Glaube ist nicht Inhalt eines Zeugnisses, sondern Erzeugnis einer Zeugung." On earlier—in fact, very early—formulations of this idea in Rosenzweig's thought, cf. above. See ibid. for early formulations also of the idea that Judaism is always already at the goal to which Christianity strives (*Der Stern*, p. 368; cf. previous note). On Rosenzweig's changing relation to Meinecke and historicism, cf. Paul Mendes-Flohr, "Franz Rosenzweig and the Crisis of Historicism," in idem., ed., *The Philosophy of Franz Rosenzweig* (Hannover and London, 1988), pp. 138–61.

41. Rosenzweig, *Der Stern*, pp. 342–72.

tual. What were his sources, what were his driving forces? And why was his position recognized as a significant theological contribution even by those who opposed it bitterly?

At first sight, it may appear as if Rosenzweig simply reverted to the traditional, preemancipatory sense of Jewish history, a sense expressed, for example, in Jehuda Halevi's *Kuzzari,* or in the writings of Loeb of Prague (known as the Maharal). Rosenzweig admired Jehuda Halevi, and later in life translated his poetry. To the traditional Jewish self-reflection, the uniqueness and the eternity of Israel were a transcendental, metahistorical premise and promise, not the outcome of history. Israel was a chosen people—not because of intrinsic merits or achievements, but because God had chosen it, and it alone, to preserve the law (literally through tradition) and to fulfill its commandments. Jehuda Halevi—in this respect exceptional—even claimed the presence of a sense of the divine, a special perceptive faculty for the divine *logos* (*al'amer 'alilahi*)[42] which only Jews possess—and only ethnically indigenous Jews, for even converts do not possess it. This pseudobiological grounding of Jewish singularity is most reminiscent of Rosenzweig, precisely because it is so exceptional within traditional and modern thought alike.

Israel alone among the nations, in this traditional perspective, is under the immediate tutelage of God. Other nations are subject to the laws of nature—be they astral, biological (growth and decay, as Halevi thought), or geophysiological. Not so Israel. Contrary to other nations, Israel neither has nor needs a guiding star, said the ancient Rabbis ("ein mazal le-Israel").[43] The topos occurs again in Yehuda Halevi: other nations obey the biological laws of growth and decay, but Israel does

---

42. Jehuda Halevi, *Sefer ha-Kuzzari* 1:4, 42, 95–96; trans. Yehudah Even-Shmuel (Tel Aviv, 1973), pp. 6, 15, 31 ff. As to the origins of the notion, cf. Julius Guttmann, *Philosophies of Judaism* (Jerusalem, 1951), p. 386, n. 353a; Herbert Davidson, "The Active Intellect in the *Cuzari* and Halevi's Theory of Causality," *Revue des études Juives* 131 (1972); and chapter 6 (possible origins in anti-Christian polemics).

43. E.g., *Babylonian Talmud, Nedarim* 32a; cf. *Shabbat* 156a: "'And he took him [Abraham] out': Said Abraham to him: Master of the World, I looked at my star and I am not to have a son. Answered He: leave your astrology—Israel has no [guiding] star." On the historical background, see Isaia M. Gafni, *The Jews in the Talmudic Era: A Social and Cultural History* (in Hebrew) (Jerusalem, 1990), p. 166 and n. 84. Jehudah Halevi, who does not quote the dictum, prefers biological metaphors for the same idea: *Kuzzari* 2:32–44. On an interesting use of the astrological idea by Rabbi Levi ben Gershon (Ralbag), cf. chapter 4, "History and Providence." Even Jean Bodin knew it: *Heptaplomeres,* ed. L. Noack (Hildesheim, 1970), p. 199.

not; its eternity is guaranteed by God. And the Maharal added: the character of every nation is shaped by the land it subsists on, on which its life depends. Exiled from its land, a nation is naturally doomed to die, except Israel, where existence in exile and dispersion is a protracted miracle, supranatural phenomenon.[44]

Furthermore, Israel's career and fortunes are utterly independent of world-historical causation, of the deeds and misdeeds of the nations among which it is scattered. The exile is a cathartic measure, a divine punishment for sins as old as the sacrifice to the golden calf at Sinai, a sin shared by all Jews, past, present, and future, because all were there. Why is it, asked the contemporary Jewish chronicler of the pogroms of the First Crusade, that our generation, so saturated with genuinely pious men (*Chassidim*), suffered so much? And he answers: precisely because of their piety, they could take upon themselves a larger portion of the collective punishment for the sin of the golden calf for which every generation must partly atone.[45] Israel's fate is determined by God and Israel alone—no other forces are at work. Nor does the existence among the nations alter the essence of Israel. Israel, said even the rationalistic-sober Rabbi Simone (Simhah) Luzzatto in the seventeenth century, is like a river whose water remains the same while only its color changes with the change of the soil it runs through.[46]

So much for the similarities between Rosenzweig and the traditional image of Jewish history. Rosenzweig would not be utterly without ground if he claimed that this was the traditional interpretation. But let us consider the differences. At least three times a day, Orthodox Jews pray for the restoration of Jewish sovereignty, the return from Exile to the land of Israel, the restoration of kings and judges. Most of them believed and still believe that all of that will happen in historical times, within a finite future, with the coming of the Messiah. Jewish eschatology—apocalyptic or realistic—traditionally held to the return of Jews to history as agents. They only differed in the question whether they are allowed "to precipitate the end," to try to bring about or pre-

44. A. F. Kleinberger, *The Educational Theory of the Maharal of Prague* (in Hebrew) (Jerusalem, 1962), pp. 37–42; M. Buber, *Bein Am Le-artzo* (Jerusalem, 1952), drew attention to similarities in the doctrine of the (later) Jean Bodin.

45. A. Habermann, ed., *Sefer Gezerot Ashkenaz ve-Tzarfat* (Jerusalem, 1945), p. 25 (Jacob ben R. Shimshon). Less than a century later, the so-called "German pietism" (*Hasidut ashkenaz*) will develop a martyrological ideology even in the private, everyday sphere. Jacob ben R. Shimshon already speaks of *Hassidim*.

46. Simone Luzzatto, *Ma'amar al Yehudei Venetziah* (Hebrew trans.) (Jerusalem, 1951), p. 106.

pare for the Messianic days by their own actions.[47] Rosenzweig must allegorize Jewish eschatology beyond recognition, as indeed he does. He is happy with the exile; one may argue that, in better times, many Jews were in fact likewise happy with their place of exile: but they were not permitted to admit it. Preemancipatory Jews regarded their status after the destruction of the Temple as a status of "captives of war" among the nations.[48] They may live in the West, but their "heart is in the East." Rosenzweig's Judaism, unlike traditional Judaism, was extraterritorial as well as extratemporal.

ROSENZWEIG, THE *WISSENSCHAFT DES JUDENTUMS*, AND ZIONISM

If Rosenzweig's outlook was decidedly not the traditional Jewish one, it was not that of Jewish liberal theologians or the nineteenth-century practitioners of the Wissenschaft des Judentums either. To the contrary: it was the rebellion against them that provided a strong impulse to Rosenzweig's views. They discovered Jewish history or historicity as a *necessary* dimension: he denied the relevance of their endeavor for the understanding of Judaism.

The *Wissenschaft des Judentums* was, throughout the nineteenth century, mainly a historical-philological discipline. It is no coincidence that, in the German language, the exact sciences and the historical-philological discipline have both been called "science" (*Wissenschaft*) since the beginning of the nineteenth century. In the perception of its practitioners, these disciplines represented exact, verifiable (or falsifiable) knowledge, empirically gained, as against the "speculative" pursuits of the metaphysicians. Like physics in the seventeenth century, history had now come into its own with the discovery of secure methodical foundations—or so they thought.

Yet the renewed interest in history, the elevation of historians virtually to a status of high priests of culture, was by no means a consequence of the discovery of a secure method. On the contrary, the outburst of historical interest in the nineteenth century caused the discovery of new modes for its articulation. The historical perspective was the discourse of the bourgeoisie. Georg Lukács and Erich Auerbach

47. Funkenstein, *Hapassiviut kesimanah shel yahadut hagolah: Mitos umeziut* (Tel Aviv, 1982), and chapter 5, "Maimonides."

48. This was still the formula used by anti-reform declarations in the nineteenth century, e.g., the collection of pamphlets entitled *Eleh divrei habrit* (Altona, 5679).

have taught us—each in his own way—how the historical interest, literary realism, and bourgeois mentality of the nineteenth century were inextricably linked.[49] The individual, the free and equal citizen that the advocates of the "civil society" (*bürgerliche Gesellschaft*) extolled was independent and dependent at the same time, agent and patient, shaping society by his labor and ingenuity, yet shaped by it and its institutions in which he (and, by proxy, she) participated. By pursuing his enlightened economic-social self-interests, the individual contributed to the commonwealth, to the harmonious balance of a society in which "private vices" led to "public virtues" as if by an "invisible hand." The *Bürgertum* saw itself as the real backbone of the modern nation-state in which all were "equal before the law": its virtue was *work* rather than pedigree or inspiration. Its history was the *real* history of the nation.

Historical research itself became solid, hard "work" rather than *otium*, or venerable tradition, methodically executed *ad majorem civitatis gloriam;* and inasmuch as the modern nation-state became a substitute religion, historians and national philologians became its high priests, discoverers and educators at one and the same time. It was this liberal-bourgeois mentality that also permeated the world of the Jews, in content and method.[50] In content, inasmuch as its goals were the enlightening of fellow-Jews and non-Jews through history about the true, historical nature of Judaism; in method, in that this was critical, "scientific" history. The still relevant aspects of Judaism could thus be separated from the obsolete and timebound ones: knowledge of history thus would serve the self-esteem of Jews and at the same time enable them to integrate into the civil society as equal citizens. If the traditional view of Jewish history saw the essence of Judaism in its absolute, even supernatural particularity, the new, liberal-national view strove to show that the essence of Judaism, even its uniqueness, lay in its universality. Even Heinrich Graetz read Jewish history as "the history of one and the same idea, the idea of pure [i.e., ethical] monotheism." The liberal-historical theology became, among Protestant and Jewish thinkers alike, a *Thron und Altartheologie* down to Herman Cohen's contention of the congruence of Judaism and "Germanhood" (*Deutschtum*).

Rosenzweig—not unlike Gershom Scholem and other German-Jewish intellectuals in the first two decades of our century—rebelled against this liberal-bourgeois Jewish complacency, rebelled against its

49. See above, pp. 248–250.
50. Perrine Simon-Nahum, *La cité investie* (Paris, 1991), chap. 1.

historicistic ideology. He did so already in his "Atheistic Theology" of 1914, drawing a brilliant parallel between the crisis of Protestant theology and what he viewed as the failure of Jewish theology.[51] Both historicized their respective revelations to the point of turning religion into anthropology. Revelatory religion, however, is and ought to remain theocentric rather than anthropocentric. God is the projection neither of natural-cosmic forces nor of ethical-political ideals; if He is seen as such, theology negates God, becomes literally atheistic, the deification of humanity. Rosenzweig's invective is not unlike Franz Overbeck's condemnation of the equation of "Christianity and Culture." Overbeck signaled the first awareness of a crisis of Protestantism, a crisis born from a hypertrophy of historical studies coupled with liberal-rational zeal.[52] Rosenzweig's later theological position was, consequently, analogous to Karl Barth's. If Judaism's essence is not the involvement in history, then no amount of critical historical studies will reveal it.

Rosenzweig could have chosen another form of rebellion against the liberal-Jewish trust in history and in the "civil society." He could have turned, as did many German-Jewish young rebels, to Zionism. There was much in Zionism that could have appealed to Rosenzweig. Like Rosenzweig, many young Zionist ideologues also refused to identify an "essence" of Judaism, either in its particularism or in its universalism. They had rebelled against the equation of Judaism with rational ethics and bourgeois values, be it the sophisticated formulations of Herman Cohen and Moritz Lazarus, or in the ridiculous sermon that made the patriarch Jacob into a prototype of a solid city councilor ("Unser Erzvater Jakob das Vorbild eines Stadtverordneten").[53] Some, like the Hebrew writer Micha Josef Berdyczewski, wanted to revive an alleged pristine Jewish mythology; others, like Scholem, claimed Judaism to be everything Jews were occupied with at any given period. The essence of Judaism was its creative spirit, for which the past was a guarantee, not a definition. An autonomous territory, the return to the land of

51. Rosenzweig, *Kelinere Schriften* (Berlin, 1937), pp. 278–90.
52. This lineage of Rosenzweig's disappointment with historicism is missing in Mendes-Flohr's excellent article, "Franz Rosenzweig and the Crisis of Historicism," op. cit. Cf. also above, pp. 260–264.
53. G. Scholem, *Devarim bego,* ed. A. Shapira (Tel Aviv, 1976), p. 398. On Rosenzweig and Zionism, see Y. Fleishman, "Franz Rosenzweig kimevaker hatzionut," in *On Franz Rosenzweig on the Occasion of the Twenty-Fifth Anniversary of His Death* (in Hebrew), ed. E. Simon et al. (Jerusalem, 1956), pp. 54–73.

Israel, would alone guarantee the renaissance of national health and creativity. Only the future could then tell what forms this creative energy would take.[54]

Much of this, in Rosenzweig's eyes, struck the right tone, except for the core of the new good message. Worse than the deification of humanity, Zionism was, in his estimate, the deification of the nation—the last station in an "atheistic theology." It is no wonder that Buber refused to publish the article of that title in *Der Jude,* to which the young Rosenzweig submitted it for publication. It was published posthumously.

ANOTHER SOURCE

Where, then, did Rosenzweig take inspiration (if at all) for his dualistic version of a profane history and a sacred non-history? A further candidate comes to mind, this time from Christian quarters: Augustine of Hippo's *De civitate Dei.* Augustine's "City of God" has no essential link, no involvement, in the "earthly city" (*civitas terrenea*) in which it dwells. The City of God has, indeed, two parts. One resides in heaven (the *civitas Dei coelestis*), whose members are there for eternity. The other part is the "City of God wandering in the lands" (*civitas Dei peregrinans in terris*). Augustine's terminology, in this his later "great and difficult work," is legal.[55]

Peregrinus is, in Roman law, a resident alien. The Christians, wherever they are on earth, are alien. Their aim is to fill the ranks of the heavenly city that were thinned out after the fall of Lucifer and his sect. Not all members of the wandering City of God—of the Church—will become members of the heavenly city: only at the end of days will it be known who deserves eternal reward. But all members of the Church want to belong to it; the will to belong makes angels and humans already members of *one* city of God now. This, too, is a legal-philosophical point: Augustine emphasizes that there exists only one City of God, even though membership in the wandering City of God does not guarantee membership in the heavenly one, because they all

---

54. Cf. D. Biale, *Gershom Scholem: Kabbala and Counter-History* (Cambridge, Mass., 1979), chapter 1; and Funkenstein, *Tzionut umada: shloshah hebetim* (Rehovot, 1985).

55. This becomes very evident when compared with his early work, *De vera religione,* where he speaks of "two human races" (*duo genera*) rather than "two cities": *De vera religione* 27.50, *Corpus Christianorum Series Latina* 32:219. Cf. E. E. Cranz, "The Development of Augustine's Ideas on Society Before the Donatist Controversy," *Harvard Theological Review* 58 (1954), pp. 255 ff.

share the will to belong to one city—they have, in Cicero's famous definition of a *respublica,* a consensus of law and a communion of interests.[56] The history of both cities, the divine and the earthly, is parallel but disjoint. The very parallelism of significant events emphasizes the separation of their career. The earthly city, driven by lust for power, makes its public appearance with Ninus (Nimrod); the City of God first becomes a community with Abraham. The earthly city achieves its goal—world-dominion and pacification—with Augustus; the divine city becomes universal with Jesus. The City of God, though by no means adverse to the *earthly* peace, has no stake in it either: whether or not the emperor is Christian is of no particular importance for its fortunes. Augustine's elaborate argument for the lack of connection between the "two cities" came as a reaction to the "political theology" prevalent among Christians since Eusebius and Constantine,[57] the assumption that the fortunes of Christianity and of the Empire are inextricably linked together. Now, in the Empire's darkest hours, it seemed that with its end, overrun by barbarian tribes, the end of Christianity, the end of the world, had also arrived. Augustine denied it.

Rosenzweig's interest in Augustine's *De civitate Dei* is well attested.[58] The similarity between their conceptions of history is striking indeed, with only one difference: where Augustine divides the "City of God" into two constituencies that will become one eternal city only at the end of days, Rosenzweig has no need for heaven or angels. His City of God is here on earth, already eternal in that it will be ever present. The end of the world will come, but it has significance only for the world and its religions, even the truest among them (Christianity), which is indeed involved in the world. Judaism will not change even in the world

56. Augustine makes it clear that he speaks of two, not four, cities (*De civitate Dei* 12.1, CCSL 48:355). This seeming paradox has occupied many interpretations since W. Kamlah, *Christentum und Geschichtlichkeit,* 2nd ed. (Stuttgart, 1951), solved it eschatologically: at the end of history the *civitas Dei coelestis* and the *civitas Dei peregrinans* (and, respectively, the *civitas terrenea* and *civitas diaboli* will become one). My solution—cf. *Heilsplan und natürliche Entwicklung* (Munich, 1965), pp. 45–48—is legal: what constitutes a *civitas* is the will of its inhabitants to belong to it, not their final fate; they may not remain in it. Cicero spoke of the city as a *consensus iuris* and *communis utilitatis* (*De republica* 1.25, ed. Ziegler, 24 ff.). On Augustine and Cicero, cf. F. G. Maier, *Augustin und das antike Rom* (Stuttgart, 1955), pp. 189 ff.

57. E. Peterson, "Der Monotheismus als politisches Problem. Ein Beitrag zur Geschichte der politischen Theologie im Imperium Romanum," in idem, *Theologische Traktate* (Munich, 1951), pp. 44 ff. The term "political theology," renewed by Carl Schmitt, was an ancient coinage: Varro, quoted by Augustine, distinguished between vulgar (mythical), political and natural theology.

58. Rosenzweig, *Der Stern,* p. 366.

to come. It represents and reenacts eternity, biologically and liturgically. Rosenzweig the political thinker went a long way from the Hegelian-historic adoration of the nation-state as the apex of world history to the rejection of states, or at least indifference to them, in the fashion of Augustine.

Personal experiences were undoubtedly decisive in this shift, experiences that Rosenzweig shared with the cohort of intellectuals of his generation who fought as front-line soldiers in the First World War. Many of them, like Rosenzweig, were thoroughly cured of national aspirations when they realized that universal death, misery, and destruction were the inevitable outcome of nationalism.[59] The nation-state revealed itself as nothing but the incarnation of the *libido dominandi*. Its peace was unstable and ephemeral in the best case. Beyond the disdain of state, politics, and history, Rosenzweig also became, through his experience as a soldier, a worshipper of life, life as such, life of and in the world. In this he certainly differed from the Christian version of *contemptus mundi*. Judaism was now in his eyes pure life, the very symbol of life, meaningful and spiritual in that it was biological, eternal in that its members died but gave life. Zest for life is the deepest drive in the *Stern der Erlösung*. It was also the secret of his ability to suffer and work throughout his debilitating illness. The point can be made briefly, yet it is more important, I think, than all of our theoretical considerations hitherto.

A curious dialectics thus permeates Rosenzweig's views of Judaism versus Christianity. On the one hand, he appropriated for Jews some of the fundamental Christian virtues—contempt for the world, or the Augustinian isolation of Christianity from world history. On the other hand, Rosenzweig willingly accepted many of the Christian characterizations of Jews and Judaism, albeit with an inverted valency, endowing them with a positive connotation. Christians since Paul viewed Jews as "Israel in the flesh"—(κατὰ σάρκα, *secundum carnem*), but Rosenzweig, as we have seen, made this into a virtue; Judaism is procreation. Christian polemics spoke of the "blindness" of the Jews (*caecitas Iudaeorum*): they are unable to detect in the old dispensation the foreshadowing of the new. Rosenzweig, too, spoke of the necessary blindness of Judaism—precisely because it is placed at the center, at the dark spot,

---

59. Cf. Stéphane Moses, *Système et Révélation: La philosophie de Franz Rosenzweig* (Paris, 1982), p. 211. While he (and others) interprets this shift as a disappointment with Hegelianism and étatisme, I would like also to emphasize the affirmation of life as such.

of the light-giving "flame" or star. Judaism, in short, is a form of existence that, in order to reflect upon itself, would have to transgress beyond itself and see itself in Christian eyes. In a letter to Hans Ehrenberg of June 1918 Rosenzweig admits that his own ability to see Judaism and Christianity as correlatives may be more Christian than Jewish and may reflect his own biography.[60] He also hints at the dialectical implications of the Jewish existence in the world and in the midst of Christianity. It may be that Judaism would not exist without Christianity. It certainly could not exist without the world.

NARRATIVE AND HISTORY

Having shed some light on the background of Rosenzweig's outlook on history, let us now consider it on its own merit. What strikes us immediately is that a very disturbing paradox lies at its threshold. It conceives Judaism, at one and the same time, as a radically historical and as a radically ahistorical phenomenon.[61] The God of Israel, Rosenzweig knew, is not a God of nature, a cosmic divinity, "ein Wind und Wettergott." He is the God of revelation, his people are the instrument of salvation within history. Revelation, redemption, dispersion were, are, and will be eminently historical, unique events. Rosenzweig—unlike medieval philosophers of religion—had some compunction asserting a miraculous *intervention* of God in history; the very existence of the natural phenomenon of life, of Israel, is a miracle[62] on the cosmic, human, and individual level. How, then, can Israel be conceived as being outside temporality?

Rosenzweig needed a structure that is temporal while defying temporality; historical, while defying historicistic relativism. He thought he had found such a structure in the idea of a perpetual creation, reve-

60. Rosenzweig, *Briefe*, ed. E. Rosenzweig and E. Simon (Berlin, 1935), p. 331.

61. Unlike Moses, *Système et Révélation,* I do not think that this is a dichotomy between a "realistic" and an "idealistic" perception. Perhaps it is the tension between the biblical and postbiblical perception of history: real involvement in history in biblical times (again desired by Zionism), accompanied by a sense of changes and events that are unique and important, as against abstention from history, accompanied by the sense that no events in the present matter much and that past events are paradigmatic and typological rather than historical. Cf. Yosef Hayim Yerushalmi, *Zakhor: Jewish Memory and Jewish History* (Seattle, 1982), and my differing interpretation above, chap. 1.

62. On his notion of miracles, see R. Wiehl, "Experience in Rosenzweig's New Thinking," in Mendes Flohr, ed., *The Philosophy of Franz Rosenzweig*, pp. 42–68, esp. 62–68.

lation and redemption; again we are reminded of Augustine's *creatio perpetua*. Creation, revelation, redemption are ever-repeated events, encoded in the liturgical cycle of the year, the driving force of nature, of the community and of the individual Jew whose (ideal) fulfillment of the commandment is an ever renewed act of will rather than mechanical obedience to the law (*Gebot* rather than *Gesetz*). The corresponding mode of articulation of these perpetual events is, therefore, not the historical reflection, but narrative—"mythos" in the original sense of the word—and reenactment. These are stations in the development of God—of truth—and instances of truth's narrative. Indeed, through the life of Jews and Christians as a community, these events tell *themselves,* speak through deed and word. Rosenzweig drew this notion of myth from Schelling.[63] It also reminds us of Mendelssohn's interpretation of Judaism as a set of symbolic acts.[64] It seems as if, beginning with Mendelssohn and ending with Rosenzweig, German-Jewish philosophy completed a full circle and returned to its starting-point, albeit much richer, much more aware of itself and its difficulties.

In Franz Rosenzweig, German-Jewish culture reached its highest moment of self-criticism and self-awareness, its highest moment of fulfillment, presaged in its beginnings. If this moment was followed by its dissolution, it was not an inevitable consequence. In the end, German-Jewish culture was destroyed by exile and murder. I am reminded of the lines Heine wrote at the end of his tortuous life:

Over your inconsistency, Lord,
Permit me that I brood:
You created the merriest poet of all—
And then you spoiled his mood.

[My trans.]

CONCLUSION

A sincere interpreter of Rosenzweig will confess that it is difficult to penetrate his vocabulary. It may be clearer now why this is

63. Rosenzweig's relation to Schelling has been thoroughly clarified by E. Freund, *Die Existenzphilosophie Franz Rosenzweigs* (Leipzig and Berlin, 1933; reprint Hamburg, 1959), pp. 12–42. From Schelling he also took the notion of "periods" of Church history (Mendes-Flohr, "Franz Rosenzweig and the Crisis of Historicism"). The notion of externalization (*sich äussern*) that Z. Levi derives from Hegel's *Entäusserung* is likewise Schelling's. See his *Precursor of Jewish Existentialism. The Philosophy of Franz Rosenzweig and Its Relationship to Hegel's System* (in Hebrew) (Tel Aviv, 1969), p. 68.

64. See above, pp. 225–226.

so. He used philosophical terms and figures of thought, inherited from different quarters, as metaphors, laden with different and sometimes ambiguous connotations. His system is "eclectic" in the sense that the various idioms employed are interchangeable; he could have conveyed his intentions with or without Hegel's dialectical language, or Cohen's techniques of establishing conceptual continuities, or Rosenstock's grammatical speculations. He actually did so in one of the most appealing of his philosophical works, *Das Büchlein vom gesunden und kranken Menschenverstand*.[65] Why Rosenzweig took the one or the other position in detail often depends on architectonic impulses or biographical circumstances rather than argument. Is the effort of deciphering his code—for a code it is—really commensurate with the yield? I can hardly imagine an interpreter of Rosenzweig altogether free from moments of such doubts. True, the complicated conceptual structures are evidence of an unusual speculative ingenuity and of a sense of order. The wealth of interpretations of institutions, events, and ideas bears witness to Rosenzweig's originality and inquisitiveness. The books manifest humor, ingenuity, and compassion. But what makes his work that which he wants it to be, a "new thinking"?

What are our expectations at the end of any protracted conceptual odyssey? We overlook, with good reason, major faults in philosophical endeavors that we choose to admire. Plato conceded that all objections in the *Parmenides* (of his creation) to his theory of ideas are irrefutable, but nonetheless he held to the theory as one that gave a richer perspective of the world. None of Descartes's terms, not even the evident *sum res cogitans,* is a clear and distinct idea, and Spinoza's ethics can be proven to rest on a *petitio principii.* Neither imprecision of terminology nor errors of reasoning are in themselves criteria of bad philosophy; although we appreciate good craftsmanship, we are willing to concede that a telephone book contains more certain truths than the best philosophical essay. What we do look for in philosophy is, I believe, akin to our expectation of a work of art: a fresh perspective, a new point of view, an unexpected way of "seeing as." Rosenzweig's *Der Stern der Erlösung,* though meager in arguments, abounds in unexpected interpretations. Many of them have a forced and artificial ring to them, and much of the interpretative terminology of Rosenzweig was not raised

65. N. Glatzer, ed. (Düsseldorf, 1964). On the problems of the notion of experience that Rosenzweig develops there, cf. N. Rottenstreich, *Sugiot befilosofiah* (Tel Aviv, 1962), pp. 290–98; and in Mendes-Flohr, ed., *The Philosophy of Franz Rosenzweig,* pp. 69–98.

in his own stables. This may be an additional reason for his admiration for Cohen's posthumous work, whose language is truly Cohen's own. But Rosenzweig turned his vices in one sense into philosophical virtues. The *Stern* consists of a continuous, conscious shift of perspective, translations of concepts of interpretation, from one *idiom* to another and from one *level* of interpretation to another. We recognized three major levels, both horizontally and vertically: (1) defining the formal structures; (2) endowing them with content; and (3) making the content meaningful as a whole. The very same concepts appear at each level "seen as" something different; and each translation is performed both with the knowledge that it is a translation and with the attempt to show how, nevertheless, any new content is foreshadowed in—can be mapped into—the old. Rosenzweig's *Stern* is a virtuous exercise in philosophical hermeneutics and, if nothing else, one of the first philosophies in our century that understands their hermeneutical character. Indeed, in his later years, when the need to create a system was satisfied and abated, Rosenzweig found his most genuine expression in creative exegesis, culminating in his translations of Halevi and of the Bible. The few theoretical articles that he published on the art of translation merit special examination; they are among the most perceptive reflections on philosophical hermeneutics, a discipline that came of age only recently.

A final remark: the method of *Der Stern der Erlösung* consists in continuous translations, a constant shift of points of view. Rosenzweig assumes, in turn, the vantage points of paganism, Christianity, and Judaism—and explains, so to say from within, the manner in which they conceive the interaction between God, World, and Man (or fail to do so). He views God from the vantage point of man, and man from the vantage point of God. He interprets Christianity and Islam in what seems to him Jewish terms, and vice versa. The book, we said, offers a progressive change of perspectives; it is a kaleidoscope of sorts. Now if, as Rosenzweig believes, Judaism is essentially uninterested in any point of view but its own—and this was indeed the traditional Jewish self-image—then his method is profoundly "un-Jewish." His claim, "das Jüdische ist meine Methode, nicht mein Gegenstand,"[66] was then simply wrong, unless he erred in his assessment of Judaism as altogether self-sufficient.

It is indeed debatable whether the strong mimetic forces that Jewish culture exhibited in various historical constellations are essential or ac-

66. Rosenzweig, *Briefe*, p. 407.

cidental. Rather than enter into such a debate with Rosenzweig, I would like to suggest that his method reflects the historical situation of German Jewry—irrespective of whether it is, in a general sense, Jewish or not. Rosenzweig saw through the illusion of consonance between *Deutschtum* and *Judentum* cultivated by so many Jews of his and his parents' generations, including Hermann Cohen. In their attempt to identify with the German culture far beyond the exigencies of good citizenship, German Jews became better Germans than any Saxonian, Bavarian or Prussian; "better" in the sense that they lived up to the ideal of a homogenous national culture more than anyone else, albeit the ideal was their own idealized image of Germany, a pure German culture of their wishes, which, as some of them believed, corresponded to the best in their own Jewish tradition. They were eager to identify with their environment, to understand Germany from *within,* even to the point of judging their own existence in terms of the environment. Rosenzweig rejected this identification and ridiculed the illusion of consonance. But he, also, wanted to understand from within the non-Jewish culture surrounding him—and be it in order to express the uniqueness of Judaism. He insisted on the right to remain alien and articulated the gap between the Jewish and non-Jewish components of his world. But he had, in a manner of speaking, to buy his right to be different by showing how well, how much from the inside, he grasped the point of view of "the other." His was also "a formidably clear sense of the time" ("ein ungeheuer helles Zeitbewusstsein") refined by his intense historical studies—in themselves an exercise in shifting points of view and in continuous translation. It seems as if only a full inside understanding, to the point of temporal identification, of "paganism," "Christianity," "Germanhood," allowed him to defy assimilation and remain Jewish by his own choice. In order to become "himself" he had to be first "the other."

9

Theological Responses
to the Holocaust

The Meaning of Meaning

That the extermination of the Jews in Europe ought to arrest the attention of theologians seems obvious. That it has actually done so, especially in the last decade, and continues to do so, is a fact. But what we mean when we ask about the theological "meaning" of the Holocaust is far from obvious. For some it means the meaning of the catastrophe in inherited theological terms: an attempt to salvage a theodicy from the rubble left by the eruption of evil as an apparently autonomous force. For others it means the meaning of the catastrophe for theology, either in a polemical vein, when they address the failure or even complicity of rival theologies, or critically, when they question the legitimacy of their own theological heritage in the shadow of the systematic destruction of human life and dignity. I shall call these trends, in turn, the direct, the polemical, and the critical-reflexive modes of theologizing about the Holocaust. And I shall argue that the first is offensive, the second hypocritical, and the third not radical enough even in its most radical manifestations.

The Holocaust as Punishment and Signal

YOEL TAITELBAUM

One of the few who dare to state that the Holocaust is perfectly comprehensible in traditional theological terms shall serve as our starting point. From the extreme case we may learn something about seemingly more reasonable attempts in the same direction.

Shortly after the foundation of the state of Israel, there appeared a book with the typical rabbinical title *And It Pleased Moses* (*Vayo'el Moshe*).[1] Its author, Rabbi Yoel Taitelbaum, was the leader of an ultra-orthodox, anti-Zionist, cohesive movement whose branch in Israel is known as the "Guardians of the City" (*neture karta*). It summarizes all known traditions in support of passive messianism—I shall explain the term immediately—and concludes that the Holocaust was an inevitable consequence of, and punishment for, a formidable sin: the transgression of the divine warning not to seek redemption by one's own hands, through human initiative. His argument is as follows: "Because of our sins we have been exiled from our land." The dispersion and oppression of the Jewish nation in the Diaspora has a punitive-cathartic function, and only God can call an end to the punishment. Those who wish to "precipitate the end" and force God's hand through human action are, whether or not they know it, rebels. Three times the Song of Songs repeats an oathlike formula: "I put you under oath, the daughters of Jerusalem, in the name of the deer and the gazelles of the field, not to hasten nor to precipitate love until it desires." An old exegetical tradition justified the inclusion of such eminently secular love songs in the canon of sacred scriptures on the grounds that it ought to be read only allegorically, as a dialogue between God and the spirit of Israel (or, in other quarters, the *ecclesia*). The three oaths, we are taught in the tractate *Ketubot* of the Babylonian Talmud, have a particular allegoresis.[2] The threefold repetition of the formula refers to the three oaths imposed on Israel and on the nations of the world after the destruction of the Temple. Israel was held by oath not to rebel against the nations

---

1. Yoel Taitelbaum, *Vayo'el Moshe* (New York, 1952; 2nd ed., 1957).
2. B. T., *Ketubot 3a*; *Cant. Rabba* 2, 7. Literally, the formula is not an oath, but a playful imitation of one: wherefore the invocation of God (*el shaddai, el teva'ot*) is replaced by the phonetical simile (*aylot ha'sade, tsviot*). Cf. R. Gordis, "The Song of Songs," in *Mordechai M. Kaplan Jubilee Volume* (New York, 1953), pp. 281–397, esp. 308–9.

among which it is held as a "prisoner of war," and not to try and "hasten the end." In return, the nations of the world were held by the third oath not to oppress Israel too much.

From these premises Taitelbaum draws an outrageous conclusion. Because, in the course of the Zionist movement, an ever growing number of Jews broke the oath and took their fate into their own hands—they wished to turn, in Herzl's words, into a political subject—the nations of the world, in turn, likewise felt themselves free of the oath not to oppress Israel too much, and oppress they did. Why did they? Taitelbaum assumes, as a matter of course, that "Esau always hates Jacob," inherently and incessantly. The Holocaust is the inevitable consequence of the Jewish spontaneous drive toward sovereignty or even autonomy. It is not even the last catastrophe: the perpetration of the sin continued with the foundation of the state of Israel. A catastrophe is imminent, after which only a few, the "remnants of Israel," will survive to witness the true redemption. Indeed, Taitelbaum's whole argument is embedded in the apocalyptical premise that the true redemption, through divine miracle, is very close at hand. The times preceding it are, in the traditional imagery, times of extreme wars and tribulations, times replete with false hopes and false messiahs.

In a curious way, Taitelbaum shares the belief that the messianic days are at the threshold with his Orthodox adversaries, the "Bloc of the Faithful" (*Gush Emunim*).[3] They too assume that hatred against Jews is inherent in the nations of the world because the choice of God fell upon Israel, or, in the more secular version of the poet U. Z. Greenberg, because Israel is "the race of Abraham, which had started on its way to become master."[4] They regard the Holocaust and the subsequent formation of the state of Israel and its wars as a divine signal for an active preparation in "the dawn of our redemption." Since our time is the time of the messianic war, and redemption has already started, it is incumbent upon Jews to conquer and hold to the promised borders of their holy land, to shape it into a *civitas dei*. For Taitelbaum the Holocaust came because Jews were too active; for the *Gush Emunim*, because Jews were too passive; for both it is a portent of the Messiah.

3. Menachem M. Kasher, *Hatekufa hagdola* (Jerusalem, 1969); it contains explicit polemics also against Taitelbaum.

4. U. Z. Greenberg, *Rehovot hanahar, Sefer ha'iliot veha'koah* (Tel Aviv, 1957), p. 7; "father of the superior race," pp. 31 passim. *Geza* is the accepted modern Hebrew term for "race"; a racial ideology will be called *torat geza*. In 1957 it had other connotations than in 1920, when Jabotinsky promised: "With blood and with sweat / A race will be born to us / proud, magnanimous, and cruel."

ACTIVE AND PASSIVE MESSIANISM

Two distinct traditions of Jewish messianism clash here in their exaggerated forms: the passive-utopian messianic tradition as opposed to active-realistic messianism. The former has been by far the predominant tradition, an antidote of the rabbinical establishment against dangerous messianic eruptions; the latter, although a minority tradition, has had a continuous career and some notable authorities on its side: Maimonides, Jacob Berab, Zvi Kalisher. Maimonides, to whom world history is a continuous history of the monotheization of the world guided by God's "cunning of reason"—that is, "Miracles of the category of the possible"—saw also in the messianic days a period within history without change in cosmic or human nature.[5] He believed that there were some ways to precipitate them through human initiative, as by the reconstruction of the old court system in the land of Israel. Jacob Berab, who tried to implement this plan through the attempt to renew the pristine ordination, was rebuked by the Jerusalemite head of the court, who insisted that the messianic days can come only as a package deal; no element of them can be taken out of its miraculous context to be implemented now.[6] Kalisher, in the nineteenth century, devoted his life to encouraging settlement in Israel or even the renewal of some sacrifices in the present for the very same reasons. Note that this "active messianism" is not a precursor of Zionism. On the contrary: Zionism started with an antimessianic claim, a desire for sovereignty irrespective of messianic expectations. Both Taitelbaum and the *Gush Emunim* represent pre-Zionistic mentalities. Both are, in different ways, fossils of the past, albeit poisonous fossils.

The ideology of passive messianism, to which Taitelbaum is an heir, should not be confused with the myth of the physical passivity of diaspora Jewry. Why did Jews not offer resistance in the face of their extermination? Raul Hilberg, in the introduction to his monumental book,[7] refers to the alleged two thousand years of mental conditioning in appeasement. Passivity, he believes, was an intrinsic mental feature of Diaspora Jewry. This is a myth as widespread as it is dangerous; dangerous it is because it suggests an artificial gap between the passive Diaspora

5. See above, pp. 147 ff.
6. Levi ben Habib, *Responsa* (Venice, 1565), appendix (*kuntres hasmikha*); on the ideological background, cf. J. Katz, "Machloket hasmicha ben Jacob Berav veha Ralbach," *Zion* 17 (1951): pp. 34 ff; see, chapter 5, "Maimonides."
7. Raul Hilberg, *The Destruction of the European Jews* (Chicago, 1967). I elaborated on some of the following remarks elsewhere *(The Passivity of Diaspora Jewry: Myth and Reality,* Aran Lecture 11, Tel Aviv, 1982).

mentality and the active, healthy mentality of the new species of Jew in Israel. Neither in antiquity nor in the Middle Ages did Jews abstain from physical resistance in the face of persecution, whenever feasible. They resisted during the Crusaders' pogroms, the Chmielnicki pogroms, and modern pogroms. Resistance during the Nazi occupation was no less than among most other occupied populations. At best, one could ask why German Jews were not more active in the resistance movement until 1939, or why there was more cooperation than necessary later. But if there was passivity, it was not a heritage of Diaspora mentality but rather of modern vintage. To the modern European Jew, who identified himself with the state he lived in, resistance against his state seemed outside the universe of discourse; nor could he conceive of a state acting against the raison d'état. The preemancipation Jew, by contrast, always saw himself as an alien, as a "prisoner of war," and was always on the alert. The legal principle, "the law of the kingdom is valid law," which was quoted by some reformers of the nineteenth century to prove the priority of state law even in Jewish terms, originally meant the opposite. It pertained to property only and delineated a *Widerstandsrecht:* only if a ruler acts in accord with the law of the land is one obliged to obey him.[8] The ideology of passive messianism is the only true nucleus of the myth of passivity: it served to emphasize the lack of acute political aspiration. In a way, then, the political emancipation and acculturation of Jews in Europe opened the way for two extreme, new possibilities: total passivity and total self-assertion. In the language of Sartre, the postemancipatory Jew may be said to live in a constant "situation" of *être-vu:*[9] he shunned it by identifying with the aggressor, or defined it by becoming Zionist.

At best, passive messianism was an ideology, not a legally binding position. It was prevalent once, but it is obsolete today even among the Orthodox. Why then dignify Taitelbaum's insult to common sense and decency with a detailed discussion? Because in theology, as in the law, much can be learned from extreme limiting cases. An overt absurdity is better than a covert one. Jewish theologians who are less extreme than either Taitelbaum or the *Gush Emunim,* such as Emil Fackenheim or E. Berkovits,[10] admit that they can see no theological

8. B. T., *Nedarim* 28*a*; *Gittin* 10*b*; *Baba Kama* 111; *Baba Batra* 54*b*–55*a*; cf. Sh. Shiloh, *Dina demalchuta dina* (Jerusalem, 1974).

9. Jean-Paul Sartre, *Réflexions sur la question juive* (Paris, 1947).

10. Emil Fackenheim, *God's Presence in History* (New York, 1970); idem, *The Jewish Return into History* (New York, 1978). E. Berkovits, *Faith After the Holocaust* (New York, 1973).

rationale to the Holocaust. The Holocaust is incomprehensible, they say, and defies all theodicies. But they do find a theological meaning in the survival of the nation and the rebirth of the state. In both they find a confirmation of the divine presence and a promise to preserve Israel.

Even these diluted versions of a theodicy are offensive. Having survived, while others—close family and friends—have not, is a terrible burden to many survivors. Haunted by excruciating memories, many of them refused to talk or reminisce in the years following internment; some of them do so only now, fearing that true memories will be lost within their generation. It may well be that the state of Israel, too, owes its establishment in part to the Holocaust; but this also is a terrible burden, not a sign of chosenness or divine grace. Similar perceptions may have moved George Steiner in his recent book, tasteless as it may otherwise be.[11] There is only one instance of theologizing in Primo Levi's account of his survival in Auschwitz. It reads:

> Now everyone is busy scraping the bottom of his bowl with his spoon so as not to waste the last drops of soup; a confused, metallic clatter, signifying the end of the day. Silence slowly prevails and then, from my bunk on the top row, I see and hear old Kuhn praying aloud, with his beret on his head, swaying backwards and forwards violently. Kuhn is thanking God because he has not been chosen.
>
> Kuhn is out of his senses. Does he not see Beppo the Greek in the bunk next to him, Beppo who is twenty years old and is going to the gas chamber the day after tomorrow and knows it and lies there looking fixedly at the light without saying anything and without even thinking any more? Can Kuhn fail to realize that the next time it will be his turn? Does Kuhn not understand that what has happened today is an abomination, which no propitiatory prayer, no pardon, no expiation by the guilty, which nothing at all in the power of man can ever clean again?
>
> If I was God, I would spit at Kuhn's prayer.[12]

Anti-Judaism and Anti-Semitism

CHRISTIANITY AND HISTORY

Recent history may or may not have a theological meaning, but it certainly carries a meaning for theology—more concretely, for Christianity. Jewish and Christian theologies devote considerable

11. George Steiner, *The Portage to St. Christobel of A. H.* (New York, 1982).
12. Primo Levi, *Survival in Auschwitz* (orig. title, *Se questo è un uomo*), trans. S. Woolf (New York, 1961), pp. 151–52.

energies to accusing, expiating, or reformulating past and present Christian attitudes toward Jews and Judaism. How deeply is Christianity implicated in the formation of the preconditions for the genocide of Jews? Is Christianity at all capable of changing its anti-Judaic attitudes without risking its very foundations?

No sincere historical interpretation doubts that anti-Jewish postures of Christianity were the single most important factor in the continuity of anti-Jewish sentiments since antiquity, that at least the silence of the churches while Jews were deprived of their legal rights, then chased and exterminated, was in part made possible by the previous theological alienation. This silence stands in contrast to the firm and effective stand of the German clergy against euthanasia. If, however, it could be shown that the antagonism between church and synagogue were not part of original Christianity, then—so we hear from some theologians—it could also be severed successfully from the main body of Christian doctrines.

This is a fallacious argument, logically as well as historically. It is logically fallacious because, hard as it may try, Christianity cannot return to the conditions of the *primitiva ecclesia:* an apocalyptic Jewish sect withdrawn from the world. The very program of *reformatio* is inaccessible. At best, one could arbitrarily choose some elements of original Christianity and declare them to be essential, while inevitably discarding others; but then one need not exclude the further history of Christianity either and distinguish sharply between "Christentum und Kultur" (Overbeck). The very same arguments which have already constituted the crisis of Protestant theology for a hundred years apply also in regard to its treatment of Judaism.

But we ought nonetheless to separate the various ingredients and driving forces in Christian anti-Jewish doctrines. It is true that the anti-Jewish ideology of the Church was not contingent upon social, political, or economic conditions only. But neither was it a product of hatred only. The Jews have always been, and remain, a *mysterium tremendum et fascinosum* to the Christian Church. The preoccupation with the phenomenon of Judaism and of continuous Jewish existence belongs to the very essence and self-definition of Christianity as a historical religion. But, contrary to common opinion, I hasten to add that the ambivalence of fascination and rejection is equally characteristic of the Jewish attitude toward Christianity more than toward any other religion, including Islam. We shall also see that some of the Christian attitudes were religious-theological in nature, while others were not even that when given a theological guise. The latter distinction may clarify the present theological situation. The historical progress of Christian attitudes toward Jews and Judaism seems to me as follows.

THE PAGAN ATTITUDE [13]

Christian anti-Judaism appears in a much sharper light when compared to its antecedents. Christianity did not inherit the anti-Jewish arguments of pagan antiquity: those were political and ethnic in origin, born in part out of the aggressive Hasmonaean policies against the Greek population of the land of Israel and in part out of competition over privileges in Egypt. Under the Roman Empire, Jewish insurrection and the menace of the missionary impact of Judaism combined to perpetuate anti-Jewish propaganda and attitudes.[14]

Christianity may have, since the second century, inherited some of the pagan anti-Jewish sentiments; it could, however, make no use of pagan anti-Jewish propaganda. Christians, for example, never denied the title Jews once had had to the land of Israel up to the time of the rise of Christianity, when the choice of God shifted from "Israel according to the flesh" to the "true Israel" (*verus Israel*), "Israel in the spirit," that is, the "Church from among the nations" (*ecclesia ex gentibus*). The keener minds among the pagan polemicists employed a typical technique: they manipulated an inverted reading of biblical passages so as to construct their own version of Jewish origins: they constructed a counterhistory, just as Jews were later to do to Christianity in the *Sefer toledot Jeshu*. The Bible itself aided pagan polemicists in their construction of a counterhistory:[15] the Hebrews were not a venerable old nation nor is their constitution authentic and worth preserving. Rather, they started out as an Egyptian leper colony, secluded and despised, which then established a reign of terror in Egypt with the aid of the Hyksos, led by a renegade Egyptian priest named Osarsiph (Moses), until they were driven out. Osarsiph gave them a constitution which was, in all respects, a plagiarized, inverted mirror image of Egyptian mores.[16]

13. The following chapter repeats and enlarges my remarks in the *Jerusalem Quarterly* 19 (1981): pp. 56–72.

14. Jochanan H. Levy, *Olamot Nifgashim* (Jerusalem, 1960), pp. 115–89 (see chapter 2, n. 50); A. Tcherikover, *Hellenistic Civilization and the Jews,* trans. S. Appelbaum (Philadelphia, 1959).

15. See above, p. 36, nn. 49–50, and I. Heinemann in Pauli-Wissowa, *Realenzyklopädie,* Supplementband V. s.v. 'Antisemitismus' (col. 3–43); J. H. Levi, op. cit., pp. 60–196.

16. Tacitus, *Hist.,* V, 4 (see chapter 2, n. 50).

And ingenious propaganda, as we said earlier, was reminiscent of what modern sociologists of knowledge describe as the formation of a "counteridentity."[17] This tradition of pagan anti-Jewish propaganda is notable for what it lacks as much as for what it contains. It would be futile to look for a religious polemic against monotheism, since most of the pagan intelligentsia was, in a manner of speaking, likewise "monotheistic." From Xenophanes through Aristotle to Plotinus, Greek philosophy developed an ever more deanthropomorphized and rarefied image of God, a natural religion (*theologia naturalis*).[18] Already Xenophanes advanced the most dominant critical argument in the history of the critique of religion until Feuerbach and Freud: that man makes his gods in his own image, that is, transfers, or projects, his (and his society's) vices and virtues upon the transcendent. The educated Greco-Roman intellectual believed, by and large, that beyond the "political cult" (*theologia politica*), religion is one of a variety of cults.

Augustine puts similar words into the mouth of Porphyrius;[19] and even our Sages let a pagan philosopher conversing with Rabbi Akiva say, "We both know in our heart that there is no reality in idolatry."[20] In other words, Church Fathers and *tana'im* alike were aware that theirs was not the only monotheistic creed among polytheistic ones. The clash between Judeo-Christian and pagan theologies was not over the number of gods but over the nature of the one God. To the Greek mind God was the embodiment of the principle of cosmic harmony, passive and self-contained: the idea of God as a moral personality active in history, an all-powerful busybody, was repulsive. That God abandoned the care of the cosmos in order to concentrate on the affairs of a small, dirty nation in the provinces seems to Celsus "a frog-and-rainworm perspective."[21]

Nonetheless, monotheism was one of the most attractive features of Judaism to the pagan mind. Was not Judaism a true philosophical reli-

17. See above, pp. 36 ff.

18. W. W. Jaeger, *Die Theologie der frühen griechischen Denker* (Stuttgart, 1964), pp. 1 ff., 50 ff. (Xenophanes). (English trans., W. W. Jaeger, *The Theology of the Early Greek Philosophers* [Oxford, 1948]).

19. Augustinus, *De civitate Dei*, X, 9 ff. 9 (in *Corpus Christianorum: Series Latina*, vol. 47, pp. 281 ff.).

20. Tractate *Avodah Zarah* 55a, in I. Epstein, ed., *The Babylonian Talmud*, sec. 4: *Seder Nezikin*, vol. 7 (London, 1935), p. 281.

21. See H. Chadwick, *Origenes: Contra Celsum*, trans. and with an introduction and notes by H. Chadwick (Cambridge, 1965), p. 199. See Andersen, *Logos und Nomos: Die Polemik des Kelsos wider das Christentum, Arbeiten zur Kirchengeschichte* 30 (1955): pp. 266 ff.

gion, worshipping a philosophical principle rather than anthropomorphic images? The very first reaction of educated Greeks to the encounter with Judaism was one of admiration.[22] No pagan polemicist could attack the monotheistic idea as such. But he could venture to show that there is nothing original or authentic in Jews or Judaism, nothing venerable and worth preserving in their laws and customs. The missionary successes of Judaism and later of Christianity proved how hopelessly unpersuasive this pagan propaganda was.

THE CHRISTIAN ATTITUDE

Christianity, we have said, had no use for the body of pagan anti-Jewish propaganda. But Christian-Jewish antagonism reaches back to the time when Christianity was still a Jewish apocalyptic sect. With other sectarian movements—for example, the Dead Sea Scrolls sect—Christians shared a hatred for the normative Jewish establishment. Already the sectarians of Qumran defined themselves as a "holy community" (*adat kodesh*) and the establishment as a "false city" (*ir shav*)—*civitas dei* against *civitas terranea*. They alone were remnants of Israel; they alone possessed the key for the eschatological "decoding" (*pesher*) of Scriptures; they were, in short, an avant-garde of the new, magnificent cosmic order in the midst of the old and corrupt one. At times, they imply that only they, "the eternal stock," will be saved at the imminent end of days. And they subsume the existing establishment under the category of "children of darkness" and are admonished "to love all children of light each according to his lot and to hate all children of darkness each according to his guilt in the vengeance of God."[23] Like them in many respects, the early Christians saw themselves as *verus Israel* and the rest of the Jews as condemned. Belief in Christ, as earlier the belief in the "Righteous Teacher" (*moreh zedek*),[24] became the true sign of salvation. Like them, early Christianity developed a hatred of the establishment of "Pharisees and Sadducees."

Soon early Christianity was to compete with the Jewish establishment in their missionary efforts—first among the God-fearing people

22. J. H. Levi, op. cit.; M. Stern, op. cit.
23. Rule of Qumran, I, 10–11; see J. Licht, *The Rule Scroll* (IQS, IQSa, and IQSb), text, introduction, and commentary (in Hebrew) (Jerusalem, 1965), p. 61. See G. Vermes, *The Dead Sea Scrolls in English* (Harmondsworth, 1962), p. 72. Also available: Theodore H. Gaster, trans., *The Dead Sea Scriptures* (Garden City, N.Y., 1956). See also chapter 3, "History as Predestination."
24. IQPHab VII, 1–5 (G. Vermes, ibid., p. 239).

(*yire'ei shamayim* or οἱ σεβόμενοι), the large groups of adorers of Judaism on the fringe of many Diaspora communities, and later among real pagans. Mutual antagonism was reinforced by the competition over proselytes. It was also reinforced by the inner conflicts in Christianity between Gentile and Jewish Christians. It was further sealed by the abstention of Christians from the second revolt (132–135 A.D.) against Rome, a revolt that, unlike the first, seems to have been unanimous. But after the second revolt against Rome and the Hadrianic persecutions that followed, Judaism lost its missionary impetus. Eventually, Christianity became the dominant imperial religion, "the kingdom became heretical," [25] and the once strong Judeo-Christian elements in the Church disappeared.

What purpose could Christian anti-Jewish doctrines have served thereafter? Why did no generation pass without leaving various anti-Jewish tracts? What is the logic behind such an enormous body of literature, which is as unsavory as it is repetitious? For it ceased to be a record of living polemics and became, more and more, a stereotypic enumeration of veiled hints in the Old Testament for the veracity of the New Testament.

The function of anti-Jewish propaganda was not external—to convert Jews—but internal. Precisely because the Church failed to convert the Jews, their very existence became a theological paradox of the first order. Not so for Islam: unlike the Church, Islam does not view its raison d'être as the individual conversion of each and every infidel. True, the world must be made "safe for Islam" through political hegemony, but under Muslim rule, the people possessing a genuine (monotheistic) revelation like Jews and Christians—the legal term is "people of the book" (*ahl al kitab*)—may retain their religious-political autonomy as a protected, second-class minority (*dhimmis*). [26] By contrast, the Christian Church proves its veracity through worldwide mission: it is an *ecclesia militans*. Yet the conversion of the Jews, who were originally the chosen people and still held to the Old Testament in its original language, was impossible either by persuasion or force.

"Israel according to the flesh" (*Israel secundum carnem*), they were called: Christianity and Judaism alike shared the fiction that the Jews

---

25. Tractate (Mishnah) *Sotah* IX, 15, in H. Danby, trans., The *Mishnah* (London, 1933), p. 306. See Michael Avi-Yonah, *The Jews of Palestine: A Political History from the Bar-Kokhba War to the Arab Conquest* (London and New York, 1976), pp. 137–57, esp. pp. 145–150.

26. E. G. von Grunebaum, *Medieval Islam* (Chicago, 1953), pp. 174–85.

were literally the descendants of Abraham; they differed only in the assessment of the value of such ethnic continuity. *Secundum carnem* also refers to the mentality of the Jews: they understood their Scriptures and laws "literally" rather than with a sublimated understanding (*spiritualis intellegentia*); they are, therefore, "blind" to the various veiled hints in the Old Testament as to the veracity of the New Testament. They are a living anachronism—"these Jews refused to change with the times"[27]—a fossil. They failed to understand that Judaism (circumcision) was "good for its time" only[28] and had to be superseded by a new dispensation for which it paved the way (Hugh of St. Victor). In short, Jews are a stubborn lot.

But then again, was not their very stubbornness also admirable? Augustine thought so,[29] and wished for Christians of his day to have some of it in the face of persecution and temptation. More than that, Jews and Judaism continued to fascinate Christians by virtue of their antiquity—that very antiquity which in theory was denigrated. Throughout its career, the Church feared Judaizers (*Judaizantes*) in its midst. After all, the very claim of the Church to be a new dispensation introduced a shift of values both in the classical world and among the converted Germanic tribes of the Middle Ages. "New" was to both mentalities a suspicious attribute: only the old was a mark of quality and authenticity. The classical political term for a dangerous revolutionary was *homo rerum novarum cupidus;* in the legal consciousness of the early Middle Ages, only old law (*altes Recht*) was good law (*gutes Recht*),[30] and Pope Gregory VII shocked his imperial adversaries when he claimed his right to establish new laws (*novas leges condere*).[31] An inherent tension was thus introduced into the European mentality between the veneration of the old and the glorification of the new. The antiquity and very existence of Jews and Judaism was used by Christians in their antipagan propaganda—to prove the authenticity of the Bible. That Judaism was the authentic monotheistic religion because it was the oldest had also been a Jewish argument—witness Jehuda Halevi's *Kuzzari;* and the few

27. See above, p. 177.

28. Hugo de Sancto Victore, *De sacramentis Christianae fidei* II, 6, 4, in Migne, *Patrologia Latina*, vol. 176, col. 450A; idem, *De vanitate mundi et rerum transeuntium usu*, IV, in Migne, op. cit., vol. 176, col. 740C. See A. Funkenstein, *Heilsplan Patrologia Latina*, pp. 52 and 165, n. 5. Hugo may have been influenced by Rashi in Genesis 6:9.

29. Bernhard Blumenkranz, *Die Judenpredigt Augustine* (Basel, 1946).

30. Kern; see above, p. 156, n. 80.

31. See above, p. 156, n. 81.

cases of medieval conversions of Judaism we know of were prompted by such sentiments.

Eventually, the Church Fathers developed a doctrine to justify the continued existence of the Jews as part of the economy of salvation,[32] and a praxis of anti-Jewish legislation to go with it. The Jews fulfill a threefold function. Their physical existence proves the authenticity of their Scriptures against pagan contentions; they guarantee the preservation of the authentic revelation and must continue to do so. Moreover, their very humiliation in dispersion is an everlasting proof (*testimonium aeternum*) of the Christian claim that, with the coming of Christ, "the scepter has ceased from Judah" and God's choice was transferred from "Israel in the flesh" to "Israel in the spirit." The present status of the synagogue as a "slave" to the Church testifies to the superiority of the latter. And finally, the Jews have an eschatological function. At the end of days their remnants will convert to Christianity en masse and perhaps even save Christianity from the Antichrist. Such was the explanation of Jewish existence, and of the relative tolerance to be extended toward them. It rested on the firm assumption that the Jews did not change; that they adhered now as before to the letter of the Bible. Perhaps even their clothes had not changed. To Anskar, we hear from his biographer, Christ appeared "tall of stature, clothed as a Jew, beautiful in appearance."[33]

NEW PATTERNS OF THE TWELFTH CENTURY

The Jews, then, were to be tolerated by the Church on the condition that they play the double role of slave and fossil. They refused to conform to either. In fact, they were a privileged minority and developed distinctly aristocratic tastes. Legally and mentally, they were all too close to the ruling powers-that-be, "pertaining to the royal palace." A Jewish boy in Germany could daydream about becoming a knight even in the twelfth century. Much later, Schlomo ibn Verga, reflecting on the Spanish Expulsion of 1492, identified the drive to reach the pinnacles of society and to boast about it as a major cause of the catastrophe. Throughout the Middle Ages, Jews were seen and saw themselves, as "prisoners of war" on alien soil, but they hardly acted like it. Nor did they agree to remain a fossil. Instead, they developed an

32. For this and for the following, see above, chapter 6 (polemics).
33. Rimbertus, *Vita Anskari*, as above, chapter 6, n. 18.

impressive, adaptable system of laws and institutions and created a vast body of interpretive and speculative literature. The discrepancy between image and reality, and the ever present reserves of popular hostility toward strangers, and Jews in particular, served as possible sources of tension.

The turning point in the history of Christian anti-Jewish doctrines came at a crucial moment of Jewish life in Europe, during the twelfth century. Several factors contributed to the deterioration of the status of Jews then: the growing independence and power of Church, the Crusades, the growth of popular religious movements, and the fact that, since the Spanish *reconquista,* the majority of Jews in Europe lived in Christian countries. Anti-Jewish doctrines changed now in quantity and in quality. Not only did they increase; they changed patterns. The new patterns created then were to last to the eighteenth century. Alongside the other categories of stereotypes, new kinds of propaganda are clearly recognizable.

Sometimes the new image could be fitted to older stereotypes. The image of Jews as economic exploiters, "usurers," was born out of new circumstances; in antiquity, Josephus only repeats a commonplace when he regrets the Jewish lack of commercial skills compared to Greeks and Phoenicians. Once born, the new stereotype comfortably adapted to old theological ones. "Israel in the flesh" is always oriented toward worldly rewards, even when keeping the precepts, and all the more so in the secular domain. Sometimes new stereotypes collided with the old or replaced them. The latter process, which led to the alienation and demonization of the Jewish image in the later Middle Ages, deserves further scrutiny.

An altogether new stereotype of this kind was the stereotype of menace and secrecy; it operated, from now on, on all levels, from the theological to the popular. Beginning with the twelfth century, more and more clergymen became acquainted with Jewish doctrines and with the massive body of postbiblical literature. Some of them turned to Hebraic studies for exegetical advice;[34] others employed it in a new brand of anti-Jewish argument. The Talmud in particular served them as evidence that the Jews were not the simple preservers of the Bible they seemed earlier, that the Jews adhered now to another, new law (*nova lex*), which superseded the biblical laws that Jews were supposed to

34. B. Smalley, *The Study of the Bible in the Middle Ages* (Oxford, 1952); H. Heilperin, *Rashi and the Christian Scholars* (Pittsburgh, 1963).

adhere to "according to the letter." Was not such a new law a heresy even in terms of Judaism proper, as understood by the Church? Was not the tolerance extended toward them based upon the premise that they did not change—and if they did and looked for a new law, then should they not look only toward the true law? Instead of both the Bible and the *lex caritatis,* they seem to have created a new law of their own making. And they adhered to it secretly, so as to appear still as the carriers of the Old Testament.

The first tract in this vein was written in the middle of the twelfth century by Peter the Venerable, abbot of Cluny. This professional peacemaker promised to "unveil" the Jewish secrets: that they had ceased to adhere to the divine law and in fact adhered to a diabolical, man-made legislation.[35] Bits and pieces of the Talmud, taken out of context, serve him to prove that, far from being a mere literal interpretation, the Talmud itself admits that even God must bow before the decisions of earthly courts, that God himself is bound by talmudic law. No longer is Judaism seen as an anachronistic, perhaps even ridiculous, but at any rate understandable, religion: its image turns into one of secret, diabolical traditions. Such were also the accusations which led to the trial and burning of the Talmud in Paris (1240).[36]

This dehumanization and demonization of the Jewish image was not confined to a few polemical tracts only. It characterizes first and foremost the popular imagination.[37] The twelfth century saw the first appearance of the blood libel. Thomas of Monmouth's narrative of the alleged case contains a reference to a converted Jew who revealed to him stipulations in "the old Scriptures of the Jews" according to which Jews are obliged to shed Christian blood at least once a year if indeed they wish to be redeemed. For this purpose a secret rabbinical synod convenes periodically from all over Europe to determine which community is in turn to commit ritual murder.[38] A clear line leads from here to the images invoked in the infamous *Protocols of the Elders of Zion.*[39]

The twelfth century thus revived—if unintentionally—the elements

---

35. Petrus Venerabilis, *Tractatus adversus Iudaeorum inveteratam duritiem,* V, as above, chapter 6, n. 33. Cf. above, chapter 6, n. 10.

36. See chapter 6, nn. 72–74.

37. See chapter 6, n. 8.

38. Thomas of Monmouth, *De vita et passione Sancti Willelmi martyris Norwicensis,* II, 9 (as above, chapter 6, n. 70).

39. N. Cohn's study *Warrant for Genocide* (above, chapter 2, n. 71), traces the literary affiliations of the *Protocols* but not the genesis of its *topoi.*

of pagan anti-Christian and anti-Jewish propaganda: accusations of secrecy and secretive mores and beliefs generated by Jewish "misanthropy" (the *odium humani generis* of Tacitus). The Jewish "secrets" (*arcanae*) are directed against the healthy social texture of their environment. Christianity was at first unable to use such arguments; they were also directed against Christians, and Christians claimed a share in the Jewish "secrets." In the later Middle Ages, beginning in the twelfth century, Jews once again became mysterious, incomprehensible, and dangerous. The popular demonic image of Jews, including the blood libel, never became the official theological stand of the Church; the Church never actually denied or confirmed those biases and, when convenient, it used them. Nor did the attack on the Talmud continue in the way it had started. How could the Church, always apprehensive of heretics who wish to turn to the "Scriptures alone" and eliminate the authoritative tradition of the Church, ask Jews to adhere to the Scriptures "without a gloss?" Not that the Church could not justify such lack of consequence, but some figures of thought become taboo in any age. The attack on the Talmud continued on the grounds, for example, that it contained blasphemies which should at least be eradicated.

Now the renewed acquaintance of Christian theologians with Jewish writings generated not only repulsion or awareness of polemical opportunities. It also heightened the fascination with Jews which we have already mentioned: fascination with Jewish exegesis (the *veritas hebraica*) and an even more intense fascination with the Kabbala later on.[40] The Kabbala is, in a particular way, an example of the dialectics of repulsion and attraction on both sides. It manifests the Jewish fascination with emanatory—even trinitarian—speculations, and early kabbalists were promptly accused of Christianizing tendencies. The kabbalists endowed hitherto heretical readings of the Bible with deep mystery—for example, the reading of "God" in Genesis 1:1 as the direct (grammatical) object, rather than subject, of the verse. To the humanists and Renaissance Platonists it seemed as if an old, secret, pre-Jewish and pre-Christian tradition of the most profound truths was unveiled through the Kabbala. The "secrecy" and "secret traditions" of the Jews thus implied not only pejorative connotations, connotations such as those captured in the word "cabal" in several European languages. To some they seemed to be of inestimable value and attraction.

---

40. Ch. Wirszubski, *Three Studies in Christian Kabbala* (in Hebrew) (Jerusalem, 1975); idem, *A Christian Kabbalist Reads the Law* (in Hebrew) (Jerusalem, 1977).

Secrecy, secret traditions, and secretive plotting may be ready attributes for the minorities in every society. In the later Christian medieval
context such popular fears may also have been a mode in which society
externalized internal fears and guilt feelings. The Church, the major
bulk of serious theologians, may not have generated such images, but
at times they succumbed to them. So much so that in later medieval
Spain even converted Jews could not avoid suspicion. The massive influx of *conversos* into Spanish society in the fourteenth and fifteenth
centuries, far from being perceived even by the Church as the fulfillment of an urgent dream, awoke in it fears of heterodoxy and secret
Jewish relapse. An unprecedented social and legal effort to lay bare the
secret elements of society poisoned the texture of Spanish life for two
centuries and more, turning it into a society obsessed with suspicion,
the first state in modern European history to be governed by racial
policies. In the name of purity of blood, *marranos* were removed from
public office or social position. In these and similar processes, which
started in the twelfth century, I do not see religious antagonism but
rather antagonisms under the guise of religious differences.

TOWARD A NON-CHRISTIAN ATTITUDE

Luther's venomous attacks notwithstanding, why did the
obsession with the Jews and Judaism abate within the Protestant horizon?[41] For one thing, relatively few Jews remained in Protestant parts
of Europe; most of them were expelled from western Europe during
the later Middle Ages. But the absence of Jews in itself had never impeded anti-Jewish propaganda earlier: it served internal functions. Another reason for the growing indifference toward Jews may be drawn
from Protestant theology itself.

The Catholic Church viewed Jews and Judaism—*mutatis mutan-
dis*—as a living example of a life *sola scriptura*, of the sorry fate of those
who adhered to the letter of the Scriptures only; it wished to show how
necessary the mediation of the Church was, of which authority Augustine once said that unless compelled by it, he would not even believe
the Sacred Scriptures. On the other hand, the Church feared, not without cause, possible impacts of this very example. Ambivalence was built
into the Christian attitude toward Jews from the outset.

41. For the following, see Shmuel Ettinger, *Modern Anti-Semitism: Studies and Essays*
(Hebrew) (Tel Aviv, 1978), esp. pp. 29 ff.; idem, in *Dispersion and Unity* 9 (1970):
pp. 17–37.

Protestantism could—but did not always successfully—overcome this ambivalence. Protestant theologies oscillated and still oscillate between two poles. Depending on the characteristics they lent to the primitive Church, they either wished to revive biblical mores and institutions—hence the swelling of literature on the "Jewish Republic"—or to separate the New Testament more emphatically from the Old. Either way, their attitude toward Jews and Judaism was much less burdened because it was less immediate. There was no *auctoritas sanctae ecclesiae* which the Jewish existence threatened to undermine or promised to confirm. In a few instances, as the late H. H. Ben-Sasson has shown,[42] some sectarian minorities even developed a sense of identification with the Jewish lot *in partibus infidelium*. In other instances, they blamed Judaism and Catholicism alike for obscuring the word of God, and the latter foe was, of course, the more formidable one.

Rationalists of the seventeenth and eighteenth centuries inherited from the Protestant attitude this basic indifference, for better or for worse. Whether a fossil or not, Judaism ceased to be a prime object of altercation.[43] At best, the lot of Jews was employed to exemplify Christian—that is, religious—intolerance. At worst, Judaism was called upon to exemplify religious ethnocentric particularism. At times, attacks on Judaism just served as a guise for attacking Christianity. In all cases, historical-cultural curiosity prevailed over theological discomfort, as we see in Schudt's *Jüdische Merkwürdigkeiten*.[44]

How much then is the rise of modern anti-Semitism rooted in the Christian tradition?

Anti-Semitic propaganda, whether extreme or moderate, has one outstanding feature.[45] Its target is not so much the traditional, Orthodox Jew who is recognizable as such. The anti-Semite fights first and foremost what he believes to be the Jew in disguise: the emancipated, assimilated Jew who is about to disrupt the healthy texture of the new nation he pretends to belong to. Whether assimilated or not, the Jew

---

42. H. H. Ben-Sasson, "Jews and Christian Sectarians," *Viator* 4 (1973): pp. 369–85.

43. See Ettinger, op. cit.; A. Hertzberg, in *The French Enlightenment and the Jews: The Origin of Modern Anti-Semitism* (New York, 1968), did not realize the older genesis of the motifs he discusses.

44. Cf. Jacob Katz, *Antisemitism: From Religious Hatred to Racial Rejection* (Hebrew) (Tel Aviv, 1979); J. J. Schudt, *Jüdissche Merkwürdigkeiten* (Frankfurt am Main and Leipzig, 1714).

45. For the following, see U. Tal, *Judaism and Christianity in the Second Reich* (Ithaca and London, 1975).

is—and remains—an alien, a dangerous, disintegrating force. Being Jewish is a *character indelebilis,* unchangeable by baptism or other external signs of changed identity. Therefore, the first political aim of the anti-Semite is to undo the original sin of nineteenth-century Europe: to revoke legal emancipation granted to Jews and, by discrimination, make them recognizable again. Moderate anti-Semitic ideologues may concede that Jews are subjectively sincere in their wish to assimilate, but in fact are incapable of doing so. More extreme anti-Semites will insist that the outward signs of Jewish identification with the surrounding society and assimilation to it are a dangerous pretext, if not even an (international) Jewish plot to take power; the most extreme anti-Semites will call not only for the annulment of emancipation, but for expulsion and genocide.

Such, in rough outline, is the phenomenology of anti-Semitic utterances. They presuppose emancipation and are directed against it, which makes them a new phenomenon altogether in Jewish history. Needless to say, the anti-Semitic aversion is again only another side of fascination. The anti-Semite appeals to the segments of the population least adapted to the modern, industrialized, capitalistic, and mobile society. He is fascinated, rightly or wrongly, by what he conceives to be Jewish adaptability, and gives it a sinister interpretation. Yet whatever its driving forces,[46] anti-Semitism seems to be worlds apart from Christian anti-Jewish attitudes. Theoretically at least, a converted Jew was, in theological terms, a Christian in all respects. On the other hand, some Protestant trends, which called upon Christianity to sever totally its links to Judaism, even to the Old Testament, needed only a modicum of secularization to become even more anti-Semitic than any Catholic doctrine. From Adolf von Harnack's adoration of Marcion to Houston Stewart Chamberlain's proof that Jesus was an Aryan, the step is a small one to take. But these may be seen as exceptions. All in all, the *ecclesia militans* fights the visible Jew and Judaism; the anti-Semite fights the invisible Jew in society (and in himself).

46. On Sartre's explanation, in his famous *Réflexions sur la question juive,* see Menachem Brinker, "Sartre on the Jewish Question: Thirty Years Later," *Jerusalem Quarterly* 10 (Winter, 1979), pp. 117–32. Sartre vividly confronted the anti-Semite and the Jews as dialectically intertwined forms of inauthentic existence. His description of the anti-Semitic mentality is the best I have ever read. His assumption that Jews persist by virtue of being seen as such revives Spinoza's contention in his *Tractatus Theologico-Politicus* (III). It also translates a psychoanalytical category from *Being and Nothingness* into terms of historical analysis: the basic situation of "être vu." But Sartre knew only the postemancipatory and assimilation-oriented Jews of his biographical experience.

Yet both theological anti-Judaism and ideological anti-Semitism draw from the same pool of popular biases accumulated over centuries; Christian theological postures, through their very continuity, provided a frame for popular biases. Some recent theologians, such as R. B. Ruether or G. G. Baum, have recognized this dependence. Moreover, from the twelfth century onward, Christian theological doctrines adjusted to popular biases and reflected them more and more: they enhanced the image of danger and secrecy beyond the demands of religious antagonism. Anti-Semitism may indeed be a secularized phenomenon, but here, as elsewhere, secularization does not follow religious attitudes as their pure counterpart. It grows within the framework of the religious mind and institutions long before it gains independence.

THEOLOGICAL CONSEQUENCES

Such then are the contours of the development of anti-Jewish doctrines, stands, and images. It is, of course, not our task to reformulate or change theological doctrines. We may, however, draw attention to two possible fallacies in the interpretation of the historical diagnosis, the one resulting from an overemphasis, the other from an underestimation, of the power of history.

First, a theologian may argue, anti-Judaism is so inherent in Christianity as a historical continuum that nothing short of an absolutely new beginning will prevent it from becoming once again a depository of anti-Jewish sentiments. Anti-Judaism, we hear from R. B. Ruether, is "the left hand of Christology."[47] The self-criticism of Baum points at the "ideology of substitution" as the source of the heritage of "contempt."[48] E. Berkovits goes even further: only Christianity, in its emphasis on salvation through Christ alone, entails an antihumanistic ethics; Judaism is immune from such abuses.[49] This is a hypocritical argument. Jewish religion regards man no less as subservient to God than does Christianity. Judaism always endorsed a *bellum deo auctore,* a war commanded by God (*milchemet chova* as opposed to *milchemet reshut*), while it took Christianity over a thousand years to find the right

47. Eva Fleischner, ed., *Auschwitz: Beginning of a New Era?* (New York, 1974), p. 75. I owe the reference to my former student, Priscilla D. Jones, with whom I had repeated discussions on the subject of this chapter.

48. G. G. Baum, *Christian Theology After Auschwitz,* Robert Waley Cohen Memorial Lecture (London, 1976), esp. pp. 7–15.

49. Berkovits, op. cit. (see above, n. 10).

formula for sanctifying war as a holy mission. Up until the Crusades, even the justified killing of an enemy in a just war (*bellum justum*) required absolution. In the case of the Amalekites and the seven Kena'anitic nations, the biblical demand comes close to a call for genocide. The Edomites were converted by coercion, the Karaites persecuted; distinctions between Israel and "the nations of the world" are no less discriminatory than the principle *nulla salus extra ecclesiam*. Berkovits's claim that from the Jewish legal point of view even a non-Jew can obtain salvation is true only in the sense that it is also true from the Christian point of view—namely, conditionally. "All those who obey the seven laws of the sons of Noah," Maimonides teaches *ex cathedra*, "are amongst the pious of the nations" and may have a portion in the world to come. But he adds: "When is this the case? If they obey the commandments because these are the will of God. Should they obey them out of rational insight (*hekhra hada'at*) only, they are not from the pious amongst the nations nor from amongst their sages." Maimonides goes even further and insists on the obligation to kill all true pagans who refuse to submit to the seven Noachidic precepts; they constitute his equivalent of the true Moslem *ahl el maut*.[50] And this obligation is not as theoretical as the obligation to exterminate the Amalekites and "the seven nations" who once inhabited Kena'an, nations now extinct in his view. Discrimination and degradation can and could be clothed in terms of both religions: to argue that only a Christian world could have led to a genocide is, to say the least, hypocritical.

Second, an underestimation of history can be just as detrimental, or at best result in arbitrary choices. Franklin Little sees the anti-Jewish postures, beginning in Christianity only after Paul, with the strong influx of non-Jews.[51] But even if he is right—and our historical remarks suggest that he is not—it makes little difference whether Christianity started to define itself in contraposition to Judaism before or after Paul. The contraposition is part of its historical self-definition. It also matters little whether the origin of antagonism was pagan; so is much of the dogmatic-philosophical language of Christianity. But the contraposition—on which, it is worth remembering, Orthodox Judaism insists on less than Christianity—need not be judged by its uncontrolled exaggerations. It need not be a malicious contraposition: my neighbor may well regard all music as cacophony, while for me it may be the very

50. Maimonides, *Mishne Tora*, Hilchot Shoftim.
51. Franklin H. Little, *The Crucifixion of the Jews* (New York, 1975).

essence and meaning of life. Yet I need not hate him for that. With some training I may even learn not to despise him. If our analysis of the course of anti-Judaic postures through history was correct, then the change came from extrareligious sources at the moment in which Judaism ceased to appear as merely an anachronistic, mistaken religious stand and instead came to be seen as a menacing, secretive plot. This evolution, though also a part of the actual history of the Church, can be separated in theory as well as in praxis, not because it came later, but because its source is not in religious images or doctrines at all.

There is one claim that divides Judaism from Christianity (or for that matter from Islam) because they share in that claim. At least in their historical manifestations, the so-called three monotheistic religions claim to possess the full, authentic, absolute revealed truths exclusively. Each of them may recognize the other monotheistic religions as incomplete, mistaken, or even falsified versions of true principles. The Jews, from the vantage point of Christianity, are fixated at an early stage of revelation. From the vantage point of Islam, both Christianity and Judaism are "people of the book" and need not be coerced to convert, as were pagans. From the vantage point of Judaism, Christianity and Islam seemed to be more or less monotheistic—"nations confined in the boundary of religion" (*'umot hagedurot bedarche hadatot*)—though the first was founded by a heretic and the second, we hear from Maimonides, by a lunatic.[52] Yet the full truth resides only in one's own religion. It is this claim that distinguishes them from classical, Greco-Roman paganism, which was tolerant of other cults because *una est religio in varietate rituum*. A pagan intellectual usually despised what Varro called *theologia mythica;* he professed allegiance to the *theologia politica,* the gods of the body politic, and believed only in the *theologia naturalis*—the philosophical truth about all positive religions. Religious intolerance was conceived and introduced rather by the monotheistic religions, though in various degrees.

Can Christianity—or Judaism—abandon the claim for absolute truth without losing its identity altogether? I do not know; but I find suggestions made by some Christian theologians that Christianity should do so, close to the conscious syncretism of later pagan antiquity. It is odd that Baum, who recommends the abandonment of the claim that *nulla salus extra ecclesiam,* at the same time blames the Holocaust on the

---

52. Cf. above, n. 5. The expression "nations restricted by the ways of religion," which J. Katz ascribes to Hameiri, is actually borrowed from Maimonides's *Guide for the Perplexed* III, 50; cf. J. Katz, op. cit., p. 115.

influx of "pagan mentality" in twentieth-century Europe. A trace of hypocrisy can be detected in such fairly common theological prejudices. Whatever "paganism" may mean, in its historical manifestations it was certainly not less humane than Christianity—or Judaism.

"Paganism" often functions, explicitly and implicitly, as synonymous with "secularism." A good many theologians blame the horrors of our century on the loss of religiosity and the triumph of "secularization." This too proves that even the most sincere theologians did not advance their self-criticism far enough. The Holocaust was no more the consequence of irreligiosity than it was the consequence of religiosity. In fact, there are good reasons to suspect theology—Jewish, Christian, or Moslem—as one of the sources for the ideological relativization of merely human values. The very blame for absolute truth and the commitment to higher than human values were paradigms for more secular ideologies. The *honor dei* which man is supposed to serve unconditionally could be, and was, transformed into an *honor patriae*. Christian and Jewish insistence on the primacy of God over man could be exchanged for other priorities, such as the working class, race, progress, or equivalent abstract objectification. True, no religious attitude should be blamed for its misrepresentation or caricaturization. The fact that Hitler often chose to speak a language saturated with religious images (*Vorsehung*—providence—being the most common) is no proof that he was, consequently, a Christian: Hermann Rauschning's *Gespräche mit Hitler* and other documents are rather a proof, to the contrary, of his strong anti-Christian sentiments. But least of all may theologians blame areligiosity for ideologies and practices of "absolute dependence" on and subservience to abstract principles—a term Schleiermacher employed to define religion. We shall return to his point later.

Reading Jacques Basnages's *Histoire de la religion des Juifs depuis Jésus Christ jusqu'a présent* (Rotterdam, 1707)—it was the very first endeavor of a Christian author to narrate the development of Jews and post-biblical Judaism in a coherent, nonpolemical vein—Heinrich Heine reacted with a poetic reflection, "To Edom" (1824). ("Edom" is a traditional Jewish metaphor for Rome and for Christianity.) The time was shortly after the Hep-Hep pogroms. It seems a fitting summary to this discussion.

TO EDOM	AN EDOM
A thousand years and more we suffer	Ein Jahrtausend schon und länger
each other, for so long an age.	Dulden wir uns brüderlich;

You—you tolerate my breathing, And I tolerate your rage	Du, du duldest dass ich atme, Das du rasest, dulde ich.
Only sometimes, in dark hours, When your curious mood just grows, With my blood you seem to color Your so neat and pious paws.	Manchmal nur, in dunkeln Zeiten Ward dir wunderlich zu Mut. Und die liebefrommen Tätzchen Färbtest du mit meinem Blut!
Our friendship now grows stronger, And increases daily too. Since I also started raging, To become almost like you!	Jetzt wird unsere Freundschaft fester Und noch täglich nimmt sie zu; Denn ich selbst begann zu rasen, Und ich werde fast wie du!

[My trans.]

The Dialectical Theology of Meaninglessness

EXAMPLES

To the most courageous among recent theologians, the very meaninglessness of the Holocaust constitutes its theological meaning. To lose faith in the face of the Holocaust constitutes its theological meaning. To lose faith in the face of the Holocaust is itself, they say, a manner of faith, a positive religious act. When, in the eleventh century, Anselm of Canterbury advanced his ontological proof of God's existence, he also gave a new meaning to the Psalm's verse: "The fool [wicked] hath said in his heart: there is no God." Since God's existence is necessarily implied by his very concept, whoever thinks of God yet denies his existence cannot but be foolish (wicked). The modern theologians I have in mind—Rahner, Baum, Rubenstein, and others—turned Anselm on his head. "A person deeply troubled by the Holocaust and made unable to affirm God's presence is caught in an essentially religious question and hence already under the influence of God's grace. If a person were shallow, or wholly pragmatic, or egotistical, or only concerned about protecting his own interests, he would not be troubled at all. He is troubled because he is religious."[53] Even atheists, Vatican II reminds us, may be touched by grace.

The admission that God—or ethical theism—died in Auschwitz be-

53. Baum, op. cit., n. 48.

cause Auschwitz defies all meaning calls, we are told, for a radical change of the most fundamental premises.

What has emerged in our theological reflection based on Karl Rahner is a rather different religious imagination. Here God is not conceived of as a lord ruling history from above, but as the vitality at the core of people's lives making them ask the important questions and moving them toward their authentic existence. God is conceived here as the ground of human existence, as the summons operative in their lives, and as the horizon toward which they move. God is not so much lord of the universe as heart of the world. What is emphasized in this theology is what theologians call Divine immanence, which in ordinary [!] language means God's being in-and-through the world. . . . God's presence to people changes them, severs them from destructive trends, and moves them towards a more creative future. . . . But the in-and-throughness of God does not leave the world as it is; it judges the world and summons it to new life."[54]

HEIDEGGER'S LANGUAGE

Yet even here, where theologians are most courageous, false tunes are unavoidable. The key phrases just mentioned point unmistakably to a definite philosophical source. Exchange "God" for "being" (*Sein*); the rest of the vocabulary is Heidegger's. Seemingly without ethical judgments, Heidegger distinguishes two modes of human existence, the inauthentic and the authentic. So does the quoted passage. *Dasein,* "Being-there" or existence, is the only form in which the elusive *Sein,* "being" (in contrast to *Seiendes,* "entities"), is concerned with itself: "[Das Dasein ist ein Seiendes], dem es in seinem Sein um dieses Sein selbst geht."[55] Yet in its first and average occurrence it is alienated from itself, lost in the world (*In-der-welt-sein*) in such a manner that it uses things in the world (*Zuhanden-sein*) and is absorbed in it. With every man are inseparably others with whom he shares the concern (*Sorge*) with the mundane. *Dasein* is inauthentic in that state, it is "man"—everyone—characterized by *Seinvergessenheit,* the lack of concern with its true self-being. It flees fear (*Angst*) rather than facing it, facing its basic feature as *Geworfen-sein,* being "thrown into" (as well as "projected into") the world. Only the authentic self, in contrast to the inauthentic "everyone" (*man*), and moved by fear and trembling, is capable of asking the question-of-being (*Daseinfrage*), the question to which there is *ipso facto* no answer because its answer is for that particular being to be no more. Here too the meaninglessness

54. Ibid., p. 19.
55. M. Heidegger, *Sein und Zeit* (Tübingen, 1960), p. 12.

of the question constitutes its very meaning. Here too it is the characteristic of the authentic self which is not "lost in trivial concerns" to ask such questions to which there is no answer. Rather than the "chatter" (*Gerede*) of "everyone" (*man*), the authentic self lets Being, which is in itself, speak for itself through its very futile question of being.

Few who read Heidegger's *Sein und Zeit* failed to be caught by its spell. The fascination with Heidegger's thought is similar in many ways to the fascination with Spinoza's *Ethics:* both have a uniquely comforting power. In both, the ultimate meaning of everything that is, resides in itself only. Spinoza's *Deus sive natura* reifies the logic of the Megarians to the utmost: only that which is, is possible; that which is not is impossible, even meaningless. Like Spinoza's God, Heidegger's being is always expressed through entities (*Seiende*), and is never capable of expressing "itself" immediately and without them; it illuminates without being seen, just as (if one may borrow a metaphor from Wittgenstein) a picture never points at itself. In contrast to Spinoza's substance, however, Heidegger insists on the necessary temporal structure of being. The acquiescence with the total immanence of the meaning of the world—including, for Heidegger, the temporality of being—means that there is no more to the life of a subject than itself; it cannot be endowed with a transcendent meaning or value; when it comes to its individual end, its meaning will be no more nor less than that and what it was. Annihilation does not deprive that which is from having meaning; it rather constitutes an integral part of that meaning.

This having been said, we turn back to the call for authenticity which some of the more courageous theological reflections on the Holocaust borrowed from Heidegger.

It is precisely at this point, namely with the distinction between authentic and inauthentic existence, that the ethical critique—a critique from the vantage point of ethics—must commence. Heidegger promises us that no moral judgment is implied in that distinction.[56] In an almost Hegelian manner, he even sees in the alienation of *Sein* in *Dasein* from itself through the flight into inauthentic existence, a necessary stage for its return (*Kehre*) unto itself. Yet consider the further attributes of inauthenticity. Only the authentic self can be said to possess conscience or even to be capable of "sinning." The anonymous "everyone" lives in a continuous degeneration and fall (*Verfall des Daseins*), a

---

56. Ibid., p. 175: "Der Titel (Das Verfallen, etc.), der keine negative Bewertung ausdrückt. . . ."

fall "into the world" (*in die Welt verfallen*). "Everyone" is, literally, interchangeable with everyone else.

Without entering a sustained discussion about the nature of moral
speech, let me assume that we ought to start with some "concrete absolutes" in an ethical discourse if we wish to navigate between relativization
and empty, formal abstractions. Let me also assume that human life and
human dignity are such absolutes—be it in a cognitive or axiomatic-
thetic, descriptive or normative sense. They command our relentless
respect; they are the "infinite right" of each subject. We may conceive of
situations, such as the necessity of self-defense, in which we would be
justified in violating them: it would be an evil act, even when justifiable.

Human life and the incommensurable value of each individual were
assaulted in infinite ways in Nazi Europe. An ethical perspective of this
sort cannot avoid being extremely narrow-minded, rigorously one-
sided. It can make no concessions to higher gods and higher values, and
it cannot permit any distinction between individuals based on the
higher values. Life, the life of each individual, must be taken to be
always meaningful in and of itself. The everyday reality of Heidegger's
"everyone," the person who never attends to the question of being but
is "lost unto the world," must be endowed from the one-sided vantage
point of ethics with mental existential truths. The man who cultivates
his garden and does all the things in the way he is supposed to cannot
be called inauthentic except by his author. From an ethical point of
view, every life is authentic, a value in and of itself, not interchangeable
with any other human life, a mode *sui generis*. Once discrimination is
permitted even in theory, its consequences are difficult to foretell. If the
person of "everyone" is interchangeable with everyone else, let alone if
he is classified a nonperson—that is, without personality—then he is
less valuable. And if less valuable, then perhaps also dispensable. Or
again, is not crisis—say, war and destruction—beneficial in Heidegger's terms, because it "calls" man to his true self? Heidegger himself
drew such conclusions after 1933.

But, you may object, the possible or even real abuses of a theory
(even by its promoter) need not be held against it: in part, this has been
my own argument. My critique, however, goes deeper than that. The
very distinction between authentic and inauthentic existences, not only
its possible career, is an intrinsic assault on the *dignitas hominis,* the
integrity and worthiness of each concrete individual life, however lived.
The latter attitude, with its difficulties and paradoxes, must constitute
the absolute center of humanistic ethical theories, even at the cost of

subscribing to a one-dimensional, flat philosophical anthropology. At best, Heidegger's distinction diverts from this focus; at the worst, it undermines it.

I do believe, however, that much of the force of Heidegger's insistence on the immanence of being, of which we spoke earlier, can be saved without redundant discriminations. An ethical monadology is conceivable in which the life of each is a unique and significant point of view of human possibilities for better and worse; each situation, individual and collective, is such that it is significant and something can be learned from it about man; and, should all human history have, finally, come to pass and leave behind no record, its meaning will be that and what it was, as replete with good and evil, the beautiful and the ugly, as it then will have been.

Mutatis mutandis, the flaws in the thought of Heidegger are also the flaws in those dialectical theologies which speak in Heidegger's idiom. Why is the person who "asks important questions," say, concerning God's presence in the face of massive evil, "more authentic" than the person who does not? And why are the questions of the *homo religiosus,* however broadly we define him, more important than the purely human questions asked by others about their experience in the concentration camps? Consider, for example, the most moving and reflective account written about the experience of Auschwitz, Primo Levi's *Se questo è un uomo* (published in English as the *Survival in Auschwitz*). It asks many questions, but none of them theological. It refuses to see the concentration camp as meaningless: "We are absolutely persuaded that no human experience is empty of meaning or unworthy of interest, and that fundamental values, even if they are not positive, can be deduced from this particular world which we are describing." Indeed, the religious-theological questions, were he to ask them, would distract from the power of Levi's reflections, which are centered around humankind, not around God.

TRUER PERSPECTIVES: THE HOLOCAUST AS A HUMAN EVENT

As against the distinction between the graced and those who lack grace, between authentic and inauthentic existences, the reality of the concentration camps taught Levi other distinctions, distinctions which are purely homocentric, such as the distinction between "the drowned and the saved."

We do not believe in the most obvious and facile deduction: that man is fundamentally brutal, egotistic and stupid in his conduct once every civilized institution is taken away, and that the Häftling is consequently nothing but a man without inhibitions. We believe, rather, that the only conclusion to be drawn is that in the face of driving necessity and physical disabilities many social habits and instincts are reduced to silence.

But another fact seems to us worthy of attention: there comes to light the existence of two particularly well-differentiated categories among men—the saved and the drowned. Other pairs of opposites (the good and the bad, the wise and the foolish, the cowards and the courageous, the unlucky and the fortunate) are considerably less distinct, they seem less essential, and above all they allow for more numerous and complex intermediary gradations.

This division is much less evident in ordinary life; for there it rarely happens that a man loses himself. A man is normally not alone, and in his rise or fall is tied to the destinies of his neighbors; so that it is exceptional for anyone to acquire unlimited power, or to fall by a succession of defeats into utter ruin. Moreover, everyone is normally in possession of such spiritual, physical and even financial resources that the probabilities of a shipwreck, of total inadequacy in the face of life, are relatively small. And one must take into account a definite cushioning effect exercised both by the law, and by the moral sense which constitutes a self-imposed law; for a country is considered the more civilized the more the wisdom and efficiency of its laws hinder a weak man from becoming too weak or a powerful one too powerful.

But in the *Lager* things are different: here the struggle to survive is without respite, because everyone is desperately and ferociously alone. If some *Null Achtzehn* vacillates, he will find no one to extend a helping hand; on the contrary, someone will knock him aside, because it is in no one's interest that there be one more "muselman" dragging himself to work every day; and if someone, by a miracle of savage patience and cunning, finds a new method of avoiding the hardest work, a new art which yields him an ounce of bread, he will try to keep his method secret, and he will be esteemed and respected for this, and will derive from it an exclusive, personal benefit; he will become stronger and so will be feared, and who is feared is, *ipso facto,* a candidate for survival. . . .

They crowd my memory with their faceless presence, and if I could enclose all the evil of our time in one image, I would choose this image which is familiar to me: an emaciated man, with head dropped and shoulders curved, on whose face and in whose eyes not a trace of thought is to be seen.

If the drowned have no story, and single and broad is the path to perdition, the paths to salvation are many, difficult and improbable.[57]

Among the "saved," then, are both the noble (such as his friend Alberto) and the ignoble, the cunning and the less cunning. Levi employs the theological idiom ironically, as if to say that being saved is not of a theological or other transcendental character; it is a most basic human property. Out of the experience of the concentration camp, Levi crys-

57. Primo Levi, op. cit., pp. 100–103.

talized the building blocks of a true philosophical anthropology, more genuine and accurate than either Heidegger's or any recent theologian's. The power of his reflections, I repeat, lies in that they are centered around the concrete man, not around a chimera of the authentic self, nor around God.

Indeed, religious questions may even be detrimental to ethical human concerns. They are detrimental, I believe, in the following sense. The assumption is made by even the most self-critical theologians that there exists a particular virtue in the commitment to values higher than human life and human integrity, that the person who lives his life *veluti pecora*, without asking existential-religious questions, lacks "grace." But the table may be turned as follows. A commitment to higher values above the sanctity of the individual not only distracts from the study of man, but can and did lead to abuses and crimes of much greater extent than selfish self-interest ever perpetrated. Granted, this is not a necessary consequence of commitments to absolutes, but it has often enough been so. Now it matters little whether the higher values were transcendent or immanent, God, fatherland, race, or the ideal society of the future. In the name of all of them crusades were fought, genocides committed, persons degraded. No major religion I know of was immune. Perhaps then dialectical theologians are not radical enough. Perhaps theology itself is one source of that very danger which they contemplate. William of Ockham, whose ethical theory recognizes very clearly the need for a concrete absolute if one wishes to navigate between the Scylla of relativization and the Charybdis of empty, formal abstractions, claimed (as once Plato's Euthyphro) that it is wrong to say that God wants that which is good. Rather, it is good because God wanted it. The God of the Bible wanted, as it were, a genocide against the Amalekites, including women, children, and cattle. A more refined God of later centuries wanted heretics to be "compelled to enter" or be abolished. An even more refined God may demand the self-sacrifice of the believer so as to sanctify the name of God. A secular age translated such demands into world-immanent terms, among them race. *Tantum religio potuit suadere malorum.*

Again, I do not argue that religious commitments do, of necessity, lead to abuse. But neither should it be argued that because of lack of religiosity (so to say, as an "outburst of paganism") concentration and extermination camps became possible. I rather argue that the focus on the religious-theological implications of the Holocaust is intrinsically the wrong focus. The question of what it teaches us about God or any other higher norms and values is insignificant beside the question of what it teaches us about man, his limits, his possibilities, his cruelty, his creativity, and his nobility. In human terms the Holocaust was not meaningless. To say that it was seems as offensive as to say that it had a theological meaning, that is, a divine purpose.

For similar reasons we ought to object to the characterization of the Holocaust as "incomprehensible." It is one of the most prevalent predicates in the theological literature about the Holocaust—and not only in the theological literature. On the contrary, historians, psychologists, sociologists, ought to be guided by the reasonable expectation that they can comprehend it. The crime committed by the Nazis was of immense proportions: the horror and the suffering transgress our capacity of imagination, but it is possible to understand them rationally. Even if the perpetrators of the crime were madmen who lost all touch with reality, a reconstruction of their mentality and patterns of action would be possible. But they were not madmen, at least not in the clinical sense of the word; if madness entails loss of the sense of reality, then no society can be called mad, because reality is a social construct through and through. The prehistory of the genocide, its necessary conditions, can be illuminated more and more. The mental mechanisms by which Nazi ideology justified mass murder can be followed step by step. Germany stood fast in its illusion of apocalyptic "total war." The Jews, they were certain, are not only an inferior race on the order of Slavs and blacks, they are even more dangerous, because they are a universal, destructive parasite which (unlike other races) cleverly adapts to become almost indistinguishable from the host society in order to destroy the healthy texture of that society from within. Their extermination was spoken of in terms of hygienic medicine: Jews were labeled a dangerous bacteria. *Entlausung* (delousing) was the terrible realization of an ideological metaphor in the concentration camps. By degrading the inmates of the camps, by robbing them of their personalities, the victims were supposed to turn into that which the Nazi ideology claimed they had always been: subhuman. It was a mechanism which functioned to concretize, to visualize, the rationale for extermination. Nor is it true that the extermination of the Jews was carried out at the cost of the war effort, as Hilberg and others once believed. We cannot excuse ourselves from the obligation to understand the Nazi mentality if we want to condemn it, let alone if we want to prevent similar crimes from being committed again.

Theologians seem to emphasize the "incomprehensibility" of the

Holocaust and the "madness" of those who caused it because they cannot find any theological meaning in it. Perhaps also it is because they hardly dare to say that if one were to believe in transcendent forces, the Holocaust would prove the autonomy of evil, an evil manifested not only or primarily by the number of its victims but by its sheer inexhaustible inventiveness, by the almost infinite number of methods found for systematic killing and degradation. If, however, we turn from God to humankind, the Holocaust is neither incomprehensible nor meaningless. It was neither bestial nor indeed pagan. It was, instead, an eminently human event in that it demonstrated those extremes which only man and his society are capable of doing or suffering. It pointed at a possibility, perhaps unknown before, of human existence, a possibility as human as the most sublime instances of creativity and compassion.

10

Zionism, Science, and History

The Themes

I wish to consider some significant trends in Zionist thought from a vantage point seldom taken, namely the relation of Zionism to science. This being a lecture to commemorate Chaim Weizmann, our first president, let us begin with the place of both in his life.[1] Zionism and science were entangled in his creative endeavors for better or worse, as contradictory and complementary moments. Again and again Weizmann complained about the fact that his political preoccupation impeded his scientific activity or, vice versa, that his scientific work removed him from the political arena. We should be careful not to assume as a matter of course that both driving forces enhanced and enriched each other. He warned us not to view the Balfour Declaration in the simplistic formula of Lloyd George as a remuneration for his contribution to the British war effort during the First World War. The Balfour Declaration does not owe its existence to acetone but rather to a protracted political labor of preparation and reorientation that began long before the war. Nevertheless, his scientific career and achievements

1. The most comprehensive biography of his early career is that of Jehuda Reinharz, *Chaim Weizmann: The Making of a Zionist Leader* (New York, Oxford, 1985).

338

rendered considerable services to his political work in that it opened some doors for him and, what is more, in that it enhanced his prestige and his self-esteem. Weizmann himself told at times how, as a student, he decided not to neglect his studies so as not to become a mere political functionary and dislocated "Luftmensch" like many of the Zionist activists and friends in Berlin and Switzerland. From early on, his scientific occupation was a refuge to him and a necessary element in the construction of his self-identity. Furthermore, Weizmann spoke about his Zionist work and its tasks with a vocabulary borrowed from the laboratory and from his image of science. Historians ought to pay attention to semantics and symbols even where they seem to be merely a rhetorical ornamentation; they reveal mentalities. Weizmann demanded time and again that things be done "methodically," that solutions be examined "cautiously." He warned both his laboratory assistants and his friends in the movement against speculative digressions, against disentangling Gordian knots by brute force. He envisioned a "synthetic Zionism," an organic consonance of means and ends. His positivistic image of science—the patient accumulation of empirical knowledge—corresponded to his perception of the course and strategy of the Zionist settlement of the land of Israel. And last, science was supposed to play a major role in the construction of the land and in the Renaissance of the national consciousness.

All of this is well known. But because not all the founding fathers of Zionism were chemists or scientists of any other discipline, one could wonder whether this dialectical interplay of science and Zionism may not have been a special, personal situation. Let me, then, review the imaginary and the real place of science in the history of Zionism from three aspects, defined briefly as (i) Zionism as science, (ii) the attitude of Zionism toward science and (iii) the demand of the Zionists for a change of values of the science of Judaism (*Wissenschaft des Judentums*). I shall try to show how these aspects, though not derivable from, still depended on, each other.

You may object that I am about to commit a mistake in category by mixing apples and oranges—the exact sciences, whose backbone is quantification practices, with other fields of investigation. Now I do not here separate science from the humanities—and not only because the German *Wissenschaft* and the Hebrew *mada* refer to both while the English language distinguishes between "science" and "scholarship." One of my purposes is to point to the commitment of several founding fathers of the Zionist movement—Achad Ha'am, Nordau, Weizmann—

to a positivistic image of science, a science presumably without pre-sumptions or presupposition, which progresses evenly and gradually through a methodical gathering of verified "facts" and the empirical conclusion derived from them. Such was the image of science through-out the nineteenth century based on this image: natural science, phi-lology, and critical history were seen as "empirical sciences," as against the "speculative sciences" represented, for example, by Hegel's system of philosophy. This image of science informed not only Zionist thinkers in the beginning of our century. Anachronistic as it may be, it still prevails within the "science of Judaism." Yet before I come to discuss this particular issue which pertains to the third aspect of my theme, let me start with its first aspect.

The Three Aspects

Zionism is not a science, nor did it ever presume to be one. This is not a trivial statement, in that Zionism emerged in an age of the apotheosis of science. A good many ideologies, right or left, appropriated to themselves the status of a science, such as Marxism, Social Darwinism, racial doctrines. Here and there we do, of course, encounter attempts to ground the solution to "the Jewish question" on a scientific basis. Already Pinsker's characterization of anti-Semitism as a disease appeared as a clinical diagnosis with the medical-psychiatric vocabulary of his times.[2] Anti-Semitism—he preferred the medical-sounding Judeophobia—has its origins in the "atavistic" fears of ghosts, a heritage from primordial humanity. Collectives behave just as individuals do. Nations may fight each other or live at peace, but they still recognize each other as being similar in nature. But the Jewish people seems to them as a ghost, as an apparition without a body among the commonwealth of "healthy" nations with a "body," that is, with a soil. Such an atavistic fear is an inevitable disease which cannot be talked away. It can be cured if and only if the Jewish people acquires a body once again. Note that Pinsker employs and inverts the folklor-istic and literary motif of the "wandering Jew" who is unable to die (as normal nations or individuals do), who is *condemned* to live eternally.[3]

Another physician, Max Nordau, won international fame and popu-

2. Leon Pinsker, *Autoemanzipation* (Berlin, 1882).
3. See A. Leschnitzer, "Der Wandernde Jude," *Festschrift H. Herzfeld* (Berlin, 1964).

larity throughout the intellectual world of his time with his diagnosis of the state of culture in the *fin de siècle*. His book, *Degeneration*[4] was translated into most European languages: it challenges the ideal of the individual genius as the source of cultural-social creativity, whose apotheosis was the heritage of the romantic movement. True, durable culture, Nordau believed, is carried on the shoulders of the middle-of-the-road bourgeoisie; the philistine guarantees the future of law, order and culture. In nature as in society, the solitary genius is but a pathological deviant, a fringe mutation. Sorry is the state of society in which the balance of cultural creativity has shifted from the center to the fringe. In the history of Social Darwinism, Nordau ought indeed to occupy a place of honor. In our context, it is evident what attracted him to the Zionist master plan of Herzl: the chance to restore physical health to the Jewish body. Only the normalization of the Jews harbors, paradoxically, a messianic chance of redemption. Unlike Herzl, Nordau did in fact employ the messianic idiom in a secular-systematic way.

There were yet other attempts to ground Zionism on a scientific basis from various directions—as Rupin and Borochov show—but they hardly determined the mainstream of Zionist thought. In most of its varieties, Zionism did not pretend to be a science or even to offer a scientific solution, but rather a concrete-practical solution to the so-called "Jewish question" or "Jewish problem." The problem was the failure or impossibility of a true emancipation—or, to use Marx's terminology, the circumstance that the political emancipation of the Jews did not generate their social emancipation.[5]

To put it more precisely, Zionism never presumed to be a comprehensive, "total ideology" in Mannheim's sense of the word—an ideology which covers all aspects of life. At best, Zionism could be, and was, grafted upon other such ideologies. In all of its trends—including the Marxist or Orthodox branch—Zionism confined its solutions to the here and now. This is certainly true of Theodor Herzl, who still believed, as he wrote his *Judenstaat,* that total assimilation would be the ideal solution to the Jewish problem—except that it is a centuries-long process which one could not await patiently, because the house of Israel is burning.[6] Had Zionism been a "total ideology" in its beginning,[7] it might have been tempted to appear as a "scientific" doctrine or as a

4. Max Nordau, *Entartung,* (Berlin, 1893).
5. See above, pp. 229–232.
6. See above, pp. 232–234.
7. The term of Karl Mannheim, *Ideologie und Utopie,* 4th edition (Frankfurt am Main, 1965), pp. 60–64, 154 ff.

messianic movement, such as seems to be the case in some Zionist quarters today. But the secret of its attraction and successes then was indeed its abstention from transcendent presumptions, at least for the time being.

But—and now we approach the second aspect of our theme—in its attitude towards science one can recognize clearly that Zionism was born in an age of the deification of science, the age of *Wissenschaftsgläubigkeit*. Zionism wanted to become a movement of renewal and rebirth, also with the aid of science. The slogan of "renewal" entailed two contradictory—yet complementary—ideals: the ideal of "normalization" of the Jewish people and the ideal of the uniqueness of Israel. On one side stood the demand to invert the occupational pyramid of Jews, so that its base will consist of a healthy agricultural and manually laboring society. Such a revolution, the early Zionists claimed, can happen only in the land of Israel because of historical memories (which will draw the masses to it) and its present condition (which will prevent them from becoming again an urban minority). Max Nordau, the most famous among the normalizers, saw therefore as the primary task of Zionism the creation of a "muscular Judaism"—*Muskeljudentum*—while postponing, true to his point of view, the construction of a Hebrew university in the land of Israel to a more distant, more affluent future. On the other side stood the faith in a specific "Jewish genius," born out of the secularization of the faith of being a chosen people, *'am segula*. Translated into secular, national or cultural terms, it could mean, as it did to Achad Ha'am, transforming the land into "a spiritual center."

Faith in the sciences shaped both of these ideals. Without science and technology—such was the almost general consensus among Zionists—there can be no normalization. Because there is not time enough to wait for the slow, organic-historical growth of a healthy agricultural society in the land of Israel, only scientific planning can secure, in the land of Israel, a massive "colonization." (The term had not yet acquired the preparation of the land for settlement under the supervision of agronomers, engineers, physicians, and economists. It is indeed a telling point that of all the dreams of Herzl in his *Altneuland,* the most daring technological ones were those realized nearly in their entirety. The book reminds us of Jules Verne's "Electric City.")

But science and technology were not thought of as merely normalizing factors. They should also, it was said, ensure that the Jewish peasant or worker will not have to give up his "superadded soul." Or, in Weizmann's words:

What form will the agricultural progress take, what will be its method? The Jew is capable of becoming a land-cultivator, provided that agronomy will assume scientific methods and reach a high level of perfection. We cannot lower the Jew, whose level of education is fairly high, to the level of the Russian peasant. We rather ought to raise agriculture to the level of the Jew.[8]

That means: conditional normalization. Most early Zionists sought only conditional normalization, not only because they feared for the "level of education" of the settlers, but also because they feared for the loss of the specific difference of Jews. In the land of Israel they saw a chance of constructing a model society precisely because of the uniqueness of the nation. Such was the basic dialectic of ideals which accompanied the Zionist aspirations from the very beginning of the movement.

This dialectic is apparent not only in the tension between those who favored the construction of a Hebrew university and those who did not, but also among the former themselves. What kind of a "spiritual center" should it be? A place in which the "Umwertung alter Werke" of Judaism should take place, by way of reflection on Judaism as a historical phenomenon? Or rather a place that should serve the practical needs of the settlement, of "building the land"? Weizmann, always in favor of organic synthesis, stood in the middle—or almost there, somewhat more on the side of practical needs. He wanted a university as a haven for Jewish intellectuals whose entry into East European universities was blocked. He also wanted it as a place to train scientists for the construction of the land. He saw in it a level with which Jews could become a real political force in the Middle East. Yet above and beyond all of these considerations, he saw in the scientific occupation a real surrogate to the traditional study of the law—*talmud tora*—which embodied the uniqueness of Israel. The historian should pay close attention to rhetoric. In his famous speech at the grounding festivity of the Hebrew University (1925) Weizmann spoke of the future university as a renewed Temple, the successor of the First and Second Temple in antiquity.

And so, almost of itself, we reached the third aspect of our theme which may be the most interesting of them. Some Zionists saw their mission in the inversion of values (*Shinuy arakhim*) within the Jewish consciousness, a revolution in the Jewish mentality. Others wanted a new "spiritual center" only. Both however, pleaded for a new outlook.[9]

8. Chaim Weizmann, *Devarim* (Tel-Aviv, 1937). See now also Derek J. Penslar, *Zionism and Technocracy* (Bloomington and Indianapolis, 1991), esp. pp. 150–154.
9. Achad Ha'am, "Shinuy Arackim," *Collected Works* (Hebrew) (Tel Aviv, Jerusalem, 1965), pp. 154 ff. The article was directed against Berditschewsky.

Of course this also meant a change of values and criteria in Jewish scholarship, in the *Wissenschaft des Judentums*. With this demand, Zionism was the successor of both the Enlightenment (*Haskala*) and the nineteenth century "science of Judaism." They, too, wished to educate the Jewish community and in part also the non-Jewish *intelligentsia,* and they wished to do so by means of a methodical self-reflection with the tools of historical-philological criticism. Here, in the study of Judaism and its history, they hoped to find a new answer to the question of what Jews, Jewish culture, and Jewish society are and what they ought to be. Here the tension between the demand for normality and the emphasis on uniqueness ought to have found a balance and a solution.

On a first glance it might seem as if no new definite answer was found. Reviewing the various trends in Jewish studies since the turn of the century, even in Israel only, we do encounter new themes: an emphasis on the manifestations of Jewish sovereignty and autonomy both in the land of Israel and in the Diaspora (Itschak Baer, Haim-Hillel Ben-Sasson, Ben-Zion Dinur); political interpretations to phenomena hitherto regarded as apolitical, such as the Pharisees or the court of Yamnia (Gedalyahu Allon); a cultivation of local archaeology almost as a national cult. We also sense a new, less apologetic style. But radically new answers to questions of Jewish existence, if they were expected, hardly emerged. And if the previous generation of scholars was still aware of the problem, the recent generation by and large ignores it and takes refuge in an obsolete positivism. The matter calls for some explanation.

The tension we spoke of between "normality" and "uniqueness" has a long pedigree in the historical consciousness of Jews. In the preemancipatory tradition, they stood in an outright contradiction to each other. Jewish existence was perceived as unique *because* it was abnormal and particular: its fate was to avoid the normal existence of other nations. R. Loeb of Prague (Maharal) articulated this disjunction most poignantly in the sixteenth century. Every nation has its own "proper place"—the Maharal translated this basic notion of Aristotelian physics into the terms of a political theory. Just as physical bodies strive to be in their "proper place," such as the earth downwards towards the center of the universe and the fire upwards above the air, so also nations. The Maharal also revived the political climatology of the ancients, not unlike Jean Bodin shortly thereafter: the soil of every nation, its earthly basis, forms the character of every nation and constitutes its lifeline. A nation taken away from its soil into exile dies a natural death; it is the law of nature. Only Israel is exempt from the laws of nature, it "has no guiding star": it is subject to God's special providence, and therefore its existence in the Diaspora, without a soil, is a perpetual miracle, an anomalous existence. The desire for normality would have amounted in his eyes to a "precipitation of the end," forbidden by the three oaths. Israel is a unique nation; it is its fate to be particular through and through.[10]

Acculturation and emancipation turned this view upside down. To prepare for the emancipation, to justify it, Western Jewish intellectuals since the beginning of the nineteenth century interpreted "universality" and "particularity," normality and uniqueness, as almost coextensive notions. The very uniqueness of Jewish tradition, they argued, lies in its universality. Judaism and Jewish history is the only history that articulates the "absolute spirit," said Nachman Krochmal, and the people of Israel are therefore exempt from the fate of all other nations that express only one, exhaustible aspect of spirituality.[11] Jewish history embodies the progress of the universal idea of pure, ethical monotheism—such was the conviction of thinkers as disparate as Graetz and Hermann Cohen. The Jewish tradition embodied and embodies the true values of humanism in its purest forms.

The common denominator to both the preemancipatory and postemancipatory definitions of the uniqueness of Judaism was indeed that both had a ready-made definition or formula. They knew what Judaism is and what its historical mission ought to be. Now, the Zionist turn in Jewish thought and deed consisted precisely in the erosion of such certainties and definitions. Zionism promised but a framework: a framework permitting development in any direction. The only faith common to all Zionists was faith in the collective creative potential of the Jews. Because of this openness to the future, no ready-made definition of the "essence of Judaism" had any real chance of being accepted. If we see the Zionist revolution in this perspective, we shall understand why the study of Judaism did not show any well-recognizable Zionist styles beyond other ideological commitments of its practitioners. Rather, the study of Judaism under the impact of Zionism reflects the very same openness towards the future. Consider, as an example, the work of Yechezkel Kaufman and Gerschom Scholem. Gerschom Scholem refused explicitly and repeatedly to accept any definition of what Judaism is. Judaism in every age consists in its creative achievements, be it law, be it myth, be it theosophy. The Kabbala was not an alien plant in an

10. Martin Buber, *Ben am le'artso* (Jerusalem, 1944), pp. 78–91; Fritz Kleinberger, *Hamachshava hapedagogit shel hamaharal miprag* (Jerusalem, 1958).

11. See above, pp. 245–246.

otherwise "rational" culture. It stood at the center of Jewish creativity from the thirteenth until at least the eighteenth century. Kaufman interpreted the emergence of monotheism in ancient Israel as a true mental revolution that has and needs no further explanation—the outburst of a truly creative force, a true mutation of mental attitudes towards the sacred. So thorough was this revolution that the biblical writers do not show an adequate notion of paganism even while condemning it—their construction of its meaning is altogether fictitious, remote from the true phenomenon. In his book *Gola venekhar*[12] Kaufman continued the same line of thought and drew conclusions for the present: it is not our task to prophesy or to prescribe where our cultural creativity shall lead us. We must guarantee a basis for it, and while not only the land of Israel is such a basis, it is a preferred one. The office of Jewish studies thus became, so to say, sanitary: to remove false perceptions, to point at the infinite creative potential of past generations as a guarantee for the future ones.

Here may be the place to say a few words about some of the controversies which Scholem's perspective generated in his lifetime and later. Recently, Eliezer Schweid repeated, with important variations, Kurzweil's contentions that the Kabbala and Sabbatianism served Scholem in a hidden agenda—the erosion of the authority of the rational-legal tradition, the *halakha*.[13] Scholem, they argued, bent history to articulate his own historiosophic prejudices. The counterarguments were, at times, carried on at an even lower level of sophistication. One of Schweid's colleagues answered him in detail: Scholem, he claimed, was merely a philologist examining the texts he encountered, drawing from them empirical conclusions impartially and with the tools of philological-historical criticism. He had no guiding philosophy of history. Joseph Dan thus not only ignores Scholem's explicit statements, namely that his very philological work has theological significance in that it is the only way, today, of giving answers to fundamental questions. His position, far from being a naive positivism as Dan depicts it, is that of reflexive positivism which does not shun philosophical-historical questions at all.[14] From the past one can learn for the future, and the lesson is precisely that of the openness of Judaism, that its creative powers have no preestablished goals. Instead of Scholem's reflexive positivism,

12. Yechezkel Kaufman, *Gola venekhar* (Tel-Aviv, 1961).
13. Baruch Kurzweil, *Bama'avak al erkhey hayahadut* (Tel Aviv, 1970), 99–240.
14. See David Biale, *Gershom Scholem: Kabbala and Counterhistory* (Cambridge, Mass., 1979).

Jewish studies again returned today either to dogmatic or to naive-positivistic attitudes, questioning the premises of neither.

To sum up: Zionism, in its beginning, called for a change in the Jewish mentality without a clear notion what it should change into, without a definite target. This very openness of Zionism allowed it to transform the previous disjunction or identification of uniqueness and normalcy, universality and particularism, into a dialectical play of complementary-contradictory poles. The uniqueness of the Jews was to obtain its assurance from the past but its meaning from an as yet un-revealed future. It made the grafting of Zionist aspirations on other ideologies or utopian movements possible.

Two Images of Humanity

I may have just used the wrong metaphor. "Grafting" may have artificial connotations. It is difficult to graft upon a historical movement elements altogether alien to it. We thus arrive at a much more fundamental level of the consideration of the tension between uniqueness and normality, and of the relation of Zionism to science. Indispensable for the understanding of Zionist thought and action is the image of humankind in which they are rooted, their anthropologi-cal presuppositions and their relation to utopian and antiutopian tra-ditions. Indeed, two main sources, again both of them contradictory and complementary, informed Zionist thoughts and aspirations: the image of a man as a *tabula rasa* susceptible to planned transformation and the image of persons as organic-historical subjects; an autonomous-rational image as against a romantic-spontaneous image. So as to re-move confusion from the outset let me emphasize that I do not mean to contrapose "humanistic" to "nationalistic" values and concerns. The matter is far more complicated and calls for an explicatory digression.

Earlier we spoke of the realist versus the utopian traditions of politi-cal theory in the West, and now, during the seventeenth century, a new brand of utopianism arose which others and myself named "realistic utopianism."[15] It neither acquiesced to the description of best govern-ment for "man as he is" nor with the description of an ideal government for "man as he should be." Realistic utopians from Campanella to Marx

15. See above, pp. 131–132.

wished to mediate between the real and the ideal in that they tried to show how the ideal social organization can and even must grow out of real or realizable starting conditions; humankind can and must change its own nature to the better if only given a realistic chance. Campanella's political thought was still anchored in Christian apocalyptic images. It differs, though, from the medieval utopian tradition (e.g., Joachim of Fiore) in one significant way in that it called for an immediate, active implementation of the *civitas solis*. The same can be said of some Puritan and other Protestant sects: they wanted a realization of the Kingdom of God in *this* world, here and now. But Campanella differed also from them in that he believed that the "sun city," once built and properly furnished, could change to the better human nature itself. It is in the power of humans to create the optional conditions for this transformation to happen. Those who believe, to the contrary, that human nature is unchangeable have no refuge but in Machiavellianism and its detestable version of *raison d'état,* a political cunning devoid of ethics which is only interested in the momentary success of the body politic. Their genealogy goes back to Aristotle, who believed that the world with all of its forms is eternal: *ex Aristotelismo Machiavellismus.*[16]

The belief in the human capacity to change nature, including human nature, with the aid of science, became, duly secularized, part of the ideology of many Enlighteners in the eighteenth century. They believed, we remember, in salvation through knowledge and in the capacity of every human being to rise to the level of the *philosophe*. Humans are, by nature, neither good nor bad, but rather a *tabula rasa* on which either prejudice or truth can be written. That both their views of nature and of society were "naive" was the contention of Marx and Marxists; their aspirations and expectations may have been more sophisticated, but they were still variations on the same theme. The very laws of history, Marx claimed, the contradictions within the bourgeois society, will of necessity generate a new society in which a human will not be alienated from his world and his fellow humans. The science of history is the guarantee that humans will be emancipated from their bondage and return to themselves as autonomous masters. Science, in this interpretation, both causes change in human nature and is changed by changes in society.

This, in a brief outline, was the genealogy of the rational-autonomous image of humankind: "man maketh his own commonwealth," even his own nature, with the aid of science; by nature, humans are a *tabula rasa*

16. See above, pp. 132, n. 2.

open to any sort of molding. It is needless to point out how profoundly Zionism was indebted to this tradition, be it through the mediation of other ideologies—such as Marxism—or even of the tradition of literal Jewish theology in the nineteenth century. On the other hand, Zionism was no less indebted to another image of man. The Romantic movement fortified the image of the individual personality that generates its specific contents spontaneously. Many trends within the Western European tradition coalesced to make it possible. That "every single human being is almost a species unto himself" was already pronounced by Dante;[17] about that time, Duns Scotus discovered individuality as a formal-constitutive (rather than material-inessential) principle of every single thing.[18] The Renaissance reintroduced the cult of the successful individual, of the *vertù,* while Montaigne discovered the complexity of his self, and the subject became ever more the beginning and end of philosophizing: "Die Substanz [ist] als Subjekt zu bestimmen" was Hegel's program.[19] The individual of the Romantic movement could be a person or a nation; in both cases it could not be exhausted by a definition: *individuum est ineffabile.* Its understanding calls for a new, different science than that of nature. A "common nature" is either a false or irrelevant notion for the comprehension of humans. Changes in the individual or in the nation obey their own, organic-intrinsic and specific laws. They create their own fate spontaneously; their future can never be mechanically construed or predicted.

It is certainly true that science of history, which stood especially in Germany under the impact of Romanticism, often served as a weapon against the ideals of the Enlightenment. Historicism served as a legitimation for the national state and as its educational instrument, sometimes in direct confrontation with the achievements and failure of the French Revolution. But just as these two images of man could be played against each other, they could also complement each other. They did so, of sorts, in the thought of Marx, which only on the surface seems committed to the rational-autonomous utopian traditions only. Closer scrutiny shows that it was no less informed by the spontaneous-individual image of the person—it underlies his (and Hegel's) notion of "alienation," and it prevented him from sketching the structure and positive contents of the "human emancipation" of the future.

And such is also the case of early Zionism. On the one hand, it

17. Dante, "De vulgari eloquentia," in *Opere,* ed. E. Moore and P. Toynbee (Oxford, 1924), p. 380.

18. Funkenstein, *Theology and the Scientific Imagination,* pp. 137 ff. (Scotus).

19. See above, p. 248.

expressed assurance that the proper education and environment could transform the Jewish mentality into a normal, "healthier" one; on the other hand, it stayed assured of the uniqueness of the Jews. On the one hand, it desired to mold "the human material" anew; on the other hand, it wished to secure freedom and space for the unfolding of individual creativity—personal and national—which obeys only inner rules. As I mentioned earlier, I do not mean the contrast between nationalistic and socialistic Zionism: in both of them we can find both elements, both images, from A. D. Gordon to Jabotinsky, from Borochov to Ben Gurion. The matter calls for a much deeper study.

I was asked whether the tension between the ideals of normality and uniqueness is still relevant in today's Israel. I fear that, instead of this constructive tension, one finds a growing polarization. One segment of Israeli society, mostly religious, fell back into a belief in a well-defined uniqueness that lacks openness or reflective criticism. Another segment abandoned, by and large, the striving for an ideal society or for uniqueness and is well satisfied with achieved accomplishments. I long for some more "synthetic Zionism"—not in the sense of harmonizing existing contradictions but in the sense of maintaining the tension between complementary oppositions, be it in everyday life, be it in Jewish studies. If I register some complaints against Amos Oz's book *Here and There in the Land of Israel,* it is because I like it. At its conclusion the author brings us to Ashdod, a town "in a human measure," without exaggerated dreams of messianism or of becoming "a light unto all nations," without monumental buildings and without an unbearable burden of history, a typical social-democratic town. He calls upon us to be content with it.[20] But perhaps we ought to keep alive the utopian element of Zionism. It belongs no less to the measure of humans that they strive for the stars, *per aspera ad astra.* Had we not dreamed exaggerated dreams we would not have built even a modest town.

20. Amos Oz, *Po va'sham be erets yisrael bi stav 1981* (Tel Aviv, 1982).

Bibliography

Abelard, Petrus. *Dialogus inter philosophum, Judaeum et Christianum*. (Migne, PL 178).

Abrabanel, Yitschak. *Perush hatora*. Warsaw, 1862.

Abraham bar Chiyya. *Sefer megillat hamegalleh*. Edited by Adolph Poznanski and Julius Guttmann. Berlin, 1924.

Abraham ben David. *A Critical Edition with a Translation and Notes of the Book of Tradition (Sefer haqabbalah)*. Edited by Gerson David Cohen. Philadelphia, 1967.

Abraham ben ha-Rambam. *Milhamot hashem*. Edited by R. Margoliot. Jerusalem, 1953.

Abraham Ibn Ezra. *Perush hatora*. 3 vols. Edited by Asher Vayser. Jerusalem, 1976.

Abraham Yosef Hakohen. *Iggrot ha-Ra'aya*. Jerusalem, 1965.

Achad Ha'am. "Shinuy Arachim," in *Collected Works*. Tel-Aviv and Jerusalem, 1965.

Agnon, Shumel Yosef. "Ben shtey 'arim," in *Samukh venir'e*. Jerusalem-Tel Aviv, 1979.

Agobard. *Epistola de Judaicis superstitionibus* (Migne, PL 104).

Alanus ab Insulis. *De fide catholica contra haereticos*. (Migne, PL 210).

Albo, Josef. *Sefer ha'iqarim*. Edited by J. Husik. Philadelphia, 1946.

Alexander of Hales. *Summa theologiae*. 4 vols. Edited by Quaracchi. Florence, 1924–1948.

Alfunsi, Petrus. *Dialogi* (Migne, PL 157).

Allen R. E. "Participation and Prediction in Plato's Middle Dialogues." In *Plato: A Collection of Critical Essays*. Edited by Gregory Vlastos. New York, 1971.

Allers, R. *Anselm von Canterbury: Leben, Lehre, Werke*. Vienna, 1936.

Alt, Albrecht. "Die Ursprünge des Israelitischen Rechts" in *Kleine Schriften*. Munich, 1953.

Altmann, A. *Moses Mendelssohn: A Biographical Study*. Philadelphia, 1973.

Ambrosius of Milan. *De Jacobo* (CSEL 32).

———. *De Paradiso*. Edited by C. Schenkel (CSEL 32).

———. *Hexaemeron*. Edited by C. Schenkel (CSEL 32).

Amulo of Lyon. *Liber contra Judaeos* (Migne, PL 116).

Anastos, Milton V. "Porphyry's Attack on the Bible." In *The Classical Tradition: Literary and Historical Studies in Honor of Harry Kaplan*. Edited by I. Wallach. Ithaca, N.Y., 1966.

Andersen, Carl. "Logos und Nomos: Die Polemik des Kelsos wider das Christentum." In *Arbeiten zur Kirchengeschichte* 30. Edited by K. Aland et al. Berlin, 1955.

Anselm of Canterbury. "Cur deus homo?" in *Anselmi Opera Omnia*. Edited by F. S. Schmitt. Edinburgh, 1946.

Anselm of Havelberg. *Dialogi* (Migne, PL 188).

Aristotle. *De caelo*. Edited by D. J. Allan. Oxford, 1936.

———. *De generatione animalium*. Edited by Drosaart-lulofs. Oxford, 1965.

———. *Politics*. Edited by E. Barker. Oxford, 1952.

Arnold, Gottfried. *Unparteyische Kirchen und Kezerhistorie*. Schaffhausen, 1740.

Ashtor, A. *The History of the Jews in Moslem Spain*. Jerusalem, 1966.

Assmann, Jan. "Kollektives Gedächtnis und kulturelle Identität." In *Kultur und Gedächtnis*. Edited by J. Assmann and T. Hölscher. Frankfurt-am-Main, 1988.

———. "Guilt and Remembrance: On the Theologization of History in the Ancient Near East." *History and Memory* 2, 1 (1990): 5–33.

Auerbach, Erich. *Scenes from the Drama of European Literature*. New York, 1959.

———. *Mimesis: Dargestellte Wirklichkeit in der abendländischen Literatur*. 2nd edition. Bern, 1959.

Augustine of Hippo. *Augustini (Sancti Aurelii) opera omnia*, ed. J. P. Migne, *Patrologia Latina cursus completus series Latina*, vol. 32–47, Paris, 1841–49.

———. *Augustini opera*, in: *Corpus scriptorum ecclesiasticorum Latinorum*, Vienna, 1887 ff.

———. *Augustini (Aurelii) opera*, in: *Corpus Christianorum, series Latina*. Turnbout, 1954 ff.

Avi-Yonah, Michael. *Biyme Roma u-Bizantion*. Jerusalem, 1946.

———. *The Jews of Palestine: A Political History from the Bar-Kokhba War to the Arab Conquest*. London and New York, 1976.

Azaria de Rossi. *Meor eynayyim*. 3 vols. Jerusalem, 1970.

———. *Azzaria di Rossi, Selected Chapters from Sefer Me'or Einayim and Matsref lakessef*. Edited by Reuven Bonfil. Jerusalem, 1991.

Baer, I. F. A., *A History of the Jews in Christian Spain*. Tel-Aviv, 1959.

———. "Lebikoret havikuchim shel rabbi Yechiel mi-Paris veshel rabbi Moshe ben Nachman." *Tarbiz* 2 (1971): 172–77. Reprinted in: *Mechkarim 'umassot betoledot am yisrael*, 2 vols., Jerusalem, 1986 II: 128–42.

———. "Don Yitschak Abravanel veyachasso el be'ayat hahistoria vehamedinah." *Tarbiz* 5 (1937): 241–259. Reprinted in *Mechkarim*: 398–416.

————. *Galut*. Translated by Robert Warshow. New York, 1947.

————. "He'arot chadshot lesefer shevet yehuda." *Tarbiz* 6 (1933): 152–79.

————. "Ein Jüdische Messias-Apokalypse aus dem Jahre 1186." *Monatsschrift für Geschichte und Wissenschaft des Judentums* 70 (1926): 113 ff.

Bamberger, Bernard Jacob. *Proselytization in the Talmud Period*. Cincinnati, 1939.

Band, Arnold. "Swallowing Jonah: The Eclipse of Parody." *Prooftexts* 10 (1990): 177–95.

Baron, Hans. *The Crisis of the Early Italian Renaissance*. Princeton, 1966.

Baron, Solo Wittmayer. "The Historical Outlook of Maimonides." In *History and Jewish Historians*. Philadelphia, 1964.

————. *A Social and Religious History of the Jews*. New York, 1952 ff.

Baum, G. G. *Christian Theology after Auschwitz*. Robert Waley Cohen Memorial Lecture. London, 1976.

Becker, Carl L. *The Heavenly City of the Eighteenth Century Philosophers*. New Haven and London, 1932.

Beda Venerabilis. *Super acta apostolorum* (Migne, PL 92).

Benin, S. D. "The Cunning of God and Divine Accommodation: The History of an Idea." *The Journal for the History of Ideas* 45 (1984): 179–91.

————. "Thou Shalt Have No Other God Before Me: Sacrifice in Jewish and Christian Thought." Ph.D. diss., University of California, Berkeley, 1980.

Benjamin, Walter. *Illuminations*. Edited by Hannah Arendt; translated by Harry Zohn. New York, 1969.

Ben Sasson, Haim Hillel. "Jews and Christian Sectarians." *Viator* 4 (1973): 369–85.

————. "Limeagamot hakhronografyah hayehudit shel yemei habeinayim uve'ayoteha" in *Historyah veaskolot historiyot*. Jerusalem, 1962.

————. *Perakim betoldot yisrael biyme habenayyim*. Tel-Aviv, 1962.

————. "Yichudam yisrael leda'at bne hamea hashtemesre," in *Peraqim lecheqer toldot yisrael* vol. 2, Schocken Institute at the HUC (1971): 145–218.

Bentzen, Aage. *Handbuch zum Alten Testament*. 2nd edition. Edited by Otto Eissfeldt. Tübingen, 1952.

Benz, Ernst. *Ecclesia Spiritualis*. Stuttgart, 1934.

Berger, Peter. *The Sacred Canopy. Elements of a Sociological Theory of Religion*. Garden City, N.Y. 1967.

————, and Thomas Luckmann. *The Social Construction of Reality*. New York, 1966.

————, and Thomas Luckmann. "Secularization and Pluralism." *International Yearbook for the Society of Religion*, 1966.

Berges, Wilhelm. "Anselm von Havelberg in der Geistesgeschichte des 12. Jahrhunderts." *Jahrbuch für die Geschichte Mittel und Ostedeutschlands* 5 (1956): 38 ff.

————. "Land und Unland in der mittelalterlichen welt." *Festschrift für H. Heimpel zum 70ten Geburtstag*. Göttingen, 1972: 399–439.

Bergmann, S. H. "The Principle of Apriority in the Philosophy of Hermann Cohen." *Knesset*, 1944.

Berkovits, E. *Faith After the Holocaust.* New York, 1973.

Beumer, Johannes. "Der theoretische Beitrag der Frühscholastik zu dem Problem des Dogmenfortschritts." *Zeitschrift für katolische Theologie* 74 (1952): 105 ff.

Biale, David. *Gershom Scholem: Kabbala and Counterhistory.* Cambridge, Mass., 1979.

———. "The Kabbala in Nachman Krochmal's Philosophy of History." *Journal of Jewish Studies* 32 (1981): 85–97.

Bildstein, J. "On Political Structures: Four Medieval Comments" in *The Jewish Journal of Sociology* 22 (1980).

Bloch, Marc. *La Société Feodale.* Paris, 1939.

Blumenberg, Hans. *Die Legitimität der Neuzeit.* Frankfurt am Main, 1966.

Blumenkranz, Bernhard. *Les auteurs Chretiens latin du moyen age sur les Juifs et le Judaisme.* Paris, 1963.

———. *Die Judenpredigt Augustins.* Basel, 1946.

Bock, Gisela. *Thomas Campanella: politisches Interesse und philosophische Spekulation.* Tübingen, 1974.

Bodin, Jean. *Methodus ad facilem historiarum cognitionem* Strassburg, 1907.

———. *Heptaplomeres.* Edited by L. Noack. Hildesheim, 1970.

Bohr, Niels. "Discussion with Einstein on Epistemological Problems in Atomic Physics," in *Albert Einstein: Philosopher-Scientist.* 3rd edition. Edited by Paul Arthur Schlipp. London, 1949.

Bousma, William J. *John Calvin: A Sixteenth Century Portrait.* New York; Oxford, 1988.

Bousset, Wilhelm. *Die Religion des Judentums im späthellenistischer Zeitalter.* 3rd edition, rev. Edited by Hugo Gressmann. Tübingen, 1966.

Box, George Herbert. "4 Ezra." In *The Apocrypha and Pseudepigrapha of the Old Testament.* 2 vols. Edited by Robert Henry Charles. Oxford, 1968.

Brinker, Menachem. "Sartre on the Jewish Question: Thirty Years Later." *Jerusalem Quarterly* 10 (1979): 117–32.

Brunner, Otto. *Land und Herrschaft. Grundfragen territorialen Verfassungsgeschichte Östereichs im Mittelalter.* Vienna, 1959.

Buber, Martin. *Bein am leartzo.* Jerusalem, 1952.

———. *Zwei Glaubensweisen.* Heidelberg, 1950.

Budde, Franz. *Historia Ecclesiastica.* 3rd edition. Jena, 1726.

Bultman, Rudolf Karl. *Das Urchristentum im Rahmen der antiken Religionen.* 2nd edition. Zürich, 1954.

Burckhardt, Jakob. *Briefe.* Edited by Max Burckhardt. Bremen, 1965.

Burdach, Conrad. *Reformation, Renaissance, Humanismus. Zwei Abhandlungen über die Grundlage Moderner Bildung und Sprachkunst.* 2nd ed. Berlin, 1926; reprint Darmstadt, 1963.

Campanella, Tommaso. *Atheismus triumphatus.* Paris, 1636.

———. *Metafisica.* Edited by Giovani di Napoli. Bologna, 1967.

———. "Rationalis philosophiae, part 5: Historiographia liber unus iuxta propria principia," in *Tutte le opere di Tommaso Campanella.* Edited by L. Firpo. Turin, 1954.

Capsali, Eliyahu. *Seder Eliyahu Zuta.* 2 vols. Jerusalem, 1979.

Caspar, Erich. (ed.) *Das Register Gregors VII.* 2 vols. MG Epistulae selectae in usum scholarum. Berlin, 1920; reprint 1967.

Cardoso, Yshac. *Las Excelencias de los Hebreos.* Amsterdam, 1679.

Cassuto, Umberto. *From Adam to Noah. A Commentary on the First Chapters of Genesis.* Jerusalem, 1944.

Censorinus. *De die natali.* Edited by F. Huftsch. Leipzig, 1897.

Chadwick, H. *Origenes: Contra Celsum.* Translated by H. Chadwick. Cambridge, 1965.

Charles, Robert Henry. (ed.) *The Apocrypha and Pseudepigrapha of the Old Testament.* 2 vols. Oxford, 1968.

Chenu, Marie Dominique. *Nature, Man and Society in the Twelfth Century.* Chicago, 1957.

Cicero. *De Oratore.* Loeb Classical Literary, Cambridge, Mass., 1967.

———. *De republica.* Edited by K. Ziegler, Leipzig, 1929.

Classen, Peter. *Gerhoch von Reichersberg.* Wiesbaden, 1960.

Cochrane, Charles Norris. *Christianity and Classical Culture: A Study of Thought and Action from Augustus to Augustine.* 2nd edition. New York, 1957.

Cohen, Bernard I. (ed.) *Puritanism and the Rise of Modern Science.* New Brunswick, 1990.

Cohen, Hermann. *Das Prinzip der Infinitissemalmethode und seine Geschichte.* Frankfurt-Main, 1968.

———. *Die Religion der Vernunft aus den Quellen des Judentums.* Berlin, 1921.

———. *Logik der reinen Erkenntnis.* 3rd. ed., Berlin, 1922.

Cohen, Gerson. "Esau as Symbol in Early Medieval Thought." In *Jewish Medieval and Renaissance Studies.* Edited by Alexander Altmann. Cambridge, Mass., 1967.

———. *The Book of Tradition by Abraham Ibn Daud.* Philadelphia, 1967.

Cohen, J. *The Friars and the Jews: The Evolution of Medieval Anti-Judasim.* Ithaca, N.Y., and London, 1982.

Cohn, Norman Rufus Colin. *The Pursuit of the Millennium.* London, 1957.

———. *Warrant for Genocide.* London, 1967.

Courtenay, W. "Necessity and Freedom in Anselm's Conception of God." *Analecta Anselmiana* 4.2 (1975): 39–64.

Cranz, E. E. "The Development of Augustine's Ideas on Society Before the Donatist Controversy." *Harvard Theological Review* 58 (1954): 255 ff.

Cross, Frank Moore. *The Ancient Library of Qumran and Modern Biblical Studies.* Revised edition. New York, 1961.

Curtius, Ernst Robert. *Europäische Literature und Lateinisches Mittelalter.* Bern, 1956.

Damiani, Petrus. "De divina omnipotentia," in *Edizione Nationale dei Classici del pensiero Italiano.* Edited by P. Brezzi and B. Nardi. Firenze, 1943.

Dan, Joseph. *Hasipur haivri biyme habenayim.* Jerusalem, 1974.

———. *Torat hasod shel chassidut Ashkenaz.* Jerusalem, 1968.

Danby, H. (trans.) *The Mishnah*. London, 1933.

Daniel, N. *Islam and the West: The Making of an Image*. Edinburgh, 1960.

Danilou, Jean. "The New Testament and the Theology of History." *Studia Evangelica* 1 (1959): 25–34.

Dante Alighieri. "De vulgari eloquentia." in *Opere*. Edited by E. Moore and P. Toynbee. Oxford, 1924.

Dassberg, Lea. *Untersuchungen über die Entwertung des Judenstatus im 11 Jahrhundert*. Paris-La Haye, 1965.

Davidson, Herbert. "The Active Intellect in the Cuzari and Halevi's Theory of Causality." *Revue des études Juives* 131 (1972): 351–96.

———. "Arguments from the Concept of Particularization." *Philosophy East and West* 18 (1968): 299 ff.

———. *Proofs for Eternity, Creation and the Existence of God in Medieval Islamic and Jewish Philosophy*. New York, 1987.

Dempf, Alois. *Sacrum Imperium. Geschichts-und Staatsphilosophie des Mittelalten und der politischen Renaissance*. München-Berlin, 1929.

Descartes, René. *Meditations*. Edited by A. Tannery. Paris, 1904.

Diestel, Ludwig. *Geschichte des Alten Testaments in der christlichen Kirche*. Jena, 1869.

Dilthey, Wilhelm. "Weltanschauung und Analyse des Menschen seit Renaissance und Reformation," in *Gesammelte Schriften*. Stuttgart, 1960.

Dimant, Devorah. "Election and Laws of History in Apocalyptic Literature," in *Chosen People, Elect Nation and Universal Mission*. Edited by Shmuel Almog and Michael Heyd. Jerusalem, 1991.

Dimitrowski, H. Z. "New Documents Regarding the Semikha Controversy in Safed." *Sefunot* 10 (1966): 115–92.

Dinur, B. Z. *Yisrael bagola*. Jerusalem, 1967.

Dubnow, S. *World History of the Jewish People*. Hebrew translation. Tel-Aviv, 1958.

Durkheim, Émile. "L'Individualisme et les intellectuélles." *Revue bleu* 4, 10 (1898): 7–13.

Düsing, Klaus. *Hegel und die Geschichte der Philosophie*. Darmstadt, 1983.

Eben-Shmuel, Jehuda. *Midreshe Geula*. Jerusalem, 1952.

Effler, R. R. "Jonn Duns Scotus and the Principle omne quod movetur ab alio movetur." *Franciscan Institute Publications, Philosophy Series* 15 (1962): 120 ff.

Efron, Joshua. *Studies of the Hasmonean Period*. Hebrew, Tel-Aviv, 1960.

Eilberg-Schwartz, Howard. *The Savage in Judaism: An Anthropology of Israelite Religion and Ancient Judaism*. Bloomington, Ind., 1990.

Eisen, Arnold. *Galut*. Bloomington and Indianapolis, Ind., 1986.

Eissfeldt, Otto. *The Old Testament: An Introduction*. Translated by P. R. Ackroyd. New York and Evanston, 1965.

Elbogen, Ismar. *Der jüdische Gottesdienst in seiner geschichtlichen Entwicklung*. 1st ed., Leipzig 1913; 3rd ed., Frankfurt-am-Main, 1931.

Eleazer of Worms. *Sefer chokhmat hanefesh*. Reprint edition. Jerusalem, 1967.

Eliade, Mircea. "Cosmic and Eschatological Renewal." In *The Two and the One*. Translated by J. M. Cohen. Chicago, 1962.

————. *Cosmos and History: The Myth of the Eternal Return.* Translated by Willard R. Trask. New York, 1959.

Elliger, Karl. *Studien zum Habakuk—Kommentar vom Toten Meer.* Tübingen, 1953.

Emden, Rabbi Jacob. *Mitpachat sefarim.* Lemberg, 1870.

Enders, A. *Petrus Damiani und die Weltliche Wissenschaft, Beitrage zur Geschichte der Philosophie des Mittelalters.* Edited by C. Bauhmer. Münster, 1910.

Entsiklopediah Mikrait. Jerusalem, 1950–76.

Entsiklopediah Talmudit le'inyene halakha [Talmudic Encyclopedia]. Edited by Meir Berlin and Shlomo Yosef Zevin. Jerusalem, 1947.

Epiphanius Panarios. (Migne, PG 41, PG 42).

Epstein, I. (ed.) *The Babylonian Talmud.* London, 1935.

Erdman, Carl. *Die Entstehung des Kreuzzugsgedankens.* 1935, reprint, Stuttgart, 1955.

Eshkoli, Aaron Ze'ev. *Hatenu'ot hameshici'yot be-Yisrael.* Jerusalem, 1956.

————. (ed.) *Sipur David Hareubeni.* Jerusalem, 1940.

Ettinger, Shmuel. "Jews and Judaism as Seen by English Deists of the Eighteenth Century." *Zion* 29 (1964).

————. *Modern Anti-Semitism: Studies and Essays.* Tel-Aviv, 1978.

Euchner, Walter. *Egoismus und Gemeinwohl: Studien zur Geschichte der bürgerlichen Philosophie.* Frankfurt-am-Main, 1973.

Eusebius of Caesarea. *Historia ecclesiastica.* 5th edition. Edited by Eduard Schwartz. Berlin, 1952.

————. *Praepartio Evangelica.* Edited by E. H. Gifford. 4 vols., Oxford, 1903.

Fackenheim, E. *God's Presence in History.* New York, 1970.

————. *The Jewish Return into History.* New York, 1978.

Febvre, Lucien Paul Victor. *Le problème de l'incroyance au XVIᵉ siècle: la religion de Rabelais.* Paris, 1942.

————. *The Problem of Unbelief in the Sixteenth Century: The Religion of Rabelais.* English translation by Beatrice Gottleib. Cambridge, Mass., 1982.

Fischer, J. *Die Erkenntnislehre Anselms von Canterbury.* Münster, 1911.

Fishbane, Michael A. *Biblical Interpretation in Ancient Israel.* Oxford, 1985.

Fishman, Talya. "New Light on the Dating and Provenance of Kol Sachal and Its Timeless Critique of Rabbinical Culture." *Tarbitz* 59 (1989/90): 178 ff.

Flasch, Kurt. *Aufklärung im Mittelalter? Die Verurteilung von 1277.* Mainz, 1989.

Fleischner, Eva (ed.) *Auschwitz: Beginning of a New Era?* New York, 1974.

Fleishman, Y. "Franz Rosenzweig kimevaker hatsiyonut." In *On Franz Rosenzweig on the Occasion of the Twenty-Fifth Anniversary of His Death.* Edited by E. Simon et al. Jerusalem, 1956.

Fletcher, Angus John Stuart. *Allegory: The Theory of Symbolic Mode.* Ithaca, N.Y., 1964.

Flusser, David. *Judaism and the Origins of Christianity.* Tel-Aviv, 1979.

Frank, Manfred. *Die Unhintergehbarkeit von Individualität: Reflexionen über Subjekt, Person und Individuum aus Anlass ihrer 'postmodernem' Toterklärung.* Frankfurt-am-Main, 1986.

Franklin, Julian H. *Jean Bodin and the Sixteenth-Century Revolution in the Methodology of Law and History.* New York, 1963.

Freudenthal, Gad. "Cosmogonie et physique chez Gersonides." *REJ* 145 (1986): 295–314.

Freund, Else. *Die Existenzphilosophie Franz Rosenzweigs.* Berlin, 1959.

Freund W. *Modernus und andere Zeitbegriffe des Mittelalters.* Köln, 1957.

Friedländer, Saul. "Die Shoah als Element in der Konstruktion israelischer Erinnerung." *Babylon.* 2 (1987): 10–22.

Friedrich, Hugo. *Montaigne.* 2nd edition. Bern and Munich, 1967.

Fuchs, Harald. *Der geistige Widerstand gegen Rom in der antiken Welt.* 2nd edition. Berlin, 1964.

Fulgentius, Fabius Planciades. "De aetatibus mundi et hominis," in *Fulgentii opera.* Edited by Rudolf Helm. Leipzig, 1898.

Funkenstein, Amos. "Anti-Jewish Propaganda: Pagan, Medieval and Modern." *The Jerusalem Quarterly,* 19 (Spring 1981): 56–72.

———. "Descartes and the Method of Annihilation," in *Sceptics, Millenarians and Jews.* Edited by D. Katz and J. Israel. Leiden, 1990.

———. "Gesetz und Geschichte: Zur historisierenden Hermeneutik bei Moses Maimonides und Thomas von Aquin." *Viator* 1 (1970): 147–78.

———. *Heilsplan und natürliche Entwicklung: Formen der Gegenwartsbestimmung im Geschichtsdenken des hohen Mittelalters.* Munich, 1965.

———. "Hermann Cohen: Philosophie, Deutschtum und Judentum." *Jahrbuch des Instituts für Deutsche Geschichte* 6 (1984): 355–365.

———. "Natural Science and Political Theory: Hobbes, Spinoza and Vico." In *Giambattista Vico's Science of Humanity.* Edited by Giorgio Tagliacozzo and D. F. Verne. Baltimore, 1976.

———. *Hapassiviut kesimanah shel yahadut hagola: Mitos umezi'ut.* Tel-Aviv, 1982.

———. "Patterns of Christian-Jewish Polemics in the Middle Ages." *Viator* 2 (1971): 373–82.

———. "Periodization and Self-Understanding in the Middle Ages and Early Modern Times." *Medievalia et Humanistica* 5 (1974): 3–23.

———. "The Persecution of Absolutes: On the Kantian and Neo-Kantian Theories of Science." *The Kaleidoscope of Science: The Israel Colloquium for the History and Philosophy of Science* 1 (1986): 329–48.

———. "Signonot befarshanut hamikra biyeme habenayim. Tel-Aviv, 1990.

———. *Theology and the Scientific Imagination: From the Middle Ages to the Seventeenth Century.* Princeton, 1986.

Funkenstein, Amos, and Steinsaltz, Adin. *Sociology of Ignorance.* Tel-Aviv, 1987.

Funkenstein, Josef. "Das alte Testament im Kampf zwischen Regnum und Sacerdotium Während des Investiturstreits." Ph.D. diss., Dortmund, 1937.

———. "Samuel und Saul in der Staatslehre des Mittelalters." *Archiv für Rechts-und Sozialphilosophie* XL/1 (1952): 129–140.

Gafni, Isaia M. *The Jews in the Talmudic Era: A Social and Cultural History.* Jerusalem, 1990.

Garnerius of Rochefort. *Contra Amaurianos*. Edited by C. Bäumker. Münster, 1926.

Gassendi, Pierre. *Exercitationes paradoxicae adversus Aristoteleos*. Edited by B. Rochot. Paris, 1959.

Gay, Peter. "The Enlightenment: A Reinterpretation." In *The Rise of Modern Paganism*. New York, 1960.

Geiger, Abraham. *Nachgelassene Schriften*. Berlin, 1875–78.

Gibbon, Edward. *The Decline and Fall of the Roman Empire*. Modern library: New York, n.d.

Gierke, Otto von. *Johannes Althusius und die Entwicklung der naturrechtlichen Staatstheorien*. Breslau, 1913.

Gilson, Étienne. *Jean Duns Scot: Introduction à ses positions fondamentales*. Paris, 1952. German trans., Düsseldorf, 1959.

Glaber, Radulfus. "Historiarum sui temporis libri quinque." In *Raoul Glaber, les cinq livres de ses Histoires*. Edited by M. Prou. Paris, 1896.

Glatzer, Nahum U. *Franz Rosenzweig: His Life and Thought*. 2nd edition. New York, 1961.

Goetschel, Roland. "Philon et le judaisme hellenistique au miroir de Nachman Krochmal." In *Hellenica et judaica*. Edited by A. Laquot et al. Paris. 1986.

Goez, Werner. *Translatio imperii: Ein Beitrag zur Geschichte des Geschichtsdenken und der politischen Theorien im Mittelalter und der frühen Neuzeit*. Tübingen, 1958.

Goldstein B. "The Hebrew Astronomical Tradition: New Sources." Isis 72 (1981): 237–51.

Goldzieher, Ignaz. *Vorlesungen über den Islam*. Heidelberg, 1910.

Good, Edwin Marshall. *Irony in the Old Testament*. Philadelphia, 1965.

Gordis, R. "The Song of Songs." In *Mordechai M. Kaplan Jubilee Volume on the Occasion of his Seventieth Birthday*. Edited by Moshe Davis. New York, 1953.

Gottleib, Ephraim. *Mechkarim besifrut haqabbalah*. Edited by Joseph Hacker. Tel-Aviv, 1976.

Graetz, Heinrich. *Die Konstruktion der jüdischen Geschichte*. Berlin, 1936.

Grafton, A. *Defenders of the Text: The Traditions of Scholarship in the Age of Science, 1450–1800*. Cambridge, Mass., 1991.

Grayzel, S. *The Church and the Jews in the XIIIth Century*. Philadelphia, 1933.

Greenberg, U. Z. *Rechovot hanahar, sefer ha'iliot vehakoach*. Tel-Aviv, 1957.

Greene, Thomas M. "History and Anachronism" in *Literature and History: Theoretical Problems and Russian Case Studies*. Edited by Gary Saul Morson. Stanford, 1986.

———. *In the Light of Troy: Imitation and Discovery in Renaissance Poetry*. New Haven, 1982.

Gregory of Rimini. *Lectura super primum et secundum sententiarum*. 6 vols. Edited by A. D. Trapp and V. Marcolino. Berlin and New York, 1979–84.

Grinz, J. M. "Ben Ugarit lekummran." *Eshkolot* IV (1962): 146–61.

Grundmann, Herbert. "Oportet et haereses esse: Das Problem der Ketzerei im

Spiegel der mittelalterlichen Bibelexegese." *Archiv für Kulturgeschichte* 45 (1963): 129–64.

———. *Studien über Joachim von Fiore.* Leipzig, 1927.

Grunebaum, E. G. von. *Medieval Islam.* Chicago, 1953.

Guttmann, Julius. "John Spencers Erklärung der biblischen Gesetze in ihrer Beziehung zu Maimonides." In *Festskrift i anleding af Professor David Simonsen 70-årige fødelsodag.* Copenhagen (1923): 258–76.

———. *Philosophies of Judism.* Translated by David W. Silverman. New York, 1964; reprint, 1973.

———. "Das Problem der Kontingenz in der Philosophie des Maimonides." *Monatsschrift für Geschchichte und Wissenschaft des Judentums* 83 (1939): 406 ff.

———. *Das Verhältniss des Thomas von Aquino zum Judentum und zur jüdischen Literatur.* Göttingen, 1891.

Gutwein, Daniel. "Marx on the Relationship Between Jews and Capitalism: From Sombart to Weber." *Zion* IV/4 (1990): 419–47.

Haberman, A. *Sefer gezerot ashkenaz vetsarfat.* Jerusalem, 1945.

Halbwachs, Maurice. *La mémoire collective.* Paris, 1950.

Harnack, Adolf von. *Marcion: Das Evangelium vom Freuden Gott.* Leipzig 1924; reprint Darmstadt, 1960.

Hauck, Karl. *Kirchengeschichte Deutschlands.* 5 vols. Berlin, 1958.

Häussler, A. "Vom Ursprung und Wandel des Lebensaltervergleiches." *Hermes* 92 (1964): 313 ff.

Hegel, Georg Wilhelm Friedrich. "Phänomenologie des Geistes." In *Sämtliche Werke.* Edited by J. Hofmeister. Hamburg, 1952.

———. *Vorlasungen über die Philosophie der Geschichte.* Edited by H. Glockner. Stuttgart, 1927.

———. *Vorlesungen über die Philosophie der Geschichte.* Edited by Friedrich Brunstädt. Stuttgart, 1961.

———. *Wissenschaft der Logik.* Nürnberg, 1812–1816.

Heidegger, Martin. *Sein und Zeit.* 9th edition, Tübingen, 1960.

Heilborn, John L. "Science in the Church." *Science in Context* 3.1 (1989): 9–28.

Heilperin, H. *Rashi and the Christian Scholars.* Pittsburgh, 1963.

Heinemann, Isaak. "Antiker Antisemitimus." In Pauli-Wissowa *Realenzyklopädie der Altertumswissenschaften,* Suplemenband V.

———. *Darche ha'aggada.* 2nd edition. Jerusalem, 1954.

———. *Ta'ame hamitsvot besifrut Yisrael.* Jerusalem, 1959.

Heinmann, Joseph. *Prayers in the Period of the Tana'im and Amora'im: Its Nature and Patterns.* Jerusalem, 1978.

Heller-Wilensky, S. O. "Isaac ibn Latif." In *Jewish Medieval and Renaissance Studies.* Edited by Alexander Altmann. Cambridge, Mass., 1967.

Helm, Rudolf. "Fulgentius, de aetatibus mundi." *Philologus* 56 (1897): 253–89.

Henrich, Dieter. "Hegels Logik der Reflexion." In *Hegel im Kontext.* Frankfurt-am-Main, 1971.

————. *Der ontologische Gottesbeweis, sein Problem und seine Geschichte in der Neuzeit*. Tübingen, 1960.

Hermann of Reichenau. *Chronicon*. Edited by G. H. Pertz. MG Script, 1844.

Hermannus quondam Judaeus. "Opusculum de conversione sua." In *Quellen zur Geschichte des Mittelalters*. Edited by G. Niemayr. Weimar, 1963.

Herodotus, *Historiae*. Vol. 1. Edited by H. B. Rosén. Leipzig, 1987.

Hertzberg, Arthur. *The French Enlightenment and the Jews: The Origin of Modern Anti-Semitism*. New York, 1968.

Hervey, Ruth E. "The Inward Wits: Psychological Theory in the Middle Ages and the Renaissance." In *Warburg Institute Surveys* 6 (1975).

Herzl, Theodore. *Der Judenstaat*. Vienna, 1934.

Hieronymus. *Chronicon Eusebii*. Edited by R. Helms. GCS 24, 1913.

————. *Epistulae*. Edited by I. Heidberg (CSEL 61/3, 1918).

Hilberg, R. *The Destruction of the European Jews*. Chicago, 1967.

Hildebertus Cenomanensis. *Sermo in septuagesima* (Migne, PL 177).

Hintikka, Jaakko. *Time and Necessity: Studies in Aristotle's Theory of Modality*. Oxford, 1973.

Horning, G. "Akkommodation." In *Wörterbuch der Philosophie*. Edited by G. Ritter et al. Darmstadt, 1971.

Hugh of St. Victor. *De sacramentis Christianae fidei* (Migne, PL 176).

————. *De scripturis* (Migne, PL 175).

————. *De vanitate mundi et rerum transeuntium usu* (Migne, PL 176).

————. *Didascalicon de studi legendi* (Migne, PL 176).

Ibn Verga, Shlomo. *Shevet Yehuda*. Edited by M. Wiener. Hannover, 1924.

Idel, M. "Hahitbodedut kerikuz bafilosofia hayehudit." *Mechkare Yerushalayim bemachshevet Yisrael* 7 (1988): 39–60.

Irenaeus of Lyons. *Libri quinque adversus haereses*. 2 vols. Edited by W. Wigan Harvey. Cambridge, 1857.

Isidore of Seville. *De fide catholica contra Iudaeos* (Migne, PL 83).

————. *De ordo creaturarum* (Migne, PL 83).

————. *Etymologiarum sive originum libri XX*. Edited by W. M. Lindsay. 1911; reprint Oxford, 1957.

Jaeger, W. W. *Die Theologische der frühen griechischen Denker*. Stuttgart, 1964.

————. *The Theology of the Early Greek Philosophers*. Oxford, 1948.

Japhet, Sara. *Emunot vede'ot besefer Divre ha-Yamim umekoman be'olam hamachshava hamikrait*. Jerusalem, 1977.

Jehuda Halevi. *Sefer hakuzzari*. Edited by Avraham Tsifroni. Tel-Aviv, 1964.

Jellineck, Adolf (ed.) *Beth hamidrash*. 3rd edition, Jerusalem, 1967.

John of Salisbury. *The Historia pontificalis of John of Salisbury*. Edited and translated by Marjorie Chibnall. London, 1956; Oxford and New York, 1986.

Jonas, Hans. *The Gnostic Religion: The Message of the Alien God and the Beginnings of Christianity*. 2nd edition, rev. Boston, 1963.

Josephon Habraicus. Edited by J. F. Breithaupt. Gotha and Leipzig, 1710.

Josephus, Flavius. "De Iudaeorum vetustate sive contra Apionem." In *Flavii Iosephi opera* 5. Edited by B. Niese, 1889; reprint Berlin, 1955.

Juster, Jean. *Les Juifs dans l'empire Romain: leur condition juridique, économique et sociale*. Paris, 1914.

Kafka, Franz. "Die Verwandlung." In *Kafkas Erzählungen*. Edited by Brigitte Flach. Bonn, 1967.

Kamin, Sarah. *Rashi: Peshuto shel mikra u-midrasho shel mikra*. Jerusalem, 1986.

———. *Jews and Christians Interpret the Bible*. Jerusalem, 1991.

Kamlah, Wilhelm. "Apokalypse und Geschichtstheologie. Die mittelalteriche Auslegung der Apokalypse vor Joachin von Fiore." In *Historische Studien* 285. Edited by W. Andreas et al. Berlin, 1935.

———. *Christentum und Geschichtlichkeit*. Stuttgart, 1951.

Kant, Immanuel. "Kritik der reinen Vernunft." In *Werke*. Edited by Wilhelm Weischedel. Wiesbaden, 1956.

Kasher, Menachem M. *Hatekufa hagdola*. Jerusalem, 1969.

Katsh, Abraham. "The Impact of Nachman Krochmal on the Development of the Zionist Movement." *Proceedings of the Ninth Congress of Jewish Studies*, 1986.

Katz, Jacob. *Anti-Semitism: From Religious Hatred to Racial Rejection*. Tel-Aviv, 1979.

———. *Ben halakha lekabbala*. Jerusalem, 1987.

———. *Ben Yehudim legoyim*. Jerusalem, 1960.

———. "Machloqet hasemikah ben Rabbi Jacob Berav vehaRalbah." *Zion* 17 (1951): 34 ff.

Kaufmann, D. *Geschichte der Attributenlehre in der judischen religiosen Philosophie des Mittelalters von Saadya bis Maimuni*. Gotha, 1877.

Kaufmann, Yechezkel. *Gola venekhar*. Tel Aviv, 1961.

Kedar, B. "Canon Law and the Burning of the Talmud." *Bulletin of Medieval Canon Law* 9 (1979): 79–82.

Kelley, Donald R. *Foundations of Modern Historical Scholarship: Language, Law and History in the French Renaissance*. New York, 1970.

———. "Klio and the Lawyers." *Medievalia et humanistica* 5 (1975): 24–49.

Kern, Fritz. *Gottesgnadentum und Widerstandsrecht im frühen Mittelalter*. 2nd edition. Darmstadt, 1954.

———. *Recht und Verfassung im Mittelalter*. Reprint, Darmstadt, 1958.

Keuck, Karl. "Historia: Geschichte des Wortes und seine Bedeutung." Ph.D. diss., University of Münster, 1934.

Kirkasani, Abu Yusuf Ya'kub. *Kitab al-anwar wal-marqib*. Edited by Leon Nemoy. New York, 1939–43.

Kisch, Guido. *Erasmus und die Jurisprudenz seiner Zeit*. Basel, 1960.

Klein-Braslawy, Sara. *Perush ha-Ramban liberi'at haolam*. Jerusalem, 1978.

Kleinberger, Fritz A. *The Educational Theory of the Maharal of Prague*. Jerusalem, 1962.

Klemperer, Viktor. *"LTI" Die Unbewältigte Sprache; aus dem Notizbuch einen Philologen*. Darmstadt, 1966.

Klempt, A. *Die Säkularisierung der Universalhistorischen Auffassung*. Göttingen, 1960.

Kluxen, W. "Literaturgeschichtliches zum lateinischen Moses Maimonides." *Rech. theol. anc. et med.* XXI (1954): 23–50.

Kohn, Martin. "Jewish Historiography and Jewish Self-Understanding in the Period of Renaissance and Reformation." Ph.D. diss., UCLA, 1979.

Kook, Rabbi Abraham Yosef Hakohen. *Ig'grot ha-Ra'aya.* 4 vols. Jerusalem, 1965.

Koselleck, Reinhart. *Vergangene Zukunft: Zur Semantik geschichtlicher Zeiten.* Frankfurt-am-Main, 1979.

Kraus, Samuel (ed.) *Das Leben Jesu nach jüdischen Quellen.* Berlin, 1902.

Kritzeck, P. *Peter the Venerable and Islam.* Princeton, 1964.

Krochmal, Nachman. "More nebuche hashem." In *The Writings of Nachman Krochmal.* Edited by S. Rawidowicz. Waltham, Mass., 1961.

Kurzweil, Baruch. *Bama'avak al erkhey hayahadut.* Tel-Aviv, 1956.

Lachover, Pinchas. *Toldot hasifrut ha'ivrit hachadasha.* Tel-Aviv, 1927.

Ladner, Gerhart. *The Idea of Reform.* New York, 1967.

Lampert of Hersfeld. *Annales.* Edited by Oswald Holder-Egger. MG script. In usu Schol. Hanover, 1894.

Landman, Leo. *Jewish Law in the Diaspora: Confrontation and Accommodation.* Philadelphia, 1968.

Langmuir, Gavin I. *Towards a Definition of Antisemitism.* Berkeley, Los Angeles, Oxford, 1990.

Lauterbach, Jacob Zallel. "The Sadducees and Pharisees." In *Rabbinic Essays.* Cincinnati, 1951.

Lazarus-Yafeh, Chava. "Ezra-'uzayr: Metamorphosis of a Polemical Motif." *Zion* LV, 3 (1986): 359–80.

Lehmann, P. "Die Heilige Einfalt." In *Historisches Jahrbuch* 1938 (58).

Leibovitz, Ieshayahu. *Yahadut, 'am yehudi 'umedinat yisrael.* Jerusalem-Tel Aviv, 1979.

———. *Emuna, historia ve-arakhim.* Jerusalem, 1982.

Leschnitzer, A. *Die Juden im Weltbild des Mittelalters.* Berlin, 1934.

———. "Der Gestaltwandel Ahasvers." In: *In Zwei Welten. Siegfried Moses zum fünfundsiebzigsten Geburtstag.* Tel-Aviv, 1962: 470–505.

———. "Der Wandernde Jude." Festschrift H. Herzfeld. Berlin, 1964.

Levi, Primo. *Survival in Auschwitz.* Translated by S. Woolf. New York, 1961.

Levi, Zeev. *Precursor of Jewish Existentialism. The Philosophy of Franz Rosenzweig and Its Relations to Hegel's System.* Tel-Aviv, 1969. (Hebrew.)

Levi ben Habib. *Responsa.* Venice, 1565.

Levinger, Jacob. *Maimonides' Techniques of Codification.* Jerusalem, 1965. (Hebrew.)

———. "Hamachshava hahalkhatit shel haRambam." *Tarbiz* 37.3 (1968): 282 ff.

Levi ben Gershon (Gersonides). *Perush al hatora al derekh habe'ur.* Venice, 1546.

———. *Sefer milchamot hashem.* Leipzig, 1866.

Levy, Jochanan. *Olamot nifgashim.* Jerusalem, 1960.

———. *Studies in Jewish Hellenism.* Jerusalem, 1960.

Licht, Jacob. "The Attitude to Past Events in the Bible and in Apocalyptic Literature." *Tarbitz* LX, 1 (1990): 1–18.

———. "Mata'at olam ve'am pedut el." In *Mechkarim bamegilot hagnuzot: sefer zikaron le-Eliezer Lipa Sukenik.* Jerusalem, 1961.

———. *Hanissayon bamikra ubayahadut shel tekufat habayit hasheni.* Jerusalem, 1973.

———. *The Rule Scroll.* Jerusalem, 1965.

Lieberman, Saul. *Sheki'in. Midreshe Teman.* Jerusalem, 1970.

Liebeschütz, Hans. "Die stellung des Judentums im Dialog des Peter Abaelard." *MGWJ* 47 (1939): 390 ff.

Limor, Ora. "The Disputation of Maiorca." Ph.D. diss. Jerusalem, 1986.

Little, Franklin H. *The Crucifixion of the Jews.* New York, 1975.

Lloyd, G. E. R. *Magic, Reason and Experience: Studies in the Origins and Development of Greek Science.* Cambridge, 1979.

———. *The Revolutions of Wisdom: Studies in the Claims and Practice of Ancient Greek Science.* Berkeley, Los Angeles, London, 1987.

Lods, A. *Jean Astruck et la critique biblique au XVIIIe siècle.* Strassburg and Paris, 1924.

Loewenberg, Peter. "The Psychohistorical Origins of the Nazi Youth Cohort." *American Historical Review,* vol. 76/5 (1971): 1457–1502.

Loewenstamm, Shlomo A. *Massoret yetsi'at Mitsrayim behishtalsheluta.* Jerusalem, 1968, 1972.

———. "Nachalat ha-Shem." In *Studies in the bible Dedicated to the Memory of U. Cassuto.* Edited by S. A. Loewenstamm. Jerusalem, 1977:149–72.

———. and J. S. Licht. "Nissayon." In *Encyclopedia Mikra'it* V. Jerusalem, 1950–76:879–83.

Löwith, Karl. *Von Hegel zu Nietzsche: Der revolutionäre Bruch im Denken des neunzehnten Jahrhunderts, Marx und Kierkegaard.* 5th edition. Stuttgart, 1964.

Lubac, Henri de. *Exégèse médiévale: les quatres sens de l'écriture.* 4 vols. Lyons, 1964.

Luce, T. J. "Ancient Views on the Causes of Bias in Historical Writing." *Classical Philology* LXXXIV, 1989: 16–31.

Lucretius. *De rerum natura.* 2nd edition. Edited by Cyrill Bailey. Oxford, 1922.

Lukács, Georg. *Der Historische Roman.* Translated by Hannah and Stanley Mitchell. Boston, 1962.

Lukes, Steven. *Emil Durkheim: His Life and Works.* New York, 1972.

Luzzatto, Simone. *Discorso circa il stato degl' Hebrei.* Venice, 1638.

Maier, Anneliese. *Metaphysische Hintergründe der spätscholastischen Philosophie.* Rome, 1955.

———. "Das Problem der Evidenz in der Scholastik des 14. Jahrhundert." In *Ausgehendes Mittelalter.* Rome, 1967. Vol. II:367–418, 519–522.

Maier, F. G. *Augustin und das antike Rom.* Stuttgart, 1955.

Maimon, Salomon. *Giv'at hamore.* Edited by S. H. Bergmann and N. Rottenstreich. Jerusalem, 1965.

——. *Geschichte des eigenen Lebens.* Berlin, 1934.

Maimonides, Moses. [Moshe ben Maimon] *Le guide des égares (Dalalat al ha'irim.)* 3 vols. Edited by S. Munk. Paris, 1856–1866.

——. *The Guide of the Perplexed.* Translated by S. Pines. Chicago, 1963.

——. *Igeret Teman. Iggrot harambam.* Edited by Josef Kafiah. Jerusalem, 1952:15–60.

——. *Ma'amar Techiat hametim.* Ibid., 63–101.

——. *Mishne tora.* Jerusalem, 1921.

——. *Perush hamishnayot.* Edited by Josef Kafiah. Jerusalem, 1963.

——. *Teshuvot harambam (Responsa).* 2 vols. Edited by Jehoshua Blau. Jerusalem, 1960.

Malcolm, N. "Anselm's Ontological Arguments." *Philosophical Review* 69 (1960): 41–62.

Manetho. "Aegyptiaca." In Josephus Flavius, *Contra Apionem.* Cambridge, Mass., 1940.

Mannheim, Karl. *Ideology and Utopia: An Introduction to the Sociology of Knowledge.* Trans. by L. Wirth and E. Shils. New York, 1955.

Marchavja, H. *Ha-Talmud bir'ei ha-natsrut.* Jerusalem, 1970.

Margaliot, Mordecai. (ed.) *Midrash Rabbah. Leviticus.* Jerusalem, 1953–56.

Martène et Durand. *Thesaurus novus anecdotarum.* Paris, 1717.

Martini, Reymundus. *Pugio fidei adversus Mauros et Judaeos.* Lipsia, 1687.

Marx, Karl. "Economic and Philosophic Manuscripts of 1844." In *Writings of the Young Marx on Philosophy and Society.* Edited and translated by Loyd D. Easton and Kurt H. Guddat. New York, 1967.

——. "Zur Judenfrage." In *Karl Marx, Friedrich Engels. Werke.* Berlin, 1956.

——. *Das Kapital.* Hamburg, 1890–1894.

Marx, Werner. *Transzendentale Logik als Wissenschafts Theorie.* Frankfurt-am-Main, 1977.

Mayer, Michael A. *Response to Modernity. A History of the Reform Movement in Judaism.* Oxford, 1988.

Mendelssohn, Moses. "Jerusalem oder über religiöse Macht und Judentum." In *Gesammelte Schriften.* Edited by G. B. Mendelsshon. Leipzig, 1843–1845.

Meinecke, Friedrich. "Die Idee der Staatsraison in der neueren Geschichte." In *Werke.* 2nd edition. Munich, 1960.

——. "Klassizismus, Romantizismus und historisches Denken im 18. Jahrhundert." In *Werke.* Edited by Eberhard Kessel. Munich, 1959.

Melancthon, Philipp. "Chronicon Carionis." In *Corpus Reformatorum* 12. Edited by Carlus Gottlieb Bretschneider. Halle IS, 1844.

Melville, Herman. *Moby-Dick; or, the Whale.* New York, 1962.

Mendes-Flohr, Paul. "Franz Rosenzweig and the Crisis of Historicism." In Mendes Flohr (ed.) *The Philosophy of Franz Rosenzweig.* Hannover and London, 1988.

Merton, Robert K. *Science, Technology and Society in Seventeenth Century England.* New York, 1970.

Miethke, Jürgen. *Ockhams Weg zur Sozialphilosophie*. Berlin, 1969.

———. "Papst, Ortsbischof und Universität in den Pariser Theologenprozessen des 13. Jahrhundert." *Miscellanea Medievalia* 10 (1978): 52–94.

Mirandola, Giovanni Pico della. *Oratio de hominis dignitate, Heptaplus, De ente et uno, e scritti vari*. Edited by E. Garin. Florence, 1946–52.

Miron, Dan. *Beyn chazon le'emet: nitsane haroman ha'ivri vehayiddi bamea ha-19*. Jerusalem, 1979.

Mitteis, Heinrich. *Der Staat des hohen Mittelalters*. 5th edition. Weimar, 1955.

Momigliano, Arnaldo. *Essays in Ancient and Modern Historiography*. Middletown, Conn., 1977.

———. "A Medieval Jewish Autobiography." In *Essays in Honor of H. R. Trevor-Roper*. Edited by H. Lloyd-Jones. Oxford, 1981.

Montaigne, Michel de. *Essais*. Edited by Maurice Rat. 2nd ed. Paris, 1962.

Moses, Stéphane. *Système et Révélation: La philosophie de Franz Rosenzweig*. Paris, 1982.

Moznayim. 1988/89.

Murray, Gilbert. *Five Stages of Greek Religion*. 3rd ed. Boston, 1951; reprint Garden City, N.Y., 1955.

Nachmanides (Moshe ben Nachman). *Torat ha-Shem temima, Kitve rabenu Mosheh ben Nachman*. Edited by Cha'im Dov Shavel. Jerusalem, 1963.

———. *Perush ha-Ramban al hatora*. Edited by Chaim Dov Chavel. Jerusalem, 1959.

———. "Vikuach ha-Ramban." In *Otsar ha-vikuchim*. Edited by J. P. Eisenstadt. New York, 1928.

Neher, André. "Copernicus in the Hebraic Literature from the Sixteenth to the Eighteenth Century." *Journal for the History of Ideas* 38 (1977): 211–26.

———. *David Gans (1541–1613) and His Times*. Translated by D. Maisel. Oxford, 1986.

Netanyahu, Benjamin Z. *Don Isaac Abravanel: Statesman and Philosopher*. Philadelphia, 1953.

Neusner, Jacob. *Judaism and Christianity in the Age of Constantine*. Chicago and London, 1987.

Nietzsche, Friedrich. "Vom Nutzen und Nachteil der Historie für das Leben." In *Werke*. Edited by K. Schlechta. 1874; München, 1960.

Niewöhner, Friedrich. *Veritas sine Varietas: Lessings Toleranzparabel und das Buch von dess Drei Betrügen*. Heidelberg. 1988.

Nock, A. D. *Conversion: The Old and the New in Religion From Alexander the Great to Augustine of Hippo*. Oxford, 1933.

———. (ed.). *Sallustius Concerning the Gods and the Universe*. Cambridge, Mass., 1926.

Nordau, Max. *Entartung*. Berlin, 1893.

Norden, Eduard. *Die antike Kunstprosa: Vom VI. Jahrhundert v. Chr. bis in die Zeit der Renaissance*. Leipzig, 1915–1918; reprint Darmstadt, 1958.

Oakley, Francis. *Omnipotence, Covenant and Order: An Excursion in the History of Ideas from Abelard to Leibniz*. Ithaca, N.Y., and London, 1984.

Oberman, Heiko Augustinus. *The Harvest of Medieval Theology: Gabriel Biel and Late Medieval Nominalism*. Cambridge, Mass., 1963.

Odo de Cambray. *Disputatio cum Judaeo*. Migne, PL 160.

Oresme, Nicole. *Le Livre du ciel et du monde*. Edited by A. D. Menut and A. J. Denomy. Madison, Wis., 1968.

Origenes. *Contra Celsum*. Edited by P. Kötzschau. GCS 30. Leipzig, 1899. Translated by Henry Chadwick. Cambridge, 1965.

――――. *De Principiis*. Edited by Herwig Görgemanns and Heinrich Karpp. Darmstadt, 1976.

――――. *Prologus in Canticum* (Migne, PG 13).

Overbeck, Franz. *Christiantum und Kultur*. Edited by C. A. Bernouli. Basel, 1919.

Oz, Amos. *Po vesham be'erets yisrael bistav 1981*. Tel-Aviv, 1982.

Parkes, James William. *The Conflict of the Church and the Synagogue: A Study in the Origins of Anti-Semitism*. London, 1934.

Paurs, J. "The Basis for the Authority of the Law According to Maimonides." *Tarbiz* 38, 1 (1969): 43 ff.

Pedaya, Haviva. "The Spiritual Versus the Concrete Land of Israel in the Geronese School of Kabbala." In *The Land of Israel in Medieval Jewish Thought*. Edited by Moshe Challamish and Aviezer Ravitzky. Jerusalem, 1991.

Penslar, Derek J. *Zionism and Technocracy*. Bloomington and Indianapolis, 1991.

Perlman, M. *Ibn Kammua's Examination of the Three Faiths*. Berkeley, 1971.

Pertz, Georgius Heinricus (ed.). *Cnutonis regis gestae: sive, Encomium Emmae reginae auctore Monacho Sancti Bertini. In usum scholarum ex Monumentis Germaniae historicis recudi fecit*. Leipzig, 1955.

Peterson, Erik. *Theologische Traktate*. (Munich, 1951).

Pfeiffer, Rudolf. *History of Classical Scholarship from the Beginnings to the End of the Hellenistic Age*. Oxford, 1968.

Philo of Alexandria. *Legum allegoriae*. Edited by G. H. Whitaker and R. Marcus. Cambridge and London, 1962.

Pines, Shlomo. "Joseph Ibn Kaspi's and Spinoza's Opinions on the Probability of a Restoration of the Jewish State." *Iyyun* 14–15 (1963–4): 289 ff.

――――. "Al hamunach ruchaniyut ve'al mishnato shel Yehuda Halevi." *Zion* 57.4 (1990): 511–540.

――――. "Hakinuy ha-irani lenotsrim veyirey hashem." In *Proceedings of the Israel Academy of Sciences* 2/7 (1966): 3–5.

――――. "Omne quod movetur necesse est ab alio movetur." *Isis* 52 (1961): 21–54.

――――. "Hasekholastiqah she-acharei Thomas Aquinas umishnatam shel Chasdai Qresqas veshel kodmav." In *Proceedings of the Israel Academy of Sciences* 1/11 (1966): 38.

Pinsker, Leon. *Autoemanzipation*. Berlin, 1882.

Pocock, John Garville Agard. *The Ancient Constitution and Feudal Law: A Study of English Historical Thought in the Seventeenth Century*. Cambridge, 1957.

Pohlenz, Max. *Die Stoa: Geschichte einer geistigen Bewegung*. 2 vols. Göttingen, 1959.

Pohlmann, Robert von. *Geschichte der sozialen Fragen und des Sozialismus in der antiken Welt*. Munich, 1912.

Polybius. *Historiae*. Edited by F. Hultsch. Berlin, 1870–1892.

Prawer, J. *A History of the Crusaders Kingdom*. Jerusalem, 1963.

Pritchard, James Bennet. *Ancient Near Eastern Texts Relating to the Old Testament*. 2nd edition. Princeton, 1955.

Quintillian. *Institutio Oratoria*. Edited by L. Radmacher. Leipzig, 1959.

Ravitzky, Aviezer. *Al da'at hamaqom: Studies in the History of Jewish Philosophy*. Jerusalem, 1991.

———. "Aristotle's *Meteorologica* and the Maimonidean Exegesis of Creation," *Jerusalem Studies in Jewish Thought* IX 1990: 225–250.

Rawidowicz, S. "War Nachman Krochmal Hegelianer?" *HUC Annual* V (1928): 535–83.

Reill, Peter Hans. *The German Enlightenment and the Rise of Historicism*. Berkeley, 1975.

———. "History and the Hermeneutics in the Aufklärung: The Thought of Johann Christoph Gatterer." *Journal of Modern History* 45 (1973): 24–51.

Reinharz, Jehudah. *Chaim Weizmann: The Making of a Zionist Leader*. New York and Oxford, 1985.

Rembaum, Joel. "The New Testament in Medieval Jewish Anti-Christian Polemics." Ph.D. diss., University of California, Los Angeles, 1975.

Remer, Gary A. "Christ as Peitho: Classical Rhetoric and the Humanist Defence of Religious Toleration." Ph.D. diss., University of California, Los Angeles, 1989.

Reuchlin, Johanus. *Augenspiegel*. Tübingen, 1511.

Reuter, Hermann. *Geschichte der religiösen Aufklärung im Mittelalter vom Ende des 8ten bis zum Anfang des 14ten Jahrhundert*. Berlin, 1875; reprint Aalen, 1963.

Rimbertus. *Vita Anskari*. Edited by G. Waitz. MG in usu schol. Hannover, 1884.

Röhr, Günter. *Platons Stellung zur Geschichte: eine methodologische Interpretationsstudie*. Berlin, 1932.

Rokéah, David. "Early Christian-Jewish Polemics on Divine Election." In *Chosen People, Elect Nation and Universal Mission*. Edited by Shmuel Almog and Michael Heyd. Jerusalem, 1991.

———. *Jews, Pagans and Christians in Conflict*. Jerusalem and Leiden, 1982.

Rosenberg, Shalom. "Land and Exile in Sixteenth-Century Jewish Thought." In *The Land of Israel in Medieval Jewish Thought*. Edited by Moshe Challamish and Aviezer Ravitzky. Jerusalem, 1991.

Rosenthal, J. (ed.) *Milchamot haShem*. Jerusalem, 1963.

———. "The Talmud on Trial: The Disputation at Paris in the Year 1240." *JQR* 47 (1956–7): 58 ff.

Rosenzweig, Franz. *Briefe*. Edited by Edith Rosenzweig. Berlin, 1935.

———. *Kleinere Schriften*. Berlin, 1937.

———. *Der Stern der Erlösung*. Frankfurt-am-Main, 1921.

———. *Briefe und Tagebucher*. Edited by Rachel Rosenzweig and Edith Rosenzweig-Scheinmann and with the collaboration of Bernhard Casper. The Hague, 1979.

Rottenstreich, N. *Jewish Thought in Modern Times*. (Hebrew). Tel-Aviv, 1945, reprint 1966.

———. *Sugiot befilosofiah*. Tel-Aviv, 1962.

Rowbotham, Arnold H. *Missionary and Mandarin in China: The Jesuits at the Court of China*. Berkeley, 1942.

Ruderman, David B. *Kabbalah, Magic and Science: The Cultural Universe of a Sixteenth-Century Jewish Physician*. Cambridge, 1988.

Sa'adia Gaon. *Sefer haemunot vede'ot*. Ibn Tibbon translation. New York, 1956.

Sacks, Oliver. *The Man Who Mistook His Wife For a Hat and Other Clinical Tales*. New York, 1985.

Saltman, Avrom. "Hermann's Opusculum de Conversione sua: Truth and Fiction." *REJ* 147/1–2 (1988): 31–56.

Sambursky, Shmuel. "The Notion of Time in the Late Newplatonic School." In *Proceedings of the Israel Academy of Sciences and Humanities* II/8 (1964).

———. "Three Aspects of the Historical Significance of Galileo." In *Proceedings of the Israel Academy of Sciences and Humanities* II(1964).

Sartre, Jean-Paul. *Réflexions sur la question juive*. Paris, 1947.

Sassportas, Jacob. *Sefer Tsitsat Novel Tsvi*. Edited by I. Tishbi. Jerusalem, 1954.

Saussure, Ferdinand de. *Cours de linguistique générale*. Paris, 1916; 4th edition. Edited by C. Bally and A. Sechehaye. Paris, 1949.

———. *Course in General Linguistics*. Trans. by W. Baskin. New York, 1959.

Scholem, Gershom Gerhard. "Franz Rosenzweig and his 'Stern der Erlösung'" in *Dvarim bego*. Edited by A. Shapira. Tel-Aviv, 1976.

———. *Major Trends in Jewish Mysticism*. New York, 1961.

———. *The Messianic Idea in Judaism and Other Essays on Jewish Spirituality*. New York, 1971.

———. *Jewish Gnosticism, Merkabah Mysticism and Talmudic Tradition*. New York, 1960.

———. *Haqabbalah be-Geronah*. Jerusalem, 1964.

———. *Haqabbalah shel sefer hatemunah veshel Avraham Abulafia*. Jerusalem, 1968.

———. *Pirke yesod behavanat haqabbalah usemaleha*. Jerusalem, 1976.

———. *Reshit haqabbalah vesefer habahir*. Jerusalem, 1968.

———. *Sabbatai Sevi: The Mystical Messiah, 1626–1676*. Translated by R. J. Zwi Werblowsky. Princeton, 1973.

———. *Ursprung und Anfänge der Kabbala*. Berlin, 1962.

———. *Von der mystichen Gestalt der Gottheit*. Zürich, 1962.

Scholz, Heinrich. *Glaube und Unglaube in der Weltgeschichte: Ein Kommentar zu Augustins De civitate Dei*. Leipzig, 1911.

Schorsch, Ismar. "The Philosophy of History of Nachman Krochmal." *Judaism* 10 (1961): 237–45.

Schreckenberg, Heinz. *Die christlichen Adversus-Judaeos Texte und ihr literarisches und historisches Umfeld* (1.–11. Jahrhundert). Frankfurt-Bern, 1982.

———. Die christlichen Adversus-Judaeos Texte (11.–13. Jh.). Mit einer

Ikonographie des Judenthemas bis zum 4. Laterankonzil. Frankfurt-Bern, 1988.

Schröder, R. "Studien zur varronischen Etymologie." In *Abhandlungen der Akademie der Wissenschaft u. Literatur Mainz, Geistes-u. Sozialwiss. Klasse* 12 (1959).

Schudt, J. J. *Jüdische Merkwürdigkeiten*. Frankfurt-am-Main and Leipzig, 1714.

Schulz, F. "Bracton on Kingship." *English Historical Review* 60 (1945): 136–76.

Schulz, Marie. *Die Lehre von der historischen Methode bei den Geschichtsschreibern des Mittelalters*. Berlin and Leipzig, 1909.

Scotus, Johannes Duns. *Opera omnia*. Edited by P. C. Balič et al., 17 vols., Vatican City, 1950 ff.

Seeberg, Erich. *Gottfried Arnold: Die Wissenschaft und die Mystik seiner Zeit*. 1923; reprint Darmstadt, 1964.

Seeberg, Reinhold. *Lehrbuch der Dogmengeschichte*. 5 vols. Berlin, 1930.

Shilo, S. *Dina demalchuta dina*. Jerusalem, 1975.

Silver, Daniel Jeremy. *Maimonides Criticism and the Maimonidean Controversy*. Leiden, 1965.

Simon, G. "Untersuchungen zur Topik der Widmungsbriefe mittelalterlicher Geschichtsschreibung bis zum Ende des 12. Jahrhunderts." *Archiv für Diplomatik* 4–6 (1958–60): 52 ff.

Simon, Marcel. *Verus Israel: étude sur les relations entre Chretiens et Juifs dans l'empire Romain (135–425)*. Paris, 1964.

Simon-Nahum, Perrine. *La cité investie*. Paris, 1991.

Smalley, Beryl. *The Study of the Bible in the Middle Ages*. Notre Dame, Ind., 1964.

Smith, Morton. *Jesus the Magician*. San Francisco, 1978.

Sorkin, David. *The Transformation of German Jewry, 1780–1840*. New York, 1987.

Spencer, John. *De legibus hebraeorum ritualibus et earum rationibus libri tres*. Cambridge, 1685.

Spinoza, *Opera quotquod reperta sunt*. Edited by J. van Vloten and J. P. N. Land. 3rd ed. The Hague, 1914.

Steiner, George. *The Portage of A. H. to San Cristobal*. New York, 1982.

Steinschneider, M. *Polemische und apologetische Literatur in arabischer Sprache zwischen Muslimen, Christen und Juden*. Leipzig, 1877.

Stern, Menachem. *Greek and Roman Authors on Jews and Judaism*. Jerusalem, 1976.

Strauss, Leo. "On Abravanel's Philosophical Tendency and Political Teaching." In *Isaac Abravanel: Six Lectures*. Edited by J. B. Trend and H. Loewe. Cambridge, 1937.

Stump, Eleanore. "Obligations." In *The Cambridge History of Later Medieval Philosophy: From the Rediscovery of Aristotle to the Disintegration of Scholasticism, 1100–1600*. Edited by Norman Kretzman et al. Cambridge and New York, 1982.

Swain, Joseph Ward. "The Theory of the Four Monarchies: Opposition History under the Roman Empire." *Classical Philology* 35 (1940): 1 ff.

————. *Historiarum libri*. Edited by K. Wellesley. Leipzig, 1989.

————. *Opera minora*. Edited by H. Turneaux and J. G. C. Anderson. Oxford, 1939.

Taitelbaum, Joel. *Vayoel Moshe*. New York, 1952.

Tal, Uriel. *Judaism and Christianity in the Second Reich*. Ithaca, N.Y., and London, 1975.

Talmon, Jacob L. *The Origins of Totalitarian Democracy*. London, 1952.

Tarn, William Woodthorpe. *Hellenistic Civilization*. 3rd ed. London, 1959.

Taubes, Jacob. "Nachman Krochmal and Modern Historicism." *Judaism* 12 (1961): 150–64.

Tcherikover, Avigdor. *Hellenistic Civilization and the Jews*. Translated by S. Appelbaum. Philadelphia, 1959.

Tertullian. "Adversus Iudaeos." In *Tertulliani Opera Omnia*. Edited by A. Kroymann. CSEL 70 (1942).

————. *Apologeticus*. Edited by Jean Pierre Waltzing. Louvain, 1910.

Theodoret of Cyrrhus. *Questions in Leviticum* (Migne, PG LXXX).

Thomas Aquinas. *Opera omnia*. Iussu impensaque Leonis XIII, PM edita. Rome, 1882 ff.

————. *Opera omnia* (Vives edition). 34 vols. Paris, 1872–1880.

Thomas of Monmouth. *De vita et passione Sancti Wilhelmi Martyris Norwicensis*. Edited by A. Jessop and M. R. James. Cambridge, 1896.

Thorndike, L. *A History of Magic and Experimental Science during the First Thirteen Centuries of Our Era*. New York, 1958.

Tierney, Brian. "The Prince Is Not Bound by the Laws." *Comparative Studies in Society and History* 5 (1963): 388 ff.

Tishbi, Isaiah. *The Doctrine of Evil and Kelippah in Lurianic Kabbala*. Jerusalem, 1943.

————. *Mishnat hazohar*. 2 vols. Jerusalem, 1957.

Toews, John Edward. *Hegelianism. The Path Toward Dialectical Humanism, 1805–1841*. Cambridge, 1980.

Trachtenberg, J. *The Devil and the Jews. The Medieval Conception of the Jews and Its Relation to Modern Anti-Semitism*. New York, 1961.

Troeltsch, Ernst. *Der Historismus und seine Probleme*. Tübingen, 1922.

Twersky, Isadore. "Josef ibn Kaspi: Portrait of a Medieval Jewish Intellectual." In *Studies in Medieval Jewish History and Literature*. Edited by I. Twersky. Cambridge, Mass., 1979.

Überweg-Geyer, Friedrich Bernhard. *Grundriß der Geschichte der Philosophie*. Basel and Stuttgart, 1960.

Urbach, Efraim Elimelech. *Ba'ale hatosafot: toldotehem, chiburehem veshitatam*. Jerusalem, 1955.

————. *Chazal: pirke emunot vedeot*. Jerusalem, 1969.

————. *The Sages, Their Concepts and Beliefs*. 2nd edition. Jerusalem, 1978.

————. "Die Staatsauflassung des Don Isaak Abrabanel." *Monatsschrift für Geschchichte und Wissenschaft des Judentums*, 81, 1937.

————. "When did Prophecy Cease?" *Tarbitz* 17 (1947): 1–11.

Vaux, Ronald de. *Ancient Israel*. 2 vols. New York and Toronto, 1965.

Venerabilis, Petrus. *Epistulae Petri Venerabilis* (RHGF 15).

————. *Tractatus adversus Judaeorum invetertam duritiem* (Migne, PL 189).

Vermes, G. *The Dead Sea Scrolls in English*. Harmondsworth, 1962.

Vico, Giambattista. *The Autobiography of Giambattista Vico*. Translated by Max Harold Fisch and Thomas Goddard Bergin. Ithaca, N.Y., 1944.

————. "La Scienza Nuova." In *Opere*. Edited by Fausto Nicolini. Bari, 1928.

————. "De Universo iuris uno principio et fine mo liber unus." In *Opere*. Edited by Fausto Nicolini. Bari, 1928.

Vidal-Naquet, Pierre. "Thesis on Revisionism." In *Unanswered Questions: Nazi Germany and the Genocide of the Jews*. Edited by François Furet. New York, 1989:304–320.

Violet, Bruno. *Die Esra Apokalypse*. 2 vols. Leipzig, 1910.

Vital, Chayim. *Ets Chayim*. Tel-Aviv, 1960.

Volkow, Shulamit. *Jüdisches Leben und Antisemitismus im 19ten und 20ten Jahrhunert*, München, 1990.

————. "The Dynamics of Dissimilation: 'Ostjuden' and the German Jews." in *The Jewish Response to German Culture*. Edited by J. Reinharz. London, 1985: 195–211.

von Fritz, Kurt. *The Theory of the Mixed Constitution in Antiquity: A Critical Analysis of Polybius' Political Ideas*. New York, 1954.

von Rad, Gerhard. "Die Anfänge der Geschichtsschreibung im alten Israel." In *Archiv für Kulturgeschichte* XXXII 1944: 1–42.

————. *Deuteronomy: A Commentary*. Philadelphia, 1966.

————. *Das Geschichtsbild des Chronistischen Werkes*. Stuttgart, 1930.

————. *The Message of the Prophets*. Translated by D. M. Stalker. New York, 1972.

Wachsmann, Meir. "Hamahshavah hafilosofit vehadatit shel Avraham bar Chiyya hanassi." In *Sefer hayovel le-H. A. Wolfson*. 3 vols. Jerusalem, 1965.

Wachtel, Alois. *Beiträge zur Geschichtstheologie des Auerlius Augustinus*. Bonn, 1960.

Wagenseil, Johann Christoph. *Tela ignea Satanae*. Altdorf, 1681.

Walbank, Frank William. *Polybius*. Sather Classical Lectures 42. Berkeley, 1972.

Watkins, J. W. N. *Hobbes' System of Ideas*. London, 1965.

Weber, Max. "Die Protestantische Ethik und der Geist des Kapitalismus." In *Gesammelte Aufsätze zur Religionssoziologie*. 3 vols. Tübingen, 1920.

Weiler, Gerschon. *Theokratia yehudit*. Tel-Aviv, 1971.

Weiss, Isaak Hirsch. *Dor dor vedorshav*. 6th edition. Wilno, 1911.

Weizmann, Chaim. *Devarim*. Tel Aviv, 1937.

Wellek, Renè and Austin Warren. *Theory and Literature*. New York, 1956.

Wendland, H. D. *Geschichtsanschauung und Geschichtes bewußtsein im Neuen Testament*. Göttingen, 1938.

Werner, Martin. *Die Entstehung des christlichen Dogmas*. Bern and Tübingen, 1953.

Westman, Robert. "The Copernicans and the Church." In *God and Nature: Historical Essays on the Encounter Between Christianity and Science*. Edited by David C. Lindberg and Ronald L. Numbers. Berkeley, Los Angeles, and London, 1986.

White, Hayden. *Metahistory: The Historical Imagination in Nineteenth-Century Europe*. Baltimore, 1973.

———. *The Content and the Form: Narrative Discourse and Historical Representation*. Baltimore and London, 1987.

Wieder, N. "The Law Interpreter of the Sect of the Dead Sea Scrolls: The Second Moses." *JJS* IV (1953): 158 ff.

Wiehl, R. "Experience in Rosenzweig's New Thinking." In *The Philosophy of Franz Rosenzweig*. Edited by Paul Mendes-Flohr. Hannover and London, 1988.

Wiener, Max. *Jüdische Religion im Zeitalter der Emanzipation*. Berlin, 1933.

Wieseltier, Meir. *Davar optimi assiyat shirim*. Tel-Aviv, 1976.

Wilkes, Michael J. *The Problem of Sovereignty in the Later Middle Ages*. Cambridge, Mass., 1964.

William of Champeau. *Dialogus inter Judaeum et Christianum* (Migne, PL 163).

Williams, A. L. *Adversus Judaeos: A Bird's-Eye View of Christian Apologiae until the Renaissance*. Cambridge, 1935.

Wippo. *Gesta Chuonradi*. Edited by H. Bresslau. MG Script. in usu Schol. 1915.

Wirszubski, Chaim. *Mequbbal notseri kore batora*. Jerusalem, 1975.

———. *Sheloshah perakim betoldot haqabbalah hanotserit*. Jerusalem, 1975.

———. *Libertas as a Political Idea at Rome During the Late Republic and Early Principate*. Cambridge, 1968.

Woolcombe, K. J. "Biblical Origins and Patristic Development of Typology." In *Essays on Typology*. Edited by Geoffrey William Hugo and K. J. Woolcombe. London, 1957.

Yadin, Yigael. "Megilot Yam ha-Melach veha'iggeret el ha-'Ivrim." In *Mechkarim bamegilot hagnuzot: sefer zikaron le-Eliezer Lipa Sukenik*. Jerusalem, 1961.

Yair ben Shabbetai da Correggio. *Herev pifiyyot*. Edited by Judah Rosenthal. Jerusalem, 1958.

Yerushalmi, Yosef Hayim. *Zakhor: Jewish History and Jewish Memory*. Seattle, 1982.

———. "The Lisbon Massacre of 1506 and the Royal Image in the Shevet Yehuda." *HUCA Supplement*. Cincinnati, 1976.

Zakovitch, Yair. *Sefer Ruth*. Tel-Aviv, 1990.

———. *"And You Shall Tell Your Son . . .": The Concept of the Exodus in the Bible*. Jerusalem, 1991.

Index

Aaron, 111

Abelard, Petrus, 173, 182–183

Abrabanel, Don Isaac, 160, 166, 199, 213 n.120; on kingship, 161–165

Abraham (Patriarch), 27, 69, 110, 148, 150 n.64, 299; trial of, 63, 64, 65

Abraham bar Chiyya, 103, 115–116, 117, 126, 199–200

Abraham Ibn Daud, 119–120 n.95

Abraham Ibn Ezra, 50, 62, 121, 246; allegoresis of, 90–93, 105; on creation, 91–92, 108, 125–126; on miracles, 107

Absolutism, 155–158, 159; of king, 160, 161–162, 163, 165; v. ordained power, 160–161, 163, 179–180

Abu-Issa movement, 134

Accommodation, 13, 14, 15, 88–98; Alfunsi on, 187–188; Augustine on, 94–95; bridges secular and sacred, 98; Christianity uses, 94–95, 98, 151–152, 250–251; divine, 187–188, 246, 250–251; Judaism on, 95–96; Krochmal on, 245, 246; in legal reasoning, 89; Maimonides on, 95–96, 140, 143 n.35, 145, 151–152; maximalistic/minimalistic, 90–91; and opportunism, 251; St. Paul on, 95; scripture and science explained by, 90–92; secularized, 96–98; Spinoza on, 96–97; Vico on, 97–98

Achad Ha'am, 247, 339, 342–343

Adam, 75, 116–117

Aegidius Colonna, 223

Aggada, 184, 185, 188, 189

Agnon, Shmuel Y., 256

Agobard of Lyons, 185, 190–191

Akiba, Rabbi, 89

Alanus ab Insulis, 173, 196–197, 198

Albo, Josef, 177 n.17, 238

Alenu leshabe'ach, 1 n.1

Alexander of Aphrodisias, 143–144 n.38

Alfunsi, Petrus, 143 n.35, 173, 183–189, 191; on divine accommodation, 187–188; on God's existence, 186, 187; on his conversion, 184–185, 188; on Islam/Mohammed, 188, 194

Allegory, 90–93, 105, 118

Allers, R., 181 n.27

Altman, A., 222 n.1

Amalekites, 128–129

Amalricans, 236

Amalrich of Bena, 126, 237

Ambrosius, 29, 110 n.72, 143 n.36

Ammonites, 56

Amulo of Lyons, 191, 196 n.75

Anachronisms, 17, 26, 121; Jews as, 177, 317

Anastos, Milton V., 96 n.24

Anselm of Canterbury, 173, 178–182; on God's existence, 180–181, 329; on God's power, 179–180; on necessity

Designer:	U.C. Press Staff
Compositor:	G & S Typesetters
Text:	10/13 Galliard
Display:	Galliard
Printer:	BookCrafters
Binder:	BookCrafters